MODERN PAINTERS

INDEX, ETC.

"Accuse me not
Of arrogance, ...
If, having walked with Nature,
And offered, far as frailty would allow,
My heart a daily sacrifice to Truth,
I now affirm of Nature and of Truth,
Whom I have served, that their Divinity
Revolts, offended at the ways of men,
Philosophers, who, though the human soul
Be of a thousand faculties composed,
And twice ten thousand interests, do yet prize
This soul, and the transcendent universe,
No more than as a mirror that reflects
To proud Self-love her own intelligence."

WORDSWORTH

Modern Painters

Vol. VI

By

John Ruskin

London : George Allen

November 1904

PREFATORY NOTE

TO THE COMPLETE EDITION OF 1888.*

THE present volume, though issued with Mr. Ruskin's sanction, has been compiled without reference to him, and he is, therefore, in no way responsible for it.

The references used in the index will be found equally applicable to all the editions of the different volumes of the work. The old index hitherto contained in the fifth volume of "Modern Painters," is omitted from the "Complete Edition," but embodied in the present index, though not always under quite the same headings.

No pains have been spared to make the following pages correct, complete, and serviceable; worthy, in fact, of the book to which they refer. In a work of this character, however, it is almost impossible that some errors and omissions should not have escaped the compiler, who will, therefore, be glad to receive any corrections which may come under the notice of persons using this volume.

A bibliography of "Modern Painters," and a collation of the main differences between the various editions, are placed at the end of the volume, and will, it is believed, be valued by collectors and students of Mr. Ruskin's works.

---

* Note to 1897 edition. This index has been slightly revised for this edition.

CONTENTS

	PAGE
GENERAL INDEX	I
BIBLIOGRAPHY	359
NOTES	369

ABBREVIATIONS

The references in this Index are double: first, to volume and page; secondly, to Part, Chapter, and paragraph, and in the case of Vols. I. and II. to Part, Section, Chapter, and paragraph. Thus, II. 200; iii. 2. 4. 16 refers to Vol. II. p. 200; Part iii. Section 2. Chapter 4. § 16; and III. 270; iv. 16. 33 to Vol. III. p. 270; Part iv. Chapter 16. § 33.

A few abbreviations almost explain themselves. Thus, (om. ed. 1. 2), after a reference, means "omitted in editions 1 and 2;" F. A. *n*, "note to *Frondes Agrestes;*" C. E., "*Cæli Enarrant;*" I. M. S., "*In Montibus Sanctis,*" etc., etc.

GENERAL INDEX

GENERAL INDEX

Aaron. *See s. Bible (b).*

Abbotsford, ugliness of, III. 282 ; iv. 16. 33.

Aberdeen granite, IV. 108 ; v. 8. 5.

Abstraction, in art, necessary when realization impossible, II. 221 ; iii. 2. 4. 16 *seqq.*

Abstractions, modern interest in, III. 158 ; iv. 11. 9–10.

Abuse of good gifts, IV. 377 ; v. 20. 17.

Acanthus, formalism of Greek, III. 222 ; iv. 14. 28.

Accessories, of a picture, not to be scamped, III. 34 ; iv. 3. 11.

Accidents, are not deeds, V. 180–81 ; viii. 1. 17.

Achilles, horses of, V. 284 ; ix. 6. 21.

    „   love of, II. 139 ; iii. 1. 14. 31.

Acrisius, father of Danaë, V. 159 ; vii. 4. 12.

Activity, definition of all perfect, as "expression of man's delight in God's work" (Dante), III. 232 ; iv. 14. 39.

    „   noble, and contemplation, III. 324 ; iv. 17. 41.

Adam, curse of, II. 125, 127 ; iii. 1. 14. 9. 11.

    „   of Brescia (Dante), III. 256 ; iv. 15. 17.

Addison's "Cato," Leigh Hunt on, II. 179 ; iii. 2. 3. 7 *n.*

    „   hymn, "The spacious firmament on high," IV. 91 *n* ; v. 6. 8.

Admetus, flocks of, V. 123 ; vii. 2. 5.

Admiration, how rightly excited, III. 11 ; iv. 1. 13.

Advent, the second, V. 385–86 ; ix. 12. 19.

Æglé, Hesperid, V. 333 ; ix. 10. 8 *n.*

    „   „   V. 348 ; ix. 11. 5.

Aerial perspective. *See s. Perspective.*

Æschylus, grand and unpopular (cf. Turner), I. xxiv ; *pref. ed* 2. 16 *n.*

    „   imagination of, II. 177 ; iii. 2. 3. 4.

3

Æschylus, *continued:*

,,   landscape of, not typical of Greek mind, III. 198 ;
        iv. 13. 27.

,,   sense of honour, V. 242 ; ix. 3. 8.

,,   works of :

        " Agamemnon " referred to, I. xxiv ; *pref. ed.* 2. 16.

        " Prometheus " ἀνήριθμον γέλασμα, I. 377 *n* ; ii. 5. 3.
                                              40 (ed. 1, 2. 39 *n*
                                              only).

        ,,   ,,   ,,   II. 164 ; iii. 2. 3. 9
                                              (ed. 1 only).

Æsthetics, definition of, II. 13, 17 ; iii. 1. 2. 1, 6.

,,   mere, have no hallowing power, II. 145 ; iii. 1. 15.
        6. and '83 *n.*

,,   modern, folly of, II. 11 ; iii. 1. 1. 10 ('83 *n*).

,,   ,,   and house decoration, II. '83 *pref.* 8, 9.

Affectation, freedom of great men from, III. 276–77 ; iv.
        16. 26.

,,   in modern painting, *ib.* ; *ib.*

Affections, capable of government, II. 22 ; iii. 1. 3. 2–3.

Agasias, l. 4 ; i. 1. 1. 2.

,,   II. 137 ; iii. 1. 14. 29.

Agassiz, unable to draw, II. 66 ; iii. 5. 6. 12. ('83 *n*).

Age, youth and, each has its ideal, II. 117 ; iii. 1. 13. 15. (*For
        the present age, see s. Modernism.*)

Agriculture, as a national industry, V. 360 *n* ; ix. 11. 22 *n.*

,,   contempt of, classical, V. 268 ; ix. 5, 6.

,,   ,,   mediæval, III. 203 ; iv. 14. 3.

,,   ,,   ,,   V. 5 ; vi. 1. 5.

,,   practice of, inspires gratitude to God, III. 205 ;
        iv. 14. 7.

Aiguilles [SYNOPSIS. IV. 182–204. 224–25. 418 *seqq.*   V. 104]:—

        angular forms of, IV. 187 *seqq.* ; v. 14. 9 *seqq.*

        cleavage of, IV. 194–96, 201 ; v. 14. 16–17. 22.

        ,,   IV. 418 *seqq.* ; App. ii. 4.

        contours of, IV. 188 *seqq.* ; v. 14. 11 *seqq.*

        ,,   IV. 200 *seqq.* ; v. 14. 21 *seqq.*

        crests and, their structure compared, IV. 224–25 ; v.
        15. 20.

        curvature of, IV. 195–96 ; v. 14. 17.

        ,,   IV. 202–3 ; v. 14. 24.

        dilapidation of, its method, IV. 193–94 and *n* ; v. 14. 15.

Aiguilles, *continued :*
  influence of, on the earth, IV. 203 ; v. 14. 24.
  lovely in their law of rending, V. 104 ; vi. 10. 11.
  various—

  > See *s.* Allée, Argentière, Bionassay, Blaitière, Bouchard,
  > Chamouni, Charmoz, Dru, Greppond, Gouté, Midi, Moine,
  > Plan, Pourri, Rouges, Sans-nom, Verte.

Air, purified and changed by the mountains, IV. 96 ; v. 7. 4.
  „   „   „   „   „   IV. 102 *seqq.*; v. 7.
                                                    8 *seqq.*

Airolo.   *See s. S. Gothard.*
Ajax, shield of, IV. 413 ; App. i. 8.
Albano (artist), prettiness of, V. 304 ; ix. 8. 1.
  „   Mr., quoted on cost of Covent Garden Theatre, IV.
           342 *n* ; v. 19. 6 *n.*
  „   Mt., country round described, storm clearing, I. 165 ;
           ii. 2. 2. 2.
  „   „   introduced into Claude's backgrounds, IV. 231 ;
           v. 15. 28.
Alcestis, love of, II. 139 ; iii. 1. 14. 31.   *See s. Euripides.*
Alchemilla, leaves of, V. 105 ; vi. 10. 13.
Alcinous, gardens of, IV. 366 ; v. 20. 2.
Aletsch glacier, I. 316 *n* ; ii. 4. 3. 12 (om. ed. 1, 2).
  „   „   IV. 191 ; v. 14. 12.
  „   „   ravine near, IV. 273 ; v. 16. 40.
Alhambra, ornaments of, IV. 289 ; v. 17. 19.
Alisma plantago, leaf of, III. 217 ; iv. 14. 23.
Alison (Sir A.), historian, distinguished from Mr. Alison, II.
           35 ; iii. 1. 4. 7 ('83 *n*).
  „   (Mr.), on beauty and association of ideas, II. 35 ; iii. 1.
           4. 7.
  „   „   on beauty, sources of, II. 41 ; iii. 1. 5. 2.
  „   „   „   his vague use of the word, II. 30 ;
           iii. 1. 3. 15.
  „   „   on unity, II. 58 *n* ; iii. 1. 6. 5 *n.*
Allée, Blanche, IV. 185 ; v. 14. 6.
  „   „   aiguille of, IV. 219 ; v. 15. 16.
Alleluia, Italian name of oxalis acetosella, I. 86 *n* ; ii. 1. 7. 9 *n*
           (om. ed. 1–4).
Allen, George, drawings for " Modern Painters " by, V. ix ; *pref.*
           6 *n.*

Allen, George, *continued :*

    ,,   ,,   drawings for " Modern Painters " by, V. 108 ; vi. 10. 19.

    ,,   ,,   engravings for " Modern Painters " by, V. '88 Epil.

    ,,   Robin, on Dürer's " Knight and Death," V. 294 *n* ; ix. 4. 16 *n.*

Allnutt (Mr. A.) owns Turner's " Bonneville," I. 141 ; ii. 1. 7. 44 (om. ed. 1, 2).

    ,,   ,,   ,,   " Sunset behind Willows," I. 156 ; ii. 2. 1. 13.

Aloe, V. 57 ; vi. 7. 4.

    ,, leaf, V. 64 ; vi. 7. 14.

Alpine flowers. *See s. Gentian, Soldanella.*

    ,, roses, colour of, III. 235 ; iv. 14. 46.

    ,,   ,, symmetry of, II. 71 ; iii. 1. 8. 3 (ed. 1, 2 only).

Alps [SYNOPSIS. I. 280, 297, 307, 395. III. 139–40, 248. IV. 114–15, 173 *seqq.*, 231, 242–44, 258–59, 260, 274–75, 297, 303–7, 329–30, 335, 367, 377. V. 90–1, 99, 104, 111, 155 *n.*, 160 *n.*, 241] :—

    aerialness of, at great distances, I. 296 ; ii. 4. 2. 9.

    buttresses of (Jungfrau and Gemmi), IV. 303–6 ; v. 17. 33–9 (pl. 46).

    cliffs of, plumb-line measures of, IV. 242–44 ; v. 16. 5.

    colour of, III. 248 ; iv. 15. 8.

    ,,   IV. 114–15 ; v. 8. 14.

    drawing of, I. 307 ; ii. 4. 2. 21.

    ,, depends on snow-drawing, I. 395 ; ii. 5. 3. 29.

    emotions roused by the sight of, III. 139–40 ; iv. 10. 8.

    gentian-belted, in spring, V. 99 ; vi. 10. 3.

    geography and structure of the, IV. 173 *seqq.* ; v. 13. 10 *seqq*

    limestone crags, their sublimity, IV. 258–59 ; v. 16. 24.

    lower gorges of, IV. 260 ; v. 16. 27.

    Paradise suggested by, IV. 367 ; v. 20. 3.

    pines on, IV. 306–7 ; v. 17. 39.

    ,,   V. 90–1 ; vi. 9. 7. 8.

    precipices of, good and bad drawing, IV. 274–75 ; v. 16. 42.

    roses on, V. 111 ; vi. 10. 22.

    signs of rain in the, V. 155 *n* ; vii. 4. 6 *n.*

    streams in, embanking, IV. 297 ; v. 17. 28.

    sunrise in, I. 280 ; ii. 3. 4. 34.

Alps, *continued :*
    Swiss character and, IV. 378 ; v. 20. 18.
    Tyrolese, V. 241 ; ix. 3. 6.
    valleys of, beauty and formation of, IV. 329–30 ; v. 18. 16.
            „   „   „   „   IV. 335 ; v. 18. 26.
    vegetation of mountain sides, IV. 305 ; v. 17. 37.
    view of, from Venice, IV. 231 ; v. 15. 27.
    winds in the, V. 160 *n* ; vii. 4. 14 *n*.   *And see s. Glaciers
        Snow, Mountains.*
Altar-tombs, mediæval and renaissance compared, II. 75 ; iii.
        1. 7. 7.
Altorf, rocks and valley of, I. 289 ; ii. 4. 1. 5.
Amalfi described, II. 244 ; Add. 4–5 (om. ed. 1).
Amazon river, IV. 99 ; v. 7. 6.
Ambition, discontent and, V. 359 *seqq.* ; ix. 11. 19 *seqq.*
    „   the true ends of, V. 387 ; ix. 12. 20.
America, Europe becoming like, IV. 398 ; v. 20. 42.
    „   its want of associations, III. 310 ; iv. 17. 21.
    „   lakes of North, IV. 101 ; v. 7. 6.
    „   pine-drawing in, V. 87 ; vi. 9. 3.
Amiens, banks of Somme at, author's diary quoted, IV. 10 *n* ;
        v. 1. 12 *n*.
    „   cathedral of, IV. 381 ; v. 20. 23.
    „   poplar groves of, III. 192 ; iv. 13. 20.
    „   „   „   IV. 369 ; v. 20. 7.
Amsterdam, no poet from, IV. 382 ; v. 20. 25.
Anachronisms of great painters and poets, III. 98 ; iv. 7.
        19–20.
Anacreon, dove of, V. 284 ; ix. 6. 21.
    „   quoted (Ode xii.), V. 243 *n* ; ix. 3. 10 *n*.
    „   „   τί πλειάδεσσι, κἀμοί ; V. 238 ; ix. 3. 1.
Anarchy, means death, V. 175 ; viii. 1. 6.
Anatomy, author's writings against, II. 102 ; iii. 1. 12. 7
        ('83 *n*).
    „   development of, only admissible in subordination to
            laws of beauty, II. 236 ; iii. 2. 5. 17.
    „   in art, not to supersede apparent fact, IV. 197 ; v.
            14. 18.
    „   study of, its effect, IV. 414 ; App. ii. 1.
Ancestry, honour of, mediæval and modern, III. 271–72 ; iv.
        16. 15.
    „   natural pride of, III. 157 ; iv. 11. 8.

Angelico [SYNOPSIS. I. 2 *n*, 86, 89. II. 47, 60 *n*, 73 *n*, 89, 129, 138,
140 *n*, 145, 187, 189; 191, 195, 229, 234–35, 237, 239,
'83 Epil. 8, 10. III. 32–3, 36, 37, 41, 45, 53–4, 60–2, 78,
81–2, 106, 131. IV. 59, 376, 379, 407. V. x. 309–12,
343] :—

"angel choirs" of, described, II. 239 ; iii. 2. 5. 21.

angels of, distinct from his men, II. 229 ; iii. 2. 5. 6.

author's study of, II. 253; '83 Epil. 10.

    „   „   V. x. ; *pref.* 7.

balanced power of (expressional and pictorial), III. 32–3 ;
iv. 3. 9.

beauty of, most sanctified, II. 145 ; iii. 1. 15. 6.

    „   occasional commonplaces enhance it, III. 37 ;
iv. 3. 14.

Christs by, II. 229 ; iii. 2. 5. 7.

colour of, V. 343 ; ix. 10. 24.

    „   pure, and expressive of the Divine, II. 234 ; iii.
2. 5. 13.

cramped by traditional treatment, II. 138 ; iii. 1. 14. 29.

decoration of, II. 234 ; ii. 2. 5. 13.

distances of, mountainous, IV. 376 ; v. 20. 16.

expressional power of (colourist), IV. 407 ; App. i. 1.

    „   its purity, III. 45 ; iv. 3. 25.

feeling of, III. 106 ; iv. 8. 7.

finish of, II. 89 ; iii. 1. 10. 4.

    „   III. 131 ; iv. 9. 18.

fog, hated by, IV. 59; v. 4. 2.

foregrounds of, oxalis acetosella in, I. 86; ii. 1. 7. 9 (om.
ed. 1, 2).

Fuseli on, III. 82; iv. 6. 8.

ideal of, III. 53–4; iv. 4. 10.

    „   III. 61; iv. 4. 20. *See below, s. temper.*

jewellery of, abstract. II. 234; iii. 2. 5. 14.

landscape of, clear, IV. 62 ; v. 4. 2.

    „   gentle, II. 47; iii. 1. 5. 10.

moral influence of a work by, III. 60; iv. 4. 19.

mountain-bred, IV. 379–80; v. 20. 21–2.

Pisan sculpture, its influence on him, IV. 379; iv. 20. 20.

popularity of, small, and why, I. 4 *n* ; i. 1. 1. 1 *n* (om. ed. 1, 2).

portraiture, in works of, II. 129; iii. 1. 14. 14.

purity of life, III. 78 ; iv. 6. 4.

religious art of, passionate ideal, III. 61; iv. 4. 20.

Angelico, *continued*:

    religious art and Bible scenes, III. 63; iv. 4. 22 (F.A. *n*).

    rendering of Paradise, II. 73; iii. 1. 7. 5 ('83 *n*).

    „   the Passion, its horrors, II. 138; iii. 1. 14, 29.

    Salvator contrasted with, V. 311; ix. 8. 14.

    size of his works, small, III. 41; iv. 3. 19.

    spiritual beauty of, III. 36; iv. 3. 12.

    „   „   V. 312; ix. 8. 15.

    temper of, III. 78; iv. 6. 4.

    variety of, II. 140 *n* ; iii. 1. 14. 31 *n*.

    Wouvermans compared with, V. 309-10; ix. 8. 12-13.

    works of :

        Annunciation (S. M. Novella, Florence), II. 187 ; iii. 2. 3. 17.

        Crucifixion (Florence Acad.), I. 86 *n* ; ii. 1. 7. 9 *n*.

        „   „   „   II. 191 ; iii. 2. 3. 20.

        „   „   „   II. 235 ; iii. 2. 5. 15.

        Infant Christ „   „   II. 237 ; iii. 2. 5. 18.

        Last Judgment „   „   I. 89 ; ii. 1. 7. 11 (om. ed. 1, 2).

        „   „   „   II. 195 ; iii. 2. 3. 23.

        „   „   „   III. 62 ; iv. 4. 20.

        Madonna (S. M. Novella, Florence), II. '83 Epil. 8.

        „   „   „   V. 309; ix. 8. 12, frontispiece.

        Paradise   „   „   „   III. 62 ; iv. 4. 20.

        St. Domenico (Fiesole), II. 61 *n* ; iii. 1. 6. 8 *n*.

        Spirits in Prison at Feet of Christ (St. Mark's fresco), II. 61 *n*.

        Vita di Christo, II. 189 ; iii. 2. 3. 18.

Angelo. *See s. Michael Angelo.*

Angels, painting of nude (cf. Cupids), II. 236 ; iii. 2. 5. 17.

Anger, right and wrong, II. 15 ; iii. 1. 2. 4.

Animals [SYNOPSIS. II. 15-16, 63 *n*, 69, 98, 101-7, 111, 116, 164, 218, 236. V. 225, 281 *seqq.*, 300 *n*] :—

    beauty of, in proportion to virtue expressed, II. 104-5 ; iii. 1. 12. 10.

    „   slothful, never very beautiful, II. 104 ; iii. 1. 12. 9.

    „   spoilt by high breeding (race-horses), II. 107 ; iii. 1. 12. 12.

    „   „   „   „   „   II. 114 ; iii. 1. 13. 10.

    ideal form in, II. 118 ; iii. 1. 13. 15.

    love of, II. 97 ; iii. 1. 12. 2.

    „   based on their happiness, II. 101 ; iii. 1. 12. 6.

Animals, *continued :*
    man's due relation to, V. 225 ; ix. 2. 1.
    modern and ancient, V. 281 *seqq.* ; ix. 6. 14 *seqq.*
    moral functions of, II. 103 ; iii. 1. 12. 8.
    no new, conceivable by us, II. 164 ; iii. 2. 2. 10.
    painting of, by Dutch, V. 281 ; ix. 6. 13. 23.
       ,,   ,,   moderns, V. 283–84 ; ix. 6. 20.
       ,,   ,,   ,,   V. 300 *n* ; ix. 7. 23.
       ,,   ,,   Venetians, V. 281–83 ; ix. 6. 14 *seqq.*
    proportions of, II. 62 *n* ; iii. 1. 6. 10 *n.*
       ,,   ,,   II. 69 ; iii. 1. 6. 16.
    rendering of, in art, abstract, II. 219 ; iii. 2. 4. 12.
       See s. Dogs, Race-horses.
Annecy, Lake of, cliffs round, IV. 260 ; v. 16. 26.
Annuals, vignettes for the, IV. 19 ; v. 2. 5.
Annunciations, rendering of, by Angelico and others, II. 187 ;
    iii. 2. 3. 17.
Anschauung, of the Germans, II. 26 ; iii. 1. 3. 7.
Anticipation, delight of, beyond the reality, III. 144 ; iv. 10. 13.
Antinous, idealism of the, II. 110 ; iii. 1. 13. 3.
Antiquity, authority of, in art, its danger and value, I. xiv–xv ;
    pref. ed. 2, 4–7.
    ,,   English and continental feeling for, IV. 4–5 ; v. 1. 5.
    ,,   reverence for, right, I. 110 ; ii. 1. 7. 26 (om. ed. 1, 2).
    ,,   ,,   ,,   true, III. 99 ; iv. 7. 21.
    ,,   ,,   ,,   ,,   V. 84 ; vi. 8. 19.
Antwerp, no poet from, IV. 382 ; v. 20. 25.
    ,,   streets of, IV. 353 ; v. 19. 22.
    ,,   works of art at :

        Adoration of Magi (Museum), I. 41 ; i. 2. 2. 7.
        Rubens' Family (Church of St. James), V. 279 ; ix. 6. 10.
        ,,   St. John, V. 277 ; ix. 6. 6.

Apelles, composition of, II. '83 Epil. 9.
    ,,   leaf-drawing of, V. 39 ; vi. 5. 2.
Apennines, barren and colourless, III. 246–48 ; iv. 15. 6–8.
    ,,   ,,   ,,   IV. 317 ; v. 17. 50.
    ,,   Lombard, III. (pl. 14).
Aphrodite, less beautiful than Madonna, I. 34 ; i. 1. 7. 3.
Apollo, arrows and lyre of, III. 67 ; iv. 5. 2.
    ,,   harmony of, V. 182 ; viii. 1. 20.
    ,,   Python and, its meaning, V. 354 *seqq.* ; ix. 11. 10 *seqq.*

Apollo, *continued*:

„ sending plagues on the Greeks, III. 183 ; iv. 13. 8.

„ "Belvidere," I. 37 ; i. 2. 1. 5.

„ „ I. 434 ; ii. 6. 2. 2.

„ „ I. 451 *n* ; ii. 6. 3. 23 *n*.

„ „ II. 238 *n* ; iii. 2. 5. 20 *n* (no divinity about it).

„ „ III. 72 ; iv. 5. 8.

Apostles' Creed, "communion of saints" and political economy, V. 379 ; ix. xii. 6. 7.

Appearances, regard for, right and wrong, V. 295 *seqq.* ; ix. 7 16 *seqq.*

Apple-blossoms, beauty of, III. 235–36 ; iv. 14. 46.

"Arabian Nights," changing princess of the, II. 152 ; iii. 2. 1. 1.

Arbor vitæ, V. 87 ; vi. 9. 2.

Architecture [SYNOPSIS. **I.** 50, 108–13, 119–20, 123–24 *n*, 147, 203, 210–11, 433. **II.** 11 *n*, 219–21, 232, '83 Epil. 5. **III.** xiii, 68, 100, 248, 270, 330. **IV.** 358, 379, 380–81. **V.** 21–2, 196, 220, 324–25]:—

age in, value of signs of, I. 110–12 ; ii. 1. 7. 26.

author's study of, begun, II. '83 Epil. 5 *n*.

„ „ to be considered in "Modern Painters," I. 137 ; ii. 1. 7. 13 (ed. 1, 2 only).

„ „ why not discussed there, I. 433 ; ii. 6. 2. 1.

bad, its influence on artists, III. 330 ; iv. 18. 8.

beauty of, as enhancing landscape, IV. 366 *n* ; v. 20. 2 *n*.

chiaroscuro, its importance, I. 112–13 ; ii. 1. 7. 27.

decline of, III. 68 ; iv. 5. 4. *See below, s. Renaissance.*

decoration and construction, II. 10 *n* ; iii. 1. 1. 9 *n*.

„ abstraction in, II. 219–21 ; iii. 2. 4. 14–15.

„ animal form in, *ib.* ; *ib.*

detail. *See below, s. effect.*

drawing of, advance in, Bellini to Prout, I. 108 *seqq.* ; ii. 1 7. 25 *seqq.* (om. ed. 1, 2).

„ conventional ruins, I. 119 ; ii. 1. 7. 31 (om. ed. 1, 2).

„ „ plans, over-distinct as pictures, I. 212 ; ii. 2. 5. 14.

„ painters and architects both to do, I. 124 *n* ; ii. 1. 7. 34 (om. ed. 1, 2).

„ rules for, I. 110 *seqq.* ; ii. 1. 7. 26 (om. ed. 1, 2).

„ „ I. 433 ; ii. 6. 2. 1.

Architecture, *continued*:

durability of, to improve with age, I. III ; ii. 1. 7. 26 (om. ed. 1, 2).

effect of, according to light and shade, I. 112–13 ; ii. 1. 7. 27.

   „   distance, I. 113 ; ii. 1. 7. 27 (om. ed. 1, 2).

   „   eye retiring, I. 202–3 ; ii. 2. 5. 2.

   „   „   I. 210 ; ii. 2. 5. 12.

flamboyant, IV. 381 ; v. 20. 23.

foundations in, I. 50 ; ii. 1. 1. 7.

good, equally effective near or far, I. 113 ; ii. 1. 7. 27 (om. ed. 1, 2).

Gothic, early influences on, IV. 379 ; v. 20. 20.

Italian painters, ideal school of, is Transalpine, II. 232 ; iii. 2. 5. 11.

life of the workman to be considered, V. 220 ; ix. 1. 7.

modern London and old Venice, V. 324–25 ; ix. 9. 18–19.

painting and, connected, I. 124 *n* ; ii. 1. 7. 34 (om. ed. 1, 2).

   „   „   III. 100 ; iv. 8. 1.

rank of, lower than sculpture or painting, and why, II. 11 *n* ; iii. 1. 1. 9 *n*.

Renaissance, expressed pride, III. 68 ; iv. 5. 4.

   „   the death of, III. 270; iv. 16. 12.

   „   „   IV. 380–81 ; v. 20. 23.

   „   monotony of modern, III. 248 ; iv. 15. 9.

   „   vulgarity of, V. 196 ; viii. 3. 3.

ruin of noble, and need of record, I. 123–24 ; ii. 1. 7. 34 (om. ed. 1, 2).

symmetry to be sacrificed to use in, III. xiii ; *pref.* 6.

tree-structure and, coincidences between, V. 21–2 ; vi. 3. 14.

Turner's, I. 433–34 ; ii. 6. 2. 1.

   See s. Acanthus, Cathedrals, Corinthian, Gothic, Greek, Ionic, Nuremberg, Palladio, Parliament, Parthenon, Proportion, Pugin, Quatrefoil, Renaissance, Restoration, Stucco, Trefoil, Venice, Whitewash, Windows, Wood.

Arcola, Napoleon I. at, V. 326 ; ix. 9. 22.

Ardon (Valais), gorge of, IV. 161 ; v. 12. 21.

   „   „   „   clefts near, IV. 273 ; v. 16. 40.

Arethusa, Hesperid, V. 333 *n* ; ix. 10. 8 *n*.

Argentière, Aiguille d', II. 159 ; iii. 2. 2. 3.

   „   „   IV. 220 *n* ; v. 15. 16 *n*.

   „   hills near, IV. 329 *n* ; v. 18. 15 *n*.

Aristocracy, fall of, through idleness and pride, III. 203;
iv. 14. 3.

Aristophanes [SYNOPSIS. I. xxiv *n*, xxvii *n*. III. 108, 198, 260,
265–66, 317. V. 157–58, 160–61, 179, 243 *n*, 284] :—
clouds disliked but studied by, I. xxvii ; *pref. ed.* 2. 19.

    ,,   ,,   ,,   ,,   III. 260 ; iv. 15. 21.
    ,,   ,,   ,,   ,,   III. 265 ; iv. 16. 3.
    ,,   ,,   ,,   ,,   V. 160–61 ; vii. 4. 15.

frogs and birds of, V. 284 ; ix. 6. 21.
jests of, bitter, III. 108 ; iv. 8. 10.
landscape of, I. xxvii *n* ; *pref. ed.* 2. 19 *n*.
    ,,   not typical of Greek mind, III. 198 ; iv. 13. 27.
thought-shop of, V. 179 ; viii. 1. 14.
works of :

Birds, "bent-clawed Graiæ," V. 157–58 ; vii. 4. 10.
    ,,   "Locks of Typhon," V. 161 ; vii. 4. 16.
Clouds, "great goddesses to the idle," III. 265–66 ; iv.
    16. 3–4.
    ,,   "speak ingeniously of smoke," *ib.* ; *ib.*
    ,,   "dethrone the gods," III. 317 ; iv. 17. 32.
    ,,   song of rain-clouds, V. 157 ; vii. 4. 10.
Frogs, on Æschylus, I. xxiv *n* ; *pref.* 2. 16 *n*.
Plutus, V. 243 *n* ; ix. 3. 10 *n*.

Aristotle [SYNOPSIS. I. 20, 62. II. '83 *pref.* 7, 14, 17, 58 *n*, 79,
95 *n*, 179 *n*. III. 324 *n*. IV. 425. V. 135] :—
method of, begins with φαινόμενα, I. 62 ; ii. 1. 3. 2.
moral system of, III. 324 *n* ; iv. 17. 41 *n*.
symmetry and ἰσότης, II. 79 ; iii. 1. 8. 3.
vapours and their colour, V. 135 ; vii. 2. 18.
works of :

Ethics, as a school book, IV. 425 ; App. iii. 3.
    ,,   "Modern Painters" based on Book x., II. 95 ; iii.
    1. 11. 4 ('83 *n*).
    ,,   on envy, temperance, etc., IV. 426 ; App. iii. 3.
    ,,   ,, habits of choice in moderation, *ib.* ; *ib.*
    ,,   ,, intemperance, II. 17 ; iii. 1. 2. 7.
    ,,   ,, pleasures, II. 14 ; iii. 1. 2. 3.
    ,,   ,, theoria, II. '83 *pref.* 7.
Rhetoric, as a school book, IV. 425 ; App. iii. 3.
    ,,   quoted, I. 20 ; i. 1. 4. 2 (om. ed. 1, 2).
    ,,   ,,   II. 58 ; iii. 1. 6. 6.
    ,,   ,,   II. 179 *n* ; iii. 2. 3. 7.

Armour, mediæval, III. 209–10 ; iv. 14. 11. 13.
   ,,   Shaksperean, IV. 387–88 ; v. 20. 30.
Armytage, engravings in " Modern Painters," I. '73 *pref.*

,,   ,,   ,,   ,,   III. x ; *pref.* 5.

,,   ,,   ,,   ,,   IV. 310 ; v. 17. 43
                                    (pl. 48).

,,   ,,   ,,   ,,   V. ix ; *pref.* 6 *n.*

,,   ,,   ,,   ,,   V. 47 ; vi. 6. 5
                                    (pl. 51).

,,   ,,   ,,   ,,   V. 110 ; vi. 10. 20.

,,   ,,   ,,   ,,   V. 125 *n* ; vii. 2.
                                    6 *n* (pl. 67).

,,   ,,   ,,   ,,   V. 134 *n* ; vii. 2.
                                    16 *n* (pl. 63).

,,   ,,   of Raphael's Holy Family, III. 332 ; iv.
    18. 12 (pl. 11).

Arno, colour of the, I. 352 ; ii. 5. 1. 8 (om. ed. 1, 2).

Arnolfo's dome, Florence, III. 277 ; iv. 16. 24.

Arona, rock of, IV. 269 ; v. 16. 37 (pl. 41).

Art * [SYNOPSIS. I. i, xvi, xxii, xxv, xxxii, xl, 8, 12, 45, 48–52, 57–8,
      85, 101, 254, 378. II. 2, 3, 4, 7, 8, 11 *n*, 116–17, 145,
      166, 207–8, 241, 245. III. vi–vii, xi, xiii, 1, 3, 14–18. 21–2,
      23–4, 28, 37, 40–2, 45, 47, 50–1, 60, 63–4, 70–1, 87, 98–9,
      103–4, 151, 164, 177, 214, 282, 334. IV. 9–10, 16–19, 69,
      83, 233 *n*, 277, 319, 353–54, 378–82. V. 151–52, 172, 177,
      194–95, 199, 213–14, 225, 226, 232, 238–39, 363, 372] :—
æstheticism and, II. 11 ; iii. 1. 1. 10 ('83 *n*).

* *See s.* Abstraction, Activity, Accessories, Aerial perspective, Æsthetics,
Affectation, Anachronism, Anatomy, Antiquity, Architecture, Artist,
Assertion, Backgrounds, Beaumont, Beauty, Blottesque, Body, Boldness,
Breadth, Brown, Brush, Caricature, Chance, Chasing, Chiaroscurists,
Chiaroscuro, China, Chinese, Choice, Christian, Classical, Clearness,
Climate, Clocks, Coarseness, Coins, Colour, Colourist, Completion, Com-
position, Conception, Contention, Contrast, Conventionalism, Copyists,
Criticism, Curvature, Daguerreotype, Dash, Deception, Decision, Design,
Detail, Distances, Distinctness, Dogmatism, Drapery, Drawing, Dress,
Effect, Effort, Enamel, Engraving, Etching, Exaggeration, Excellence,
Execution, Expression, Evanescence, Facility, Facsimile, Facts, Falsity,
Fancy, Figure, Finish, Flemish school, Flesh, Florence, Foreground, Fore-
shortening, Form, Freedom, French, Fresco, Galleries, Generalization,
German, Glass, Gold, Gothic, Gradation, Greece, Grotesque, Harmony,
Heraldry, Historical, House-decoration, Idealism, Illumination, Imagina-
tion, Imitation, Inadequacy, Indecision, Indistinctness, India, Infinity,
Inspiration, Intaglio, Invention, Italy, Jewellery, Landscape, Landscapist,

Art, *continued*:

aim of, to interpret nature, not to take her place, I. xvi ; *ed.* 2. *pref.* 7.

„ „ „ „ „ III. 149 ; iv. 10. 19.

„ to praise God, not display man's dexterity, I. xxv ; *ed.* 2. *pref.* 17.

„ the expression of thought and truth, I. 48–52 ; ii. 1. 1. 2 *seqq.*

allegorical, III. 103–4 ; iv. 8. 6.

architecture below sculpture and painting, II. 11 *n* ; iii. 1. 1. 9 *n.*

bad, evil effects of its habitual use, IV. 353–54 ; v. 19. 23.

Christian, fails by denying man's animal nature, V. 226 ; ix. 2. 4.

climate and, V. 151–52, vii. 4. 2.

„ V. 238–39 ; ix. 3. 2. 3.

coldness, a sign of feebleness, I. 51 ; ii. 1. 1. 9.

completeness in itself of a true piece of, I. xl ; *ed.* 2. *pref.* 35.

conventionalism to be dreaded in, I. xvi ; *ed.* 2. *pref.* 8.

criticism, 1848, its abuse of colour, II. 242 ; Add. i. '83 *n* (om. ed. 1).

„ is art-faculty essential to ? III. xi ; *pref.* 5.

deception of, III. 18 *seqq.* ; iv. 2. 1 *seqq.* See s. *Deception, Imitation.*

defined as "the expression of delight in God's work," V. 225 ; ix. 2. 1.

detail and breadth in, I. xxxi–xxxiii ; *pref. ed.* 2. 24–5.

dilettanteism in, II. 2 ; iii. 1. 1. 2.

Law, Lindsay, Lines, Mannerism, Manuscripts, Master, Mediæval, Mimicry, Models, Moderation, Modern, Moorish, Mosaic, Motive, Mystery, Naturalist, Nature, Niggling, Ninevite, Normandy, Northern, Novice, Nude, Oil-painting, Old masters, Ornament, Outline, Painter, Painting, Pallet-knife, Pencil, Perception, Perfectness, Personification, Perspective, Pharisaism, Photography, Pictures, Picturesque, Popularity, Portraiture, Power, Pre-Raphaelites, Profane, Proportion, Purism, Purple, Rapidity, Realism, Reality, Realization, Reformation, Relation, Religious, Repose, Rescue, Rest, Restoration, Romanesque, Rome, Ruins, Rules, Scale, Sensibility, Sensuality, Shadow, Sight, Simplicity, Sincerity, Size, Sketches, Sky-painting, Snow, Softness, Strangeness, Style, Supernatural, Symbolism, Symmetry, Sympathy, Subject, Sublimity, Success, Taste, Technical, Textures, Theoria, Thirteenth century, Tone, Treatment, Truth, Tuscan, Ugliness, Unity, Urbino, Utility, Vanity, Variety, Vehicles, Venice, Water-colour.

Art, *continued :*

    early, want of shade in, I. 57 ; ii. 1. 2. 6.

    English, 1843, I. 1 ; *pref.* 1.

    evil confronted and conquered by great, V. 232 ; ix. 2. 13.

          „   „   „   „   I. xxiii. ; *pref. ed.*
        2. 14.

    execution (1400 *seqq.*) increased, as feeling decreased, III.
        334 ; iv. 18. 14.

    facts, *i.e.* truth, the basis, not the crown, of all, I. 50 ; ii. 1. 1. 7.

    falsity in, unpleasurable (pathetic fallacy), III. 164 ; iv. 12. 4.

          „   „   „   „   III. 176–77 ; iv.
        12. 15.

    great, "art of dreaming," IV. 382 ; v. 20. 24.

      „   "common nature" in, III. 15 ; iv. 1. 18.

      „   confesses man as both animal and spiritual, V. 226 ;
            ix. 2, 4.

      „   delicate always, III. 42 ; iv. 3. 20.

      „   details carefully given in, III. 16 ; iv. 1. 19.

      „   distinct, how far, III. 40 ; iv. 3. 17.

      „   errors as to what makes, III. 28–9 ; iv. 3. 3.

      „   essentials of (noble subject, beauty, sincerity, inven-
            tion), *ib.* ; *ib.* ; *seqq.*

      „   expression of spirits of great men, III. 47 ; iv. 3. 28.

      „   „   „   „   „   V. 199 ; viii. 3. 8.

      „   „   „   „   „   V. 214; viii. 4. 21.

      „   freedom of, V. 194 ; viii. 2. 15.

      „   general characteristics, V. 199 ; viii. 3. 8.

      „   grasp and breadth of, III. 41 ; iv. 3. 18.

      „   invention in all, III. 43 ; iv. 3. 21.

      „   „   „   IV. 16 ; v. 2. 1.

      „   never fortuitous or contentious, V. 194 ; viii. 2. 15.

      „   "of things seen and believed," III. 87 ; iv. 7. 5.

      „   points out the most beautiful in nature, III. 37 ; iv.
            3. 13.

      „   produced by men of high feeling, III. 14 ; iv. 1. 17.

      „   thought, not execution, the true test of, I. 11 ; i. 1. 2. 7.

    greatest, that with most greatest ideas, I. 8 *seqq.*; i. 1. 2. 1 *seqq.*

        „   „   „   „   I. 12 ; i. 1. 2. 9.

        „   „   „   „   III. 3 ; iv. 1. 3.

        „   „   „   „   III. 45 ; iv. 3. 24.

    greatness in, cannot be taught or acquired, III. 47 ; iv. 3. 27.

      „   is a gift, III. 151 ; iv. 10. 22.

Art, *continued :*

 high, meaning of the term, III. 3 *seqq.* ; iv. 1. 3 *seqq.*

  „ and low, how distinguished, III. 28 *seqq.* ; iv. 3. 3 *seqq.*

  „ modern ideal of, III. 70–1 ; iv. 5. 7.

 highest, appeals to the mind, not the senses only, I. 48
     seqq. ; ii. 1. 1. 3 *seqq.*

  „ „ to the few only, I. 49 ; ii. 1. 1. 6.

  „ purely imaginative, III. 44 ; iv. 3. 22.

  „ sympathy the basis of, IV. 10 ; v. 1. 12.

 historical and imaginative, III. 43–4 ; iv. 3. 21 *seqq.*

  „   „ III. 98–9 ; iv. 7. 21.

  „ poetical, IV. 16 ; v. 2. 2.

 history of, in England, France, and Italy, IV. 380–81 ; v.
  20. 23–4.

 ideality of, II. 116–17 ; iii. 1. 13. 13.

 imaginative and topographical, IV. 17–18 ; v. 2. 4 *seqq.*

 imitative, perfection of, described, III. 22–3 ; iv. 2. 7.

  „ symbolic and, III. 215 ; iv. 14. 19.

  „ time of early, III. 215 ; iv. 14. 19.

 infinity, a test of truth in, I. 254 ; ii. 3. 3. 22.

 invention, essential to, V. 177 ; viii. 1. 10.

 knowledge and feeling as tests of, IV. 233 *n* ; v. 15. 29 *n.*

 language, art a kind of, I. 8 ; i. 1. 2. 2.

 laws or rules of, exist, III. vi ; *pref.* 2.

  „ the safeguard of the unimaginative, II. 166 ; iii. 2.
    2. 12.

 love of, the only effective patronage, II. 3 ; iii. 1. 1. 2.

 luxury supports, IV. 378 ; iv. 20. 19.

 man in relation to, V. 225 *seqq.* ; ix. 2. 1 *seqq.*

 minuteness of, V. 195 ; viii. 3. 2.

 modern, advance of, 1848–83, II. 246 ; Add. 6. '83 *n*
  (om. ed. 1).

  „ developments of, III. xv. ; *pref.* 6.

  „ ignorance of, *temp.* Scott, III. 282 ; iv. 16. 33.

  „ indistinctness of subjects and treatment, IV. 319 ;
    v. 18. 1.

 moral influence of, too little realized in history, I. xxiii ;
  pref. ed. 2. 14.

 morality of, II. 144 ; iii. 1. 15. 5.

  „ III. 45 ; iv. 3. 24.

 mountain influence on, IV. 378 ; v. 20. 19.

 mysterious or indistinct, IV. 58 *seqq.* ; v. 4. 1 *seqq.*

B

Art, *continued :*

    national decline (sensuality) and, III. 71 ; iv. 5. 7.

         „   „   and neglect of art, II. 144 ; iii. 1. 15. 5.

         „   pursuit of arts, its effect, V. 363 ; ix. 11. 25.

    naturalist, its denial of man's spirit, V. 226 ; ix. 2. 4.

    neglect of works of, II. 6–8 *n* ; iii. 1. 1. 7.

    noble, according to artist's aim, III. 24–5 ; iv. 2. 8.

    perfection of, I. 378–79 ; ii. 5. 3. 4.

    pleasure in, its sources, III. 1 ; iv. 1. 1.

    popularity greatest of what kind of art, I. 49 ; ii. 1. 1. 5–6.

    position of true, lofty, II. 2–3 ; iii. 1. 1. 2.

    production of good, possible to every age, I. xv ; *pref. ed.* 2. 6.

    profane, III. 71 ; iv. 5. 7.

    realization, all art is, II. 208 ; iii. 2. 4. 3.

         „   its growth, III. 51 *seqq.* ; iv. 4. 7 *seqq.*

    religion and, inverse ratio of technique and devotion, I. xxiii ; *pref. ed.* 2. 14.

         „   and, inverse ratio of technique and devotion, III. 334 ; iv. 18. 14.

         „   misuse of art in (Bible pictures), III. 63–4 ; iv. 4. 23.

    sacred, its general influence, III. 48 *seqq.* ; iv. 4. 1 *seqq.*

         „   „   „   III. 60–1 ; iv. 4. 19.

    service of, to man, V. 172 ; viii. 1. 1.

    size in, sometimes a sign of baseness, V. 196 ; viii. 3. 3.

    students, aim at clearness, IV. 70 ; v. 4. 16.

         „   „   „   IV. 83 ; v. 5. 20.

         „   general advice to, "selecting nothing, etc.," V. 199 ; viii. 3. 8.

    style in, its meaning, I. 101 ; ii. 1. 7. 20.   *See s. Style.*

    subjects not attainable by, II. 208 ; iii. 2. 4. 3.

         „   recommended, IV. 19–20 ; v. 2. 6.

         „   reference to man compulsory in all, V. 226 ; ix. 2. 3.

    success in, how found, V. 199 ; viii. 3. 8.

    talk of, and ignorance of nature, I. 59 ; ii. 1. 2. 7.

         „   vanity of modern, II. 2 ; iii. 1. 2 ('83 *n*).

    transcendental, its use questioned, V. 372 ; ix. 12. 1.

    truth, a sign of beauty in, I. 51 ; ii. 1. 1. 9.

         „   a test of greatness and thought in, I. 52 ; ii. 1. 1. 10.

         „   does a work of art add to recorded truth ? a test, I. 85 ; ii. 1. 7. 8 (om. ed. 1, 2).

Art, *continued*:

    usefulness of, II. 3–4 ; iii. 1. 1. 3 *seqq.*

       „   „   III. 21–2 ; iv. 2. 6.

Art Journal, Sept. 1, 1854, criticism of "Modern Painters,"
    III. 137 *n* ; iv. 10. 5 *n.*

—— Union, engraving, I. 129 ; ii. 1. 7. 36 (om. ed. 1, 2).

   „   „   "Pilgrim's Progress," Christian and Apollyon, en-
    graving of ideal stones, IV. 325 ; v. 18. 10.

Artichoke, leaf of, V. 64 ; vi. 7. 14.

Artists * [Synopsis. **I.** xxiv–v, xxxi, xxxvii–viii *n*, xlvi–vii, 8–10,
    12, 48, 62, 68–70, 78, 89, 124 *n*, 130–32, 139 *n*, 229,
    325, 335, 347, 360, 447–50. **II.** 3, 46, 116, 166, 184
    seqq., 222. **III.** 24, 30–1, 46, 98, 104, 149. **IV.** 9–15,
    16–17, 48, 73–4, 197–98, 389, 413–14. **V.** 199, 202,
    209–15, 221, 225–26] :—

    aim of, to produce a connected series of works, I. xlvi ; *pref.
    ed.* 2. 40.

   „   truth and deception, I. 78 ; ii. 1. 7. 1.

   „   true aim of, I. 448 *seqq.* ; ii. 6. 3. 22 *seqq.*

* Foreign Schools :—Albano, Angelico, Apelles, Arnolfo, Backhuysen,
Bandinelli, Bartolomeo, Basaiti, Bassano, Bellini, Berghem, Bonifazio,
Bosch, Both, Botticelli, Bronzino, Canaletto, Canova, Caracci, Caravaggio,
Castagna, Catena, Carpaccio, Cellini, Cima da Conegliano, Cimabue,
Claude, Correggio, Cuyp, Da Vinci, De Hooghe, Denner, Dolci, Domeni-
chino, Dow, Dürer, Dutch School, Fabriano, Fischer, Francia, Gaddi,
Ghiberti, Ghirlandajo, Giorgione, Giotto, Giulio Romano, Gozzoli, Greuze,
Guardi, Guercino, Guido, Hobbima, Holbein, Jan Steen, Laurati, Lippi,
Lombardo, Loutherbourg, Luca della Robbia, Luini, Mantegna, Masaccio,
Memling, Memmi, Michael Angelo, Mino da Fiesole, Murillo, Orcagna,
Overbeck, Palma, Perugino, Pesellino, Phidias, Pinturicchio, Pisano,
Pisellino, Potter, Poussin (N. and G.), Praxiteles, Procaccini, Raphael,
Rembrandt, Rethel, Rosselli, Rubens, Ruysdael, Salvator, Schon-
gauer, Snyders, Solazzino, Spagnoletto, Tempesta, Teniers, Tintoret,
Titian, Uccello, Vandevelde, Vandyck, Van Eyck, Velasquez, Vernet (H.),
Veronese, Verrocchio, Volterra, Wouvermans, Zeuxis, Zuccaro.

English Schools :—Barret, Barry, Bennet, Blacklock, Blake, Brett,
Callcott, Cattermole, Collins, Constable, Cox, Creswick, Cruikshank,
Davidson, Dawson, De Wint, Dighton, Drummond, Etty, Fielding, Flax-
man, Fuseli, Gainsborough, Girtin, Goodall, Haghe, Harding, Haydon,
Hook, Hunt (H.), Hunt (W.), James, Landseer, Lauder, Lawrence,
Lee, Leech, Leighton, Leslie, Lewis, Linnell, Mackenzie, Maclise, Martin,
Millais, Morland, Mulready, Nash, Nesfield, Palmer, Pickersgill, Pre-
Raphaelites, Prout, Pyne, Reynolds, Richmond, Roberts, Robson, Romney,
Rossetti, Severn (J.), Stanfield, Stothard, Tayler, Turner (J. M. W.),
Turner (W.), Uwins, Varley, Wallis, Watts, Webster, Wilkie, Wilson.

Artists, *continued :*

aim of young, truth alone, I. 447–48 ; ii. 6. 3. 20.

architects and painters, artists to be both, I. 124 *n* ; ii. 1
  7. 34 *n* (om. ed. 1, 2).

aspects, the science of, IV. 413–14 ; App. ii. 1.

backgrounds as tests of power, II. 45 ; iii. 1. 5. 6.

calmness, essential to, V. 213–14 ; viii. 4. 20. 21.

classes of, mainly two, I. 78 ; ii. 1. 7. 1.

duty of, to be preachers, I. xlvii–viii ; *pref. ed.* 2. 42.

   „ to interpret nature, I. 69–70 ; ii. 1. 4. 4.

   „   „   „ III. 149 ; iv. 10. 19.

"effects" of, I. 229 ; ii. 3. 2. 1.

facility and indecision, I. xxxi ; *pref. ed.* 2. 24.

   „ and number of works, I. 448–9 ; ii. 6. 3. 22.

foresight in composition of great, V. 202 ; viii. 4. 4.

   „   „   „ V. 209–10 ; viii. 4. 15–16.

grasp of subject by, V. 213 ; viii. 4. 20.

great, as their aim is great, III. 24 ; iv. 2. 8.

   „ according to choice of subject, III. 29–30 ; iv. 3. 5.

   „ are painter-poets, I. 9 ; i. 1. 2. 3.

   „ forget themselves in their subjects, I. 89; ii. 1. 7. 10.

   „   „   „ and are forgotten, I. 325 ; ii. 4.
                  3. 26.

   „ mere painters are only "writing-masters," I. 11 ; i.
          1. 2. 6.

   „ symbolism loved by, III 104 ; iv. 8. 6.

   „ sympathy of, IV. 9–13 ; v. 1. 12. 13.

   „   „   „ IV. 14–15 ; v. 1. 16.

   „   „   „ V. 221 ; ix. 1. 9.

   „   „   „ V. 225–26 ; ix. 2. 1. 2. *See below, s.
                subjects.*

greatest, they who give most greatest ideas, I. 12 ; i. 1. 2. 9.

   „ the noblest thinkers, V. 199 ; viii. 3. 7. *See s. Art.*

greatness, no one combines all its elements, III. 46 ; iv. 3. 26.

ideal of, in striking essence of anything, II. 116–17 ; iii. 1.
  13. 13.

imaginative and unimaginative, II. 166 ; iii. 2. 2. 12.

knowledge of, of what it should be, I. xxxvi–viii *n* ; *pref.
  ed.* 2. 30. 33.

   „   „ technical and intellectual, I. 8 ; i. 1. 2. 1.

   „   „ water-painting, as illustrative, I. 358 ; ii. 5. 1.
         16 (om. ed. 1, 2).

Artists, *continued:*

    license of great, I. 358 ; ii. 5. 1. 16 (om. ed. 1, 2).

    masters and novices distinguished, I. 336 ; ii. 4. 4. 15.

    method of all true, straightforward, V. 210 ; viii. 4. 16.

    qualities needed by, and fatal to, V. 213–15 ; viii. 4. 20–3.

    right mind for an, II. 3 ; iii. 1. 1. 2 ('83 note).

    scenery and its influence on, IV. 73–4 ; v. 5. 5–6.

    See s. Dürer, Giorgione, Titian, Turner (home and surroundings).

    self-control essential to, V. 213–14 ; viii. 4. 20.

    selfishness and vanity fatal to, V. 213–14 ; viii. 4. 20–1.

    sight, keenness of, IV. 197–98 ; v. 14. 18.

    subjects, choice of, I. xlvi ; *pref. ed.* 2. 40. *See s. Choice.*

    „   „   beauty and character, I. 48 ; ii. 1. 1. 2.

    „   „   compared to hospitality, IV. 48 ; v. 3. 17.

    „   religious, by different artists, II. 186 *seqq.*; iii. 2.
                   3. 16 *seqq.*

    „   „   landscape in, II. 231 *seqq.*; iii. 2. 5. 9 *seqq.*

    „   to be various, not to repeat themselves, I. 70 ; ii.
                   1. 4. 4.

    „   „   „   as they are apt to do, I. 449 ; ii. 6.
                   3. 22.

    „   „ emphasize the most important and *vice versâ*,
                   I. 62 ; ii. 1 3. 1.

    „   „ give nature's constant truths, not her rare
                   violations of truth, I. 68 ; ii. 1. 4. 1.

    „   „   „ nature's moments of highest beauty, I. 68 ;
                   ii. 1. 4. 1.

    „   „ make artist and spectator self-forgetful, 1.
                   xxiv–v ; *pref. ed.* 2. 16.

    „   „ paint what they see, I. 347–48 ; ii. 5. 1. 4 (om.
                   ed. 1, 2).

    „   „   „   „   IV. 16–17 ; v. 2. 2. 3.

    „   „   „   „   contentedly, IV. 389 ; v.
                   20. 32.

    „   „   „   „   in their own age I. 130–2 ;
                   and country, ii. 1. 7. 37.

                            I. 139 *n*; ii.
    „   „   „   „   „   „   I. 7. 42 *n*
                          (om.ed.1,2).

    „   „   „   „   „   „   III. 98 ; iv.
                   7. 19.

Artists, *continued*:

  unconscious, may be so of the laws he works by, III. 93–4 ;
      iv. 7. 12.
Arve, plain of (Sallenches), I. 289 ; ii. 4. 1. 5.
  „   valley of the, IV. 260 ; v. 16. 26.
  „   „   débris in, IV. 297 ; v. 17. 28.
Arveron, source of the, IV. 214 ; v. 15. 11.
Asceticism, effect on the body of, II. 123–24 ; iii. 1. 14. 7.
  „   IV. 373 ; v. 20. 12.
  „   errors of, V. 225–26 ; ix. 2. 2.
  „   forms of (religious, military, monetary), V. 357–59 ;
             ix. 11. 17–18.
Ash, leaf of mountain-, V. 25 ; vi. 4. 6.
Aspects, a science of, as of essences, III. 325–26 ; iv. 17. 43.
Aspen, forms of, V. 29 ; vi. 4. 8.
  „   renderings of, IV. 79 *seqq.* ; v. 5. 16 *seqq.* (pl. 27–8).
          See s. Homer.
Asphalt colourists, III. 250 ; iv. 15. 11.
Assaissement, geological, IV. 223 *n* ; v. 15. 17 *n.*
Assertion, its growth in art, III. 51 ; iv. 4. 8.
Assisi, IV. 373 ; v. 20. 12.   *See s. Giotto.*
Association [SYNOPSIS. II. 36–9, 49, 160. III. 19, 307, 310, 329] :—
  charm of, peculiarly modern and European, III. 310 ; iv.
      17. 21.
  „   Turner influenced by, III. 329 ; iv. 18. 7.
  of ideas, accidental and rational, II. 36 *seqq.* ; iii. 1. 4. 8 *seqq.*
  „   beauty independent of, II. 35 ; iii. 1. 4. 7.
  „   conscience gains force from, II. 37–8 ; iii. 1. 4. 10.
  „   enjoyment of landscape and, III. 307 ; iv. 17. 14.
  „   power of, II. 49 ; iii. 1. 5. 13.
  „   „   III. 19 ; iv. 2. 2.
  „   „   V. 241 ; ix. 3. 6.
  „   unconscious, II. 36–7 ; iii. 1. 4. 9.
  „   value to the artist of, II. 160 ; iii. 2. 2. 5.
Atheism, modern, III. 158 ; iv. 11. 9.
  „   of large cities, IV. 355 ; v. 19. 24.   *See s. Infidelity.*
Athene, Pallas, Greek idea of, III. 180 ; iv. 13. 5.
  „   „   Mars' contest with, III. 182 ; iv. 13. 7.
  „   „   shield and Gorgon of, V. 242 ; ix. 3. 8.
Athenæum, art criticism of the, I. xlix ; *pref. ed.* 2. 46.
  „   (Feb. 10, 1844) on generalization in art, I. xxxiv ;
          pref. ed. 2. 27.

Athens, mountains from, IV. 372 ; v. 20. 11.

Athleticism, natural and forced, II. 120–21 ; iii. 1. 14. 3.

    ,,   to be made serviceable, V. 360–61 ; ix. 11. 22.

Atlas, Hesperides the daughters of, V. 330 ; ix. 10. 4.

    ,,   V. 387 ; ix. 12. 20.

Atmosphere, perfect clearness of, rare everywhere, IV. 71–2 ;
    v. 5. 2.

    ,   effects of, in modern landscape, III. 264 *seqq.* ;
    iv. 16. 2 *seqq.*

Atrides, ivory skin of, III. 158 ; iv. 11. 9.

    ,,   strong and gentle, V. 289 ; ix. 7. 5.

Attention, all God asks of us, V. 166 ; vii. 4. 25.

Aucuba, stem of the, V. 19 ; vi. 3. 12.

    ,,   ,,   V. 32 ; vi. 4. 11.

Aurora borealis, II. 36 ; iii. 1. 4. 8 ('83 *n*).

Austrian generals in Italy, V. 357–58 ; ix. 11. 17.

Authority, great art and, V. 194 ; viii. 2. 15.

Author :—

    [SYNOPSIS. I., II., III. I. i, 26, 94, 96, 165, 205, 351, 354, 365,
      367. II. '83 *pref.*, §§ 3, 6, 8, 9 ; p. 24, 27, 29, 43, 49, 61, 66,
      73, 76, 84, 88, 92, 120, 242, 246, '83 Epil. §§ 1, 3, 4, 6, 7, 8,
      10, 12, 13, 14. III. vi–viii, x, xi, xii, xiii, xv–xvi, 62, 66, 94,
      96, 243, 268–69, 307–10, 321–22, 334–35, 341 *n*, 359–60. IV.
      vii, 10 *n*, 59–60, 142, 181 *n*, 190 *n*, 197, 201, 219 *n*, 236–38, 299 *n*,
      365, 377, 398–99, 420 *n*, 422. V. v, vii, ix, x, xi, 87, 105, 111 *n*,
      115, 121, 144 *n*, 162, 173, 199, 220, 230–32, 298 *n*, 311, 356–57,
      366 *n*, 372, 385] :—

    I. Personal, Character, Life, etc. II. His Work and
        Teaching. III. Miscellaneous. IV. His Books—
        (a) Their Style : (b) Quoted or referred to.

    I. Personal.

        as a child, at the sea, II. 43 ; iii. 1. 5. 3.

        Bible-training of, II. '83 Epil. 7.

        birthday dinner-party, II. '83 Epil. 14.

        born in London, earliest years, III. 307–8 ; iv. 17. 14.

        earliest recollection, Friar's Crag, etc., III. 307 ;
          iv. 17. 13.

        father's wine business, II. 25 ; iii. 1. 36 ('83 *n*).

        his character, II. '83 ; *pref.* 9.

        imaginative power decreased, 1846–83, II. 60 ; iii. 1.
          6. 8 ('83 *n*).

Author, *continued :*

    love of mountains and nature, III. 307 ; iv. **17.** 13 *seqq.*

    ,,   ,,   IV. 365 ; v. 20. 1.

    modesty of, II. 27 ; iii. 1. 3. 11 ('83 *n*).

    not inventive, III. 96 ; iv. 7. 16 (F.A. *n*).

    ,,   ,,   III. 308 ; iv. **17.** 17.

    religious feelings :

        as a child, III. 308 ; iv. **17.** 16.

        early life, V. 164 ; vii. 4. 22 (F.A. *n*).

        evangelical education, II. 29 ; iii. 1. 3. 13 ('83 *n*).

        ,,   outburst instanced, II. 120 ; iii. 1. 14. 2.

        faith, 1845, II. '83 Epil. 7.

        liberal, III. 242 ; iv. 14. 53.

        on Protestantism and Rome, III. 268-70 ; iv. 16. 20.

his health, delicate, 1841, II. '83 Epil. 1.

his movements

    1840. Rome, crossing the Campagna, I. 165 ; ii. 2. 2. 2.

    ,,   ,,   II. 73 ; iii. 1. 7. 5 ('83 *n*).

    ,,   ,,   V. ix ; *pref.* 7.

    1842. Switzerland, II. '83 Epil. 3, 4.

        Bruges, I. 26 ; i. 1. 5. 5.

    1844. Switzerland, II. '83 Epil. 3, 4.

    1845. Florence, II. '83 Epil. 10.

        Geneva (diary on Rhone), I. 354 ; ii. 5. 1. 10 (om. ed. 1, 2).

        Venice, I. 351 ; ii. 5. 1. 7 (om. ed. 1, 2).

    ,,   Lucca, II '83 Epil. 6.

    ,,   Pisa, *ib.*; *ib.* 6-7.

    1847. Scotland, II. 246 ; Add. 8 (om. ed. 1).

    1849. Switzerland

    ,,   Cascade des Pélerins } IV. 299 *n* ; v. 17. 30 *n*.

    1850. Venice, IV. 347 ; v. 19. 14.

    1851. Matlock (diary), V. 230-31 ; ix. 2. 12.

    1853. Edinburgh, IV. 423 ; App. iii. 2.

    1856. Denmark Hill, III. xiii ; *pref.* 6.

    ,,   ,,   ,,   IV. vii ; *pref.* 4.

    1856-60. Various, V. v ; *pref.* 1.

    1858. Germany (studying Titian), V. vii-viii ; *pref.* 4.

    ,,   Turin, V. vii ; *pref.* 4.

    ,,   Rheinfels (Basle), V. 367 *n* ; ix. 11. 30 *n*.

    1874. Rome, II. '83 Epil. 13.

    1882. Pisa, II. 76 ; iii. 1. 7. 7 ('83 *n*).

    ,,   ,,   II. 88 ; iii. 1. 10. 3 ('83 *n*).

    1883. Oxford (re-acceptance of chair), II. '83 Epil. 12.

    1888. Chamouni, V. '88 Epil.

Author : books of, *continued :*

"Pre-Raphaelitism," on Turner's Highland drawings, III. 251 ; iv. 15. 12.

,,   ,,   ,,   ,,   recollection of early impressions, IV. 30 ; v. 2. 18.

,,   ,,   ,,   ,,   Yorkshire hills, IV. 259 ; v. 16. 25.

"Proserpina," II. 110, 113 ; iii. 1. 13. 3. 8 ('83 *n*).

"Queen of the Air," II. 238 ; iii. 2. 5. 20 ('83 *n*).

"Sesame and Lilies," "Mystery of Life," II. 73 ; iii. 1. 7. 5 ('83 *n*).

"Seven Lamps," II. 10 *n* ; iii. 1. 1. 9 *n* ('83 Add.).

,,   ,,   "Lamp of Memory," II. 37 ; iii. 1. 4. 9 ('83 *n*).

,,   ,,   great art is of things seen, III. 86–7 ; iv. 7. 5.

,,   ,,   Chap. IV., § 3, III. 233 ; iv. 14. 41.

,,   ,,   ,,   § 9, V. 298 *n* ; ix. 7. 21 *n*.

,,   ,,   on desire for greatness, V. 196 ; viii. 3. 3.

"Stones of Venice," II. 11 *n* ; iii. 1. 1. 9 *n* ('83 Add.).

,,   ,,   its connection with "Modern Painters," III. 100 ; iv. 8. 1.

referred to, Vol. I. 1. 14 . . . I. 92 *n* ; ii. 1. 7. 12 *n* (om. ed. 1–4).

,,   19. 14 . . . II. '83 Epil. 5 *n*.

,,   20. 15–16 . . III. 233 ; iv. 14. 41.

,,   ,, 19 (pl. 7) . IV. 195 ; v. 14. 16.

,,   23. 5 . . . I. 121 *n* ; ii. 1. 7. 32 *n* (om. ed. 1–4).

Author : books of, " Stones of Venice," referred to, *continued* :

         Vol. I. 27. 33 (pl. 17) . . V. 53 ; vi. 6. 12.

         „   30. 5 . . . . . I. 51 *n* ; ii. 1. 1.
                            7 *n* (Add. ed.
                            5).

         „   App. xi . . . . I. 92 *n* ; ii. 1. 7.
                            12 *n* (om. ed.
                            1–4).

         „   „   . . . . I. 130 *n* ; ii. 1. 7.
                            37 *n*. (om. ed.
                            1–4).

         „   App. xvii . . . I. 15 *n* ; i. 1. 3. 2
                            n (om. ed. 1–4).

         Vol. II. 5, 30–34 (sanctity of colour), III. 233 ;
                            iv. 14. 42.

         „   „   „   „   IV. 53 ;
                            v. 3. 23.

         „   6 (Nature of Gothic) III. 77 ; iv. 6. 2.

         „   „   „   III. 292 ; iv. 16. 43.

         „   „ 51 (on evil) . III. ix ; *pref.* 4.

         Vol. III. 1. 9 (on curves) IV. 284 ; v. 17. 10.

         „   1–2 (Renaissance) IV. 392 ; v. 20. 34.

         „   3 (grotesque Renaissance) III. 100–
                            2 ; iv. 8. 1–4.

         „   3, 74 . . . . . IV. 408 ; App. i. 3.

         „   4. 3 *seqq.* . . . V. 299 *n* ; ix. 7. 21 *n*.

         „   „ 7–21 . . . . III. 45 *n* ; IV. 3. 24 *n*.

         „   „ 21 . . . . . III. 148 *n* ; iv. 10. 18 *n*.

Turner Notes, 1857, V. 328 *n* ; ix. 10. 1 *n*.

   „   „   „   „ 363 *n* ; ix. 11. 26 *n*.

   „   „   1858, „ 328 *n* ; ix. 10. 1 *n*.

   „   „   1878 (Splugen), II. '83 Epil. 3.

   „   „   „ (" Modern Painters " quoted), V. 359 *seqq.* ; ix. 11. 18 *seqq.*

Authors, imaginative and the reverse, II. 178 ; iii. 2. 3. 6 ('83 *n*).

Autumn pensiveness, V. 85 ; vi. 8. 20.

Avignon, III. 299 ; iv. 17. 4.

Avon, Shakspeare and mountain-influence, IV. 382, 385 ; v. 20.
  25. 29.
Awe, fear distinct from, II. 135–36 ; iii. 1. 14. 26.

Backgrounds, light and dark, their value, II. 45 ; iii. 1. 5. 6.
Backhuysen's clouds, I. 235 ; ii. 3. 3. 19 (ed. 1 only).
  „   libels on the sea, I. 348–49 ; ii. 5. 1. 4–5 (om. ed.
          1, 2).
  „   seas of, I. 365 ; ii. 5. 1. 21.
  „   work of (Dulwich Gallery, 75), I. 235 ; ii. 3. 3. 19
          (ed. 1 only).
Bacon [SYNOPSIS. II. 140. III. 296, 302, 314, 326, 357. IV. 383–84,
  396. V. 158, 194]:—
  anecdote of, his reply as a child to the Queen, IV. 383–84 ;
          v. 20. 27.
  „   „   „   „   „   IV. 396 ; v.
                                                20. 38.
  character and breeding of (compared with Pascal's), IV.
          383–84 ; v. 20. 27.
  „   „   his servility, III. 314 ; iv. 17. 27.
  first philosopher of material nature, III. 296 ; iv. 16. 45.
  study and love of nature by, III. 302 ; iv. 17. 7.
  to be studied, III. 357 ; App. 2.
  Turner gives aspects, Bacon essences, III. 325–26 ; iv.
          17. 43.
  works of :

          "Advancement of Learning," V. 158 ; vii. 4. 12.
          "do it by a kind of felicity," V. 194 ; viii. 2. 15.
          on ideal beauty, II. 140 ; iii. 1. 14. 32.

Bad men, of use in rousing indignation, III. 279 ; iv. 16. 28.
Balaam, avarice of, II. 147 ; iii. 1. 15. 8.
Balaclava. See s. Crimea.
Balance, true and false, mediæval and modern, III. 210 ; iv.
  14. 12.
Ball, girl burnt to death at a. See s. De la Vigne.
Ballad, "Blythe, Blythe, Blythe," V. 297 ; ix. 7. 19.
  „   "Twa Corbies," III. 262 ; iv. 15. 21.
Balzac, absence of religion in, III. 269 ; iv. 16. 10.
  „   characteristics of, III. 276 ; iv. 16. 23 and F.A. n.
  „   finish of, affected, III. 277 ; iv. 16. 26.

Bandinelli [SYNOPSIS. I. 442. II. 112 *n*, 132, 198] :—
    I. 442 ; ii. 6. 3. 9.
    size of ideals, II. 112 ; iii. 1. 13. 6 ('83 *n*).
    want of imagination (his Hercules and Cacus), II. 198 ; iii
        2. 3. 27.
    works of :

          Christ, vulgar, II. 132 ; iii. 1. 14. 20.
          statue, St. Croce, Florence, II. 198 ; iii. 2. 3. 27.

Banks, author's use of the term, IV. 305 ; v. 17. 37.
     ,,   earth-, miniature mountains, I. 334–35 ; ii. 4. 4. 11–12.
     ,,   formation of, IV. 277 ; v. 17. 1.
     ,,   mountain and hill side, IV. 291 *seqq.* ; v. 17. 21.
     ,,   vegetation of, luxuriant, IV. 132 ; v. 10. 5.
Barret, George, fine light and tone of, I. 163 *n* ; ii. 2. 1. 21 *n*.
     ,,   ,,   foliage and twilight of, I. 439 ; ii. 6. 3. 3.
     ,,   ,,   ,,   ,,   I. 448 ; ii. 6. 3. 22.
     ,,   ,,   praise of, IV. 79 ; v. 5. 15.
Barry, huge works of, V. 196 ; viii. 3. 3.
     ,,   quoted, on chiaroscuro, I. 191 ; ii. 2. 3. 9.
     ,,   ,,   ,,   formation of judgment, I. 4 ; i. 1. 1. 2.
     ,,   ,,   ,,   want of truth in early art, I. 58 ; ii. 1. 2. 6.
Bartolomeo, Fra [SYNOPSIS. I. 163, 189. II. 2 *n*, 129, 236, 239, Epil
        5. 6] :—
    holy feeling and light of, I. 163 ; ii. 2. 1. 22.
    no original power in, II. '83 Epil. 6.
    not popular, and why, I. 2 *n* ; i. 1. 1 *n* (ed. 1, 2 only).
    works of :

          Angels (Lucca), II. 236 ; iii. 2. 5. 17.
          Last Judgment (Florence, Ospedaletto), II. 195 ; iii. 2. 3. 23
          Magdalen (Lucca), II. '83 Epil. 5. 6.
          portraiture of Savonarola, II. 129 ; iii. 1. 14. 14.
          St. Stephen, II. 239 ; iii. 2. 5. 21.

Basaiti, Marco, all religious works, V. 246 ; ix. 3. 17.
     ,,   ,,   work (Venice Acad.), its golden sky, I. 89 ; ii. 1
        7. 11 (om. ed. 1, 2).
Bassano, cattle-pieces of, V. 285–86 ; ix. 6. 23.
     ,,   colour without form (jewels), II. 216 ; iii. 2. 4. 10.
     ,,   ,,   ,,   ,,   V. 350 ; ix. 11. 8 *n*.
Battle, god of, Greek idea, II. 238 ; iii. 2. 5. 20.
Baxter, R., quoted on truth, I. xix ; *pref. ed.* 2. 12.

Beaumont, Sir G., "Where do you put your brown tree?" I. xliv *n* ; *pref. ed.* 2. 39 *n*.

Beauty [SYNOPSIS. I. xxxiii *n* 14, 25–7, 45–6, 51, 55, 441. II. '83 *pref.* 4, 13, 18–21 *seqq.*, 29–33, 35, 39–42, 49–50, 67, 73, 90, 94–7, 100, 104–7, 108 *seqq.*, 116, 123, 142–44, 145, 148. III. 1, 26–7, 35 *n*, 37–8, 66, 73–4, 158–59, 208–9, 270–71, 302 *seqq.*, 325. IV. 138–39, 202, 277 *seqq.*, 348–49, 356–57. V. 59, 81–3, 232, 357]:—

   absolute or the result of custom ? II. 33 ; iii. 1. 4. 3.   *See s.*
                                  Custom.
       „   „   „   III. 26–7 ; iv. 3. 1. 2.
   association of ideas not the basis of, II. 35 ; iii. 1. 4. 7.
   Christian and pagan sense of, compared, II. 19 ; iii. 1. 2. 9. 10.
   contrast essential to, III. 37–8 ; iv. 3. 14.
   definition of, I. 29–30 ; i. 1. 6. 1.
      „   „   II. '83 *pref.* 4.
      „   „   is not truth, II. 32 ; iii. 1. 4. 1.
      „   „   or usefulness, II. 33 ; iii. 1. 4. 2.
   different degrees of, necessary and serviceable, II. 94 ; iii. 1. 11. 2.
   differently seen by different persons, II. 39–40 ; iii. 1. 4. 12.
   division into typical and vital, II. 31 ; iii. 1. 3. 16.
   enjoyment of, destroyed by satiety, IV. 138–39 ; v. 11. 7.
   everything (even an ugly thing) has some, III. 38 ; iv. 3. 15.
   expression (moral) and, II. 104–5 ; iii. 1. 12. 10.
   faces gain beauty by virtue, II. 123 ; iii. 1. 14. 6.
     „   real and ideal beauty of, III. 73–4 ; iv. 5. 11.
   false ideas about, II. 32 *seqq.*; iii. 1. 4. 1. *seqq.*
   form and, curves essential, II. 65 ; iii. 1. 6. 12.
     „   IV. 277 *seqq.*; v. 17. 3 *seqq. See s. Form.*
   fulfilment of function as basis of, II. 108 *seqq.* ; iii. 1. 13. 1 *seqq.*
     „   „   „   „   II. 116 ; iii. 1. 13. 12.
   God's gift to man, not a necessity, II. 17 ; iii. 1. 2. 6.
     „   seal on His works, II. 39 ; iii. 1. 4. 12.
   happiness and, go together, II. 97 ; iii. 1. 12. 1.
   ideal, its meaning, I. 31 ; i. 1. 6. 6.
   ideas of, I. 14 ; i. 1. 3. 1.
     „   I. 29 *seqq.* ; i. 1. 6. 1 *seqq.*

Beauty, *continued :*

 ideas of, object of their study, I. 46 ; i. 2. 3. 6.

  „ instinctive, II. 49 ; iii. 1. 5. 14.

  „   „ III. 1–2 ; iv. 1. 1.

 indifference to. *See below, s. modern.*

 intellectual, meaning of, I. 30 ; i. 1. 6. 4.

 littleness of some, I. 45 ; i. 2. 3. 4.

 love of, artists ranked according to, III. 35–7 ; iv. 3.
  12 *seqq.*

  „ authors ranked according to, III. 302 *seqq.*; iv. 17.
  7 *seqq.*

  „ essential to great art, *ib.; ib.*

  „ „ „ knowledge of beauty, V. 356–7 ; ix. 11. 15.

  „ not unscientific, III. 325 ; iv. 17. 42.

 mediæval and ancient love of, III. 208–10 ; iv. 14. 11–12.

 moderation essential to, II. 90 ; iii. 1. 10. 6.

 modern disregard of manly, III. 158–59 ; iv. 11. 9.

  „ indifference to, V. 357 ; ix. 11. 15.

 moral, not sensual, II. 13 ; iii. 1. 2. 1.

  „ qualities of, II. 18–19 ; iii. 1. 2. 8. *See below, s.
  physical.*

 morality and, their connection, II. 144 ; iii. 1. 15. 5. *See s.
  Goodness.*

 nature of, *the* subject of " Modern Painters," IV. 202 ;
  v. 14. 24.

 not created by man, but a necessity of God's work, II. 94 ;
  iii. 1. 11. 2.

 perfect, how far conceivable by man, II. 143 ; iii. 1. 15. 2.

  „ existent on earth, *ib.; ib.*

  „ man not to live amid, IV. 138 ; v. 11. 7.

 physical, more perceptible than moral, III. 72–3 ; iv. 5. 8–10.

  „ nobility of, III. 73 ; iv. 5. 10. *See s. Body, Physical
  beauty, etc.*

 principles of universal, asserted to exist, I. xxxiii *n* ;
      pref. ed. 2. 26 *n.*

  „   „ demonstrable, II. 29 ; iii. 1. 3. 14.

 pursuit of, and truth, I. 51 ; ii. 1. 1. 9.

  „ reckless, III. 27 ; iv. 3. 2.

  „ vulgar, III. 73 ; iv. 5. 10. *See s. Death.*

 rarity of extreme, II. 29 ; iii. 1. 3. 13 ('83 *n*).

 repose, a test of, II. 73 ; iii. 1. 7. 5.

  „ „ II. 116 ; iii. 1. 13. 12.

Beauty, *continued* :

 ruin of, by man, V. 357 ; ix. 11. 15.

 self-sacrifice, the parent of, V. 59 ; vi. 7. 7.

 sense of, based on what, II. 107 ; iii. 1. 12. 12.

  „ deficient, in many good men, II. 148–9 ; iii. 1. 15. 9

  „ an eye for beauty, like ear for music, I. 55 ; ii. 1. 2. 3.

  „ „ „ „ „ II. 145 ; iii. 1. 15. 6.

  „ degraded, if not based on morality, II. 18–19 ; iii. 1. 2. 8–9.

  „ healthy and morbid, II. 21 *seqq.*; iii. 1. 3. 1 *seqq.*

  „ how exalted, how debased, V. 232 ; ix. 2. 13.

  „ keenest in youth, II. 42 ; iii. 1. 5. 2.

  „ no incentive to duty (Schiller), II. 148 ; iii. 1. 15. 9.

  „ rudeness of life and, IV. 356–57 ; v. 19. 26.

 sensuality and love of, connected, II. 18 ; iii. 1. 2. 8.

  „ „ consistent, IV. 348–49 ; v. 19. 17.

 sign of truth in art, I. 51 ; ii. 1. 1. 9.

 sources of, all conceivable, are visibly, II. 142 ; iii. 1. 15. 1.

  „ „ divine, II. 144 ; iii. 1. 15. 4.

 sublimity of highest, I. 45 ; i. 2. 3. 4.

 sympathy and, II. 100 ; iii. 1. 12. 5.

 trees, their fellowship and, V. 81–3 ; vi. 8. 17–18.

 truth essential to, I. 27–8 ; i. 1. 5. 6.

  „ „ I. 51 ; ii. 1. 1. 9.

  „ „ I. 441–42 ; ii. 6. 3. 7.

  „ „ but distinct in art, III. 35 *n* ; iv. 3. 12 *n.*

     See above, s. definition.

  „ sacrifice of to, III. 66 ; iv. 5. 1.

  „ „ III. 270 ; iv. 16. 12.

 typical, II. 41 *seqq.*; iii. 1. 5. 1 *seqq.*

 vital, analysed, II. 96 *seqq.*; iii. 1. chaps. 12–14.

 word, Alison's use of, vague, II. 30 ; iii. 1. 3. 15.

  „ author's use of, excludes sexual reference, II. 30 ; iii. 1. 3. 15 ('83 *n*).

    See s. Alison, Curvature, Greek, Gutter, Nature (love of), Spirals, Straight lines, Transparency, Utility.

Beauvais, Cathedral of, sunset, V. 129 ; vii. 2. 12 (pl. 66).

  „ old houses at, destroyed, II. 6 *n* ; iii. 1. 1. 7 *n.*

Beddgelert, IV. 383 ; v. 20. 27.

Belief, and knowledge, in religion, V. 276 *n* ; ix. 6. 2 *n*.

Believers, old meaning of, V. 179 ; viii. 1. 14.

Bell, Sir Charles ("Essays on Expression," "On the Hand"),
     quoted :—

   II. 64 *n* ; iii. 1. 6. 10 *n*.

   II. 69 ; iii. 1. 6. 16 ('83 *n*).

   II. 74 ; iii. 1. 7. 6. *n* (on the Laocoon).

   II. 105 ; iii. 1. 12. 10 (on the mouth).

   II. 123 ; iii. 1. 14. 4 (on facial expression).

   II. 202 *n* ; iii. 2. 3. 28 *n*.

   II. 223 ; iii. 2. 4. 19 (on the Medici Chapel).

Bellini, Gentile, architecture of, I. 90 ; ii. 1. 7. 11 (om. ed. 1, 2).

  "   "   "   "   I. 108–9 ; ii. 1. 7. 25 (om. ed. 1,2).

  "   "   "   "   I. 114 ; ii. 1. 7. 28 (om. ed. 1, 2)

  "   "   landscape of, I. 90 ; ii. 1. 7. 11 (om. ed. 1, 2).

  "   "   works of :

      Madonna (Brera, Milan), I. 90 ; ii. 1. 7. 11.

      portraits of Dandolo, II. 129 ; iii. 1. 14. 14.

      St. Mark's (Venice Academy), I. 114 ; ii. 1. 7. 2⁇
       (om. ed. 1, 2).

     "   "   "   II. 220 ; iii. 2. 4.
            14.

Bellini, Giovanni [SYNOPSIS. I. 90–1, 108, 130. II. 48, 89, 129,
     170, 230. III. 33, 56, 131. IV. 40, 59, 376–
     77, 407. V. 246] :—

  architecture of, I. 90 ; ii. 1. 7. 11 (om. ed. 1, 2).

   "   "   I. 108–9 ; ii. 1. 7. 25 (om. ed. 1, 2).

  backgrounds of, mountains, IV. 376–77 ; v. 20. 16.

  balanced powers (expressional and pictorial) of, III. 32 ;
   iv. 3. 9.

  colour purer than Titian's, I. 91 ; ii. 1. 7. 11 (om. ed.
   1, 2).

  erba della Madonna, III. 131 ; iv. 9. 18.

  expressional power, colourist, IV. 407 ; App. i. 1.

  finish of, II. 89 ; iii. 1. 10. 4.

   "   III. 131 ; iv. 9. 18.

  landscape of, I. 90 ; ii. 1. 7. 11 (om. ed. 1, 2).

   "   IV. 40 ; v. 3. 7.

   "   clear (hatred of fog), IV. 59 ; v. 4. 2.

  luminous skies of, II. 48 ; iii. 1. 5. 11.

  Madonnas of, Venetians, not Jewesses, I. 130 ; ii. 1. 7. 37
   (om. ed. 1, 2).

Bellini, Giovanni, *continued :*

pictures of, all religious, III. 56 ; iv. 4. 14.
,,   ,,   V. 246 ; ix. 3. 17.
portraiture in his works, II. 129 ; iii. 1. 14. 14.
refinement and gradation, I. 90 ; ii. 1. 7. 11 (om. ed. 1, 2).
symmetry of, II. 71 ; iii. 1. 8. 4 (ed. 1 only).
works of :

figures in the Camuccini Titian, II. 170 ; iii. 2. 2. 19.
landscape in S. Francesco della Vigna, Venice, I. 90 ; ii. 1.
    7. 11 (om. ed. 1, 2).
S. Jerome (Venice, S. Grisostomo), I. 90-1 ; ii. 1. 7. 11 (om.
    ed. 1, 2).
,,   ,,   ,,   ,,   II. 129 ; iii. 1. 14. 14.
,,   ,,   ,,   ,,   II. 230 ; iii. 2. 5. 8.

Ben Lomond, IV. 170 ; v. 13. 8.
Benedictine monastery, IV. 399 ; v. 20. 44.
Benevolence, wise purchase is the truest, V. 360 *n* ; ix. 11. 22 *n.*
Bennett, foliage of, I. 427 *n* ; ii. 6. 1. 28 *n* (om. ed. 1–4).
Benvenue, IV. 365 ; v. 20. 2 (F.A. *n*).
Beranger, smiling blasphemy of, III. 269 ; iv. 16. 10.
Bergen-op-Zoom, no poet from, IV. 383 ; v. 20. 27.
Berghem [SYNOPSIS. I. 6, 41, 42, 79, 186. III. 135. IV. 377.
        V. 75–6, 218, 305, 309]:—
author's depreciation of, I. 6 ; i. 1. 1. 4.
clouds generalized, I. 231 ; ii. 3. 3. 13 (ed. 1, 2 only).
display, too great love of, I. 42 ; i. 2. 2. 9.
landscape, hybrid, V. 218 ; ix. 1. 3.
,,   ,,   V. 305 ; ix. 8. 2.
,,   ,,   V. 309 ; ix. 8. 11.
light on drapery, III. 135 ; iv. 10. 3.
Marmontel mistaking picture by, for window, I. 79 ; ii.
    1. 7. 2.
mountains of, IV. 377 ; v. 20. 17.
shadows of, I. 186 ; ii. 2. 3. 4.
works of :

Dulwich Gallery, 132, I. 41 ; i. 2. 2. 7.
,,   ,,   I. 180 ; ii. 2. 3. 13 (ed. 1, 2 only).
,,   ,,   160 (tree-drawing), V. 75–6 ; vi. 8. 10.

Berlin, Rubens at, instance of sunlight, V. 346 *n* ; ix. 11. 3 *n.*
,, Titian's Lavinia, V. viii ; *pref.* 4.
,,   ,,   ,,   V. 100 ; vi. 10. 4.

Berlin, *continued :*
    „   wool of, better than its philosophy, V. 179 ; viii. 1. 14.
Berne, cathedral of, sky behind, V. 144 ; vii. 3. 12.
    „   country from Fribourg to, IV. 139 *seqq.* ; v. 11. 8.
    „   „   „   IV. 367 ; v. 20. 3.
    „   inventive power of people, IV. 383 ; v. 20. 27.
    „   no poet from, IV. 382 ; v. 20. 25.
    „   pines round, V. 93 ; vi. 9. 10.
Bernese Alps (Oberland), valley of the, IV. 173 ; v. 13. 9.
Bettering oneself, V. 359 ; ix. 11. 20.
Bible [SYNOPSIS. I. xl, 45, 63, 80, 86, 112, 217, 436. II. '83 *pref.*
    4–6, 18–20, 23, 27, 54–5, 71, 73 *n*, 86, 103–4, 115, 127–
    28, 130, 136, 138, 142, 144, 146–47, 150, 168, 186–87, 190–92,
    226–27. III. 21, 38, 51, 57–8 *n*, 62–4 *n*, 72 *n*, 75, 87, 103,
    115, 121, 152, 171, 174, 183, 207, 214, 230–31, 239, 240,
    242–43, 309, 317, 318, 323, 358. IV. 5, 9, 18, 54, 55, 73,
    86–7, 88 and *n*, 89, 90–4, 96, 99, 104, 126, 147, 149–50, 164,
    177, 252, 335, 346, 349, 362, 364, 374, 400–6, 424–25. V. 1,
    9, 22, 85, 105, 115, 126, 155, 158, 164–69, 175 and *n*, 181,
    195, 217, 223, 225, 233 *n*, 235, 236, 244, 245, 248, 256, 263,
    265, 266, 268, 290, 294, 295, 327, 335, 339, 343, 350–51 and *n*,
    355 *n*, 359, 375, 378, 381, 383, 384, 385, 386, 387]—(*a*)
    Generally; (*b*) *Incidents and persons in;* (*c*) *Passages
    quoted :—*

(*a*) *Generally :*
        angels appearing to Abraham, Jacob, Joshua, etc., III.
          183 ; iv. 13. 8.
        dragon, the scriptural, V. 355 ; ix. 10. 11.
        "fighting with the world," very little in it about, V.
          385 ; ix. 12. 18.
        firmament, IV. 87 ; v. 6. 5.
          „   IV. 88*n*–89 ; v. 6. 8*n*–9.
        God appearing in the clouds, IV. 88 ; v. 6. 5.
        grass, herbs, flax, etc., of what typical, III. 241–42 ;
          iv. 14. 53.
        illustrations to, unreal, III. 63 ; iv. 4. 22.
          „   „   (Brown's, 1840), *ib.* 64 *n* ; *ib.* 23 *n.*
        mountains in the, IV. 400 *seqq.* ; v. 20. 45 *seqq.*
        pathetic fallacy in, III. 169–70 ; iv. 12. 11.
          „   „   III. 173–74 ; iv. 12. 14.
        reading of, literally, as a practical guide, IV. 400 ; v.
          20. 44.

Bible : (a) *Generally, continued :*

    reading of, methods, V. 164–66 ; vii. 4. 22–5.

       ,,   V. 166–71 ; vii. 4. 26 *seqq.*

    sacred chord of colour in, IV. 54–5 ; v. 3. 24.

       ,,   ,,   ,,   V. 350–51 ; ix. 11. 8.

    story of lady's remark on, to Mr. Cameron, I. 63 ; ii. 1. 3. 3.

    teaching of, on right conduct (no doctrine), III. 318 ; iv. 17. 33.

    words in, spoken direct by God to man, their general tenor, III. 318 ; iv. 17. 33.

  (b) *Incidents and persons, etc., in :**

    Aaron's death, III. 207 ; iv. 14. 10.

       ,,   ,,   IV. 401–2 ; v. 20. 46. *See s. Trans-figuration.*

    Babylon, mystery of the great, IV. 73 ; v. 5. 4.

    Balaam (Numb. xxii.–v.), V. 381 ; ix. 12. 10.

    Christ at Emmaus, III. 21 ; iv. 2. 5.

       ,, in the mountains, III. 207 ; iv. 14. 10.

       ,, the Magdalen and, III. 21 ; iv. 2. 5.

    Creation, IV. 86 ; v. 6. 2.

    David on Gilboa, II. 147 ; iii. 1. 15. 8.

    Eldad and Medad, IV. 18 ; v. 2. 4.

    Elijah and Mt. Horeb, II. 226 ; iii. 2. 5. 2.

       ,, at Cherith, III. 207 ; iv. 14. 10.

    Fiery furnace of Dura (Dan. iii. 1. 25), II. 142 ; iii. 1. 15. 1.

    Gilgal, deadly gourds of, II. 145 ; iii. 1. 15. 6.

    Good Samaritan, V. 383 ; ix. 12. 14.

    Herod's death, V. 355 *n* ; ix. 11. 11 *n.*

    Isaac scenting Esau, II. 18 ; iii. 1. 2. 7.

    Isaiah, spasmodic, V. 268 ; ix. 5. 5.

    Israel at Sinai, III. 207 ; iv. 14. 10.

    Jehoram, death of, V. 355 *n* ; ix. 11. 11 *n.*

    Jephthah's daughter, III. 207 ; iv. 14. 10.

    Job, sum of its teaching, III. 318 ; iv. 17. 33.

       ,, spasmodic, V. 268 ; ix. 5. 5.

    Judas' death, V. 355 *n* ; ix. 11. 11 *n.*

---

* *See s.* Aaron, Adam, Balaam, Christ, Daniel, David, Ecbatana, Eden, Job, Judas, Lazarus, Moses, Noah, Psalms, Reed, Samaria, Saul, Scarlet, Septuagint, Transfiguration, Vulgate.

Bible : (b) *Incidents and persons, etc., in, continued :*

 Lazarus, II. 140 ; iii. 1. 14. 31.

 Leah and Rachel (cf. Dante), III. 230–31 ; iv. 14. 37.

 Mary's spikenard, II. 18 ; iii. 1. 2. 7.

 Moses and the burning bush, II. 226 ; iii. 2. 5. 2.

  „ at Horeb, III. 207 ; iv. 14. 10.

  „ his death on the mountains, IV. 401–3 ; v. 20.
   46–47.

 Ornan, threshing-floor of, II. 140 ; iii: 1. 14. 31.

 Proverbs of Solomon, III. 357 ; App. ii.

 Psalms, delight in the law in the, V. 165 ; vii. 4. 22.

 Rahab's scarlet thread, IV. 55 ; v. 3. 24.

 Revelation, colours of the, II. 86 ; iii. 1. 9. 9.

  „ S. John's visions of heaven, II. 142 ; iii. 1.
   15. 1.

 Saul, disobedience of, II. 147 ; iii. 1. 15. 8.

 Sermon on the Mount, its practical value, III. 358 ;
  App. ii.

 Shimei, II. 130 ; iii. 1. 14. 16.

 Sinai, IV. 400 ; v. 20. 45.

 Sodom, bread of, V. 359 ; ix. 11. 20.

 Song of Solomon, spasmodic, V. 268 ; ix. 5. 5.

 Tabernacle, its colours, IV. 54 ; v. 3. 24.

 Transfiguration, III. 207 ; iv. 14. 10.

  „ IV. 403 *seqq.*; v. 20. 47 *seqq.*

(c) *Passages quoted :*

 Gen. i. 2—"Earth without form and void," IV. 147 ; v. 12. 4.

  „ i. 2—" „ „ „ " V. 386 ; ix. 12. 19.

  „ i. 9—"Let the dry land appear," IV. 94 *seqq.*; v. 7. 1
   seqq.

  „ i. 11—"Herb yielding seed," III. 242 ; iv. 14. 53.

  „ i. 11—" „ „ „ " V. 105 ; vi. 10. 15.

  „ ii. 1—"Thus the heavens and the earth were finished,"
   IV. 91 ; v. 6. 8.

  „ ii. 10—"To water the garden," III. 214 ; iv. 14. 17.

  „ ii. 15—"To dress it and keep it," V. 1 ; vi. 1. 1.

  „ iii. 1—"Serpent more subtle," V. 295 ; ix. 7. 15.

  „ iii. 18—"Thorns also and thistles shall it bring forth,"
   V. 263 ; ix. 4. 15.

  „ iii. 19—"Dust thou art, and unto dust shalt thou return," IV. 96 ; v. 7. 3.

  „ iii. 24—"At the east . . . a flaming sword," V. 1 ;
   vi. 1. 1.

Bible : (c) *Passages quoted, continued :*

Gen. iv. 10—" Thy brother's blood crieth from the ground,"
IV. 412 ; App. i. 6.

  ,,   v. 3—"In His likeness, after His image," V. 221 *seqq.*;
ix. 1. 9 *seqq.*

  ,,   vii. 11) "Fountains of the great deep,") V. 159 ; vii.

  ,,   viii. 2) "Windows of heaven,"   )   4. 13.

  ,,   viii. 4—"Ark rests on Ararat," IV. 400 ; v. 20. 45.

  ,,   ix. 13—"I do set My bow in the clouds," IV. 92 ; v.
6. 9.

  ,,   xviii. 19—"To do judgment and justice," V. 373 ; ix.
12. 2.

  ,,   xix. 17–19—"Escape to the mountain . . . lest some
evil overtake me," IV. 400 ; v. 20. 45.

  ,,   xxii. 4—"Abraham . . . saw the place afar off," *ib.* ; *ib.*

Exod. xiii. 21, etc.—"Pillar of cloud," IV. 88 *n* ; v. 6. 5 *n.*

  ,,   xiv. 13—"Stand still and see the salvation of God,"
II. 72 ; iii. 1. 7. 4.

  ,,   xix. 18—"Sinai . . . on a smoke," IV. 149 ; v. 12. 6.

  ,,   xx. 25—"If thou lift up thy tool," III. 121 ; iv. 9. 6.

  ,,   xxiv. 1–10—Nadab and Abihu, "body of heaven in
its clearness," IV. 364 ; v. 19. 33.

  ,,   xxviii. 2—"For glory and for beauty," I. 336 ; ii. 4.
4. 15.

  ,,   xxxiii. 22—"Vision of Moses," II. '83 *pref.* 4 *n.*

Lev. xiv. 4 { "Scarlet and hyssop," IV. 54–5 ; v. 3. 24.
            { "   ,,   ,,   " V. 350–1 and *n* ; ix. 11.
                                   8 and *n.*

  ,,   xvi. 2—"The cloud upon the mercy-seat," IV. 88 *n* ;
v. 6. 5 *n.*

  ,,   xix. 36—II. '83 *pref.* 6.

Numb. x. 34—"The cloud of the Lord," IV. 88 *n* ; v. 6. 5 *n.*

  ,,   xi. 15—Moses, "let me not see my wretchedness,"
IV. 402 ; v. 20. 47.

  ,,   xv. 38—"Fringes of blue." III. 58 *n* ; iv. 4. 16 *n.*

  ,,   xxiv. 4–16—"Vision of God, falling into a trance,
but having His eyes open," II. 147 ; iii. 1.
15. 8.

Deut. xiv. 29—"Eat and be satisfied," V. 359 ; ix. 11. 20.

  ,,   xxi. 4—"Rough valley . . . neither eared nor sown,"
IV. 335 ; v. 18. 26.

  ,,   xxxii. 4—"God . . . just and right is He," V. 223 ;
ix. 1. 13.

  ,,   xxxii. 49—"Get thee up into this mountain," IV. 402 ;
v. 20. 47.

Bible : (c) *Passages quoted, continued* :

    Josh. ix. 21—"Hewers of wood, drawers of water," II. 5;
        iii. 1. 1. 5.

    Judg. v. 4—"The earth trembled," etc., IV. 88 *n* ; v. 6.
        5 *n.*

      ,,   v. 30—"Have they not sped?" (Sisera), IV. 412 ; App.
        i. 6.

    2 Sam. i. 24—"Saul who clothed you with scarlet and other
        delights," IV. 55 ; v. 3. 24.

      ,,   xii. 5, 6—"The man shall die . . . he had no pity,"
        V. 290 ; ix. 7. 6.

    1 Kings viii. 10—"The cloud filled the house of the Lord,"
        IV. 88 *n* ; v. 6. 5 *n.*

      ,,   viii. 38—"The plague of his own heart," IV. 349 ;
        v. 19. 18.

      ,,   xix. 12—"A still small voice," I. 218 ; ii. 3. 1. 3.

    2 Kings ii. 23—"Go up, thou bald head," V. 381 ; ix. 12. 10.

      ,,   v. 27—(Gehazi) "leper white as snow," IV. 55 ; v.
        3. 24.

      ,,   ix. 31—"Had Zimri peace?" V. 385 ; ix. 12. 16.

      ,,   xxiii. 18—"Let no man move his bones," III. 171 ;
        iv. 12. 11.

    Job iv. 15—(Eliphaz) "The hair of my flesh stood up," II.
        '83 *pref.* 5.

    ,,   v. 21—"Afraid of destruction when it cometh," IV. 335 ;
        v. 8. 26.

    ,,   xi. 7—"By searching find out God . . . perfection," IV.
        89 ; v. 6. 7.

    ,,   xiv. 18-19 { "Mountain falling cometh to nought," IV.
        96 *n* ; v. 7. 3 *n.*
        { "Mountain falling cometh to nought," IV.
        335 ; v. 18. 26.

    ,,   xix. 26—"Though after my skin worms destroy my
        body," I. 45 ; i. 2. 3. 2.

    ,,   xxviii. 10—"Cutteth out rivers among rocks," II. 115 ;
        iii. 1. 13. 10.

    ,,   xxxv. 8—"Hurt a man as thou art," IV. 413 ; App. i. 8.

    ,,   xxxvi. 24-7—"Remember thou magnify His work," etc.,
        V. 168 ; vii. 4. 29.

    ,,   xxxvi. 29 { "Spreadings of the clouds . . . tabernacle,"
        IV. 91 *n* ; v. 6. 8.
        { "Spreadings of the clouds . . . tabernacle,"
        V. 155 ; vii. 4. 7.

    ,,   xxxvi. 32—"With clouds He covereth the light," *ib.* ; *ib.*

    ,,   xxxvii. 6—"The great rain of His strength," V. 156 ; *ib.* 8.

Bible : *(c) Passages quoted, continued :*

Job xxxvii. 16—" The balancings of the clouds," V. 115 ; vii.
1. 3.

„ xxxvii. 16—" Wondrous work of Him which is perfect in
knowledge," *ib.* ; *ib.*

„ xxxviii.-xli.—On God in nature, III. 318 ; iv. 17. 33.

„ xxxviii. 1 ⎫ " The Lord answered Job out of the whirl-
„ xl. 6 ⎭ wind," III. 317 ; iv. 17. 32.

„ xxxviii. 33—" Knowest thou the ordinances of heaven ? "
IV. 91 *n.* ; v. 6. 8.

„ xl. 18—" His bones as pieces of brass," V. 339 ; ix. 10. 17.

„ xli. 18—" By his neesings a light doth shine," V. 339 ;
ix. 10. 17.

„ xli. 18—" His eyes are like the eyelids of the morning,"
III. 323 ; iv. 17. 40.

„ xli. 29–30 ⎧ " Laugheth at the shaking of a ⎫ V. 336 ; ix.
spear," ⎪
⎨ ⎬ 10. 13.
" Sharp stones are under him," ⎭

„ xlii. 5—" I have heard of Thee . . . mine eye seeth
Thee," II. '83 *pref.* 4–5.

Psalm viii. 1—" How excellent is Thy name," V. 169 ; vii.
4. 31.

„ viii. 53 ⎧ " There is no God," IV. 90 ; v. 6. 7.
⎨
⎩ „ „ „ " V. 378 ; ix. 12. 5.

„ xviii. 9–11—" He bowed the heavens also . . . thick
clouds of the skies," IV. 88–9 ; v. 6.
5. 6.

„ xix. 1 ⎧ " The heavens declare," V. 167 *seqq.* ; vii. 4.
⎪ 27 *seqq.*
⎨
⎪ " „ „ " V. 217 ; ix. 1. 1.
⎩

„ xix. 4—" Set a tabernacle for the sun," IV. 92 ; v. 6. 9.

„ xix. 10—" Sweeter than honey and honeycomb," V.
165 ; vii. 4. 22.

„ xxiv. 4—" Lifted up their souls unto vanity," V. 235 ;
ix. 2. 18.

„ xxvii. 1—" Of whom shall I be afraid ? " II. 136 ; iii.
1. 14. 27.

„ xxxvi. 5—" Thy faithfulness reacheth unto the clouds,"
IV. 88 ; v. 6. 5.

„ xxxvi. 6—" Thy righteousness is like great mountains," IV. 104 ; v. 7. 10.

„ xlii. 7—" Deep calleth unto deep," IV. 99 ; v. 7. 6.

„ xlviii. 2—" The city of the great King," V. 386 ; ix. 12. 20.

„ lxviii. 8—" The earth shook, the heavens also dropped,"
IV. 92 ; v. 6. 9.

Bible : (c) *Passages quoted, continued :*

Psalm lxviii. 34—"His strength is in the clouds," IV. 88 ; v. 6. 5.

,,   lxxii. 3—"The mountains shall bring peace," IV. 364 ; v. 19. 33.

,,   lxxii. 6-16—"He shall come down like rain," etc., V. 164; vii. 4. 21.

,,   lxxiv. 13—"Thou brakest the heads of the dragons," V. 335 ; ix. 10. 11. (See LXX.)

,,   lxxv. 8—"In the hand of the Lord is a cup . . . red," V. 233 *n*; ix. 2. 14 *n*.

,,   lxxvii. 17—"The clouds poured out water," IV. 88 ; v. 6. 5.

,,   xc. 10—"Yet is their strength labour and sorrow," V. 265 ; ix. 4. 18.

,,   xcii. 1 *seqq.*—"It is a good thing to give thanks," etc., III. 230 ; iv. 14. 36.

,,   xcv. 4—"The strength of the hills is His also," IV. 335 ; v. 18. 26.

,,   xcv. 5—"His hands prepared the dry land," IV. 94 ; v. 7. 1.

,,   xcvii. 2—"Clouds and darkness round about Him," IV. 88 ; v. 6. 5.

,,   civ. 3—"Who makest the clouds His chariot," IV. 89 ; v. 6. 6.

,,   cxiv. 5—"What ailed Thee, O thou sea . . . fleddest," IV. 164 ; v. 12. 23.

,,   cxix. 38—"Devoted to Thy fear," II. 136 ; iii. 1. 14. 27.

,,   cxxi. 1 { "Hills, from whence cometh my help," IV. 364 ; v. 19. 33.
{ "Hills, from whence cometh my help," IV. 400 ; v. 20. 45.

,,   cxxi. 6—"Sun shall not smite by day," V. 237 ; ix. 2. 20.

,,   cxxxix. 16—"See my substance, being yet imperfect," IV. 177 ; v. 13. 14.

,,   cxlvii. 8—"Who maketh grass to grow upon the mountains," III. 240 ; iv. 14. 51.

,,   cxlvii. 17—"He casteth forth His ice like morsels," V. 158; vii. 4. 11.

Prov. iii. 3—"Bind them about thy neck," V. 373 ; ix. 12. 2.

,,   xxx. 15—"Three things that are not satisfied," V. 359 *n*; ix. 11. 19 *n*.

,,   xxxi. 21—"All her household clothed with scarlet," IV. 55 ; v. 3. 24.

Bible : (c) *Passages quoted, continued :*

Eccl. iii. 11—"Everything beautiful in his time," II. 5 ; iii.
   1. 1. 5.

,,   iv. 11—"How can one be warm alone ?" II. 55 ; iii.
   1. 6. 2. (F.A. *n*).

,,   ix. 10—"Whatsoever thy hand findeth to do," V.
   265 ; ix. 4. 19.

Song of Solomon iv. 3—"Lips like a thread of scarlet," IV.
   55 ; v. 3. 24.

,,   ,,   v. 5—"Myrrh on the handles of the lock,"
   II. 18 ; iii. 1. 2. 7.

,,   ,,   vi. 10—"Who is he that looketh forth as the
   morning ?" II. 181 ; iii. 2. 3. 8.

Isaiah i. 18—"Though your sins be as scarlet," IV. 55 ;
   v. 3. 24.

,,   ii. 2—"The mountain of the Lord's house . . . above
   the hills," IV. 364 ; v. 19. 33.

,,   iii. 24—"Instead of well-set hair, baldness," IV. 346 ;
   v. 19. 12.

,,   xiv. 8—"Yea, the fir-trees rejoice," III. 174 ; iv. 12. 14.

,,   xxii. 13—"Let us eat and drink, for to-morrow we
   die," V. 266 ; ix. 5. 2.

,,   xxv. 8 { "Death swallowed up in victory," V. 236 ; ix.
   2. 20.
   "   ,,   ,,   ,,   ,, " V. 256 ; ix.
   4. 3.

,,   xxxii. 5—"The vile person no more liberal, nor the
   churl bountiful," V. 290 ; ix. 7. 7.

,,   xxxiv. 4—"Heavens rolled together as a scroll," IV.
   91 ; v. 6. 8.

,,   xxxv. 7—"Grass, with reeds and rushes," III. 242 *n* ;
   iv. 14. 53.

,,   xl. 6—"All flesh is grass," *ib*. ; *ib*.

,,   xl. 15—"The isles as a little thing," V. 195 ; viii. 3. 1.

,,   xlii. 3—"Smoking flax shall He not quench," III. 243 ;
   iv. 14. 53.

,,   li. 8—"From generation to generation," IV. 5 ; v. 1. 5.

,,   liii. 9—"He made His grave with the wicked," II.
   187 ; iii. 2. 3. 16.

,,   lv. 8 { "My thoughts not your thoughts," etc., IV.
   90 ; v. 6. 7.
   "   ,,   ,,   ,,   ,, " V. 223 ;
   ix. 1. 14.

,,   lv. 12—"Mountains break forth into singing," III.
   174 ; iv. 12. 14.

Bible : (c) *Passages quoted, continued :*

Isaiah lvii. 5–6—"Among the smooth stones . . . is thy portion," IV. 335 ; v. 18. 26.

  ,,   lx. 17—"Thy officers peace, and thine exactors righteousness," V. 387 *n* ; ix. 12. 20 *n*.

  ,,   lxi. 11—"As the earth bringeth forth her bud, righteousness and praise spring forth," V. 22 ; vi. 3. 14.

  ,,   lxv. 22—"As the days of a tree are the days," etc., V. 85 ; vi. 8. 19.

Jer. i. 13—"I see a seething pot," etc., III. 103 ; iv. 8. 5.

  ,,   iii. 6—"Upon every mountain, under every green tree," IV. 364 ; v. 19. 33.

  ,,   iv. 24—"Mountains trembled, all the hills moved lightly," IV. 126 ; v. 9. 6.

  ,,   xviii. 6—"As clay in the hands of the potter," V. 384 ; ix. 12. 16.

Ezek. i. 4—"A whirlwind . . . a great cloud," IV. 88 *n* ; v. 6. 5 *n*.

  ,,   i. 10–16—Vision of wheeled eagles, III. 115 ; iv. 8. 21.

  ,,   xxiii. 14—"Images pourtrayed with vermilion," III. 72 *n* ; iv. 5. 7 *n*.

  ,,   xxxvii. 7—"Behold a shaking, and the bones came together," II. 168 ; iii. 2. 2. 15.

  ,,   xl. 3—"A line of flax . . . and a measuring reed," III. 243 ; iv. 14. 53.

Daniel iv. 25—"Eat grass like oxen," II. 5 ; iii. 1. 1. 6.

  ,,   vii. 13—"Son of man came with the clouds of heaven," IV. 88 *n* ; v. 6. 5 *n*.

Hosea iv. 12–19—"My people ask counsel," etc., III. 75 *n* ; iv. 5. 13.

  ,,   x. 8—"To the mountains, cover us," IV. 364 ; v. 19. 33.

  ,,   xiii. 5—"I did know thee . . . land of drought," V. 164 ; vii. 4. 21.

  ,,   xiii. 15—"East wind . . . up from the wilderness," *ib.* ; *ib.*

  ,,   xiv. 4–6—"Heal their backsliding . . . Lebanon," *ib.* ; *ib.*

Joel ii. 8—"They shall walk every one in his path," V. 126 ; vii. 2. 7.

  ,,   iii. 13—"Put in the sickle, for the harvest is ripe," V. 327 ; ix. 9. 24.

Amos vi. 12—"Shall horses run upon the rock," IV. 335 *n* ; v. 18. 26 *n*.

Bible : *(c) Passages quoted, continued :*

   Micah iv. 1—" Mountain of the house of the Lord," IV. 364 ;
       v. 19. 33.

    ,,   vi. 2—" Hear ye, O mountains, the Lord's controversy,"
       IV. 364 ; v. 19. 33.

   Matt. iv. 1—" Led into the wilderness . . . to be tempted,"
       II. 190 ; iii. 2. 3. 19.

    ,,   iv. 2—" Fasted forty days . . . an hungred," IV. 424 ;
       App. iii. 2.

    ,,   iv. 16—" People in darkness saw great light," IV. 405 ;
       v. 20. 48.

    ,,   v. 1 ⎰ " Sermon on the Mount," III. 318 ; iv. 17. 33.
      seqq. ⎱ "   ,,   ,,   ,," III. 323–24 ; iv. 17. 40.
         "   ,,   ,,   ,," III. 358 ; App. ii.

    ,,   v. 5—" The meek . . . inherit the earth," V. 359 ; ix.
       11. 19.

    ,,   v. 6—" Hunger after righteousness," V. 359 ; ix. 11. 20.

    ,,   v. 8—" Blessed are the pure in heart," II. 20 ; iii. 1.
       2. 10.

    ,,   v. 8—" *Happy* are the pure in heart," II. '83 *pref.*
       4, 5.

    ,,   v. 14—" City set on a hill," V. 225 ; ix. 2. 1.

    ,,   v. 29–30—" Pluck it out, and cast it from thee," I. 85 ;
       ii. 1. 7. 8 (om. ed. 1, 2).

    ,,   v. 34—" Swear not . . . neither by heaven," IV. 92 ;
       v. 6. 9.

    ,,   vi. 5—" Pray . . . that they be seen of all," V. 245 ;
       ix. 3. 16.

    ,,   vi. 9—" Our Father, which art in heaven," IV. 93 ; v.
       6. 9.

    ,,   vi. 10—" Thy kingdom come," V. 386 ; ix. 12. 19–20.

    ,,   vi. 16—" When ye fast . . . of a sad countenance,"
       IV. 424 ; App. iii. 2.

    ,,   vi. 25—" Life more than meat . . . raiment," II. 4 ;
       iii. 1. 1. 5.

    ,,   vi. 26—" Your heavenly Father feedeth them," II. 104 ;
       iii. 1. 12. 8.

    ,,   vi. 28 ⎰ " Consider the lilies . . . they toil not," III.
          243 ; iv. 14. 53.
        ⎱ " Consider the lilies . . . they toil not," III.
          323 ; iv. 17. 40.

    ,,   vi. 30—" If God so clothe the grass," etc., III. 239 ;
       iv. 14. 51.

    ,,   vii. 1—" Judge not, that ye be not judged," V. 373 ;
       ix. 12. 2.

Bible : (c) *Passages quoted, continued :*

Matt. vii. 4–5—"The beam in thine own eye," III. 358 ; App. ii.

,,   viii. 20—" Son of man hath not where to lay His head," II. 104 ; iii. 1. 12. 8.

,,   ix. 28—"Believe ye that I am able," V. 381 ; ix. 12. 10.

,,   x. 14—"Shake off the dust of your feet," I. 79 ; ii. 1. 7. 2.

,,   x. 16—"Wise as serpents, harmless as doves," V. 295 ; ix. 7. 15.

,,   x. 29–31—"More value than many sparrows," V. 195 ; viii. 3. 1.

,,   xi. 14—"If ye will receive it, this is Elias," V. 386 ; ix. 12. 20.

,,   xi. 28—"Come unto Me, all ye that labour," II. 71 ; iii. 1. 7. 1.

,,   xii. 20—"Smoking flax shall he not quench," III. 243 ; iv. 14. 53.

,,   xii. 30—"He that gathereth not . . . scattereth," I. xl ; *pref. ed.* 2. 35.

,,   xii. 50—" My brother, sister, and mother," V. 387 ; ix. 12. 20.

,,   xiv. 19—"Sit down on the grass," III. 239 ; iv. 14. 51.

,,   xvii. 1—"Into an high mountain apart," IV. 404 ; v. 20. 48.

,,   xvii. 5—"Hear ye Him" (Transfiguration), IV. 406 ; v. 20. 49.

,,   xx. 14—"Unto this last, as unto thee," II. 126 ; iii. 1. 14. 10.

,,   xxii. 37—"Thou shalt love the Lord thy God," II. 23 ; iii. 1. 3. 2.

,,   xxiv. 15—"Abomination of desolation," I. 112 ; ii. 1. 7. 26 (om. ed. 1, 2).

,,   xxiv. 30—"Son of man coming in the clouds with power" (see xxvi. 64), IV. 88 n; v. 6. 5n. V. 386 ; ix. 12. 19. 20.

,,   xxiv. 38—"Marrying and giving in marriage," V. 236 ; ix. 2. 19.

,,   xxiv. 41—"Two women grinding at the mill," IV. 9 ; v. 1. 11.

Mark iv. 19—"The cares of this world," III. 309 ; iv. 17. 19.

,,   ix. 29—"This kind . . . by prayer and fasting," IV. 424 ; App. iii. 2.

Luke ii. 7—"Wrapped Him in swaddling clothes," III. 51 ; iv. 4. 9.

Bible : (c) *Passages quoted, continued :*

Luke vi. 44 { "Every tree known by its fruit," V. 244 ; ix. 3. 13–14.
" " " " " V. 373 ; ix. 12. 3.

„   viii. 15—"An honest and good heart," II. 27 ; iii. 1. 3. 9.

„   ix. 29–32—"As He prayed . . . two men stood with Him," IV. 405 ; v. 20. 49.

„   ix. 48—"The least shall be greatest," V. 195 ; viii. 3. 1.

„   x. 31—"Passed by on the other side," IV. 362 ; v. 19. 32.

„   xii. 47—"Beaten with many stripes," IV. 363 ; v. 19. 32.

„   xvi. 19—"Clothed in purple and fine linen," IV. 55 ; v. 3. 24.

„   xxiii. 30 { "To the hills, Cover us," I. 45 ; i. 2. 3. 2.
" " " " " IV. 364 ; v. 19. 33.

John i. 17—"Law by Moses ; grace and truth by Christ," V. 164 ; vii. 4. 22.

„   iii. 16—"God so loved the world," V. 385 ; ix. 12. 18.

„   iv. 13—"Whoso drinketh of this water shall thirst again," { IV. 378 ; v. 20. 18. V. 359 ; ix. 11. 20.

„   viii. 12—"I am the light of the world," V. 385 ; ix. 12. 18.

„   xvi. 13—"When He, the Spirit of truth, is come," V. 256 ; ix. 4. 2.

„   xvii. 21—"All one, as Thou in Me and I in Thee," II. 54 ; iii. 1. 6. 1.

Acts xvii. 18—"What will this babbler say ?" III. 152 ; iv. 10. 22.

„   xvii. 23—"Whom ye ignorantly worship," V. 343 ; ix. 10. 24.

Rom. v. 3—"Tribulation . . . worketh patience," V. 248 ; ix. 3. 20.

„   v. 5—"Hope maketh not ashamed," V. 248 ; ix. 3. 20.

„   xi. 16—"If the firstfruit be *holy* (helpful)," V. 175 *n* ; viii. 1. 5 *n.*

„   xii. 9—"Love without dissimulation," etc., II. 5 ; iii. 1. 1. 6 *n.*

1 Cor. i. 23—"Stumblingblock, to Greeks foolishness," I. 436 ; ii. 6. 2. 4.

„   i. 28—"The things which are not," III. 144 ; iv. 10. 13.

Bible : *(c) Passages quoted, continued :*

    1 Cor. viii. 1—"Knowledge puffeth up," V. 158 ; vii. 4. 12.

      „   ix. 26—"Fight as one that beateth the air," IV. 425 ; App. iii. 3.

      „   x. 24—"Let no man seek his own," etc., III. 351 ; iv. 18. 38.

      „   xiii. 7—"Charity proveth (?) all things," II. 26 ; iii. 1. 3. 9.

      „   xiii. 12—"Through a glass darkly," V. 224 ; ix. 1. 15.

      „   xv. 32—"Eat and drink, for to-morrow we die," V. 266 ; ix. 5. 2.

      „   xv. 54—"Death swallowed up in victory." *See s.* Isaiah xxv. 8.

    Eph. ii. 12—"Having no hope, and without God in the world," III. 268 ; iv. 16. 10.

      „   iv. 8—"Alienated from the life of God," II. 18 ; iii. 1. 2. 8.

    Phil. iv. 8—"Whatsoever things are pure," III. 38 ; iv. 3. 15.

    Col. i. 17—"By whom all creatures . . . consist," V. 175 ; viii. 1. 5.

    1 Thess. iv. 17—"Pray without ceasing," IV. 88 *n* ; v. 6. 5 *n.*

    1 Tim. i. 15—"Faithful saying and worthy of all acceptation," V. 181 *n* ; viii. 1. 17 *n.*

      „   iv. 3—"Forbidding to marry . . . abstain from meats," IV. 424 ; App. iii. 2.

    Heb. iv. 15—"Tempted in all things as we are," IV. 404–6 ; v. 20. 47. 49.

      „   xi. 34—"Out of weakness made strong," IV. 252 ; v. 16. 17.

    James i. 23—"Beholding his natural face in a glass," II. 119 ; iii. 1. 14. 1.

      „   iv. 8—"Cleanse your hands . . . ye doubleminded," II. '83 *pref.* 6.

      „   v. 4—"The cries of them which reaped," V. 175 *n* ; viii. 1. 5 *n.*

      „   v. 12—"Let your yea be yea," II. '83 *pref.* 6.

    1 Peter i. 12—"Angels desire to look into," IV. 73 ; v. 5. 4.

    2 Peter iii. 8—"A thousand years as one day," V. 195 ; viii. 3. 1.

      „   iii. 10–12—"Elements melt in fervent heat," IV. 91 ; v. 6. 8.

    1 John i. 5—"God is light, and in Him is no darkness at all," II. 81 ; iii. 1. 9. 1.

      „   iv. 8—"God is love," V. 223 ; ix. 1. 12.

    Jude 12—"Clouds without water," V. 386 ; ix. 12. 19.

Bible : (c) *Passages quoted, continued :*

      Jude 13—" Raging waves . . . foaming at their own shame,"
            III. 170 ; iv. 12. 11.

      Rev. i. 7—" Behold, He cometh with }   IV. 88 *n* ; v. 6. 5 *n.*
            clouds, and every eye {   V. 386 ; ix. 12. 19.
            shall see Him,"

    ,, i. 19—" Write the things thou hast seen," III. 87 ; iv.
            7. 5.

    ,, iv. 7—" Holy, holy, holy," V. 175 ; viii. 1. 5.

    ,, v. 6—" Seeming of slaying " ("as it had been slain "),
            II. 142 ; iii. 1. 15. 1.

    ,, vii. 2—" Angel ascending from the east," II. 128 ; iii.
            1. 14. 12.

    ,, xiv. 13—" Their works do follow them," II. 73 *n* ; iii.
            1. 7. 4 *n.*

    ,, xviii. 16—" Fine linen, and scarlet," IV. 55 ; v. 3. 24.

    ,, xxi. 1—" New heaven and new earth," V. 386 ; ix.
            12. 19.

    ,, xxi. 20—" Chrysoprasus," etc., I. xx *n* ; *ed. 2 pref.* 13 *n.*

    ,, xxii. 3–4—" No more curse . . . see His face," II.
            150 ; iii. 1. 15. 12.

    ,, xxii. 6—" Faithful and true," V. 181 ; viii. 1. 17.

Bietsch-horn, peak and clefts on the, IV. 187 ; v. 14. 10.
    ,,   ,,   ,,   ,,   IV. 191 ; v. 14. 12.
    ,,   ,,   ,,   ,,   IV. 273 ; v. 16. 40.
Bicknell, E., his Turner's Calder Bridge, I. 141 ; ii. 1. 7. 44
            (om. ed. 1, 2).
    ,,   ,,   ,,   Port Ruysdael, I. 402 ; ii. 5. 3. 37
            (om. ed. 1, 2).
    ,,   ,,   ,,   Venice, Campo Santo, V. 132 *n* ;
            vii. 2. 15 *n.*
Bingen, vine-terraces of, IV. 261 ; v. 16. 27.
Bionnassay, Aiguille de, IV. 220 ; v. 15. 16.
Birch-tree, bud of the, V. 83 ; vi. 8. 18.
    ,,   in Scotland, V. 93 ; vi. 9. 11.
Bird, flying, how drawn, V. 25 ; vi. 4. 5.
Birth, value of long descent, V. 288 *n* ; ix. 7. 3 *n.*
Black Prince, the, III. 156 ; iv. 11. 6.
Black realization of white, III. 356 ; App. 2.
    ,,   ,,   ,,   IV. 37 *n* ; v. 3. 1. 2 *n.*
Blacklock, W. J., hill-drawing of, I. 327 ; ii. 4. 3. 28 (om. ed. 1–4).
Black spruce, V. 86–7 ; vi. 9. 1–3.
Blackthorn, branch of, V. 81 *n* ; vi. 8. 14 *n.*

Blackwood's Magazine, its criticism of "Modern Painters,"
         I. xx ; *pref. ed.* 2. 13.
  "   "   "   "   I. xlix–l ; *ib.* 46.
  "   "   "   "   III. 341 *n* ; iv. 18. 26 *n*.
  "   "   on Keats, Turner, and the Czar's death,
         IV. 411–12 ; App. i. 6.
  "   "   on Turner's colour, I. 152 ; ii. 2. 2. 1
         (ed. 1, 2 only).
Blaitière, Aiguille, IV. 172 *n* ; v. 13. 8 *n*.
  "   "   IV. 194–98 ; v. 14. 16. 18.
  "   "   IV. 221 *n* ; v. 15. 16 *n*.
  "   "   IV. 421–22 ; App. ii. 4, 5.
Blake's colour, III. 106 ; iv. 8. 8.
  "   grotesque power (Job), *ib.* ; *ib.*
  "   sincere, but morbid, III. 270 *n* ; iv. 16. 10 *n*.
Blanc, Mont, aiguilles surrounding, IV. 221 *n* ; v. 15. 16 *n*.
  "   "   angles of slopes near, IV. 329 ; v. 18. 15.
  "   "   beds under, parallel, IV. 416 ; App. ii. 3.
  "   "   chain of, its formation, IV. 183 *n* ; v. 14. 3 *n*.
  "   "   "   geography, IV. 185 *seqq.* ; v. 14. 6 *seqq.*
  "   "   "   IV. 209–10, 214 ; v. 15. 7. 11.
  "   "   cirrus clouds shadowing, I. 232 ; ii. 3. 2. 6.
  "   "   cloud-cap over, V. 139 ; vii. 3. 4 (pl. 69).
  "   "   form of, IV. 216–22 ; v. 15. 14. 16.
  "   "   gneiss-beds under, straightness and regularity,
         IV. 217–22 ; v. 15. 16.
  "   "   granite of, IV. 112 ; v. 8. 11.
  "   "   mountain round, IV. 223 ; v. 15. 19.
  "   "   position of, IV. 171 ; v. 13. 8.
  "   "   "silver flame" of, III. 145–46 ; iv. 10. 15.
  "   "   streams' action on, IV. 145–46 ; v. 12. 2. 3.
Blindness to and neglect of God's warnings, IV. 362 ; v. 19. 32.
Blitzius, V. 362 ; ix. 11. 24. *See s. Gotthelf.*
Blossoms, apple and cherry, V. 7 ; vi. 2. 2.
Blottesque, modern style, IV. 82–3 ; v. 5. 19–20.
Blue, colour exists though unseen, III. 161–62 ; iv. 12. 1–2.
  "   place of, as a colour, V. 349 ; ix. 11. 7.
—— bell of Scotland, II. 68 ; iii. 1. 6. 15.
Body, beauty of the, to the true artist, V. 252–53 ; ix. 3. 30.
  "   effect of the mind on the, II. 121 *seqq.* ; iii. 1. 14. 4 *seqq.*
  "   ideal rendering of the human, II. 235 *seqq.* ; iii. 2. 5. 16
    seqq.

Boileau's Pluto "tout . . . beau dans les dictionnaires," II. 198 ; iii. 2. 3. 26.

Boldness in art, generally a vice, I. 42–3 and *n* ; i. 2. 2. 9 and *n*.
,,   ,,   ,,   ,,   III. 42 ; iv. 3. 20.
,,   ,,   no merit in itself, III. 278 ; iv. 16. 27.

Bologna Gallery, Domenichino's Madonna del Rosario, I. 93 *n* ; ii. 1. 7. 13 *n* (om. ed. 1, 2).
,,   ,,   ,,   ,,   Martyrdom of St. Agnes, *ib.* : *ib.* (*ib.*).
,,   ,,   Francia's, sky of the, I. 89 ; ii. 1. 7. 11 (om. ed. 1, 2).
,,   ,,   Perugino's Annunciation, II. 47 ; iii. 1. 5. 10.
,,   ,,   ,,   ,,   II. 232 ; iii. 2. 5. 11.
,,   ,,   Raphael's St. Cecilia, *ib.* ; *ib.*
,,   ,,   ,,   ,,   ,,   III. 59 *n* ; iv. 4. 17 *n*.
,,   ,,   ,,   ,,   St. Paul, *ib.* ; *ib.*

Bolton Abbey, Turner's drawing and love of, IV. 261 *seqq.* ; v. 16. 28. 30 *seqq. See s. Wharfe.*

Bonifazio, colour of, perfect, IV. 324 ; v. 18. 9.
,,   first to try and give real sun, III. 338 ; iv. 18. 22.
,,   no profane works by, V. 246 ; ix. 3. 17.
,,   Titian followed by, III. 360 ; App. iii.
,,   work by, Israelite Camp (Ven. Libr. Vecch.), III. 338 ; iv. 18. 22.

Bonneville, plain of, IV. 152 ; v. 12. 12.

Books, drawing of, *mystery* to be shown in, IV. 63 ; v. 4. 7.
,,   of Beauty, III. 72 ; iv. 5. 9. *See s. Literature, Writers.*

Boone's Turner catalogue, V. 329 *n* ; ix. 10. 3 *n*.

Bosch, E., picture of dog and boy, V. 284 ; ix. 6. 20.

Bossons, Glacier des, IV. 223 ; v. 15. 18.

Botanist's love of flowers, cp. artist's and poet's, I. xxxvi–vii ; *pref. ed.* 2. 30.

Botany,* author's division of plants and trees, V. 7 *seqq.* ; vi. 2. 2. 3 *seqq.*

---

* *See s.* Alchemilla, Alisma, Alleluia, Aloe, Alpine flowers, Apple, Arbor vitæ, Artichoke, Ash, Aspen, Aucuba, Birch, Blackthorn, Black-spruce, Blossom, Blue Bell, Brooklime, Buds, Carob-tree, Cedar, Chestnut, Cole-wort, Coltsfoot, Columbine, Cowslip, Crocus, Daisy, Dogwood, Elm leaf, Endogenous, Fir, Flowers, Foliage, Forests, Foxglove, Fruit, Gentian, Gooseberry, Grapes, Grass, Harvey, Hawthorn, Heather, Herbage, Hollyhock, Horse-chestnut, Horticulture, Hyacinth, Iris, Ivy, Laburnum, Larch, Laurel, Leaves, Lichen, Lilac, Lily, Lindley, Link, Linnæus, Magnolia.

Botany, *continued :*
  „   classifications and questions in, V. 7 ; vi. 2. 1.
  „   flowers at Sion, IV. 361 *n* ; v. 19. 31 *n.*
  „   mediæval (12–1400), III., pl. 8, 9.
  „   nomenclature of, fatal to its study, V. 56; vi. 7. 3.
Both, author's depreciation of, I. 6 ; i. 1. 1. 4.
  „   leafage of, I. 422; ii. 6. 1. 22.
  „   sunshine and imperfect colour of, V. 346; ix. 11. 3.
  „   work of (Dulwich Gallery, 41), foreground, I. 311; ii. 4. 4.
       17 (ed. 1, 2 only).
Botticelli, author first to show his supremacy, II. '83 Epil. 13.
  „   „   ignorant of (1856), III. 63; iv. 4. 22 (F.A. *n*).
  „   Life of Moses (Sistine), II. '83 Epil. 7.
Bouchard, Aiguille, its form, crest, cleavage, etc., IV. 41 *n* ; v
             3. 8 *n* (pl. 25).
  „   „   IV. 214–23; v. 15. 11. 19.
  „   „   IV. 234–36 ; v. 15. 31.
  „   „   morning light on the, V. 150 *n*; vii. 3. 17 *n*
                      (pl. 69).
Boughs, downward tendency of all, I. 309–10; ii. 4. 3. 4.
  „   growth of, V. 58 *seqq.*; vi. 7. 6 *seqq.*
  „   spreading of, V. 62; vi. 7. 11. *See s. Branch, Trees.*
Box-tree, leaf of, V. 34; vi. 4. 14.
Boydell's engravings from Claude, Rubens, III. 122–23; iv. 9. 8–9.
  „   „   Salvator's Apollo and Sibyl, V. 78 *n*;
                      vi. 8. 11 *n.*
Boys, T., illustrations to " Modern Painters " by, III. xii ; *pref.* 6.
Bramble, leaf of a, III. 218 ; iv. 14. 24.
Branch aspect [SYNOPSIS. V. 44 *seqq.*, 54, 69–70, 75] :—
    conditions of (spring, caprice, fellowship), V. 69 *seqq.*; vi.
      8. 2 *seqq.*
    balanced elasticity of, V. 70; vi. 8. 4.
    curvature, V. 44 ; vi. 6. 1.
      „   V. 69–70 ; vi. 8. 3.
      „   V. 75; vi. 8. 10 (pl. 58).
    structure, V. 44 *seqq.*; vi. 6. 1 *seqq.*

Manna, Maple-tree, Mosses, Nomenclature, Oak, Olive, Oxalis, Palms,
Pansy, Parnassia, Parsley, Pea-pods, Phillyrea, Pillar-plants, Pines, Plane,
Plant, Plantain, Poplar, Ramification, Ranunculus, Resilience, Rhodo-
dendrons, Roots, Rose, Sails, Sap, Sapling, Savoy, Seed, Shoots,
Sisymbrium, Soldanella, Strawberry, Sunflower, Thistle, Toad-flax, Trees,
Trefoil, Trunk, Vegetation, Vine, Violet, Watercress, White, Willow.

Branch, *continued* :
    thickening in growth, V. 54 ; vi. 7. 1. *See s. Trees.*
Bread of righteousness, V. 359 ; ix. 11. 20.
Breadth in art, is not vacancy, I. 208 ; ii. 2. 5. 10.
   ,,   ,, great art, III. 41 ; iv. 3. 18.
Breath, visibility of, on a cold day, V. 146–47 ; vii. 3. 15.
Brêche de Roland, IV. 180 ; v. 13. 18.
Breeding, good, its meaning and value, V. 287–88 and *n* ; ix.
    7. 1 *seqq.* and *n.*
Brenta, embankments on the, III. 224 ; iv. 14. 29.
Brett, John, on vulgarity, V. 302–3 ; ix. 7. 24.
   ,,   ,, work of, "Val d'Aosta" (1859), V. 302 ; ix. 7.
    24.
Breven, Mont, IV. 41 *n* ; v. 3. 8 *n.*
   ,,   ,, form of, IV. 219 ; v. 15. 16.
   ,,   ,, pine-forests of, IV. 368 *n* ; v. 20. 4 *n.*
   ,,   ,, precipice of summit, IV. 241–42 and *n* ; v. 16. 4
    and *n.*
   ,,   ,, rocks of, IV. 113 ; v. 8. 13.
   ,,   ,, slope of, IV. 329 *n* ; v. 18. 15 *n.*
Brieg, IV. 191 ; v. 14. 12.
   ,, ravine near, IV. 273 ; v. 16. 40.
Bristol, cliffs of, IV. 155 ; v. 12. 15.
British Institution, pictures in, before 1848, II. 241 ; Add. (ed.
    1, note 4).
——— Museum, Claude's sketches, I. 414 ; ii. 6. 1. 12.
   ,,   ,, Egyptian lions, II. 218 ; iii. 2. 4. 12.
   ,,   ,, MSS. Cotton (aspen), IV. 80 ; v. 5. 17.
   ,,   ,,   ,, (rock), III. 255 ; iv. 15. 16.
   ,,   ,,   ,, Harleian (sun), III. 338 ; iv. 18. 22.
   ,,   ,,   ,,   ,,   ,, (German art), IV. 349 ;
    v. 19. 18.
   ,,   ,,   ,, Sloane (aspen), IV. 80 ; v. 5. 16.
   ,,   ,,   ,, various (tree), III. 215 ; iv. 14. 19.
   ,,   ,,   ,, (rocks), IV. 267 ; v. 16. 35.
Bronzino, base grotesques of, III. 106 ; iv. 8. 8.
   ,, work of "Christ and Spirits in Prison" (Flor. Uff.),
    vulgar, II. 61 ; iii. 1. 6. 8.
   ,, work of "Christ and Spirits in Prison," II. 230 *n* ; iii.
   ,,   2. 5. 7 *n.*
Brooklime, Derbyshire, V. 231 ; ix. 2. 12.
Brotherhood, IV. 370 ; v. 20. 7.

Brown (colour), its use, III. 248–51; iv. 15. 9–12.
            See s. Beaumont, Dante.

,,   ,,   none in nature, *ib.* ; *ib.*

,,   ,,   ,,   ,,   IV. 143 ; v. 11. 11.

,,   ,,   the ugliest of colours, *ib.* ; *ib.*

———, Dr., Lect. xcii. on Unity, II. 54 ; iii. 1. 6. 1.

———, Rawdon, "Four Years at Court of Henry VIII.," IV 359 *n* ; v. 19. 29 *n.*

Browning, E. B., feeling of, III. 269 ; iv. 16. 10.

———, Robert, concentration of, IV. 392 ; v. 20. 34.

,,   ,,   ,,   ,,   IV. 390–92.

,,   ,,   his grasp of mediævalism, IV. 390 *seqq.* ; v. 20. 32 *seqq.*

,,   ,,   rugged rhymes of, IV. 390 ; v. 20. 32.

,,   ,,   works of :
        St. Praxed's church, on sculpture, IV. 391–92 ; v. 20. 32–3.

Bruges, author at (1842), and French pictures, I. 26 ; i. 1. 5. 5.

,,   Cathedral, Madonna, I. 26 ; i. 1. 5. 5.

,,   sea-embankments of, III. 224 ; iv. 14. 29.

Bruno, St., IV. 377 ; v. 20. 17.

Brush, pencil and, their use by artists, I. 265–66 ; ii. 3. 4. 10.

Brussels, Rubens' works at, Christ and St. Francis, etc., V. 277 ;
        ix. 6. 6.

,,   ,,   ,,   Veronese's Holy Family, V. 250 ;
        ix. 3. 25.

Buds, growth of, V. 11 *seqq.* ; vi. 3. 1–4 *seqq.*

,,   sections of, V. 18 ; vi. 3. 11.

,,   spiral succession of, V. 16 ; vi. 3. 8.

,,   united growths of, V. 58 *seqq.* ; vi. 7. 6 *seqq*

,,   youth typified by, III. 217–18| ; iv. 14. 24.
        See s. Horse-chestnut, Oak.

Buet, Mt., IV. 131 ; v. 10. 4.

,,   ,,   IV. 158 ; v. 12. 18.

,,   ,,   IV. 254 ; v. 16. 20.

Bulicame, baths of, III. 224 ; iv. 14. 29.

Bunsen, on German philosophy, III. 356 ; App. ii.

Bunyan's "Pilgrim's Progress," Slough of Despond, V. 230 ;
    ix. 2. 11.

Buoyancy of things, on what dependent, V. 117 *n* ; vii. 1. 6 *n.*

Burke, "Sublime and Beautiful" :
    its high value, II. 67 ; iii. 1. 6. 14 ('83 *n*).

Burke, "Sublime and Beautiful," *continued :*

    its theory criticised, I. 44 *seqq.* ; i. 2. 3. 2.

    quoted (i. 16) on imitation, I. 19 ; i. 1. 4. 1.

        „   (ii. 8) „ number and symmetry, I. 232 ; ii. 3. 2. 6.

        „   „   „ proportion, II. 64 ; iii. 1. 6. 10.

        „   „   „   „   II. 67–8 ; iii. 1. 6. 14–15.

Burns, study and love of nature by, III. 302 ; iv. 17. 7.

Business, proper, of a man in the world, III. 48–9 ; iv. 4. 2.

      „   „   „   III. 356 ; App. ii.

           See s. Pursuits.

Busybody, has no invention, III. 96 ; iv. 7. 16.

Buttercup leaf, form of, V. 103–4 ; vi. 10. 11.

    „   „   „   V. 105 ; vi. 10. 13.

Byfield, Miss, her woodcuts for "Modern Painters," III. xii ;

                                       pref. 6.

  „   „   „   „   „ V. ix *n*; *pref.* 6 *n.*

  „   „   „   „   „ V. 108 ; vi. 10. 19.

Byron [Synopsis. I. xviii *n*, xl *n*, 3 *n*, 449. II. 182, '83 Epil. 7. 13.

    III. 8, 250, 269, 274, 279, 283, 287, 302, 305, 312–15.

    IV. 205. V. 363–64, 383]:—

    author's knowledge of, at Pisa, II. '83 Epil. 7.

    blasphemy of, its sadness, III. 269 ; iv. 16. 10.

    colouring of, bright and pure, III. 250 ; v. 15. 11.

        „   „   „   III. 274 ; iv. 16. 18.

    death without hope, V. 383 ; ix. 12. 14.

    desperate, not melancholy, III. 283 ; iv. 16. 34.

    details, his use of, III. 8 ; iv. 1. 8.

    emotional, heads sentimental literature, III. 279 ; iv. 16. 29.

    female characters noble (Angiolina, Marina, Myrrha), III. 313 ; iv. 17. 27.

    illustrations to. *See s. Finden, Harding, Turner.*

    indignant at pain and injustice, III. 315 ; iv. 17. 28.

    lonely joy in Jura storm, III. 314 ; iv. 17. 27.

    love of nature, II. '83 Epil. 13.

        „   „   selfish, III. 287 ; iv. 16. 38.

        „   „   III. 302 ; iv. 17. 7.

        „   „   III. 305 ; iv. 17. 10.

    passionateness of, III. 312 ; iv. 17. 26.

    popularity of, I. 4 *n* ; i. 1. 1 *n.*

    public neglect of, V. 383 ; ix. 12. 14.

    sense of beauty, V. 363–64 ; ix. 11. 26.

Byron, *continued :*

   works of, quoted or referred to :

      Childe Harold, and Turner's pictures, V. 363–64; ix. 11. 26.

    ,,   ,,   iii. 71. "Love earth only for its earthly sake," III. 305; iv. 17. 10.

    ,,   ,,   iv. 75. Soracte's crest, "wave about to break," IV. 205; v. 15. 2.

    ,,   ,,   iv. 29. Twilight, "'tis gone, and all is grey," III. 250; iv. 15. 11.

      Don Juan, "A green field," etc., I. xl *n* ; *pref. ed.* 2. 34 *n.*

    ,,   on versatility of artists, I. 449; ii. 6. 3. 22.

      Marino Faliero, on vice and virtue, I. xvii *n* ; *pref. ed.* 2. 10 *n* (ed. 2, 3 only).

      on tenderness of Dante, II. 182; iii. 2. 3. 9.

      Prisoner of Chillon, III. 8; iv. 1. 8.

      Siege of Corinth, "'Tis midnight; on the mountains brown," III. 250; iv. 15. 11.

Cab-horses, sufferings of, IV. 363 ; v. 19. 32.

Caen, cathedral of, its influence, IV. 379 ; v. 20. 20.

Cagliari. *See s. Veronese.*

Calabria, banditti of, IV. 377 ; v. 20. 17.

Calais, church, picturesque old tower (symbolism), IV. 2–3 ; v. 1. 2. 3.

    ,,   ,,   ,,   ,,   IV. 6–7 ; *ib.* 7–9.

    ,,   ,,   spire (Prout), IV. 14 ; v. 1. 15.

Calame, chalk-drawing of, IV. 82 ; v. 5. 19.

Caliban (idealism), II. 110 ; iii. 1. 13. 3. *See s. Shakspere.*

Caligula, I. xiii ; *pref. ed.* 2. 3.

    ,,   -like pleasures, II. 29 ; iii. 1. 3. 13.

Callcott, Sir A. [SYNOPSIS. I. i, 100, 155, 163 *n*, 200, 369, 402, 426. V. 382]:—

    far below Turner, I. viii ; *pref.* 2.

    foliage of, I. 396 ; ii. 6. 1. 27 (ed. 1, 2 only).

    hill-scenery of, I. 303 ; ii. 4. 3. 28 (ed. 1, 2 only).

    mediocrity of (not destined to live), I. 100 ; ii. 1. 7. 18 (om. ed. 1, 2).

    no eye for colour, I. 163 *n* ; ii. 2. 1. 21 *n.*

    place of, in National Gallery catalogue, V. 382 : ix. 12. 11.

    seas of, I. 402 ; ii. 5. 3. 37 (om. ed. 1, 2).

    want of tone, I. 155 ; ii. 2. 1. 12.

Callcott, *continued*:

    water-painting of, I. 343 ; ii. 5. 2. 2 (ed 1, 2 only).

    works of :

        the best in gallery of Sir J. Swinburne, I. 100 ; ii. 1. 7. 18 (om. ed. 1, 2).

        "Trent," I. 200 ; ii. 2. 4. 6.

          ,,   *ib.* ; *ib.* 7 (ed. 1, 2 only).

Callirhoë, V. 335–36 ; ix. 10. 12.

Calmness, essential to an artist, V. 313–14 ; viii. 4. 20. 21.

Calvin, dislike of art, III. 59–60 ; iv. 4. 18.

Calypso, "the concealer," V. 234 ; ix. 2. 17.

Cambium, its action in trees, V. 45 *n* ; vi. 6. 3 *n*.

Cambridge canals, weeds in, III. 279 ; iv. 16. 28.

Camels, eyes of, II. 105 ; iii. 1. 12. 10 ('83 *n*).

Camera obscura, effect of, I. 150 ; ii. 2. 1. 4.

Campagna, Rome, described, I. xlii ; *pref. ed.* 2. 37 (F.A. *n*). *See s. Rome.*

Campo Felice, Vesuvius, I. 290 ; ii. 4. 1. 5.

Canaletto [SYNOPSIS. I. *ed.* 3 *pref.*, 6, 81, 118, 211, 348, 357, 362–65, 369, 387. V. 218] :—

    author's depreciation of, I. *pref. ed.* 3 (ed. 3 only).

       ,,   ,,   I. 6. ; i. 1. 1. 4.

    canals of, I. 348 ; ii. 5. 1. 4 (om. ed. 1, 2).

    chiaroscuro of his architecture, accurate, I. 332 ; ii. 5. 1. 2 (ed. 1, 2 only).

    mechanism of, I. 76 ; ii. 1. 7. 8 *n* (ed. 1, 2 only).

    picturesque landscape of, V. 218 ; ix. 1. 3.

    vacancy and falsehood of, I. 211 ; ii. 2. 5. 14.

    Venices of, I. 76 ; ii. 1. 7. 7 (ed. 1, 2 only).

    vileness of (heartless, mechanical, untrue), I. 117 *seqq.* ; ii. 1. 7. 30 (om. ed. 1, 2).

    water-painting of, its colour false, I. 364 ; ii. 5. 1. 19.

       ,,   ,,   ,, reflections, I. 362–64 ; ii. 5. 1. 18–19.

       ,,   ,,   ,, ripples, I. 369 ; ii. 5. 2. 1.

       ,,   ,,   ,, want of truth, I. 387 ; ii. 5. 3. 17.

    work of, St. Mark's (Palace Manfrini), vacancy of, I. 211 ; ii. 2. 5. 14.

Canova, ball-room sentiment of, II. 198 ; iii. 2. 3. 27.

    ,,   tombs by, II. 75 ; iii. 1. 7. 7.

    ,,   vile classicality of, I. 131 ; ii. 1. 7. 37 (om. ed. 1, 2).

    ,,   want of imagination, II. 198 ; iii. 2. 3. 27.

    ,,   work of, "Perseus," tassels in the, I. 67 ; ii. 1. 3. 8.

Canterbury, High Street, small houses in, IV. 4 ; v. 1. 5.

Capacity, doing one thing well is not great, III. 339 ; iv. 18. 23.

Capella de' Medici, Twilight and Day, I. 37 ; i. 2. 1. 5. *See s.
    M. Angelo.*

Capri, introduced into Claude's backgrounds, IV. 231 ; v
    15. 28.

Caprice, of branch growth, V. 76 *seqq.* ; vi. 8. 11 *seqq.*

Caracci, coarseness of the, II. 179 *n* ; iii. 2. 3. 7.

    „   portraiture of, II. 129 ; iii. 1. 14. 14.

    „   vile landscape of, III. 337 ; iv. 18. 20.

    „   worthlessness of, IV. 79 ; v. 5. 15.

Caravaggio, morbid brutality of, II. 146 ; iii. 1. 15. 7

    „   sombre colour of, III. 274 ; iv. 16. 18.

    „   ugly subjects of, III. 37 ; iv. 3. 12.

Caretto, tomb of Ilaria di.   *See s. Quercia.*

Cargneule, rock called, IV. 219 *n* ; v. 15. 16 *n*.

Caricature, impossible of virtue, in middle ages, III. 271 ; iv.
    16. 14.

    „   may be subtle, never perfect, IV. 57 ; v. 3. 24.

    „   modern effect and methods of, IV. 409 ; App. i.
                3 *seqq.*

    „   poetry and, IV. 409 ; App. i. 5.

    „   value of, IV. 409 ; App. i. 4.

Carleton, Sir D., letter of Rubens to, V. 278 ; ix. 6. 8.

Carlo Dolci.   *See s. Dolci.*

Carlyle, T., author's debt to, III. 359 ; App. 3.

    „   „   „   style influenced by, III. 359 ; App. 3.

    „   „   pure lightning of, III. 180 ; iv. 13. 4–5.

    „   „   thought and anger of, III. 269 ; iv. 16. 10.

    „   „   „   "seer-" ship of, III. 279 ; iv. 16. 28.

    „   „   to be studied, III. 357 ; App. 2.

    „   „   work of, "Sartor Resartus," boy watching scroll
                (clouds), V. 120 *n* ; vii. 1. 9 *n*.

Carmini Chapel, Tribute Money fresco, III. 334 ; iv. 18. 14.

Carob-tree, I. 408 ; ii. 6. 1. 2.

Carpaccio, author first to appreciate, II. '83 Epil. 13.

    „   drawing of architecture by, I. 114 ; ii. 1. 7. 28 (om.
            ed. 1, 2).

    „   luminous skies of, II. 48 ; iii. 1. 5. 11.

Carrara, hills of (in Dante), III. 255–57 ; iv. 15. 17–18.

    „   „   IV. 317 ; v. 17. 50 (pl. 47).

    „   „   IV. 379 ; v. 20. 20.

Carriages, English, finish of, III. 118 ; iv. 9. 4.

Carthage, fall of, its lesson, V. 368–69 ; ix. 11. 31.

Carthusian monasteries, IV. 399 ; v. 20. 44.

Cary's Dante, quoted, III. 20–1 ; iv. 2. 5 (Purg. xii. 64 : ideal of art).

  ,,   ,,   ,,   III. 230 ; iv. 14. 37 (Leah).

  ,,   ,,   ,,   III. 256 *seqq.* ; iv. 15. 18 *seqq.* (mountain).

  ,,   ,,   ,,   IV. 115 *n* ; v. 8. 15 *n* (symbolic colour of stone).

  ,,   ,,   ,,   V. 337 ; ix. 10. 14 (Geryon). *See s. Dante.*

Cascade des Pélerins, ruined, IV. 299 *n* ; v. 17. 30 *n.*

  ,,   ,,   ,,   slope above, IV. 310 ; v. 17. 44 (pl. 48).

Castagno, Andrea del, rocks of, III. 254 ; iv. 15. 16 (pl. 10).

Castle life, loneliness of mediæval, III. 214 ; iv. 14. 8.

Catena, Vincenzo, no profane work by, V. 246 ; ix. 3. 17.

Cathedral, entrance of, five-doored, III. 222 ; iv. 14. 27.

  ,,   French and English, the finest named, IV. 380–81 ; v. 20. 23.

         See s. Amiens, Beauvais, Berne, Caen, Chartres, Cologne, Coutances, Dumblane, Lichfield, Lincoln, Lucca, Magdeburg, Milan, Paris, Parma, Peterborough, Pisa, Rheims, Rome, Roslin, Rouen, Venice, Verona, Wells, Westminster.

Catlin, story of Indians and drawing by, I. 57–8 ; ii. 1. 2. 6.

Cattermole, G., decline of, I. 122 *seqq.* ; ii. 1 7. 33 *seqq.* (om. ed. 1, 2).

  ,,   ,, driven into doing small sketches, I. xlv *n* ; *pref. ed.* 2. 40 *n.*

  ,,   ,, foliage of, I. 431 ; ii. 6. 1. 33.

  ,,   ,, "spongy breadth" of, I. 245 , ii. 3. 4. 7 (ed. 1, 2 only).

  ,,   ,, works of :

         Fall of Clyde, I. 123 ; ii. 1. 7. 33.
         Glendearg, *ib.* ; *ib.*

Cattle-pieces, V. 285–86 ; ix. 6. 23.

Caves, Homeric, III. 196 *seqq.* ; iv. 13. 24 *seqq.*

Cayley's Dante, III. 89 ; iv. 7. 8 (Rue de Fouarre).

  ,,   ,, III. 229 ; iv. 14. 35 (Countess Matilda).

  ,,   ,, III. 247 *n* ; iv. 15. 7 (Malebolge rock).

  ,,   ,, IV. 334 ; v. 18. 25 (landslip near Trent).

Cedar, "flaked breadth" of, V. 86 ; vi. 9. 1.

Celibacy, of mediæval clergy, V. 241 ; ix. 3. 7.

Cellini, Benvenuto, on mist of Italian skies, I. 57 ; ii. 1. 2. 5.

       ,,   ,,   ,, Pope's seal, II. 229 ; iii. 2. 5. 7.

Cenis, Mt., clouds on, V. 147–48 ; vii. 3. 17.

      ,,   ,, V. 161 ; vii. 4. 17.

Ceres, and marriage, V. 333 ; ix. 10. 8.

   ,, mysteries of, from Egypt, V. 159 ; vii. 4. 12.

Cervantes, Don Quixote, appreciation of, by different minds, I. 3 *n* ; i. 1. 1 *n*.

      ,,   ,,   ,, love of nature in, III. 315 ; iv. 17. 29.

      ,,   ,,   ,, no vulgarity in his emaciation, V. 297 ; ix. 7. 20.

      ,,   ,,   ,, Sancho referred to, I. xxi ; *pref. ed* 2. 13.

Cervin, Mt. *See s. Matterhorn.*

Ceto, daughter of Nereus, V. 157 *seqq.* ; vii. 4. 9 *seqq.*

      ,,   ,,   ,, V. 333–35, 337 ; ix. 10. 9–11, 15. *See s. Gorgons.*

Chain, IV. 285 ; v. 17. 12. *See s. Curves (catenary).*

Châlets, beauty of Swiss, V. 93 ; vi. 9. 10.

Chambéry, mountains near, IV. 260 ; v. 16. 26.

Chamouni [SYNOPSIS. I. 242, 316. IV. 115, 128, 169, 185, 192 244, 251, 298, 345, 398. V. 91, 147] :—

   aiguilles of, IV. 169 *seqq.* ; v. 13. 6 *seqq.*

      ,, IV. 192 ; v. 14. 13.

      ,, IV. 244 ; v. 16. 6.

      ,, IV. 251 ; v. 16. 16. *See s. Aiguilles.*

   disfigured by quarrying, IV. 128 ; v. 9. 10.

   "fairies' hollow" at, V. 91 ; vi. 9. 8.

   mountains of, their colour, IV. 115 ; v. 8. 14.

      ,, Grandes Jorasses, clouds on, I. 242 ; ii. 3. 3. 4

      ,, Montagne du Côté, I. 293 ; ii. 4. 3. 12 (ed. 1, 2 only).

      ,,   ,, de Taconay, I. 316 ; ii. 4. 3. 12 (om. ed. 1, 2).

   pine-wood glen at, now ruined, V. 91 ; vi. 9. 8 (F.A. *n*)

   rain-clouds at, V. 147 ; vii. 3. 16.

   ruin of, by tourists, IV. 398 ; v. 20. 41.

   valley of, described, IV. 169 *seqq.* ; v. 13. 6 *seqq.*

      ,,   ,, IV. 185 ; v. 14. 6.

      ,, lines of, IV. 298 ; v. 17. 30 (pl. 35).

Chamouni, *continued* :

    valley of, picture of tormented souls in, IV. 345 ; v. 19. 11.

Champagne, plains of, IV. 367 ; v. 20. 3.

      „   want of invention in people, IV. 383 ; v. 20. 27.

Chance, great art leaves nothing to, V. 194 ; viii. 2. 15. *See s Fors.*

Change, influence and love of, II. 58–9 ; iii. 1. 6. 6.

      „   too much, becomes monotonous, III. 311 ; iv. 17. 23.

      „   very little is enough, *ib.* ; *ib.*

      „   violent and sudden, V. 22 ; vi. 3. 14.

Character, how far predetermined, and outside education, III. 46 ; iv. 3. 26.

Charenton, the Seine at, IV. 366 ; v. 20. 2.

Charity, essence of, defined as perfection of theoretic faculty, II. 97 ; iii. 1. 12. 2.

      „   influence of, on countenance, II. 123 ; iii. 1. 14. 6.

      „   rendering of, by Giotto and Reynolds, III. 105 ; iv. 8. 7.

      „   „   „   Veronese, V. 248 ; ix. 3. 20.

Charlemagne, the greatest of kings, III. 352 ; iv. 18 (39).

Charmoz, Aiguille, IV. 144 ; v. 12. 1.

      „   „   IV. 186 ; v. 14. 8 (sharp horn of).

      „   „   IV. 193–95 ; *ib.* 13 *seqq.*

      „   „   IV. 199*n*–202 ; *ib.* 20*n*–22.

      „   „   IV. 217 ; *ib.* 15. 15.

      „   „   IV. 220 *n* ; *ib.* 16 *n.*

      „   „   IV. 222 *n* ; *ib.* 17 *n.*

      „   glacier, IV. 421 ; App. ii. 5.

Chartres cathedral, IV. 379 ; v. 20. 20.

      „   „   IV. 381 ; v. 20. 23.

      „   „   sculpture, leaf and figure, V. 39 ; vi. 5. 4.

      „   „   statues, II. 220 ; iii. 2. 4. 14.

      „   „   window, sea in painted, I. 366 ; ii. 5. 1. 22 (om. ed. 1, 2).

Chartreuse, " crocused slopes " of, III. 208 ; iv. 14. 10.

      „   IV. 260 ; v. 16. 26.

      „   IV. 274 ; v. 16 42.

      „   remark of monk about mountains, V. 357 ; ix. 11. 17.

Chasing, art of (armour), III. 209 ; iv. 14. 11.

Chasms, mountain, I. 316 ; ii. 4. 3. 12.

Chasteness. *See s. Moderation.*

Chaucer, as illustrator of nature, II. '83 Epil. 13.

Chaucer, *continued* :

„   love of woods by (Canacé, "Squire's Tale," II. 46),
     III. 227 ; iv. 14. 33.

„   studies his own age, III. 98 ; iv. 7. 19.

„   the "sainted child" of, II. 167 ; iii. 2. 2. 13.

Chède, Lac de (Switz.), its beauty and ruin (1840), I. 353 *n* ;
     ii. 5. 3. 5 *n* (ed. 1, 2 only).

Cheerfulness, essential Christian virtue, III. 240–41 ; iv. 14. 51–2.

Chemistry, illustrations of the imagination from, II. 162–63 ;
     iii. 2. 2. 8.

Chess, mystery of the game, compared with Turner's methods,
     IV. 68 ; v. 4. 14.

Chestnut, sweeping, V. 111 ; vi. 10. 23.

„   sweet, symmetry of the, II. 79 ; iii. 1. 8. 3. *See s.
     Horse-chestnut.*

Chiaroscurists, colourists and, comparative merits, etc., of,
     IV. 49–50 ; v. 3. 19–20.

„   give no absolute truth, IV. 50 ; v. 3. 20.

Chiaroscuro [SYNOPSIS. I. 73-4, 77, 150, 184, 190–93, 430.
     III. 150 *n.* IV. 42–3, 45–7] : —

colour less important than, I. 75 ; ii. 1. 5. 8.

contrasts of systems of, IV. 42–3 ; v. 3. 10–11.

deceptive, debasing, I. 77 ; ii. 1. 6. 2.

fatal influence of effort after, III. 150 *n* ; iv. 10. 20 *n.*

"imperceptible gradations" from light to dark, untrue,
     I. 193 ; ii. 2. 3. 12.

laws of, I. 184 *seqq.* ; ii. 2. 3 *seqq.*

nature's arrangement of, I. 190 *seqq.* ; ii. 2. 3. 8 *seqq.*

„   contrasted with man's, I. 150–52 ; ii. 2. 1. 4–5.

necessity of, in expressing form, I. 74–5 ; ii. 1. 5. 7–8.

„   in high art, I. 192 ; ii. 2. 3. 10.

of old masters, I. 180 ; ii. 2. 3. 13–41 (ed. 1, 2 only).

Venetian colourists and, IV. 45–7 ; v. 3. 14.

value of, in learning to draw, I. 429 ; ii. 6. 1. 31 (om. ed. 1, 2)

writers on, ignorant, I. 191 ; ii. 2. 3. 9.

Childlike-ness, value of, IV. 51–2 ; v. 3. 21.

„   perception, IV. 74 *n* ; v. 5. 5 *n.*

Children, "child father to the man," I. xxxi ; *pref. ed.* 2. 24.

„   education of, V. 361 *n* ; ix. 11. 22 *n.*

„   how to read the Bible, V. 166–67 ; vii. 4. 25–6.

„   instinct of, about space, II. 42–3 ; iii. 1. 5. 3.

„   picture-books and, III. 51 ; iv. 4. 7.

Chillon, Hotel Biron to be omitted from sketch of, IV. 21 ; v. 2. 7.
China, consummation of clay in porcelain, V. 176 ; viii. 1. 9.
  „   figures, love of, bad taste, II. 88 ; iii. 1. 10. 3.
  „   monsters, II. 203 ; iii. 2. 3. 29.
  „   shepherdesses, III. 71 ; iv. 5. 7.
  „   value of rare, V. 272–73 ; ix. 5. 16.
Chinese art, fine colours of, III. 94 ; iv. 7. 14.
  „   no sense of perspective, I. 57 ; ii. 1. 2. 6.
  „   opium-eaters (example in particular truth argument),
         I. 63–4 ; ii. 1. 3. 4.
Chlorite, composition of, IV. 120-21 ; v. 9. 2.
Choice, danger of a spirit of, II. 28 and *n* ; iii. 1. 3. 12 and *n.*
  „   loving and insolent, II. 146 ; iii. 1. 15. 7.
  „   must be sincere, III. 30 ; iv. 3. 6.
  „   „   „   III. 38–9 ; iv. 3. 16.
  „   of subject, by artists, to paint } II. 233 ; iii. 2. 5. 12.
         what they love,   }
  „   „   „   „   III. 30 ; iv. 3. 6.
  „   „   „   „   III. 38 ; iv. 3. 16.
  „   „   „   „   IV. 18–19 and *n* ; v. 2.
                                     5–6 and *n.*
  „   open to us in all things, IV. 364 ; v. 19. 33.
Christ, baptism of, by Giotto and others, II. 189 ; iii. 2. 3. 18.
  „   buffeting of, sceptre of reed, etc., III. 242 ; iv. 14. 53.
  „   divinity and humanity of, IV. 404 *seqq.* ; v. 20. 47.
  „   life of, imagination needed to realize, III. 50 ; iv. 4. 5.
  „   never well portrayed in art, II. 229 ; iii. 2. 5. 7.
  „   Transfiguration of, IV. 403 *seqq.* ; v. 20. 47 *seqq.*
  „   victory over spiritual death, V. 384 ; ix. 12. 16.
  „   walking on the sea, Raphael and the reality, III. 57–8 ;
         iv. 4. 16.
Christian art, chronology of, III. 215–16 ; iv. 14. 20.
  „   „   imitative and symbolic, III. 215 ; iv. 14. 19.
  „   „   immortality of soul and early, V. 227 ; ix. 2. 7.
  „   character, coldness to beauty, II. 148–50 ; iii. 1.
         15. 9–11.
  „   „   denied the flesh, V. 226 ; ix. 2. 4.
  „   church, ideal, V. 276 ; ix. 6. 3.
  „   Greek and, ideas of God, II. 238 *seqq.* ; iii. 2. 5. 20.
  „   moral system, its spirit, II. 27 ; iii. 1. 3. 10.
  „   virtues, cheerfulness, and humility, III. 240–41 ; iv.
         14. 52.

Chrysaor, angel of lightning, V. 159 ; vii. 4. 12.
    „   „   „   V. 335 ; ix. 10. 12.
Chrysoprase, its colour, I. *ed.* 2. *pref.* 13 ; II. 91 ; iii. 1. 10. 7.
Church, going to, English propriety and, III. 151–52 ; iv. 10. 22.
    „   „   regularly, V. 245 ; ix. 3. 16.
    „   limited modern meaning of word, III. 243 ; iv. 14. 53.
    „   prayer in fine and old churches, V. 187 ; viii. 2. 6.
Cima da Conegliano, foregrounds and flowers, I. 86 ; ii. 1. 7. 9
                                            (om. ed. 1, 2).
    „   „   „   „   I. 89 ; ii. 1. 7. 10
                                            (om. ed. 1, 2).
    „   „   landscape of, III. 138 ; iv. 10. 5.
    „   „   works of :
                            Louvre, No. 173, rocks, IV. 268 ; v. 16. 36.
                            Mad. dell' Orto, Venice, I. 86 ; ii. 1. 7. 9
                                            (om. ed. 1, 2).

Cimabue, great in idea, I. 11 ; i. 1. 2. 7.
    „   mosaic at Pisa, II. 220 ; iii. 2. 4. 14.
    „   not popular, and why, I. 2 *n* ; i. 1. 1 *n* (ed. 1 and 2).
Cincinnatus, in his garden, III. 203 ; iv. 14. 3.
Cinqfoil, simplest expression of proportion, IV. 207 ; v. 15. 4.
    „   trees and architecture, V. 21 ; vi. 3. 14.
Circe, meaning of, V. 235 ; ix. 2. 17.
Circle, curves of a, IV. 282 ; v. 17. 7.
Cities, atheism of large, IV. 355 ; v. 19. 24.
    „   life in, IV. 382 ; v. 20. 26.
    „   „   its influence and origin (mediævalism), V. 4–5 ;
                            vi. 1. 5.
    „   necessity for manufacturing, V. 358 ; ix. 11. 18.
    „   streets of, to be beautiful with art, III. 274 ; iv. 16. 19.
Civilization, ideal life of, V. 268 ; ix. 5. 6.
    „   of savages, its use questioned, III. 320–21 ; iv.
                            17. 36.
Clairmont, coteaux of, IV. 261 ; v. 16. 27.
Classical architecture, V. 268 ; ix. 5. 6.
    „   art, prejudices created by, II. 41 ; iii. 1. 5. 2.
    „   „ proper, V. 266 *seqq.* ; ix. 5. 1 *seqq.*
    „   „ want of faith in, V. 267 ; ix. 5. 3.
    „   landscape, III. 178 *seqq.* ; iv. 13. 1 *seqq.*
    „   „   its features and influence, V. 268–69 ; ix
                            5. 6–8.
    „   life, ideal of, V. 268 ; ix. 5. 6

Classicalism, deities of, V. 269 ; ix. 5. 8.

Claude [SYNOPSIS. I. xvii, xxiv–vi, 6, 26, 33, 63, 80–1, 94, 132, 138,
142, 156, 161, 163, 169–70, 179, 186, 189, 206, 213 n, 218,
220, 222 seqq., 236, 239, 241, 245, 248–52, 287, 296–98, 302,
318, 322–23, 337, 343, 348–49, 360, 366, 410–13, 414, 422–23,
426, 433, 443. II. 48, 159, 170. III. 19, 123–27, 133, 198,
336–43, 344–45, 353–54. IV. 1, 2, 59, 202, 231, 266–69,
274, 313, 327, 376–77. V. 52, 136, 266–73, 345–46, 382]:—

admiration for, how far justified, V. 272 ; ix. 5. 16.
appreciation of, demanded, III. 19 ; iv. 2. 3.
architecture of, its errors, I. 433 ; ii. 6. 2. 1.
art-teaching in days of, IV. 313 ; V. 17. 47.
author's depreciation of, I. pref. ed. 3 (only).

,,   ,,   ,, I. 6 ; i. 1. 1. 4.

backgrounds of, places introduced, IV. 231 ; v. 15. 28.
character, power, and works of, I. 94 ; ii. 1. 7. 14 (om. ed.
1, 2).

,,   ,,   ,, III. 337–38 ; iv. 18. 20. 21.
,,   ,,   ,, (summary), V. 267 ; ix. 5. 3.
,,   ,,   ,,   ,, V. 269 seqq. ;
                                                 ix. 5. 10 seqq.

chiaroscuro, I. 186 ; ii. 2. 3. 4.
      ,,   I. 189–90 ; ii. 2. 3. 7.
      ,,   I. 180 ; ii. 2. 3. 15 (ed. 1, 2 only).
classicalism, I. 132 ; ii. 1. 7. 38 (om. ed. 1, 2).
colour of, false, I. 170 ; ii. 2. 2. 6.
      ,,   imperfect, V. 346 ; ix. 11. 3.
clouds, I. 236 ; ii. 3. 2. 11.
      ,,   I. 238–39 ; ii. 3. 2. 14.
      ,,   I. 241 ; ii. 3. 3. 3.
      ,,   generalized, I. 248–52 ; ii. 3. 3. 13–17.
      ,,   unspacious, ib. ; ib.
      ,,   untrue, V. 136 ; vii. 2. 19.
conceptions of, their absurdities, III. 340 ; iv. 18. 26.
delicacy of, V. 345 ; ix. 11. 2.
distances of, I. 184 ; ii. 2. 4. 6 (ed. 1, 2 only).
      ,,   I. 296–97 ; ii. 4. 2. 8–9.
      ,,   I. 423 ; ii. 6. 1. 24.
falsity of, I. 443–44 ; ii. 6. 3. 11–13.
feebleness of, due to deficient love of nature, I. 81–2 ; ii. 1
7. 5 (om. ed. 1, 2).
feebleness of, II. 48 ; iii. 1. 5. 12.

Claude, *continued* :

    filmy, futile, IV. 59 ; v. 4. 2.

    foolish elegance in, III. 344 ; iv. 18. 31.

    foregrounds, I. 189 ; ii. 2. 3. 7.

            „   assumed nearness of, I. 213 *n* ; ii. 2. 5. 15 *n* (om. ed. 1, 2).

            „   I. 337 ; ii. 4. 4. 17 (ed. 1, 2. 21).

            „   edges of, I. 343 ; ii. 4. 4. 27 (ed. 1, 2. 31).

            „   eulogized ! I. 349 ; ii. 5. 1. 5 (om. ed. 1, 2).

            „   "making out" in, I. 396 ; ii. 6. 1. 27 (ed. 1, 2 only).

    form, his sense of beauty of, useless, I. 80 ; ii. 1. 7. 3.

    idealism (classical), I. xxv ; *pref. ed.* 2. 17.

    imagination, deficient, II. 170 ; iii. 2. 2. 18.

    influences on, Florentine and Venetian, III. 340–42 ; iv. 18. 25–7.

    "juicy," "pulpy," praised as ! I. 222 ; ii. 3. 1. 11.

    landscape of, III. 197–98 ; iv. 13. 26.

            „   IV. 202 ; v. 14. 23.

            „   IV. 267 ; v. 16. 35.

            „   IV. 376 ; v. 20. 16.

    leafage, I. 422–23 ; ii. 6. 1. 22–4.

    mist of, III. 343 ; iv. 18. 28.

    mountains of, distant hills, I. 287 ; ii. 4. 1. 2.

            „   false, I. 297–98 ; ii. 4. 2. 10–11 (ed. 1, 2. 12, 13).

            „   ignorance of structure, IV. 231 ; v. 15. 28.

            „   IV. 274 ; v. 16. 41.

            „   IV. 377 ; v. 20. 17.

    National Gallery catalogue on, V. 382 ; ix. 12. 11.

    no moral influence, I. xxiii–xxvi ; *pref. ed.* 2. 15–17.

    pastoralism of, III. 345 ; iv. 18. 31.

    perspective, aërial, I. 296–97 ; ii. 4. 2. 9 (ed. 1, 2, § 11).

            „   example of false, I. 433 ; ii. 6. 2. 1.

    picturesqueness, first distinct in, IV. 1 ; v. 1. 1.

            „   Ghirlandajo compared, IV. 2 ; v. 1. 1 (pl. 18).

    reflections of, I. 360 ; ii. 5. 1. 17 (om. ed. 1, 2).

    rocks of, III. 342 ; iv. 18. 27.

            „   IV. 266–67 ; v. 16. 35.

            „   IV. 327 ; v. 18. 11.

    sameness of, I. 63 ; ii. 1. 3. 2.

Claude, *continued :*

"scientific ideals" (waterfalls), I. 318 ; ii. 4. 3. 16.

seas of, compared with nature's, I. 81 ; ii. 1. 7. 5.

    „   „ praised, I. 366 ; ii. 5. 1. 21 (ed. 1, 2, § 27).

    „ and waves, V. 270 ; ix. 5. 11.

shadows of, I. 186–87 ; ii. 2. 3. 4.

skies of, clear, I. 141–42 ; ii. 1. 7. 44 (om. ed. 1, 2).

    „   fine and true, I. 220 ; ii. 3. 1. 9. *See above, s. clouds*

stone-drawing of, IV. 327; v, 18. 11.

sunshine, first painted by, I. 94 ; ii. 1. 7. 14 (om. ed. 1, 2).

    „   I. 223 *seqq.* ; ii. 3. 1. 13–15 *seqq.*

    „   III. 133 ; iv. 10. 2.

    „   III. 337–39 ; iv. 18. 22–3.

    „   unequalled, even by Turner, III. 339–40 ; iv. 18. 25.

    „   V. 346 ; ix. 11. 3.

tone of, compared with Turner's, I. 156 ; ii. 2. 1. 13.

    „   I. 161 ; ii. 2. 1. 20.

    „   untrue, I. 162 ; ii. 2. 1. 21.

trees of, never right, I. 94 ; ii. 1. 7. 14 (om. ed. 1, 2).

    „   I. 218 ; ii. 3. 1. 4.

    „   I. 413 ; ii. 6. 1. 10.

    „   III. 125–26 ; iv. 9. 11.

    „   III. 353–54 ; App. i.

    „   V. 52–3 ; vi. 6. 11–12 (bough drawing. *See pl.* 4).

Turner, chief master of, III. 337 ; iv. 18. 22.

    „   excels him, I. xvii ; *pref. ed.* 2. 9.

    „   intellectual inferiority of Claude, I. 33 ; i. 1. 7. 2.

    „   sun-painting of, III. 339–40 ; iv. 18. 25.

    „   tone of, compared, I. 156 ; ii. 2. 1. 13.

    „   works of, resembling, I. 138 ; ii. 1. 7. 42 (om. ed 1, 2).

waterfalls, "scientific ideals," I. 318 ; ii. 4. 3. 16.

water-painting, I. 348 ; ii. 5. 1. 5 (om. ed. 1, 2).

works of :

    British Museum sketches, I. 414; ii. 6. 1. 12 (ed. 1, 2, § 11).

    Campagna, Rome, I. xlii ; *pref. ed.* 2.

    Dulwich Gallery, No. 241, I. 220 ; ii. 3. 1. 9.

    „   „   „ 244, I. 302 ; ii. 4. 2. 17 (ed. 1, 2, § 19).

    „   „   „ 260, mountains of, I. 322 ; ii. 4. 3.

Claude : works of, *continued :*

  Enchanted Castle (poss. Lord Wantage), fine sky, I. 220 ; ii.
                3. 1. 9.

  Florence, Uffizii, two works of, I. 360 ; ii. 5. 1. 17 (om. ed.
                1, 2).

  "Liber Veritatis," No. 140, III. 124–27 ; iv. 9. 9–11 (tree
                stems, pl. 4).

      „   „   „   180, III. 341 ; iv. 18. 26 (Æneas).
      „   „   „   „   *ib.* ; 340 (Moses).
      „   „   „   145, III. 342 ; iv. 18. 27.
      „   „   „   „   III. 354 ; App. i.
      „   „   „   86, IV. 231 ; v. 15. 28 (hill-draw-
                ing).

      „   „   „   91, IV. 265–67 ; v. 16. 34–6
                (rocks).

      „   „   „   5, IV. 327 ; v. 18. 11 (stones).

  Marriage of Isaac and Rebecca (Nat. Gall., 12) :

      I. 168 ; ii. 2. 2. 5 (ed. 1, 2, § 6).
      a copy, I. 220 ; ii. 3. 1. 9.
        „   I. 296 ; ii. 4. 2. 8 (ed. 1, 2, § 10).
      chiaroscuro of, I. 186 ; ii. 2. 3. 4.
      distance, I. 206 ; ii. 2. 5. 7.
      mountains, I. 296 ; ii. 4. 2. 8 (ed. 1, 2, § 10–11).
      trees in, I. 412 ; ii. 6. 1. 9.

  Mill (Nat. Gall.), I. xl *seqq.* ; *pref. ed.* 2. 36 *seqq.*
      „   „   II. 159 ; iii. 2. 2. 4.
      „   „   V. 270 ; ix. 5. 11.
  Molten Calf, III. 123 ; iv. 9. 8.
      „   „   V. 271–72 ; ix. 5. 14.
  Morning Scene, Cephalus and Procris (Nat. Gall.), I. 337–38 ;
                ii. 4. 4. 17–18.
      „   „   „   „   „   „   I. 318 ; ii. 4.
                4. 27 (ed. 1, 2
                only).

  Moses and Burning Bush (Ellesmere Gall.), III. 340 ; iv.
                18. 26.
  Narcissus (Nat. Gall., 19), "boa-constrictor" tree, I. 410–11 ;
                ii. 6. 1. 7. 9.
  Pisa, IV. 2 ; v. 1. 1.
  Rome, fine skies of works in, I. 220 ; ii. 3. 1. 9.
  St. George and Dragon, V. 271 ; ix. 5. 13.
  Seaport (Nat. Gall., 5), clouds false, I. 245 ; ii. 3. 3. 8.
      „   „   „   I. 161 ; ii. 2. 1. 20.
      „   („   „   14), architecture, I. 433 ; ii. 6. 2. 1.

Claude : works of, *continued :*

    Seaport (Nat. Gall., 14), chiaroscuro, I. 180 ; ii. 2. 3. 15 (ed. 1, 2 only).

    ,,   ,,   ,,   figures, I. 26 ; i. 1. 5. 5.

    ,,   (,,   ,,   30), architecture, I. 433 ; ii. 6. 2. 1.

    ,,   ,,   ,,   fine sky of, I. 220 ; ii. 3. 1. 9.

    Simon before Priam (Nat. Gall., 5), I. 179 ; ii. 2. 2. 16 (ed. 1, 2, § 18).

    ,,   ,,   ,,   ,,   mountains and trees in, I. 296 ; ii. 4. 2. 8.

    ,,   ,,   ,,   ,,   trees in, I. 413 ; ii. 6. I. 11.

Clay, china and sapphire, the consummation of, V. 176–77 ; viii. I. 9.

Clearness, nothing is clearly seen, IV. 60 *seqq.* ; v. 4. 4 *seqq.*

    ,,   students to aim at, IV. 70 ; v. 4. 16.

    ,,   ,,   ,,   IV. 83 ; v. 5. 20.

    ,,   turns mysterious in its infinity, IV. 84 ; v. 5. 21.

Cleavage [SYNOPSIS. **IV.** 113, 123 *n*, 133, 234, 413, 418–21]:—

    aiguilles, IV. 418 *seqq.* ; App. ii. 4.

    granite, IV. 421 ; *ib.* 5.

    leading lines of mountain, IV. 234 ; v. 15. 31.

    rock, IV. 413 *seqq.* ; App. ii. 1 *seqq.*

    slaty, IV. 113 ; v. 8. 13.

    ,,   IV. 123 *n* ; v. 9. 6 *n.*

    ,,   IV. 133 ; v. 10. 7.

    ,,   IV. 413 ; App. ii.

Clergyman, only one, ever drawn by Turner, V. 322 *n* ; ix. 9. 13 *n.*

Cleverness, no artist made by mere, V. 214 ; viii. 4. 22.

Cliffs, few English, of great unbroken height, I. 320 ; ii. 4. 3. 18.

    ,,   formation of, IV. 154–55 ; v. 12. 15–16.

    ,,   ,,   IV. 157 ; v. 12. 18.

    ,,   ,,   IV. 166–67 ; v. 13. 2.

    ,,   ,,   IV. 254 ; v. 16. 20.

    ,,   mistake respecting, IV. 314 ; v. 17. 48.

    ,,   of lower Alps, described, IV. 254–55 ; v. 16. 20–1.

    ,,   overhanging, IV. 268 *seqq.* ; v. 16. 37–9.

    ,,   precipitous, IV. 272–73 ; v. 16. 40.

    See s. Alps, Precipices.

Climates, art produced by different, V. 152 ; vii. 4. 2.

Climates, *continued :*

   ,,   V. 238–39 ; ix. 3. 2–3.

Clocks, real, in pictures, III. 339 ; iv. 18. 24.

Cloudiness, some in all landscape, IV. 71–2 ; v. 5. 2.

Clouds [SYNOPSIS. I. 68, 219, 229 *seqq.*, 234, 238, 240–50, 253–54,
        257, 260–64, 266–67. III. 222–23, 258, 260, 264 *seqq.*
        IV. vi, 37–8, 71–2, 88–93, 319, 370. V. 3, 113, 115, 118–50,
        151–71] :—

-balancings, V. 113–20 ; vii. 1. 1 *seqq.*

brighter than the sky, or whitest paper, IV. 37–8 ; v. 3. 4.

    ,,   their lustre, V. 135–36 ; vii. 2. 18.

buoyancy, why do they float? V. 115 *seqq.* ; vii. 1. 4 *seqq.*

central (cumulus) :

    character of, I. 240 *seqq.* ; ii. 3. 3. 1, 4 *seqq.*

    cirrostratus and, combined, I. 252 ; ii. 3. 3. 19.

    colours changing, I. 260–61 ; ii. 3. 4. 2.

    depth and size of, I. 245–46 ; ii. 3. 3. 9–11.

    explanation generally given of, V. 137–38 ; vii. 3. 2.

    formation of, I. 241–44 ; ii. 3. 3. 4–6.

        ,,   when they form, V. 137 *seqq.* ; vii. 3. 1
             seqq.

    unpaintable, *ib.* ; *ib.* 2.

    variety of their masses, I. 246–48 ; ii. 3. 3. 11–12.

chiaroscuro of, IV. 38 ; v. 3. 4–5.

cirrus (or upper) :

    characteristics of, I. 230–33 ; ii. 3. 2. 4–8.

    common forms of, I. 230–31 ; ii. 3. 2. 4.

    many colours of, I. 238 ; ii. 3. 2. 14.

    never painted till Turner, I. 233–34 ; ii. 3. 2. 9–10.

    number of, at sunrise, calculated, V. 123 ; vii. 2. 5.

    ordered marshalling of, V. 125–26 ; vii. 2. 7.

cloudlessness, rarity of total, IV. 71–2 ; v. 5. 2.

colour of, how caused, V. 118–19 ; vii. 1. 8.

    ,,   ,,   V. 134–36 ; vii. 2. 17–19.

connected *with* the sky, not separate, I. 219 ; ii. 3. 1. 6.

creation of, Bible account, IV. 88–93 ; v. 6. 5 *seqq.*

curves in, all curves, rare, I. 68–9 ; ii. 1. 4. 1.

    ,,   how caused, V. 3 ; vi. 1. 3.

    ,,   usual conditions, V. 131 and *n* ; vii. 2. 13 and *n.*

Dante on, III. 259 ; iv. 15. 20.

defined, I. 219 ; ii. 3. 1. 5.

divisions of. *See below, s. kinds.*

Clouds, *continued* :

 drawing of, mediæval symbol, wave-band, III. 223 ; iv.
    14. 28.

   „   modern (1843) English, I. 258 ; ii. 3. 3. 28
     (and note ed. 5 *seqq.*).

   „   modern, III. 264 *seqq.* ; iv. 16. 1 *seqq.*

   „   „ and ancient, IV. 319 ; v. 18. 1.

   „   principles, rules, and methods, V. 125 *n* ; vii.
     2. 6 *n.*

   „   requisite knowledge, V. 131 ; vii. 2. 14.

   „   "use pencil point," V. 132 ; vii. 2. 15.

 edges often darker than centres, I. 254 ; ii. 3. 3. 21.

 engraving of, V. 125 *n* ; vii. 2. 6 *n.*

 formation of, affected by damp, heat, and cold, V. 146–49 ;
   vii. 3. 14 *seqq.*

 generalization of, I. 247–48 ; ii. 3. 3. 12.

 God appearing in, in the Bible, IV. 88 ; v. 6. 5.

 highest, may deposit moisture, I. 260 ; ii. 3. 4. 1.

 infinity and variety of, I. 232–33 ; ii. 3. 2. 8.

   „ „ „ I. 251–52 ; ii. 3. 3. 17.

   „ „ „ V. 123–24 ; vii. 2. 6.

   „ „ „ V. 125–26 ; vii. 2. 7.

 kinds of, upper (cirrus), central (cumu- ⎱ I. 230 ; ii. 3. 2. 2.
  lus, stratus), and lower (rain-cloud), ⎰ V. 113 *seqq.* ; vii. 1. 2.

 kinds of (massive, striated, etc.), V. 121–22 ; vii. 2. 2–3.

 "leeside" Alpine, V. 139–40 ; vii. 3. 4.

 level, early painters' love of, III. 259 ; iv. 15. 21.

 love of, Egyptian, Greek, and Jewish, III. 260–61 ; iv.
   15. 21.

   „ English, justifiable, IV. 71 ; v. 5. 1.

   „ modern, III. 259, 262 ; iv. 15. 20, 24.

 "mare's tails," I. 231 ; ii. 3. 2. 4.

 mediæval symbolism of, III. 223 ; iv. 14. 28.

 mistaken for mountains, V. 134 and *n* ; vii. 2. 17 and *n.*

 motion of, its laws, V. 119–20 ; vii. 1. 9.

 mountains and, apparently motionless on, I. 241–42 ; ii. 3.
   3. 4.

   „ „ cloud-capped, V. 139 *seqq.* ; vii. 3. 4 *seqq.*

   „ „ fine association of, III. 258–59 ; iv. 15. 20.

   „ „ in lowland scenery and, IV. 370–71 ; v.
     20. 8.

   „ „ sorts of, on, V. 141–42 ; vii. 3. 7–10.

Clouds, *continued* :

> mountains and, wet weather and, V. 144–46 ; **vii. 3. 13.**
>
> mystery of, V. 119–20 ; vii. 1. 9.
>
> nearness of, IV. vi *n* ; *pref.* 3 *n.*
>
> "of relaxation," V. 147 ; vii. 3. 16.
>
> office of the, IV. 92–3 ; v. 6. 9.
>
>   „   „   their service to man, V. 113 ; vii. 1. 1.
>
> opaque character of, V. 135 ; vii. 2. 17.
>
> outline of, changes every moment, I. 229 ; ii. 3. 2. 1.
>
>   „   how regulated, V. 119 ; vii. 1. 9.
>
> perspective of, V. 128 *seqq.*; vii. 2. 10 *seqq.* (pl. 64).
>
> rain, formation of clouds in and after, V. 146 ; vii. 3. 14.
>
> rain-clouds :
>
> > angels of the sea, V. 151–71 ; vii. 4 *seqq.*
> >
> > colour of, heavy and monotonous, I. 261 ; ii. 3. 4. 2.
> >
> > elevation of, I. 260 *n* ; ii. 3. 4. 1 *n.*
> >
> > form of, I. 261 ; ii. 3. 4. 3.
> >
> >   „   horseshoe (Col de Balme), I. 262 ; ii. 3. 4. 4.
> >
> > functions, etc., of, V. 153–56 ; vii. 4. 5 *seqq.*
> >
> > never given by old masters, I. 263 ; ii. 3. 4. 6.
> >
> > pure blue sky seen only through, I. 272 ; ii. 3. 4. 20.
> >
> > rendering of, by Turner and Fielding, I. 265–66 *seqq.* ;
> >   ii. 3. 4. 10–12 *seqq.*
> >
> > velocity of, I. 262 ; ii. 3. 4. 4.
> >
> > wonderful effects of, value to artist, I. 262 ; ii. 3. 4. 5.
>
> scientific knowledge of, how far advanced, V. 115 ; vii. 1. 3.
>
> shadows of, V. 130 ; vii. 2. 13.
>
> spray, "white or purple," V. 134 *seqq.*; vii. 2. 17 *seqq.*
>
> sunset among the high, I. 170 ; ii. 2. 2. 7.
>
> transparency of, I. 248–49 ; ii. 3. 3. 14.
>
> truth of, I. 229–81 ; ii. 3. 2. 1 *seqq.*
>
> variety of, at different elevations, I. 230 ; ii. 3. 2. 2.
>
> waters divided from waters by, IV. 88 ; v. 6. 5.
>
> wind, its action on, V. 121 ; vii. 2. 1. *See s. Graiæ, Sky, Storm.*

Clown, implied reproach of word, V. 4 ; vi. 1. 4.

Cluse, valley of, IV. 152 ; v. 12. 12.

    „   „   IV. 260 ; v. 16. 26.

Coarseness, a sign of bad art, III. 42 ; iv. 3. 20.

    „   distinct from work done to be seen far off, *ib.* ; *ib*

Coast scenery. *See s. Stanfield.*

Cockney dialect, why vulgar, V. 297 ; ix. 7. 19.

Cocytus, of modern England, V. 343 ; ix. 10. 24. 25.

„   „   „   V. 347 ; ix. 11. 4.

" Cœcus adulator," etc., I. 165 *n* ; ii. 2. 2. 2.

Cœur de Lion, Saladin sending horses to, IV. 410 ; App. i. 5.

Coherent rocks, author's use of term, IV. 109 ; v. 8. 7.

Coins, lettering of Greek and English, V. 298 ; ix. 7. 21. *See
    s. Greek coins.*

Col d'Anterne, IV. 131 ; v. 10. 4.

„   „   IV. 254 ; v. 16. 20.

„ de Bonhomme, IV. 220 ; v. 15. 16.

„   „   „   IV. 367 ; v. 20. 3.

„   „ Ferret, IV. 131 ; v. 10. 4.

„   „   „   IV. 175 ; v. 13. 11.

Coleridge, S. T., on imitation and copying in art, I. 19 ; i. 1. 4. 1.

„   „   „   „   „   „   I. 443 ; ii. 6. 3.
                                                                                11.

„   „   quoted :

> "A man all light," etc., II. 141 *n* ; iii. 1. 14. 32.
>
> "Brown . . . . as the ribbed sea sand," III.
>   235 *n* ; iv. 14. 45 *n*.
>
> "Never to blend our pleasure or our pride,"
>   II. 98 ; iii. 1. 12. 2.
>
> "The one red leaf," etc., III. 166–67 ; iv. 12.
>   6–7.
>
> "The thin blue flame," etc., II. 212 ; iii. 2.
>   4. 6.
>
> Tricks her hair in lovely plight " (Geraldine,
>   "Christabel," ii. 34), V. 124 ; vii. 2. 6.

Colewort, in Raphael's pictures, I. xxx ; *pref. ed.* 2. 23.

Collins, sea-shore by, II. 241 ; Add. ed. 1. note 4.

Cologne, Rubens' " S. Peter " at, V. 277 ; ix. 6. 6.

Colonos, forest of, III. 226–28 ; iv. 14. 33–5.

Colour [SYNOPSIS. I. 71–5, 83–4, 103–4, 111, 142, 149–50, 168,
        170–72, 173, 179, 183, 440. II. 47–8, 57, 81, 86 *n*, 94–5,
        133, 216–17, 234. III. 35, 94–5, 107–8, 161–62, 233 *seqq.*,
        267, 273–74. IV. 37, 47–8, 53–7, 67–9, 113–15, 131, 255,
        258, 284, 368–69, 407. V. 210–12, 347–54] :—

    all beautiful, mingled, IV. 113–14 ; v. 8. 14. *See below, s.
        single.*

    best among half-savage people, III. 94–5 ; iv. 7. 14.

    -blindness, I. 73 ; ii. 1. 5. 6.

        „   V. 349 ; ix.-11. 7.

Colour, *continued :*

    brilliancy of, bad if violent, II. 91–2 ; iii. 1. 10. 8.

    chiaroscuro before, I. 74–5 ; ii. 1. 5. 8.

    chords of perfect, III. 107–8 ; iv. 8. 9.

       „   „   III. 292 ; iv. 16. 43.

       „   „   IV. 54 ; v. 3. 24.

       „   „   V. 346, 348 ; ix. 11. 4 *seqq.*

    contrasts, IV. 42 ; v. 3. 11.

    delight in, natural and right, IV. 55 ; v. 3. 24.

       „   of all great artists, III. 35 ; iv. 3. 11.

    dignity of, V. 348 *seqq.* ; ix. 11. 5 *seqq.*

    distance, its effect on, IV. 67–9 ; v. 4. 13 *seqq.*

    expression and, powers of, go together, IV. 407 ; App. i. 1.

    fact, not mere sensation, III. 161–62 ; iv. 12. 1–2.

    falsifying, its effect, V. 351–52 *n* ; ix. 11. 8 *n.*

    form, and abstract, V. 349 *n* ; ix. 11. 8 *n.*

   „   before, I. 72 ; ii. 1. 5. 3.

   „   „   IV. 56*n*–57 ; v. 3. 24 and *n.*

   „   colour without, how far desirable, II. 216–17 ; iii. 2. 4. 10.

   „   more pleasurable than, I. 75 ; ii. 1. 5. 9.

   „   senses of, often distinct, I. 440 ; ii. 6. 3. 4.

    gradations of, II. 51 ; iii. 1. 5. 16.

       „   eye trained to see, IV. 73–4 ; v. 5. 5.

       „   IV. 284–85 ; v. 17. 10–11.

    laying of different, in a picture, V. 210–12 ; viii. 4. 17–18.

    local, its exact hue difficult to determine, I. 74–5 ; ii. 1. 5. 8.

    love typified by, V. 353–54 ; ix. 11. 8–9.

    mellowed always by age, I. 111 ; ii. 1. 7. 26 (om. ed. 1, 2).

    melodies of, II. 86 *n* ; iii. 1. 9. 9 *n.*

    modern and mediæval, III. 273–74 ; iv. 16, 18.

   „   sentimental school lacks, III. 35 ; iv. 3. 11.

   „   „   „   sombre, III. 267 ; iv. 16. 8.

   „   „   „   „   III. 273–74 ; iv. 16. 18.

    moisture expressed by fulness of, IV. 258 ; iv. 16. 24.

    nature's brilliancy, unattainable, I. 170–71 ; ii. 2. 2. 7.

   „   „   „   I. 173–74 ; ii. 2. 2. 10.

   „   moderation of, to be observed by artists, II. 91–2 ; iii. 1. 10. 7–8.

   „   sign of life in all things, IV. 130–31 ; v. 10. 3.

   „   want of, a sign of death, *ib.* ; *ib.* (cf. III. 35 ; iv. 3. 11. IV. 53–4 ; v. 3. 23).

Colour, *continued* :

objects of one kind, seldom distinguished by, I. 73 ; ii. 1. 5. 4.

painting, colour the essence of, V. 347 ; ix. 11. 5.

    ,,   ,, *the* gift in, V. 350 *n* ; ix. 11. 8 *n*.

pale, deepest in shade, IV. 47 ; v. 3. 16.

pleasure derived from, I. 12 ; i. 1. 2. 8.

power of, implies all other art-power, V. 350 *n* ; ix. 11. 8 *n*.

powerful, generally a little conventional, I. 83 ; ii. 1. 7. 7 (om. ed. 1, 2).

primitive, the three, V. 349 ; ix. 11. 7.

principles of, recapitulated, V. 349 *n* ; ix. 11. 8 *n*.

pure, its use, to express the supernatural, II. 234 ; iii. 2. 5. 13. *See below, s. red.*

purity of, its essence, II. 81–2 ; iii. 1. 9. 2.

    ,,   ,, II. 85–6 ; iii. 1. 9. 8.

qualities of, absolute and real, IV. 37 ; v. 3. 3.

    ,, as affected by light, I. 149–50 ; ii. 2. 1. 2.

    ,, relative, I. 73 ; ii. 1. 5. 5.

realism compelled by, V. 353 *n* ; ix. 11. 8 *n*.

realization and, III. 148 ; iv. 10. 18.

red, the loveliest pure, IV. 47–8 ; v. 3. 16.

sanctity of, loss of modern feeling for, III. 267 ; iv. 16. 8.

    ,, colour of precious things, IV. 53–4 ; v. 3. 23–4.

    ,, V. 350–52 ; ix. 11. 8.

sense of, Greek and mediæval, III. 233 *seqq.* ; iv. 14. 42 *seqq.*

sensuality connected with impurity, II. 133 ; iii. 1. 14. 21 *seqq.*

single, more beautiful than patched, II. 57 ; iii. 1. 6. 5.

subordination, a law of, I. 170 ; ii. 2. 2. 22 (ed. 1, 2 only).

sun-colour and sunshine, V. 346 *seqq.* ; ix. 11. 3 *seqq.*

-system, no single, I. 142–43 ; ii. 1. 7. 45 (om. ed. 1, 2).

tenderness of, IV. 368 ; v. 20. 4.

truth of, distinct from feeling, I. 169 ; ii. 2. 2. 5.

    ,, or falsehood, necessary, V. 349–50 *n* ; ix. 11. 8 *n*.

use of, crude, bright, and subdued, I. 103–4 ; ii. 1. 7. 21 (om. ed. 1, 2).

    ,, pure, II. 234 ; iii. 2. 5. 13.

    ,, purple in excess, and too little yellow, I. 179 ; ii. 2. 2. 17.

warm and cold, II. 86 *n* ; iii. 1. 9. 9 *n*.

Colour, *continued :*

 wet, always most brilliant, IV. 258 ; v. 16. 24.
   See s. Brown, Green, Water.

Colourists, chiaroscurists and, IV. 49–50 ; v. 3. 19–20.
  ,, flatness of great, *ib.* ; *ib.*
  ,, give some absolute truth, *ib.* ; *ib.*
  ,, good, always have some other power, IV. 57 ; v
    3. 24.
  ,, the seven supreme, named, V. 350 *n* ; ix. 11. 8. *n.*
  ,, tone of great, I. 157 ; ii. 2. 1. 14.
  ,, use of green by, I. 168 *n* ; ii. 2. 2. 5 *n.*

Coltsfoot, leaf of, V. 105 ; vi. 10. 14.

Columbine, in Titian's "Bacchus and Ariadne," I. xxx ; *pref.
 ed.* 2. 23.

Columbus, V. 382 ; ix. 12. 11.

Comasque Alps (Il Resegone), IV. 162 ; v. 12. 21.

Commandment, law *v.*, V. 169 ; vii. 4. 32.

Common things, beauty of even, if we will see it, I. 347 ; ii. 5.
 1. 4 (om. ed. 1, 2).

Communities, large and small (men and leaves compared), V.
 28–9 ; vi. 4. 8.

Como, author's love of, IV. 366 ; v. 20. 2.

Competition, a law of death, V. 175, 177 ; viii. 1. 6. 9.

Completion, of a picture, what, V. 200 *seqq.* ; viii. 4. 1 *seqq.*
 See s. Finish, Portraiture.

Composition [SYNOPSIS. **I.** xxxix *seqq.*, 208. **II.** 159, 161, 244.
    III. 56, 84 *seqq.*, 93–4. **IV.** 20, 290–91. **V.** 173 *seqq.*
    177–78, 184 *seqq.*, 191–92, 198–99, 202, 210] :—

 in art, analyzed, etc., I. 208 ; ii. 2. 5. 10.
  ,, II. 159 ; iii. 2. 2. 4.
  ,, III. 56 ; iv. 4. 15.
  ,, breadth of, V. 198–99 ; viii. 3. 7.
  ,, described as poetry, V. 178 ; viii. 1. 13.
  ,, easier than faithful imitation, IV. 20 ; v. 2. 7.
  ,, every part essential to a great, V. 184 ; viii. 2. 1.
  ,, ,, ,, ,, V. 191–92 ; viii. 2. 13–14
  ,, false and true, IV. 20 *seqq.* ; v. 2. 7 *seqq.*
  ,, ,, ,, V. 173 *n* ; viii. 1. 2 *n.*
  ,, ,, ,, V. 177–78 ; viii. 10–13.
  ,, generalization is not, I. xxxix ; *pref. ed.* 2. 34.
  ,, harmony of, with true rules, II. 161 ; iii. 2. 2. 6.
  ,, ,, ,, ,, **III.** 93–4 ; iv. 7. 12.

Composition in art, *continued* :

  „ imagination distinct from, II. 159 ; iii. 2. 2. 3.

  „ instinctive, V. 173 ; viii. 1. 3.

  „ law of perfectness, V. 210 ; viii. 4. 16.

  „ motive of, V. 184 *seqq.* ; viii. 2. 1 *seqq.*

  „ noble, III. 84 *seqq.* ; iv. 7. 1. *seqq.*

  „ picturesque and poetical, II. 244 ; Add. 4 (om. ed. 1).

  „ technical, V. 172 *seqq.* ; viii. 1. 2 *seqq.*

  „ transgression of laws of, IV. 290–91 ; v. 17. 20.

  „ use of determinant sketches, V. 202 ; viii. 4. 5.

  „ value of, I. xxxix *seqq.* ; *pref. ed.* 2. 34 *seqq.*

Conceit, defined, always vulgar, V. 296 ; ix. 7. 18.

  „ instance of misplaced, in poetry, III. 166–7 ; iv. 12. 6. 7.

Conception [SYNOPSIS. II. 144, 157–58, 164, 206–7, 229. V. 209–10, 213]:—

 artists foresee the whole work, II. 163 ; iii. 2. 2. 9.

  „ „ „ V. 209–10 ; viii. 4. 15–16.

  „ „ „ V. 213 ; viii. 4. 20.

 connection with verbal knowledge, II. 157 ; iii. 2. 2. 1.

 fancy distinct from, II. 207 ; iii. 2. 4. 3.

 kinds of, II. 158 *n* ; iii. 2. 2. 2 *n.*

 limits of, II. 143 ; iii. 1. 15. 2.

  „ II. 229 ; iii. 2. 5. 7.

 meaning of, II. 157 ; iii. 2. 2. 1.

 vagueness of, II. 206 ; iii. 2. 4. 2.

Conscience, aided by association of ideas, II. 37–8 ; iii. 1. 4. 10.

Consistence, of inanimate things, V. 174 *seqq.* ; viii. 1. 5 *seqq.*

Constable [SYNOPSIS. I. xliv *n*, 99–100, 190. III. 126–27 and *n*, 128, 133–36, 150 *n*, 355. IV. 39, 82]:—

 aspen by, IV. 82 ; v. 5. 19.

 author's criticism on, III. 355 ; App. i.

 chiaroscuro of, I. 190 ; ii. 2. 3. 8.

  „ "Though my pictures have nothing else, they shall have chiaroscuro," III. 150 ; iv. 10. 20 *n.*

 feeling of, for his art, I. xliv *n* ; *pref. ed.* 2. 39 *n.*

 foliage of, III. 128 ; iv. 9. 15.

 showers, III. 133–36 ; iv. 10. 2. 3.

 spots and splashes of, IV. 39 ; v. 3. 6.

 works generally (Fuseli on them), I. 99 ; ii. 1. 7. 18 (om. ed. 1, 2).

  Helmingham Park, III. 128 ; iv. 9. 15.

  Lock on the Stour, III. 126–27 and *n* : iv. 9. 15 and *n.*

Constantin quoted, on use of colour, II. 234 ; iii. 2. 5. 13.

Contemplation, true happiness in, III. 321–25 ; iv. 17. 36–42.

   ,,   value of, V. 358–59 ; ix. 11. 18. *See s. Theoria.*

Contention, great art owes nothing to, V. 194 ; viii. 2. 15.

Contentment, beyond wealth, V. 359 ; ix. 11. 18.

   ,,   essential to true possession, V. 359 ; ix. 11. 19 *seqq*

   ,,   meekness and, *ib.* ; *ib.*

Continent, antiquity in England and on the, IV. 4–5 ; v. 1. 5.

Contrast, a principle of art, III. 37 ; iv. 3. 14.

   ,,   ,,   ,,   III. 85 ; iv. 7. 3.

   ,, law of, in all things, IV. 363–64 ; v. 19. 33.

Controversy, religious, of Protestantism, V. 275 ; ix. 6. 2.

Conventionalism, mediæval, *e.g.* heraldry, III. 210–11 ; iv. 14. 13

   ,,   wilful, in art, IV. 80 and *n* ; v. 5. 16 and *n.*

Convulsions, mountain, extent of original, IV. 162–64 ; v. 12. 22–3

Cooper, Fenimore, " Miles Wallingford," storm in, I. 403 *n* ; ii. 5. 3. 38 *n* (om. ed. 1, 2).

Co-operation, a law of life, V. 175, 177 ; viii. 1. 6. 9.

Copyists in art, contemptible, I. 450 ; ii. 6. 3. 22.

   ,, of Raphael, I. 5 ; i. 1. 1. 2.

Coral animals, how they build, V. 69 ; vi. 8. 1.

Corinth, mountain outline from, IV. 372 ; v. 20. 11.

Corinthian capitals, IV. 289 ; v. 17. 19.

Cormayeur, town of, IV. 185 ; v. 14. 6.

   ,,   ,, IV. 219 ; v. 15. 16

Corniche road, Dante's similes from its scenery, III. 246 ; iv. 15. 6.

   ,,   ,,   ,,   ,,   ,, III. 252 ; iv. 15. 13.

Correggio [SYNOPSIS. II. 51, 134, 146, 186, 222 *n.* III. 32, 36, 46, 68, 105–6, 335. IV. 59, 64, 380. V. 39, 40, 100, 154 *n*, 304, 350 *n*, 351 *n*, 383] :—

 author's sympathy with, V. 304 ; ix. 8. 1.

 characteristics and subjects of, III. 32 ; iv. 3. 8.

 chiaroscuro, I 180 ; ii. 2. 3. 14 (ed. 1, 2 only).

 choice of background, III. 335 ; iv. 18. 16.

 colour perfect, V. 350 *n* ; ix. 11. 8 *n.*

 flesh-painting, III. 106 ; iv. 8. 7.

 gradations of, refined, II. 51 ; iii. 1. 5. 17.

 landscape, III. 335 ; iv. 18. 16.

 leaf-drawing of, V. 39 ; vi. 5. 2. 3.

 life and surroundings of, III. 335 ; iv. 18. 15. 16.

 morbidezza of, V. 350–51 *n* ; ix. 11. 8 *n.*

 mystery and softness of, IV. 64 ; v. 4. 9.

Correggio, *continued*:

    mystery and softness of, V. 383 ; ix. 12. 13.

    no new school originated by, IV. 380 ; v. 20. 21.

    only, could have painted rain-cloud, V. 154 *n* ; vii. 4. 6 *n.*

    physical beauty of, III. 36 ; iv. 3. 12.

    sensuality of, II. 134 ; iii. 1. 14. 24.

        ,,   II. 146 ; iii. 1. 15. 6.

    sidelong grace of, III. 32 ; iv. 3. 8.

    tenderness, III. 46 ; iv. 3. 26.

    vagueness of landscape, IV. 59 ; v. 4. 2.

    "vulgar sentimentalism," II. 186 ; iii. 2. 3. 16.

    works of :

        Antiope (Louvre), III. 68 ; iv. 5. 4.
        ,,   foliage, V. 40 ; vi. 5. 5.
        ,,   ,,   V. 100 ; vi. 10. 5.
        ,,   hair, V. 154 *n* ; vii. 4. 6 *n.*
        Charioted Diana, II. 134 ; iii. 1. 14. 24.
        Dresden works, foliage, V. 100 ; vi. 10. 5.
        Mad. dell' Incoronazione (Parma), II. 134 ; iii. 1. 14. 24.
        ,   della Scudella   ,,   II. 222 *n* ; iii. 2. 4. 16 *n.*
        Parma works, II. 186 ; iii. 2. 3. 16.
        St. Catherine of the Giorno (Parma), II. 134 ; iii. 1. 14. 24.
        St. George (Dresden), V. 100 ; vi. 10. 5.

Corrie-nan-shian, V. 91 ; vi. 8. 8 (F.A. *n*).

Corruption, human, II. 119 *seqq.* ; iii. 1. 14. 1–2.

    ,,   of the best, worst (optimi pessima) in art, III. 29 ;
        iv. 3. 3.

    ,,   ,, things animate and inanimate, V. 174 ; viii. 1. 4.

Côte, Montagne de la, its crest, IV. 217 ; v. 15. 15.

    ,,   ,,   ,,   ,,   ,,   IV. 218–19 *n* ; v. 15. 16.

    ,,   ,,   ,,   ,,   ,,   IV. 223–24 *n* ; v. 15. 18–19 *n*
        (pl. 35–6).

    ,,   ,,   ,,   ,,   ,,   IV. 298 ; v. 17. 30.

    ,,   ,,   ,,   ,, slope, IV. 329 *n* ; v. 18. 15 *n.*

    ,,   ,,   ,,   ,, strata or beds, IV. 422 ; App. ii. 5.

    ,,   ,,   ,,   ,,   V. 149 ; vii. 3. 17.

Cotytto, I. 176 ; ii. 2. 2. 13 (ed. 1, 2, 14).

Couloir, meaning of Savoyard word, IV. 22 and *n* ; v. 2. 9 and *n.*

Countenance, as affected by mind and soul, II. 119 *seqq.* ; iii. 1.
    14. 1 *seqq.*

    ,,   ideal, free from sinning, not from sin, II. 126–28 ;
        iii. 1. 14. 11–12.

Countenance, *continued :*

　　　,,　　　signs of evil on, commonest (pride, sensuality,
　　　　　　　fear, cruelty), II. 128, 131 *seqq.* ; iii. 1. 14. 18.
　　　　　　　　　See s. Face, Features.

Country-folk, implied reproach of term, IV. 4 ; vi. 1. 4.

　　　,,　　-house, English and continental, IV. 5 ; v. 1. 6.

　　　,,　　-life, its influence on men, V. 5–6 ; vi. 1. 7.

Courage, a sign of good breeding, V. 299 ; ix. 7. 22.

Cousen, John, engravings to " Modern Painters," I. 1873 *pref.*

　　,,　　　,,　　　,,　　　,,　　　,,　　III. 128 *n* ; iv.
　　　　　　　　　　　　　　　　　　　　　9. 15 *n.*

　　,,　　　,,　　　,,　　　,,　　　,,　　V. ix *n* ; *pref.*
　　　　　　　　　　　　　　　　　　　　　6 *n.*

　　,,　　　,,　　　,,　　Turner's " Rivers of France," I. 183
　　　　　　　　　　　n ; ii. 2. 2. 20 *n* (om. ed. 1, 2).

Coutances, Cathedral of, its influence, IV. 379 ; v. 20. 20.

Couttet, Joseph, author's Swiss guide, II. '83 Epil. 4.

　　,,　　　,,　　　,,　　　,,　　　,, IV. 298 *n* ; v. 17. 30 *n.*

Covent Garden Theatre, burnt, 1856, its costliness, IV. 342 *n* ;
　　v. 19. 6 *n.*

Covetousness, Dante on, V. 337 ; ix. 10. 15.

Cowslip, V. 54 ; vi. 7. 4.

Cox, David [SYNOPSIS. I. xlv *n*, 101–3, 264, **273**, 327 *n*, 430, 439.
　　　　　IV. 79] :—

　　eulogy, etc., of, I. 76 ; ii. 1. 7. 6 (ed. 1, 2 only).

　　　,,　　　,,　　I. 102–3 ; ii. 1. 7. 20 (om. ed. 1, 2).

　　　,,　　　,,　　I. 327 *n* ; ii. 4. 3. 28 *n* (om. ed. 1–4).

　　　,,　　　,,　　IV. 79 ; v. 5. 15.

　　execution of, accidental, I. 104 ; ii. 1. 7. 22 (om. ed. 1, 2).

　　foliage of, I. 430 ; ii. 6. 1. 33 (om. ed. 1, 2). Cf. *pref. ed.*
　　　2. xlv *n* ; 40 *n*

　　" loose and blotted handling" of, I. 102 ; ii. 1. 7. 20 (om.
　　　ed. 1, 2).

　　paints too many small pictures, I. *pref. ed.* 2. xlv *n.* ; 40 *n.*

　　　,,　　　,,　　　,,　　　,,　　I. 103 ; ii. 1. 7. 20 (om. ed.
　　　　　　　　　　　　　　　　　　　　1, 2).

　　rain blue of his water colours, I. 273 ; ii. 3. 4. 21 (ed. 1–4, 24).

　　storms of, I. 264 ; ii. 3. 4. 7.

　　wild weedy banks of, I. 439 ; ii. 6. 3. 3.

　　works of :

　　　(1) Water Colour Exhib., 1843, I. xlv *n* ; *pref. ed.* 2. 40 *n.*
　　　(2) " Red Sunset," I. 103 ; ii. 1. 7. 20 (om. ed. 1, 2).

Cozens, J. R., landscape of, III. 346 ; iv. 18. 32.

Crabbe, "Patron," quoted, "Cold grew the foggy morn," IV. 56 *n* ; v. 3. 24 *n*.

Creation, Biblical account of the, IV. 86–7 ; v. 6. 2.

,, meaning of, "life-giving," V. 182–83 ; viii. 1. 19–20.

Creature, none can conceive what is more than, II. 229 ; iii. 2. 5. 7.

Cremona-violin-coloured foregrounds, III. 250 ; iv. 15. 11.

Cremorne, Chamouni becoming like, IV. 398 ; v. 20. 41.

Crests, mountain, IV. 205 *seqq.* ; v. 15. 1 *seqq.*

,, ,, beauty of, dependent on radiant curvature, IV. 212 ; v. 15. 8.

,, ,, formation of, IV. 208–9 ; v. 15. 5–6.

,, ,, ,, compared with aiguilles, IV. 224–25 ; v. 15. 20.

,, ,, precipices and, IV. 240–41 *n* ; v. 16. 2 *n*.

,, ,, sometimes like flakes of fire, I. 295 ; ii. 4. 2. 6. *See s. Mountains.*

Creswick, foliage and tree-painting, I. 421–22 ; ii. 6. 1. 20–21 (ed. 1, 2. 19–20)

,, ,, ,, ,, I. 431 ; ii. 6. 1. 34.

,, works of :

Nut-Brown Maid, *ib.* I. 421–22 ; ii. 6. 1. 20–21 (ed. 1, 2, 19–20).

Weald of Kent, I. 431 ; ii. 6. 1. 34 (om. ed. 1, 2).

Crichtoun, III. 328 ; iv. 18. 4.

Crimean war, II. 6 ; iii. 1. 1. 6 ('83 *n*).

,, ,, its causes and lessons, III. 346 *seqq.* ; iv. 18 (33 *seqq.*).

,, ,, Russian generals, "January," etc., IV. 410 ; App. i. 5.

Criticism [SYNOPSIS. I. xiv–xviii, 1, 5–6, 12, 52, 358, 438 *seqq.*, 443. III. vii–viii, 18, 24–5. IV. 411 *seqq.*] :—

as a criterion of excellence, I. 1 ; i. 1. 1. 1.

contemptible, when most so, I. 358 ; ii. 5. 1. 16.

evil of base, IV. 411 *seqq.* ; App. i. 6.

executive power distinct from (no critic is a great artist, or great artist critic), III. xi ; *pref.* 5.

fault-finding more read than praise, I. xiv ; *pref. ed.* 2. 4.

judicious, its duty, I. 11 ; i. 1. 2. 7.

modern, I. 438 *seqq.* ; ii. 6. 3. 1 *seqq.*

Criticism, *continued* :

    modern, incapable and inconsistent, I. 443–4 ; ii. 6. 3. 12–13.
       „   its general tone, III. 18 ; iv. 2. 1.
    of living and dead masters, I. xiii ; *pref. ed.* 2. 3.
       „   points to be considered, I. xvi–xix ; *pref. ed.* 2. 9–11.
    slowness to praise living merit, why ? I. xiv ; *pref. ed.* 2. 4.
    sympathy, its true basis, III. 25 ; iv. 2. 8.
    technical knowledge essential to, I. 4 ; i. 1. 1. 2.
    truth, its importance in, I. 52 ; ii. 1. 1. 10.
    work and knowledge essential to just, III. vii–viii ; *pref.* 3.
            See s. Press.

Crocodile, of Ganges, V. 339 ; ix. 10. 18.
Crocus, "spendthrift," III. 164 ; iv. 12. 4.
Cross, not cross-bones, V. 380 ; ix. 12. 8.
Crucifixion, renderings of, common, II. 191 ; iii. 2. 3. 20.
Cruelty, ill-bred, V. 290 ; ix. 7. 7.
Cruikshank (George), genius of, IV. 409–10 ; App. i. 4–5 *n.*
    „   „   neglected by his age, V. 293 and *n* ; ix. 7. 11 *n.*
    „   „   works of :

            Irish Rebellion, *ib.* ; *ib.*
            Jack Sheppard, *ib.* ; *ib.*
            Noah Claypole ("Oliver Twist"), *ib.* ; *ib.*

Crustaceans, beauty of, II. 100 ; iii. 1. 12. 4.
      „   V. 87 ; vi. 9. 2.
Crystal Palace (1851), I. 454 ; ii. 6. 3 postscript (om. ed. 1–4
    „   „   „   Alhambra Courts, IV. 54 *n* ; v. 3. 24 *n.*
Crystalline, compact and slaty, IV. 105 *seqq.* ; v. 8. 1 *seqq.*
    „   „   „   IV. 107 *seqq.* ; v. 8. 4 *seqq.*
    „   „   „   IV. 112 *seqq.* ; v. 8. 12 *seqq.*
    „   „   „   IV. 120 *seqq.* ; v. 9. 1 *seqq.*
    „   curvature in slaty, IV. 158 ; v. 12. 19.
    „   rocks, author's use of term, IV. 109–11 *seqq.* ; v. 8. 7–10 *seqq.*
Crystallization, aqueous, IV. 413 *seqq.* ; App. ii. 1 *seqq.*
    „   of mountains, IV. 107 *seqq.* ; v. 8. 4 *seqq.*
Crystals, formation and growth of leaves and, compared, V. 36–7 ; vi. 4. 17–18.
    „   from water, V. 176–77 ; viii. 1. 9.
Cuff, R., engravings to "Modern Painters," I. *pref.* '73.

Cuff, R., *continued :*
  „ engravings to "Modern Painters," V. ix ; *pref.* 6 *n.*
Cumberland hills, Glaramara, I. 293 ; ii. 4. 3. 12 (ed. 1, 2
                only).
  „   „   Saddleback, I. 316 ; *ib.* (om. ed. 1, 2).
  „   „   their moorland, IV. 97 ; v. 7. 4.
  „   „   „   vegetation, IV. 305 ; v. 17. 37.
  „   lakes, colour of, III. 249 ; iv. 15. 9.
Cunning, V. 240 ; ix. 3. 5.
  „   vulgarity of, V. 294 ; ix. 7. 11.
Cupids, angels and, not to be confused, II. 236–37 ; iii. 2.
       5. 17.
Curiosities, value of, V. 272–73 ; ix. 5. 16.
Curse or purse, no good work done for, V. 381 ; ix. 12.
       10.
Curtius, V. 196 ; viii. 3. 4.
Curvature, curves [SYNOPSIS. I. 334, 392, 424. II. 49–51, 65–7,
               91. IV. 203–4, 212, 277–78, 279–81, 283–88,
               298–301 *n*, 304, 321. V. 21, 62–3, 351 *n*]:—
  beauty of, analyzed, which most and least lovely, IV. 279
               seqq. ; v. 17. 4 *seqq.*
  „   II. 49–50 ; iii. 1. 5. 14.
  „   compared with straight lines, IV. 278 *seqq.* ; v.
               17. 3 *seqq.*
  „   essentials of, IV. 288 ; v. 17. 18.
  „   laws of, IV. 212 ; v. 15. 8.
               See below, s. spirals.
  catenary, IV. 285–86 *n* ; v. 17. 12 *n.*
  essential to beauty of form, II. 66 ; iii. 1. 6. 12.
       „   „   „   IV. 277–78 ; v. 17. 3.
  is to lines, as gradation to colour, II. 51 ; iii. 1. 5. 16.
       „   „   „   V. 351 *n* ; ix. 11. 8 *n.*
  law of, throughout nature, II. 65–6 ; iii. 1. 6. 12.
       „   „   „   IV. 203–4 ; v. 14. 25.
  laws of change and delicacy in, IV. 301 ; v. 17. 31 *n.*
  leaf curvature, IV. 287 *seqq.* ; v. 17. 16 *seqq.* (pl. 42–4).
  "look for curves and you will see them," and *vice versâ*,
       IV. 321 ; v. 18. 4.
  mountain débris, IV. 298–301 ; v. 17. 30.
       „   „   IV. 302 ; v. 17. 31 (pl. 35).
       „   example of complexity, IV. 304 ; v. 17. 35.
  mortal and immortal, IV. 283 ; v. 17. 8.

Curvature, curves, *continued*:

    natural lines, all more or less curved, II. 50; iii. 1. 5. **15** (and '83 *n*).

       „   „   continuity of, I. 335; ii. 4. 4. 13.

       „   „   moderation in curvature of, II. 91–2; iii. 1. 10. 7–8.

    parabolic, IV. 286; v. 17. 13.

    proportion in, II. 65; iii. 1. 6. 11.

    quantity of, measurable, IV. 285 *n*; v. 17. 11 *n*.

    radiation of, IV. 209 *seqq.*; v. 15. 7–8 *seqq.*

    spirals and conics, the most beautiful, II. 65; iii. 1. 6. 11.

    trees and, I. 424; ii. 6. 1. 25.

       „   „   *e.g.* of stems, V. 21; vi. 3. 14.

       „   „   „   „   V. 62–3; vi. 7. 12.

    water, curves of running, I. 392; ii. 5; iii. 24.

    "well-composed," IV. 287–89; v. 17. 16–18.

Custom [SYNOPSIS. II. 26–7, 33–4, 58. III. 27, 310–11] :—

    beauty, independent of, II. 33 *seqq.*; iii. 1. 4. 3 *seqq.*

       „   not the mere result of, III. 27; iv. 3. 2.

    deadens us to pain and wrong (*e.g.* in art), II. 26; iii. 1. 3. 8.

       „   „   sensation, confirms affection, II. 33; iii. 1. 4. 4.

    effect of, on our pleasures, II. 58; iii. 1. 6. 6.

       „   „   „   deadening, III. 310–11; iv. 17. 23.

Cuyp [SYNOPSIS. I. 6, 80, 97, 157, 159–61, 163, 186, 222, 227, 239, 240, 336, 361, 368. III. 332–33, 343, 344. V. 39, 41, 217, 275 *seqq.*, 279, 280–81, 286, 346 *seqq.*] :—

    animals of, V. 280–81; ix. 6. 12–13.

    author's depreciation of, I. 6; i. 1. 1. 4.

    calm water, good, I. 368; ii. 5. 1. 23 (om. ed. 1, 2).

    cattle-pieces, V. 286; ix. 6. 23.

    chiaroscuro of, I. 157; ii. 2. 1. 14. *See below, s. sun-light.*

       „   I. 186; ii. 2. 3. 4.

       „   I. 180; ii. 2. 3. 15 (ed. 1, 2 only).

    clouds of, cirrus, I. 238–39; ii. 3. 2. 14.

       „   generalized, I. 231; ii. 3. 3. 13 (ed. 1, 2 only).

    colour of, I. 157; ii. 2. 1. 14.

       „   imperfect, V. 346; ix. 11. 3.

    foregrounds of, I. 336–37; ii. 4. 4. 16 (ed. 1, 2. 20)

Cuyp, *continued :*
 landscape of, and Pre-Raphaelite work, III. 332–33 ; iv.
     18. 12.
   „   heads pastoral landscape, V. 217 ; ix.
     1. 2.
 leaf-drawing of, V. 39 ; vi. 5. 3.
   „   V. 41 ; vi. 5. 7.
 merit of, I. 97 ; ii. 1. 7. 16 (om. ed. 1, 2).
 powerful, but no sense of beauty, I. 80 ; ii. 1. 7. 3.
 powers of, V. 280 ; ix. 6. 12.
 Rubens and, V. 275 *seqq.* ; ix. 6. 1 *seqq.*
 shadows of, I. 186 ; ii. 2. 3. 4.
 skies of, I. 227 ; ii. 3. 1. 20.
 sunlight of, I. 157 ; ii. 2. 1. 14.
   „ discords in tone, I. 159–61 ; ii. 2. 1. 19–20.
   „ V. 280 ; ix. 6. 12.
   „ V. 346–47 ; ix. 11. 3–4.
 tone untrue, I. 162 ; ii. 2. 1. 21.
 truthful, but limited, III. 344 ; iv. 18. 31.
   „ covering other faults, V. 286 ; ix. 6. 23.
 Turner as influenced by, III. 343 ; iv. 18. 29.
 unspiritual, V. 279 ; ix. 6. 10.
 works of :

  Dulwich Gallery (No. 169), I. 160 ; ii. 2. 1. 19.
   „   „   „ large, central clouds, I. 240 ; ii.
               3. 3. 1.
   „   „   „ „ false sky, I. 222 ; ii. 3. 1.
               11.
   „   „   „ „ Hazlitt's praise of its
             "downiness," *ib.* ; *ib.*
   „   „ (No. 83), reflections in water of, I. 361 ; ii.
           5. 1. 17 (om. ed. 1, 2).
   „   „   „ I. 338 ; ii. 5. 1. 19 (ed. 1, 2 only).
   „   „ (No. 163), leaf-drawing, V. 41 ; vi. 5. 7.
  National Gallery (No. 53), I. 160 ; ii. 2. 1. 19.
   „   „   „ foliage, V. 41 ; vi. 5. 7.
  Waterloo etchings, I. 97 ; ii. 1. 7. 16 (om. ed. 1, 2).

Cycloid, curves, IV. 283 ; v. 17. 7.
  „ „ IV. 301 *n* ; v. 17. 31 *n.*
Cypress-spire, V. 86 ; vi. 9. 1.
Cyrene, scenery of, V. 330 ; ix. 10. 4. *See s. Hesperides.*
Cytheræa, III. 67 ; iv. 5. 2. *See s. Venus.*

Da Vinci, Leonardo [SYNOPSIS. I. xlviii, 6, 93–5, 120, 124, 144.
II. 88, 129, 179 *n*, 189, 229. III. 30, 41–2,
46, 130, 254, 278, 354, 361. IV. 45, 48–50,
59, 321, 379–80, 408. V. 39, 135, 202–3,
277, 285, 350 *n*] :—

author's reverence for, I. xlviii, *pref. ed.* 2. 42.
     „   „   „ I. 6 ; i. 1. 1. 4.
characteristics of :
    architecture, masonry in, I. 120 ; ii. 1. 7. 31 (om. ed.
       1, 2).
        „   nobly designed, I. 124 ; ii. 1. 7. 34 (om.
           ed. 1, 2).
    caricaturist elements, IV. 408 ; App. i. 3.
    colour and chiaroscuro (contrasted masses), IV. 45 ; v.
       3. 13.
      „   „   „ IV. 48–9 ; v. 3. 16. 18.
      „   „   „ V. 350 *n* ; ix. 11. 8 *n*.
    dignity, II. 179 *n* ; iii. 2. 3. 7.
    executive excellence of, IV. 379–80 ; v. 20. 21–2.
    figures of, less than life-size in best works, III. 41–2 ;
      iv. 3. 19.
    finish, II. 88–9 ; iii. 1. 10. 4.
      „ and detail, III. 130 ; iv. 9. 18.
      „   „ ease, III. 278 ; iv. 16. 27.
    horse introduced into sculpture by, V. 285 ; ix. 6. 22.
    landscape, I. 93–5 ; ii. 1. 7. 13–14 (om. ed. 1, 2).
      „   clear, IV. 59 ; v. 4. 2.
    leaf-drawing, V. 39 ; vi. 5. 2.
    love of beauty, III. 46 ; iv. 3. 25.
    methods of, IV. 49 and *n* ; v. 3. 19 and *n*.
      „   false for study, *ib.* ; *ib.*
      „   Turner's compared, *ib.* ; *ib.*
    mountain influence on, IV. 379–80 ; v. 20. 21–2.
    originated no new school, *ib.* ; *ib.*
    perfection, I. 144 ; ii. 1. 7. 45 (om. ed. 1, 2).
    portraiture in works of, II. 129 ; iii. 1. 14. 14.
    rock-drawing, III. 254 ; iv. 15. 16 (pl. 10).
      „   III. 354 ; App. i.
      „   law of transmitted light, V. 135 ; vii. 2.
        18.
  popularity, greatest of his feeblest points, I. 4 *n* ; i. 1.
  1. 1 *n*.

Da Vinci, Leonardo, *continued :*
  sketches of, V. 202–3 ; viii. 4. 6.
  works of :

      angel by, in Verrocchio's Baptism of Christ, II. 189 ; iii. 2. 3.
        18.
      Cenacolo (Milan), II. 229 ; iii. 2. 5. 7.
        „   „   III. 30 ; iv. 3. 5.
        „   „   III. 361 ; App. iii.
        „   „   V. 277 ; ix. 6. 5.
      Christs by, II. 229 ; iii. 2. 5. 7.
      drapery study (Louvre), IV. 45, 50 ; v. 3. 13. 20.
      foliage study (Florence, Uffizii), I. 93 ; ii. 1. 7. 13 (om. ed.
        1, 2).
      Holy Family (Louvre), I. 93 ; ii. 1. 7. 13 (om. ed. 1, 2).
      Madonna (Milan, Brera), I. 90 ; ii. 1. 7. 11 (om. ed. 1, 2).
      St. Anne (Louvre), agates in, III. 131 ; iv. 9. 18.
        „   „   „   IV. 321 ; v. 18. 3.

Daguerreotype, use of, in architectural drawing, I. 114 ; ii. 1. 7.
                  28 (om. ed. 1, 2).
      „   „   „ recording architectural detail, I. 118 ;
                  ii. 1. 7. 30 (om. ed. 1, 2). *See s.*
                  Photography.

Daisy, V. 111 ; vi. 10. 23.
Danaë, myth of, V. 158–59 ; vii. 4. 12.
Danaides, myth of, *ib.* ; *ib.*
Dancing, motion of, V. 70 ; vi. 8. 3.
      „   till dawn, III. 274 ; iv. 16. 19.
Danger, contemplation (not fear) of, sublime, I. 45 ; i. 2. 3. 3.
Daniel, II. '83 *pref.* 5.
Dannaeker's Ariadne, III. 71 ; iv. 5. 7.
Dante [SYNOPSIS. **II.** 73, 137–38, 176, 177, 196. **III.** 20, 27 *n*, 75,
      105, 115, 116, 156, 165 *n*, 192 *n*, 199, 223–26, 227–30,
      231–33, 235, 237–38, 241–43, 245–47, 249, 251–60,
      275, 278, 283–84, 289, 292, 293, 304 *n*, 327, 359. **IV.** 29,
      78, 115–16 *n*, 253, 265, 317, 326, 334, 387, 389. **V.** 255,
      283, 312 *n*, 317, 337, 364] :—
  (1) *General notes on :*
      accuracy minute, III. 253 ; iv. 15. 13.
      ambiguity of, IV. 78 ; v. 5. 12.
      author's debt to, III. 359 ; App. iii.
        „   first study of, II. 73 ; iii. 1. 7. 5 ('83 *n*).
      colour carefully defined by, III. 238 ; iv. 14. 49.

Dante, (1) *General notes on, continued :*

  colour, subtle, III. 289 ; iv. 16. 42.

    ,, symbolic use of (hewn rock), IV. 115–16 *n* ; v. 8. 15 *n. See below, s.* (3) *subjects.*

  creative power, III. 165 *n* ; iv. 12. 6 *n.*

  definiteness of, III. 223–26 ; iv. 14. 29–32.

    ,, III. 238 ; iv. 14. 50.

  description, orderly (Paradise), III. 225 ; iv. 14. 31.

  editions of, Flaxman's engraving of stones, IV. 326 ; v. 18. 10.

    ,, Norton's "Vita Nuova," V. 312 *n* ; ix. 8. 15 *n.*

    ,, renderings of (Inferno), II. 137 ; iii. 1. 14. 29. *See s. Cary, Cayley.*

  finish and ease, III. 278 ; iv. 16. 27.

  Giotto's portrait of, II. 129 ; iii. 1. 14. 14.

    ,, relation o, III. 276 ; iv. 16. 22.

    ,, (cf. Turner and Scott), III. 327 ; iv. 18. 2.

  greatest of all poets, III. 20 ; iv. 2. 5.

    ,, no second, IV. 317–18 ; v. 17. 51.

  Homer and Virgil's influence on, III. 199 ; iv. 13. 27

  imagination of, II. 177–78 ; iii. 2. 3. 4. 5.

    ,, greater than Milton's, III. 224–25 ; iv. 14. 30.

    ,, often involuntary remembrance, IV. 29 ; v. 2. 17.

  "inspired exponent of religious teaching," III. 243 ; iv. 14. 53.

  landscape, feeling for, III. 156 ; iv. 11. 6.

  Milton and, III. 223 *seqq.* ; iv. 14. 29.

  repose of, II. 73 ; iii. 1. 7. 5 (and '83 *n*).

  Scott compared with, III. 283 ; iv. 16. 34.

  self-command, III. 169 ; iv. 12. 10.

  sense of truth, V. 364 ; ix. 11. 26.

  Shakspere and, compared, IV. 394-95 *n* ; v. 20. 38 and *n.*

  spiritual personification, III. 105 ; iv. 8. 7.

  sternness of (supposed), III. 160 ; iv. 12. 10.

  subject of, his own time, III. 97–8 ; iv. 7. 18. 19.

  symbolism of, IV. 115–16 *n* ; v. 8. 15 *n.*

  tenderness of, unrivalled. II. 182 ; iii. 2. 3. 9.

Dante, (1) *General notes on, continued*:

    Turner and, compared, V. 320 ; ix. 9. 9.

        „   „   V. 364 ; ix. 11. 26.

    typical of his own time, III. 198–99 ; iv. 13. 27.

        „   mediæval mind, III. 275 ; iv. 16. 21.

    universality of (Straw Street and Seventh Heaven), III. 89 ; iv. 7. 8.

(2) *Persons and places*:

    Adam of Brescia, III. 256 ; iv. 15. 17.

        „   „   and Sinon, IV. 385 ; v. 20. 29.

    Alps, III. 255–57 ; iv. 15. 17. 19.

        „   Dante "a bad climber," III. 253 ; iv. 15. 13.

        „   "Qual' è quella ruina," etc., IV. 334 ; v. 18. 25.

    Apennines, III. 257 ; iv. 15. 19.

    Beatrice, III. 230–32 ; iv. 14. 37–8.

        „   gazing on the sun, III. 259 ; iv. 15. 20.

    Buonconte da Montefeltro, III. 261–62 ; iv. 15. 21.

    Casella, V. 364 ; ix. 11. 26.

    Casentino, III. 256 ; iv. 15. 17.

    Chiron (Centaur), III. 87 ; iv. 7. 6.

    Countess Matilda, III. 229 *seqq.*; iv. 14. 35–9.

    Fésole, III. 256 ; iv. 15. 17.

    Forli, falls of (Inf. xvi. 99), III. 247 ; iv. 15. 6.

    Francesca di Rimini, II. 178 ; iii. 2. 3. 5.

        „   „   IV. 56 *n*; v. 3. 24 *n*.

    Geryon (or fraud), V. 336–37 ; ix. 10. 13–14.

    Lethe, III. 229 ; iv. 14. 36.

        „   "a bleak and Alpine cliff," III. 257 ; iv. 15. 18.

        „   called brown, III. 249 ; iv. 15. 9.

    Lucan, III. 256 ; iv. 15. 17.

    Malebolge, arches of, III. 246–47 ; iv. 15. 5. 7.

    Medusa, III. 237 ; iv. 14. 48.

    Paduans, Chiarentana, III. 257 ; iv. 15. 18.

    Penestrino, IV. 395 *n*; v. 20. 38 *n*.

    Phlegethon, III. 224 ; iv. 14. 29.

    Rachel and Leah, vision of, III. 230–31 ; iv. 14. 37.

    Sigier, "who while in Rue de Fouarre," etc., III. 89 ; iv. 7. 8.

    Solomon (Par. x. 109 ; xiii. 95), II. 103 ; iii. 1. 12. 8 ('83 *n*).

    Tabernicch, Pietra-pana, III. 247 ; iv. 15. 6–7.

Dante, (2) *Persons and places, continued*.

      Ugolino, II. '83 Epil. 7.

       „   dream of, III. 256 ; iv. 15 17.

  (3) *Subjects in :*

      abyss of seventh circle, III. 252–53 ; iv. 15 13.

      Alps, etc. *See above, s.* (2) *places.*

      anger, imaged by Alpine clouds, III. 259 ; iv. 15. 20.

      art, imitative, III. 20 ; iv. 2. 5.

       „ likeness, III. 116 ; iv. 9. 2.

       „   „   IV. 389 ; v. 20. 31.

      boat of the condemned, II. 196 ; iii. 2. 3. 24.

      colours in, III. 233, 235 *seqq.* ; iv. 14. 42. 46 *seqq.*

       „   "less than roses, more than violets," III. 235 ; iv. 14. 46.

       „   list of, III. 237–38 ; iv. 14. 49.

       „   stones of Purgatory gate, IV. 116 *n* ; v. 8. 15 *n*.

       „   use of "brown" waves, twilight, III. 249 ; iv. 15. 9.

      courage of, joyful, III. 283 ; iv. 16. 34.

      demons in, V. 283 ; ix. 6. 19.

      dragon of, V. 337 ; ix. 10. 15.

      dress, love of beautiful, IV. 387 ; v. 20. 30.

      evil-pits in (Inf. vii.), III. 245–47 ; iv. 15. 4. 7.

      flame, "Feriami 'l Sole . . . parer la fiamma," II. 176 ; iii. 2. 3. 2.

      grass, "green enamel," III. 237–38 ; iv. 14. 48.

       „   "green herb," III. 237 ; iv. 14. 49.

       „   significant use of, III. 238–41 ; iv. 14. 51–3.

      happiness higher and lower in, III. 231–32 ; iv. 14. 38.

      heathens before Christ, damnation of, V. 255 ; ix. 4. 1.

      hell in, detail of, III. 223–25 ; iv. 14. 29–32.

       „   and in Milton, *ib.* ; *ib.*

      humility symbolized by, III. 240–41 ; iv. 14. 52.

      inscription in obscure colour. III. 249 ; iv. 15. 9.

      landscape in (Inf.), flat and trenched, III. 225–26 ; iv. 14. 32.

       „   ideal landscape in, III. 227 *seqq.* ; iv. 14. 34.

       „   typical of mediævalism, III. 199 ; iv. 13. 27.

Dante : (3) *Subjects in, continued :*

   light loved by, III. 258–59 ; iv. 15. 20.

   Love in, picture of, suggested, III. 105 ; iv. 8. 7.

   mediæval faith as declared by, III. 232 ; iv. 14. 39.

   mountains in (Purg.), III. 225–26 ; iv. 14. 32.

            ,,   abodes of misery, III. 245 ; iv. 15. 3.

            ,,   forms, as grasped by, III. 255–57 ; iv. 15. 17–18.

            ,,   his dislike of steep places, III. 252–53 ; iv. 15. 13.

            ,,   named. *See above, s. (2) Tabernicch.*

   pit of Inferno, cloudy bottom, III. 258 ; iv. 15. 20.

   Psalm xcii. referred to, III. 230 ; iv. 14. 36.

   rain, III. 258–59 ; iv. 15. 20.

   rocks, colour of, III. 246 *seqq.* ; iv. 15. 6 *seqq.*

    ,,   disliked, III. 292 ; iv. 16. 43.

    ,,   ,,   (cf. "Marriage"), III. 304 *n* ; iv. 17. 9 *n.*

    ,,   epithets of, III. 253–54 ; iv. 15. 14.

    ,,   ,,   "cut rocks," IV. 253 ; v. 16. 19.

    ,,   ,,   "erto," "sconcio," etc., III. 253 ; iv. 15. 14.

    ,,   ,,   "iron-grained," IV. 265 ; v. 16. 33.

    ,,   ,,   "maligno," III. 253 ; iv. 15. 14.

    ,,   ,,   "stagliata," *ib.* ; *ib.*

    ,,   ,,   ,,   III. 258 ; iv. 15. 19.

    ,,   frangible substance of, III. 252 ; iv. 15. 13.

    ,,   rocky scenery (Apennine), III. 246 *seqq.* ; iv. 15. 6 *seqq.*

   rush gathering, emblem of humility, III. 241; iv. 14. 53.

   singing birds, III. 293 ; iv. 16. 44.

   sky and clouds in, III. 258 *seqq.* ; iv. 15. 20 *seqq.*

   sunlight in, III. 258 ; iv. 15. 20.

   twilight, "brown" (Inf. xi. 1), III. 249 ; iv. 15. 9.

   waves, "brown," *ib.* ; *ib.*

   woods in, thought terrible, III. 226–27 ; iv. 14. 33.

       ,,   *e.g.* Paradise and Inferno, III. 228–29 ; iv. 14. 34.

 (4) *Various quotations :*

   "aer nero . . . maligno," III. 249 ; iv. 15. 9.

   "as dead leaves flutter" (spirits falling), III. 166 ; iv. 12. 6.

   "   ,,   ,,   ,,   ,, III. 192 *n* ; iv. 13. 20 *n.*

Dante : *Various quotations, continued :*

"as flakes of snow" (blasphemers), III. 256 ; iv. 15. 18.

"as one mountain-bred," III. 256 ; iv. 15. 17.

"as snow . . . amidst the living rafters," III. 257 ; iv. 15. 19.

"bello ovile, dov' io dormii agnello " (Par. xxv. 5), V. 317 ; ix. 9. 3.

'   „   „   „   „   „   „   „   V. 364 ; ix. 11. 26.

"bianca aspetto di cilestro," III. 258 ; iv. 15. 20.

"climbed with heart of proof the adverse steep," IV. 326 ; v. 18. 10.

"color ferrigno," III. 251 ; iv. 15. 13.

"del 'nò,' per lì danar, vi 'sì' far ita," III. 27 *n* ; iv. 3 2 *n*.

"fummo acerbo," III. 258 ; iv. 15. 20.

"il gran nemico" (Pluto), V. 337 ; ix. 10. 15.

"loco Alpestro," IV. 334 ; v. 18. 25.

"thou art beyond all art," III. 228 ; iv. 14. 34.

"Qual di pennel fu maestro, e di stile " (Purg. xii. 64), III. 20 ; iv. 2. 5.

"Quel giorno più non vi leggemmo avante," II. 178 ; iii. 2. 3. 5.

"Sopra lor vanità, che par persona," III. 75 ; iv. 5. 13.

"Sweet air made gladsome by the sun," III. 258 ; iv. 15. 20.

"tanta rossa" (Love), III. 105 ; iv. 8. 7.

"That pacific Oriflamb," III. 260 ; iv. 15. 21.

"Thick clouds . . . Thaumantian iris," III. 259 ; iv. 15. 20.

"tremola della marina" (dawn), III. 258 ; iv. 15. 20.

"tutto di pietra, e di color ferrigno," III. 247 *n* ; iv. 15. 7 *n*.

"   „   „   „   „   „   " III. 251 ; iv. 15. 13.

"Venga Medusa, s'il farem di Smalto," III. 237 ; iv. 14. 48.

Dark ages, are they now or in the past ? III. 298 ; iv. 16. 9.

Darkness and light, mingling of, IV. 278, 304 ; v. 17. 3. 36.

Dart, banks of the, IV. 315 ; v. 17. 48.

Darwinism, II. 93 ; iii. 1. 11. 1 ('83 *n*.).

Dash and facility in art, IV. 69–70 ; v. 4. 16.

David, character and descent of, V. 290 ; ix. 7. 6.

„   fair and ruddy, II. 124, 126 ; iii. 1. 14. 7. 10.

„   Nathan and, V. 290 ; ix. 7. 6.

„   "ruddy cheeks" of, III. 158 ; iv. 11. 9.

——— (artist), works of, III. 97 ; iv. 7. 18.

Davidson, foliage of, I. 427 *n* ; ii. 6. 1. 28 *n* (om. ed. 1–4).

Dawn, dancing till, III. 274 ; iv. 16. 19.

Dawn, *continued*:

,, moment of, described, I. 278–79; ii. 3. 4. 31 (ed. 1–4. 35).

,, over sea, emotional beauty of, II. 43–4; iii. 1. 5. 4.

,, rose-colour, in the hills, IV. 368; v. 20. 4. *See s. Sunrise.*

Dawson (artist), picture by (1851), cirrus-clouds in, I. 258 *n*; ii. 3. 3. 28 *n* (om. ed. 1–4).

Dazio Grande, rocks at, IV. 311 *seqq.*; v. 17. 45.

De Hooghe, quiet painting of, V. 309; ix. 8. 11.

,, Turner's study of, III. 343; iv. 18. 29.

De la Roche, picture by (R.A. 1844), I. 106 *n*; ii. 1. 7. 22 *n*.

De la Vigne (Casimir), "Toilette de Constance," quoted, III. 172–73; iv. 12. 13.

De la Vigne (Casimir), "Toilette de Constance," quoted, III. 180; iv. 13. 6.

De Saussure, author's master in geology, IV. 180 *n*; v. 13. 18 *n*.

,, ,, ,, ,, V. 138–39; vii. 3. 4.

,, discovery of fan shape of central mountains, I. 293; ii. 4. 2. 3.

,, on Lake Leman, III. 8 *n*; iv. 1. 8 *n*.

,, ,, Matterhorn, IV. 246–47; v. 16. 10.

,, ,, rocks of Dazio Grande, IV. 311–12; v. 17. 45–6.

,, story of woman at Argentière, III. 12 *n*; iv. 1. 14 *n*.

,, ,, ,, ,, III. 44; iv. 3. 22.

,, work in Alps (curved cleavage), IV. 201; v. 14. 22.

,, ,, ,, and love of, IV. 415 *seqq.*; App. ii. 2 *seqq.*

,, works of, on aiguilles, IV. 183 and *n*; v. 14. 3 and *n*.

,, ,, IV. 222 *nn*; v. 15. 17 *nn*.

De Stendhal, Vie de Metastasio, Haydn, etc., quoted, III. 64 *n*; iv. 4. 24 *n*.

De Stendhal, Vie de Metastasio, Haydn, etc., quoted, III. 92–3; iv. 7. 11–12.

De Wint, fields of, III. 133–34; iv. 10. 2.

,, lowland rivers of, I. 375; ii. 5. 2. 12.

,, storms of, I. 264; ii. 3. 4. 7.

,, tone of, I. 163 *n*; ii. 2. 1. 21 *n*.

,, water-painting of, I. 343; ii. 5. 2. 2 (ed. 1–4 only).

De Wint, *continued* :

,,   winter scenes of, I. 303 ; ii. 4. 2. 19 (om. ed. 1, 2).

,,   works of, I. 107 ; ii. 1. 7. 23 (om. ed. 1, 2).

Dead, the, can receive our honour, not our gratitude, I. 7 ; i. 1. 1. 5.

,,   speak no ill of, why not of the living? IV. 411 *seqq.* ; App. i. 6–8.

Death [SYNOPSIS. I. 7, 44. IV. 344, 347, 412. V. 58–9, 175, 227, 257, 262–64, 302–3, 325–26, 368–69, 384] :—

contemplation of, I. 44 ; i. 2. 3. 2.

,,   by Dürer and Salvator, V. 257 ; ix. 4. 4.

,,   ,,   ,,   V. 262–64 ; ix. 4. 15 *seqq.*

Dance of, Lucerne Bridge, IV. 344 ; v. 19. 10–11.

,,   Reformation and, V. 256 ; ix. 4. 3.

follows vain pursuit of wealth, power, or beauty (cf. Carthage, Rome, Venice), V. 368–69 ; ix. 11. 31.

human brotherhood asserted by, not by life, IV. 412 ; App. i. 6.

life through (in tree growth), V. 58–9 ; vi. 7. 7.

means separation, V. 175 ; viii. 1. 6.

modern horrors of, V. 325–26 ; ix. 9. 22–3.

morbid love of, a sign of weakness, IV. 347–48 ; v. 19. 15–16.

renderings of, early Christian, V. 227 ; ix. 2. 7.

remorse at that of wronged or neglected friends, I. 7 ; i. 1. 1. 5.

swallowed up in victory, V. 384 ; ix. 12. 16.

vulgarity, a form of, V. 302–3 ; ix. 7. 24. *See s. Decay, Ruin.*

"—— and the Cobbler" (Venetian opera, 1850), IV. 347 ; v. 19. 14–15.

Débris curvature, IV. 301–2 ; v. 17. 31 (pl. 35).

,,   lines taken by, IV. 295 *seqq.* ; v. 17. 26 *seqq.*

,,   ,,   IV. 328–29 *n* ; v. 18. 13 *seqq.*

Decay, mingled with beauty, in Italy, IV. 345–46 ; v. 19. 12–13.

Deceit, a gentleman's scorn of, V. 293 ; ix. 7. 11.

Deception in art, I. 20 ; i. 1. 4. 3.

,,   ,,   absence of truth and, therefore, of beauty in, I. 28 ; i. 1. 5. 6.

,,   ,,   bad art, I. 35 ; i. 2. 1. 1.

Deception in art, *continued :*

" " chiaroscuro and, I. 77 ; ii. 1. 6. 2.

" " its low aim, I. 78 *seqq.* ; ii. 1. 7. 1 *seqq.*

" " III. 18 *seqq.* ; iv. 2. 1 *seqq.*

Decision, a quality of execution, I. 40 ; i. 2. 2. 5 *seqq.*

Decoration, architectural effects of light on, I. 112 ; ii. 1. 7. 27.

" use of, in representing the supernatural, II. 234 ; iii. 2. 5. 13.

Deed, what is implied by a, V. 179–80 ; viii. 1. 15 *seqq.*

Deflection, law of, in trees, V. 27–9 ; vi. 4. 8.

Deformities, bodily, when vulgar, V. 297 ; ix. 7. 20.

Deïphobe (Cumæan Sibyl), V. 355 ; ix. 11. 12.

" " " V. 363 *n* ; ix. 11. 26 *n.*

" " " V. 371 ; ix. 11. 32.

Deity. *See s. God.*

Delicacy, of great art, III. 42 ; iv. 3. 20.

Delights, objects of healthy, IV. 371 ; v. 20. 9.

Delphi, Apollo's shrine at, IV. 372 ; v. 20. 11.

Deluge, early Christian renderings of the, V. 227 ; ix. 2. 7.

" in the Louvre, II. 137 ; iii. 1. 14. 29.

Denner, contemptible detail of, I. xxxiii ; *pref.* 2. 26.

" -like portraiture, I. xxxvi ; *pref.* 2. 29.

Dent d'Erin, IV. 249 ; v. 16. 13.

—— de Morcles (Valais), form of, IV. 160 ; v. 12. 21.

" " " " IV. 168 ; v. 13. 5.

" " slope of, IV. 329 *n* ; v. 18. 15 *n.*

—— du Midi (of Bex), IV. 168 ; v. 13. 5.

" " " IV. 254 ; v. 16. 20.

" " " IV. 329 *n* ; v. 18. 15 *n.*

Derbyshire hills, formation of limestone, IV. 106 ; v. 8. 2.

" valleys, IV. 315 ; v. 17. 48.

Derwent, banks of, IV. 315 ; v. 17. 48.

" water, Friar's Crag, author's earliest recollection, III. 307 ; iv. 17. 13.

Desert, art and intellect produced in a, V. 152 ; vii. 4. 2.

" essence of, V. 220–21 ; ix. 1. 8.

" existence of, its meaning, IV. 101 ; v. 7. 6.

Design, by machinery, IV. 289–90 ; v. 17. 19.

" in nature, to be studied, IV. 110–11 ; v. 8. 9.

Desire, no natural, quite frustrate, II. 95 ; iii. 1. 11. 4.

" for what is denied, greatest, IV. 139 ; v. 11. 8.

" the true objects of, V. 386–87 ; ix. 12. 20.

Destruction, of beautiful things for commercial reasons, II. 6-8;
    iii. 1. 1. 7. *See s. Chamouni, Quarries, Scenery.*
Detail and breadth in art, I. xxxii ; *pref.* 2. 24-5.
    „   over-painting of, I. 214; ii. 2. 5. 17.
    „   poetry and, III. 7-10 ; iv. 1. 8 *seqq.*
    „   Reynolds (Sir J.) on, *ib.* ; *ib.*
    „   treatment of, careful by great men, III. 130 ; iv. 9. 18.
    „   „   false, by old masters, I. 79 ; ii. 1. 7. 3. *See
        s. Finish.*
Detraction from greatness, its spirit, I. xiii ; *pref.* 2. 3.
Devil, the, held by some to be the world's lawgiver, V. 378
    ix. 12. 5.
Devonshire, valleys of, IV. 315 ; v. 17. 48.
Diablerets, the, IV. 161 ; v. 12. 21.
    „   „   IV. 254 ; v. 16. 20.
Diagrams in "Modern Painters," V. 66 ; vi. 7. 16.
Dialect, vulgarities of, V. 296-97 ; ix. 7. 17-19.
Diamond, consummation of soot, V. 176 ; viii. 1. 9.
Diana, V. 123 ; vii. 2. 5.
    „   Greek idea of, III. 183-85 ; iv. 13. 7. 9.
    „   Juno's contest with, *ib.* ; *ib.*
Diary, author's, quoted. *See s. Author.*
    „   of woman of fashion on art, III. 72 ; iv. 5. 9.
Dickens [SYNOPSIS. I. 219-20, 403. III. 269, 275, 360. V. 293
    297-98] :—
    influence of, on modern writing, III. 360 ; App. iii.
    love of natural scenery in, III. 275 ; iv. 16. 19.
    religious teaching of, III. 269 ; iv. 16. 10.
    works of, referred to :

        American Notes, "looking through the sky," I. 220 ; ii. 3. 1. 7.
        Chadband, vulgarity of, V. 297 ; ix. 7. 20.
        David Copperfield, III. 275 ; iv. 16. 19.
        „   „   storm at sea in, I. 403 ; ii. 5. 3. 38 (F.A. *n*).
        Mrs. Gamp, vulgarity of, V. 297 ; ix. 7. 19.
        Oliver Twist (Cruikshank's "Noah Claypole"), V. 293 ;
        ix. 7. 11.
        Quilp, vulgarity of, V. 297 ; ix. 7. 20.
        Uriah Heap, vulgarity of, *ib.* ; *ib.*

Dido and Æneas (Nat. Gall.), I. 414-15 ; ii. 6. 1. 12.
Difficulty, conquest of, its pleasure, I. 17 ; i. 1. 3. 5.
Digby, Sir K., author's debt to, V. 302 *n* ; ix. 7. 23 *n.*

Digby, Sir K., *continued* :

,,   ,,   Broad Stone of Honour, *ib.* ; *ib.*

,,   ,,   Children's Bower, *ib.* ; *ib.*

Dighton, W. E., "Hayfield in a shower" (1847), II. 246 ; Add. 7 (om. ed. 1.).

,,   ,,   "Haymeadow corner" (1848), *ib.* ; *ib.* (*ib.*).

Dijon, twisted spire of, V. 21 ; vi. 3. 14.

Diluvium, author's use of the term, IV. 109 ; v. 8. 7.

Diomed, Mars and, III. 183 ; iv. 13. 8.

Discontent, ambition and, V. 359 ; ix. 11. 19.

"Discord," in Homer, Spenser, and Turner, V. 340 *seqq.* ; ix 10. 20 *seqq.*

Disease and gloom go together, IV. 355 ; v. 19. 25.

Disobedience, evil of, V. 82 ; vi. 8. 18.

Disorder, vulgarity of, V. 299 ; ix. 7. 22.

Dissecting nature, often as proper as dreaming over her, III 302 ; iv. 17. 7.

Dissimilarity, good of, V. 83 ; vi. 8. 18.

Distance, aërial effect of, on mountains, I. 295 ; ii. 4. 2. 6.

,,   ,,   ,,   ,,   I. 298–99 ; ii. 4. 2. 12.

,,   art done to be seen at a, not "coarse" work, III. 42 ; iv. 3. 20.

,,   effect of, given more by drawing than tone, I. 196–97 ; ii. 2. 4. 1.

,,   ,,   infinity in art, II. 46–7 ; iii. 1. 5. 8–9.

,,   ,,   objects approaching the eye, or as the eye retires from them, I. 202 *seqq.* ; ii. 2. 5. 1 *seqq.*

,,   expression of infinity in, II. 44 ; iii. 1. 5. 5.

,,   outline of objects at a, I. 301–2 ; ii. 4. 2. 16.

,,   painting of mountain and lowland, IV. 376–77 ; v. 20. 16.

,,   pictorial colour affected by, IV. 67 ; v. 4. 13.

,,   truth of, I. 196 *seqq.* ; ii. 2. 4. 1 *seqq.*

,,   ,,   I. 202 *seqq.* ; ii. 2. 5. 1 *seqq.*

,,   value of luminous, in otherwise vulgar pictures, II. 48 and *n* ; iii. 1. 5. 12 and *n*.

Distinctness, of drawing in great art, III. 40 ; iv. 3. 17.

Dogmatism, in art, III. vi ; *pref.* 2.

Dogs, introduction of, into Venetian pictures, V. 249 ; ix. 3. 22

,,   ,,   ,,   especially by Veronese, V. 281 *seqq.* ; ix. 6. 14 *seqq.*

Dogwood, bud of, V. 82 ; vi. 8. 18.

Dolci, Carlo, polished into inanity, I. 11 ; i. 1. 2. 7.

  ,, ,, smoothness of, I. 43 *n* ; i. 2. 2. 9 *n*.

  ,, ,, ,, ,, III. 121–22 ; iv. 9. 7.

  ,, ,, work of, St. Peter (Pitti, Florence), II. 219 ; iii. 2. 4. 13.

Dolon, wolf-skin helmet of, V. 141 ; vii. 3. 6.

Dome du Gouté, IV. 172 *n* ; v. 13. 8 *n*.

  ,,   ,, cloud cap of, V. 139 ; vii. 3. 4.

Domenichino, angels of, II. 236 ; iii. 2. 5. 17.

  ,,   baseness of, I. 93–4 *n* ; ii. 1. 7. 13 *n* (om. ed. 1, 2).

  ,,   vile landscape of, III. 337 ; iv. 18. 20.

  ,,   works of :

      " Madonna del Rosario," I. 93–4 *n* ; ii. 1. 7. 13 *n* (om. ed. 1, 2).

      " Martyrdom of St. Agnes," II. 236 ; iii. 2. 5. 17.

Dominic, St., IV. 373 ; v. 20. 12.

Dominion, love of, deprecated, III. 159 ; iv. 11. 9.

Don Quixote. *See s. Cervantes.*

Doron, Mt., IV. 254 ; v. 16. 20.

Dover cliffs, IV. 165 ; v. 13. 1.

Dow, Gerard, I. 10 ; i. 1. 2. 7 (ed. 1, 2 only).

  ,, ,, I. 87 ; ii. 1. 7. 10 (om. ed. 1, 2).

  ,, ,, III. 20 ; iv. 2. 4.

Downs, English south, IV. 97 ; v. 7. 4.

  ,,   ,,   ,, IV. 160 ; v. 12. 20.

Dragon, England's god, V. 343–44 ; ix. 10. 24–5.

  ,, of the Hesperides, V. 330 ; ix. 10. 4.

  ,,   ,,   ,, V. 333–34 ; ix. 10. 9–10.

  ,, Retsch's and Turner's, II. 183–84 ; iii. 2. 3. 12–13.

  ,, Turner's, V. 331–56 ; ix. 10. 5 *seqq.* (*passim*).

     See s. Bible, Dante, Greeks, Turner.

Drama, public opinion a fair judge of the, I. 3 *n* ; i. 1. 1. 1 *n*.

     See s. Opera, Stage, Theatre.

Dranse, Martigny, course of the river, I. 392 ; ii. 5. 3. 23.

Drapery, curves of, IV. 285 ; v. 17. 12.

  ,, drawing of, I. 396 ; ii. 5. 3. 29 (om. ed. 1, 2).

  ,, kinds of, and particular truth, I. 64–5 ; ii. 1. 3. 5.

  ,, pre-Raphaelite, severity of old, II. 236 ; iii. 2. 5. 17.

Drawing, always useful, writing generally useless, III. 316–17 ; iv. 17. 31.

Drawing, *continued:*

,,   children to learn, III. 316–17 ; iv. 17. 31.

,,   ,,   ,,   V. 361 *n* ; ix. 11. 22 *n.*

,,   delicate and good, distinguished, IV. 228 ; v. 15. 25.

,,   distinctness of all good, III. 40 ; iv. 3. 17.

,,   ,,   ,,   ,,   IV. 58 ; v. 4. 1.

,,   faithful, rarity of, V. 71 ; vi. 8. 5.

,,   needs quiet, V. viii–ix ; *pref.* 6.

,,   recipe for (Encycl. Brit.), IV. 312–13 ; v. 17. 47.

,,   treatises on, IV. 320 ; v. 18. 3.

          See s. Architecture, Art, Clouds, Landscapes, Moun-
               tains, Turner.

Dreaming over and dissecting nature, III. 302 ; iv. 17. 7.

Dreams, grotesque, IV. 28–9 ; v. 2. 16.

Dresden Gallery, Correggio's "St. George," etc., V. 100 ; vi.
          10. 5.

,,   ,,   Rembrandt's Wife and himself, V. 279 ; ix.
          6. 10.

,,   ,,   Titian's "Lavinia," etc., V. viii ; *pref.* 4.

,,   ,,   ,,   ,,   V. 100 ; vi. 10. 4.

,,   ,,   Veronese's "Ascent to Calvary," V. 251 ; ix.
          3. 26.

,,   ,,   ,,   "Europa," V. 100 ; vi. 10. 5.

,,   ,,   ,,   His own Family, V. 247–49 ; ix.
          3. 19–21.

Dress, consistent and graceful, III. 274 ; iv. 16. 19.

,,   importance of, in art, increased (Veronese), V. 219 ; ix.
          1. 5. 6.

,,   modern, decline of beauty ⎰ II. 35 ; iii. 1. 4. 6.
               in (cf. mediæval and ⎱ III. 270–72 ; iv. 16. 12–15.
               oriental),   ⎰ V. 301 *n* ; ix. 7. 23 *n.*

,,   national, its value, V. 361 *n* ; ix. 11. 22 *n.*

,,   "sad-coloured," III. 251 ; iv. 15. 13.

,,   Shakspere and Dante on, IV. 387–88 ; v. 20. 30.

Drought (1854), IV. 145 ; v. 12. 2.

Dru, Aiguille, IV. 202 ; v. 14. 23.

,,   ,,   IV. 220 *n* ; v. 15. 16 *n.*

,,   ,,   clouds on, V. 121 ; vii. 2. 2 (pl. 69).

,,   ,,   ,,   V. 140–41 ; vii. 3. 5. 8.

Drummond, H., "Banditti on the Watch" (R.S.A., '48), II. 246 ;
          Add. 8 (om. ed. 1).

Dryad's crown, V. 40 ; vi. 5. 5 (pl. 53).

    ,,   toil, V. 13 ; vi. 3. 5 (pl. 51).

    ,,   waywardness, V. 79 ; vi. 8. 12 (pl. 59).

Dubois, M. Hippolyte, drawing for "Modern Painters" by, V.
    74 n ; vi. 8. 8 n.

Dulwich Gallery [SYNOPSIS.   I. xxxi, 41, 96, 154, 158, 160, 175, 205,
                    220–22, 240, 244–45, 255, 270, 302, 312, 313,
                    322, 331, 335, 361, 379.   V. 40, 41, 75–6, 79 n,
                    273] :—

much referred to in "Modern Painters," I. i ; pref. 4.

works in :

    Backhuysen (75), clouds of, I. 235 ; ii. 3. 3. 19 (ed. 1 only).

    Berghem (132), I. 41 ; i. 2. 2. 7.

        ,,   ,, its chiaroscuro, I. 180 ; ii. 2. 3. 13 (ed. 1, 2
                      only).

        ,,   (160), tree-drawing, V. 75–6 ; vi. 8. 10.

    Both (41), foreground of, I. 311 ; ii. 4. 4. 17 (ed. 1, 2 only).

    Claude (241), a copy, I. 220 ; ii. 3. 1. 9.

        ,,   (244), I. 302 ; ii. 4. 2. 17.

        ,,   (260), mountains of, I. 322–23 ; ii. 4. 3. 22.

    Cuyp (163), large, false sky, I. 222 ; ii. 3. 1. 11.

        ,,   ,,   ,, its central clouds, I. 240 ; ii. 3. 3. 1.

        ,,   ,,   ,, ,, leaf-drawing, V. 41 ; vi. 5. 7.

        ,,   ,,   ,, ,, tone, I. 159–60 ; ii. 2. 1. 19.

        ,, (83), ib. ; ib.

        ,,   ,, reflections, I. 361 ; ii. 5. 1. 17.

    Hobbima (131), Water Mill, its foliage, V. 40 ; vi. 5. 5 (pl. 54).

        ,,   ,,   ,, tree in, V. 79 n ; vi. 8. 12 n.

    Potter, Paul (176), reflections in, I. 361 ; ii. 5. 1. 17 (om. ed.
        1, 2).

    Poussin, G. (269), Niobe, rocks in, I. 313 ; ii. 4. 3. 9.

    ———, N. ,, Inspiration of Poet, V. 273 ; ix. 5. 17.

        ,   ,, Nursing of Jupiter, I. xxxi ; pref. 2. 23.

        ,,   ,,   ,,   ,, V. 273 ; ix. 5. 17.

        ,,   (260), I. 153 ; ii. 2. 1. 8.

        ,,   ,, I. 205 ; ii. 2. 5. 6.

        ,,   (295), I. 184 n ; ii. 2. 4. 6 n (ed. 1, 2 only).

        ,,   (212), so-called work, its clouds, I. 245 ; ii. 3. 3. 8.

    Rubens (175), I. 175 ; ii. 2. 2. 12.

        ,,   ,, rainbow, I. 96 ; ii. 1. 7. 15 (om. ed. 1, 2).

    Salvator (159), I. 244 ; ii. 3. 3. 7.

        ,,   ,, its clouds, I. 270 ; ii. 3. 4. 17.

        ,,   ,, rock in foreground, I. 331 ; ii. 4. 4. 7.

        ,,   (220), clouds of, false, I. 245 ; ii. 3. 3. 8.

Dulwich Gallery : *works in, continued :*

    Salvator (220), clouds of, monotonous, I. 255 ; ii. 3. 3. 23

       ,,   ,,   mountains in, I. 312 ; ii. 4. 3. 8.

       ,,   ,,   rock in foreground, I. 331 ; ii. 4. 4. 7.

    Teniers (139), painting of ground in, I. 335 ; ii. 4. 4. 13.

    Titian's "Europa," I. 158 ; ii. 2. 1. 15.

    Vandevelde (113), reflections in, I. 361–62 ; ii. 5. 1. 17 (om. ed.
        1, 2).

       ,,   ,,   shadow of ship on water, I. 361 ; ii. 5. 3. 6.

Dumas, study and love of nature, III. 302 ; iv. 17. 7.

    ,,   work of, Monte Cristo, murder in, IV. 348 ; v. 19. 16.

Dumblane Cathedral, V. v ; *pref.* 1.

Dürer, A. [SYNOPSIS. I. 95, 131, 183, 417. II. 243. III. xii, 36–7,
        46, 101, 104, 106, 124, 131, 150, 277. IV. 49 *n*, 56, 59,
        63, 66, 83, 131, 197, 211 and *n*, 228 *seqq.*, 348, 353. V.
        73–4, 108, 207 *n*, 232, 255 *seqq.*, 260, 263–65, 313,
        325–26, 344, 349–50 *n*, 368 *n*, 379] :—

    I. 131 ; ii. 1. 7. 37 (om. ed. 1, 2).

    animal and hair-painting of (cf. Mulready), II. 243 ; Add.
        3 (om. ed. 1).

    author's facsimiles from, V. 207 *n* ; viii. 4. 7 *n*.

    decision of, II. 243 ; Add. 3 (om. ed. 1).

       ,,   IV. 83 ; v. 5. 20.

    definiteness of, IV. 66 ; v. 4. 12.

    detail of, "gloomily minute," I. 95 ; ii. 1. 7. 15 (om. ed. 1,
        2).

    disdain of colour in his drawings, V. 352 *n* ; ix. 11. 8 *n*.

    education of, V. 257 ; ix. 4. 5 *seqq.*

    engraving without colour, IV. 56 ; v. 3. 24.

    etching, I. 183 *n* ; ii. 2. 2. 20 *n* (om. ed. 1, 2).

    finish, III. 46 ; iv. 3. 26.

       ,,   III. 131 ; iv. 9. 18.

    foliage of, V. 73–4 ; vi. 8. 7 *seqq.*

       ,,   V. 108 ; vi. 10. 19.

       ,,   tree-drawing, I. 417 ; ii. 6. 1. 14 (om. ed. 1, 2).

       ,,   ,,   in his wood-cuts, IV. 197 ; v. 14. 18.

    form and light, no colour, V. 349–50 *n* ; ix. 11. 8 *n*.

    grotesque idealism of, III. 150 ; iv. 10. 21.

    indifference to beauty of, III. 36–7 ; iv. 3. 12.

       ,,   ,,   ,,   cf. IV. 353 ; v. 19. 22.

    landscape of, clear, IV. 59 ; v. 4. 2.

    lines, always noble, IV. 211 *n* ; v. 15. 8 *n*.

Dürer, A., *continued:*

melancholy side to, V. 232 ; ix. 2. 13.
method, follows Da Vinci, IV. 49 ; v. 3. 19.
mountain-drawing, IV. 228–29 ; v. 15. 25–6.
mystery of, IV. 63 ; v. 4. 8.
price of "a plate of figs," V. 379 ; ix. 12. 7.
Reformation and, V. 257 *seqq.* ; ix. 4. 4 *seqq.*
reply of, " Sir, it cannot be better done," III. 277 ; iv. 16. 24.
   „   „   „   „   „   IV. 131 ; v. 10. 4
                                     (F.A. *n*).
Salvator and, V. 255 *seqq.* ; ix. 4. 1 *seqq.*
sea, in his works, V. 260 ; ix. 4. 9.
skeletons of, V. 368 *n* ; ix. 11. 31 *n.*
strength of, IV. 353 ; v. 19. 22.
style of, anti-blottesque, IV. 83 ; v. 5. 20.
"sunny gleams" of, V. 326 ; ix. 9. 24.
temper of, V. 311–12 ; ix. 8. 15.
view of life and death, V. 263–65 ; ix. 4. 16–19.
   „   „   V. 325–26 ; ix. 9. 22.
wood-cuts from ("Modern Painters," vol. iv.), III. xii ;
   pref. 6.
works of :

Adam and Eve, III. 124 ; iv. 9. 9.
   „   „   branch in, V. 73–4 ; vi. 8. 7. 9 (pl. 57).
Bishop by, V. 313 ; ix. 8. 15 (fig. 100).
Cannon, V. 259 ; ix. 4. 7.
Dragon of Apocalypse (mountain background), IV. 228 *seqq.* ;
   v. 15. 25 *seqq.*
Fall of Lucifer, wood-cut, IV. 211 ; v. 15. 8.
Knight and Death, III. 101 ; iv. 8. 2.
   „   „   III. 106 ; iv. 8. 8.
   „   „   V. 260, 263 ; ix. 4. 10. 16.
Melancholia, III. 104 ; iv. 8. 6.
   „   IV. 49 *n* ; v. 3. 19 *n.*
   „   V. 264–65 ; ix. 4. 17–19.
   „   V. 344 ; ix. 10. 25.
S. Hubert, leaf-cluster, V. 108 ; vi. 10. 19.
   „   V. 260 ; ix. 4. 9.
S. Jerome, V. 260 ; ix. 4. 9.

Düsseldorf, Bosch's "Boy and Dog" at, V. 284 ; ix. 6. 20.
   „   Rubens' Madonna, V. 277 ; ix. 6. 6.
Dust, visible in sunshine, I. 224 ; ii. 3. 1. 13.

Dust, *continued :*

„   visible, V. 118 ; vii. 1. **7.**

Dutch :

no poet produced by the, IV. 382–83 ; v. 20. 25. 27.

school of painting [SYNOPSIS. **I.** xxxiii, 6, 11, 97, 186, 205,
223, 228, 240, 364, 401–2. **II.** 243. **III.**
5, 19–20, 43, 121–22, 193, 344–45. **IV.**
380. **V.** 40–3, 75–6, 79, 218, 279 *seqq.*,
283, 286, 304–5, 308–9]:—

author just even to them, II. 243 ; Add. 2 (om. ed.
1), '83 *n.*

„   has no sympathy with, V. 304 ; ix. 8. 1.

barren technique of (except Rubens, Rembrandt, and
Vandyck), I. 11 ; i. 1. 2. 7.

battle-pieces, V. 308–9 ; ix. 18. 10.

cattle-pieces, V. 286 ; ix. 6. 23.

character of landscape, III. 344–45 ; iv. 18. 31.

deceptive imitation of, III. 19–20 ; iv. 2. 4.

details of, contemptible, I. xxxiii ; *pref.* 2. 26.

„   every brick painted, I. 205 ; ii. 2. 5. 5.

„   mean and minute, V. 40 ; vi. 5. 5.

dogs in, unclean, V. 283 ; ix. 6. 19.

feeling deficient, and lowland life, IV. 380 ; v. 20. 22.

„   „   insensitive, V. 304–5 ; ix. 8. 1.

first totally irreligious art, V. 279 ; ix. 6. 11.

finish of, smooth, III. 121–22 ; iv. 9. 7.

infinity lacked by, V. 42 ; vi. 5. 7.

influence of, evil, I. 97 ; ii. 1. 7. 16 (om. ed. 1, 2).

„   on modern (especially English) art, V.
309 ; ix. 8. 11.

leaf-painting of, V. 41 ; vi. 5. 7 (pl. 54).

„   „   V. 43 ; vi. 5. 9.

manufactory of pictures, V. 305 ; ix. 8. 2.

never gives mountains, III. 193 ; iv. 13. 20.

Reynolds on, III. 5 ; iv. 1. 5 *seqq.*

sea-painting, "libellers of the sea," I. 6 ; i. 1. 1. 4.

„   I. 364 ; ii. 5. 1. 20 (om. ed. 1, 2).   *See s.
Backhuysen, Vandevelde.*

„   I. 401–2 ; ii. 5. 3. 37 (om. ed. 1, 2).

shadow-painting of, I. 185–86 ; ii. 2. 3. 3.

sight of, deficient, V. 305 ; ix. 8. 1.

skies of backgrounds (early school), I. 223 ; ii. 3. 1. **12.**

Dutch : *school of painting, continued :*

   skies of backgrounds (early school), I. 228 ; ii. 3. 1. 20.

    „ central clouds, I. 240–41 ; ii. 3. 3. 1.

   street views, V. 218 ; ix. 1. 3.

   subjects of, trivial, III. 43 ; iv. 3. 21.

   temper of the, V. 279 *seqq.* ; ix. 6. 11 *seqq.*

   tree-drawing of, V. 75–6 ; vi. 8. 10.

    „ „ foreshortening, V. 79 ; vi. 8. 12.

   vulgarity of, V. 305 ; ix. 8. 2.

   workmanship of, good, V. 304 ; ix. 8. 1.

Duty, everyone has some gift and some, I. 85 ; ii. 1. 7. 8 (om.
   ed. 1, 2).

 „ power of choice always implies a, II. 2 ; iii. 1. 1. 1.

 „ „ „ *e.g.* in case of the senses, II. 25 ; iii. 1. 3. 6.

 „ sense of beauty no incentive to (Schiller), II. 148 ; iii. 1.
   15. 9.

Earlom, engraving of Claude by, IV. 2 ; v. 1. 1 (pl. 18).

Earth, colours of the, IV. 40 ; v. 3. 7.

 „ creation and sculpturing of the, IV. 94 *seqq.* ; v. 7. 1 *seqq.*

 „ „ are we nearer it, or its end, IV. 146–47 ; v. 12. 4.

 „ form of, changed since creation, and still changing ? IV.
   147–48 ; v. 12. 5.

 „ general structure, I. 286 ; II. iv. 1. 1.

 „ „ „ mountains its action, plains its repose,
      I. 288 ; II. iv. 1. 3. *See s. Plains,
      Mountains.*

 „ geological divisions of, I. 290–91 ; II. iv. 1. 7.

 „ noblest scenes of, seen by few, I. 216–17 ; ii. 3. 1. 1.

 „ painting of, by old masters, I. 334 ; II. iv. 4. 11 (ed.
   1, 2. 13).

 „ preparation of, for man, V. 3 ; vi. 1. 3.

 „ the whole, not habitable, IV. 101 ; v. 7. 6. *See s. Man,
   Scenery.*

——— -fall, beneficent power of, IV. 103 ; v. 7. 10.

  „   „   „ IV. 302 ; v. 17. 31.

——— -veil, the, of vegetation and its ministry to man, V. 2–3 ;
  vi. 1. 2–3.

Ease, appearance of, a sign of greatness, III. 278 ; iv. 16. 27.
  See s. Facility.

Ecbatana, III. 224 ; iv. 14. 29.

Echidna, meaning of Greek, V. 335–37 ; ix. 10. 12–15.

Economy.

> *See s.* Competition, Destruction, Labour, Machinery, Manufacturer,
> Money, Utility, Valuable, War, Wealth, Work.

Eden, garden of, accepted mediæval symbolism of, III. 213;
     iv. 14. 17.
  "   "   no longer possible? V. 2; vi. 1. 2.
Edgeworth, Maria, admiration for Dr. Johnson on education,
  II. 151; iii. 2. 1 ('83 Introd. Note, § 2).
Edinburgh, preacher at, on fasting (1853), IV. 423–24; App. iii. 2.
  "   Salisbury crags, IV. 157; v. 12. 18.
  "   town of:
    college tower, II. '83 Epil. 5 *n.*
    new town, its dull formality, III. 282; iv. 16. 33.
Education [SYNOPSIS. I. 29. II. ix–x, 46, 73, 316–17. IV. 13,
  383–84, 426. V. 5, 267, 288 *n*, 294–95, 361–62 and *n*]:—
 author's experiments in, V. 361 *n*; ix. 11. 22 *n.*
 breeding and, V. 288 *n*; ix. 7. 3 *n.*
 children's, what they should learn, *ib.*; *ib.*
 classicalism and modern, V. 267; ix. 5. 5.
 country and town (Pascal and Bacon), IV. 383–84; v. 20. 27.
 develops, does not alter character (*e.g.* currant into apricot),
  III. 46; iv. 3. 26.
 essence of, in training character, not in knowledge, V.
  360–62; ix. 11. 22–3.
 examples of.

> *See s.* Bacon, Dürer, Giorgione, Pascal, Salvator, Scott,
> Turner.

 love of picturesque, a means of, IV. 13; v. 1. 14.
 mediæval, "syllogism and sword," V. 5; vi. 1. 5.
 mistakes of, irremediable, IV. 426; App. iii. 4.
 persons of simple life, what they should know, V. 361 *n*,
  362; ix. 11. 23.
 subjects of:
  drawing essential, III. 316–17; iv. 17. 31.
  love of nature to be cultivated, *ib.*; *ib.*
  practical logic necessary, III. viii–ix; *pref.* 4.
    "   "   " IV. 426; App. iii. 1.
 taste and distaste as affected by, I. 29; i. 1–6. 1.
  " as trained by modern, III. 69–70; iv. 5. 6.
 truth, how to inculcate respect for it, V. 294–95; ix. 7. 14.
 vulgarity of, the worst of all, III. 73; iv. 5. 10.

Education, *continued* :

 what it is and what it should be, IV. 424–26 ; App. iii. 3.
   See s. Children, Singing, Teaching.

Effect, in art, meaning of, I. 148 ; ii. 1. 7. 47 (ed. 1, 2, § 13).

Effort. *See s. Ease, Facility.*

Egeri, Lake of, Swiss victory at, V. 95 ; vi. 9. 13.

  ,, ,, ,, V. 369 *n* ; ix. 11. 31 *n.*

Egotism, sometimes a good thing, III. 306 ; iv. 17. 12.

Egyptian colossal statues, II. 220 ; iii. 2 ; iv. 14.

  ,,   ,,   ,, IV. 117 ; v. 8. 17. *See s. British
              Museum.*

  ,, landscape, V. 227 ; ix. 2. 5.

  ,,   ,, and sculpture, III. 202 ; iv. 14. 1.

  ,, mummy, its symmetry, III. 210 ; iv. 14. 12.

  ,, mysteries of Ceres, V. 159 ; vii. 4. 12.

  ,, mythology, animals in, V. 284 ; ix. 6. 21.

Eiger, the, Grindelwald, IV. 175 ; v. 13. 11.

  ,,   ,,   ,, its cliffs, IV. 272 ; v. 16. 39.

  ,,   ,,   ,, V. 144 ; vii. 3. 12.

Einsiedeln, and sale of indulgences, V. 95 ; vi. 9. 14.

Electricity, cloud form and, V. 119–20 ; vii. 1. 9.

  ,,   ,,   ,, V. 125–26 ; vii. 2. 7.

  ,,   ,,   ,, V. 137–38 ; vii. 3. 1. 3.

  ,,   ,,   ,, V. 140–41 ; vii. 3. 6.

Elephant, nobility of an, V. 289 ; ix. 7. 5.

Elgin marbles, grander for want of colour, etc., II. 216 ; iii.
              2. 4. 9.

  ,,   ,,   ,,   ,,   ,, II. 219 ; iii.
              2. 4. 14.

  ,, ,, ideal size of, II. 223 ; iii. 2. 4. 19.

  ,, ,, modern sculpture of lace, and the, I. xxxvi, 29 ;
         pref. ed. 2.

  ,, ,, the Theseus, II. 223 ; iii. 2. 4. 19.

Elizabethan England, IV. 380–81 ; v. 20. 23.

  ,, ,, art and character, contempt of fine dress
                IV. 386–88 and *n*
                v. 20. 30 and *n.*

  ,, ,,   ,,   ,, IV. 389 ; v. 20. 31.

  ,, ,, decoration, II. 79 ; iii. 1. 8. 3.

  ,, ,, garden, its carved trees, V. 91 ; vi.
           9. 8.

  ,, ,, literature. *See s. Shakspere.*

Ellesmere Gallery, Claude's " Moses and Burning Bush," III. 340 ; iv. 18. 26.

,,   ,,   Turner's Sea-piece, I. 402 ; ii. 5. 3. 37 (om. ed. 1, 2).

Ellipse, curves of an, IV. 283 ; v. 17. 7.

Elm-leaf, III. 217 ; iv. 14. 23.

,,   curves of an, IV. 287 ; v. 17. 16.

,,   structure of, V. 29 ; vi. 4. 8.

Elpenor, sluggishness of (Homer), V. 234 ; ix. 2. 16.

Embankment, of Alpine streams, IV. 297 ; v. 17. 28.

Emerson's essays, on vulgarity, V. 302 *n* ; ix. 7. 23 *n*.

,,   poems, III. 359 ; App. 3.

,,   quoted, "The light-outspeeding telegraph," III. 320 *n* ; iv. 17. 36.

Emmenthal, pines of the, V. 93 ; vi. 9. 10.

Emotions, abuse of, in frivolous pleasure, IV. 39 ; v. 3. 6.

,,   acuteness of moral, and imagination, II. 204–5 ; iii. 2. 3. 31.

,,   analysis of literary (Byron, etc.), III. 279–80 ; iv. 16. 29.

,,   control of, and incapacity for, distinct, III. 303 ; iv. 17. 9.

,,   four noblest, III. 11 ; iv. 1. 13.

,,   intellect and, struggle between, III. 167–68 ; iv. 12. 8. 9.

,,   three orders of mind, III. 303–4 ; iv. 17. 9.

,,   works of high emotion require sympathy to understand them, I. 90 ; ii. 1. 7. 11 (om. ed. 1, 2).

                    See s. Pathetic fallacy.

Enamel, described, III. 236–37 ; iv. 14. 48.

Enamelled grass (mediæval poets), III. 236–38 ; iv. 14. 47–50.

Enamelling, art of, III. 209 ; iv. 14. 11.

Encyclopædia Britannica, article on "Drawing" quoted, IV. 312–13 ; v. 17. 47.

Endogenous trees, V. 9 *n* ; vi. 2. 4 *n*.

Energy, high moral feeling, I. 14–15 ; i. 1. 3. 2.

,,   implied by repose, II. 72 ; iii. 1. 7. 3.

,,   its expression in plants, a source of pleasure, II. 99 ; iii. 1. 12. 4.

,,   purity, a type of, II. 81–2 ; iii. 1. 9. 2.

,,   ,,   of matter expresses, II. 85 ; iii. 1. 9. 7.

Engelberg (hill of angels), V. 96 ; vi. 9. 15.

England [SYNOPSIS. I. 87–8, 97, 443–44. II. 72, '83 Epil. 13.
            III. 268–70, 350 *seqq.* IV. 4–5, 71, 165, 314–15, 340,
            366, 378–81, 392. V. 93, 267, 276, 285, 343–44, 355
            358, 377–78, 379–80, 383] :—

architecture of, IV. 378 ; v. 20. 20.

art in, appreciation of ! (Turners in National Gallery
                    cellars), II. '83 Epil. 13.

   „   „   public easily misled, I. 443–44 ;
                                ii. 6. 3. 13.

   „   climate and, IV. 71 ; v. 5. 1.

   „   culminates, 12–1300, IV. 381 ; v. 20. 23.

   „   landscapists, want of balance, I. 88 ; ii. 1. 7. 10
                                (om. ed. 1, 2).

   „   „   „   detail, *e.g.* specific flowers,
                                I. 87 ; ii. 1. 7. 9 (om.
                                ed. 1, 2).

   „   „   I. 97 *seqq.* ; ii. 1. 7. 17 *seqq.*

   „   "religious" art, III. 268–70 ; iv. 16. 10.

   „   sudden decline after 1400, IV. 378–81 ; v. 20. 20–23.

   „   *temp.* Elizabeth. *See s. Elizabeth.*

cathedrals of, which finest, IV. 381 ; v. 20. 23. *See s.
    Cathedrals.*

continent and, compared, IV. 4–5 ; v. 1. 4–6.

cottager of, his bright life, IV. 340 ; v. 19. 5.

cottages, steep roofs of, V. 259 ; ix. 4. 7.

expects every man to do his duty, V. 379–80 ; ix. 12. 7–8.

France and, relations of (1856), III. 350 *seqq.* ; iv. 18.
    37 *seqq.*

literature, since 1600, classical revival, V. 267 ; ix. 5. 5.

madonna of, the mammon-dragon, V. 343–44 ; ix. 10. 24–5.

modern, V. 355 ; ix. 11. 12.

   „   destiny of, to be the world's furnace and work-
                    shop ? V. 358 ; ix. 11. 18.

   „   faith and obedience obsolete, II. 72 ; iii. 1. 7. 4
                    ('83 *n*).

   „   infidelity, V. 377–78 ; ix. 12. 5. *See s. Infidelity.*

   „   iron- (not lion-) hearted now, V. 383 ; ix. 12. 14.

   „   merry England no more, III. 268 ; iv. 16. 9.

   „   treatment of her great men, "the Levite passing
                    by," V. 383–84 ; ix. 12. 14–15.

people of, their character :

   „   formalism, V. 276 ; ix. 6. 3.

England : people of, *continued*:

" "Hearts of Oak," IV. 392 ; v. 20. 35.

" precision and spruceness, IV. 5 ; v. 1. 6.

scenery, author's love of it, IV. 366 ; v. 20. 2.

" continent compared with, IV. 4 ; v. 1. 5.

" downs, IV. 165 ; v. 13. 1.

" homesteads, IV. 141 ; v. 11. 9.

" smallness of, IV. 4 ; v. 1. 5.

sport in, V. 285 ; ix. 6. 22. *See s. Sport.*

valleys of, their formation, IV. 314-15 ; v. 17. 48.

woods of, oak and elm, V. 93 ; vi. 9. 11.

Engravers.

See s. Allen, Armytage, Boydell, Boys, Byfield, Cousen, Cuff, Earlom, Flaxman, Goodall, Holl, Laing, Lasinio, Le Keux, Lefebre, Meulemeester, Miller, Shaw, Volpato, Woollett.

Engraving [SYNOPSIS. **I.** 43 *n*, 107, 182 *n*, 272, 275-76. **III.** x, 122-23. **V.** 42-3, 109-10, 125 *n*, 351 *n*]:—

colour cannot be given by ; what it *can* give, I. 182 *n* ; ii. 2. 2. 20 *n* (om. ed. 1, 2).

" cold colour as rendered by, I. 272 ; ii. 3. 4. 19 (ed. 1-4, § 21).

" touches of colour given by pure lines, III. x ; *pref.* 5.

curvature, its loss in, V. 351 *n* ; ix. 11. 8 *n*.

finish in, exemplified by tree-stems, III. 122-23 ; iv. 9. 8.

influence of, on artists, *e.g.* Harding, I. 107-8 ; ii. 1. 7. 24 (om. ed. 1, 2).

modern (1843) condemned, I. 43 *n* ; i. 2. 2. 9 *n* (esp. ed. 1 and 2).

of sky and cloud, V. 125 *n* ; vii. 2. 6 *n*.

of storms, faults of and ironical rules for, I. 276 ; ii. 3. 4. 26 (ed. 1-4, § 31).

of Turner's pictures, generally, I. 182 *n* ; ii. 2. 2. 20 *n* (om. ed. 1, 2).

" " " V. 42-3 ; vi. 5. 9.

" " " V. 109-10 ; vi. 10. 20.

See s. Turner, Woodcutting.

Enjoyment, true and vulgar, III. 320-23 ; iv. 17. 36-8.

" work enjoyed by worker, V. 301 *n* ; ix. 7. 23 *n*.

Enthusiasm, faith of, impure, IV. 373 ; v. 20. 12.

Enuo, one of Graiæ, V. 158 ; vii. 4. 10.

Epictetus, epitaph on "poor and rich and beloved of the gods,"
    IV. 12 ; v. 1. 13.

Epicurism, and Christian sense of beauty, compared, II. 19–20 ;
    iii. 1. 2. 9–10.

Epitaph. *See s. Epictetus, Lacedæmonians.*

Equality, evil of, V. 83 ; vi. 8. 18.

    ,,   impossible, *e.g.* of intellect, III. 151 ; iv. 10. 22.

Eris, goddess of discord, V. 339–41 ; ix. 10. 19–22.

Erytheia (Hesperid), V. 333 *n* ; ix. 10. 8 *n*.

    ,,   ,,   V. 348 ; ix. 11. 5.

Escape, lines of, IV. 291–92, 295–96 ; v. 17. 21. 27.

Essex marshes, no ballads from the, IV. 383 ; v. 20. 27.

Etala, passage on the Charmoz, IV. 221 *n* ; v. 15. 16 *n*.

Etching, French, praised, I. 426 ; ii. 6. 1. 27 (om. ed. 1, 2).

Ethical subjects.

    See s. Ambition, Anticipation, Anger, Asceticism, Cheerfulness,
    Childishness, Conceit, Conscience, Contemplation, Content-
    ment, Countenance, Courage, Covetousness, Cruelty, Cunning,
    Death, Deceit, Desire, Difficulties, Discontent, Disease, Dis-
    obedience, Disorder, Dominion, Duty, Egotism, Emotions,
    Energy, Enjoyment, Enthusiasm, Evil, Excitement, Faults,
    Fool, Frankness, Gentleman, Good, Goodness, Great, Great-
    ness, etc., Grief, Habit, Happiness, Hardship, Health, Help,
    Horror, Humanity, Humility, Indifference, Indignation, In-
    sensibility, Jealousy, Judging, Judgment, Jest, Kindness,
    Knavery, Landscape, Laughter, Law, Levity, Liberty, License,
    Lie, Life, Lives, Living, Love, Loyalty, Luxury, Lying, Man,
    Meekness, Melancholy, Mercy, Mischief, Misuse, Modera-
    tion, Mortal, Nobility, Novelty, Obedience, Obscurity, Pain,
    Passions, Peace, Pity, Pleasure, Pride, Purity, Recklessness,
    Refinement, Religion, Remorse, Restraint, Rivalry, Scoffing,
    Scorn, Self, Selfishness, Sensuality, Seriousness, Silence, Sin,
    Sinlessness, Social, Soldier, Sorrow, Spirits, Submission,
    Suffering, Sympathy, Talk, Taste, Temperance, Terrible,
    Terror, Thinkers, Thought, True, Trust, Truth, Truthfulness,
    Uncertainty, Vanity, Veneration, Vice, Virtue, Vulgarity,
    Work, World, Youth.

Etruscan kings, burial of, I. 117 ; ii. 1. 7. 30 (om. ed. 1, 2).

Etty [SYNOPSIS. I. 156. II. 134, 218, 245. IV. 59] :—
    colour of, breadth of treatment, II. 218 ; iii. 2. 4. 11.
    misty vagueness of, IV. 59 ; v. 4. 2.
    nude studies of, II. 134 ; iii. 1. 14. 24 (and '83 *n*).

Etty, *continued:*
    want of tone, I. 156 ; ii. 2. 1. 12.
    works of :

        Morning Prayer, II. 245 ; Add. § 6 (om. ed. 1).
        St. John, *ib.*; *ib.*; *ib.*
        Still Life, *ib.*; *ib.*; *ib.*

Euripides, Alcestis, central idea of Greek drama, V. 234 *n*; ix.
    2. 15 *n*. *See s. Alcestis.*
    „   quoted ἡ γλῶσσ' ᾽ὀμώμόκ᾽, etc., V. 294 ; ix. 7. 13.
    „   „   on Hesperides and dragon, V. 335 ; ix. 10. 12.
    „   „   „   „   „   V. 341–42 ; ix. 10.
        22.

Europa, V. 366 ; ix. 11. 30.
Europe, architecture of, ruined buildings instanced, II. 6–7 *n*;
    iii. 1. 1. 7 *n*.
    „   art of, its main sources, IV. 378–79 ; v. 20. 20.
    „   future of, what we are coming to, IV. 398–99 ; v. 20. 42.
    „   *temp.* Napoleon I., V. 326 ; ix. 9. 23.
    „   unbelief of modern (London and Paris), III. 269 ; iv.
    16. 10.
Euryale, Gorgon, V. 158 ; vii. 4. 11.
Eurybia, child of Nereus, V. 157 ; vii. 4. 9.
    „   tidal force of sea, V. 334 ; ix. 10. 10.
Evanescence, the law of, IV. 74–5 ; v. 5. 7 (pl. 26).
Evangelicalism, bad art and music of, III. 63–4 ; iv. 4. 23.
    „   contempt of art by, V. 276 ; ix. 6. 4.
Evaporation, clouds, etc., V. 147–50 ; vii. 3. 17.
Evil [Synopsis. **III.** ix, 115, 324. **IV.** 363–64, 423. **V.** 83, 180-81,
    232, 241, 312] :—
    accidental, V. 180–81 ; viii. 1. 17.
    conquest of, confronted, the basis of great art, V. 232 ;
        ix. 2. 13.
        „   exemplified, V. 312 ; ix. 8. 15.
    contemplation of, in mediæval religion, V. 241 ; ix. 3. 7.
    continuance of, probable (cf. "Stones of Venice"), III.
        ix, *pref.* 4.
    free thought and the origin of, IV. 423 ; App. iii. 1.
    good and, co-existent, IV. 364 ; v. 19. 33.
        „   extremes of, in many things, III. 324 ; iv. 17. 41.
        „   sources of, V. 83 ; vi. 8. 18.
    indisputable fact of, IV. 363 ; v. 19. 32.

Evil, *continued :*

    self-destroying, III. 115 ; iv. 8. 21.

        See s. Good, Sin.

Evolena, valley of, IV. 174 ; v. 13. 10.

     ,,   ,,   character of its people, V. 94 ; vi. 9. 13.

Eyck, Van. *See s. Van Eyck.*

Eye, beauty of, in animals and men, II. 104–5 ; iii. 1. 12. 10.

  ,, focus of, altered in looking at reflections, I. 376–77 ; ii.
        5. 3. 2.

  ,,   ,, truth of space dependent on, I. 196 *seqq.* ; ii. 2.
        4. 1 *seqq.*

  ,, keenness of artists', IV. 73–4 ; v. 5. 5.

  ,,   ,, how tested, IV. 197 ; v. 14. 18.

  ,, "watchfires" of the, III. 73 ; iv. 5. 11.

        See s. Sight.

Exaggeration in art, its laws and limits, II. 222–23 ; iii. 2. 4. 19.

     ,,   ,, necessary in a diminished scale, II. 225 ;
        iii. 2. 4. 21.

Excellence, artistic, perceived by artists, beauty by men of taste,
        I. 17 ; i. 1. 3. 4.

  ,, meaning of the word, I. 16 and *n* ; i. 1. 3. 3 and *n.*

  ,,   ,,   ,, connotes conquered difficulty,
        I. 17 ; i. 1. 3. 5.

  ,, obscurity essential to the highest, IV. 65 ; v. 4. 9.

  ,, public opinion as a test of, I. 1–2 ; i. 1. 1. 1.

  ,, technical, III. 30–1 ; iv. 3. 6.

        See s. Execution, Expression.

Excitement, morbid craving for, IV. 348 ; v. 19. 16.

Execution [SYNOPSIS. I. 39 *seqq.*, 42, 214–15, 371. II. 88 *n*, 200 *n*.
        III. 33–4, 54, 70. V. 297–98 and *n*] :—

    faults of, due to false imagination, II. 220 *n* ; iii. 2. 3. 28 *n.*

    feeling and, neither to be sacrificed   } III. 33–4 ; iv. 3. 10–11.
        to the other,   }

     ,,   ,,   ,,   ,, III. 54 ; iv. 4. 11.

     ,,   ,,   ,,   ,, III. 70 ; iv. 5. 6.

    methods and vices of, II. 220 *n* ; iii. 2. 3. 28 *n.*

    mystery of, necessary to give space, I. 215 ; ii. 2. 5. 18.

    precision in, V. 297–98 and *n* ; ix. 7. 21 and *n.*

    qualities essential to, I. 39 *seqq.* ; i. 2. 2. 1 *seqq.*

  ,, (*a*) great, (*b*) attractive, I. 42 ; i. 2. 2. 8.

    rude, when a source of noble pleasure, II. 88 *n* ; iii. 1. 10.
    3 *n.*

Execution, *continued:*

swift, I. 40 ; i. 2. 2. 6.

   ,,   I. 42 ; i. 2. 2. 9.

   ,,   best gives perfect detail, I. 214 ; ii. 2. 5. 17.

kinds of, II. 200 *n* ; iii. 2. 3. 28 *n*. *See above, s. qualities.*

water, drawing of, demands, I. 371 ; ii. 5. 2. 4.

      See s. Art, Drawing, Niggling.

Exhibition, International, 1851, I. 454 ; ii. 6. 3, postscript (om. ed. 1–4).

Expression and colour, perfect expression demands colour, IV. 56 *n* ; v. 3. 24 *n*.

   ,,   ,,   powers of, go together, IV. 407 ; App. i. 1.

   ,,   dignity of, *ib.* ; *ib.*

   ,,   influence of moral, in animal form, II. 104–5 ; iii. 1. 12. 10.

   ,,   of inspiration, II. 227 *seqq.* ; iii. 2. 5. 4 *seqq.*

   ,,   ,, superhuman character, *ib.* ; *ib.*

   ,,   schools of (Great, Pseudo, Grotesque), IV. 407 ; App. i. 1.

   ,,   subtle, how reached, IV. 56 *n*, 57 ; v. 3. 24 and *n*.

   ,,   technique and, their place in great art, III. 32 *seqq.* ; iv. 3. 9 *seqq.*

      See s. Execution and Feeling.

Ezzelin, V. 290 ; ix. 7. 7.

Fabriano, Gentile da, "Adoration of Magi" ruined, II. 8 *n* ; iii. 1. 1. 7 *n*.

Face, as affected by intellect, morals, etc., II. 121 ; iii. 1. 14. 4.

   ,,   proportion and symmetry in a, II. 79 ; iii. 1. 8. 2.

      See s. Beauty.

Facility in art, I. 39 ; i. 2. 2. 1

   ,,   ,,   its value, II. 200 *n* ; iii. 2. 3. 28 *n*.

      See s. Ease, Execution.

Facsimile, difficulty of, IV. 82 *n* ; v. 5. 18 *n*.

Facts, artists to study not effects but, III. 95–7 ; iv. 7 15–17.

   ,,   character as affected by study of, *ib.* ; *ib.*

   ,,   in poetry, value of pure, III. 169–72 ; iv. 12. 11–12.

Faido (St. Gothard), pass of, IV. 22 ; v. 2. 9 (pl. 20, 21).

   ,,   ,,   ,,   (Turner's), IV. 233 ; v. 15. 30.

Fairy tales, if moral, seldom imaginative, III. 101 ; iv. 8. 3.

Faith [SYNOPSIS. **II.** 72–3, 122–23, 126. **III.** 317. **IV.** 373. **V.**
    181, 228–29, 247–48, 255, 275–76] :—
    defined (its etymology), V. 181 ; viii. 1. 17.
    derivation of (πίστις), V. 275–76 ; ix. 6. 2.
    love of nature and, III. 317 ; iv. 17. 32.
    meaning of, II. 72–3 ; iii. 1. 7. 4.
    mistress of imagination, II. 126 ; iii. 1. 14. 10 ('83 *n*).
    mountain influence on, IV. 373 ; v. 20. 12.
    reason and intellect below, II. 122 ; iii. 1. 14. 5 ('83 *n*).
          „   „   „   V. 228–29 ; ix. 2. 9–10.
    the Reformation and, V. 255 ; ix. 4. 1.
    Veronese's rendering of, V. 247–48 ; ix. 3. 20.
    want of. *See s. Greek, Infidelity.*
Fall, lines of, IV. 291 *seqq.* ; v. 17. 21 *seqq.*
Fallacy. *See s. Pathetic fallacy.*
Falsehood, always revolting, I. 51 ; ii. 1. 1. 8.
Falsity, fatal to art, V. 214–15 ; viii. 4. 23.
    „   of sight or speech, V. 178–79 ; viii. 1. 14.
Familiarity and strangeness, as a cause of delight, II. 58–9 ;
    iii. 1. 6. 6. *See s. Custom.*
Fancy [SYNOPSIS. **I.** 413. **II.** 97, 151, 152 *seqq.*, 160, 179, 181, 182,
    and *n*, 183, 205, 207, 209, 214. **III.** 164 *n*. **IV.** 342–43] :—
    conception and, distinct, II. 207–8 ; iii. 2. 4. 3.
    contemplative (pathetic fallacy), III. 164 *n* ; iv. 12. 4.
    detailing operation of the, II. 183 ; iii. 2. 3. 12.
    function of the, which the noblest, II. 209–10 ; iii. 2. 4. 5.
    imagination and, work distinct, I. 414 ; ii. 6. 1. 11 (om. ed.
                                       1, 2).
      „   „   „   II. 151 ; iii. 2. 1 (Introd.
                                      Note '83, § 2).
      „   „   „   II. 152 *seqq.* ; iii. 2. 1. 2 *seqq.*
      „   „   „   II. 160 ; iii. 2. 2. 5.
      „   „   „   II. 181 *seqq.* ; iii. 2. 3. 9 *seqq.*
      „   „   „   II. 205 ; iii. 2. 3. 33.
      „   „   „   II. 209–10 ; iii. 2. 4. 5.
    morbid or nervous, II. 214–15 ; iii. 2. 4. 7.
    never serious, II. 182 and *n* ; iii. 2. 3. 9 and *n*.
    restless, imagination quiet, II. 182–83 ; iii. 2. 3. 11.
    ridiculous, if the reality is impossible, IV. 342–43 ; v. 19. 8.
    sees outside, imagination the heart, II. 179 ; iii. 2. 3. 7.
      „   II. 181 ; iii. 2. 3. 8.
Faraday, Prof., III. vi ; *pref.* 2.

Farnley, Turner's drawings at, I. 134 ; ii. 1. 7. 39 (om. ed. 1, 2).
"   "   "   I. 137 ; ii. 1. 7. 41 (om. ed. 1, 2).
"   "   "   (Valley of Chamouni), *ib.* ; *ib.*
                        (ed. 3, 4 only).

Fashion, authority of, II. 26 ; iii. 1. 3. 8–9.
"   follies of, II. 33 ; iii. 1. 4. 3 ('83 *n*).
"   influence of, on our appreciation of things, II. 87 ; iii.
          1. 10. 2.

Fasting, Presbyterian sermon on, IV. 423–24 ; App. iii. 2.

Fate, in Dante and Shakspere, IV. 395 *n* ; v. 20. 38 *n*.
"   " Greek poetry and Shakspere, V. 233–34 ; ix. 2. 14 *seqq.*
"   " "short withering" (Hesiod), V. 331 ; ix. 10. 7.
"   " the three fates, V. 331–32 ; ix. 10. 7.

Faulhorn, the, IV. 173 ; v. 13. 9.

Faults, some stamp a man for ever, whatever else he does, I.
         93 and *n* ; ii. 1. 7. 13 *n* (om. ed. 1, 2).

Fawkes. *See s. Farnley.*

Fear, awe distinct from, II. 135–36 ; iii. 1. 14. 26.
"   holy, distinct from terror, II. 136 ; iii. 1. 14. 27.
"   junction of ferocity and, II. 136 ; iii. 1. 14. 28.
"   of God, testimony and, V. 169–70 ; vii. 4. 33.

Features, Greek and Northern (mediæval), compared, III.
          208–9 ; iv. 14. 11.

Feeling, always indescribable, III. 309 ; iv. 17. 19.

Fellowship, of branches, V. 81 *seqq.* ; vi. 8. 15 *seqq. See s. Unity.*

Fences, mediæval, great importance of, III. 213–14 ; iv. 14.
         16–17.

Fenelon, study and love of nature, III. 302 ; iv. 17. 7.

Ferocity. *See s. Fear.*

Feuillet, Octave, "La Crise," "Il y aurait des gens assez bêtes,"
          etc., III. 311 ; iv. 17. 24.

Fever, delirium of, IV. 347 ; v. 19. 15.

Février, General, IV. 410 ; App. i. 5–6. *See s. Punch.*

Fiction, the best, is in reality, III. 74 ; iv. 5. 13.

Field-sports. *See s. Sport.*

Fielding, Copley [SYNOPSIS. **I.** 103 *seqq.* 199, 264–65, 326, 327 *n*,
          369–70, 372–73, 375, 397, 431. **III.** 259, 345.
          IV. 59, 71, 78] :—
     analysis of his work, I. 103 *seqq.* ; ii. 1. 7. 21 (om. ed. 1, 2).
     "bad weather" of, IV. 71 ; v. 5. 1.
     "breaking waves" of, I. 397 ; ii. 5. 3. 30 (om. ed. 1, 2).
     characteristics, I. 327 *n* ; ii. 4. 3. 28 *n* (om. ed. 1–4).

Fielding, Copley, characteristics, *continued :*

     „   I. 369 ; ii. 5. 2. 1, 3 (ed. 1–4 only).

  cloudiness of, IV. 59 ; v. 4. 2.

     „   IV. 78 ; v. 5. 14.

  distance and space well expressed by, I. 199 ; ii. 2. 4. 6.

  downs of, III. 345 ; iv. 18. 31.

  faults of, as a colourist, I. 103–4 ; ii. 1. 7. 21 (om. ed. 1, 2).

  foliage of, I. 431 ; ii. 6. 1. 33.

  foregrounds highly finished, I. 104–5 ; ii. 1. 7. 22 (om. ed.
                    1, 2).

     „   „   „   I. 311 ; ii. 4. 4. 16 (ed. 1, 2
                    only).

  hills of, I. 280 ; ii. 4. 22 (ed. 1, 2 only).

  lakes and calm water of, I. 369 ; ii. 5. 2. 1.

  mountains of, I. 326 ; ii. 4. 3. 27.

  praise of, I. 76 ; ii. 1. 7. 6 (ed. 1, 2 only).

  rain of, I. 249 ; ii. 3. 4. 16 (ed. 1, 2 only). *See below,
    showery skies.*

  seas of, fully described, I. 372–74 ; ii. 5. 2. 6–9.

     „   "desolated," I. 375 ; ii. 5. 2. 12.

  showery skies, their dexterous truth, I. 264–65 *n* ; ii. 3. 4.
        8–10 and *n.*

     „   and showers, III. 259 ; iv. 15. 20.

  weakness of, uses pencil too little, brush too much, I. 265–
    66 ; ii. 3. 4. 9–10

  works of :

        Bolton Abbey (R.A. 1843) badly hung, I. 106 *n* ; ii. 1. 7.
               22 *n* (om. ed. 1, 2).

           „   „   its foreground, I. 311 ; ii. 4.
                    4. 16 (ed. 1, 2 only).

Fields, glorious significance of the, III. 239–40 ; iv. 14. 51.

Figs, a plate of, the price of a Dürer. *See s. Dürer.*

Figure and leaf, drawing and sculpture of, their rise and fall,
  V. 39 ; vi. 5. 4.

Finch (painter), I. 327 *n* ; ii. 4. 3. 28 *n* (om. ed. 1–4).

Finden's Bible. *See s. Turner.*

   „   Byron. *See s. Stanfield, Turner.*

Finish [SYNOPSIS. I. 87–9, 120, 204, 212, 214, 427. II. 85, 88 *n*,
     88–90. III. 116–18, 119, 120, 121–25, 128, 130, 131–32,
     148, 324 *n.* V. 200–1, .98–99 *n*, 300 *n*] :—

  artistic, I. 427 ; ii. 6. 1. 29 (om. ed. 1, 2).

Finish, *continued*:

    continental and English, III. 117–18 ; iv. 9. 4.

    defined, in the completion, not a part of beauty, II. 89 ; iii.
          1. 10. 4.

      „   „   complete expression of ideas, III. 121–23 ;
          iv. 9. 7. 8.

      „   means "added fact or more truth," III. 121–23 ;
          iv. 9. 7. 10.

      „   „   „   „   „   III. 128, 130 ;
          iv. 9. 15. 18.

    for finish sake, bad, III. 121 ; iv. 9. 7.

    function and, always relative, I. 120 ; ii. 1. 7. 31 (om. ed.
          1, 2).

    God alone can give perfect, III. 120 ; iv. 9. 5.

    good and bad, III. 324 *n* ; iv. 17. 41 *n.*

    harmony essential to artistic, V. 200–1 ; viii. 4. 2.

    in landscape foregrounds, I. 212 ; ii. 2. 5. 15.

    infinite, in God's work, II. 90 ; iii. 1. 10. 4.

    kinds of, (1) workmanship, (2) work, III. 117 ; iv. 9. 3.

    landscape needs more than figures, I. 214–15 ; ii. 2. 5. 18.

    limits of, right, III. 116 *seqq.* ; iv. 9. 1 *seqq.*

      „   „   III. 148 ; iv. 10. 18.

    love of, in works of art, II. 88 ; iii. 1. 10. 3.

      „   „ all great artists, II. 88–9 ; iii. 1. 10. 4.

      „   „   „   III. 130 ; iv. 9. 18.

      „   „   „   V. 300 *n* ; ix. 7. 22 *n.*

    mysteriousness of, I. 204–5 ; ii. 2. 5. 4.

    principles of perfect, V. 298–99 *n* ; ix. 7. 21 *n.*

    too much in portraits, repulsive, I. 214 ; ii. 2. 5. 18.

    useful and useless, III. 119 ; iv. 9. 5.

    want of, right or wrong according to its motive, I. 87–9 ; ii. 1.
          7. 10 (om. ed. 1, 2).

      „   „   „   „ II. 89 *n* ; iii. 1. 10. 3 *n.*

      „   „   „   „ III. 121–24 ; iv. 9. 7. 9.

Finsteraarhorn, I. 292 ; ii. 4. 2. 1.

      „   IV. 167 *n* ; v. 13. 3 *n.*

      „   IV. 173 ; v. 13. 9.

      „   IV. 187 ; v. 14. 10.

Fir, spruce, author's favourite tree, V. 87 ; vi. 9. 3.

    „   „ foreshortening of its shoot, V. 80–1 ; vi. 8. 14.

    „   „ pyramid of, V. 86 ; vi 9. 1.

Fir-cone, V. 65 ; vi. 7. 15.

Fire-wood, stems destined for, V. 61 ; vi. 7. 10.

Firmament, meaning of the word, IV. 86 *seqq.* ; v. 6. 1 *seqq.*

  „   „   „   V. 167 ; vii. 4. 27.

First-fruits, value of the idea, III. 205 ; iv. 14. 7.

Fischer, Magdeburg cathedral, shrine, V. 258 *n* ; ix. 4. 6 *n.*

  „ Nuremberg fountain, *ib.* ; *ib.*

  „   „ Shrine of St. Sebald, *ib.* ; *ib.*

Fish, ugliness of flat, II. 78 ; iii. 1. 8. 1.

Fissures, curvilinear and straight, IV. 197–98 ; v. 14. 18.

Flattery, net of, IV. 306 ; v. 17. 38.

Flaxman's Dante, engraving of stones, IV. 325–26 ; v. 18. 10.

Flégère, pine forests of, IV. 368 *n* ; v. 20. 4 *n.*

Fleming, quoted, on uses of mountains, IV. 98 ; v. 7. 5.

  „   „   „   „ IV. 371 ; v. 20. 9.

Flemish school [SYNOPSIS. I. xxv, 95 *seqq.*, 119, 303, 368. III.
    193, 335. IV. 353, 376] :—

 architectural details of, good, I. 118 ; ii. 1. 7. 30 (om. ed.
  1, 2).

 calm water of, best of old masters, I. 368 ; ii. 5. 1. 23.

 distances of, IV. 376 ; v. 20. 16.

 early landscape, I. 95 *seqq.* ; ii. 1. 7. 15 *seqq.* (om. ed. 1, 2).

 landscape, III. 335 ; iv. 18. 16.

  „ IV. 376 ; v. 20. 16.

 mountains of, III. 193 ; iv. 13. 20.

 sense of beauty, deficient, IV. 353 ; v. 19. 22.

 subjects of, I. xxv ; *ed.* 2. *pref.* 17.

 winter scenes, I. 303 ; ii. 4. 2. 19 (om. ed. 1, 2).

Flesh, beauty of human, II. 84 ; iii. 1. 9. 5.

 „ painting of, its colour, II. 132 *seqq.* ; iii. 1. 14. 20 *seqq.*

Flint, hardness of, IV. 109 ; v. 8. 8.

 „ way it breaks up, IV. 116 ; v. 8. 16.

Floods, fertilizing value of heavy, IV. 103 ; v. 7. 9.

Florence [SYNOPSIS. I. 37, 93–6, 108–9, 314 *n*, 360, 366, 368, 414.
   II. 7 *n*, 48 *n*, 60 *n*, 75 *n*, 88 *n*, 133, 137–38, 145–46,
   170–71, 187, 188–89, 198–99, 216–20, 223, 229–30,
   232–33, 235, '83 Epil. 8. III. 225, 255, 331–32. IV. 133,
   372, 378–79. V. 221, 238–40, 251–52, 305, 309–10] :—

 Arno. *See s. v.*

 art of, compared with Greek art, V. 238 ; ix. 3. 1.

  „   „   „ Venetian art, V. 239–40 ; ix. 3. 4.

  „ indifference to natural scenery in, V. 221 ; ix. 1. 9.

 frescoes of Federigo Zuccaro, II. 220 ; iii. 2. 4. 14.

Florence, *continued :*
    mosaic, materials of, IV. 133 ; v. 10. 6.
        „   Dutch pictures and, V. 305 ; ix. 8. 2.
    mountains from, IV. 372 ; v. 20. 11.
    Pisan sculpture at, IV. 379 ; v. 20. 21.
    public buildings of, destroyed or neglected, II. 7 *n* ; iii. 1.
        1. 7 *n.*
    works of art, etc., in :

        Academy, Angelico's Crucifixion, II. 235 ; iii. 2. 5. 15.
            „   Giotto's "Baptism of Christ," II. 188–89 ; iii. 2.
                3. 18.
            „   Perugino's "Assumption," II. 47 ; iii. 1. 5. 10.
            „   „   „   II. 8 *n* ; iii. 1. 1. 7 *n.*
            „   pictures restored in, *ib.* ; *ib.*
            „   Vita di Cristo, II. 60 *n* ; iii. 1. 6. 8 *n.*
        Albizzi Palace, Perugino's fresco, II. 235 ; iii. 2. 5. 15.
        Baptistery mosaics, II. 220 ; iii. 2. 4. 14.
        Bronze Boar of, II. 218 ; iii. 2. 4. 12.
        Church of L'Annunziata, II. 187 ; iii. 2. 3. 17.
        Medici Chapel, I. 37 ; i. 2. 1. 5.
            „   „   II. 223 ; iii. 2. 4. 19.
        Or San Michele. *See s. Orcagna.*
        Pitti and Strozzi palaces, noble architecture of, II. 89 *n* ; iii.
            1. 10. 3 *n.*
            „   C. Dolci's St. Peter, II. 219 ; iii. 2. 4. 13.
            „   Rubens', I. 96 ; ii. 1. 7. 15 (om. ed. 1, 2).
            „   Salvator's, I. 314 *n* ; ii. 4. 3. 9 *n* (om. ed. 1, 2).
            „   „   I. 366 ; ii. 5. 1. 21 (om. ed. 1, 2).
            „   „   II. 137 ; iii. 1. 14. 29.
            „   „   Diogenes, II. 170 ; iii. 2. 2. 19.
            „   „   Peace and arms of War, I. 413–14 ; ii. 6. 1.
                11 (om. ed. 1, 2).
            „   „   St. Anthony, II. 48 *n* ; iii. 1. 5. 12 *n.*
            „   „   sea-piece, II. 188 *n* ; iii. 2. 3. 18 *n.*
            „   Titian's Magdalen, II. 133 ; iii. 1. 14. 22.
            „   „   „   V. 251–52 ; ix. 3. 28–29.
            „   „   Marriage of St. Catherine, I. 96 ; ii. 1. 7. 15
                (om. ed. 1, 2).
        Ricardi Palace, B. Gozzoli's frescoes, II. 232 ; iii. 2. 5. 10.
        S. Ambrogio, Cosimo Rosselli's fresco, II. 60 *n* ; iii. 1. 6.
            8 *n.*
            „   Mino da Fiesole's altar-piece, *ib.* ; *ib.*
        Santa Croce, modern tomb in, II. 76 *n* ; iii. 1. 7. 7 *n.*
            „   „   statue by Bandinelli in, II. 198 ; iii. 2. 3. 27.

Florence, works of art, etc., in, *continued :*

    S. Maria Maddalena, Perugino's fresco, I. 368 ; ii. 5. 1. 23
                                  (om. ed. 1, 2).

        ,,   ,,   ,,   ,,   II. 232; iii. 2. 5. 11.

    S. Maria Novella, II. 137 ; iii. 1. 14. 29.

       ,,   ,,   II. '83 Epil. 8.

       ,,   ,,   Angelico's Annunciation, II. 187 ; iii. 2.
                                 3. 17.

       ,,   ,,   Angelico's Annunciation, V. 309–10 ; ix.
                                   8. 12 (frontispiece).

       ,,   ,,   Ghirlandajo's Salutation, I. 109 ; ii. 1. 7
                                   25 (om. ed. 1, 2).

       ,,   ,,   Ghirlandajo's square window, *ib.* ; *ib.*

       ,,   ,,   Memmi (Simon), picture of the Duomo,
                                   I. 109 ; ii. 1. 7. 25 (om. ed. 1, 2).

       ,,   ,,   Memmi (Simon), picture of the Duomo,
                                   II. 60 *n* ; iii. 1. 6. 8 *n.*

       ,,   ,,   pulpit of, gilded, II. 216 ; iii. 2. 4. 9.

    S. Miniato, III. 225 ; iv. 14. 31.

       ,,   view from, III. 255 ; iv. 15. 17.

    Uffizii, Bronzino's "Christ and Spirits in Prison," II. 61 ; iii. 1.
                                     6. 8.

       ,,   ,,   ,,   ,,   ,,   II. 230 ; iii.
                                     2. 5. 7 *n.*

       ,,   Claude's, water in, I. 360 ; ii. 5. 1. 17 (om. ed. 1, 2).

       ,,   Da Vinci's sketch, foliage, I. 93 ; ii. 1. 7. 13 (om. ed.
                1, 2).

       ,,   Filippino Lippi, II. 234–35 ; iii. 2. 5. 14.

       ,,   Ghirlandajo's "Adoration of Magi," II. 233 *n* ; iii.
                                 2. 5. 11 *n.*

       ,,   ,,   ,,   ,,   III. 331 ; iv.
                                  18. 10.

       ,,   Perugino's portrait of himself, II. 145 ; iii. 1. 15. 6.

       ,,   ,,   ,,   ,,   II. 233 ; iii. 2. 5. 11.

       ,,   Raphael's "Holy Family," III. 332 ; iv. 18. 12 (pl.
                11).

Flowers [SYNOPSIS. I. xxxvii, 105, 199, 286, 334, 344, 419–21, 425.
      II. 98–9, 180–81. III. 204, 235, 241, 302. IV. 258,
      368–70. V. 56 *seqq.*, 98–102, 107 *n*] :—

    Alpine, V. 99 ; vi. 10. 3.

    beauty of form in, V. 107 *n* ; vi. 10. 19 *n.*

    colour of, its origin, V. 98 ; vi. 10. 1.

    greatest minds careless of, but not of *thorns*, V. 101–2 ; vi.
        10. 7.

Flowers, *continued :*

 herbage and, general characteristics of all, V. 102 *seqq.* ; vi. 10. 10–11.

 love of, and sympathy with, II. 98–9 ; iii. 1. 12. 3.

  „ mediæval, III. 204 ; iv. 14. 6.

  „ rare, V. 98 ; vi. 10. 2.

  „ the kind of people having (poets), V. 101 ; vi. 10. 7.

 never sublime, V. 101 ; vi. 10. 7.

 often as properly dissected as dreamt over, III. 302 ; iv. 17. 7.

 painting of, by great artists, careless, V. 99 *seqq.* ; vi. 10. 4 *seqq.*

  „ „ „ „ V. 102 ; vi. 10. 9.

  „ not to be too imitative, V. 102 ; vi. 10. 8.

 Savoyard name (Pain du Bon Dieu), IV. 369 *n* ; v. 20. 5.

 Shakspere's and Milton's, II. 180–81 ; iii. 2. 3. 7.

  „ „ Shelley's, I. xxxvii ; *pref.* 2. 31.

 " the faith that every flower enjoys the air it breathes," II. 98 ; iii. 1. 12. 3.

 trees and, growth of, V. 56 *seqq.* ; vi. 7. 4 *seqq.*

 trefoil to six-foil, V. 107 *n* ; vi. 10. 19 *n.*

 typical of excellence and brevity of life, III. 242 ; iv. 14. 53.

  „ fine colour, III. 235–36 ; iv. 14. 46.

   See s. Botany.

Foam, cannot be really drawn, I. 395–96 ; ii. 5. 3. 29 (om. ed. 1, 2).

 „ characteristics of, I. 403–4 ; ii. 5. 3. 38 (ed. 1, 2. 37).

   See s. Schaffhausen.

Foliage, drawing of, ancient landscape, I. 407 ; ii. 6. 1. 1.

 „ „ on the Continent and by pre-Raphaelites, I. 425 *seqq.* ; ii. 6. 1. 27.

 „ „ R.A. 1846, very bad, I. 426 ; ii. 6. 1. 28.

 „ element of mountain glory, IV. 369–70 ; v. 20. 7.

 „ regularity, unity, variety of, I. 418–19 ; ii. 6. 1. 16.

   See s. Leaf.

Fontainebleau, author's love of, IV. 366 ; v. 20. 2.

Fool's power for evil, IV. 411 *n* ; App. i. 6 *n.*

Forbes' "Travels Through the Alps" quoted, IV. 68 ; v. 4. 13.

 „ „ „ „ IV. 194 ; v. 14. 16.

 „ works, glacier theory, IV. 180 *n* ; v. 13. 18 *n.*

 „ „ map of Alps, IV. 41 ; v. 3. 8.

 „ „ Matterhorn, IV. 189–90 ; v. 14. 11–12.

Forbes' works, *continued :*

„ „ Matterhorn and Riffel, IV. 245 *n* ; v. 16. 9 *n.*

„ „ „ IV. 247–48 ; v. 16. 10–11.

Forefathers, we imitate without honouring our, III. 271–72 ; iv. 16. 15.

Foreground, detail in nature, I. 212 ; ii. 2. 5. 15.

„ „ *e.g.* leafage, III. 128–29 ; iv. 9. 16.

„ edges and round surfaces in, I. 343 *seqq.*; ii. 4. 4. 27.

„ importance of, I. 335–36 ; ii. 4. 4. 14 (ed. 1, 2. 18).

„ increasedly lovely when wet, IV. 258 ; v. 16. 24.

„ lesson given by all, I. 344 ; ii. 4. 4. 30.

„ mountain, attractiveness of, I. 105 ; ii. 1. 7. 22.

„ must sometimes yield to distance, I. 198 ; ii. 2. 4. 4. *See s. Turner.*

„ of old masters, I. 328 ; ii. 4. 4. 1.

„ „ „ I. 334 ; ii. 4. 4. 11.

„ „ „ I. 336–37 ; ii. 4. 4. 16.

„ vagueness of modern as opposed to mediæval, III. 265–66 ; iv. 16. 4.

Foreign words, use of, in English, IV. 391 *n* ; v. 20. 33 *n.*

Foreshortening, in tree-drawing (Dutch, Turner, etc.), V. 79–81 ; vi. 8. 12–14.

Forests, art and intellect produced by, V. 152–53 ; vii. 4. **2**

„ beauty of, I. 379 ; ii. 6. 1. 1 (ed. 1, 2 only).

„ best, all of same trees, II. 57 ; iii. 1. 6. 5.

„ southern and northern writers on (Homer, Dante, Shakspere, etc.), III. 226–27 ; iv. 14. 33.

Form [SYNOPSIS. **I.** 72–5, 297, 440. **II.** 216–17. **III.** 217–18. **IV.** 56 *n*, 57, 76, 277–79. **V.** 349 *n*] :—

abstract, without colour, II. 216 ; iii. 2. 4. 9.

beauty of, its essentials, IV. 277–79 ; v. 17. 3.

blindness, unknown, I. 74–5 ; ii. 1. 5. 8.

colour and, form more pleasurable, I. 75 ; ii. 1. 5. 9.

„ „ important, I. 72–3 ; ii. 1. 5. 3.

„ „ „ IV. 56 *n*, 57 ; v. 3. 24 and *n.*

„ „ „ V. 349 *n* ; ix. 11. 8 *n.*

„ sense of, often dissociated, I. 440 ; ii. 6. 3. 4.

importance of, I. 76 ; ii. 1. 6. 2.

laws of, inviolable, I. 297 ; ii. 4. 2. 10.

means outline and chiaroscuro, I. 74 ; ii. 1. 5. **7.**

Form, *continued* :

> rendering of, insisted on, and why, IV. 76 ; v. 5. 10.

> sacrifice of, to colour, II. 216–17 ; iii. 2. 4. 10.

> typical, value of its recurrence in nature, III. 217–18 ; iv. 14. 24.

> > *See s. Curvature.*

Formazza Val, De Saussure on the, IV. 417, 422 ; App. ii. 3. 5.

Foxglove, V. 57–8 ; vi. 7. 4. 5.

France [SYNOPSIS. I. 136–37. III. 192–93, 350 *seqq.* IV. 97, 160, 314, 366, 374, 379, 380–81. V. 276, 378] :—

> architecture of, IV. 379 ; v. 20. 20.

> art of. *See s. French art.*

> best country to teach grace to artists, I. 136 ; ii. 1. 7. 41 (om. ed. 1, 2).

> cathedrals of, finest, IV. 380–81 ; v. 20. 23.

> England and, their relation, 1856, III. 350 *seqq.* ; iv. 18. 37 *seqq.*

> landscape of, author's love of (except Champagne), IV. 366 ; v. 20. 2.

> > „ coteaux of, IV. 97 ; v. 7. 4.

> > „ „ IV. 160 ; v. 12. 20.

> > „ „ IV. 366 ; v. 20. 2.

> > „ enhanced by its architecture, IV. 366 *n* ; v. 20. 2 *n.*

> > „ foliage of, its beauty, I. 136 ; ii. 1. 7. 41 (om. ed. 1, 2).

> > „ poplars of (Amiens), III. 192–93 ; iv. 13. 20.

> > „ „ V. 93 ; vi. 9. 11.

> > „ valleys of, beauty of, I. 136 ; ii. 1. 7. 41.

> > „ „ how formed, IV. 314 ; v. 17. 48.

> religious temper of, how formed, IV. 374 ; v. 20. 13.

> > „ „ blasphemy, V. 276 ; ix. 6. 3.

> > „ „ irreligion, V. 378 ; ix. 12. 5.

> Turner's feeling for, I. 136 ; ii. 1. 7. 41 (om. ed. 1, 2). *See s. French art, etc.*

Francia [SYNOPSIS. I. 89, 109. II. 47, 71, 121, 239. III. 52, 56, 131. IV. 409] :—

> architecture of, I. 109 ; ii. 1. 7. 25 (om. ed. 1, 2).

> finish of, III. 131 ; iv. 9. 18.

> "insipid faces" of (Leslie quoted), IV. 409 ; App. i. 3.

> landscape (open skies) of, II. 47 ; iii. 1. 5. 10.

> Madonnas of, II. 239 ; iii. 2. 5. 21 (and '83 *n*).

Francia, *continued:*

    religious pictures of (backgrounds), III. 52 ; iv. 4. 9.

        ,,   ,,   III. 56 ; iv. 4. 14.

    skies of (Bologna Gallery), I. 89–91 ; ii. 1. 7. 11 (om. ed. 1, 2).

    symmetry of, II. 71 ; iii. 1. 8. 4 (ed. 1 only).

    work of (National Gallery), II. 121 ; iii. 1. 14. 23 (ed. 1 only).

Francis, St., IV. 373 ; v. 20. 12.

        ,,   "Lady Poverty," IV. 375 ; v. 20. 15. *See s. St. Francis.*

Franconia, scenery of, V. 259–60 ; ix. 4. 7. 9.

Frankness, of true gentlemen, V. 292 ; ix. 7. 10.

Free thought, origin of evil and, IV. 423 ; App. iii. 1.

Freedom of great art, V. 194 ; viii. 2. 15.

Freestone, IV. 134 ; v. 11. 1. *See s. Sandstone.*

French [SYNOPSIS. I. 26–7, 89, 112, 130, 425–26. II. 30, 37, 145, 237. III. 270, 276, 277–78. IV. 348, 381. V. 267, 304] :—

    art, decline of, sudden after 1400, IV. 381 ; v. 20. 23.

    ,, effect of antique study on, evil, I. 130 ; ii. 1. 7. 37 (om. ed. 1, 2).

    ,, etching good, I. 426 ; ii. 6. 1. 27 (om. ed. 1, 2).

    ,, godless, I. 130 ; ii. 1. 7. 37 (om. ed. 1, 2).

    ,, Greek art, its influence on, II. 237 ; iii. 2. 5. 19.

    ,, landscape, evils of, II. 145 ; iii. 1. 15. 6.

    ,, modern school, I. 26–7 ; i. 1. 5. 5.

    ,,   ,,   ,, chiaroscuro of, deceptive, I. 425–26 ; ii. 6. 1. 27 (om. ed. 1, 2).

    ,,   ,,   ,, merits and failings of, *ib.* ; *ib.* (*ib.*).

    ,,   ,,   ,, powers and learning of, III. 276 ; iv. 16. 23.

    ,, morbid horror of, II. 137 ; iii. 1. 14. 29.

    ,, religious school, III. 270 ; iv. 16. 10.

    ,, sensuality of, II. 30 ; iii. 1. 3. 15 ('83 *n*).

    ,,   ,, V. 304 ; ix. 8. 1.

    ,, vicious through its vanity, I. 89 ; ii. 1. 7. 10 (om. ed. 1, 2).

    books, good illustrations to, I. 426 ; ii. 6. 1. 27 (om. ed. 1, 2).

    "Libertas" on St. Michele of Lucca, I. 111–12 ; ii. 1. 7. 26 (om. ed. 1, 2).

    literature, affectation of, III. 277–78 ; iv. 16. 26.

        ,,   classical revival and, V. 267 ; ix. 5. 5.

        ,,   novels, III. 276 ; iv. 16. 23.

French, *continued :*

    literature, novels, morbid horrors of, IV. 348 ; v. 19. 16.

Fresco painting, outside walls, I. 116, 117 ; ii. 1. 7. 30 (om. ed. 1, 2).

Fribourg (Switz.), country round, IV. 139 *seqq.* ; v. 11. 8.

      ,,   ,,   railroad, ruins of, IV. 398 ; v. 20. 41.

      ,,   ,,   towers and walls of (author's drawing), IV. 33 ; v. 2. 23 (pl. 24–5).

Friends, gradual recognition of approaching, I. 203–4 ; ii. 2. 5. 3.

Frohn-alp (Bay of Uri), V. 97 ; vi. 9. 16.

Fruit, definition of a, V. 105–6 ; vi. 10. 15 *seqq.*

  ,, -painting, and high art, III. 31 ; iv. 3. 6.

Frütigen (Berne), valley of, V. 95 ; vi. 9. 14.

Fungi, colours of, IV. 54 and *n* ; v. 3. 23 and *n.*

Funnels, mountain crests formed like, IV. 213–14 ; v. 15. 10.

Furca del Bosco, Saussure quoted, IV. 418 ; App. ii. 3.

Fuseli [SYNOPSIS. **I.** xxxii *n*, 19, 99, 192. **II.** 64 *n*, 89 *n*, 164, 183, 192 *n*, 194 *n*, 203. **III.** 82. **V.** 353 *n*] :—

    art of, "poor fumigatory," III. 82 ; iv. 6. 8.

    grey spectra of, V. 353 *n* ; ix. 11. 8 *n.*

    quoted, on artistic conception, II. 164 ; iii. 2. 2. 9.

      ,,   ,, Angelico. III. 82 ; iv. 6. 8.

      ,,   ,, chiaroscuro, I. 192 ; ii. 2. 3. 10.

      ,,   ,, Constable, I. 99 ; ii. 1. 7. 18 (om. ed. 1, 2).

      ,,   ,, deception in art, I. xxxii *n* ; *pref.* 2. 24 *n.*

      ,,   ,, "Greek alone is grand," II. 64 *n* ; iii. 1. 6. 10 *n.*

      ,,   ,, imitation and copying, I. 19 ; i. 1. 4. 1.

      ,,   ,, invention and fancy, II. 183 ; iii. 2. 3. 12.

      ,,   ,, negligence the shadow of energy, II. 89 *n* ; iii. 1. 10. 3 *n.*

      ,,   ,, Raphael's "Holy Innocents," II. 192–93 ; iii. 2 3. 21.

      ,,   ,, Tintoret's Crucifixion, II. 192 *n* ; iii. 2. 3. 20 *n.*

      ,,   ,,   ,, "Holy Innocents," II. 194 *n* ; iii. 2. 3. 22 *n.*

      ,,   ,, Zeuxis' Centaur, II. 203 ; iii. 2. 3. 29.

Future state, imagination given us to realize our, III. 50 ; iv. 4. 5.

Gaddi, Taddeo, gentle landscape of, II. 47 ; iii. 1. 5. 10.

Gainsborough [SYNOPSIS. **I.** xxi *n*, 87, 97–8, 131, 141–43. **III.** 344. **V.** 318, 353 *n*] :—

    characteristics of, I. xxi *n* ; *pref.* 2. 13 *n.*

Gainsborough, *continued :*
    characteristics of, I. 141 ; ii. 1. 7. 44 (om. ed. 1, 2).
    colour and truth of, V. 353 *n* ; ix. 11. 8 *n.*
    failings, etc., of, I. 98 ; ii. 1. 7. 17 (om. ed. 1, 2).
    finished detail, deficient, I. 87 ; ii. 1. 7. 9 (om. ed. 1, 2).
    method and vehicles of, unknown, I. 143 ; ii. 1. 7. 45 (om.
        ed. 1, 2).
    purity of, I. 131 ; ii. 1. 7. 37 (om. ed. 1, 2).
    squirearchy of, V. 318 ; ix. 9. 7.
    Turner's study of, III. 344 ; iv. 18. 30.
    work by, given by him to R.A., I. 98 ; ii. 1. 7. 17 (om. ed.
        1, 2).
Galileo, V. 382 ; ix. 12. 11.
" Galleria delle belle Arti " (book) referred to, II. 189 ; iii. 2. 3.
    18.
Galleries.

    See s. Berlin, Bologna, Dresden, Dulwich, Ellesmere, Louvre,
        Munich, National, Turin, Venice, Windus.

Ganges, the river, IV. 99 ; v. 7. 6.
Gardens, Homeric, III. 191–92 ; iv. 13. 18. 19.
    „   in mediæval landscape, III. 202–3 ; iv. 14. 2.
    „   love of, mediæval and Greek, III. 204 ; iv. 14. 6.
Garter, ribbon of the (gentian), V. 99 ; vi. 10. 3.
Gaveston, Piers, place of his execution, pine-trees at, IV. 394 ;
    v. 20. 38.
Gemmi, Mt., IV. 254–55 ; v. 16. 20.
    „   „   clefts in the, IV. 273 ; v. 16. 40.
    „   „   IV. 303 ; v. 17. 33.
Generalization in art, absurdity shown, I. xxxiv–v ; *pref.* 2. 27–8.
    „   „   „   „   I. xxxix ; *pref.* 2. 33.
    „   „   based on ignorance of nature, I. xxxviii ;
                pref. 2. 32.
    „   „   composition distinct from, I. xxxix ; *pref.*
                2. 34.
    „   „   defined, I. 208 ; ii. 2. 5. 10.
    „   „   „   III. 137 *n* ; iv. 10. 5 *n.*
    „   „   idealism opposed to, II. 116–17 ; iii. 1.
                13. 13.
    „   „   so-called, I. 296 ; ii. 4. 2. 7.
Geneva, colour of Rhone at (author's diary), I. 254–55 ; ii. 5. 1.
    10 (om. ed. 1, 2).

Geneva, *continued :*

,,   lake of, railroad at head, IV. 398 ; v. 20. 41.

,,   wooden loggias at, destroyed, II. 7 *n* ; iii. 1. 1. 7 *n.*

Genèvre, Mt., religion of people, IV. 376 ; v. 20. 15.

Genius, always teaches some lesson, I. 439 ; ii. 6. 3. 2.

,,   not the result of education, III. 47 ; iv. 3. 27.

,,   public reception of, original, I. xviii–xix ; *ed.* 2. *pref.* 11.
      See s. Criticism.

Genlis, Mme. de, her criticism of art quoted, IV. 257–58 ; v. 16.
      23–4.

Genoa, art and climate of, V. 239 ; ix. 3. 2.

,,   Pietà (M. Angelo), II. 89 ; iii. 1. 10. 4.

Genteel, a word exclusively English, IV. 4 ; v. 1. 4.

Gentian, belts of, on Alps in spring, V. 99 ; vi. 10. 3.

,,   blue still, though unseen, III. 162 ; iv. 12. 2.

,,   of the Jura, III. 235 ; iv. 14. 46.

,,   ,,   IV. 368 ; v. 20. 5.

Gentility, English, "a genteel house to let," IV. 4 ; v. 1. 4.

Gentleman, characteristics of the true, V. 287–89 *seqq.* ; ix. 7.
      1. 5. *seqq.*

Genuineness, offensive to modern temper, IV. 411 ; App.
      i. 6.

Geology,* author's early study of, I. xxxiv–v ; *pref. ed.* 2.
      27–8.

,,   ,,   later study of, IV. 180 *n* ; v. 13. 18 *n.*

,,   curvature in nature, II. 65–6 ; iii. 1. 6. 12.

,,   formation of new mountains (theory), IV. 147 ; v.
      12. 4.

,,   joints of mountain beds, I. 309 ; ii. 4. 3. 2.

,,   stones and rocks, geologist's view of, I. xxxvii ; *pref.*
      2. 32.

,,   study of, its nature, I. xxxviii–ix ; *ib.* 33.

,,   ,,   its use, I. 322 ; ii. 4. 3. 21.

* *See s.* Agassiz, Aiguilles, Aletsch, Alps, Apennines, Assaissement,
Banks, China, Chrysoprase, Clay, Cleavage, Cliffs, Coherent rocks, Con-
vulsions, Crystalline, Crystallization, Crystals, Curvature, De Saussure,
Débris, Diamond, Diluvium, Earth, Fissures, Fleming, Flint, Forbes,
Freestone, Glacier, Gneiss, Granite, Hornblende, Hutton, Jedburgh,
Joints, Lamination, Langholme, Limestone, Magnesia, Marble, Mica,
Minerals, Mont Blanc, Montanvert, Mountains, Opal, Plains, Porphyries,
Protogine, Rhine, Rocks, Sandstone, Sapphire, Sharpe, Slate, Slaty, Soil,
Soot, Stone, Stones, Strata, Streams, Strid, Thomson, Undulation, Valleys,
Yorkshire, Zumloch.

Gerard Dow. *See s. Dow.*

German [SYNOPSIS. I. 84–6, 95 *seqq.*, 131, 223, 414, 425. II. 26, 235. III. 34, 37, 65, 74, 80, 82–3, 146, 161–63 *n*, 269, 276, 278, 356. IV. 52, 63, 249, 348–49, 353, 355, 356–57, 410. V. 87, 94, 179, 276, 304] :—

architecture. *See s. Nuremberg.*

art, early landscape, I. 95 *seqq.* ; ii. 1. 7. 15 *seqq.* (om. ed. 1, 2).

„ modern school :

affected want of technique, III. 34 ; iv. 3. 11.

author's depreciation of it, III. 356 ; App. ii.

„   knowledge of it, I. 425 ; ii. 6. 1. 27 (om. ed. 1, 2).

barber's-block beauty, III. 37 ; iv. 3. 14.

heroics of, V. 304 ; ix. 8. 1.

idealism of, III. 74 ; iv. 5. 12.

landscape (Venetian Acad.), I. 96 *seqq.* ; ii. 1. 7. 15 *seqq.* (om. ed. 1, 2).

purism, its self-conceit, III. 82–3 ; iv. 6. 9.

religious school, bad colour, II. 235 ; iii. 2. 5. 15.

„   „   „   III. 65 ; iv. 4. 24.

„   „   historical and, III. 276 ; iv. 16. 23.

„   „   vanity of, III. 269 ; iv. 16. 10.

sickliness of, I. 131 ; ii. 1. 7. 37 (om. ed. 1, 2).

vileness of, I. 223 ; ii. 3. 1. 12.

„ old school, love of ugliness, etc., I. 414 ; ii. 6. 1. 11 (om. ed. 1, 2).

„   „   „   „   IV. 348–49 ; v. 19. 17.

„   „   sense of beauty, deficient, IV. 353 ; v. 19. 22.

„   „   want of mystery, IV. 63 ; v. 4. 8.

character, gloom of, and sedentary life, IV. 355 ; v. 19. 25.

literature, affectation, III. 278 ; iv. 16. 26.

„   grotesque in poetry, IV. 410 ; App. i. 5. *See below, s. philosophy.*

missal (1450) figure of St. Peter, IV. 356–57 ; v. 19. 26. *See s. Schongauer.*

painter, ideal sketches of young, seen by author, III. 80 ; iv. 6. 6.

German, *continued :*

    philosophy, Anschauung of, II. 26 ; iii. 1. 3. 7 ('83 *n*).

        „   conceit of, III. 146 ; iv. 10. 15.

        „   depreciated, III. 276 ; iv. 16. 23.

        „   „   III. 356 ; App. ii.

        „   metaphysical contempt of colour, IV. 52 ; v. 3. 22.

        „   modern, its harmfulness, V. 179; viii. 1. 14.

        „   nomenclature, IV. 249 ; v. 16. 13.

        „   rationalism, V. 276 ; ix. 6. 3.

        „   "subjectivity" parodied, III. 161–63 *n* ; iv. 12. 1–3 *n*.

    pine-trees, drawing of, V. 87 ; vi. 9. 3.

        „   influence of, in the North, V. 94 ; vi. 9. 12.

Geryon, Dante on, V. 336–37 ; ix. 10. 13–14.

    „   oxen of, V. 337–39 ; ix. 10. 14–19.

Getting on in the world, V. 385 ; ix. 12. 18.

Ghent, sea-embankments of, III. 224 ; iv. 14. 29.

Ghiberti, leaf-mouldings of, V. 39 ; vi. 5. 4.

    „   rocks of, III. 255 ; iv. 15. 16.

Ghirlandajo [SYNOPSIS. **I.** 87, 108, 130. **II.** 48, 80, 129, 233 *n*, '83 Epil. 10. **III.** 41, 61–2, 254–55, 331, 333, 341–42. **IV.** 2, 381. **V.** 39, 100] :—

    architecture of, I. 108 ; ii. 1. 7. 25 (om. ed. 1, 2).

    author's study of (1845), II. '83 Epil. 10.

    backgrounds of fruit and flowers, V. 100 ; vi. 10. 5.

    characteristics of, IV. 381 ; v. 20. 23.

    copied by Claude, III. 341–42 ; iv. 18. 27.

    desire to paint walls of Florence, III. 41 ; iv. 3. 19.

    ferns in works of, I. 87 ; ii. 1. 7. 9 (om. ed. 1, 2).

    landscape of, III. 341–42 ; iv. 18. 27.

        „   anti-picturesque, IV. 2 and *n* ; v. 1. 1 and *n* (pl. 18).

        „   gentle, II. 47 ; iii. 1. 5. 10.

    Madonnas of, Florentines, not Jewesses, I. 130 ; ii. 1. 7. 37 (om. ed. 1, 2).

    portraiture in his works, II. 129 ; iii. 1. 14. 14.

    reality of conception, III. 61–2 ; iv. 4. 20–1.

    religious art of, *ib.* ; *ib.*

    rocks of, III. 254–55 ; iv. 15. 16 (pl. 10). *See below, s works.*

Ghirlandajo, *continued* :
    symmetrical groups of, II. 80 ; iii. 1. 8. 4.
    works of :

        Adoration of Magi (Florence, Uffizii), II. 233 *n* ; iii. 2. 5
            11 *n*.
            „   „   its background, III. 331 ; iv. 18. 10.
        Baptism of Christ, rock in, III. 333 ; iv. 18. 13.
        Salutation (S. Maria Novella, Florence), I. 109 ; ii. 1. 7. 25
            (om. ed. 1, 2).
        square window („   „   „   ), *ib.* ; *ib.* (*ib.*).
        view of Pisa, IV. 2 ; v. 1. 1.

Gibraltar, V. 326 ; ix. 9. 22.
Giorgione [SYNOPSIS. I. 90–1, 95, 104, 116, 129, 364. II. 48, 132–
            33, 179 *n*, 216. III. 345–46. V. 39, 253, 312 *seqq*., 321,
            350 *n*, 370 and *n*] :—
    I. 129 ; ii. 1. 7. 36 (om. ed. 1, 2).
    colour and light of, I. 104 ; ii. 1. 7. 21 (om. ed. 1, 2).
        „   of Venetian fishermen, I. 364 ; ii. 5. 1. 19 (om. ed.
            1, 2).
        „   qualities of, II. 179 *n* ; iii. 2. 3. 7.
        „   „   perfect, V. 350 *n* ; ix. 11. 8 *n*.
    flatness of masses (colour without form), II. 216 ; iii. 2
        4. 10.
    flesh tints of, II. 216 ; iii. 2. 4. 9.
    frescoes of, in ruins (Venice, Fondaco de' Tedeschi), I
            116 ; ii. 1. 7. 30 (om. ed. 1, 2).
        „   „   V. 370 and *n* ; ix. 11. 32 and *n*.
            See below, s. work of.
    home of, and of Turner compared, V. 315 *seqq*. ; ix. 9. 1.
        seqq.
    landscape, quaint and solemn, I. 90, 91 ; ii. 1. 7. 11 (om. ed
        1, 2).
        „   I. 95 ; ii. 1. 7. 14 (om. ed. 1, 2).
    leaf-drawing of, V. 39 ; vi. 5. 2.
    nude figures of, II. 133–34 ; iii. 1. 14. 22.
        „   „   V. 253 ; ix. 3. 30.
    portraiture of, its modesty, II. 132 ; iii. 1. 14. 19.
    religious feeling of, V. 321 ; ix. 9. 11–12.
    rivalry of Titian and, III. 345–46 ; iv. 18. 32.
    skies of, luminous, II. 48 ; iii. 1. 5. 11.
    temper of (modesty), II. 132–33 ; iii. 1. 14. 19–22.

Giorgione, *continued :*

    temper of (spirit, sense, and intellect), V. 312 ; ix. 8. 15.

    work of, " Hesperid Æglé," V. 312 ; ix. 8. 15 (pl. 79).

Giotto [SYNOPSIS. I. xxiii, 4 *n*, 11, 93. II. 7 *n*, 11 *n*, 47, 80, 129,
         140 *n*, 188–89, 191, 195, 198, 230 *n*, 232, 234, '83 Epil.
         7. III. 21, 33, 62, 104, 105, 276, 327. IV. 376–77, 379,
         380. V. 298–99 *n*] :—

    balanced powers of, III. 33 ; iv. 3. 9.

    breaks barbarism of Byzantine schools, I. xxiii ; *pref.* 2. 14.

    cramped by tradition, II. 191 ; iii. 2. 3. 20.

    Crucifixions by, *ib.*; *ib. See below, s. works of.*

    Dante's portrait by, II. 129 ; iii. 1. 14. 14.

       ,,   relation to, III. 276 ; iv. 16. 22.

       ,,   ,,   cf. Turner and Scott, III. 327 ; iv. 18. 2.

    distances of, mountainous, IV. 376–77 ; v. 20. 16.

    great in ideas, I. 11 ; i. 1. 2. 7.

    greatest painter of his age, III. 21 ; iv. 2. 5.

       ,,   works in painting, not architecture, II. 11 *n* ; iii.,
         1. 1. 9 *n*.

    jewel-painting, abstract, II. 234 ; iii. 2. 5. 14.

    landscape of, gentle, II. 47 ; iii. 1. 5. 10.

    limited, II. 232 ; iii. 2. 5. 10.

    mountain-bred, IV. 379–80 ; v. 20. 21–2.

    Pisan sculpture, its influence on, IV. 379 ; iv. 20. 20.

    popularity of, small, and why, I. 4 *n* ; i. 1. 1 *n*.

    purity of, II. 188 ; iii. 2. 3. 18.

    reality of conception, III. 62 ; iv. 4. 21.

    religious art of, *ib.* ; *ib.*

    rocks of, III. 254–55 ; iv. 15. 16 (pl. 10).

    symmetrical grouping of, II. 80 ; iii. 1. 8. 4.

    variety of, II. 140 *n* ; iii. 1. 14. 31 *n*.

    works of :

        at Assisi, III. 104 ; iv. 8. 6.

       ,, Florence, Dante's portrait, II. 129 ; iii. 1. 14. 14.

       ,,   ,,   Baptism of Christ (Acad.), II. 188–89 ; iii. 2. 3.
           18.

       ,,   ,,   Campanile, V. 298–99 *n*; ix. 7. 21 *n*.

       ,,   ,,   Santa Croce, tempera picture, II. 198 ; iii. 2.
           3. 27.

       ,, Padua, III. 104 ; iv. 8. 6.

       ,,   ,,   colour of frescoes, II. 235 ; iii. 2. 5. 15.

       ,,   ,,   Charity, III. 105 ; iv. 8. 7.

Giotto : works of, *continued* :
     at Padua, Inferno, II. 137 ; iii. 1. 14. 29.
     ,,   ,,   Last Judgment, II. 195 ; iii. 2. 3. 23.
     ,, Pisa, Sacrifice for the Friends (Job), I. 93 ; ii. 1. 7. 13
                             (om. ed. 1, 2).
     ,,   ,,   ,,   ,,   II. '83 Epil. 7.
     ,,   ,,   Satan before God, II. 7 *n* ; iii. 1. 1. 7 *n*.
     ,,   ,,   ,,   ,,   II. 230 *n* ; iii. 2. 5. 7 *n*.
     ,, Venice, St. Mark's Convent, Crucifixion, II. 138 ; iii. 1.
            14. 29.

Girtin, T., landscape of, III. 346 ; iv. 18. 32.
Giulio Romano, architecture of, bad, IV. 390 ; v. 20. 33.
Glacier de Taconay, IV. 223 ; v. 15. 18.
     ,,   des Bois, IV. 118–19 and *n* ; v. 15. 16 and *n*.
     ,,   ,,   IV. 223 ; v. 15. 17.
     ,,   des Bossons, IV. 298 ; v. 17. 30.
Glaciers, action of, on mountains, IV. 178–79 ; v. 13. 17.
     ,,   dirt-bands in, IV. 67–68 ; v. 4. 13.
     ,,   motion of, IV. 144 ; v. 12. 1.
     ,,   ,,   perceived by Turner, V. 89–90 ; vi. 8. 6–7.
     ,,   streams, IV. 144 ; v. 12. 1.
     ,,   tourists on Swiss, III. 267 ; iv. 16. 6.
     ,,   tracks of old, on mountains, IV. 178 *n* ; v. 13. 16.
Gladiator, the dying, II. 137 ; iii. 1. 14. 29.
Glaramara, Cumberland hill, I. 293 ; ii. 4. 3. 12 (ed. 1, 2 only).
Glass, artist's mind to be like finely blown, I. 51 ; ii. 1. 1. 7.
—— -painting, decline of, IV. 381 ; v. 20. 23.
—— -roof, mistaken by author for an Alp, III. 139 ; iv. 10. 8.
Glenfarg (Kinross), author's visit, as a child, to, III. 307 ; iv.
     17. 13. 14.
Gloom, disease and, go together, IV. 355 ; v. 19. 25. *See s.*
     Mountain-life.
Gneiss, of Matterhorn, IV. 168 ; v. 13. 5.
     ,,   what it is, IV. 216 ; v. 15. 15.
     ,,   ,,   IV. 217–20 ; v. 15. 16.
                 See s. Montanvert.
God [SYNOPSIS. I. 29, 60–1, 344. II. 53, 68–9, 84–5, 90, 94, 136,
     205, 229, 237 *seqq.* III. 179 *seqq.*, 185, 187, 205, 267, 317–
     18, 316. IV. 88–92, 110, 149, 362. V. 221–24] :—
     appearance of, in clouds, in the Bible, IV. 88–92 ; v. 6.
     5–9.
     children of, II. 136 ; iii. 1. 14. 27 ('83 *n*).

God, *continued:*

communications of truth to men, II. 146–47 ; iii. 1. 15. 8.

conception of, childlike and simple, IV. 90 ; v. 6. 7.

    „   and of "man in his likeness," V. 221–24 ; ix. 1. 9 *seqq.*

faith and trust in, II. 205 ; iii. 2. 3. 33 (F.A. *n*).

gratitude to, how diminished by mediæval views of nature, III. 204 ; iv. 14. 7.

Greek idea of, as seen in art, II. 238 *seqq.* ; iii. 2. 5. 20.

    „   „   „   III. 179 *seqq.* ; iv. 13. 4 *seqq.*

infinity of, not mysterious but unfathomable, II. 53 ; iii. 1. 5. 19.

intentions, not to be questioned, but His law accepted, II. 68–9 ; iii. 1. 6. 15–16 ('83 *nn*).

knowledge of, possible only if we know ourselves, V. 224 ; ix. 1. 14.

love of nature helps faith in, III. 317–18 ; iv. 17. 32.

manifestations of, in nature, I. 60 ; ii. 1. 2. 8.

    „   „   I. 344 ; ii. 4. 4. 30.

    „   „   and in man, III. 316 ; iv. 17. 31.

    „   „   „   V. 221 ; ix. 1. 9.

man's taste healthy when illustrative of, I. 29 ; i. 1. 6. 1.

modern endeavour to realize, not to obey, III. 185 ; iv. 13. 11.

    „ idea of, as separate from nature, III. 187 ; iv. 13. 13.

mountains built by, IV. 149 ; v. 12. 8.

not seen in nature by moderns, III. 267 ; iv. 16. 7.

purity expresses his energy, etc., II. 84–5 ; iii. 1. 9. 6 *seqq.*

purposes of, in nature to be studied by man, IV. 110 *n* ; v. 8. 9.

    „   inscrutable, IV. 362 ; v. 19. 32.

representation of, in art, II. 229 ; iii. 2. 5. 7.

revealed in all things great and small, I. 344 ; ii. 4. 4. 30.

    „ though best so, in man to man, V. 224 ; ix. 1. 14.

work, all perfectly finished, II. 89 ; iii. 1. 10. 4.

    „   „   „   and necessarily so, II. 94 ; iii. 1. 11. 2.

Goethe [Synopsis. III. 276–77] :—

evil influence of. III. 276 ; iv. 16. 23 (F.A. *n*).

Goethe, *continued:*
    jealousy and conceit of, III. 277 ; iv. 16. 25.
    works of :

        "Conversations," III. 277 ; iv. 16. 25.
        "Faust," unintelligible, III. 276 ; iv. 16. 23 and F.A. *n.*
        "Wilhelm Meister," dulness of, III. 276; iv. 16. 23 and
            F.A. *n.*

Gold, colour, why liked, II. 86 *n* ; iii. 1. 9. 9 *n* ('83 *n*).
  ,, use of, in pictures (Bellini, Tintoret, etc.), I. 114–15 ; ii.
           1. 7. 28 (om. ed. 1, 2).
  ,,   ,, in Venetian architecture, I. 117 *n* ; ii. 1. 7. 30 *n*
           (om. ed. 1, 2).
Goldau, valley of, IV. 331 ; v. 18. 20 (pl. 50). *See s. Turner.*
Golden, author's use of the word, II. 86 *n* ; iii. 1. 9. 9 *n*
      ('83 *n*).
———— Legend, epilogue of, V. 154 *n* ; vii. 4. 6 *n.*
Goldsmith, bright wit of, II. 33 ; iii. 1. 4. 3 ('83 *n*).
     ,,   improvidence of, III. 314 ; iv. 17. 27.
     ,,   study and love of nature, III. 302 ; iv. 17. 7.
     ,,   work quoted, "Citizen of the World," on beauty and
           custom, III. 27 ; iv. 3. 2.
Gondola, reflections of, in water, I. 331 ; ii. 5. 1. 10 (ed. 1, 2
    only).
Good, evil and, co-existent, IV. 363–64 ; v. 19. 33.
    ,,   ,, extremes of both, in many things, III. 324–25 ;
          iv. 17. 41.
    ,,   ,, sources of, V. 83 ; vi. 8. 18.
    ,, of evil doer, accidental, V. 180–81 ; viii. 1. 17.
    ,,   ,, often unconscious, II. 147 ; iii. 1. 15. 8.
    ,,   ,, rejection of, a mistake, II. 147 ; iii. 1. 15. 8.
          See s. Goodness.
Goodall, engravings of Turner ⟩ I. 183 *n* ; ii. 2. 2. 20 *n* (om.
  (Rogers' Poems),   ⟩   ed. 1, 2).
     ,,   ,,   ,, IV. 81 ; v. 5. 18.
Goodall, work by (1848), Brit. Inst., II. 219 ; Add. ed. 1.
    note 4.
Goodness, beauty and, can bad men do beautiful work? II.
          144 ; iii. 1. 15. 5.
    ,,   ,, insensibility to beauty, in highly moral
          men, *ib.* ; *ib.*
Gooseberry, thorns of, V. 81 *n* ; vi. 8. 14 *n.*

Gorgons, V. 156–58 ; vii. 4. 9–11.
    ,,   their birth, V. 333–35 ; ix. 10. 9–11.
Gothard.   *See s. Saint Gothard.*
Gothic, and Greek art, author's love of former, II. 219 ; iii. 2.
             4. 14.
    ,,   architecture, apse cannot be accurately painted, IV.
               273 ; v. 16. 41.
    ,,   ,,   moral value of, III. 107 ; iv. 8. 9.
    ,,   ,,   mouldings, II. 220 ; iii. 2. 4. 14.
    ,,   ,,   mountains less Greek than Gothic, II
               64 *n* ; iii. 1. 6. 10 *n.*
    ,,   ,,   use of trefoil, etc., in, V. 21 ; vi. 3. 14.
Gotthelf, Swiss writer, IV. 142–43 ; v. 11. 10.
    ,,   ,,   V. 362 ; ix. 11. 24.
Goûté, Aiguille du, IV. 172 *n* ; v. 13. 8 *n.*
    ,,   ,,   IV. 217 ; v. 15. 15.
    ,.   ,,   IV. 220 *n* ; v. 15. 16 *n.*
Government, a law of life, V. 175 ; viii. 1. 6.
Gower Street.   *See s. London.*
Gozzoli, Benozzo, choice of subject, Pisa, III. 31–2 ; iv. 3. 8.
    ,,   ,,   landscape of, II. 47 ; iii. 1. 5. 10.
    ,.   ,,   II. 232 ; iii. 2. 5. 10.
    ,,   ,,   reality of conception, III. 62 ; iv. 4. 21.
    ,,   ,.   religious art of, *ib.* ; *ib.*
    ,,   ,,   works of :

             Campo Santo, Pisa, II. '83 Epil. 7.
             ,,   ,,   ,,   II. 228 ; iii. 2. 5. 5.
             Ricardi Palace fresco, II. 232 ; iii. 2. 5. 10.

Grace, law and, V. 164–65 ; vii. 4. 22.
Gracefulness.   *See s. Poplar, Willow.*
Gradation, beauty and need in art of, II. 51–2 ; iii. 1. 5. 16. 18.
    ,,   effects of, seen by cultivated eyes, IV. 73–4 ; v. 5
             5–6 *seqq.*
    ,,   infinity of, I. 222 ; ii. 3. 1. 11.
    ,,   necessity of, in painting, I. 158 ; ii. 2. 1. 17.
             See s. Rose, Sky, Turner.
Graiæ. birth of, V. 334 ; ix. 10. 11.
    ,,   mountain clouds, V. 142 ; pl. 70.
    ,,   origin of, V. 157 *seqq.* ; vii. 4. 10 *seqq.*
    ,,   story of, V. 348 ; ix. 11. 5.
Grand style in art, common idea of, IV. 51 ; v. 3. 21.

Grande Jorasse (Col de Ferret), the, IV. 175 ; v. 13. 11.

Granite, Aberdeen, IV. 108 ; v. 8. 5.

　　"　　breakage and chiselling of, IV. 116–17 ; v. 8. 16–17.

　　"　　cannot be sculptured like marble, IV. 117 ; v. 8. 17.

　　"　　characteristics of, IV. 113 seqq. ; v. 8. 14 seqq.

　　"　　colours of, IV. 143 ; v. 11. 11.

　　"　　-countries, character of people, IV. 118 ; v. 8. 18.　See
　　　　　s. Guttannen.

　　"　　formation of, IV. 108–9 ; v. 8. 6.

Grapes, structure of bunch of, V. 64 ; vi. 7. 14.

Grass, "enamelled" (in mediæval poets, Dante, etc.), III.
　　　236–38 ; iv. 14. 47–50.

　　"　　its glory and significance in poetry and fact, III. 238
　　　　　seqq. ; iv. 14. 51–2.

　　"　　" lessons of cheerfulness and humility and love, III.
　　　　　240–41 ; iv. 14. 52.

　　"　　" lessons of cheerfulness and humility and love, V.
　　　　　107 ; vi. 10. 17.

　　"　　mystery in, I. 336 ; ii. 4. 4. 15.

　　"　　" III. 129 ; iv. 9. 16.

　　"　　Venetian drawing of, III. 336 ; iv. 18. 18.
　　　　　　See s. Greek.

Gratitude, cannot be paid to the dead, I. 7 ; i. 1. 1. 5.

　　"　　how it arises, II. 17 ; iii. 1. 2. 6.

Great art.　See s. Art.

Great men [Synopsis. I. 3 n, 7. III. 94, 198, 269, 275–77, 281,
　　　287, 327, 345, 362. IV. 18, 78, 318. V. 214] :—

　　better to discover others than to be one oneself, IV. 18 ;
　　　v. 2. 4.

　　early influences on, to be studied, III. 327 ; iv. 18. 1.

　　epitomize the national mind, III. 198 ; iv. 13. 27.

　　　"　　their own age, III. 275 ; iv. 16. 21.

　　gentle courtesy of, V. 214 ; viii. 4. 21.

　　get help and good from everything, III. 345 ; iv. 18. 32.

　　　" and the greatest, the most help, III. 362 ; App. iii.

　　how produced, III. 287–88 ; iv. 16. 39.

　　humility of, just estimate of self, III. 276–77 ; iv. 16. 24.

　　infidelity of nearly all, nowadays, III. 269 ; iv. 16. 10.

　　　"　　"　　"　　" III. 281 ; iv. 16. 31.

　　intelligibility necessary to, IV. 78 ; v. 5. 13.

　　loneliness of, IV. 318 ; v. 17. 51.

　　mercifulness of, III. 277 ; iv. 16. 24.

Great men, *continued :*

    neglect of, in their lives, I. 7 ; i. 1. 1. 5.

    never jealous of others, III. 277 ; iv. 16. 25.

    public appreciation of, I. 3–4 *n* ; i. 1. 1. *n.*

    seriousness of, III. 275 ; iv. 16. 20.

    silent reserve of, V. 214 ; viii. 4. 21.

    simplicity of, III. 94 ; iv. 7. 13.

Great work, done once for all by one man, IV. 318 ; v. 17. 51.

      ,,   must always stand alone, V. 173 ; viii. 1. 2.

Greatness, acknowledged by centuries of praise, I. xiii ; *pref. ed.* 2. 3.

           ,,   long, generally real, I. 1–2 ; i. 1. 1. 1.

    estimated justly only by equals and superiors, I. 2 ; i. 1. 1. 1.

    in art and literature, shown by authors' self-annihilation, I. xxiv ; *ed.* 2. *pref.* 16.

    instinctive character of its essence, III. 287–88 ; iv. 16. 39.

    interest in small things indicates, I. 343 ; ii. 4. 4. 28.

    love of, in art, V. 196 ; viii. 3. 3.

    relativity of, V. 195 ; viii. 3. 1–2. *See s. Great men.*

Greek [SYNOPSIS. I. xxii, 34. II. 64 *n*, 110, 121, 135, 219, 237–38, 243. III. 154, 179–84, 185–90, 198–201, 203, 206, 208–9, 222, 227, 233–34, 236, 238–39, 260–61, 267. IV. 205, 207, 212, 288–89, 372 *seqq.* V. 40, 156 *seqq.*, 219, 221, 227, 233 *seqq.*, 238, 241–42, 284, 372, 378] :—

    art :

        colour, sense of, III. 233–35 ; iv. 14. 42. 46.

        design, its simplicity, V. 219 ; ix. 1. 5.

        Florentine and, opposed, V. 238 ; ix. 3. 1.

        formalism, III. 222 ; iv. 14. 28.

        heroic spirit of, V. 233 *seqq.* ; ix. 2. 14 *seqq.*

        ideal of the body in, II. 121 ; iii. 1. 14. 3.

        idealism dull, II. 110 ; iii. 1. 13. 3 ('83 *n*).

        indifference of, to natural scenery, V. 221 ; ix. 1. 9. *See below, s. feeling for nature.*

        influence of, on Italian and French schools, II. 237 ; iii. 2. 5. 19 *seqq.*

        no landscape painting in, III. 154–55 ; iv. 11. 3.

        ,,   ,,   ,,   V. 227 ; ix. 2. 5.

        sculpture, its perfection, I. xvi ; *pref. ed.* 2. 9 (note ed. 2–4 only).

Greek : art, *continued :*

      statue, divine only as an expression of divinity, I 34 ;
           i. 1. 7. 3.

      studies of the nude, II. 135 ; iii. 1. 14. 25.

      Venetian and divine influences, V. 241–42 ; ix. 3. 6–8.

  architecture :

      author's preference of Gothic, II. 220 ; iii. 2. 4. 14.

      honeysuckle ornament, IV. 207 ; v. 15. 3.

           ,,   ,,   IV. 288 ; v. 17. 18.

      mouldings, IV. 289 ; v. 17. 19.

      nature's mountains more Gothic than Greek, II. 64 *n* ;
           iii. 1. 6. 10 *n.*

  coins, arrangement of hair on, II. 243 ; Add. 3 (om. ed. 1).

    ,,   muscles on, V. 40 ; vi. 5. 6.

  feeling :

      for animals, V. 284 ; ix. 6. 21.

      ,, nature, III. 188 *seqq.*; iv. 13. 14. *seqq.*

      ,,   ,,   compared with mediæval (use *v.* beauty),
                III. 238 ; iv. 14. 51.

      ,,   ,,   does not personify nature, but puts a God
                in her, III. 179–81 ; iv. 13. 3. 6.

      ,,   ,,   horror of barren hills, III. 208 ; iv. 14. 10.

      ,,   ,,   indifference to nature, III. 222 ; iv. 14. 28.

      ,,   ,,   ,,   ,,   V. 221 ; ix. 1. 9.

      ,,   ,,   landscape, III. 199 ; iv. 13. 28. *See s.*
                Homer.

      ,,   ,,   love of clouds and rain, III. 260 ; iv. 15. 21.

      ,,   ,,   ,,   grass, III. 238 ; iv. 14. 51.

      ,,   ,,   ,,   marshy land, III. 236–38 ; iv. 14.
                47–9.

      ,,   ,,   ,,   woods, III. 226 ; iv. 14. 33.

      ,,   ,,   mountain-feeling and intellectual lead of
                Greece, IV. 372 ; v. 20. 11.

      ,,   ,,   preference of human beauty, III. 188–89 ;
                iv. 13. 14. 15.

  helmet, mountain form and, IV. 205 ; v. 15. 1.

      ,,   ,,   ,,   IV. 212 ; v. 15. 9.

  idea of death and after death, V. 235–36 ; ix. 2. 19.

  life, beautiful natural surroundings, III. 188 ; iv. 13. 14.

    ,, enjoyments of a, III. 203 ; iv. 14. 4.

    ,, healthy, not morbid, III. 186 ; iv. 13. 12.

    ,,   ,,   ,,   III. 188–89 ; iv. 13. 14.

Greek, *continued :*

   life, little travelling in, III. 206 ; iv. 14. 9.
   mind (cf. old Scotch borderer), III. 199–200 ; iv. 13. 28.
   „   intellectual lead, IV. 372 *seqq.*; v. 20. 11 *seqq.*
   poetry. *See s. Æschylus, Fate.*
   religion :
      chief ideas of, V. 235–37 ; ix. 2. 19–20.
      faith and, III. 199–200 ; iv. 13. 28.
      idea of God, II. 238 ; iii. 2. 5. 20.
         „   „   Christian compared, II. 238 ; iii. 2. 5. 20.
         „   „   III. 179 *seqq.* ; iv. 13. 4 *seqq.*
         „   „   III. 181–84 ; iv. 13. 7–8.
         „   „   familiar, III. 185–87 ; iv. 13. 11–12.
         „   „   *in* nature, and nature, therefore, living,
                     III. 187 ; iv. 13. 13.
      irreligion, V. 378 ; ix. 12. 5.
      rain-myths, V. 156 *seqq.* ; vii. 4. 9 *seqq.*
      wood-gods, III. 267 ; iv. 16. 7.
   word for "sin," V. 372 ; ix. 12. 2.
Green, use of, by great colourists, I. 168 *n* ; ii. 2. 2. 5 *n.*
Greenwood trees, in English literature, III. 227 ; iv. 14. 33.
Grenoble, mountains near, IV. 260 ; v. 16. 26.
   „   IV. 383 ; v. 20. 27.
Greppond, Aiguille, IV. 194 ; v. 14. 16. *See s. Blaitière.*
Greta, Turner's love of, IV. 261 ; v. 16. 28.
Greuze, low-necked dresses of, III. 71 ; iv. 5. 7.
Grief, when noble and when base, II. 138–39 ; iii. 1. 14. 30.
   „   when unselfish, is compassion, III. 11 ; iv. 1. 13.
   „   wildness of, instanced, III. 175 ; iv. 12. 15. *See s. Re-*
            morse.
Gries, pass of the, IV. 417 ; App. ii. 3.
Griffin, true and false, III. 109 *seqq.* ; iv. 8. 11 *seqq.* (pl. 1).
   „   „   „   IV. 236–37 ; v. 15. 32.
   „   „   „   IV. 261 ; v. 16. 27.
Grimsel, Mt., IV. 217, 422 ; App. ii. 3. 5.
Grindelwald, cliffs of, IV. 274 ; v. 16. 42.
   „   Eiger, V. 144 ; vii. 3. 12.
   „   rain-clouds at, V. 147 ; vii. 3. 16.
   „   valley, IV. 173–75 ; v. 13. 9. 11.
Grotesque [SYNOPSIS. III. 77, 100–2, 106–9, 115. IV. 54 *n*, 407] :—
   character and kinds of, in art, III. 100–15 ; iv. 8. 1 *seqq.*
   concentrated symbolism of, III. 102 ; iv. 8. 5.

Grotesque, *continued:*

    expression not to be elaborate, III. 106–7 ; iv. 8. 8.

    false, III. 108–9 ; iv. 8. 10.

    meaning of, III. 77 ; iv. 6. 2.

    modern, IV. 54 *n* ; v. 3. 24 *n.*

        „   IV. 407 *seqq.* ; App. i. 1 *seqq.*

    use of colour in expressing, III. 106–8 ; iv. 8. 8–9.

        See s. Février, Punch, Spenser.

Gruyère, scenery of the, V. 260 ; ix. 4. 9.

Guadagni Palace, Salvators in the, I. 414 ; ii. 6. 1. 11 (om. ed.
    1, 2).

  „   „   „   „   II. 170 ; iii. 2. 2. 19.

  „   „   „   (Baptism), II. 188 *n*; iii. 2. 3. 18 *n.*

Guardi, picturesque landscape of, V. 218 ; ix. 1. 3.

Guardian, 86th paper, on imagination, II. 177 *n* ; iii. 2. 3. 3
    (om. ed. 1).

Guercino's Hagar (Brera, Milan), II. 139 ; iii. 1. 14. 30.

Guido [Synopsis. II. 129, 134, 146, 179 *n.* V. 256]:—

    coarseness of, II. 179 *n* ; iii. 2. 3. 7 *n.*

    fading sanctity of, V. 256 ; ix. 4. 4.

    portraiture of, II. 129 ; iii. 1. 14. 14.

    sensuality of, II. 146 ; iii. 1. 15. 6.

    works of, "Susannah" (Nat. Gal.), II. 134 ; iii. 1. 14. 24.

  ——— da Como, pulpit of (San Bartolomeo, Pisa), II. 216 ;
    iii. 2. 4. 9.

Guttannen granite, IV. 418, 422 ; App. ii. 3, 5.

Gutter, beauty in a, if we will but see it, I. 347 ; ii. 5. 1. 4 (om.
    ed. 1, 2).

Habit, force of, *e.g.* streams on mountains, IV. 227 ; v. 15. 23.
    See s. Custom.

Haghe, imitator of Prout, I. 120 ; ii. 1. 7. 31 (om. ed. 1, 2).

    „   works of, architectural drawings, I. 122 ; ii. 1. 7. 33
    (om. ed. 1, 2).

Hair, arrangement of, in spiritual pictures, II. 237 ; iii. 2. 5. 18.

Hakewell's Italy, Turner's drawings for, I. 134 ; ii. 1. 7. 39
    (om. ed. 1, 2).

Halifax manufacturers, V. 358 ; ix. 11. 17.

Happiness, author's view of, II. '83 *pref.* 7.

    „   beauty and, go together, II. 97 ; iii. 1. 12. 1.   *See s.*
        Health.

    „   duty of, III. 48 ; iv. 4. 2.

Happiness, *continued* :

„   essentials of, V. 359 ; ix. 11. 18.

„   higher and lower, Dante on, III. 231–32 ; iv. 14. 38.

„   mediæval (in God's service) and Greek ideas of, III. 232 ; iv. 14. 40.

„   true sources of, and modern pleasures, III. 321–23 ; iv. 17. 36–8.

Hapsburg, the Swiss and the house of, V. 95 ; vi. 9. 13.

Harding, J. D. [SYNOPSIS. I. 106 *n*, 107, 190, 200, 305, 307, 327, 333, 371, 375, 411, 421, 425, 428–30. II. 245–46, '83 Epil. 11–12. **IV.** 59, 82]:—

character of his work, I. 76 ; ii. 1. 7. 6 (ed. 1, 2 only).

„   „   I. 107–8 ; ii. 1. 7. 24 (om. ed. 1, 2).

„   „   II. '83 Epil. 12.

chiaroscuro of, good, I. 190 ; ii. 2. 3. 7.

„   „   I. 429 ; ii. 6. 1. 31 (om. ed. 1, 2).

clearness and definiteness of, IV. 59 ; v. 4. 2.

distance of, I. 200 ; ii. 2. 4. 6.

execution of, IV. 82 ; v. 5. 19.

„   „   sharpness of touch, I. 402 ; ii. 6. 1. 35 (ed. 3, 4 only).

foliage of, next best to Turner's, I. 411 ; ii. 6. 1. 8.

„   I. 421 ; ii. 6. 1. 20.

„   I. 425 *seqq.* ; ii. 6. 1. 27–32.

„   aspen by, IV. 82 ; v. 5. 19.

„   favourite tree, form, V. 68 *n* ; vi. 7. 18 *n*.

mountain drawing of, I. 280 ; ii. 4. 2. 21 (ed. 1, 2 only).

„   „   urged to draw the Alps, I. 307 ; ii. 4. 2. 21.

„   „   I. 327 ; ii. 4. 3. 28.

rock drawing of, I. 333 ; ii. 4. 4. 10.

seas of (R.A. 1842), I. 371 ; ii. 5. 2. 5.

torrents of, I. 375 ; ii. 5. 2. 12.

water of, I. 371 ; ii. 5. 2. 4–5.

with author in Italy, 1845–46, II. '83 Epil. 11.

works of :

Alpine sunrise, 1844, I. 108 ; ii. 1. 7. 24 (om. ed. 1, 2).

book on use of pencil, I. 429 ; ii. 6. 1. 31 (om. ed. 1, 2).

Illustrations to Byron, " Chamouni " and " Wengern Alp," I. 305 ; ii. 4. 2. 19.

"Park and Forest," I. 411 ; ii. 6. 1. 8.

„   „   I. 428 ; ii. 6. 1. 30.

Harding, J. D. : works of, *continued :*

      picture, R.A. 1843-44, badly hung, I. 106 *n* ; ii. 1. 7. 22 *n* (om. ed. 1, 2).

        ,,   ,,   1848,   ,,   II. 245-46 ; Add. 6 (om. ed. 1).

      ,,   in B. G. Windus' possession, I. 100 ; ii. 1. 7. 24 (ed. 3, 4 only).

Hardship, its effect on the body, II. 120-21 ; iii. 1. 14. 3.

    ,,   sense of beauty deadened by, IV. 356-58 ; v. 19. 26-7.

Harlech, sands of, III. 206 ; iv. 14. 8.

Harmony, artistic, perfects by combination things imperfect alone, II. 161 ; iii. 2. 2. 6 (and '83 *n*).

    ,,   invention and, V. 182-83 ; viii. 1. 20.

Harvey, Alex., "Trees and their Nature," V. 45 ; vi. 6. 3 *n.*

Hastings, crags of, IV. 165 ; v. 13. 1.

Hawthorn shoot, V. 28 ; vi. 4. 8.

Haydn, anecdote of, on rules of music, III. 92-3 ; iv. 7. 12.

Haydon, size of his works, V. 196 ; viii. 3. 3.

Hazlitt, praise of Cuyp's "nectarine" sky (Dul. Gall.), I. 222 ; ii. 3. 1. 11.

Health and cheerfulness go together, IV. 355 ; v. 19. 25.

    ,,   as a part of education, III. 274 ; iv. 16. 19.

    ,,   and modern nervous illness, III. 271 ; iv. 16. 14.

Hearing, pleasure of, II. 16-17 ; iii. 1. 2. 5-6.

Heather, IV. 368 ; v. 20. 5.

    ,,   at sunset, III. 235 ; iv. 14. 46.

Heaven, brightness of, how to be realized, IV. 39-40 ; v. 3. 6. 7.

    ,,   infinity and fitfulness of, I. 142 ; ii. 1. 7. 44.

    ,,   presence of God in, IV. 92 ; v. 6. 9.

    ,,   relation of, to our globe, IV. 90-1 ; v. 6. 8.

    ,,   the word, its biblical use, IV. 86 *seqq.* ; v. 6. 2 *seqq.*

    ,,   ,,   ,, origin and meaning, V. 167 *seqq.* ; vii. 4. 27 *seqq.*

             See s. Firmament, Sky.

Hector, death of, V. 235 ; ix. 2. 18.

Help, law of, in life. V. 174 *seqq.* ; viii. 1. 4 *seqq.*

    ,,   source of good, V. 83 ; vi. 8. 18.

Helpfulness of inventive power, V. 215 ; viii. 4. 23.

Helps, Sir A., author's debt to, III. 359 ; App. 3.

    ,,   ,,   ,,   ,,   V. 312 *n* ; ix. 8. 15 *n.*

Helps, Sir A., *continued*:

,,   ,,   his "quiet English," III. 360 ; Add. 3.

,,   ,,   thinker and seer, III. 279 ; iv. 16. 28.

,,   ,,   to be studied, III. 357 ; App. 2.

,,   ,,   works of, " Friends in Council " quoted, V. 264 *n* ; ix. 4. 18 *n*.

Hemlock, V. 57–8 ; vi. 7. 4. 5.

Henley, scenery of, IV. 263 ; v. 16. 31.

Henry III., England *temp.*, IV. 380 ; v. 20. 23.

Heosphorus, V. 387 ; ix. 12. 20.

Heraldry, balance of, in missal-painting, IV. 79–80 ; v. 5. 16.

,,   mediæval, its effect on art, III. 210–11 ; iv. 14. 13.

,,   rejects all doubtful lines, *ib.* ; *ib.*

Herbage, general characteristics of all, V. 103 *seqq.* ; vi. 10. 10–11.

Herbert, Dr., on solitary vegetation (*Journal Hort. Soc.*, Pt. i.), II. 114 ; iii. 1. 13. 10.

————, George, author's debt to, III. 359 ; App. 3.

,,   ,,   not popular, and why, I. 4 *n* ; i. 1. 1. 1 *n*.

,,   ,,   quoted :

"A good digestion turneth all to health," II. 28 *n* ; iii. 1. 3. 12 *n*.

"Fool not, for all may have . . . a glorious life," I. 85 ; ii. 1. 7. 8 (om. ed. 1, 2).

"God's creatures leap not," etc., II. 119 ; iii. 1. 14. 1.

"Some men are full of themselves," etc., III. 136 ; iv. 10. 5.

Hercules, *agonizing* strength of, V. 333 ; ix. 10. 8.

,,   killing Geryon, V. 337 ; ix. 10. 14.

,,   Ladon and, V. 354 ; ix. 11. 10.

Heredity, of temper, etc., III. 288 ; iv. 16. 39.

Hermon, Mt., scene of the Transfiguration, IV. 405 ; v. 20. 48.

Herodotus, inspired by Marathon, III. 98 ; iv. 7. 21.

,,   landscape in, III. 199 ; iv. 13. 27.

,,   noble history, III. 43 ; iv. 3. 21.

,,   referred to :

cloud of Eleusis before Salamis, III. 260 ; iv. 15. 21.

colour of Ecbatana battlements, IV. 54 ; v. 3. 24.

Book I. 31, V. 237 *n* ; ix. 2. 20 *n*.

Herodotus, referred to, *continued* :

        Book I. 59, V. 243 *n* ; ix. 3. 10 *n.*

           ,,   V. 37, cut down like pine trees, V. 89 *n* ; vi. 8. 5 *n.*

           ,,   VII. 221, V. 237 *n* ; ix. 2. 20 *n.*

Hesiod, Theog. 664, δωτῆρες ἐάων, V. 233 *n* ; ix. 2. 14 *n.*

   ,,   on the Hesperides, V. 331 ; ix. 10. 6.

   ,,   ,,   ,,   V. 335 ; ix. 10. 12.

   ,,   on Nereus, V. 334 ; ix. 10. 9.

Hesperid Æglé, V. 161 *n* ; vii. 4. 17 *n.*

   ,,   ,,   V. 330 *seqq.* ; ix. 10. 1 *seqq.*

   ,,   ,,   V. 364 ; ix. 11. 27 and '78 *n.*

   ,,   ,,   title of chapter, why, V. 370 *n* ; ix. 11. 32 *n.*

Hesperides, the garden of the, IV. 366 ; v. 20. 2.

   ,,   ,,   ,,   V. 330 *seqq.* ; ix. 10. 4 *seqq.*

   ,,   ,,   ,,   V. 348 ; ix. 11. 5.

   ,,   ,,   ,,   V. 387 ; ix. 12. 20.

Hestia, Hesperid, V. 333 ; ix. 10. 8.

Highland valley described, V. 229–30 ; ix. 2, 11. *See s. Scotland.*

Hill, Miss O., help to author in "Modern Painters" plates, V. ix *n* ; *pref.* 6 *n.*

Hills, author's intense love of, IV. 365 ; v. 20. 1.

   ,,   formation of lower, I. 308–10 ; ii. 4. 3. 1–4.

   ,,   "pure and holy," I. 307 ; ii. 4. 2. 21 (ed. 1, 2. § 23).

               See s. Alps, Earth, Mountains.

Himalaya, snow on the, I. 260 ; ii. 3. 4. 1.

Hippocrene, Pegasus and, V. 159 ; vii. 4. 13.

Historical art, knowledge of man its basis, I. xxxv ; *pref. ed.* 2. 29.

   ,,   ,,   noble and base, III. 43–4 ; iv. 3. 21.

   ,,   ,,   ,,   ,,   and the imagination, III. 44 ; iv. 3. 22.

   ,,   ,,   present age, always its best subject, III. 98 ; iv. 7. 19.

History, poetry and, different statement of same facts, III. *seqq.* ; iv. 1. 8 *seqq.*

         See s. Napoleon, Nelson, Nero, Thermopylæ, Waterloo, Winkelried, Zurich.

Hobbima [SYNOPSIS. I. 6, 214, 349, 422. III. 20. V. 39–42, 79 *n*] :—
author's depreciation of, I. 6 ; i. 1. 1. 4.
characteristics of, III. 20 ; iv. 2. 4.

Hobbima, *continued :*
  distances of, I. 214 ; ii. 2. 5. 16–17.
  leafage of, I. 222–23 ; ii. 6. 1. 22–23.
    „   V. 39–41 ; vi. 5. 3–6.
  niggling of, I. 214 ; ii. 2. 5. 17.
    „   V. 42 ; vi. 5. 8.
  popular, I. 349 ; ii. 5. 1. 5 (om. ed. 1, 2).
  work of :

    " Mill " (Dulwich Gallery, 131), I. 338 ; ii. 5. 1. 18 (ed. 1,
                                              2 only).
      „   „   „   V. 40 ; vi. 5. 5.
      „   „   „   V. 79 *n* ; vi. 8. 12 *n* (tree
                                              in it).

Hogarth, English character of, I. 131 ; ii. 1. 7. 37 (om. ed. 1, 2).
  „   variety of, II. 140 *n* ; iii. 1. 14. 31 *n*.
Holbein [Synopsis. I. 87, 131. II. 132. III. 101. V. 39, 100, 232,
        257, 353 *n*, 368 *n*] :—
  colour and truth of, V. 353 *n* ; ix. 11. 8 *n*.
  essentially of his own time and country, I. 131 ; ii. 1. 7. 37
        (om. ed. 1, 2).
  finish of, I. 87 ; ii. 1. 7. 10 (om. ed. 1, 2).
  leaf- and flower-drawing of, V. 39 ; vi. 5. 2.
    „   „   „   V. 100 ; vi. 10. 4.
  melancholy of, V. 232 ; ix. 2. 13.
  portraits of, their " glorious severity," II. 132 ; iii. 1. 14.
        19.
  Reformation and, V. 257 ; ix. 4. 4.
  skeletons by, V. 368 *n* ; ix. 11. 31 *n*.
  work of, " Dance of Death," III. 101 ; iv. 8. 2.
Holl, engraving by, " Ancilla Domini," II. '83 Epil. 8.
    „   „   „   V. frontispiece.
Holland, low country, author's dislike of, IV. 365 ; v. 20. 1.
    „   „   feelings of people, IV. 372 ; v. 20. 11.
  ———, J., water-painting of, I. 343 ; ii. 5. 2. 2 (ed. 1–4
        only).
Hollyhock, II. 90 ; iii. 1. 10. 4.
    „   black, V. 259 ; ix. 4. 8.
Holmes, O. W., quoted, " The spendthrift crocus," etc., III.
        164 ; iv. 12. 4.
Holy, means helpful, V. 175 ; viii. 1. 5.
Holyrood, III. 328 ; iv. 18. 4.

Homer [SYNOPSIS. I. xxvii *n.* II. 74, 83, 177, 207. III. 14, 86, 90,
      156, 165–66, 171–72, 178–79, 182, 184–86, 190–99, 203,
      226, 234, 238, 241, 247–48, 254–55, 260, 276, 284, 293.
      IV. 79, 253, 268, 317–18. V. 233 and *n*, 234–36, 236 *n*,
      242, 284, 293–94] :—

general characteristics, etc. :

    cheerfulness, III. 283 ; iv. 16. 34.

    creative power, III. 165 ; iv. 12. 6 *n.*

    death "purple," III. 234 ; iv. 14. 44.

    faithfulness and truth of, III. 194 *n* ; iv. 13. 21 *n.*

    fate in, V. 233–36 ; ix. 2. 14–16 *seqq.*

    Greek army, compared to flowers in spring, III. 241 ;
        iv. 14. 53.

    „   mind, typified in, III. 198–99 ; iv. 13. 27.

    „   „   „   III. 275 ; iv. 16. 21.

    heroic spirit in, V. 235–37 ; ix. 2. 19 *seqq.*

    idealism (Achilles), III. 86 ; iv. 7. 4.

    imagination of, II. 177 ; iii. 2. 3. 4.

    influence of, on Dante, Virgil, etc., III. 199 ; iv. 13. 27.

    Michael Angelo compared to, by Sir J. Reynolds, III.
        14 ; iv. 1. 16.

    nature in. *See below.*

    no second, possible, IV. 317–18 ; v. 17. 51.

    Phidias and, their relation, III. 276 ; iv. 16. 22.

    realism of, III. 195 ; iv. 13. 23.

    sea-birds in, "having care of the ⎱ III. 191 ; iv. 13. 17.
        works of the sea," ⎰

    „   „   „   „   III. 293 ; iv. 16. 44.

    scenes of horror in, impossible to painter, II. 207 ; iii.
        2. 4. 2.

    sense of horror, V. 242 ; ix. 3. 8.

    "sharp," use of word (Od. xi. 333), III. 197 ; iv. 13. 25.

    symmetry loved by, III. 191 ; iv. 13. 18.

    truth of (pathetic fallacy), III. 171–72 ; iv. 12. 12.

love of nature, etc. :

    generally, I. xxvii *n* ; *pref. ed.* 2. 19 *n.*

    „   III. 15 ; iv. 1. 18.

    landscape, III. 190 *seqq.* ; iv. 13. 16–27.

    „   orderliness of, *ib.* ; *ib.*

    „   subservience to man, *ib.* ; *ib.*

    „   „   „   III. 195 ; iv. 13. 23.

Homer : love of nature, etc., *continued :*
  nature viewed as dead, III. 284 ; iv. 16. 36.
  no sense of the picturesque, III. 198 ; iv. 13. 26.

  particular details :

   aspens. *See below, s. poplars.*
   asphodel meadows (Od. xi. 571 and xxiv. 13), III.
    194 *n* ; ix. 13. 21 *n.*
   earth "life-giving," III. 171 ; iv. 12. 12.
   flowers in, III. 241 ; iv. 14. 53.
   gardens in, III. 191–92 ; iv. 13. 18–19.
   grass loved in, III. 238 ; iv. 14. 51.
   marsh-nourished parsley (Il. ii. 776), III. 190 ; iv.
    13. 16.
   marsh-plants loved in, III. 194 ; iv. 13. 21.
   plains loved in, III. 193 ; iv. 13. 20.
   poplar-groves of Proserpine, III. 192 ; iv. 13. 20.
    „ aspen-poplar, IV. 79 ; v. 5. 16.
   rocks and caves in, III. 196 *seqq.* ; iv. 13. 24 *seqq.*
    „ „ III. 247–48 ; iv. 15. 7.
    „ cut and sculptured (cf. Dante), III. 254–55 ;
     iv. 15. 15–16.
    „ cut and sculptured (cf. Dante), IV. 253 ; v.
     16. 19.
    „ over-roofed and hanging, IV. 268 ; v. 16. 37.
   sea and waves in, III. 178–79 ; iv. 13. 2–3.
    „ wine-coloured, III. 234 ; iv. 14. 43.
   woods, pleasure in, III. 194 ; iv. 13. 22.
    „ thought sacred in, III. 226 ; iv. 14. 33.

  persons or incidents referred to :

   Achilles, III. 86 ; iv. 7. 4.
    „ "cutting chops," III. 86. 90 ; iv. 7. 4. 10.
    „ speech of, to Priam, V. 233 *n* ; ix. 2. 14.
   Alcinous' garden, III. 191 ; iv. 13. 18.
   Alecto, III. 86 ; iv. 7. 4.
   Argus, Ulysses' dog, V. 284 ; ix. 6. 21.
   Atrides, anger of, at broken sword, III. 185 ; iv. 13. 11.
   Ceres' couch, a ploughed field (Od. v. 127), III. 194 *n* ;
    iv. 13. 21 *n.*
   child frightened at helmet, III. 15 ; iv. 1. 18.
   Cyclops' landscape (Od. ix. 132), III. 196 ; iv. 13. 24.

Homer : persons or incidents referred to, *continued*:
    Elpenor's death, III. 166 ; iv. 12. 6.
    Helen, III. 86 ; iv. 7. 4.
       ,,   reply of, to Venus, III. 186 ; iv. 13. 11.
    Ithaca described, rain of, III. 197 ; iv. 13. 26.
       ,,   ,,   ,,   III. 260 ; iv. 15. 21.
    Juno and Diana, III. 184 ; iv. 13. 9.
    Laertes' garden, III. 191 ; iv. 13. 18.
       ,,   ,,   III. 203 ; iv. 14. 3.
       ,,   recognizing Ulysses, III. 191 ; iv. 13. 19.
    Nausicaa, compared to a palm-tree, III. 192 ; iv. 13. 19.
    Pallas receiving Ulysses, V. 293–94 ; ix. 7. 12.
    Scamander, river-god, III. 182 ; iv. 13. 7.
       ,,   Vulcan restraining, III. 194 ; iv. 13. 21.
    Simois struck by Ajax, III. 192 ; iv. 13. 20.
    Telemachus, Atrides' gift of horses to, III. 194 ; iv. 13. 21.
    Thersites, III. 86 ; iv. 7. 4.
    Ulysses, saved from the raft, III. 193–95 ; iv. 13. 21–22.
       ,,   on the rushes, III. 241 ; iv. 14. 53.

              See s. Apollo, Atrides, Diana, Diomed, Discord, Juno, Helen, Mars, Scamander.

  various quotations :
    II. 74 ; iii. 1. 7. 5 ('83 *n*).
    III. 156 ; iv. 11. 6.
    ὡς δ' ὅτε τίς τ' ἐλέφαντα, etc., II. 83 *n* ; iii. 1. 9. 5.
    Iliad (iv. 141), "blood-stained flesh, purpled ivory," III. 189 ; iv. 13. 15.
       ,,   (ix. 209), III. 86 ; iv. 7. 5.
    Odyssey (viii. 325), δωτῆρες ἐάων, V. 233 *n* ; ix. 2. 14 *n*.
       ,,   (x. 495), V. 236 *n* ; ix. 2. 19 *n*.
       ,,   (xii. 357), sacrifice with leaves for corn, III. 195 ; iv. 13. 22.

Hood, T., "Song of a Shirt," IV. 409–10 ; App. i. 5.
Hook, J. C., pastoral works of, V. 286 ; ix. 6. 23.
Hooker, R. [SYNOPSIS. I. xiv. II. 10, 15, 26, 54, 59, 88, 90, 140, 242] :—
    author's imitation of, II. 242 ; Add. 1 and '83 *n* (om. ed. 1).
    quoted, on "contemplative fancy" (Eccl. Pol., i. 6. 2), II. 26 ; iii. 1. 3. 7.

Hooker, R., quoted, *continued :*

„   on exactness of nature, II. 88 ; iii. 1. 10. 3.

„   „ good in and from all things, II. 54 ; iii. 1. 6. 1.

„   „ ideal beauty (Eccl. Pol., V. 1. 2), II. 140 ; iii. 1. 14. 32.

„   „ law and moderation, II. 90 ; iii. 1. 10. 5.

„   „ praise of past (Eccl. Pol., V. 7. 3), I. xiv ; *ed. 2, pref.* 5.

„   „ various (Eccl. Pol., II. ii. 2), II. 10 ; iii. 1. 1. 8.

„   „   „ („   „ I. 7), II. 15 ; iii. 1. 2. 4.

„   „   „ II. 59 ; iii. 1. 6. 6 ('83 *n*).

Hope, springs eternal, IV. 139 ; v. 11. 8.

„   Veronese's rendering of, V. 248 ; ix. 3. 20.

Hornblende (mineral), IV. 121 ; v. 9. 3.

Horror, morbid love of, sign of weakness, IV. 347–48 ; v. 19. 15 16.

„   scenes of, in poetry, impossible in painting, II. 207 ; iii. 2. 4. 2.

Horses, to be guided, not flogged, III. 95 ; iv. 7. 15 (F.A. *n*).

„   nervous temper of, V. 284 *n* ; ix. 6. 21 *n*.

„   rendering of, in art, *ib.* ; *ib., seqq.*
              See s. Cab-horse, Hunting.

Horse-chestnut, leaf of, III. 217 ; iv. 14. 23.

„   „   „   quatrefoil type, V. 20, 21 ; vi. 3. 12. 13.

„   „   „   size of, V. 29–31 ; vi. 4. 9–11.

„   „   „   V. 104 ; vi. 10. 12.

Horticulture, plants spoiled by, II. 107 ; iii. 1. 12. 12.

„   „   „   II. 114–15 ; iii. 1. 13. 10.

Hospitality, compared to choice of truths by artists, IV. 48 ; v. 3. 17.

Hotels, modern, and old-fashioned inns, IV. 397 *n* ; v. 20. 40 *n*.

House-decoration, author's home and, II. '83 *pref.* 8. 9.

Howard, relief of sufferers, III. 300 ; iv. 17. 5.

„   small study and love of nature, III. 302 ; iv. 17. 7.

Howitt's "Rural Scenery," III. 360 ; App. 3.

Human form, Greek study of the, III. 188–90 ; iv. 13. 14–15.

Humanity, corruption of, II. 119 *seqq.* ; iii. 1. 14. 1–2.

Humboldt, author owes nothing to, III. 361 ; App. 3.

„   forests mentioned by, V. 152 ; vii. 4. 2.

Humility, essential Christian virtue, III. 240–43 ; iv. 14. 52–3.
              See s. Grass.

„   inculcated by science, III. 272 ; iv. 16. 16.

Humility, *continued :*

,,   necessary to enjoyment of nature, III. 286 ; iv. 16. 37.

,,   ,,   ,,   ,,   IV. 73 ; v. 5. 4.

,,   of great men, in just estimate of self, III. 276–77 ; iv. 16. 24.

         See s. Invention.

Hunt, Holman [SYNOPSIS. I. 445 *n.* III. 30, 33, 44, 62, 82, 97, 278, 361. IV. 63-4 *n.* V. 380]:—

early work of, I. 445 *n* ; ii. 6. 3. 16 *n* (om. ed. 1–4).

public neglect of, in his youth, V. 380 ; ix. 12. 9–10.

unaffected, III. 278 ; iv. 16. 26.

works of :

     Awakening Conscience, III. 97 ; iv. 7. 18.

     Christ in Temple, V. 380 ; ix. 12. 9–10.

     Claudio and Isabella, III. 30 ; iv. 3. 5.

     Light of the World, III. 33 ; iv. 3. 9 (execution and feeling, both perfect).

     ,,   ,,   ,,   III. 44 ; iv. 3. 23 (how far imaginative).

     ,,   ,,   ,,   III. 62 ; iv. 4. 20 (ideal religious art).

     ,,   ,,   ,,   III. 82 ; iv. 6. 8.

     ,,   ,,   ,,   III. 361 ; App. 3 (not a plagiarism).

     ,,   ,,   ,,   IV. 63-4 *n* ; v. 4. 8 *n* (author's letter to *Times* on it).

——, Leigh, " Imagination and fancy " referred to, II. 179 and *n* ; iii. 2. 3. 7 *n*, 8.

——, William [SYNOPSIS. I. 121, 303, 327 *n*, 431, 440. II. 111, 218. III. 90, 94, 278. IV. 24]:—

I. 327 *n* ; ii. 4. 3. 28 *n* (om. ed. 1–4).

anecdote of, " aiming at his effect," III. 94 ; iv. 7. 13.

colour of, brilliant, I. 121 ; ii. 1. 7. 32 (om. ed. 1, 2).

,,   broad treatment of, II. 218 ; iii. 2. 4. 11.

commonplaces of, not vulgar (" Farmer's girl "), III. 90 ; iv. 7. 9.

foliage, I. 431 ; ii. 6. 1. 34 (om. ed. 1, 2).

fruit of, IV. 24 ; v. 2. 13.

keen truth of, I. 440 ; ii. 6. 3. 5.

oyster, drawing by, of an, II. 111 ; iii. 1. 13. 5.

unaffected, but without invention, III. 278 ; iv. 16. 26.

winter-scenes of, I. 303 ; ii. 4. 2. 19 (om. ed. 1, 2).

Hunting, ruin of horses in, IV. 363 ; v. 19. 32. *See s. Sport.*

Hutton, geology of, IV. 416 ; App. ii. 2.

Hyacinths, wood and grape, IV. 368 ; v. 20. 5.

Idealism and the ideal [Synopsis. **I.** xxvi–viii, xlii, xliii, 31, 58, 425. **II.** 111–13, 116–18, 126, 128–29, 215–20, 226 *seqq.*, 228. **III.** 48 *seqq.*, 53, 66 *seqq.*, 74–6, 84, 95–8. **IV.** 202, 325–26, 340–41, 342. **V.** 226]:—

common notion of, false, III. 48 ; iv. 4. 2.
definition of the true, I. xxviii ; *pref. ed.* 2. 20.
 „ „ „ I. 31 ; i. 1. 6. 6.
essentials, love, II. 130 ; iii. 1. 14. 16.
 „   never egotistic, III. 96 ; iv. 7. 16.
everything at all stages has its ideal, II. 116–17 ; iii. 1. 13. 13–15.
 „ „ „ „ II. 126 ; iii. 1. 14. 10.
false, dulls perception of truth, III. 51 *seqq.* ; iv. 4. 9. *seqq.*
 „ its final baseness, III. 74–5 ; iv. 5. 13.
 „ religious and profane, III. 48 *seqq.* ; iv. 4. 1 *seqq.*
 „ stage-pastorals, IV. 340 *seqq.* ; v. 19. 6 *seqq.*
 „ stones and, IV. 325–26 ; v. 18. 10.
form of, almost the most beautiful, I. 396 ; ii. 6. 1. 26 (ed. 1, 2 only).
 „ in vegetables and animals, II. 111 *seqq.* ; iii. 1. 13. 5 *seqq.*
kinds of (purist, naturalist, grotesque), III. 76 *seqq.* ; iv. 6. 1 *seqq.*
landscape and classical art, I. xxvi ; *pref. ed.* 2. 18.
 „ *e.g.* Claude's Mill, I. xli ; *pref. ed.* 2. 36.
 „ its effect on the heart, I. xliii ; *pref. ed.* 2. 38.
mountain-drawing, IV. 202 ; v 14. 23. *See s. Aiguilles.*
naturalist, III. 84 *seqq.* ; iv. 7. 1 *seqq.*
 „ historical art and, III. 95 *seqq.* ; iv. 7. 15 *seqq.*
 „ landscape produces the heroic, V. 226 ; ix. 2. 4.
nature hints at, never realizes, I. 58 ; ii. 1. 2. 7.
operation of true, III. 84–5 ; iv. 7. 1–2.
profane, results of pursuing, III. 66 *seqq.* ; iv. 5. 1 *seqq.*
pursuit of, modern, III. 48 ; iv. 4. 2 *seqq.*
 „ „ III. 70 *seqq.* ; iv. 5. 7 *seqq.*
realism and, II. 215 ; iii. 2. 4. 9.
 „ *e.g.* Landseer and Veronese, II. 217 ; iii. 2. 4. 11.
rendering of, by abstraction of form and colour, II. 216 ; iii. 2. 4. 9.

Idealism and the ideal, *continued*:

    size of the ideal, not above average, II. 112 ; iii. 1. 13. 6
        ('83 *n*).

    superhuman ideal, II. 226 *seqq.* ; iii. 2. 5. 1 *seqq.*

        ,,   ,,   expressed by utmost human beauty, II.
        228 ; iii. 2. 5. 6.

    truth sacrificed to, III. 74 ; iv. 5. 12.

    word ideal ; its twofold meaning (1, imagination ; 2, type),
        II. 109 *seqq.* ; iii. 1. 13. 2 *seqq.*

    youth and age, idealism of each, II. 117 ; iii. 1. 13. 15.

Ideas, receivable from works of art, I. 14 ; i. 1. 3. 1. *See s.*
    Beauty, Imitation, Power, Relation, Truth.

Idiosyncrasies, generally defects, I. 66 ; ii. 1. 3. 7.

Idleness, evil example of, III. 279 ; iv. 16. 28.

    ,,   gentlemanship and, V. 287–88 ; ix. 7. 1 *seqq.*

    ,,   mediæval pride in, III. 203 ; iv. 14. 3.

Idler, The, Sir J. Reynolds' papers in, III. 3 *seqq.* ; iv. 1. 4 *seqq.*
    See s. Johnson.

Idolatry, modern shadow, III. 75 ; iv. 5. 13.

Illiterateness, vulgar, and why, V. 297 ; ix. 7. 19.

Illumination, art of, its character and value, III. 107–8 ; iv.
    8. 9.

    ,,   ,,   its decline, IV. 381 ; v. 20. 23.

    ,,   ,,   pigments used in, III. 237–38 ; iv. 14. 49.

    ,,   ,,   representation of the sun in, III. 338 ; iv.
    18. 22.

                See s. Manuscripts.

Images of things, how conceived by the mind. *See s. Conception.*

Imagination [SYNOPSIS. **I.** xlv *n*, 56–7, 325, 413, 441, 451. **II.** 11,
    143, 151–53, 155–56, 157, 161–69, 172–78, 181–86,
    200 *n*, 201–6, 209, 222. **III.** 43, 44, 49, 76–7, 84,
    86–7, 101, 113–14, 138, 140, 141–45, 146–47, 224–25,
    238–39, 298–99. **IV.** 18, 29, 31, 48 *seqq.*, 83, 139,
    196–97, 236–38, 342–43, 373–74] :—

    analysis of, in " Modern Painters," still incomplete, II. 151 ;
        iii. 2. 1. 1 ('83 *n*).

    characteristics, etc., of :

        activity loved by it, III. 146–47 ; iv. 10. 16.

        appeals *to* imagination, II. 186 ; iii. 2. 3. 15.

        based on moral feelings, independence of mind, re-
        ference to nature, II. 204–5 ; iii. 2. 3. 31–3.

Imagination : characteristics, etc., of, *continued :*

    companion of knowledge, I. 441 ; ii. 6. 3. 7.

        „   „   „   and of industry, II. 205 ; iii. 2. 3. 33.

    conventional ideas do not control, II. 204 ; iii. 2. 3. 32.

    creates only by combining, III. 44 ; iv. 3. 23.

    detail asserted, a sign of it, III. 224–25 ; iv. 14. 30.

    foresight and insight of true, III. 86–7 ; iv. 7. 5.

        „   „   „   IV. 31 ; v. 2. 21.

    genius' open Sesame, II. 177 ; iii. 2. 3. 4.

    highest intellectual power, *ib.* ; *ib.*

    intuitive, not taught or acquired, II. 161 ; iii. 2. 2. 6.

        „   II. 177 ; iii. 2. 3. 4.

    involuntary remembrance, IV. 29 ; v. 2. 17.

    irresistible, if noble, IV. 18 ; v. 2. 4.

    knows no laws, and violates none, II. 166 ; iii. 2. 2. 13.

    love of nature aided by it, III. 298–99 ; iv. 17. 3–4.

    makes use of accumulated knowledge, III. 44 ; iv. 3. 23.

    noble only if it conceives truly, III. 141 ; iv. 10. 8.

    repeats itself never, II. 166 ; iii. 2. 2. 13.

    rightness of, and its reasons, III. 113–14 ; iv. 8. 18–19.

    roused easily by very little, III. 141 ; iv. 10. 9.

        „   and easily jaded, III. 144–45, 147-48 ; iv. 10. 14. 18.

    self-forgetfulness of, I. 325 ; ii. 4. 3. 26.

    serious, II. 182 ; iii. 2. 3. 9.

        „   and playful, III. 101 ; iv. 8. 2.

    strengthened by feeding on truth and nature,   I. 450–52 ; ii. 6. 3. 23.

        „   „   „   II. 205 ; iii. 2. 3. 33.

    tests of, II. 166 *seqq.* ; iii. 2. 2. 13 *seqq.*

        „   II. 221–22 ; iii. 2. 4. 17.

    truth and, II. 200 *n* ; iii. 2. 3. 28 *n.*

        „   no false work imaginative, II. 173 ; iii. 2. 2. 22. *See below, s. function.*

    unconscious truth of noble, IV. 236–38 ; v. 15. 32-3.

    vague drawing may appeal to it, IV. 83 ; v. 5. 20.

        „   „   as it fills up the gaps, III. 141–42 ; iv. 10. 9. 10.

    variety and life given by it, II. 168 ; iii. 2. 2. 15.

Imagination : characteristics, etc., of, *continued* ·

    visions of lofty, II. 151 ; iii. 2. 1 ('83 Introd. Note 3).

    wrong, if false, IV. 342–43 ; v. 19. 8.

    common ideas and errors about it, II. 10–11 ; iii. 1. 1. 10.

       ,,   ,,   ,,   ,,   II. 203–4 ; iii. 2. 3. 30.

    definition of. *See below, s. kinds of.*

    errors of :

        "audacious liberty" of, I. xlv *n* ; *ed.* 2. *pref.* 40 *n.*

        may lead senses into error (seeing what we think we
           see), I. 56–7 ; ii. 1. 2. 5–6.

    fancy and :

        distinct, I. 414 ; ii. 6. 1. 11 (om. ed. 1, 2).

          ,,   II. 151 ; iii. 2. 1 ('83 Introd. Note 1).

          ,,   II. 152 *seqq.* ; iii. 2. 1. 2 *seqq.*

          ,,   II. 160 ; iii. 2. 2. 5.

          ,,   II. 179 ; iii. 2. 3. 7 (fancy sees the outside ;
               imagination the heart).

          ,,   II. 181 *seqq.* ; iii. 2. 3. 9 *seqq.* (fancy restless ;
               imagination quiet).

          ,,   II. 205 ; iii. 2. 3. 33.

          ,,   II. 209 *seqq.* ; iii. 2. 4. 5–7.

    function and power of :

        adds a charm to what is denied, IV. 139 ; v. 11. 8.

        lawful uses, and abuses of, III. 49 *seqq.* ; iv. 4. 5
          seqq.

        in conceiving perfect beauty, II. 143 ; iii. 1. 15. 2.

        in glorifying visible things, III. 141–42 ; iv. 10. 9. 10.

          ,,   ,,   ,,   III. 298–99 ; iv. 17. 3.

        in grasping instinctively the ⎫
          essence of truth,   ⎬ II. 176 ; iii. 2. 3. 3.
                        ⎭

          ,,   ,,   ,,   II. 201–3 ; iii. 2. 3. 29.

          ,,   ,,   ,,   IV. 236 ; v. 15. 32.

        invention, as a subject of, III. 76–77 ; iv. 6. 2.

        noblest function, III. 76 *seqq.* ; iv. 6. 1 *seqq.*

        triple function of (associate, contemplate, penetrate),
          II. 155 ; iii. 2. 1. 6. *See below, s. works of art.*

    kinds of :

        associative, II. 157 *seqq.* ; iii. 2. 2. 1 *seqq.*

          ,,   defined, II. 161–62 ; iii. 2. 2. 7.

          ,,   dignity and grasp of, II. 163 ; iii. 2. 2. 9.

          ,,   limits of (no one can conceive a new
               animal), II. 164 ; iii. 2. 2. 10.

Imagination : kinds of, associative, *continued :*

    „   tests of, harmony, simplicity, truth, II 172 ; iii. 2. 2. 22.

    „   work of, in naturalist idealism, III. 84 : iv. 7. 1.

    contemplative, II. 206 *seqq.* ; iii. 2. 4. 1 *seqq.*

    penetrative, II. 175 *seqq.* ; iii. 2. 3. 1 *seqq.*

    „   III. 140 ; iv. 10. 8.

penetrative and creative, III. 144 ; iv. 10. 13.

meaning of the word, limited, II. 151 ; iii. 2. 1 ('83 Introd. Note 2).

mountain influence on, IV. 373–74 ; v. 20. 12–13.

theoretic faculties and, connections of, II. 168 ; iii. 2. 2. 16.

works of art and :

    "addressing the imagination" as the end of art, III. 142–43 ; iv. 10. 10. 12.

    essential to great art, III. 43 ; iv. 3. 21.

    function of, in art, II. 151 ; iii. 2. 1. 1.

    historical and imaginative art distinct, III. 44 ; iv. 3. 22.

    judgment and, imaginative persons bad judges of art, and why, III. 141 *seqq.* ; iv. 10. 9 *seqq.*

    rarity of, amongst artists, II. 169 ; iii. 2. 2. 17.

    suggestiveness distinct from, II. 184–85 ; iii. 2. 3. 14.

    want of, involves monotony, II. 167 ; iii. 2. 2. 14.

Imitation [SYNOPSIS. I. 14, 19–23, 27–8, 35, 78, 173–74, 440. II. 220. III. 18 *seqq.*, 210–11, 215. V. 101] :—

art and :

    architectural ornament and, II. 220 ; iii. 2. 4. 15.

    change from symbolism to, III. 215 ; iv. 14. 20.

    easy, I. 22 ; i. 1. 4. 6.

    growth of, 12–1300, III. 20–1 ; iv. 2. 5.

    „   „   III. 210–11 ; iv. 14. 13.

    how far to be deceptive, III. 18 *seqq.* ; iv. 2. 1 *seqq.*

    ideas of, I. 14 ; i. 1. 3. 1.

    „   I. 22 ; i. 1. 4. 6.

    „   the destruction of art, I. 28 ; i. 1. 5. 6.

    „   need not be studied, I. 35 ; i. 2. 1. 1.

    „   source of pleasure, I. 173 ; ii. 2. 2. 10.

    of flowers, impossible, V. 101 ; vi. 10. 7.

    pleasure of, I. 20–1 ; i. 1. 4. 3.

    „   contemptible, and why, I. 21–2 ; i. 1. 4. 4–6.

Imitation : art and, *continued :*

        subjects capable of, always ignoble and small, I. 21–2 ; i. 1. 4. 5.

        trickeries of, I. 440 ; ii. 6. 3. 5.

        truth and, distinguished, I. 24 *seqq.* ; i. 1. 5. 2 *seqq.*

             ,,   inconsistent, I. 27–8 ; i. 1. 5. 6.

             ,,   motives of, I. 78 ; ii. 1. 7. 1.

    dramatic, noble, and why, I. 22 ; i. 1. 4. 6.

    real meaning of the word, I. 20 ; i. 1. 4. 2.

                   See s. Symbolism.

Immortality, Greek hope of, V. 267 ; ix. 5. 3.

Impressions, artist's mental, how formed, IV. 21–2 ; v. 2. 8–9.

        ,,   first childlike, generally the truest, IV. 51–2 ; **v.** 3. 21.

Inadequacy, a quality of execution, I. 40 ; i. 2. 2. 5.

Inconsistency, modern, III. 273 ; iv. 16. 17.

Indecision, a sign of base art, III. 40 ; iv. 3. 17.

Independence. *See s. Mind.*

India, art of, colours of, fine, III. 94 ; iv. 7. 14.

     ,,   ,,   *e.g.* shawls, V. 349 *n* ; ix. 11. 8 *n.*

     ,,   ,,   intellect of, V. 152 ; vii. 4. 2.

     ,,   ,,   pleasure in, due to its laboriousness, I. 15 ; i. 1. 3. 2.

     ,,   people of, keen sight, but none for art, I. 57–8 ; ii. 1. 2. 6.

Indifference to suffering, its selfishness, IV. 362–63 ; v. 19. 32.

Indignation, how rightly roused, III. 11 ; iv. 1. 13.

        ,,   usefully so, by bad men, III. 279 ; iv. 16. 28.

Indistinctness of conception, how far an added charm, II. 206–7 ; iii. 2. 4. 2–3.

Infidelity, modern, its causes, III. 268–69 ; iv. 16. 10.

       ,,   ,,   the fault of the age, III. 281 ; iv. 16. 31.

       ,,   ,,   its spirit ("God is, but cannot rule"), V. 347–48 ; ix. 12. 4–5.

Infinity [Synopsis. I. 254–56. II. 44–53. **IV.** 35 *seqq.*, 60, 84] :—

    consists in variety, not in number, I. 256 ; ii. 3. 3. 25.

    distance expressive of, II. 44 ; iii. 1. 5. 5.

    idea of, necessary and powerful in art, II. 45 ; iii. 1. 5. 6.

    its influence over the heart, II. 49 ; iii. 1. 5. 13.

    modes in which it is felt (curvature, gradation), II. 49 *seqq.* ; iii. 1. 5. 13 *seqq.*

    mystery of, IV. 60 ; v. 4. 4.

    sought by artists, II. 46 ; iii. 1. 5. 8.

    test of truth in art, I. 254 ; ii. 3. 3. 22.

Infinity, *continued:*

    typical of redeemed life, IV. 84 ; v. 5. 21.

    vastness does not imply, II. 52–3 ; iii. 1. 5. 19. *See s. Infinity.*

Ingleborough, wind on, V. 160 *n* ; vii. 4. 14 *n.*

Innkeepers, old and modern, IV. 397 *n* ; v. 20. 40 *n.*

Innocents, Holy, Raphael's and Tintoret's, II. 192–93 ; iii. 2. 3. 21.

Innspruck, IV. 398 ; v. 20. 41.

Insects, visible by virulence, I. xiii ; *pref. ed.* 2. 3.

Insensibility of vulgarity, V. 291 *seqq.* ; ix. 7. 9 *seqq.*

Inspiration, how to be expressed (as distinct from divinity), II. 228–29 ; iii. 2. 5. 6.

    „   prophetic, its nature, III. 168 ; iv. 12. 9.

    „   revelations made by, II. 142 ; iii. 1. 15. 1

    „   sometimes given through evil men, II. 146–48 ; iii. 1. 15. 8.

    „   wide meaning of, III. 151–52 ; iv. 20. 22.

Instinct. *See s. Invention.*

Intaglio, II. 158 ; iii. 2. 2. 2.

Intellect, climates productive of, V. 151–52 ; vii. 4. 2.

    „   features affected by, II. 121 ; iii. 1. 14. 4.

    „   orders of, struggle of emotion and, III. 167–68 ; iv. 12. 8–9.

    „   superiority of one over another, III. 151–52 ; iv. 10. 22.

Intellectual lead of a nation, IV. 372 ; v. 20. 11.

Intemperance. *See s. Temperance.*

Interest of great minds in little things, I. 343 ; ii. 4. 4. 28 (ed. 1, 2. 32).

Interlachen valley, I. 289 ; ii. 4. 1. 5.

Inundations, of Rhone, and in Alps, IV. 297 ; v. 17. 28.

Invention [SYNOPSIS. **I.** 123, 325. **III.** 43, 90–1, 94–5, 277–78. **IV.** 17, 21–2. **V.** 172–73, 177, 183, 210, 214–16, 349 *n*]:—

    artist to decide if he has it, and how, IV. 17 ; v. 2. 3.

    essential to great art, III. 43 ; iv. 3. 21.

    „   „   III. 277–78 ; iv. 16. 26.

    „   „   V. 210 ; viii. 4. 16.

    evil of misapplied, I. 123–24 ; ii. 1. 7. 34.

    greatest, when not apparent, I. 325 ; ii. 4. 3. 26.

    high place of, V. 183 ; viii. 1. 20.

    imaginative and unimaginative artists, their, IV. 21–2 ; v. 2. 8–9.

Invention, *continued*:

    instinctive, not by rule, III. 90 ; iv. 7. 10.

       „   *e.g.* eastern art, III. 94–5 ; iv. 7. 14–15.

    kinds of, formal or material, V. 172 *seqq.* ; viii. 1. 1 *seqq.*

       „   spiritual, V. 216 *seqq.* ; ix. 1. 1 *seqq.*

    limits of, in proportion, II. 66 ; iii. 1. 6. 13.

    of form, higher than of colour, V. 349 *n* ; ix. 11. 8 *n.*

    power of, needs no rules, III. 90–1 ; iv. 7. 10–11.

    sincerity, humility, and truth, essential to, V. 214–15 ; viii. 4. 23.

    the greatest quality of art, V. 177 ; viii. 1. 10.

    value set on, may be too high, when there is so much to be *recorded*, I. 124 ; ii. 1. 7. 34 (om. ed. 1, 2).

    young artists not to aim at, V. 177 ; viii. 1. 10.

Investigation, accurate, always of use, V. 195 ; viii. 3. 3.

Ionic capitals, IV. 289 ; v. 17. 19.

Iris, blue (aquilegia), in Titian's Bacchus and Ariadne, I. xxx, xxxiii ; *pref. ed.* 2. 23, 26.

Irreligion. *See s. Infidelity.*

Ischia, introduced into Claude's backgrounds, IV. 231 ; v. 15. 28.

Isère, hills of, IV. 261 ; v. 16. 27.

Isolation, implies imperfection, II. 54 ; iii. 1. 6. 1. *See s. Unity.*

Italy [Synopsis. **I.** 57, 263. **III.** 81, 248–49. **IV.** 84, 345 *seqq.,* 352–53, 372. **V.** 261]:—

    art in. *See below, s. Italian school.*

    beggars in, IV. 345 ; v. 19. 12.

    character of the people, IV. 345 *seqq.* ; v. 19. 12 *seqq.*

       „   „   IV. 352–53 ; v. 19. 22.

    drama in, skull-mask, IV. 347 ; v. 19. 14.

    modern, its political condition, III. 81 ; iv. 6. 7.

    mountains of (and intellectual power of Rome), IV. 372 ; v. 20. 11.

    palaces of, their desolation, IV. 345–46 ; v. 19. 12.

       „   modern whitewash, III. 248–49 ; iv. 15. 9.

    rain-clouds in (Rome, Sorrento), I. 263 ; ii. 3. 4. 5.

    scenery of South, described, V. 261 ; ix. 4. 12.

    skies of, less blue than French, I. 57 ; ii. 1. 2. 5.

    twilight in, described, IV. 84 ; v. 5. 21.

        See s. Names of places.

Italian school [SYNOPSIS. I. 10, 82–93, 131, 163, 184, 206, 223,
          227, 244, 407, 410. II. 47–8, 60–1, 232, 237,
          '83 Epil. 6. III. 5 *seqq.*, 16, 259, 344. IV. 381.
          V. 43, 53, 151, 246]:—

    characteristics :
          architecture of ideal painters, Transalpine, II. 232 ; iii.
              2. 5. 11.
          clouds of (1600–1700), false, I. 244–45 ; ii. 3. 3. 8.
              „   „   „   V. 151 ; vii. 4. 1 *seqq.*
          distances of, idea of infinity, II. 46–7 ; iii. 1. 5. 9.
          early period, burning messages of prophecy, I. 11 ; i.
                      1. 2. 7.
              „   „   holy light and feeling of, I. 163 ; ii. 2.
                      1. 22.
          earnestness and truth of feeling, II. 47–8 ; iii. 1. 5.
                      9–10.
              „   „   „   II. 60 ; iii. 1. 6. 8.
          foliage, a chief feature, I. 407 ; ii. 6. 1. 1.
              „   conventional leaf-drawing, V. 43 ; vi. 5. 9.
          foregrounds, I. 86 ; ii. 1. 7. 9 (om. ed. 1, 2).
          Greek art, its influence, II. 237 ; iii. 2. 5. 19.
          landscape of early, I. 82–4 ; ii. 1. 7. 6 *seqq.* (om. ed.
                      1, 2).
              „   school, III. 344 ; iv. 18. 31.
          lines of early, hard, I. 185 *n* ; ii. 2. 4. 7 *n* (ed. 2 only).
          religious, abstract, V. 246 ; ix. 3. 18. *See s. Artists'
              names.*
          Reynolds on the, III. 5 *seqq.* ; iv. 1. 5 *seqq.*
          sculpture (branch, San Zeno), V. 53 ; vi. 6. 12.
          serene summer of, III. 259 ; iv. 15. 21.
          shadows, painting of, I. 185 ; ii. 2. 3. 2.
          skies of, I. 89 ; ii. 1. 7. 11.
              „   I. 223, 227–28 ; ii. 3. 1. 12. 20.
          spaces in, dead, I. 205 ; ii. 2. 5. 5.
          trees of, *e.g.* View near Albano (Nat. Gall.), I. 410 ;
              ii. 6. 1. 7.
          virtues of, summed up, II. '83 Epil. 6.
    modern school :
          heartless detail of landscape, I. 88–9 ; ii. 1. 7. 10 (om.
              ed. 1, 2).
          Venetian Academy examples, I. 84 ; ii. 1. 7. 7 (om.
              ed. 1, 2).

Italian school : modern school, *continued*

        vileness of, I. 131 ; ii. 1. 7. 37 (om. ed. 1, 2).

    rise of, IV. 381 ; v. 20. 23.

    total decline, 1759, III. 16 ; iv. 1. 19.

              See s. Landscapes (mediæval).

Ivy, curvature, IV. 287–88 ; v. 17. 17.

  ,,   -leaf, example of law of composition, III. 222 ; iv. 14. 27.

James, J. A., book by, "Anxious Inquirer," IV. 423 ; App. iii. 1.

Jameson, Mrs., remark about Bible to, I. 63 ; ii. 1. 3. 3.

    ,,   ,,   works of, referred to, II. 239 ; iii. 2. 5. 21 ('83 *n*).

Jan Steen's painting of pans, I. 349 ; ii. 5. 1. 5 (om. ed. 1, 2).

Jealousy, a sign of littleness, III. 277 ; iv. 16. 25.

Jedburgh, sandstone of, IV. 138 ; v. 11. 6.

    ,,   the Abbey, V. v ; *pref.* 1.

Jest, elaborate always painful, III. 107 ; iv. 8. 8.

  ,, true and false, III. 108 ; iv. 8. 10.

Jesuitism, spirit of, V. 294 ; ix. 7. 13.

Jewellery, abstract painting of, by Angelico and others, II. 234 ;

           iii. 2. 5. 14.

    ,,   painting of a clasp and drop, V. 211–12 ; viii. 4. 18.

Job, II. '83 *pref.* 4–5.

Johnson, Dr., connection of Mr. Lowe with, III. 345 *n* ; iv. 18. 31.

    ,,   ,,   love and study of nature by, III. 302 ; iv. 17. 7.

    ,,   ,,   indolence of, III. 314 ; iv. 17. 27.

    ,,   ,,   stern sense, II. 33 ; iii. 1. 4. 3 ('83 *n*).

    ,,   ,,   style of, imitated by author, II. 242 ; Add. 1 and

            '83 *n* (om. ed. 1).

    ,,   ,,   works of, quoted :

              on beauty as the result of custom, III. 27 ; iv. 3. 2.

              ,, criticism (Idler), IV. 411 *n* ; App. i. 6 *n.* *See*

                 s. Idler.

              ,, education, II. 151 ; iii. 2. 1 ('83 Introd. Note 2).

              ,, "excellent," definition of word, I. 16 *n* ; i. 1.

                 3. 3 *n.*

Joints, geological, I. 309 ; ii. 4. 3. 2.

Joy, necessary to ideas of beauty, II. 18 ; iii. 1. 2. 8.

  ,,   ,,   ,,   ,,   II. 31 ; iii. 1. 3. 16.

  ,, noble emotion, II. 16–17 ; iii. 1. 2. 5–6.

  ,,   ,,   ,,   III. 11 ; iv. 1. 13.

  ,, of humble life, V. 359–60 ; ix. 11. 21.

Joy, *continued* :
  „ youthful, typified in flowers, III. 218 ; iv. 14. 24.
  „   „   „   „   III. 241 ; iv. 14. 53.
Judas, I. 65 ; ii. 1. 3. 6.
Judging others, "judge not," V. 373 ; ix. 12. 2.
Judgment, difficulty of forming a true, in art, I. 4 ; i. 1. 1. 2.
  „   „   „   „   „   I. 53–61 ; ii. 1. 2. 1
                                                         seqq.
  „   „   „   „   „   II. 26 ; iii. 1. 3. 8–9.
  „   sense of beauty and moral, II. 103 ; iii. 1. 12. 8.
  „   statute and, V. 170 ; vii. 4. 34.
  „   substituted for admiration, V. 267 ; ix. 5. 3.
  „   taste distinct from, I. 30 ; i. 1. 6. 3. *See s. Taste.*
  „   unconscious association affecting, II. 36–7 ; iii. 1. 4. 9.
  „   universal equality of, in Shakspere, IV. 384 ; v. 20. 28.
Jungfrau, chain of the, IV. 303 ; v. 17. 33.
  „   cliffs of the, IV. 272 ; v. 16. 39.
  „   high, but secondary mountain, I. 292 ; ii. 4. 2. 1.
Juno, Diana's contest with, III. 184 ; iv. 13. 9.
  „   sphere and meaning of, V. 333 ; ix. 10. 8.
Jupiter, sphere of, V. 333 ; ix. 10. 8.
Jura, crests of the, III. 206 ; iv. 14. 8.
  „   limestone of, colour, IV. 137 ; v. 11. 5.
  „   „   „   IV. 160 ; v. 12. 20.
  „   „   „   IV. 165 ; v. 13. 1.
Juvenal (IV. xi. 102), "Ut phaleris gauderet equus," I. xxiii ;
    ed. 2, *pref.* 14.

Kaleidoscope, symmetrical beauty of, II. 79 ; iii. 1. 8. 3.
Kant, III. 357 ; App. 2.
Keats [SYNOPSIS. **II.** 210. **III.** 165 *n*, 169, 178, 180, 274, 280,
          283, 284, 287, 302, 313. **IV.** 411 and *n*. **V.** 92 *n*, 253,
          320, 364, 383] :—
    author's intense admiration for, V. 92 *n* ; vi. 9. 9 *n.*
    death of, IV. 411 and *n* ; App. i. 6.
    public neglect of, V. 383 ; ix. 12. 14.
    qualities, etc., of :
          colouring, III 274 ; iv. 16. 18.
          conception, V. 253 ; ix. 3. 31.
          exquisite sincerity, III. 167 *n* ; iv. 12. 7 *n.*
          few human characters in, III. 313 ; iv. 17. 27.
          love of nature, III. 3c2 ; iv. 17. 7.

Keats : qualities, etc., of, *continued :*

  passion altering nature, III. 284, 287 ; iv. 16. 36, 38.

  reflective, III. 165 *n* ; iv. 12. 6 *n.*

  sadness, III. 283 ; iv. 16. 34.

  second order of poets (pathetic fallacy), III. 169 ; iv. 12. 10.

  sense of beauty, V. 364 ; ix. 11. 26.

  sentimental writing, III. 280 ; iv. 16. 29.

  Turner's mind and his compared, V. 320 ; ix. 9. 9.

  wayward indolence, III. 180 ; iv. 13. 6.

 works of, quoted :

  " bursts joy's grape against his palate fine," III. 287 ; iv. 16. 38.

  " dewy rosary on the eglantine " (" Isabella," xxiv), II. 210 ; iii. 2. 4. 5.

  " How cam'st thou over the unfooted sea ? " III. 167 *n* ; iv. 12. 7 *n.*

  (on a wave) " Down whose green bank the short-lived foam " III. 178 ; iv. 13. 2.

  Ode to Psyche, on the pine, V. 92 *n* ; vi. 9. 9 *n.*

" Keepsake," Turner's " Florence " in, I. 140 ; ii. 1. 7. 43 (om. ed. 1, 2).

   ,,   ,, Schaffhausen, V. 188 ; viii. 2. 8.

   ,,   ,, study of trees, I. 137 ; ii. 1. 7. 41 (om. ed. 1, 2).

        See s. Turner.

Kent, flint walls of, IV. 116 ; v. 8. 16.

 ,, scenery of, and Shakspere, IV. 383 ; v. 20. 27.

Kepler, work of, did not pay, V. 379, 382 ; ix. 12. 7. 11.

Keswick, IV. 383 ; v. 20. 27.

Kindness, a mark of good breeding, V. 290 ; ix. 7. 7.

Kings formerly chosen for manly beauty, III. 158–59 ; iv. 11. 9.

Kingsley, Charles, " Alton Locke," farmer in, on hills and plains, III. 193 ; iv. 13. 20.

  ,,   ,,   ,, " cruel crawling foam," III. 164, 169 ; iv. 12. 5. 11.

——, Rev. W., of Sidney Sussex college, anecdote of Turner's " Storm," V. 375 *n* ; ix. 12. 4 *n.*

Knavery, on a large and small scale, still one, V. 288 ; ix. 7. 2.

Knight, mediæval, enjoyments of a, III. 203–4 ; iv. 14. 4.

Knight, mediæval, *continued :*

> „ „ love of light and fine weather, III. 260 ; iv. 15. 21.

> „ „ pilgrimages and gloomy life, III. 206 ; iv. 14. 8 *seqq.*

> „ „ young, riding forth, described, III. 208–10 ; iv. 14. 11–12.

—— (Payne), on Virgil's Laocoon, II. 74 *n* ; iii. 1. 7. 6. *n.*

Knowledge, coldness of (Minerva's Gorgon), V. 158 ; vii. 4. 12.

> „ communication of (railways, etc.), III. 320–21 ; iv. 17. 36.

> „ hinders pleasure in beauty, III. 325 ; iv. 17. 42.

> „ imagination and, in art, go together, I. 441 ; ii. 6. 3. 7.

> „ influence of, on art, I. 49–51 ; ii. 1. 1. 5 *seqq.*

> „ „ „ I. 253 ; ii. 3. 3. 20.

> „ necessary to right art judgment, I. 128 ; ii. 1. 7. 36.

> „ „ „ „ „ I. 435–36 ; ii. 6. 2. 4.

> „ „ „ „ „ I. 443 ; ii. 6. 3. 11.

> „ noble or ignoble according to the motive seeking it, I. xxxvi–vii ; *pref. ed.* 2, 30.

> „ of our own ignorance, V. 115 ; vii. 1. 3.

> „ pride of, IV. 72–3 ; v. 5. 4.

> „ refusal of, a form of asceticism, V. 357 ; ix. 11. 17.

> „ sight and, connected, I. 57–8 ; ii. 1. 2. 6.

> „ thought and, I. 52 ; ii. 1. 1. 10.

> „ trust, its highest form, V. 181 ; viii. 1. 17.

> *See s. Education.*

Knox (John), his dislike of art, III. 59 ; iv. 4. 18.

La Riccia, storm clearing over, described, I. 165–66 ; ii. 2. 2. 2. *See s. Poussin, G.*

Labour, degrading, if mechanical, IV. 9 ; v. 1. 11.

> „ „ not otherwise, V. 288 ; ix. 7. 2.

> „ no man to have more than is healthy, V. 360–61 ; ix. 11. 22.

> „ Turner's view of, V. 364–65 ; ix. 11. 28

Laburnum, branch structure, V. 50 ; vi. 6. 9.

> „ leaf, curves of, IV. 287 ; v. 17. 16 (pl. 42).

La Côte, clouds over, V. 149 ; vii. 3. 17.

> „ form of, IV. 218–19 and *n* ; v. 15. 16 and *n.*

Lac de Combal, IV. 219 ; v. 15. 16.

Lacedæmonian epitaph, V. 181–82 ; viii. 1. 18.

Lady-like manners, Homeric and modern, III. 184–85; iv. 13. 9.

Laing, J. J., help in illustrations to " Modern Painters," III. xii ; *pref.* 6.

Laisser-aller, a false principle, III. 49 ; iv. 4. 2.

Lamartine, "Harmonies," illustrated edition, I. 426 *n* ; ii. 6. 1. 27 *n* (om. ed. 1, 2).

Lamination of mountain beds, I. 309 ; ii. 4. 3. 3.

    „   „   slate, IV. 130 ; v. 10. 2. *See s. Cleavage, Geology, Strata.*

Lands, kinds of. *See s. Climates.*

Landscape [SYNOPSIS. **I.** xxiii, xxvi, xxviii, xxxv–vi, xl, 47–8, 78–93, 100–1, 132, 149, 166, 207–8, 233, 248–49, 263, 272, 295, 306 *n*, 318, 418 *seqq.*, 425. **II.** 80, 145, 170, 190, 231–33 *n.* **III.** viii–ix, 30–1, 137– 38, 153 *seqq.*, 161 *seqq.*, 178 *seqq.*, 190–91, 198, 202, 213 *seqq.*, 215, 264 *seqq.*, 296, 297 *seqq.*, 310, 312–13, 323 *seqq.*, 331–32, 344–45. **IV.** 16 *seqq.*, 41 *seqq.*, 59, 85, 312–13, 367–68. **V.** 216 *seqq.*, 221, 226–27, 267–73] :—

    author's wide use of term, III. 178 ; iv. 13. 1.

    choice of, and national feeling, I. 132 ; ii. 1. 7. 38.

    classical, described and defined, III. viii ; *pref.* 4.

    „   „   „   „   III. 178 *seqq.*; iv. 13. 1 *seqq.*

    „   „   „   „   V. 268–69 ; ix. 5. 6–8 *seqq.*

    „   hackneyed type of (Renaissance), III. 198 ; iv. 13. 26.

    „   headed by Nicolo Poussin, V. 217 ; ix. 1. 2.

    clearness and mistiness of early and later, IV. 59 ; v. 4. 2.

    colours of distant, cannot be truly painted, IV. 41 *seqq.* ; v. 3. 8 *seqq.*

    „   flat and mountain, IV. 367–68 ; v. 20. 4.

    conventional, recipe for a, I. 44 ; ii. 1. 1. 3 (ed. 1, 2 only).

    „   „   „   (cf. *Encycl. Brit.*), IV. 312–13 ; v. 17. 47.

    Dutch. *See s. v.*

    evil, how far expressible in, II. 145 ; iii. 1. 15. 6.

    finish and detail of, I. xxxiv–v ; *ed.* 2. *pref.* 27–8.

    „   fulness of nature, essential to, I. 207–8 ; ii. 2. 5. 9.

    generalization in, condemned, I. xxxviii–ix ; *pref.* 2. 21.

Landscape, *continued :*

  growth of, with use of sky as background, III. 215–16 ; iv. 14. 20.

  heroic, V. 217 ; ix. 1. 2.

  high art and, III. 31 ; iv. 3. 6.

  history of, I. 82 *seqq.* ; ii. 1. 7. 6 *seqq.* (om. ed. 1, 2).

        ,,   up to Raphael, III. 331–33 ; iv. 18. 10–12.

  Homeric, III. 190 *seqq.* ; iv. 13. 16. 27.

  ideal character and specific truth, I. xxvii–viii ; *pref. ed.* 2. 19–20.

  imaginative, four examples of, named, II. 170–71 ; iii. 2. 2. 19.

  instinct for, analyzed from author's own feelings, III. 309–10 ; iv. 17. 20.

  interest in, dependent on human life, V. 217 *seqq.* ; ix. 1. 4 *seqq.*

        ,,   gives importance to painter over poet, III. 265 ; iv. 16. 22.

  kinds of (heroic, classical, pastoral, contemplative, picturesque, hybrid), V. 217 *seqq.* ; ix. 1. 2 *seqq.*

        ,,   their periods, V. 226 ; ix. 2. 4.

        See above, s. classical, *and below, s.* mediæval, modern, old masters.

  limits of, and nature's vastness, I. 80–1 ; ii. 1. 7. 4.

  love of, opposed to all evil passion, III. 312 ; iv. 17. 26.

  mediæval (early religious, Italian) :

      I. 82 *seqq.* ; ii. 1. 7. 6 *seqq.* (om. ed. 1, 2).

      III. viii ; *pref.* 4.

      III. 136–38 ; iv. 10. 5.

      III. 202 ; iv. 14. 1 *seqq.*

      III. 213 *seqq.* ; iv. 14. 16 *seqq.*

      III. 223 ; iv. 14. 28.

      III. 233 ; iv. 14. 41.

      IV. 79–80 ; v. 5. 16 *seqq. See s. Manuscripts.*

      its infinite, clear distances, IV. 84 ; v. 5. 21.

      ,, symmetry, II. 230–33 *n* ; iii. 2. 5. 8–11 *n.*

  modern :

      aim of, superior to old masters, I. 81 ; ii. 1. 7. 4.

      characteristics of (cloudiness, liberty, mystery, profanity, sombre colour), III. 264 *seqq.* ; iv. 16. 1 *seqq.*

Landscape : modern, characteristics of, *continued :*

       " (want of earnestness and complete-
                ness), I. 449 ; ii. 6. 3. 22.

    continental schools, author's knowledge of, I. 425 ; ii.
                6. 1. 27 (om. ed. 1, 2).

    "   " no true school, I. 306 *n* ; ii. 4. 2.
                20 *n* (om. ed. 1, 2).

    growth of, from mediæval formalism, III. 331 *seqq.* ;
                iv. 18. 10.

    pathetic fallacy only in, III. 178–79 ; iv. 13. 1. 2

    tendency of (1843), I. 100–1 ; ii. 1. 7. 19 (om. ed. 1, 2).

    Turner heads and begins, I. xxxvi ; *pref. ed.* 2. 29.

    "   "   " I. 84 ; ii. 1. 7. 7 (om. ed.
                1, 2).

  novelty of, III. 154 *seqq.* ; iv. 11. 3 *seqq.*

  objects of, to state nature's facts, artist's thoughts, I. 47–8 ;
          ii. 1. 1. 1.

    " for picture's sake, and for nature's, III. 345 ; iv.
          18. 31.

    " how far to merely copy nature, IV. 16 *seqq.* ; v.
          2. 1 *seqq.*

  of old masters :

    aim, merits, and faults, I. 79–80 ; ii. 1. 7. 3
    " at deception, I. 78 ; ii. 1. 7. 2.

    black patchwork of, I. 169 ; ii. 2. 2. 5 (om. ed. 1)

    Claude and his school, their fatal effect, I. *ed.* 3. *pref.*
        (ed. 3 only).

    clouds of, generalized, I. 248 ; ii. 3. 3. 13.

    " opaque, *ib.* ; *ib.* 14.

    " rain-cloud never given, I. 263 ; ii. 3. 4. 6

    foregrounds of sacred painters, never give near water
        or rock, II. 189 ; iii. 2. 3. 18.

    idealism of, false, I. xxvi ; *pref. ed.* 2. 18.

    " *e.g.* Claude's "Mill," I. xli ; *pref. ed.* 2. 36.

    leafage of, I. 418 *seqq.* ; ii. 6. 1. 16 *seqq.*

    monotonous repetition, I. 79 ; ii. 1. 7. 3.

    mountain-drawing (no distant ranges), I. 295–96 ; ii. 4.
          2. 7.

    "   " I. 318 ; ii. 4. 3. 15.

    skies of, no fleecy skies, I. 233 ; ii. 3. 2. 9.

    "   " gradations, I. 272 ; ii. 3. 4. 20 (ed. 1–4, 23).

    tone of, unequalled, I. 149 *seqq.* ; ii. 2. 1. 1 *seqq.*

Landscape, *continued*:

    pastoral, headed by Cuyp, V. 217 ; ix. 1. 2.

        „   V. 279 *seqq.* ; ix. 6. 10 *seqq.*

    picturesque, V. 218 ; ix. 1. 3.

    science, its relation to, III. 323 *seqq.* ; iv. 17. 39 *seqq.*

    sculpture and, III. 202 ; iv. 14. 1.

    symmetry in, II. 80 ; iii. 1. 8. 4.

    sympathy with humanity essential to, V. 221 ; ix. 1. 9.

    value of, as a moral influence, I. xxiii ; *pref. ed.* 2. 15.

      „   „   „   „   III. 153 *seqq.* ; iv. 11. 1 *seqq.*

      „   „   „   „   III. 294–96 ; iv. 16. 45.

      „   „   „   „   III. 297 *seqq.* ; iv. 17. 1 *seqq.*

      „   „   „   „   IV. 142 ; v. 11. 10.

      „   „   „   „   V. 216 *seqq.* ; ix. 1. 1 *seqq.*

Landscapists, aim of great, I. 47–8 ; ii. 1. 1. 1.

    „   „   „   IV. 23–4 ; v. 2. 11.

    „   at their best in their native land, I. 130 ; ii. 1. 7.

                37 (om. ed. 1, 2).

    „   choice of truths by, I. 78 *seqq.* ; ii. 1. 7. 1 *seqq.*

    „   seventeenth century, vicious } I. 78 ; ii. 1. 7. 1.

           and false style,   }

    „   „   „   „   I. 196 ; ii. 2. 4. 1.

    „   „   „   „   I. 348 ; ii. 5. 1. 5.

    „   „   „   „   I. 410 ; ii. 6. 1. 7.

    „   to paint what they *love* in nature, II. 233 ; iii. 2.

              5. 12.

Landseer, Sir E. [SYNOPSIS. I. 9, 73, 125, 156. II. 88, 217 and *n*,

         242. V. 108, 284, 292–93] :—

    I. 73 ; ii. 1. 5. 6.

    colour of, false, II. 242 ; Add. 2 (om. ed. 1).

    dogs of, and of Veronese, II. 217 ; iii. 2. 4. 11.

      „   their character, V. 283–84 ; ix. 6. 20.

    powers and qualities of, II. 217 *n* ; iii. 2. 4. 11 *n*.

    reputation of, European, I. 125 ; ii. 1. 7. 35 (om. ed. 1, 2).

    sporting subjects of, II. 88 ; iii. 1. 12. 2 (ed. 1 only).

    want of tone (R.A. 1848), I. 156 ; ii. 2. 1. 12.

    works of :

        Ladies' Pets, grass in, V. 108 ; vi. 10. 19.

        Low Life, V. 292–93 ; ix. 7. 11.

        Old Cover Hack (R.A. 1848), II. 242 ; Add. 2 (om. ed. 1).

        Otter Hunt, II. 8 ; iii. 1. 12. 2 (ed. 1 only).

        Random Shot (R.A. 1848), *ib.* ; *ib.* (*ib.*).

Landseer, Sir E. : works of, *continued :*
　　Shepherd's Chief Mourner, I. 9 ; i. 1. 2. 4.
　　　　　,,　　　,,　　　,,　　I. 33 ; i. 1. 7. 3.
　　　　　,,　　　,,　　　,,　　II. 217 *n*; iii. 2. 4. 11 *n.*
　　　　　,,　　　,,　　　,,　　V. 284 ; ix. 6. 20.
　　Shoeing, II. 196 *n* ; iii. 2. 4. 11 *n* ; (ed. 1 only).

Langholme, sandstone of, IV. 138 ; v. 11. 6.
Language, accuracy of, liable to misinterpretation, III. 5–6 ; iv. 1. 5.
　,,　　ambiguity of, in great writers, IV. 77–8 ; v. 5. 12–13.
　,,　　art a kind of, I. 8, 9 ; i. 1. 2. 2.
　,,　　decorative and expressive, distinguished, I. 10 ; i. 1. 2. 6.
　,,　　fine, is not great writing (matter *v.* style), I. 8, 9 ; i. 1. 2. 2.
　,,　　,,　　,,　　,,　　,,　　,,　I. 10 ; i. 1. 2. 5.
　,,　　,,　　,,　　,,　　,,　　,,　I. 33 ; i. 1. 7. 3.
Lanslebourg, V. 161 ; vii. 4. 17.
Laocoon, knowledge displayed in the, I. 32 ; i. 2. 1. 3 (ed. 1, 2 only).
　,,　　want of repose in it, II. 74 ; iii. 1. 7. 6 and *n.*
Laodamia, love of, II. 139 ; iii. 1. 14. 31.
Larch-tree, growth of stem, V. 56 ; vi. 7. 3.
　,,　　under sunset, V. 93 *n* ; vi. 9. 10 *n.*
Lasinio, engravings of, bad, III. 333 ; iv. 18. 13.
　,,　　,,　　vile and vulgar, IV. 2 *n* ; v. 1. 1 *n.*
Last Judgment, renderings of the, II. 194–95 ; iii. 2. 3. 23. *See s.*
Laudatio temporis acti, in art and criticism, I. xiv ; *pref. ed.* 2. 4.
Lauder, picture by, its sky (1848), II. 219 ; Add. (ed. 1. note 4).
Lauffen, castle of, V. 189 ; viii. 2. 10 (pl. 75).
Laughter, mean and shallow jests of modern life, II. 182 ; iii. 2. 3. 9–10.
　,,　　something serious in everything, *ib.* ; *ib.*
Laurati, gentle landscape of, II. 47 ; iii. 1. 5. 10.
Laurel, curves of, IV. 287 ; v. 17. 16 (pl. 43).
　,,　　growth of the, I. 412 *n* ; ii. 6. 1. 9 *n* (om. ed. 1, 2).
　,　　leaves, V. 29 ; vi. 4. 8.
Lausanne, Turner's sketch of, V. 207–8 ; viii. 4. 8–11.
Lauterbrunnen, cliffs of, IV. 157 ; v. 12. 18.

Law, commandment v., V. 169 ; vii. 4. 32.

,,   grace and, V. 164–65 ; vii. 4. 22.

,,   obedience to moral, author's insistence on, II. '83 *pref.* 6.

,,   ,,   ,,   its delight, V. 165 ; vii. 4. 23.

,,   observance and violation of, in art, I. 416–17 ; ii. 6. 1. 14 (om. ed. 1, 2).

,,   of lines, what transgression of, permissible, IV. 290–91 ; v. 17. 20.

,,   of nature, if of life, is that of loveliness, V. 104 ; vi. 10. 11.

Lawrence, Sir T., "Satan" of, II. 223 ; iii. 2. 4. 19.

Lazarus, Christian religion and, V. 241–42 ; ix. 3. 8.

Le Keux, engravings to "Modern Painters" by, III. x ; *pref.* 5.

,,   ,,   ,,   ,,   ,,   IV. 33, 66 ; v. 4. 12 (pl. 25).

,,   ,,   ,,   ,,   ,,   IV. 303 n ; v. 17. 33 n.

,,   ,,   ,,   ,,   ,,   V. 259 n ; ix. 4. 7 n (pl. 76).

,,   ,,   ,,   ,,   ,,   V. 368 n ; ix. 11. 30 n.

Le Sage, "Gil Blas," III. 314 ; iv. 17. 28.

,,   no love of nature in, III. 314–16 ; iv. 17. 28–30.

Lear, Edward, "Voyage of Violet, Guy, and Lionel" ("Quangle Wangle"), II. 164 ; iii. 2. 2. 10 ('83 n).

Leaves [SYNOPSIS. I. 422, 425 *seqq.* III. 216. IV. 207, 287 *seqq.* V. 9–10, 23–9, 35–9, 45–6, 74, 84–5, 105, 110–11] :—

drawing of, I. 418 *seqq.* ; ii. 6. 1. 16–18.

,,   ancient and modern, V. 39 *seqq.* ; vi. 5. 2 *seqq.*

,,   conventional till Turner, V. 74 ; vi. 8. 9.

,,   figure-drawing and, co-existent, V. 39 ; vi. 5. 4

,,   full size in foreground, V. 40 ; vi. 5. 5.

,,   "If you can paint one leaf, you can paint the world," V. 39 ; vi. 5. 2.

feed the plant, V. 35 ; vi. 4. 15.

,,   tree-shoots, V. 45–6 ; vi. 6. 2–3.

form, alternation of, V. 105 ; vi. 10. 13 *seqq.*

,,   and structure of, IV. 207 ; v. 15. 3.

,,   crystals and, formation and growth compared, V. 36–7 ; vi. 4. 17–18.

,,   curvature, IV. 287 *seqq.* ; v. 17. 16 *seqq.* (pl. 42–4).

,,   growth (mediæval view), III. 216 *seqq.* ; iv. 14. 21.

,,   intricacy and unity of, I. 422 ; ii. 6. 1. 21.

Leaves : form, *continued* :

　　　,,　laws of deflection, succession, and resilience, V. 28
　　　　　　seqq. ; vi. 4. 8 *seqq.*

　　　,,　orders of, shield and sword, V. 9–10 ; vi. 2. 5.

　　　,,　　　,,　　studding-sails and mainsails, V. 25–7 ; vi.
　　　　　　4. 6–7.

　　　,,　radiation, V. 29 ; vi. 4. 8.

　　　,,　rending of, V. 104 ; vi. 10. 12 (pl. 60).

　　　,,　structure, V. 23 *seqq.* ; vi. 4. 1 *seqq.*

　　　,,　symmetry of, V. 24–5 ; vi. 4. 4.

　　　,,　　　,,　　　V. 38 ; vi. 5. 1.

　　　,,　torn and jagged, V. 103 *seqq.* ; vi. 10. 11 *seqq.*
　　　　　　(pl. 60).

　　　,,　wings of a, V. 25 ; vi. 4. 5.

　　　leaflets and, distinguished, V. 26 ; vi. 4. 7.

　　　lesson of reverence for the past from, V. 84–5 ; vi. 8. 19.

　　　monuments of, V. 85 ; vi. 8. 20.

　　　motionless, V. 110–11 ; vi. 10. 22.

　　　seek the sun, V. 35 ; vi. 4. 15.

　　　　　　　　See s. Trees.

Lee, F. R. (painter), I. xxii *n* ; *pref. ed.* 2. 13 *n*.

Leech, J., powers of, IV. 409 ; App. i. 4.

Lefèbre, engravings of Titian (Peter Martyr, S. Jerome), V. 80 ;
　　　　　　vi. 8. 13.

　　　,,　　　　,,　　　　,,　and Veronese, V. 190 ; viii. 2. 12.

Leicestershire, flatness of, IV. 366–67 ; v. 20. 2–3.

Leighton, Sir F., author and, II. '83 Epil. 14.

Leonardo. *See s. Da Vinci.*

Leonidas, choice of, III. 180 ; iv. 13. 5.

　　　,,　　　,,　　V. 196 ; viii. 3. 4.

Leopard, mediæval, III. 211 ; iv. 14. 13.

Leslie, George (elder), at author's birthday-dinner, II. '83 Epil.
　　　　　　14.

　　　,,　　　,,　　　,,　subjects of, III. 30 ; iv. 3. 5.

　　　,,　　　,,　　　,,　Life of Constable, III. 126–27 ; iv. 9. 13.

　　　,,　　　,,　　　,,　　　,,　　　,,　III. 150 *n* ; iv. 10.
　　　　　　20 *n*.

　　　,,　　　,,　　　,,　　　,,　　　,,　III. 355 ; App. i.

　　　,,　　　,,　　　,,　　　,,　　　,,　IV. 82 ; v. 5. 19.

　　　,,　　　,,　　　,,　quoted, "insipid faces of Francia," IV.
　　　　　　409 ; App. i. 3.

Lettering on coins, V. 298 and *n* ; ix. 7. 21 and *n*.

Levity, modern, III. 270 ; iv. 16. 11.

,,   ,,   III. 282 ; iv. 16. 34.

,,   not characteristic of great men, III. 275 ; iv. 16. 20.

Lewis, John, estimate of (climax of water-colour), I. 38 ; i. 2. 1. 8.

,,   ,,   foreign (especially Spanish) studies of, I. 131 ; ii. 1. 7. 37 (om. ed. 1, 2).

,,   ,,   limited number of his works, I. 449 ; ii. 6. 3. 22.

,,   ,,   sketches of animals, *e.g.* horses, V. 285 *n* ; ix. 6. 22 *n*.

Liberty, author's use of the word, III. 319 ; iv. 17. 34 (F.A. *n*).

,,   formalism and, in modern landscape, III. 266 ; iv. 16. 5.

,,   restraint and, II. 90 ; iii. 1. 10. 5 *seqq.*

,,   Scott's love of, III. 287 ; iv. 16. 38. *See s. Mill.*

License, of great artists defended, I. 359-60 ; ii. 5. 1. 16 (om. ed. 1, 2).

Lichen, colour of, in rocks, IV. 115 ; v. 8. 14.

,,   mosses and, IV. 137-38 ; v. 1⋫. 5. 6.

,,   ,,   IV. 322 ; v. 18. 7.

,,   ,,   V. 111-12 ; vi. 10. 23. 25. *See s. Moss-lands.*

Lichfield, cathedral of, IV. 381 ; v. 20. 23.

Lie, power of a, IV. 413 ; App. i. 8. *See s. Lying.*

Life, choice of, V. 386-87 ; ix. 12. 20.

,,   help and, V. 174 *seqq.* ; viii. 1. 4 *seqq.*

,,   ideal happiness of, "where hope and memory are as one," II. 73 *n* ; iii. 1. 7. 4 *n.*

,,   nothing, unless nobly lived, II. 8 ; iii. 1. 1. 7.

,,   "rose and cankerworm," V. 356 *seqq.* ; ix. 11. 13 *seqq.*

,,   shortness of, I. 110 ; ii. 1. 7. 26 (om. ed. 1, 2).

,,   true pleasures of humble, V. 359-60 ; ix. 11. 21.

        See s. Colour, Man.

—— size, greatest art below, III. 41-42 ; iv. 3. 19.

Light, always slightly coloured, I. 159 ; ii. 2. 1. 18.

,,   effects of, on colour, I. 157 ; ii. 2. 1. 14.

,,   ,,   ,,   landscape, I. 188-89 ; ii. 2. 3. 6.

,,   gradations of, never destroyed by distance, IV. 75-6 ; v. 5. 8.

,,   highest light possible to artist, and the sun's, IV. 35-6 ; v. 3. 1.

,,   love of, universal, II. 81 ; iii. 1. 9. 1.

,,   mingling of darkness and, IV. 278, 304 ; v. 17. 3. 36.

Light, *continued :*
„   symbol of the divine, II. 81 ; iii. 1. 9. 1.
          See s. Chiaroscuro, Tone.
Likes and dislikes, individual feelings, II. 39–40 ; iii. 1. 4. 12.
Lilac branch, V. 76–8 ; vi. 8. 10. 11 (pl. 58).
Lilies, Greek formalism of, III. 222 ; iv. 14. 28.
Lily of valley, II. 90 ; iii. 1. 10. 4.
    „   „   (Jura), III. 235 ; iv. 14. 46.
Limestone, characteristics of, I. 329 ; ii. 4. 4. 2.
    „   „   „   IV. 134 *seqq.* ; v. 11. 1 *seqq.*
    „   cliffs (Bonneville), IV. 152, 155, 160 ; v. 12. 12. 15. 21.
    „   colour of rocks, III. 247–48 ; iv. 15. 7.
    „   of Jura, IV. 165 ; v. 13. 1.
    „   „ Valais, IV. 272 ; v. 16. 40.
Lincoln, cathedral of, IV. 380–81 ; v. 20. 23.
Lincolnshire fen-country, IV. 365–66 ; v. 20. 1. 2.
Lindley, Professor, "Introd. to Botany," V. 16 *n* ; vi. 3. 8 *n.*
    „   „   „   „   „   V. 24 *n* ; vi. 4. 4 *n.*
    „   „   „   „   „   V. 45 *n* ; vi. 6. 3 *n.*
Lindsay, Lord, "Christian Art," II. 73 ; iii. 1. 7. 5 ('83 *n*).
    „   „   „   „   II. '83 Epil. 7.
    „   „   „   „   V. 226 ; ix. 2. 4.
Linen, significance of, in priesthood, III. 242 ; iv. 14. 53.
Lines, governing, their nature, IV. 197 ; v. 14. 18.
    „   horizontal and undulating, V. 184 ; viii. 2. 1.
    „   in faces, II. 123 ; iii. 1. 14. 5.
    „   proportion of, II. 67 ; iii. 1. 6. 13.
    „   qualities of, in nature, I. 40 ; i. 2. 2. 6.
    „   simplicity and grandeur of, IV. 261 ; v. 16. 27.
    „   system and laws of mountain, IV. 290 *seqq.* ; v. 17. 20.
          See s. Curvature, Escape, Fall, Mountain, Projection,
          Rest.

Link, Mr., botanical nomenclature, V. 56 ; vi. 7. 3.
Linlithgow, III. 328 ; iv. 18. 4.
Linnæus, "Systema Naturæ," quoted, II. '83 *pref.* 4 and *n*, 5.
Linnell, cumulus clouds, I. 258 *n* ; ii. 3. 3. 28 *n* (om. ed. 1–4).
    „   engravings after M. Angelo, II. 241 ; Add. 1 (om. ed. 1).
    „   works of :
          I. 402 ; ii. 6. 1. 35 (ed. 3, 4 only).
          II. 241 ; Add. 1 (om. ed. 1).
          Eve of Deluge, *ib.* ; *ib.* (*ib.*).
          Forest Scene, *ib.* ; *ib.* (ed. 1, note 4).

Lion, eye and mouth of, their beauty, II. 105 ; iii. 1. 12. 10.
Lippi, Filippino, innovations of, III. 334 ; iv. 18. 14.
     „   „   jewel-painting of, II. 234–35 ; iii. 2. 5. 14.
     „   „   works·of :

                     Carmini Chapel, III. 334 ; iv. 18. 14.
                     Uffizii, Florence, II. 235 ; iii. 2. 5. 14.

———, Filippo, author's study of, II. '83 Epil. 10.
     „   „   „   ignorance of (1856), III. 63 ; iv. 4. 22
                           (F.A. n).
     „   „   portraiture of, II. 117 ; iii. 1. 14. 14 (ed. 1 only).
Lips, descriptions of, II. 179–80 ; iii. 2. 3. 7 (fancy and imagina-
    tion).
Literature, classical school of taste or restraint, V. 267 ; ix. 5. 5.
     „   history of (age of Dante ends in Italy as that of
               Shakspere rises in England), IV. 381 ; v. 20. 23.
     „   imaginative and unimaginative, II. 177–78 ; iii. 2.
               3. 5.
     „   modern temper, III. 269 ; iv. 16. 10.
     „   „   „   III. 277 seqq. ; iv. 16. 26 seqq.
     „   narrative higher than sentimental, III. 279 ; iv.
               16. 29.
     „   no great intellectual, from high religious temper,
               V. 228–29 ; ix. 2. 9.
     „   reputation for, on what dependent, I. 1 ; i. 1. 1. 1.
     „   scenery most productive of (mountain-influence),
               IV. 382 ; v. 20. 25.

            See s. Narrative, Pathetic, Plagiarism, Poetry, Poets,
            Spasmodic, Thinkers, Writers, Writing.

Lithography, common, and by Prout, I. 119 ; ii. 1. 7. 31 (om.
    ed. 1, 2).
Living and dead, trampling on, IV. 411 ; App. i. 6.
Loch Leven, III. 328 ; iv. 18. 4.
Locke, definition of an idea, I. 12 ; i. 1. 2. 8.
     „   on perception, I. 54 ; ii. 1. 2. 2.
     „   „   primary and secondary qualities of bodies, I. 71–3 ;
             ii. 1. 5. 1–6.
Logic, true power of, rare, III. ix ; pref. 4.
     „   want of, in education, IV. 411 ; App. iii. 1.
Logs, persons compared to, V. 180 ; viii. 1. 16.
Loire, description of the, V. 184 seqq. ; viii. 2. 2.

Loire, *continued :*
„   its wooded reaches, IV. 369–70 ; v. 20. 7.
Lombard griffin, III. 109 *seqq.* ; iv. 8. 11 *seqq.* (plate).
Lombardo, Pietro and Tullio, architecture of, III. 52 *n* ; iv. 4. 9.
Lombardy, plain of, I. 290 ; ii. 4. 1. 5.
    „   „   IV. 365 ; v. 20. 1.
    „   „   IV. 367 ; v. 20. 3.
    „   stones and gravel of, IV. 320–21 ; v. 18. 3.
London :—
    buildings in :
        Army and Navy Club, base of, III. 120 *n* ; iv. 9. 6.
        Covent Garden, Turner's home, V. 316–25 ; ix. 9. 2 *seqq.*, 19.
        Gower Street, the climax of ugliness, III. 270–71 ; iv. 16. 12. 13.
        London Bridge, "mysterious forest below," V. 319 ; ix. 9. 7. 8.
        St. Paul's Churchyard, and place of St. Mark's, Venice, V. 317 ; ix. 9. 4.

    love of money in, V. 357 ; ix. 11. 17.
    religion of, in Turner's youth, V. 322 ; ix. 9. 13. 14.
    smoke, and sunrise, V. 122–23 ; vii. 2. 4.
    suburbs, filthy débris of, I. xli ; *pref. ed.* 2. 36.
Longfellow, "Golden Legend," "The stooping sun up-gathers his spent shafts," III. 185 *n* ; iv. 13. 10 *n.*
    „   "Dance of Death," IV. 344 ; v. 19. 10.
    „   „   „   IV. 390 ; v. 20. 32.
    „   "Hiawatha," its lessons in nature, II. '83 Epil. 13.
Lord's Prayer, "Thy kingdom *come*," V. 386 *seqq.* ; ix. 12. 19–20.
Louis IX., France *temp.*, IV. 380 ; v. 20. 23.
—— XIV.,   „   „   *ib.* ; *ib.*
    „   „   his court, IV. 39 ; v. 3. 6.
Loutherbourg, Turner's study of, III. 344 ; iv. 18. 30.
Louvre, the (Paris).
    See s. Cima da Conegliano, Correggio, Da Vinci, Poussin (N.), Rubens, Ruysdael, Titian, Veronese.

Love, basis of good art, I. 87–9 ; ii. 1. 7. 10 (om. ed. 1, 2).
    „   best work done only for, II. 140 ; iii. 1. 14. 32.
    „   „   „   „   V. 379–80 ; ix. 12. 7–8.

Love, *continued :*

   ,,   characteristic of all great men, II. 97–9 ; iii. 1. 12. 2–3.

   ,,   colour typifies, V. 352 *n*, 354 ; ix. 11. 8 *n*, 9.

   ,,   essential to right drawing, IV. 34 ; v. 2. 24.

   ,, - grows in giving, II. 97 ; iii. 1. 12. 3 ('83 *n*).

   ,,   ideal attainable only by, II. 130 ; iii. 1. 14. 16.

   ,,   noble emotion, III. 11 ; iv. 1. 13.

   ,,   perception quickened by, I. 56 ; ii. 1. 2. 4.

   ,,   reason below, II. 122 ; iii. 1. 14. 5.

   ,,   scorn or, which to be cultivated ? V. 262 ; ix. 4. 14.

   ,,   source of unity, II. 54–5 ; iii. 1. 6. 1–2.

   ,,   trust and, the only mother's milk of the soul, V. 381 ; ix. 12. 10.

   ,,   vital beauty and, II. 96–7 ; iii. 1. 12. 1–2.

   ,,   want of, in some old masters, I. 82 ; ii. 1. 7. 5.

Lowe, Mr., Turner's first drawing-master, III. 345 ; iv. 18. 31.

Lowell, J. R., author's debt to, V. 312 *n* ; ix. 8. 15 *n*.

   ,,   ,,   friend and teacher, V. 380 ; ix. 12. 10.

   ,,   ,,   quoted, "Disappointment's dry and bitter root," *ib.* ; *ib.*

Lowlands, art of, want of feeling, IV. 380 ; v. 20. 22.

   ,,   influence on character, IV. 381 ; v. 20. 24.

   ,,   lowlander proud of his ("Alton Locke"), III. 193 ; iv. 13. 20.

Loyalty, in highest sense, V. 95 ; vi. 9. 13.

Luca della Robbia, I. 131 ; ii. 1. 7. 37 (om. ed. 1, 2).

   ,,   ,,   coloured porcelains of, painful, II. 216 ; iii. 2. 4. 9.

Lucan, in Dante, III. 256 ; iv. 15. 17.

Lucca, Fra Bartolomeo's works in, II. 236 ; iii. 2. 5. 17.

   ,,   Pisan sculpture at, IV. 379 ; v. 20. 21.

   ,,   San Frediano, sea mosaic, I. 366 ; ii. 5. 1. 22 (om. ed. 1, 2).

   ,,   ,,   II. '83 Epil. 5.

   ,,   San Michele, ruinous condition of, I. 111–12 ; ii. 1. 7. 26 (om. ed. 1, 2).

   ,,   ,,   II. '83 Epil. 5.

   ,,   tomb of Ilaria di Caretto, II. 76 ; iii. 1. 7. 7.

Lucerne, character of people round, V. 94 ; vi. 9. 13.

   ,,   Dance of Death on bridge, IV. 344 ; v. 19. 10–11.

   ,,   destruction of, by tourists, IV. 398 ; v. 20. 41.

Lucerne, *continued:*

„ large hotel near, to be omitted from sketch of, IV. 20–1 ; v. 2. 7.

„ Mt. Pilatus and, V. 139 ; vii. 3. 4.

„ Tell's Chapel on lake of, V. 97 *n* ; vi. 9. 16 *n.* *See s. Uri.*

Lucian, Micyllus dialogue, V. 243 *n* ; ix. 3. 10 *n.*

„ „ „ V. 337 ; ix. 10. 15.

Lucrezia Borgia, V. 290 ; ix. 7. 7.

Luini, author's ignorance of (1856), III. 63 ; iv. 4. 21 (F.A. *n*).

„ supremacy of, first shown by author, II. '83 Epil. 13.

„ work of, S. Catherine, II. 239 ; iii. 2. 5. 21 ('83 *n*).

Lustre, beauty and, II. 83–4 ; iii. 1. 9. 5.

Luther, dislike of art, III. 59 *n* ; iv. 4. 18 *n.*

Luxury, art supported by, IV. 378 ; v. 20. 19.

„ certain degree of, refining, II. 121 ; iii. 1. 14. 3.

„ enervating influence of, V. 357 ; ix. 11. 16.

„ evil of, V. 83 ; vi. 8. 18.

„ modern private, II. 7 ; iii. 1. 1. 7.

„ „ III. 321 ; iv. 17. 36.

Lying, honourable and base, V. 293–95 ; ix. 7. 12–14. *See s. Lie.*

Lyme, crags of, IV. 165 ; v. 13. 1.

Lyons, the Rhone at, IV. 176 ; v. 13. 12.

Macaulay, Lord, on mediæval missals, III. 213–14 ; iv. 14. 17.

„ „ „ „ III. 224 ; iv. 14. 29.

Macchiavelli, subtlety of, V. 295 ; ix. 7. 15.

Machinery, evils of, V. 162 and *n* ; vii. 4. 17 and *n.*

„ „ degradation of worker, V. 360 *n* ; ix. 11. 22 *n.*

„ imitation of good designs by, IV. 290 ; v. 17. 19.

Maclise, criticism of, in "Modern Painters," I. xliv *n* ; *pref. ed.* 2. 45 *n* (ed. 2 only).

„ Hamlet of, I. 4 *n* ; i. 1. 1 *n.*

„ „ I. 413 *n* ; ii. 6. 3. 13 *n* (ed. 1, 2 only).

„ Ophelia, *ib.* ; *ib.* (*ib.*).

Mackenzie, imitator of Prout, I. 119 ; ii. 1. 7. 31 (om. ed. 1, 2).

Madonna, England's, V. 343 ; ix. 10. 24.

„ in pictures and in reality, III. 53 ; iv. 4. 9.

„ „ "Mater Dolorosa," III. 55–6 ; iv. 4. 13.

Madonna, *continued*:

,,   never painted as a Jewess by mediævals, I. 130 ; ii.
          1. 7. 37 (om. ed. 1, 2).

,,   Venetian Madonna in the house, V. 247 ; ix. 3. 19
          seqq.

Maga (*Blackwood*), criticism of " Modern Painters," Vol. I., by,
    I. xx ; *pref. ed.* 2. 13.

Magdalen, Renaissance, III. 67, 68 ; iv. 5. 2. 5.

Magdeburg cathedral, shrine by Fischer in, V. 258 *n* ; ix. 4.
    6 *n.*

Maggiore, Lago, disfigured by quarry near it, IV. 128 ; v. 9. 10.

Maglans, fountain of, and débris near, IV. 329 *n* ; v. 18. 15 *n.*

Magnesia, in rocks, IV. 120–21 ; v. 9. 2.

Magnitude, relativity of, V. 195 ; viii. 3. 1. *See s. Size.*

Magnolia, curvature of leaves, IV. 287, 288 ; v. 17. 16. 18 (pl.
    42).

Maidenhead, scenery of, IV. 263 ; v. 16. 31.

Maize-blossom, V. 57 ; vi. 7. 4.

Majority, opinion of the, its value, I. 2 *n* ; i. 1. 1. 1 *n.*

Malakhoff-like summit of Riffelhorn, IV. 245 ; v. 16. 8.

Malaria, in the Valais, IV. 359 ; v. 19. 30.

Mallet, quoted by Turner, under a picture, V. 329 ; ix. 10. 3.

Man [SYNOPSIS. I. 59–60, 216. II. 4, 119, 124–25. III. 48–9, 157–
    60, 168. IV. 138–39. V. 1, 224–26, 358–59, 363] :—

    animal *and* spiritual, V. 226 ; ix. 2. 3.

    beauty (vital) in, II. 119 *seqq.* ; iii. 1. 14. 1 *seqq.*

    ,,   not good for him to live } I. 216 ; ii. 3. 1. 1.
    ,,   amid perfect,

    ,,   ,,   ,,   ,,   IV. 138–39 ; v. 11. 7

    change between ancient and modern, III. 157–60 ; iv. 11.
    7–10.

    characteristics of, now and formerly, *ib.* ; *ib.*

    duty of (knowledge, happiness, reform), III. 48–9 ; iv. 4. 2.
    ,,   (to dress the earth), V. 1 ; vi. 1. 1.

    end and aim of his life, V. 363 ; ix. 11. 25.

    ,,   ,,   ,,   to find something beyond his powers,
          III. 168 ; iv. 12. 8.

    function and use of, II. 4 ; iii. 1. 1. 4.

    God's best revelation, V. 224 ; ix. 1. 14.

    ,,   ,,   V. 225 ; ix. 2. 1.

    happiness of, in what, V. 358–59 ; ix. 11. 18. *See s. Happi-
    ness.*

Man, *continued :*

    ideals of, no single, as in animals, II. 124–26 ; iii. 1. 14.
        9–10.

    isolation of, above all creation, its errors, V. 225–26 ; ix.
        2. 2.

    moods of, various, I. 60 ; ii. 1. 2. 8.

    natural beauty, its lessons to, V. 165–66 ; vii. 4. 23–5.

    noble spirit in, how perceived, IV. 18 ; v. 2. 4–5.

    noblest tone and reach of life, V. 363 ; ix. 11. 25.

    orders of, three, III. 303–4 ; iv. 17. 9.

    perfection of, threefold, V. 358–59 ; ix. 11. 18.

    pursuits of, how divided, II. 9–10 ; iii. 1. 1. 8.

        „   „   „   V. 178–79 ; viii. 1. 14 *seqq.*

    society necessary to his development, II. 124 *n* ; iii. 1.
        14. 9.

    sublimest scenery spoilt by his presence, I. 217 ; ii. 3. 1. 1.

    sun of the world, V. 224 ; ix. 1. 15.

        „   „   V. 225 ; ix. 2. 1.

    type of, no single, as in animals, II. 124–25 ; iii. 1. 14. 9.

        See s. Business, Ethical subjects, Great men, Idiosyncrasies,
        Idleness, Life, Men, Ugliness, Work.

Manchester, Art Treasures Exhibition 1858, V. v ; *pref.* 1.
    „   cottons, III. 322 ; iv. 17. 38.
    „   love of money, V. 357 ; ix. 11. 17.

Manifestations, of God to man, in the Bible, II. 226–27 ; iii. 2.
    5. 2.

Manna, French "pain de Dieu" flower, I. 87 *n* ; ii. 1. 7. 9 *n*
    (om. ed. 1–4).

Mannerism, affectation and, in great men, III. 277–78 ; iv.
    16. 26.
    „   in art, distinct from style, I. 101–2 ; ii. 1. 7. 20
        (om. ed. 1, 2).

Mantegna, backgrounds of, fruit and flowers, V. 100 ; vi. 10. 5.
    „   jewel-painting of, II. 234 ; iii. 2. 5. 14.
    „   stones   „   IV. 321 ; v. 18. 3.

Manufacturers, asceticism of, V. 357–58 ; ix. 11. 17–18.
    „   the modern poets (makers), V. 178 ; viii. 1. 14.

Manuscripts, aspen in, 1200–1300, IV. 79 ; v. 5. 16.
    „   backgrounds of mediæval (1200–1500), golden,
        chequered sky, III. 215 ; iv. 14. 19.
    „   chequers of noble, IV. 350 ; v. 19. 19 (pl. 7)

Manuscripts, *continued* :

,,   coarse German (1450), tender French (1250), IV. 356–57 ; v. 19. 26.

,,   colours of, IV. 54 ; v. 3. 24.

,,   engraving from 1200–1300, III. 51 ; iv. 4. 9.

,,   floral ornament, 1200–1400, III. 218 *seqq.* ; iv. 14. 25 *seqq.*

,,   landscape of, III. 213 *seqq.* ; iv. 13. 16 *seqq.*

,,   ,,   IV. 266–67 ; v. 16. 35.

,,   Madonna and S. Peter in early, IV. 356–57 ; v. 19. 26.

,,   rocks in, III. 254–55 ; iv. 15. 16.

,,   ,,   IV. 267 ; v. 16. 35.

,,   scroll-curves of, IV. 290 ; v. 17. 19.

See s. British Museum, Illumination, Schongauer, Yolande.

Maple-tree, leaf form of, V. 32 ; vi. 4. 11.

Marble, coloured (opaque), white (translucent), IV. 134–35 ; v. 11. 2.

,,   qualities of, IV. 134–35 ; v. 11. 2.

,,   use of, in house and home, IV. 392 ; v. 20. 35.

Mary of Egypt, Saint, III. 68 ; iv. 5. 5.

Marmontel, mistaking a Berghem for a window, I. 79 ; ii. 1. 7. 2.

,,   Tales of, quoted on taste, III. 46 ; iv. 3. 26.

"Marriage" quoted, III. 304 *n* ; iv. 17. 9 *n*.

Mars, contest with Athena, its meaning, III. 182 ; iv. 13. 7.

,,   Diomed and, III. 183 ; iv. 13. 8.

Martigny, air round, IV. 359 ; v. 19. 30.

,,   author at, IV. 61 ; v. 4. 5.

,,   buttress of Alps, IV. 303 ; v. 17. 33 (pl. 46).

,,   country near, described, IV. 337 ; v. 19. 3.

,,   gneiss above, glacier tracks on, IV. 178 *n* ; v. 13. 16 *n*.

Martin, cirrus clouds in his works, V. 141 ; vii. 3. 9.

,,   work of, Canute (R.A. 1843), I. xxxvi, xxxviii *n* ; *pref. ed.* 2. 29. 33 *n*.

Masaccio [SYNOPSIS. I. 90, 100. II. 129, 233 *n*, 237, '83 Epil. 10. III. 98, 334. IV. 316–17] :—

author's study of, II. '83 Epil. 10.

early death of, IV. 317 ; v. 17. 51.

Masaccio, *continued*:

 landscape of, I. 100 ; ii. 1. 7. 19 (om. ed. 1, 2).

 mountain form of, IV. 316–17 ; v. 17. 50. 51 (pl. 13).

 paints his own age (vital truth from vital present), III. 98 ;
  iv. 7. 19.

 portraiture in his works, II. 129 ; iii. 1. 14. 14.

 Raphael influenced by his innovations, III. 334 ; iv. 18. 14.

 works of :

  Deliverance of St. Peter, II. 237 ; iii. 2. 5. 18.

  Tribute Money, Carmini Chapel (landscape in), I. 90 ; ii. 1
   7. 11 (om. ed. 1, 2).

  Tribute Money, Carmini Chapel (landscape in), I. 100 ; ii.
   1. 7. 19 (om. ed. 1, 2).

  Tribute Money, Carmini Chapel (landscape in), II. 233 *n* ;
   iii. 2. 5. 11 *n*.

  Tribute Money, Carmini Chapel (landscape in), III. 334 ; iv.
   18. 14.

Master and novice in art, distinguished, I. 336 ; ii. 4. 4. 15 (ed.
 1, 2, § 19).

Materialism, rise of modern, V. 276 ; ix. 6. 3.

Matilda, Countess (in Dante), III. 230–31 ; iv. 14. 37.

Matlock, cliffs of, IV. 155 ; v. 12. 15.

 „ via Gellia, author at (1851), V. 230 ; ix. 2. 12.

Matterhorn [SYNOPSIS. II. 224. IV. 161, 167–68, 189–92, 244–52,
   259, 275, 415]:—

 beds of the, IV. 415 ; App. ii. 1.

 daring form of, II. 224 ; iii. 2. 4. 20.

  „ „ IV. 161 ; v. 12. 21.

  „ „ IV. 167–68 ; v. 13. 3. 5.

 form of, IV. 189–92 ; v. 14. 11. 12.

  „ IV. 244–52 ; v. 16. 7. 17.

  „ IV. 259 ; v. 16. 25.

 impression of as perpendicular, IV. 247–48 ; v. 16. 11. 12.

 mica flakes of, IV. 251–52 ; v. 16. 16. 17.

  „ „ IV. 275 ; v. 16. 42.

    See s. Riffel, Zermatt.

Meauves, coteaux of, IV. 261 ; v. 16. 27.

Mediævalism [SYNOPSIS. III. 154–55, 158–60, 203–7, 210–13,
   222–24, 232, 233, 235, 238, 244–45, 248–49,
   255–56, 259, 268. IV. 319, 373, 400. V. 5,
   357]:—

 disdain of agriculture, III. 203 ; iv. 14. 3.

Mediævalism, *continued* :

definiteness, III. 222–23 ; iv. 14. 28.

feeling for nature, compared with the Greek (beauty *v.* use), III. 238 ; iv. 14. 51.

,, ,, dread of thick foliage, III. 227 ; iv. 14. 33.

,, ,, inaccuracies in, III. 212 ; vi. 14. 14 *seqq.*

,, ,, ,, ,, III. 244 ; iv. 15. 2 *seqq.*

,, ,, love of colour, fatal to love of southern hills, { III. 233 *seqq.*; iv. 14. 43 *seqq.* III. 248–49 ; iv. 15. 9.

,, ,, mountains, awe-inspiring, III. 204 ; iv. 14. 6.

,, ,, ,, ,, III. 207 ; iv. 14. 10.

,, ,, ,, ,, III. 245 ; iv. 15. 3.

,, ,, ,, ,, IV. 373 ; v. 20. 12.

,, ,, ,, ,, IV. 400 ; v. 20. 45.

,, ,, neglect of earth's beauty, III. 154 ; iv. 11. 3.

,, ,, ,, ,, ,, V. 5 ; vi. 1. 6.

,, ,, sentimental, III. 203 ; iv. 14. 4.

,, ,, summed up, III. 203 *seqq.* ; iv. 14. 4 *seqq.*

,, ,, ,, ,, III. 212 ; iv. 14. 15 *seqq.*

landscape, no landscape painting, III. 154–55 ; iv. 11. 3. 4.

life, solitude of castle-life, III. 206–7 ; iv. 14. 8.

,, brighter and happier than to-day's, III. 268 ; iv. 16. 9.

,, not the dark ages, III. 258 ; iv. 16. 9 (om. ed. 1, 2).

mind opposed to Greek, III. 204 ; iv. 14. 6.

religious asceticism, V. 357 ; ix. 11. 17.

,, faith, III. 231–32 ; iv. 14. 38–9.

rock-drawing, III. 254–55 ; iv. 15. 15. 16 (pl. 10).

rugged stone, dislike of, IV. 319–20 ; v. 18. 2.

sky and clouds, III. 259–60 ; iv. 15. 21.

spirit, and modern change from it, III. 158–60 ; iv. 11. 9–10.

symbolism of clouds and water, III. 222–23 ; iv. 14. 28.

symmetry, love of, III. 210 ; iv. 14. 13.

want of gratitude, III. 205 ; iv. 14. 7.

Mediævalism, *continued :*
    war, the earth one battlefield, V. 5 ; vi. 1. 5. 6.

        See s. Beauty, Cities, Education, Gardens, Knight, Landscape, Modernism, Shakspere.

Mediterranean, colour of the, I. 352 ; ii. 5. 1. 8 (om. ed. 1, 2).
Medusa, meaning of, V. 158–59 *n* ; vii. 4. 11. 13 *n*.
    ,,   Venga, V. 338 ; ix. 10. 17 (pl. 71).
Meekness, contentment and, V. 359 ; ix. 11. 19.
Meillan, Mont, fortress of, IV. 260 ; v. 16. 26.
Melancholy, modern morbid, III. 189 ; iv. 13. 14.
Melrose, III. 328 ; iv. 18. 4.
    ,,   Scott's love of, III. 282 ; iv. 16. 33.
Membership, unity of, II. 56 ; iii. 1. 6. 3.
Memling, finish of, III. 131 ; iv. 9. 18.
    ,,   moral influence of a work by, III. 60 ; iv. 4. 19.
Memorials, destruction of all old, IV. 398 ; v. 20. 42.
Memory, drawing from, II. 206 ; iii. 2. 4. 1.
    ,,   essential to perception of truth, I. 56 ; ii. 1. 2. 5.
Memmi, Simon :—
    works by :

        Duomo of Florence (S. M. Novella), I. 109 ; ii. 1. 7. 25 (om. ed. 1, 2).
        ,,   ,,   ,,   ,,   II. 60 *n* ; iii. 1. 6. 8 *n*.
        frescoes in Spanish Chapel, III. 104 ; iv. 8. 6.
        Petrarch's portrait, II. 129 ; iii. 1. 14. 14.

Men, classified according to their employments, V. 178 *seqq.* ; viii. 1. 14 *seqq.*
    ,, the greatest ignored till they are gone, IV. 216 ; v. 15. 13.
        See s. Man.
Mer de Glace, IV. 178 ; v. 13. 16.
    ,,   ,,   IV. 199 ; v. 14. 20.
    ,,   ,,   IV. 214 ; v. 15. 11.
    ,,   ,,   by Turner and others, compared, IV. 202 ; v. 14. 23.
Mercy, a sign of good breeding, V. 290 ; ix. 7. 7.
Metaphor, abuse of, in bad writing, III. 174 ; iv. 12. 15.
Metaphysics, author's inclination to, III. 279 ; iv. 16. 28.
    ,,   harmfulness of, III. 279 and *n* ; iv. 16. 28 and *n*.
    ,,   on imagination, II. 152 ; iii. 2. 1. 2.

Metaphysics, *continued :*

    „   study of, III. 356–57 ; App. 2.

            See s. Fancy, Fear, Features, Hear, Imagination, Impressions, Intellect, Infinity, Invention, Mind, Nation, Novelty, Reason, Recollection, Reflection, Relation, Zest.

Metastasio, death of, III. 64 ; iv. 4. 24.

Mettenberg, Bernese Oberland, IV. 173 ; v. 13. 9.

Metternich, Prince, subtlety of, V. 295 ; ix. 7. 15.

Meulemeester, his engraving of Raphael's "Burning Bush," III. 123 ; iv. 9. 8.

Meyringen, valley of, I. 289 ; ii. 4. 1. 5.

Mica, colour and qualities of, IV. 112 ; v. 8. 12.

  „   composition of, IV. 120 *seqq.* ; v. 9. 2 *seqq.*

  „   flakes of the Matterhorn, IV. 252 ; v. 16. 17.

  „   type of strength out of weakness, *ib.* ; *ib.*

Michael Angelo [SYNOPSIS. I. xxiii, xlviii, 4 n, 6, 34, 36–7, 67, 77, 367 n, 434, 442. II. 11 n, 16, 73, 74 n, 75, 88 and n, 112, 133, 134, 195, 196, 198–200 and n, 205 n, 218, 220, 223, 229, 230, 236, 241. III. 7, 14, 47, 104, 130, 135–36. IV. 377, 379. V. 277, 350 n] :—

  author's early reverence for, I. 6 ; i. 1. 1. 4.

      „   study for, II. 73 ; iii. 1. 7. 5 ('83 n).

  characteristics of :

    anatomy lessens his divinity, II. 236 ; iii. 2. 5. 17.

    certainty of execution, II. 200 n ; iii. 2. 3. 28 n.

    chiaroscuro, I. 77 ; ii. 1. 6. 2.

      „   I. 180 ; ii. 2. 3. 14 (ed. 1, 2 only).

    execution, II. 200 n ; iii. 2. 3. 28 n.

    finish of, and "impetuous") II. 79–80 n ; iii. 1. 10. 3 n
      want of it,   )   (ed. 1 only), 4.

      „   „   „   III. 130 ; iv. 9. 18.

    grasp of truth, III. 135 ; iv. 10. 3.

    lines of, perfect, I. 185 ; ii. 2. 4. 7 (ed. 2 only).

    repose of, II. 73–4 ; iii. 1. 7. 5–6 (and '83 n).

  engravings after, by Linnell, II. 241 ; Add. 1 (om. ed. 1).

  fiends of, II. 230 n ; iii. 2. 5. 7 n.

  greatest work of, not in architecture, II. 11 n ; iii. 1. 1. 9 n ('83 n).

  greatness of, I. xlvii–viii ; *pref. ed.* 2. 42–3.

Michael Angelo : greatness of, *continued :*

    „   I. 442 ; ii. 6. 3. 9.

    „   transcends evil, II. 133 ; iii. 1. 14. 20.

human inspiration given by him alone, II. 229 ; iii. 2. 5. 6.

mountains, not loved by, IV. 377 ; v. 20. 16.

    „   „   IV. 379 ; v. 20. 20.

nudities of, not sensual, II. 132–34 ; iii. 1. 14. 20–3.

panegyric on, II. 198–200 ; iii. 2. 3. 28.

perfection of, I. xvi ; *pref.* 2. 9 (note in ed. 2–4 only).

popularity greatest of his feeblest work, I. 4 *n* ; i. 1. 1. 1. *n*.

power of, cannot be taught, III. 47 ; iv. 3. 27.

Reynolds, Sir J., on, III. 7, 14 ; iv. 1. 7, 16.

sculpture of, colossal statues, II. 222–23 ; iii. 2. 4. 19.

    „   "non ha l'ottimo scultore," II. 197 ; iii. 2. 3. 26.

    „   nude figures of, II. 134 ; iii. 1. 14. 23.

    „   pictures less expressive than, II. 199 *n* ; iii. 2. 3. 28 *n.*

    „   Pisan sculpture's influence on, IV. 379 ; v. 20. 20.

seas of, I. 367 ; ii. 5. 1. 22 *n* (om. ed. 1, 2).

sense of power given by, I. 36 ; i. 2. 1. 4.

size of ideal in, II. 112 ; iii. 1. 13. 6 ('83 *n*).

spiritual power of, seizes very heart of angels, II. 200 *n* ; iii. 2. 3. 28 *n.*

symbols, use of, II. 230 ; iii. 2. 5. 7.

temper of, II. 205 *n* ; iii. 2. 3. 32 *n.*

tombs after, II. 75 ; iii. 1. 7. 7.

Torso of Vatican superior to his work, I. 434 ; ii. 6. 2. 2.

works of :

    Adam (Sistine), II. 198 ; iii. 2. 3. 28.

    Adam and Eve, Creation, II. 230 ; iii. 2. 5. 7.

    Bacchus (Florence), I. 37 ; i. 2. 1. 5.

        „   „   II. 199 *n* ; iii. 2. 3. 28 and *n.*

    Daniel (Sistine), I. 67 ; ii. 1. 3. 8.

    Dawn and Twilight (Medici Chapel), I. 37 ; i. 2. 1. 5.

        „   „   „   „   II. 73 ; iii. 1. 7. 5.

    Duke Lorenzo, II. 199–202 *n* ; iii. 2. 3. 28.

    Jonah, fish in, II. 218 ; iii. 2. 4. 12.

    Last Judgment, I. xxiii ; *pref. ed.* 2. 14.

        „   „   II. 195 ; iii. 2. 3. 23.

        „   „   II. 198 ; iii. 2. 3. 28.

        „   „   V. 277 ; ix. 6. 6.

Michael Angelo : works of, *continued :*

Medici Chapel, II. 223 ; iii. 2. 4. 19.

Night and Morning, *ib.* ; *ib.*

,, ,, his best statues, III. 104 ; iv. 8. 6.

Pieta of Florence, II. 199 ; iii. 2. 3. 28.

,, ,, Genoa, its exquisite finish, II. 88–9 ; iii. 1. 10. 4.

,, ,, ,, II. 202 *n* ; iii. 2. 3. 28 *n.*

Plague of fiery serpents, II. 74 *n* ; iii. 1. 7. 6 *n.*

S. Matthew, II. 199 ; iii. 2. 3. 28.

Sistine Chapel, ceiling, I. 34 ; i. 1. 7. 3.

,, ,, ,, II. 220 ; iii. 2. 4. 14.

,, ,, colours of, V. 350 *n* ; ix. 11. 8 *n.*

various works mentioned, II. 198–99 ; iii. 2. 3. 28.

Michael, the Archangel, renderings of, in art, II. 238 ; iii. 2. 5. 20.

Michelet, quoted, " ce damné Salvator," V. 262 ; ix. 4. 14.

,, ,, Du Prêtre, II. 137 *n* ; iii. 1. 14. 29 *n.*

,, ,, L'Insecte, V. 196–97 ; viii. 3. 4. 5.

Midi, Aiguille du, IV. 172 *n* ; v. 13. 8 *n.*

,, ,, IV. 221 *n* ; v. 15. 16 *n.*

Milan, art-school of, IV. 379–80 ; v. 20. 21.

,, Cathedral, statues, II. 220 ; iii. 2. 4. 14.

,, ,, sunset behind it, V. 134 ; vii. 2. 17 (pl. 68).

,, mountains from, IV. 379 ; v. 20. 20.

,, pictures in, Brera, Camillo Procaccini, II. 138 ; iii. 1. 14. 29.

,, ,, ,, Guercino's Hagar, II. 139 ; iii. 1. 14. 30.

,, ,, ,, Madonna, I. 90 ; ii. 1. 7. 11 (om. ed. 1, 2).

,, ,, ,, Salvator's S. Jerome, II. 170 ; iii. 2. 2. 19.

,, ,, ,, Titian's S. Jerome, I. 91 ; ii. 1. 7. 12 (om. ed. 1, 2).

,, ,, ,, ,, ,, II. 170, 173 ; iii. 2. 2. 19, 22.

,, ,, ,, ,, ,, IV. 377 ; v. 20. 16.

,, ,, Leonardo's Cenacola, II. 229 ; iii. 2. 5. 7.

Military asceticism, V. 357 ; ix. 11. 17–18.

Mill, J. S., " Liberty " referred to, V. 194 ; viii. 2. 15.

——. *See s. Windmill.*

Millais, J. E., early works of, I. 445 *n* ; ii. 6. 3. 16 *n* (om. ed. 1–4).

,,   ,,   " Huguenot," III. 97 ; iv. 7. 18.

Miller, engravings of Turner (esp. Scott Illust.), I. 183 *n* ; ii. 2. 2. 20 *n* (om. ed. 1, 2).

,,   ,,   best of his engravers, III. 123 *n* ; iv. 9. 8 *n*.

,,   ,,   Turner's Grand Canal, V. 125–26 *n* ; vii. 2. 6 *n*.

,,   ,,   ,,   Modern Italy, III. 123 ; iv. 9. 8.

Milnes' (Lord Houghton) " Life of Keats," IV. 411 *n.* ; App. i. 6 *n*.

Miltiades, III. 156 ; iv. 11. 6.

Milton [Synopsis. II. 99 *n*, 153–54, 175, 180–81, 208, 224, 236, 238. III. 196 *n*, 223–24, 238, 302, 314. IV. 87 *n*. V. 124, 329, 338, 379] :—

Dante and, descriptions of flame, II. 175–76 ; iii. 2. 3. 2.

,,   and hell, III. 223 *seqq.* ; iv. 14. 29 *seqq.*

Death in, II. 208 ; iii. 2. 4. 3.

Eden described (want of imagination), II. 153–54 and *n* ; iii. 2. 1. 4.

imagination of, II. 153 and *n* ; iii. 2. 1. 4.

,,   III. 224 ; iv. 14. 30.

price paid for " Paradise Lost," V. 379 ; ix. 12. 7.

severity of, III. 314 ; iv. 17. 27.

study and love of nature, III. 302 ; iv. 17. 7.

Turner's vignettes to, II. 224 ; iii. 2. 4. 20.

works of, quoted :

    " And like a comet burned . . . Ophiuchus huge,"   II. 154 ; iii. 2. 1. 5.

    "   ,,   ,,   ,,   " II. 208 ; iii. 2. 4. 4.

    " Bring the rathe primrose," II. 180 ; iii. 2. 3. 7.

    " Edged with poplar pale," III. 196 *n* ; iv. 13. 24 *n*.

    " enamelled " (use of word), III. 238 ; iv. 14. 50.

    " God made the firmament . . . expanse," IV. 87 *n* ; v. 6. 4 *n*.

    " His face Deep scars of thunder," II. 236 ; iii. 2. 5. 16.

    " Like Teneriff or Atlas, unremoved," II. 209 ; iii. 2. 4. 4.

    " Mammon, the least erected fiend that fell," V. 338 ; ix. 10. 17.

    " Many a frozen, many a fiery Alp," III. 224 ; iv. 14. 29.

    " Missing thee, I walk unseen " (Pens. 66), II. 155 ; iii, 2. 1. 5.

    " Opening eyelids of the morn " (Lyc. 2), *ib.* ; *ib.*

Milton : works of, quoted, *continued :*

    "Play in the plighted clouds," V. 124 ; vii. 2. 6.

    "Rears from off the pool," etc., II. 175 ; iii. 2. 3. 2.

    "They at her coming sprung" (flowers), II. 99 *n* ; iii. 1. 12. 3 *n*.

    "With hostile brow and visage all inflamed" (Michael), II. 238 ; iii. 2. 5. 20.

    "Ye mists and exhalations," etc. (Turner, Coniston Fells), V. 329 ; ix. 10. 3.

Mimicry, art not to be mere, III. 149–50 ; iv. 10. 20.

Mind, effect on the body, II. 121 *seqq.* ; iii. 1. 14. 4 *seqq.*

   ,,   government of, its importance, III. 95–6 ; iv. 7. 15 (F.A. *n*).

   ,,   independence of, II. 199 ; iii. 2. 3. 28.

Mineral, formation of a, V. 36 ; vi. 4. 17.

Minerva, shield of, its meaning, V. 158 ; vii. 4. 12.

Mino da Fiesole, I. 131 ; ii. 1. 7. 37 (om. ed. 1, 2).

   ,,   ,,   II. 60 *n* ; iii. 1. 6. 8 *n* (altar-piece, St. Ambrogio, Florence).

   ,,   ,,   II. 198 ; iii. 2. 3. 27 (his truth and tenderness).

   ,,   ,,   II. 216 ; iii. 2. 4. 9 (two statues, St. Catherine, Pisa).

   ,,   ,,   IV. 381 ; v. 20. 23.

Minorities, to be considered ? II. 12 ; iii. 1. 1. 11 (note at end).

Minuteness. *See s. Size.*

Mirage, effect of, IV. 72 ; v. 5. 2.

Mirror, the dark, V. 221 *seqq.* ; ix. 1. 9 *seqq.*

Miserliness, an ill-bred thing, V. 290 ; ix. 7. 7.

Missionary work, III. 320–21 ; iv. 17. 36.

Mist, defined, I. 219 ; ii. 3. 1. 5.

   ,,   more or less in all landscapes, IV. 71–2 ; v. 5. 2.

   ,,   morning, V. 113–14 ; vii. 1. 2.

   ,,   mystery and, happiness of, IV. 72 ; v. 5. 3.

   ,,   Scotch, V. 117 ; vii. 1. 6.

   ,,   visibility of, I. 223 ; ii. 3. 1. 13 *seqq. See s. Clouds, Fielding (cloudiness).*

Mistakes, pride at bottom of all great, IV. 52 ; v. 3. 22.

Misuse, of best gifts, IV. 377 ; v. 20. 17.

Models, in art and literature, their use and abuse, I. xvi ; *pref. ed.* 2. 8.

Moderation, analysis of, II. 87 *seqq.* ; iii. 1. 10. 1 *seqq.*

Moderation, *continued* :

 „ described, II. 90 ; iii. 1. 10. 5.
 „ in curves and colours, II. 91 ; iii. 1. 10. 7.
 „ the guide of beauty, II. 90–1 ; iii. 1. 10. 6.
 „ „ most difficult virtue, II. 91–2 ; iii. 1. 10. 8.

Modern art, indistinctness of subjects and treatment, IV. 319 ;
 v. 18. 1. *See s. Art, Landscape, etc.*

Modernism [Synopsis. II. 182. III. 153, 158–60, 178, 188, 266–68,
 270–71, 281, 282–83, 319 *seqq.* IV. 389, 398–99, 411.
 V. 6, 356–57, 377–78, 384–85] :—

 calamitous, III. 153 ; iv. 11. 1.
 characteristics, III. 267–68 ; iv. 16. 7–8.

 „ III. 270 ; iv. 16. 11.
 „ III. 281 ; iv. 16. 31.

 commercial spirit, V. 6 ; vi. 1. 7.
 ennui and faithlessness of, III. 268–69 ; iv. 16. 9. 10.
 infidelity of, III. 268 ; iv. 16. 10. 12. *See s. Infidelity.*

 „ V. 377–78 ; ix. 12. 4. 5.

 levity and melancholy of, II. 182 ; iii. 2. 3. 10.

 „ „ „ III. 282–83 ; iv. 16. 34.

 love of the past, III. 271–72 ; iv. 16. 15.
 mechanical impulses, III. 319 *seqq.* ; iv. 17. 35 *seqq.*
 mediæval spirit compared with, III. 158 *seqq.* ; iv. 11.
 9–10.

 „ „ „ „ III. 266 ; iv. 16. 5.

 monetary asceticism, V. 357 ; ix. 11. 17.
 neglect of beautiful things, V. 356–57 ; ix. 11. 15.
 offended at genuine work, IV. 411 ; App. i. 6.
 pathetic fallacy characteristic of, III. 178 ; iv. 13. 2.
 pride of knowledge and progress, IV. 398–99 ; v. 20.
 42.

 „ „ „ V. 384–85 ; ix. 12. 17.

 smoke nuisance, III. 188 ; iv. 13. 14.
 want of splendour, IV. 389 ; v. 20, 32.

 See s. Criticism, Dress, Idolatry, Infidelity, Inconsistency,
 Landscape.

Moine, Aiguille du, IV. 199 *n* ; v. 14. 20 *n*.
Moisture, fulness of colour expresses, IV. 258 ; v. 16. 24.
Mole, Mont, V. 139 ; vii. 3. 4.
Molecules of water, and clouds, V. 116–17 ; vii. 1. 5. 6.
Molière, natural wisdom of, III. 315 ; iv. 17. 29. 30.

Molière, *continued :*
   „   some love of nature in, *ib.* ; *ib.*
   „   works of :

       "J'aime mieux ma mie" (Wordsworthian), *ib.* ; *ib.*
       "Misanthrope" and "Tartuffe" perfect plays, *ib.* ; *ib.*

Momus, spirit of blame, V. 332 ; ix. 10. 7.
Monasticism, mountains and, IV. 400–1 *seqq.* ; v. 20. 45 *seqq.*
   „   „   „   III. 208 ; iv. 14. 10.
   „   value of its peace, as compared with activity, V.
       310–11 ; ix. 8. 13.
Money, "best work done for nothing," V. 379, 380–81 ; ix. 12.
       7. 10.
   „   expenditure of, directs labour, V. 360 *n* ; ix. 11. 22 *n.*
   „   modern love of, V. 357 ; ix. 11. 17. *See s. Wealth,*
       Work.
Monk's dress, gloomy colour, III. 249 ; iv. 15. 9.
   „   learning, mere words, V. 5 ; vi. 1. 5.
   „   opera-going, in religious art, III. 61 ; iv. 4. 19.
Mont Blanc, etc. *See s. Blanc and names of different mountains.*
Montagne, meaning of word, III. 253 ; iv. 15. 14.
   „   de la Côte, IV. 172 *n* ; v. 13. 8 *n.*
   „   „   top of, IV. 217 ; v. 15. 15.
   „   „   IV. 298 ; v. 17. 30.
   „   de Saas, IV. 173 ; v. 13. 10.
Montanvert, the, IV. 199 ; v. 14. 20
   „   „   IV. 214 ; v. 15. 11.
   „   „   IV. 222 ; v. 15. 17.
   „   „   IV. 225 ; v. 15. 21.
   „   „   Aiguille Charmoz and, IV. 144 ; v. 12. 1.
   „   „   gneiss, IV. 122 *n* ; v. 9. 5. *n.*
   „   „   „   IV. 216, 219 *n* ; v. 15. 15. 16.
   „   „   pine-forests of, IV. 368 *n* ; v. 20. 4 *n.*
   „   „   slope of, IV. 329 *n* ; v. 18. 15 *n.*
   „   „   view from, IV. 185–87 ; v. 14. 6–8.
Monte, meaning of Italian, III. 253 ; iv. 15. 14.
   „   Rosa, IV. 173 ; v. 13. 10.
   „   „   V. 134 ; vii. 2. 17 (pl. 85).
   „   „   V. 372 ; ix. 12. 1 (pl. 85).
   „   St. Angelo, in Claude's backgrounds, IV. 231 ; v. 15. 28.
   „   Viso, IV. 187 ; v. 14. 10.
   „   „   IV. 373 ; v. 20. 12.

Montreux, author at (peasant quoting Bible), IV. 377–78 ; v. 20. 18

Moonlight scenes, painting of, I. 303 ; ii. 4. 2. 19 (om. ed. 1, 2).

Moorish ornament, IV. 289 ; v. 17. 19.

Moral feelings, as affecting the features, II. 123 ; iii. 1. 14. 5.

Morality, deadened moral sense implies dulness of perception, I. 56 ; ii. 1. 2. 4.

Moralizing, on nature, instead of confessing God in nature, III. 295–96 ; iv. 16. 45.

      „   earliest type in Jaques, *ib.* ; *ib.*

Morgarten, V. 369 *n* ; ix. 11. 31 *n.*

Morland, Turner's study of, III. 344 ; iv. 18. 30.

Mortal, divine the real opposite of, V. 183 *n* ; viii. 1. 20 *n.*

"Mortiferousness" of mind, IV. 352 ; v. 19. 21. *See s. Schongauer.*

Mosaic, improved by age, I. 111 ; ii. 1. 7. 26 (om. ed. 1, 2).

Moscow, V. 326 ; ix. 9. 22.

Moses, on descent from the Mount, II. 227 ; iii. 2. 5. 2.

      „   death of, and presence at Transfiguration, IV. 400–6 ; v. 20. 46–9.

Moss-lands, art and intellect produced by, V. 151–52 ; vii. 4. 2. 4. *See s. Lichen.*

Motive, in a picture, its meaning, I. 82 and *n* ; ii. 1. 7. 6 and *n.*

      „   „   „ *e.g.* in Turner's Loire side, V. 184 *seqq.* ; viii. 2. 1 *seqq.*

Mountaineer, dislike of country by, III. 193 ; iv. 13. 20.

      „   false stage ideal, IV. 340–41 ; v. 19. 6.

      „   term of reproach, in Dante, III. 255–57 ; iv. 15. 17–18.

      „   „   „ in Shakspere, III. 193 ; iv. 13. 20.

      See s. Mountains : (5) *life among.*

Mountains [SYNOPSIS. I. 167, 287–88, 290–302, 305, 308 *seqq.*, 314–18, 319–20, 324–27. III. 192–93, 202–3, 207, 218, 225, 248, 253, 258, 267. IV. 94–9, 102–4, 105, 111, 131–32, 146–50, 156, 158, 166–68, 176–77, 183–85, 187, 192–93, 197–204, 205–6, 212 *seqq.*, 216, 223–27, 241–42, 245, 251, 256, 264, 274, 291, 292–94, 301–2, 304, 329–32, 334–39, 343, 352–53, 357–58, 362, 365–74, 377, 379 *seqq.*, 381, 399 *seqq.*, 406. V. 114 *seqq.*, 138 *seqq.*, 141–42, 357–58] :—

(1) *aspect, structure, etc., of :*
      beauty of, described (metaphor from sea and waves) IV. 205–6 ; v. 15. 2.

Mountains : (1) *aspect, structure, etc., of, continued :*

    beauty of, essential to the world's beauty, IV. 96 ; v. 7. 4.

        „   give extremes of beauty, and of ugliness, IV. 357–58 ; v. 19. 27.

        „   lowlands and, compared, IV. 367–71 ; v. 20. 4. 9.

    bones of the earth, I. 288 ; ii. 4. 1. 4.

    central and inferior, I. 291 ; ii. 4. 1. 7.

        „   not always highest, I. 292 ; ii. 4. 2. 1.

        „   universal formation of, I. 292–93 ; ii. 4. 2. 1–3.

    chain, its unity, IV. 206 *seqq.* ; v. 15. 2 *seqq.*

    convulsions, often fertilize the plain, IV. 102–3 ; v. 7. 9.

    creation of the, IV. 94 *seqq.* ; v. 7. 1 *seqq.*

    crests, curvature, how reached, IV. 304 *seqq.* ; v. 17. 35.

    curvature, *ib.* ; *ib.*

        „   complexity and harmony of, IV. 304 ; v. 17. 35.

        „   undulation and, IV. 158 ; v. 12. 19 *seqq.*

    destruction and after-repose, IV. 335 ; v. 18. 26.

    distant, characteristics of, I. 298–302 ; ii. 4. 2. 12–16.

    effect of, on scenery, IV. 365 ; v. 20. 1 *seqq.*

    falling of (Bergfall), IV. 185 ; v. 14. 5.

    fissures, curvilinear and straight, IV. 198 ; v. 14. 18.

    form and structure, I. 288 ; i. 4. 1. 3.

        „   „   I. 319–20 ; ii. 4. 3. 18.

        „   bedded structure, IV. 166 ; v. 13. 2.

        „   changeable and changed? IV. 146–48 ; v. 12. 4. 6.

        „   „   what the original? IV. 176–77 ; v. 13. 13.

        „   kinds of, IV. 205 ; v. 15. 1.

        „   typical (falling for vital force), III. 218 ; iv. 14. 24.

    growth of, IV. 94 *seqq.* ; v. 7. 1 *seqq.*

        „   IV. 227 ; v. 15. 23.

        „   IV. 291–93 ; v. 17. 21 *seqq.*

    higher peaks, smaller now than formerly, IV. 177 ; v. 13. 15.

    highest, always have multiplied formation, I. 297–99 ; ii 4. 2. 10–12.

Mountains : (1) *aspect, structure, etc., of, continued :*

    highest pasturages, the best, IV. 104 *n* ; v. 7. 10 *n.*

       „   poor soil and keen climate round, IV. 167 ; v. 13. 3.

       „   "Titan hands" of, I. 288 ; ii. 4. 1. 3.

    hills and, a purely English distinction, III. 254 ; iv. 15. 14.

    inferior, beds how formed and divided, I. 308 *seqq.* ; ii. 4. 3. 1 *seqq.*

       „   disintegration of, I. 315 ; ii. 4. 3. 11.

       „   no high precipices or steep slopes, I. 320 ; ii. 4. 3. 18.

    lines of, rest, IV. 328 *seqq.* ; v. 18. 15 *seqq.*

       „   system of, IV. 290 *seqq.* ; v. 17. 20.

    materials of, I. 288 ; ii. 4. 1. 4.

       „   IV. 95–6 ; v. 7. 3.

       „   IV. 105 *seqq.* ; v. 8. 1 *seqq.*

       „   not adamantine, by design, IV. 110 ; v. 8. 9.

       „   „ everlasting, IV. 146 ; v. 12. 3.

       „   teachings of their decay, IV. 334–35 ; v. 18. 26.

    outlines of, I. 314–15 ; ii. 4. 3. 10.

       „   I. 324 ; ii. 4. 3. 24. *See above, s. lines.*

    peaks, rarity of real, IV. 187 ; v. 14. 10.

    -ranges, characteristics of (mass and detail), I. 316–18 ; ii. 4. 3. 13–14.

       „   classes of, IV. 150 ; v. 12. 9.

    security of structure, IV. 184–85 ; v. 14. 4.

    slopes, degree of, I. 320 ; ii. 4. 3. 18.

    stratified and unstratified, IV. 150 ; v. 12. 9.

       „   three forms of, IV. 156 *seqq.* ; v. 12. 18 *seqq.*

    water, action of, on :

       aqueous erosions of inferior, I. 315 ; ii. 4. 3. 11.

       small streams and mountain-growth, IV. 226–27 ; v. 15. 23.

       torrents and ravines, I. 316 ; ii. 4. 3. 12. *See s. Streams, Torrents.*

  (2) *clouds and :*

    association of, fine, III. 258 ; iv. 15. 20.

    cloud-cap of, V. 139 *seqq.* ; vii. 3. 4 *seqq.*

Mountains : (2) *clouds and, continued* :

    clouds round, kind of, V. 141–42 ; vii. 3. 7–10

    drift-cloud, V. 142 ; vii. 3. 11.

    lowlands and, compared, IV. 369–71 ; v. 20. 7 8.

    mist, V. 114 *seqq.* ; vii. 1. 2.

(3) *drawing of* :

    by ancient and modern landscapists, I. 287 ; ii. 4. 1. 2.

         "   "   "   "   I. 304–5 ; ii. 4.
                                              2. 19.

         "   "   "   "   I. 325–26 ; ii. 4
                                              3. 26.

    " Claude and others, IV. 274 ; v. 16. 41.

    " Salvator and Titian (false colour), I. 167 ; ii. 2. 2. 4

    difficulty of painting, IV. 198–200 ; v. 14. 19–21.

    distances, a test of artist's temper, IV. 376 ; v. 20. 16.

    good and bad, test of, IV. 376–77 ; v. 15. 20. 24.

    precipices, IV. 256 ; v. 16. 22–3.

    -ranges, none by old masters, I. 295–6 ; ii. 4. 2. 6–7.

(4) *feeling for* :

    " cathedrals of the earth," IV. 371 ; v. 20. 9.

        "   "   "   IV. 399 ; v. 20. 43.

    in the Bible, III. 207 ; iv. 14. 10.

    " inhabited by the beasts," IV. 98 ; v. 7. 5.

        "   "   "   IV. 371 ; v. 20. 9.

    lowlanders' love of, as highlanders of plains, III. 192–
    93 ; iv. 13. 20.

    mediæval landscape and, III. 202–3 ; iv. 14. 2.

        "   views of, sanctity and terror, III. 207 ; iv. 14.
                                             10.

        "   "   "   "   III. 225 ; iv. 14.
                                             32.

        "   *See s. Dante* (III. 244–45 ; iv. 15. 3).

    modern landscape and, III. 266 ; iv. 16. 5.

    monkish view of, IV. 400 *seqq.* ; v. 20. 45 *seqq.*

        "   "   cf. III. 225 ; iv. 14. 32.

    " We do not look at the mountains," modern cry, V.
    358 ; ix. 11. 17.

(5) *life among* :

    calamities incident to, IV. 357–58 ; v. 19. 27.

Mountains : (5) *life among, continued :*

    character as affected by, IV. 343 *seqq.* ; v. 19. 9 *seqq.*
        ,,   ,,   ,, IV. 352 *seqq.* ; v. 19. 22 *seqq.*
      ,,   its gloom, IV. 362 ; v. 19. 32.
    gloomy, *e.g.* the Swiss, IV. 339–40 ; v. 19. 4–5.

(6) *influence of :*

    on art, IV. 378–82 ; v. 20. 19–24.
    ,, character, IV. 381–82 ; v. 20. 24.
    ,, imagination and religion, IV. 373–74 ; v. 20. 12–13.
    ,, intellectual lead of Greece and Rome, IV. 372 ; v. 20. 11.
    ,, literary power, IV. 382 ; v. 20. 25.

(7) *ministry of :*

    to man, IV. 336 *seqq.* ; v. 19. 1 *seqq.*
    ,,   IV. 371 ; v. 20. 9.

(8) *office and use of :*

    IV. 96 *seqq.* ; v. 7. 4 *seqq.*
        (1) to give motion to water, IV. 99 ; v. 7. 6.
        (2) ,,   ,,   air, IV. 102 ; v. 7. 8.
        (3) to change the ground, IV. 102–3 ; v. 7. 9.

(9) *scenery :*

    basis of author's love of all scenery, IV. 365–66 and *n* ; v. 20. 1–2 and *n.*
    beauty of, compared with lowlands, IV. 367–71 ; v. 20. 4–9.
    ,, the most beautiful of all, if healthy, IV. 367 ; v. 20. 3.
    colours of, IV. 367–68 ; v. 20. 4.
    clouds and trees of lowlands and of, IV. 369–71 ; v. 20. 7–8.
    lakes and torrents of, IV. 369 ; v. 20. 6.
    southern and northern, compared, III. 248 ; iv. 15. 8.

        See s. Aiguilles, Alps, Apennines, Bietsch-horn, Blanc, Breven, Buet, Cenis, Chambery, Chamouni, Col, Comasque, Côte, Crests, Cumberland, Dent d'Erin, Derbyshire, Diablerets, Dôme du Goûté, Doron, Eiger, Emmenthal, Faulhorn, Finsteraarhorn, Frohn-Alp, Gemmi, Genèvre, Geology, Grande

Mountains : (9) *scenery, continued :*

> Jorasse, Himalaya, Jungfrau, Jura, Matterhorn, Montagne, Montanvert, Mont, Peaks, Precipices, Pyramidal, Ravines, Religion, Resegone, Riffelhorn, Rigi, Rochers des Fys, Rossberg, Saddleback, Salève, Schreckhorn, Simmenthal, Sixt, Snow, Snowdon, Splugen, Tabor, Taconay, Tapia, Vesuvius, Volcanic, Vosges, Weisshorn, Wetterhorn.

Mouth, beauty of, in animals and men, II. 105–6 ; iii. 1. 12. 10
Mozart, melody of, V. 178 ; viii. 1. 12.
Mud, in streets of manufacturing town, V. 175–76 ; viii. 1. 7. 8.
Mulready, at author's birthday-dinner, II. '83 Epil. 14.

„   clear and definite, IV. 59 ; v. 4. 2.
„   foliage of, I. 427 ; ii. 6. 1. 28 (om. ed. 1, 2).
„   mannerisms of, II. 243 ; Add. 4 (om. ed. 1).
„   works of :

> "Burchell and Sophia" (1848), dogs in, II. 243 ; Add. 3 (om. ed. 1).
> "Butt" (1848), dogs in, *ib.* ; *ib.* (*ib.*).
> "Choosing the Wedding Gown," spaniel in, *ib.*; *ib.*(*ib.*).
> "Children at Play," IV. 15 ; v. 1. 17.
> "Gravel Pit," (1848), II. 244 ; Add. 4 (om. ed. 1).

Munich, Rubens' "Last Judgment," V. 277 ; ix. 6. 6.
„   Titian's portrait of an admiral, V. viii ; *pref.* 4.
„   Wouvermans, No. 208, V. 305–6 ; ix. 8. 2–5.
Murano, mosaics of, II. 220 ; iii. 2. 4. 14.
Murillo, gipsy Madonnas of, V. 256 ; ix. 4. 4.
„   slurred lines of, I. 185 ; ii. 2. 4. 7 *n* (ed. 2 only).
„   „   „   II. 88 ; iii. 1. 10. 3.
Muses, harmony of, V. 182 ; viii. 1. 20.
Music [Synopsis. I. xxvi. II. 61, 66–7. III. xi, 63–4, 92. IV. 56 and *n*, 73, 138–39, 284] :—

analogy from, IV. 284 ; v. 17. 10–11.
ear for, its delicacy, IV. 73 ; v. 5. 5.
enjoyment of, lost with satiety, IV. 138–39 ; v. 11. 7.
Evangelical Church-, purposely bad, III. 63–4 ; iv. 4. 23.
false note justly hissed, though one cannot sing, III. xi ; *pref.* 5.
great moral power ; why not painting ? I. xxvi ; *pref.* 2. 17.
no one melody best, II. 67 ; iii. 1. 6. 13.

Music, *continued:*
    rules of, genius needs and violates none, III. 92 ; iv. 7.
      11.
    unity of sequence in, II. 61 ; iii. 1. 6. 9.
    words and, relative value, IV. 56 and *n* ; v. 3. 24 and *n*
Mystery, advantages of, over perfect knowledge, IV. 72 ; v. 5. 3.
    „   a quality of execution, I. 40 ; i. 2. 2. 4.
    „   mistiness in art and nature, IV. 58 *seqq.* ; v. 4. 2 *seqq*
    „   modern love of, III. 265 ; iv. 16. 3.
    „   noble and ignoble, III. 324 *n* ; iv. 17. 41 *n.*
    „   „   „   IV. 76–8 ; v. 5. 10. 12.
    „   Turnerian, IV. 58–60 ; v. 4. 1 *seqq.*
    „   wilful, IV. 71 *seqq.* ; v. 5. 1. *seqq.*
      See s. Nature.

Mythology.

    See s. Achilles, Acrisius, Admetus, Æglé, Aphrodité, Apollo,
    Arethusa, Athena, Atlas, Callirhoë, Calypso, Ceres, Ceto,
    Chrysaor, Circe, Danaë, Danaides, Deiphobe, Delphi, Diana,
    Dido, Diomed, Dolon. Eris, Euryale, Eurybia, Europa, Fates,
    Gorgons, Graiæ, Hector, Hercules, Hesperid, Hestia, Hippo-
    crene, Juno, Jupiter, Mars, Medusa, Minerva, Muses, Nar-
    cissus, Neptune, Nereid, Nereus, Pallas, Parnassus, Pegasus,
    Pephredo, Perseus, Persephone, Phorcys, River-gods,
    Scamander, Scylla, Sibyl, Steino, Thaumas, Typhon, Venus,
    Vesta.

Nant d'Arpenaz, III. 145–46 ; iv. 10. 15.
Naples, Salvator's native place, V. 257 ; ix. 4. 5.
    „   soil round, its colour, I. 179 ; ii. 2. 2. 16 (ed. 1, 2. 18).
Napoleon I., death-scatterer, V. 326 ; ix. 9. 22.
——— III., a great emperor, III. 350 ; iv. 18. 37.
Narcissus, III. 235 ; iv. 14. 46 (Vevay).
    „   V. 107 *n* ; vi. 10. 19 *n.*
Narrative, rarity of simple, III. 278 ; iv. 16. 28.
Nash, Joseph, architectural drawing of, I. 122 ; ii. 1. 7. 33
    (om. ed. 1, 2).
Nation, growth of a, based on reverence, V. 84 ; vi. 8. 19.
    „   „   compared with that of a tree, V. 84–5 ;
            vi. 7. 5.
    „   „   its temper, III. 288 ; iv. 16. 39.
    „   true mind of a, always summed-up in that of its greatest
        men, III. 198 ; iv. 13. 27.

National Gallery :—
  catalogue (1860) on Callcott, Claude, Turner, V. 382 ; ix.
      12. 11.
  pictures in.

      See s. Claude, Cuyp, Francia, Guido, Poussin, Raphael,
        Reynolds, Rubens, Salvator, Titian, Turner, Uccello,
        Veronese, Wilson.

Natural history, modern anatomist, II. 151 ; iii. 2. 1 (Introd.
      Note 1883).
  „   „   to be taught to children, V. 361 *n* ; ix. 11. 22 *n.*
  „   science, inventions of, III. 322 ; iv. 17. 37.
  „   „   relations of, to landscape art, III. 323 *seqq.* ;
                iv. 17. 39 *seqq.*
Naturalists in art, III. 77 ; iv. 6. 2.   *See s. Idealism.*
Nature [SYNOPSIS. I. xvi, 31, 36, 40, 52, 53, 58, 60–1, 62–3, 166,
      174, 175–79, 204, 210, 232, 238, 309–10, 333 *n*, 422, 439,
      450 *n.* II. 36–8, 169, 172. III. 23, 76, 129–30, 188, 203,
      212, 267, 270–71, 286, 298–300, 302–3, 308–10, 312–14,
      316–18. IV. 16, 20, 27 *n*, 32, 53–4, 60, 69, 84, 129,
      283–85. V. 2–5, 165, 220, 356] :—
  art and :
      art to interpret, not take the place of nature, I. xv–xvi ;
        pref. ed. 2. 6.
      artists to study nature, I. 333 *n* ; ii. 4. 4. 10 *n* (om. ed.
        1, 2).
      fidelity to, I. 439 ; ii. 6. 3. 3.
      imitation of, not easy, III. 22 ; iv. 2. 7 (F.A. *n*).
      improvement of, and copying nature in landscape art,
                IV. 16 *seqq.* ; v. 2. 1 *seqq.*
        „   „   IV. 27 *n* ; v. 2. 16 *n.*
        „   „   spoils her, I. 450 *n* ; ii. 6. 3. 23 *n.*
      knowledge of nature, needed to supply necessary defects
        of art, I. 174 ; ii. 2. 2. 10.
      subjects of art, not in nature's occasional violations of
                truth, I. 68 ; ii. 1. 4. 1.
        „   „   though in her singular applications of
                        principles, I. 69 ; ii. 1. 4. 2.
      transcends the artist's power, I. 52 ; ii. 1. 1. 10.
        „   „   he cannot paint her brightness, I. 166 ;
                        ii. 2. 2. 3.
        „   „   or the whole of anything, IV. 20–1, 32 ;
                        v. 2. 7. 22.

Nature, *continued:*

 characteristics of :

  beauty of simple nature, constant, I. 31 ; i. 1. 6. 5 (cf.
    I. 68 ; ii. 1. 4. 1).

    „ greatest when indicating human life, II. 37 ;
     iii. 1. 4. 9.

    „ highest, evanescent, I. 69 ; ii. 1. 4. 2–3.

    „ lessons taught by its study, V. 165 ; vii. 4.
     23–4.

    „ terrible when desert, V. 220–21 ; ix. 1. 8.

  colours of, brightest used on innocent things, IV. 53 ;
    v. 3. 23.

    „ unpaintable, I. 166 ; ii. 2. 2. 3.

    „ variety of, infinite (cf. Turner), I. 177–78 ;
     ii. 2. 2. 15.

  curves of, the favourite, IV. 284–86 ; v. 17. 9. 12.

  detail and delicacy of, III. 129–31 ; iv. 9. 16. 18.

  God, the soul of, I. 60 ; ii. 1. 2. 8. *See s. God.*

  gradations throughout, imperceptible, IV. 129 ; v.
    10. 1.

  ideal and imperfect, I. 450 *n* ; ii. 6. 3. 23 *n.*

  imaginative always, II. 169, 172 ; iii. 2. 2. 17. 21 ('83 *nn*).

  laws of, "universal tendencies graced by exceptions,"
    I. 309–10 ; ii. 4. 3. 4.

    „ violation of, rare, I. 68 ; ii. 1. 4. 1.

  lessons from, never quite clear, IV. 53 ; v. 3. 23.

  mysterious, I. 40 ; i. 2. 2. 4.

    „ IV. 60–1 ; v. 4. 4.

    „ IV. 69–70 ; v. 4. 16.

    „ IV. 84 ; v. 5. 21.

  never monotonous, I. 178 ; ii. 2. 2. 16.

    „ vacant, never distinct, I. 204 ; ii. 2. 5. 4.

  rightness of, constant, but for our disobedience, II. 37 ;
    iii. 1. 4. 9 ('83 *n*).

    „ „ III. 76 ; iv. 6. 1.

  ruin of, by man, V. 357 ; ix. 11. 15.

  scenery often ugly, II. 169 ; iii. 2. 2. 17 ('83 *n*).

  ugliness sometimes allowed in, I. 68 ; ii. 1. 4. 1.

  unity of, I. 422 ; ii. 6. 1. 21.

  variety of, infinite, I. 58 ; ii. 1. 2. 7.

    „ „ I. 69 ; ii. 1. 4. 4.

    „ „ I. 178–79 ; ii. 2. 2. 16.

Nature : characteristics of, *continued :*

    variety of, infinite, I. 209 ; ii. 2. 5. 10.

        ,,   ,,   I. 232–33 ; ii. 3. 2. 8.

        ,,   ,,   I. 238 ; ii. 3. 2. 14

        ,,   ,,   I. 309–10 ; ii. 4. 3. 4.

        ,,   ,,   V. 2–5 ; vi. 1. 2 *seqq.*

  feeling for :

    author's youthful ecstasy, III. 307–9 ; iv. 17. 14–19.

    balanced powers of mind needed for full admiration of,
        III. 298–300 ; iv. 17. 3–5.

    by Greeks, III. 188 *seqq.* ; iv. 13. 14 *seqq.*

        ,,   Venetians, Turner, etc., V. 356 ; ix. 11. 14.

    mediæval, not classical, III. 203–4 ; iv. 14. 4.

        ,,   summarized, III. 212 ; iv. 14. 15 *seqq.*

    modern art, secular, III. 267 ; iv. 16. 7.

    reaction from Renaissance, III. 270–71 ; iv. 16. 13.

  ignorance of, common, I. 53 ; ii. 1. 2. 1.

    ,,   ,,   and talk about art, I. 59 ; ii. 1. 2. 7.

  love of, absent in some high intellects, III. 301–5, 314 ; iv.
        17. 7–9. 28.

    ,,   checked in modern education, III. 316 ; iv. 17. 31.

    ,,   development of, and its results, III. 318–19 ; iv. 17.
        34.

    ,,   distinct from moral principle, III. 312 ; iv. 17. 26.

    ,,   dreamer's (list of poets, etc.), III. 302 *seqq.* ; iv. 17.
        7 *seqq.*

    ,,   faith in God and, III. 317, 319 ; iv. 17. 32, 34.

    ,,   moral qualities implied in, III. 316 ; iv. 17. 30.

    ,,   ,,   *e.g.* power of admiration of good,
        III. 313–14 ; iv. 17. 27.

    ,,   poets and, *e.g.* Scott, Byron, etc., III. 386–87 , iv.
        16. 38.

    ,,   unconscious thoughts inspired by, III. 298 *seqq.* ;
        iv. 17. 3 *seqq.*

  to be studied, not dreamt over, III. 302 ; iv. 17. 7.

  warrior spirit neglects her beauty, V. 4–5 ; vi. 1. 5–6.

    See s. Botany, Flowers, Geology, Mountains, Scenery, Stones,
    Torrents, Water, etc.

Neatness, modern love of, III. 117 ; iv. 9. 3.

    ,,   ,,   ,,   IV. 3–6 ; v. 1. 3.

    ,,   vulgarity of extreme, V. 297 ; ix. 7. 21

Neglect, of great men, while living, I. 7 ; i. 1. 1. 5.
    „   „   „   III. v, vi ; *pref.* 1.

Nelson, sailors and shipping in his time, V. viii ; *pref.* 5.
    „   Turner's three subjects, V. 319 ; ix. 9. 8.

Neptune, horse and, V. 159 *n* ; vii. 4. 13 *n*.
    „   rule of, V. 156 ; vii. 4. 9.

Nereid's guard, the, V. 328 *seqq.*, 305 ; ix. 10. 1 *seqq.*, 4 (pl. 78)

Nereus, Greek sea-god, V. 156–57 ; vii. 4. 9.
    „   meaning, parentage, and progeny of, V. 333–34 ; ix. 10. 9–10.

Nero, I. xiii ; *ed.* 2. *pref.* 3.

Nesfield, "radiant cataracts" of, I. 375 ; ii. 5. 2. 12.
    „   waterfall and seas of, praised, I. 370 ; ii. 5. 2. 3.

Newspaper, criticism of art, expresses, does not guide, public opinion, I. xix–xx ; *pref. ed.* 2. 13.

Newton, Isaac, I. 63, 65 ; ii. 1. 3. 3. 6.
    „   „   III. 277 ; iv. 16. 24.
    „   „   apple of, red or withered ? III. 300 ; iv. 17. 5.
    „   „   feeling for and study of nature, III. 302, 305 ; iv. 17. 7. 10.

—— ——, John, Life of, V. 134 *n* ; vii. 2. 17 *n*.

Niagara, channel of, IV. 100 ; v. 7. 6.

Niesen, Mont, V. 139 ; vii. 3. 4.

"Niggling," misuse of the word, V. 40–1 ; vi. 5. 6–7. *See s. Hobbima.*

Night, modern pleasures taken at, III. 274 ; iv. 16. 19.

Ninevite landscape sculpture, III. 202 ; iv. 14. 1.

Noah, II. '83 *pref.* 5.

Nobility, sensitiveness *the* sign of, V. 289–90 ; ix. 7. 5–6. *See s. Aristocracy.*

Nomad nations, art and intellect of, V. 152 ; vii. 4. 2.

Nomenclature, author's botanical, V. 8 ; vi. 2. 3.
    „   botany oppressed by, V. 56 ; vi. 7. 3.

Noonday described, I 279 ; ii. 3. 4. 32 (ed. 1–4. 36).

Normandy, central source of European art, IV. 379 ; iv. 20. 20.
    „   imagination of people, IV. 374 ; v. 20. 13.
    „   influence in South Europe, *ib.* ; *ib.*
    „   inventive power, IV. 383 ; v. 20. 27.

North, Christopher, editor of *Blackwood*, 1843, I. xxii ; *pref. ed.* 2. 13.

Northern art, feeling of early, compared with Italian, I. 95–6 ; ii. 1. 7. 15 (om. ed. 1, 2).

Northern art, *continued :*

„   „   seeks truth only, indifferent to beauty, III. 36–7 ; iv. 3. 12.

„   character, and the pine, V. 93–4 ; vi. 9. 11–12.

„   „   and southern, as to sense of beauty, IV. 353 ; v. 19. 22.

„   Europe and southern, religious temper, IV. 374 ; v. 20. 13.

Northumberland, valleys of, IV. 315 ; v. 17. 48.

Norton, C. E., author's drawings of flowers, in his possession, II. '83 Epil. 2.

„   „   „   friend, V. 312 *n* ; ix. 8. 15 *n*.

„   „   "Travels in Italy" and "Vita Nuova," *ib.* ; *ib.*

Novelty, its effect on pleasure, II. 58–9 ; iii. 1. 6. 6.

„   „   „   III. 310 ; iv. 17. 22.

„   sources of, to be preserved, III. 310–12 ; iv. 17. 23. 25.

„   vulgar love of, I. 110 ; ii. 1. 7. 26 (om. ed. 1, 2).

„   „   „   by the weak- and hard-hearted, II. 59 ; iii. 1. 6. 7.

Novice, and master in art, I. 336 ; ii. 4. 4. 15 (ed. 1, 2. 19).

Nude, in art, the human body a less subject of art than the mind, I. 33–4 ; i. 1. 7. 3.

„   „   painting of, by old masters and others, II. 133–35 ; iii. 1. 14. 22–5.

„   „   „   best given where it is common in life, *ib.* ; *ib.*

„   „   „   by the Venetians, V. 253 ; ix. 3. 30.

Number most felt when symmetrical, I. 232 ; ii. 3. 2. 6.

Nuremberg described, V. 257 *seqq.* ; ix. 4. 5 *seqq.*

„   Dürer's home, V. 257–58 ; ix. 4. 5 (pl. 76).

„   funeral in old, V. 326 ; ix. 9. 23.

„   streets of, IV. 353 ; v. 19. 22.

„   toys, and modern German philosophy, V. 179 ; viii. 1. 14.

Oak, analysis of form and structure of a spray of, V. 13–15 ; vi. 3. 5–6.

„   branches of an, their curves, I. 425 *n* ; ii. 6. 1. 26 *n* (ed. 1, 2. 25 *n*).

„   „   „   ramification, V. 63 *seqq.* ; vi. 7. 13 *seqq.*

„   -bud, V. 82 : vi. 8. 18.

Oak, *continued* :
  ,,   -leaf, engraving of cluster, V. 40 ; vi. 5. 5 (pl. 53).
  ,,   ,,   size of, various, V. 29–30 ; vi. 4. 9–10.
  ,,   ,,   structure of, V. 104 ; vi. 10. 12.
  ,,   least graceful of trees, V. 47 ; vi. 6. 5.
  ,,   park and wild, ideals of, II. 112–14 ; iii. 1. 13. 7–9.
  ,,   type of cinqfoil tree-structure, V. 21 ; vi. 3. 13.
Oban, bed of clay slate near (Kerrera), IV. 123 *n* ; v. 9. 5 *n.*
Obedience, glory and law of, V. 165 ; vii. 4. 23.
  ,,   highest, V. 181 ; viii. 1. 17.
  ,,   methods of, V. 373 ; ix. 12. 2.
  ,,   peace of, V. 387 ; ix. 12. 20.
Oberwesel, vine-terraces of, IV. 261 ; v. 16. 27.   *See s. Turner.*
Objective, useless word, III. 161–63 ; iv. 12. 1–3.
Obscenity, sign of no spiritual power, V. 283 ; ix. 6. 19.
Obscurity, law of, IV. 62–3 ; v. 4. 7.
  ,,   unintelligible and intelligible, IV. 78 ; v. 5. 13.
            See s. Mystery.
Ogygia, " ancient," V. 235 ; ix. 2. 17.
Oil-painting, methods of, forgotten, III. 340 ; iv. 18. 25.
  ,,   water-colour less difficult than, I. 227 ; ii. 3. 1. 19.
Old masters, guides, not ideals, I xvi ; *pref. ed.* 2. 7.
  ,,   masters, though not true to nature, I. *pref. ed.* 1. 3.
  ,,   truth of tone in the, I. 149 *seqq.* ; ii. 2. 1. 1 *seqq.*

         See s. Dutch, Italians, Venetians, and the names of
           different artists.

Olive-trees, V. 93 ; vi. 9. 11.
Opal, colours of, how caused, V. 98 ; vi. 10. 1
  ,,   vary on different days, I. 157 ; ii. 2. 1. 14.
  ,,   consummation of sand, V. 176 ; viii. 1. 9.
Opera, costliness of modern, worse than useless, IV. 341 and *n* ;
    v. 19. 6 and *n.*
Opinions, change of, in old age, back to earliest youth, I.
             xxxi–ii ; *pref. ed.* 2. 24.
  ,,   ,,   necessary and right, V. x ; *pref.* 8.
  ,,   value of, men never justly estimated by their in-
           feriors, I. 2 ; i. 1. 1. 1.
Opposition, simplest expression of, IV. 208 ; v. 15. 4.
Optics, knowledge of, destroys pleasure in the rainbow, III.
    325 ; iv. 17. 42.
Oratorio, emotion of the frivolous at an, IV. 39 ; v. 3. 6.

Orcagna [SYNOPSIS. I. 4 *n*. II. 106, 137, 195, 216, 230 *n*. III. 32-3, 62, 104. IV. 351, 379-80, 407. V. 227] :—

characteristics and subjects of, III. 32 ; iv. 3. 8.

balanced powers of, III. 33 ; iv. 3. 9.

expressional power of (colourist), IV. 407 ; App. i. 1.

corruption and death in his works, V. 227 ; ix. 2. 7.

fiends of, II. 230 *n* ; iii. 2. 5. 7 *n*.

influence of mountains on, IV. 379-80 ; v. 20. 22.

    „   „ Pisan sculptures on, IV. 379 ; v. 20. 20.

not popular, and why, I. 4 *n* ; i. 1. 1. 1 *n* (om. ed. 1, 2).

works of :

    Campo Santo, Pisa, II. '83 Epil. 7.

      „   „   „ Inferno, II. 137 ; iii. 1. 14. 29.

      „   „   „   „ mouth of demon in, II. 106 ; iii. 1. 12. 10.

      „   „   „   „ repainted, IV. 351 ; v. 19. 20.

    Last Judgment, II. 195 ; iii. 2. 3. 23.

      „   „ III. 62 ; iv. 4. 20.

    Or San Michele, coloured statues of Madonna, II. 216 ; iii. 2. 4. 9.

    Trionfo della Morte, III. 62 ; iv. 4. 20.

      „   „   „ III. 104 ; iv. 8. 6.

Orderliness, English and continental, IV. 5 ; v. 1. 6.

Originality, consists in genuineness, not novelty, II. 178 ; iii. 2. 3. 6.

    „   of all greatness, I. xvi–xviii and *n* ; *pref. ed.* 2. 8. 10 *n*.

    „   public reception of noble, I. xviii–xix ; *pref. ed.* 2. 11.

    „   value of, III. 362 ; App. iii.

Ornament, Angelico's use of abstract, II. 234 ; iii. 2. 5. 14.

    „   animal form, its use in, II. 218–19 ; iii. 2. 4. 12.

    „   architectural, I. 110–13 ; ii. 1. 7. 26–27.

    „   „   I. 205 ; ii. 2. 5. 5–6.

    „   backgrounds and, III. 214–16 ; iv. 14. 19–20.

    „   curvature in, IV. 289–90 ; v. 17. 19.

    „   "doggrel" and formal, IV. 288–89 ; v. 17. 18. 19.

    „   dress and, IV. 387–88 ; v. 20. 30.

    „   floral in missals (12–1300), III. 218 *seqq.* ; iv. 14. 25 *seqq.*

    „   language of, and expression, I. 10–11 ; i. 1. 2. 6.

    „   symbolic, II. 219 *seqq.* ; iii. 2. 4. 14 *seqq.*

    „   symmetrical, III. 218–19 ; iv. 14. 25–6.

Ornament, *continued :*

„   typical, III. 217–18 ; iv. 14. 23–4.

„   vulgar. *See above, s.* "*doggrel.*"

Osma, desert of, IV. 373 ; v. 20. 12.

Ostrich, action of, II. 102 ; iii. 1. 12. 7.

Outline, clearness of distant, I. 301–2 ; ii. 4. 2. 16 (ed. 1 and 2, 18).

„   -drawing, qualities of good, IV. 230 ; v. 15. 26.

„   sketching in, in a picture, III. 122 ; iv. 9. 8.

„   „   „   „   V. 210–11 ; viii. 4. 17.

„   soft and slurred, a sign of vice in art, I. 199 ; ii. 2. 4. 6.

Overbeck, errors of, in choice of subject, III. 31 ; iv. 3. 7.

Oxalis acetosella, "Pain du bon Dieu" flower, of Savoy,   } I. 87 *n* ; ii. 1. 7. 9 *n.*

„   „   „   „   „   IV. 369 *n* ; v. 20. 5 *n.*

Oxford, author's Professorship, re-accepted, II. '83 Epil. 12.

„   „   drawings at, *ib., ib.* 1.

„   drawing schools, drawings lent by P.R.A. to, *ib., ib.* 14.

„   Queen's College façade, ugly but venerable till restored, I. 110 ; ii. 1. 7. 26 (om. ed. 1, 2).

Oyster, ideal of an, II. 111 ; iii. 1. 13. 5.

Padua, Arena Chapel, neglected state of, II. 8 *n* ; iii. 1. 1. 7 *n.*

„   „   „   pictures in, II. 138 ; iii. 1 14. 29.

„   „   „   „   II. 235 ; iii. 2. 5. 15.

      See s. Giotto.

Pagan, sense of beauty, II. 19–20 ; iii. 1. 2. 9–10.

„   virtues, proud and sorrowful, III. 241 ; iv. 14. 53.

Pain, discipline of, II. 5 ; iii. 1. 1. 6.

Pain de Sucre (Vevay), its slope, IV. 329 *n* ; v. 18. 15 *n.*

Painter, character of a, "a painter of saints a saint himself," II. 120 ('83 *n*) ; iii. 1. 14. 2.

„   duty of, to paint well first, III. 32–3 ; iv. 3. 9.

„   „   „   „   *i.e.* to colour, IV. 56–7 ; v. 3. 24.

„   „   „   „   „   „   V. 347 ; ix. 11. 5

„   nature's preacher, I. 70 ; ii. 1. 4. 5.

„   no needless colour to be used, II. 85 ; iii. 1. 9. 8.

„   place of, raised by interest in landscape, III. 275 ; iv. 16. 22.

      See s. Artists.

Painting [SYNOPSIS. I. 166. II. 88. III. 13, 16, 68, 100, 141. IV. 49, 56-7, 66. V. 210, 347] :—

   architecture and, both to be studied, III. 100 ; iv. 8. 1.

   bold coarse work in, II. 88 ; iii. 1. 10. 3.

   classification of, III. 13 ; iv. 1. 14.

•   colouring the essence of, IV. 56-7 ; v. 3. 24.

        „   „   „   V. 347 ; ix. 11. 5.

   ground of, what best, V. 210 ; viii. 4. 17.

   methods of,   „   V. 210-11 ; viii. 4. 16-17.

   naturally, difficulty of, III. 16 ; iv. 1. 19.

   nature's brightness beyond, I. 166 ; ii. 2. 2. 3.

   perfect, is indistinct, IV. 60 ; v. 4. 12.

   poetry includes, III. 13 ; iv. 1. 15.

   poets bad judges of, and why, III. 141 ; iv. 10. 9.

   Renaissance, III. 68 ; iv. 5. 5.

   schools of, divided : (1) local colour, (2) chiaroscuro, IV. 49 ; v. 3. 18.

           See s. Art, Illumination, Landscape, etc.

Palgrave, W. G., "Arabia," II. 105 ; iii. 1. 12. 10 ('83 n).

Palladio, architecture of, III. 68 ; iv. 5. 4.

   „   „   „   IV. 360 ; v. 19. 31.

Pallas.   See s. Athena.

Pallet-knife, its use, I. 143 ; ii. 1. 7. 45.

Palms, described, V. 9 n ; vi. 2. 4.

Palmas, no profane pictures by the, V. 246 ; ix. 3. 17.

Palmer, S., works of, praised, I. 402 ; ii. 6. 1. 35 (ed. 3, 4 only).

Pansy, V. 57 ; vi. 7. 4.

Paper, experiment with white, illustrating light, IV. 35-7 ; v. 3. 1. 2.

Parabola, IV. 286 ; v. 17. 13.   See s. Curves.

Paradise, best image of, in nature, IV. 367 ; v. 20. 3.

      „   mediæval representations of, clouds in, III. 259 ; iv. 15. 21.

Paris, love of, II. 139 ; iii. 1. 14. 31.

—— Notre Dame, IV. 379 ; v. 20. 20.

   „   Sainte Chapelle, IV. 380 ; v. 20. 23.

           See s. Louvre.

Parliament, Crimea and, III. 349-50 ; iv. 18. (36).

      „   levity of, III. 275 ; iv. 16. 20.

      „   modern, V. 178 ; viii. 1. 14.

      „   "talking tabernacle," V. 380 ; ix. 12. 9.

      „   Houses of, architecture of, II. 221 n ; iii. 2. 4. 15 n.

Parliament, Houses of, *continued*:

　　　,,　　　　　,,　　　　architecture of, V. 380 ; ix. 12. 9. 10.
　　　,,　　　　　,,　　　　cartoons for (1844), I. 131 ; ii. 1. 7. 37
　　　　　　　　　　　　　　　(om. ed. 1, 2).
Parma, Baptistery, mosaics, II. 220 ; iii. 2. 4. 14.
　　　,,　　Cathedral, Correggios in, clouds bad, II. 222 *n* ; iii. 2.
　　　　　　　　　　　　　　　　4. 17 *n.*
　　　,,　　Gallery　　　,,　　　　,,　　II. 186 ; iii. 2. 3. 16.
　　　,,　　　　,,　　　　　,,　　　　,,　　II. 134 ; iii. 1. 14. 24.
　　　,,　　　　,,　　　　Tintoret's " Entombment," II. 186 ; iii. 2.
　　　　　　　　　　　　　　　3. 16.
　　　,,　　mountains from, IV. 380 ; v. 20. 21.
Parnassia palustris (flower), V. 8 ; vi. 2. 3.
Parnassus, Apollo's throne on, IV. 372 ; v. 20. 11.
Pars, William (1783), engraving of " Mer de Glace," IV. 202 ;
　　　v. 14. 23.
Parsey's " Convergence of Perpendiculars " quoted, I. 360 *n* ;
　　　ii. 5. 1. 17 *n* (om. ed. 1, 2).
Parsley, leaves of, V. 105 ; vi. 10. 13.
Parthenon, author's view of the, II. 219–20 ; iii. 2. 4. 14.
　　　,,　　friezes, I. 37 ; i. 2. 1. 5.
　　　,,　　pure lines of, I. 110 ; ii. 1. 7. 26 (om. ed. 1, 2).
Pascal, character and life of, IV. 383–84 ; v. 20. 27–8.
　　　,,　　study and love of nature, III. 302 ; iv. 17. 7.
Passion, analysis of, in literature, its value, III. 279 – 80 ; iv.
　　　16. 29.
　　　,,　　base and noble, II. 138–39 ; iii. 1. 14. 30.
　　　,,　　rendering and value of, in art, II. 139–40 ; iii. 1. 14. 31.
　　　,,　　the four sacred passions, III. 11 ; iv. 1. 13.
　　　,,　　　,,　　lower passions, ministered to by art, III. 71 ; iv.
　　　　　　　　　5. 7.
　　　　　　　　　　　　　See s. Temperance.
Past, over-value of, in modern life, III. 271–74 ; iv. 16. 15, 19.
　　　,,　　present and, sadly sundered, IV. 4–5 ; v. 1. 5.
Pastoralism, dramatic, IV. 340 *seqq.* ; v. 19. 6 *seqq.*
　　　,,　　in landscape, III. 345 ; iv. 18. 31.
Pathetic fallacy, the, III. 161–77 ; iv. 12. 1 *seqq.*
　　　,,　　　　,,　　referred to, III. 285 ; iv. 16. 37.
Patriotism of all great men, I. 130 ; ii. 1. 7. 37 (om. ed. 1, 2).
Patronage of art, buying of pictures, I. xlv *n* ; *pref. ed.* 2.
　　　　　　　　　　40 *n.*
　　　,,　　　　　,,　　its false taste, I. xlviii ; *pref. ed.* 2. 43.

"Paul and Virginia," illustrated French edition, I. 426 ; ii. 6. 1. 27 (om. ed. 1, 2).

Pavillon, the (plain of Arve), I. 268 ; ii. 4. 1. 5 (ed. 1 only).

Pay, "best work for nothing," V. 379, 381 ; ix. 12. 7. 10. *See s. Work.*

Pea-pods, edible, V. 106 *n* ; vi. 10. 15 *n*.

Peace, moral decline during prolonged, II. 5 ; iii. 1. 1. 6.

    ,,   true and false, V. 384 *seqq.* ; ix. 12. 17 *seqq.* *See* plate 84, V. 370 ; ix. 11. 32.

                  See s. Monasticism, Obedience.

Peacock's feather, colour of, V. 98 ; vi. 10. 1.

Peaks, rarity of real, in mountain form, IV. 187 ; v. 14. 10.

Peasant, aged, pathetic appearance of, IV. 6 ; v. 1. 7.

    ,,   education of a, what he should know, V. 362 ; ix. 11. 23.

    ,,   life of, English and Swiss, real and stage, IV. 338 *seqq.* ; v. 19. 4–6.

    ,,   Montreux, quoting Bible, IV. 377–78 ; v. 20. 18.

Pegasus (lower rain-clouds), V. 158–60 ; vii. 4. 12–14.

Pélerins, Cascade des (Chamouni), IV. 298 ; v. 17. 30.

    ,,   ,,   ,,   IV. 330 ; v. 18. 18.

Pencil, use of the, how to be taught, I. 429–30 ; ii. 6. 1. 31 (om. ed. 1, 2).

    ,,   ,,   in making sketches, V. 126 *n* ; vii. 2. 7 *n*.

Pephredo, one of the Graiæ, V. 158 ; vii. 4. 10.

Perception, acuteness of, may be increased, IV. 321–22 ; v. 18. 5.

    ,,   ,,   *e.g.* by love, I. 56 ; ii. 1. 2. 4.

    ,,   truth of, rare (men see what they expect), I. 56–7 ; ii. 1. 2. 5.

                  See s. Locke, Sight.

Perfectness in art, its meaning, V. 200–1 *seqq.* ; viii. 4. 2 *seqq.*

Perrault, I. xiii ; *pref. ed.* 2. 3.

Persephone, III. 67 ; iv. 5. 2.

Perseus, myth of, its meaning, V. 158–59 ; vii. 4. 12.

    ,,   sculptor of the, I. xxiii ; *pref. ed.* 2. 14.

Personification, its place in painting, III. 103–4 ; iv. 8. 6.

Persons, useless, *deed*less, V. 180 ; viii. 1. 16.

Perspective, aerial, defined, distinct from tone, I. 150 ; ii. 2. 1. 3.

    ,,   ,,   I. 196–97 ; ii. 2. 4. 1.

    ,,   ,,   in modern landscape, III. 264–65 ; iv. 16. 2.

    ,,   ,,   sometimes violated by nature, I. 297 ; ii. 4. 2. 10.

Perspective, *continued :*

„   despised in 12-1300 art, III. 20 ; iv. 2. 5.   *And see
                s. Chinese.*
„   of clouds and sky, V. 128 *seqq.* ; vii. 2. 10 *seqq.*
„   „   „   as expressive of buoyancy, V. 134 *n* ; vii.
                2. 16 *n.*
„   „   mountains, IV. 198 ; v. 14. 19.
„   Turner's lectures on, V. 376 *n* ; ix. 12. 4 *n.*
Perugia, art of, IV. 379 ; v. 20. 21.
Perugino [SYNOPSIS. I. xvii, 4 *n*, 87, 115, 163, 368. II. 47, 89,
        145, 191, 229, 232-33, 234, 235, 238. III. 52, 55, 60,
        131, 334. IV. 59, 376-77, 380, 407. V. 228, 343] :—

    architecture of, Transalpine, not Italian, II. 232 ; iii. 2.
        5. 11.
    backgrounds of religious pictures of, III. 52 ; iv. 4. 8.
    character of (Vasari on), II. 145 ; iii. 1. 15. 6.
    colour of, V. 343 ; ix. 10. 24.
    distances of, mountainous, IV. 376-77 ; v. 20. 16.
    excelled by Raphael, I. xvii ; *pref. ed.* 2. 9.
    expressional power of (colourist), IV. 407 ; App. i. 1.
    faces of, their beauty, II. 145 ; iii. 1. 15. 6.
    finish of, I. 87 ; ii. 1. 7. 10 (om. ed. 1, 2).
        „   II. 89 ; iii. 1. 10. 4.
        „   III. 131 ; iv. 9. 18.
    holy feeling and light, I. 163 ; ii. 2. 1. 22.
    jewel-painting, abstract, II. 234 ; iii. 2. 5. 14.
    landscape of, II. 47 ; iii. 1. 5. 10.
        „   II. 232 ; iii. 2. 5. 10-11.
        „   formal, taken by Raphael, III. 334 ; iv. 18. 14.
        „   its clearness, IV. 59 ; v. 4. 2.
    lines, of hard, I. 185 ; ii. 2. 4. 7 *n* (ed. 2 only).
    moral influence of his work, III. 60 ; iv. 4. 19.
    mountain influence on, IV. 380 ; v. 20. 22.
    not popular, and why, I. 4 *n* ; i. 1. 1 *n.*
    religious temper of, and intellect weak, V. 228 ; ix. 2. 9.
    superhuman ideal of, II. 238 ; iii. 2. 5. 20.
    symmetry of, II. 71 ; iii. 1. 8. 4 (ed 1 only).
    use of real gold by, I. 115 ; ii. 1. 7. 28 (om. ed. 1, 2).
    water-painting, I. 368 ; ii. 5. 1. 23 (om. ed. 1, 2).
    works of :

        Annunciation (Bologna), II. 47 ; iii. 1. 5. 10.
        Assumption (Florence Academy), *ib.* ; *ib.*

Perugino : works of, *continued :*
        Bologna Gallery, II. 233 ; iii. 2. 5. 11.
        Christs, II. 229 ; iii. 2. 5. 7.
        Crucifixion, II. 191 ; iii. 2. 3. 20.
        fresco, Albizzi Palace, II. 235 ; iii. 2. 5. 15.
          „   S. Maddalena, Florence, I. 368 ; ii. 5. 1. 23 (om. ed.
                                      1, 2).
          „   „   „   II. 232 ; iii. 2. 5. 11.
        Michael Archangel, II. 238 ; iii. 2. 5. 20.
        Nativities, III. 52 ; iv. 4. 9.
        portrait of himself (Florence, Uffizii), II. 145 ; iii. 1. 15. 6.
          „   „   „   „   II. 233 ; iii. 2. 5. 11.
        Queen Virgin, III. 55 ; iv. 4. 12.

Pesellino, Filippo, rocks of, III. 254 ; iv. 15. 16 (pl. 10).
Peterborough, cathedral of, IV. 381 ; v. 20. 23.
Petrarch, Simon Memmi's portrait of, II. 129 ; iii. 1. 14. 14.
Pharisaism, artistical, III. 65 ; iv. 4. 24.
Phidias, I. 4 ; i. 1. 1. 2.
    „   V. 350 *n* ; ix. 11. 8 *n.*
    „   Homer and, their relation, III. 276 ; iv. 16. 22.
    „   idealism of, III. 87 ; iv. 7. 5.
    „   perfection of, I. 144 ; ii. 1. 7. 45 (om. ed. 1, 2).
    „   repose of, *e.g.* in the Theseus, II. 73 ; iii. 1. 7. 5 (and
            '83 *n*).
Phillips, Prof., letter to author on geology of Strid, IV. 264–66 ;
        v. 16. 33–4.
Phillyrea, shoot of, V. 28 ; vi. 4. 8.
Philology, author's contempt of, III. 279 *n* ; iv. 16. 28.
Philosophers, harmfulness of, *ib.* ; *ib.*
    „   meaning of, V. 179 ; viii. 1. 14.
Philosophy, dangers of, V. 179 ; viii. 1. 14.
    „   sensationalist, III. 161–62 ; iv. 12. 1.
    „   what to read in, III. 357 ; App. 2.
        See s. Germans, Metaphysics, Socrates, Subjective.
Phorcys, son of Nereus, V. 157 *seqq.* ; vii. 4. 9 *seqq.*
    „   „   „   V. 333–35 ; ix. 10. 9, 11.
    „   „   „   V. 337 ; ix. 10. 15.
            See s. Gorgons.
Photography [SYNOPSIS. I. 82, 114, 118. III. x–xi, 22. IV. 33
        and *n*, 65, 253, 312]:—
    advance of, III. x–xi ; *pref.* 5.
    architecture and, I. 114 ; ii. 1. 7. 28 (om. ed. 1, 2).

Photography, *continued :*
     architecture and, I. 118 ; ii. 1. 7. 30 (om. ed. 1, 2).
     calotypes, daguerreotypes, I. 82 ; ii. 1. 7. 5.
     exaggerated shadows of, IV. 312 ; v. 17. 46.
     of snow mountains, IV. 253 ; v. 16. 18.
     "sun-stains" of, III. 22 ; iv. 2. 7.
     topographical value of, IV. 33 and *n* ; v. 2. 23 and *n.*
     Turnerian distinctness of, IV. 65 ; v. 4. 11.
                    See s. Daguerreotype.
Physical beauty, mediæval perfection of, III. 209 ; iv. 14. 11
     „   „   „   worship of, III. 271 ; iv. 16. 14.
     „   „   modern neglect of, *ib.* ; *ib.*
Picardy, people of, their want of invention, IV. 383 ; v. 20. 27.
Pickersgill's "Contest of Beauty," R.A. 1848, II. 245 ; Add. 6
     (om. ed. 1).
Pictures [SYNOPSIS. I. xlvi, 11, 70, 443-46. II. 197. III. 22, 133
          seqq., 147-50. IV. 20, 67-8. V. 101, 210-11, 212-13] :—
     "all is wrong till all is right" in, V. 212 ; viii. 4. 19.
     completeness as a test of value, I. 11 ; i. 1. 2. 7.
          „   „   „   I. 445 ; ii. 6. 3. 15.
     effect of distance on, IV. 67-8 ; v. 4. 13.
     „   „   greatest pictures to be seen at a distance,
                    V. 101 ; vi. 10. 6.
     finish, to be as much as possible, I. 446-47 ; ii. 6. 3. 18.
     great landscape, to give rare instances of general truth, I
          70 ; ii. 1. 4. 5.
     ideal, as distinct from studies, I. xlv-xlvi ; *pref. ed.* 2. 40.
     inventful, plenty of, III. 150 ; iv. 10. 21.
     likeness not to dispense with imagination, III. 147 ; iv.
          10. 17.
     method of painting, the best (Venetian), V. 210-11, 212-13 ;
          viii. 4. 17. 19.
     noble, inspired ideals, III. 149 ; iv. 10. 19.
     powerful according as imagination pierces the heart of the
          subject, II. 197 ; iii. 2. 3. 25.
     price of, a fair test of merit, I. 443 ; ii. 6. 3. 9.
          „ I. 445-46 ; ii. 6. 3. 16-18.
     spirit of artist to be seen in, III. 149 ; iv. 10. 19.
     suggestion of artist's written notes to accompany their, IV.
          20 ; v. 2. 7.
     unfinished, modern love of, I. 445-46 ; ii. 6. 3. 15 *seqq.*
     uninventive artists', III. 22 ; iv. 2. 7.

Pictures, *continued :*

unreality of, its advantage, III. 147 *seqq.* ; iv. 10. 17 *seqq.*

use of, III. 133 *seqq.* ; iv. 10. 1 *seqq.*

whole to be foreseen from the first, V. 213 ; viii. 4. 20.

Picturesque [SYNOPSIS. I. 100. II. 80. III. 198. IV. 1 *seqq.*, 5–6, 9–13 *seqq.*] :—

definition of the, IV. 2 ; v. 1. 1.

essence of, "nobly borne unconscious suffering," IV. 5–6 ; v. 1. 7.

landscape, V. 218 ; ix. 1. 3.

love of, its indifference to misery, IV. 10–12 ; v. 1. 12–13.

,, a modern feeling, I. 100; ii. 1. 7. 19 (om. ed. 1, 2).

modern art and Turner, and the, IV. 1 *seqq.*; v. 1. 1. *seqq.*

none in Homer, III. 198 ; iv. 13. 26.

sense of sublimity, IV. 6 ; v. 1. 8.

sympathy distinguishes high and low, IV. 9–10 ; v. 1. 12.

,,   ,,   ,,   ,, IV. 13 *seqq.* ; v. 1. 15 *seqq.*

symmetry not to be sacrificed to the, II. 80 ; iii. 1. 8. 4.

treatment of stones, IV. 320 ; v. 18. 3.

See s. Calais spire.

—— *Annual,* Stanfield's "Innspruck," I. 280 ; ii. 4. 2. 22 (ed. 1, 2 only).

Pilatus, Mount, IV. 238 ; v. 15. 34.

,,   ,, V. 139 ; vii. 3. 4.

Pilgrimages, mediæval travels and, III. 206–7 ; iv. 14. 9.

"Pilgrim's Progress," Art Union edition, engraving of stones, IV. 325 ; v. 18. 10.

Pillar-plants, *e.g.* palms, V. 9–10 ; vi. 2. 4. 6.

Pine [SYNOPSIS. III. 124, 300–1. IV. 142, 306–7, 368 *n.* V. 9–10, 57, 88–93]:—

author's use of the word, V. 9–10 ; vi. 2. 5.

described, IV. 142 ; v. 11. 9 (and F.A. *n*).

,,   delicacy, V. 93 ; vi. 9. 10.

,,   fineness of the, "fringes the sky," V. 92 *seqq.* ; vi. 9. 9.

,,   formal outline, V. 88 ; vi. 9. 4.

,,   grandeur of, V. 90 ; vi. 9. 7.

,,   roundness and straightness, V. 88 ; vi. 9. 4 *seqq,*

,,   ,,   ,, compactness, V. 91 ; vi. 9. 8.

dew on the, V. 92 ; vi. 9. 9.

Pine, *continued :*

    -forests, colour of, purple, IV. 368 *n* ; v. 20. 4 *n.*

         „   no gloom in, felt by author, V. 91 ; vi. 9. 8.

    Herodotean simile, V. 89 *n* ; vi. 9. 5 *n.*

    influence of, on northern and Swiss character, V. 93–4 ;
         vi. 9. 11. 12.

    lowland trees, compared with the, V. 88 *seqq.* ; vi. 9. 4 *seqq*

    painting of, must be patient, IV. 307 ; v. 17. 40.

         „   IV. 368 *n* ; v. 20. 5 *n.*

         „   V. 87 ; vi. 9. 3.

    service of, to man, V. 88–9 ; vi. 9. 5.

    Shakspere on, IV. 394 ; v. 20. 38.

         „   V. 92 ; vi. 9. 9.

    stone-pine, growth of a, V. 57 ; vi. 7. 5.

         „   head of, V. 86 ; vi. 9. 1.

    strength of old, III. 124 ; iv. 9. 9 (pl. 3).

    sunlight on, V. 92 ; vi. 9. 9.

    varied and balanced interest in, III. 300–1 ; iv. 17. 6.

                 See s. Fir-cone.

Pinturicchio, finish of, II. 89 ; iii. 1. 10. 4.

         „   tenderness of, II. 179 *n* ; iii. 2. 3. 7.

         „   works of, Madonnas, II. 239 ; iii. 2. 5. 21.

Pisa, author at (1845), II. '83 Epil. 6.

     „   „   (1882), II. 76 ; iii. 1. 7. 7 ('83 *n*).

     „   „   II. 88 ; iii. 1. 10. 3 ('83 *n*).

     „   Baptistery, restorations, II. 88 ; iii. 1. 10. 3.

     „   „   ruin of, II. 7 *n* ; iii. 1. 1. 7 *n.*

     „   Campo Santo, Benozzo Gozzolis in, II. 228 ; iii. 2. 5. 5.

     „   „   „   III. 31–2 ; iv. 3. 8.

     „   „   Giotto's "Sacrifice of Job" (attributed to
                                         him), II. '83 Epil. 7.

     „   „   „   "Satan," II. 230 *n* ; iii. 2. 5. 7 *n.*

     „   „   Orcagna's Inferno, II. 137 ; iii. 1. 14. 29.

     „   „   „   repainted, IV. 351 ; v.
                                         19. 20.

     „   „   ruin of the, II. 7 *n* ; iii. 1. 1. 7 *n.*

     „   Cathedral, central source of European art, IV. 379 ; iv.
         20. 20.

     „   Cimabue's mosaic at, II. 220 ; iii. 2. 4. 14.

     „   Maremma and art at, V. 238–39 ; ix. 3. 2.

     „   mountains from, IV. 372 ; v. 20. 11.

     „   „   „   IV. 379 ; v. 20. 20.

Pisa, *continued*:

„ sculpture of, its area and influence, IV. 379–80 ; v. 20. 20–21.

„ S. Caterina, statue of Mina da Fiesole, II. 216 ; iii. 2. 4. 9.

„ Spina, S. M. della, restored, II. 88 ; iii. 1. 10. 3 ('83 *n*).

Pisano, Nicolo, good influence of study of antique on, I. 130 ; ii. 1. 7. 37 (om. ed. 1–3).

————, Nino, good influence of study of antique on, *ib.* ; *ib.* (*ib.*).

Πίστις, its derivation, V. 275–76 ; ix. 6. 2.

Pistoja, Baptistery, restoration, II. 88 ; iii. 1. 10. 3.

„ Pisan sculpture at, IV. 379 ; v. 20. 21.

„ San Bartolomeo, Guido da Como's pulpit, II. 216 ; iii. 2. 4. 9.

Pitti Gallery, Florence, Salvator's "Umana Fragilità," grey spectre in, V. 262 ; ix. 4. 14.

Pity, a sign of good breeding, V. 289–90 ; ix. 7. 6–7.

Places, etc., named :—

See s. Abbotsford, Aiguilles, Airolo, Albano, Aletsch, Allée Blanche, Alps, Altorf, Amalfi, Amiens, Annecy, Apennines, Ardon, Arve, Arveron, Assisi, Avignon, Beauvais, Berne, Bolton, Bingen, Bonneville, Brenta, Brieg, Bristol, Bruges, Brussels, Bulicame, Canterbury, Capri, Calabria, Calais, Cambridge, Campagna, Carrara, Cathedrals, Chambéry, Chamouni, Champagne, Charenton, Chartreuse, Chède, Chillon, Clairmont, Cluse, Como, Corinth, Cormayeur, Corniche Road, Corrie-nan-shian, Cumberland, Cyrene, Dart, Dazio Grande, Derbyshire, Derwent, Devonshire, Dijon, Dusseldorf, Edinboro', Eiger, Engelberg, England, Faido, Florence, Fontainebleau, Formazza, France, Fribourg, Geneva, Genoa, Ghent, Gibraltar, Glacier, Glaramara, Glenfarg, Goldau, Grenoble, Greppond, Greta, Gries, Grimsel, Grindelwald, Gruyère, Harlech, Hastings, Henley, Holland, Holyrood, Ingleboro', Innspruck, Interlachen, Ischia, Isère, Italy, Jedburgh, Jura, Kent, Keswick, La Côte, La Riccia, Lac de Combal, Langholme, Lauffen, Lausanne, Lauterbrunnen, Leicestershire, Lincolnshire, Linlithgow, Loch Leven, Loire, Lombardy, London, Lucca, Lucerne, Lyme, Lyons, Maggiore, Maglans, Manchester, Martigny, Matlock, Meauves, Melrose, Mediterranean, Mer de Glace, Mettenberg, Meyringen, Milan, Montreux, Morgarten, Moscow, Munich, Murano, Nant d'Arpenaz, Naples, Niagara, Normandy, Northumberland, Nuremberg, Oban, Osma,

Places, etc., named, *continued*:

> Oxford, Padua, Paris, Parma, Pélerins, Picardy, Pisa, Pistoja, Provence, Reuss, Resegone, Rheinfelden, Rhine, Rhone, Rochdale, Rokeby, Rome, Romney, Roslin, Rotterdam, Runnymede, Salève, Sallenches, San Miniato, Savoy, Scandinavia, Schaffhausen, Seine, Shrewsbury, Siena, Sierra, Sion, Sixt, Sorrento, Spanish Chapel, Sparta, Staffordshire, Stratford, Strid, Suffolk, Switzerland, Tête Noire, Thames, Torcello, Tours, Trient, Turin, Tyrol, Ulm, Urbino, Uri, Val d'Aosta, Val Ferret, Valais, Vallombrosa, Valorsine, Vatican, Vaud, Veiento, Venice, Verona, Vevay, Villeneuve, Via Mala, Virginia Water, Vindonissa, Wales, Warwickshire, Wells, Westminster, Westmoreland, Wharfe, Yorkshire, Zermatt, Zmutt.

Plagiarism, III. 320 *n* ; iv. 17. 35 *n*.
,,   III. 359 *seqq*. ; App. 3.
,,   III. 361 ; App. 3.
Plains, author's dislike of, IV. 365 ; v. 20. 1
,,   formation of, I. 289 ; ii. 4. 1. 5.
,,   interest in, of mountaineers, and *vice versâ*, III. 193 ; iv. 13. 20.
,,   mountains, essential to, IV. 97 ; v. 7. 4.
,,   trees, IV. 369 ; v. 20. 7.
Plan, Aiguille du, IV. 172 *n* ; v. 13. 8 *n*.
,,   ,,   ,,   IV. 196 ; v. 14. 17.
,,   ,,   ,,   IV. 221 *n* ; v. 15. 16 *n*.
,,   ,,   ,,   IV. 422 ; App. ii. 5.
Plane-tree, leaf of American, III. 217 ; iv. 14. 22.
Plants, adaptation to man's needs, V. 2–3 ; vi. 1. 2–3.
,,   beauty of, in proportion to its vitality, II. 99 ; iii. 1. 12. 4.
,,   constructive proportion and, II. 68 ; iii. 1. 6. 15.
,,   delight in, is in their happiness and strength, II. 100–1 ; iii. 1. 12. 5.
,,   ideal of, II. 112 *seqq*. ; iii. 1. 13. 7 *seqq*.
,,   law of succession in, V. 29–30 ; vi. 4. 9.
,,   less lovable than animals, and why, II. 106–7 ; iii. 1. 12. 11.
,,   life of, law of help, V. 174 ; viii. 1. 4.
,,   proportion in, Burke quoted, II. 68 ; iii. 1. 6. 15.
,,   roots of, V. 46 ; vi. 6. 4.
,,   seed of, V. 106 ; vi. 10. 16.
,   sympathy with, II. 98–9 ; iii. 1. 12. 3.

Plants, *continued:*
,, "tented" and building, earth and pillar, V. 8 ; vi. 2. 2–3.
,, typical of virtues, III. 241–43 ; iv. 14. 53.
,, uses of, V. 2–3 ; vi. 1. 2–3.
See s. *Botany, Flowers,* etc.
Plantain, seed vessel of, IV. 61–2 ; v. 4. 5.
Platæa, battle of, II. 238 ; iii. 2. 5. 20.
Plato, jests of, bright and playful, III. 108 ; iv. 8. 10.
,, no landscape or love of the country in, III. 199 ; iv.
13. 27.
,, seer and thinker, III. 279 ; iv. 16. 28.
,, study of, recommended, III. 357 ; App. 2.
,, works of, quoted :

Hippias, I. xlviii–xlix ; *pref. ed.* 2. 44.
,, V. 243 *n* ; ix. 3. 10 *n.*
Laws (on rejoicing), V. 182 and *n* ; viii. 1. 20 and *n.*
Phædo, V. 183 *n* ; viii. 1. 20 *n.*
Timæus, on unity, II. 57 ; iii. 1. 6. 4.

Pleading, special, in the pulpit, IV. 423–24 ; App. iii. 2–3.
Pleasures [SYNOPSIS. II. 13–17, 27–9. III. 1, 144, 274, 310–11.
V. 359–60] :—
Aristotle on the rank of the, II. 14–16 ; iii. 1. 2. 3–5.
artistic, its sources, III. 1 ; iv. 1. 1.
custom and novelty as affecting, III. 310–11 ; iv. 17. 22–3.
future and present, III. 144 ; iv. 10. 13.
God's seal visible in all true sources of, II. 27 ; iii. 1. 3. 10
night made deadly with our, III. 274 ; iv. 16. 19.
nobleness of various, II. 13–14 ; iii. 1. 2. 2.
of sight, always open to everybody, II. 29 ; iii. 1. 3. 13.
temperance and intemperance in, II. 14–16 ; iii. 1. 2. 3–5
true, of humble life, V. 359–60 ; ix. 11. 21.
See s. *Taste.*
Poetry [SYNOPSIS. I. 9, 56. II. 177. III. 7–13, 24, 88–9, 141,
164–73, 275. IV. 31–2, 288–89, 374, 389–90. V. 102,
178, 181 *seqq.*] :—
common words finely used in, III. 88–9 ; iv. 7. 7. 8.
definition, etc., of, III. 10–12 ; iv. 1. 12–14.
,, ,, III. 24 ; iv. 2. 8.
,, ,, V. 178 ; viii. 1. 13.
,, ,, V. 181 *seqq.* ; viii. 1. 18 *seqq.*
first-rate only, to be read, III. 165 *n* ; iv. 12. 6 *n.*

Poetry, *continued :*

history and, different statement of same facts by, III.
7 *seqq.*; iv. 1. 8 *seqq.*

modern, dwells on the past, IV. 389–90 ; v. 20. 32.

noble sensibility the source of, I. 55 ; ii. 1. 2. 3.

painters and versifiers included in, I. 9 ; i. 1. 2. 3.

„ III. 13; iv. 1. 15.

pathetic fallacy and, III. 164 ; iv. 12. 4.
See s. Pathetic fallacy.

pure fact, its value in, III. 169–72 ; iv. 12. 11. 12.

reading aloud of, IV. 288–89 ; v. 17. 18.

second-rate, of *no* value, III. 165 *n* ; iv. 12. 6 *n.*

superstition, often merely a form of, IV. 374 ; v. 20. 13.
See s. Detail.

Poets, bad judges of painting, and why, III. 141 ; iv. 10. 9.

„ facts better stated by, than by economists, IV. 31–2 ; v
2. 21.

„ greatest, command of feeling, III. 169 ; iv. 12. 10.

„ „ depth of feeling, III. 173–74 ; iv. 12. 14.

„ imagination of, its nature, II. 177 ; iii. 2. 3. 4.

„ interest in landscape and in man, III. 275 ; iv. 16.
22.

„ love of flowers by, V. 102 ; vi. 10. 7.

„ meaning of, V. 178 ; viii. 1. 14.

„ orders of, two only : (1) creative, (2) reflective, III. 165 *n* ;
iv. 12. 6 *n.*

„ temperament of, III. 167–68 ; iv. 12. 8–9.

Political economy, irreligion of modern, V. 378 ; ix. 12. 5.

„ „ used to justify cheating, V. 288 ; ix. 7. 2.

„ „ valuable things, III. 319–20 ; iv. 17. 35.
See s. Labour, Machinery, Work.

Political science, true basis of, IV. 109 ; v. 8. 6.

Politics, no religion in modern, III. 268–69 ; iv. 16. 10.

Pomona, cherries of, III. 2 ; iv. 1. 2.

Poor. *See s. Peasant.*

Pope, A., classicalism of, V. 267 ; ix. 5. 5.

„ cold-hearted, III. 174 ; iv. 12. 15.

„ „ „ only in his pastorals, V. 267 *n* ; ix. 5. 5 *n.*

„ ingenious fabulist, III. 179–80 ; iv. 13. 4.

„ love of nature, moderate, III. 315 ; iv. 17. 20.

„ morality, II. 59 ; iii. 1. 6. 6 ('83 *n*).

„ wisdom of, V. 267 *n* ; ix. 5. 5.

Pope, A., *continued :*

    „   works of :

             Homer, death of Elpenor (unimaginative), III. 166 ; iv. 12. 6.

             "Where'er you walk," III. 175 ; iv. 12. 15.

Pope, the, struggle of Venice with, V. 238–39 ; ix. 3. 2–3.

    „   „   „   „   V. 244 ; ix. 3. 12.

Poplars, an element in lovely landscape, I. 137 ; ii. 1. 7. 41.

    „   „   „   „   III. 196 ; iv. 13. 25.

                           See s. Homer.

    „   French lines of, III. 192–93 ; iv. 13. 20.

Popularity, as a true sign of greatness, I. 3–4 *n* ; i. 1. 1. 1 *n.*

    „   of works appealing to the passions, *ib.* ; *ib.*

Porphyries, characteristics of, IV. 113 *seqq.* ; v. 8. 14 *seqq.*

    „   colours of, IV. 115–16 ; v. 8. 15.

Portraiture, dress to be subordinate in, I. 66 ; ii. 1. 3. 8.

        „   generalization fatal to, II. 128 ; iii. 1. 14. 13.

        „   likeness, various recognition of, I. 59–60 ; ii. 1. 2. 8

        „   „   „   „   „   I. 307 ; ii. 4. 2. 21.

        „   modern (1846) aims at prettiness, not character, II. 129 ; iii. 1. 14. 15.

        „   „   and Venetian idea of a gentleman's, V. 245 ; ix. 3. 15.

        „   of great idealists complete, III. 85 ; iv. 7. 3.

        „   „   „   „   III. 98 ; iv. 7. 20.

        „   old masters' introduction of, II. 128–29; iii. 1. 14. 14.

        „   pride and, II. 132 ; iii. 1. 14. 19.

        „   thundercloud, backgrounds of, IV. 256–57 ; v. 16. 23.

                  See s. Vandyck, Veronese.

Potter, Paul, author's depreciation of, I. 6 ; i. 1. 1. 4.

    „   „   cattle of, admired, I. 349 ; ii. 5. 1. 5 (om. ed. 1, 2).

    „   „   leaf-drawing of (cf. Hobbima, Ruysdael), V. 39 ; vi. 5. 3.

    „   „   powers of, V. 280 ; ix. 6. 12.

    „   „   works of :

             Dulwich Gallery (176), water in, I. 361 ; ii. 5. 1. 17 (om. ed. 1, 2).

             „   „   „   „   I. 338 ; ii. 5. 1. 20 (ed. 1, 2 only)

             Lord Westminster's Gallery, II. 242 ; Add. 2 (om. ed. 1).

Pourri, Aiguille, Chamouni, IV. 206 and *n* ; v. 15. 2 and *n*.

    „   „   „   IV. 225 ; v. 15. 21.

Poussin, G. and N., art-teaching in their days, IV. 313 ; v. 17. 47.

    „   „   landscape of, IV. v ; *pref.* 1.

    „   „   Richard Wilson influenced by, I. 97 ; ii. 1. 7. 17 (om. ed. 1, 2).

————, Gaspar [SYNOPSIS. I. xlviii, 6, 63, 80–1, 95, 98, 164, 168, 186, 189, 206–7, 209, 214, 221, 228, 236, 241, 245, 248–49, 263, 274, 313, 409–10, 413, 414–15, 418–20, 422, 444. II. 48, 170. III. 270, 343–45. IV. v, 39–40, 44, 258, 313. V. 274] :—

    author's depreciation of, I. xlviii ; *pref. ed.* 2. 42.

       „   „   „   I. *pref.* 3 (ed. 3 only).

       „   „   „   I. 6 ; i. 1. 1. 4.

    chiaroscuro of, I. 186, 189 ; ii. 2. 3. 4. 7.

       „   „   I. 180 ; ii. 2. 3. 15 (ed. 1, 2 only).

    climax of ugliness, III. 270 ; iv. 16. 12.

    clouds of, I. 236 ; ii. 3. 2. 11.

       „   I. 241 ; ii. 3. 3. 3.

       „   generalized, unspacious, I. 248–50 ; ii. 3. 3. 13–15.

    colour and light of, IV. 44 ; v. 3. 12.

    distances of, clever tricks, I. 209 ; ii. 2. 5. 10.

       „   I. 214 ; ii. 2. 5. 16.

    dull dignity of, III. 344 ; iv. 18. 31.

    effective, to the ignorant, IV. 39–40 ; v. 3. 6–7.

    falsity of, I. 443–44 ; ii. 6. 3. 11–13.

    feebleness, due to no love of nature, I. 80–2 ; ii. 1. 7. 3–5 (om. ed. 1, 2).

    generalization of, I. 214 ; ii. 2. 5. 18.

    imagination of, feeble, II. 170 ; iii. 2. 2. 18.

    landscape of, generally, I. 95 ; ii. 1. 7. 14 (om. ed. 1, 2).

       „   „   „   I. 184 and *n* ; ii. 2. 4. 6 and *n* (ed. 1, 2 only).

    leafage of, its false regularity, I. 419–20 ; ii. 6. 1. 17–19 (ed. 1, 2. § 16–18).

       „   I. 422 ; ii. 6. 1. 22–3 (ed. 1, 2. § 21–2).

    mannerisms of, II. 48 ; iii. 1. 5. 12.

    moral sense, but none of beauty, I. 80 ; ii. 1. 7. 3.

    pastoralism of, III. 345 ; iv. 18. 31.

    sameness of, I. 63 ; ii. 1. 3. 2.

Poussin, Gaspar, *continued :*
  skies of, untrue, I. 221 ; ii. 3. 1. 10.
      „   „   I. 228 ; ii. 3. 1. 20.   *See above, s. clouds.*
  sublimity of, false, IV. 258 ; v. 16. 24.
  tone of, low, V. 274 ; ix. 5. 18.
  tree-drawing, I. 413 ; ii. 6. 1. 10.
      „   I. 415 ; ii. 6. 1. 13.
  Turner influenced by, III. 343 ; iv. 18. 28.
  works of :

      La Riccia (Nat. Gall., 98), I. 164 ; ii. 2. 2. 1.
          „   „   „   tree in it, I. 409-10 ; ii. 6. 1. 6.
          „   „   „   „   I. 389 ; ii. 6. 1. 13 (ed.
                                                  1, 2 only).
          „   „   „   „   II. 170 ; iii. 2. 2. 18.
      Dido and Æneas (Nat. Gall., 95), clouds of, I. 274 ; ii. 3. 4. 23
                                                  (ed. 1-4. 26).
          „   „   „   „   I. 414-15 ; ii. 6.
                                                  1. 12.
          „   „   „   „   II. 170 ; iii. 2. 2. 18.
      Niobe (Dulwich, 269), rocks of, I. 313 ; ii. 4. 3. 9.
      Sacrifice of Isaac (Nat. Gall., 31), clouds, "ropy wreath," I.
                                                  245 ; ii. 3. 3. 8.
          „   „   „   „   clouds and foliage, II. 170 ;
                                                  iii. 2. 2. 18.
          „   „   „   „   distance, I. 207 ; ii. 2. 5. 8.
          „   „   „   „   sky untrue (though it is
                                                  one of his best works),
                                                  I. 221 ; ii. 3. 1. 10.
          „   „   „   „   trees in, I. 168 ; ii. 2.
                                                  2. 5.
      Two Storms (Nat. Gall., 36, 161), I. 263 ; ii. 3. 4. 6.
          „   „   „   „   I. 114-15 ; ii. 6. 1. 12.
      View near Albano (Nat. Gall., 68), leafage, I. 410 ; ii. 6. 1. 7.
          „   „   „   „   „   I. 420 ; ii. 6. 1.
                                                  19.

Poussin, Nicolo [SYNOPSIS. I. xx *n*, xxviii, xxxi, 6, 95, 131, 153,
                  163, 168, 186, 205, 221, 228, 245, 274, 302, 366,
                  425 *n.* II. 137, 170, 221. III. 343. IV. 257-
                  58. V. 217, 267, 273, 274]:—
  battle-pieces of, V. 273 ; ix. 5. 18.
  chiaroscuro of, I. 180 ; ii. 2. 3. 15 (ed. 1, 2 only).
  classical landscape headed by, V. 217 ; ix. 1. 2.
  Claude and. *See below, s. temper.*

Poussin, Nicolo, *continued:*

    colour of, instance of false, I. 169 ; ii. 2. 2. 5.

    distances of, I. 302 ; ii. 4. 2. 17.

    great in feeling, I. 205 ; ii. 2. 5. 6.

    heartless, I. 131 ; ii. 1. 7. 37 (om. ed. 1, 2).

    intellectual mind of, I. 153 ; ii. 2. 1. 8.

    landscape of, generally, I. 95 ; ii. 1. 7. 14 (om. ed. 1, 2).

        ,,   ,,   I. 184 and *n* ; ii. 2. 4. 6 and *n* (ed. 1, 2 only).

        ,,   ideal, I. xxviii ; *pref. ed.* 2. 20.

        ,,   imaginative, II. 170 ; iii. 2. 2. 19.

        ,,   praised by author, when fine, I. 6 ; i. 1. 1. 4.

        ,,   Turner influenced by, III. 343 ; iv. 18. 28.

    "learned," why so called, I. xx *n* ; *pref. ed.* 2. 13 *n*.

    qualities of, III. 343 ; iv. 18. 28.

    religious works of, V. 273 ; ix. 5. 18.

    sensibility deficient, *ib.* ; *ib.*

    skies untrue, I. 221, 228 ; ii. 3. 1. 10, 20.

    temper of, V. 267, 273 ; ix. 5. 3. 17 *seqq.*

    Titian excels all he does, V. 273 ; ix. 5. 17.

    tone of, untrue, I. 163 ; ii. 2. 1. 22.

    trees of, symmetrical, I. 425 *n* ; ii. 6. 1. 26 *n*.

    water-painting of, I. 366 ; ii. 5. 1. 22.

    works of :

        Apollo (Nat. Gall.), II. 221 ; iii. 2. 4. 16.

        Death of Polydectes, V. 273 ; ix. 5. 18.

        Deluge (Louvre), I. 366 ; ii. 5. 1. 22 (om. ed. 1, 2).

        ,,   ,,   II. 137 ; iii. 1. 14. 29.

        ,,   ,,   false sublimity of, IV. 257–58 ; v. 16. 23–4.

        ,,   ,,   ,,   ,,   V. 274 ; ix. 5. 18.

        Dulwich Gallery, 212 (attributed work), I. 245 ; ii. 3. 3. 8.

        ,,   ,,   ,, its false clouds, *ib.* ; *ib.*

        ,,   ,,   260, I. 154 ; ii. 2. 1. 8.

        ,,   ,,   I. 205 ; ii. 2. 5. 6.

        ,,   ,,   295, I. 184 *n* ; ii. 2. 4. 6 *n* (ed. 1, 2 only).

        Inspiration of the Poet (Dulwich), V. 273 ; ix. 5. 17.

        Nursing of Jupiter (Dulwich), fine detail, I. xxxi ; *pref. ed.* 2. 23.

        ,,   ,,   ,,   V. 273 ; ix. 5. 17.

        Phocion (Nat. Gall., 40), clouds in, I. 274 ; ii. 3. 4. 23 (ed. 1–4, § 26).

        ,,   ,,   ,,   false colour of sky, I. 168 *n* ; ii. 2. 2. 5 *n*.

Poussin, Nicolo : works of, *continued :*

    Phocion (Nat. Gall., 40), shadows in, I. 186 ; ii. 2. 3. 4.

        ,,   ,,   ,, truth of tone, I. 153–54 ; ii. 2. 1. 8.

        ,,   ,,   ,, Turner's Mercury and Argus com-
                              pared, I. 154 ; ii. 2. 1. 9.

    Plague, V. 273 ; ix. 5. 18.

    Triumph of David, *ib.* ; *ib.*

    Triumph of Flora (Louvre), III. 343 ; iv. 18. 28.

Powder and patches, age of, III. 270 ; iv. 16. 12.

Power, delight in work of art and ideas of, I. 14 *seqq.* ; i. 1. 3.
    2 *seqq.*

  ,,   desire for, V. 387 ; ix. 12. 20.

  ,,   display of, rather than of truth, by artists, I. 42–3 ; i. 2.
    2. 9–11.

  ,,   duty implied by, even of the senses, II. 24–5 ; iii. 1. 3. 6.

  ,,   great, only great objects call forth, I. 15–16 ; i. 1. 3. 3.

  ,,   ideas of, I. 14 *seqq.* ; i. 1. 3. 2 *seqq.*

  ,,   ,,   how far to be studied, I. 35 *seqq.* ; i. 2. 1. 1 *seqq.*

  ,,   never wasted, I. 18 ; i. 1. 3. 5.

  ,,   seen and unseen, I. 36 ; i. 2. 1. 3 *seqq.*

  ,,   sensation of, and its intellectual perception, I. 37 ; i. 2.
    1. 7.

Prayer, fine churches and, V. 187 ; viii. 2. 6.

Praxiteles, I. 33 ; i. 1. 7. 3.

Preaching, *both* sides to be stated, IV. 423 ; App. iii. 2–3.

  ,,   Presbyterian and Romanist, *ib.* ; *ib.*

Precipices [SYNOPSIS. I. 308, 310, 319–20. IV. 154–55, 209, 240
    seqq., 253–55, 259–60, 275–76] :—

  author's use of the term, IV. 209 ; v. 15. 6.

  beauty of, IV. 274 ; v. 16. 42.

  crests distinct from, IV. 241 *n* ; v. 16. 2 *n.*

  cut rocks of (Homer and Dante), IV. 253 ; v. 16. 19.

  formation of, I. 308 ; ii. 4. 3. 1.

        ,,   I. 310 ; ii. 4. 3. 4.

        ,,   IV. 154–55 ; v. 12. 15–16.

        ,,   IV. 240 *seqq.* ; v. 16. 2 *seqq.*

  forms of, which safest, IV. 241 ; v. 16. 3.

       ,,   ,, usual, IV. 259–60 ; v. 16. 26 *seqq.*

  height of, IV. 240 ; v. 16. 1.

       ,,   no high ones in lower hills, I. 320 ; ii. 4. 3. 18.

  in lower Alps, desolateness, IV. 254–55 ; v. 16. 20–21.

  materials of, soft stone (slaty coherents), IV. 254 ; v. 16. 20.

Precipices, *continued :*
    painting of, difficult, IV. 256 ; v. 16. 22.
        „   patience needed, IV. 275–76 ; v. 16. 43.
                    See s. Cliffs.
Predicate, subject and, relative importance in art, I. 63–4 ; ii. 1
    3. 3 *seqq.*
Pre-Raphaelite—Pre-Raphaelitism [SYNOPSIS. I. 64–5, 427 *n*,
                                445 *n*. II. '83 Epil. 2, 14.
                                III. 33, 63, 82 *n*, 136–38,
                                150, 270 *n*, 278. IV. 19,
                                59, 63, 306–8, 365, 407.
                                V. 38–40, 102, 197] :—
Pre-Raphaelite Brethren (P.R.B.) :
    author's influence on, V. 102 ; vi. 10. 8.
    criticized falsely as puerile, III. 63 ; iv. 4. 23.
    detail of, patient, IV. 306–8 ; v. 17. 39–41.
        „   V. 197 ; viii. 3. 5.
        „   IV. 19 ; v. 2. 5.
    execution, definite and clear, IV. 59 ; v. 4. 2.   *See s.*
        Mystery.
    expressional and colourist power, IV. 407 ; App. i. 1.
    flower-painting of, V. 102 ; vi. 10. 8.
    foliage of, I. 427 *n* ; ii. 6. 1. 28 *n* (om. ed. 1–4).
        „   V. 40 ; vi. 5. 5.
    greatest modern school, IV. 59 ; v. 4. 2.
    morbid choice of subject, IV. 19 ; v. 2. 5.
    name and objects of, I. 445–46 *n* ; ii. 6. 3. 16 *n* (om. ed. 1–4).
        „   an unfortunate one, I. 427 *n* ; ii. 6. 1. 28 *n* (om. ed.
            1–4).
    naturalist, not purist movement, III. 82 *n* ; iv. 6. 8.
    pictures of, transcripts from nature, III. 150 ; iv. 20. 21.
    powers of, III. 33 ; iv. 3. 9.
    praised, I. 427 *n* ; ii. 6. 1. 28 *n* (om. ed. 1–4).
    preference of marsh to mountain by, IV. 365 ; v. 20. 2
        (F.A. *n*).
    principles of, right, V. 38–9 ; vi. 5. 2.
    schism of, II. '83 Epil. 14.   *See s. Pre-Raphaelitism.*
Pre-Raphaelitism :
    author's first ideas of, II. '83 Epil. 2.
    modern, not representative of modern (1856) school, III.
        278 ; iv. 16. 26.
        „   III. 270 *n* ; iv. 16. 10 *n*.

Pre-Raphaelitism, *continued :*
  mystery of, IV. 63 ; v. 4. 8.
  Turner and, not opposed, III. 136–38 ; iv. 10. 5–6.
  unaffected, III. 278 ; iv. 16. 26.
Presbyterianism, illogical sermon, IV. 423 ; App. iii. 2.
Present, modern neglect of, and study of past, III. 49 ; iv. 4. 3.
Press, duty of, in art-criticism, I. 443 ; ii. 6. 3. 10–11.
Pride [SYNOPSIS. **II.** 120, 131. **III.** 64, 68, 203. **IV.** 52, 72–3 **V.** 296]:—
  analyzed, original vice of all, II. 131 ; iii. 1. 14. 18.
  baseness of, III. 68 ; iv. 5. 4.
  cause of all great mistakes, IV. 52 ; v. 3. 22.
  countenance as affected by, II. 131 ; iii. 1. 14. 18.
  criminality of, II. 132 ; iii. 1. 14. 19 (and '83 *n*).
  "desert island" of, II. 120 ; iii. 1. 14. 2 (*ib.*).
  in idleness, mediæval, III. 203 ; iv. 14. 3.
  of knowledge, IV. 72–3 ; v. 5. 4.
  portraiture and, II. 132 ; iii. 1. 14. 19. *See s. Portraiture.*
  religious, the worst of all, III. 64 *n* ; iv. 4. 24.
  right and wrong, V. 296 ; ix. 7. 18.
  sensuality and, fostered by renaissance, III. 68 ; iv. 5. 4.
            See s. Venice : (c) landscape.
Prism-coloured clouds, I. 279 *n* ; ii. 3. 4. 32 *n*.
Procaccini, Camillo, martyrdom by (Brera, Milan), II. 138 ; iii 1. 14. 29.
Profane art, its growth, III. 66–7 ; iv. 5. 1–2.
  „   modern feeling for nature, III. 267 ; iv. 16. 7.
Progress, modern, universal ? III. 271–72 ; iv. 16. 15.
  „   of gradual growth (cf. trees), V. 21–2 ; vi. 3. 14.
Projection, effect of, in a picture, a cheap trick, I. 77 ; ii. 1 6. 3.
  „   lines of, IV. 291, 295 ; v. 17. 21. 26.
Pronunciation, vulgarity of over-precise, V. 296–97 ; ix. 7 17–18.
Prophets, meaning of, V. 178 ; viii. 1. 14.
Proportion [SYNOPSIS. **II.** 61–9, 78. **IV.** 207]:—
  apparent and constructive, II. 61 *seqq.* ; iii. 1. 6. 10 *seqq.*
  constructive or expedient, II. 68 *seqq.* ; iii. 1. 6. 15.
  errors about, Burke and, II. 64 ; iii. 1. 6. 10.
  lines and, II. 66 ; iii. 1. 6. 13.
  principles of, summarized, II. 69 ; iii. 1. 6. 17.
  simplest expression of, cinqfoil, IV. 207 ; v. 15. 4.

Proportion, *continued :*
    size in relation to, II. 66 *n* ; iii. 1. 6. 10 *n.*
    symmetry and, distinct, II. 78–9 ; iii. 1. 8. 2.
          See s. Curvature.
Prosperity, evil of prolonged, II. 4–5 ; iii. 1. 5 *seqq.*
Protestantism, art disliked by, III. 59–60 ; iv. 4. 18.
      ,,   belief in God's presence, IV. 354 ; v. 19. 23.
      ,,   errors of, V. 275 ; ix. 6. 2.
      ,,   lowland and mountain, IV. 375–76 ; v. 20. 14. 15
      ,,   over-anxiety of, II. 149 ; iii. 1. 15. 10–11.
      ,,   Romanism and, bitterness of, IV. 354–55 ; v.
                              19. 23.
      ,,   ,,   ,,   divisions of, III. 269; iv. 16. 10.
      ,,   ,,   ,,   temper of, compared, IV.
                                375–76 ; v. 20. 14.
      ,,   self-condemnation of, II. '83 *pref.* 5.
Protogine, rock of Mont Blanc, IV. 216 ; v. 15. 15.
Prout, S. [Synopsis. I. 102, 108, 119–22, 327 *n.* II. '83 Pref. and
      Epil. III. 310. IV. 11 *n*, 14] :—
    architectural work of, I. 108 ; ii. 1. 7. 25 (om. ed. 1, 2).
      ,,   ,,   ,,   I. 121–22 ; ii. 1. 7. 31–2 (*ib.*).
      ,,   ,,   ,,   I. 327 *n* ; ii. 4. 3. 28 *n.* (om. ed. 1–4).
    at author's birthday dinner, II. '83 Epil. 14.
    author's early imitation of, II. '83 Epil. 1.
    character of, II. '83 *pref.* 9.
    colour of, sunny, I. 121 ; ii. 1. 7. 32 (om. ed. 1, 2).
    early drawings of (noble picturesque), IV. 14 ; v. 1. 15.
    figures, cleverly placed, I. 121 ; ii. 1. 7. 32 (om. ed. 1, 2).
    imitation of. *See s. Haghe, Mackenzie.*
    lithographs (Flanders, Italy, Switzerland), I. 120 ; ii. 1. 7.
      31 (*ib.*).
    noble picturesque of, IV. 14 ; v. 1. 15.
    pre-eminent in his own line, I. 119–20 ; ii. 1. 7. 31 (om. ed.
      1, 2).
      ,,   his imitation, *ib.* ; *ib.* (*ib.*).
    outline touch of, I. 102 ; ii. 1. 7. 20 (*ib.*).
    romantic associations as affecting, III. 310 ; iv. 17. 21.
    various sketches of (Brussels, Calais, Cologne, Flanders,
                   Germany, Gothic cell at Ratisbon,
                   Italy, Louvain, Nuremberg, Sion,
                   Switzerland, Tours), I. 120–22 ; ii.
                   1. 7. 31–2 (om. ed. 1, 2).

Prout, S., *continued :*
    views of Amiens, IV. 11 *n*; v. 1. 12 *n*.
      „   Venice, I. 76 ; ii. 1. 7. 8 and *n* (ed. 1, 2 only).
Provence, inventive power of people of, IV. 383 ; v. 20. 27.
Provision, means "foresight," V. 360 *n* ; ix. 11. 21 *n*.
Psalms, doggrel versions of the, III. 64 *n* ; iv. 4. 23 *n*. *See s.*
    Bible.
Public opinion, as a criterion of excellence, I. 1 ; i. 1. 1. 1. *See*
    s. Patronage.
Pugin, author owes nothing to, III. 361 ; App. 3.
Punch, "Février turned traitor" (modern grotesque), IV. 410 ;
    App. i. 5.
    „   skye terrier in, II. 243 ; Add. 3 ('83 *n*) (om. ed. 1).
Punishment, eternal, V. 255 ; ix. 4. 1.
Purchase. *See s. Benevolence.*
Purism, in art, III. 76–7 ; iv. 6. 2.
    „   idealism of, *ib.* ; *ib.* 3.
    „   noble when instinctive, III. 82 ; iv. 6. 9.
    „   school of, and Angelico, V. 309–10 ; ix. 8. 12.
Puritanism, bitter short-sight of, as to Greek religion, III.
            179–80; iv. 13. 4–5.
    „   III. 269 ; iv. 16. 10.
    „   character of, IV. 354 ; v. 19. 23.
    „   sternness of, IV. 374 ; v. 20. 13.
            See s. Protestantism.
Purity, analysis of its nature, II. 81 *seqq.* ; iii. 1. 9. 2 *seqq.*
    „   implies help and consistence, V. 175 ; viii. 1. 6.
    „   of colour, II. 85 ; iii. 1. 9. 8.
    „   of heart, its true meaning, II. '83 *pref.* 5.
    „   type of divine energy, II. 81 ; iii. 1. 9. 2.
    „   „   sinlessness, II. 84 ; iii. 1. 9. 6.
            See s. Apollo, Nude.
Purple, in natural scenery, IV. 368 and *n* ; v. 20. 4 and *n*.
    „   popularity of, III. 234 ; iv. 14. 44.
    „   "wine-coloured," in Greek poets, *ib.* ; *ib.* 43 *seqq.*
    „   yellow and, use of, I. 179 ; ii. 2. 2. 17.
Purpose, want of, in most actions, V. 180 ; viii. 1. 16.
Purse or curse, no good work done for, V. 381 ; ix. 12. 10.
Pursuits of men : (1) subservient, (2) objective, II. 9 ; iii. 1.
        1. 8.
    „   „   practical and noble, II. 9–10 ; *ib.*
          See s. Business, Work.

Pyne, J. B., rock-drawing by, I. 333 ; ii. 4. 4. 10 (ed. 1, 2.
§ 12).
Pyramidal mountain form, rare, IV. 187–89 ; v. 14. 10–11.
Python. *See s. Apollo.*

Qualities of things, Locke on, I. 71 ; ii. 1. 5. 1.
Quarries, beautiful scenery destroyed by, IV. 128 ; v. 9. 10.
            See s. Chamouni, Maggiore.
Quatrefoil, architecture, and in trees, V. 21 ; vi. 3. 14.
    „   leaf-form, V. 31–2 ; vi. 4. 11.
Quercia, tomb of Ilaria di Caretto (Lucca) by :—
    „   „   author's first (1845) sight of it, II. '83 Epil.
                5. 6.
    „   „   description of it, II. 76 ; iii. 1. 7. 7.
"Quivi Trovammo," V. 328 ; ix. 10. 1 (pl. 78).

Race, value of, in animals and men, V. 287 ; ix. 7. 1.
——horses, loss of beauty in special breeding, II. 107 ; iii. 1.
    12. 12.
Racing, ruin of horses in, IV. 363 ; v. 19. 32.
Radclyffe, Mrs., her study and love of nature, III. 302 ; iv.
    17. 7.
    „   „   III. 313 ; iv. 17. 27.
Radiation of curves, IV. 210 *seqq.* ; v. 15. 7–8 *seqq.*
Railings, English love of iron, IV. 5 ; v. 1. 6.
Railways [SYNOPSIS. I. 132. II. 6, 12. III. 311, 320 *seqq.*, 322.
            IV. 397–98. V. vii, 357]:—
    art and, I. 132 ; ii. 1. 7. 37 (om. ed. 1, 2).
    England (1846) being torn up by, II. 6 ; iii. 1. 1. 7.
    in lake-district, Wordsworth and author on, II. 12 ; iii. 1.
        1. 11 (note at end).
    only make the world smaller, III. 320 *seqq.* ; iv. 17. 35
        seqq.
    ruin, and modernism, V. vii ; *pref.* 3.
        „ in Switzerland, IV. 397–98 ; v. 20. 41.
    speed, III. 322 ; iv. 17. 37.
    travelling, not travelling at all, III. 311 ; iv. 17. 24.
        „   V. 357 ; ix. 11. 15.
Rain, angel of the sea, V. 153 ; vii. 4. 5.
    „ beauty of, V. 151 ; vii. 4. 1.
    „ darkness of, but colours heightened, IV. 257–58 ; v.
        16. 24.

Rain, *continued :*
   „   drop of, its buoyancy, V. 117 n ; vii. 1. 6 n.
   „   fall of, its effect on barren rocks, I. 268 ; ii. 3. 4. 14 (ed.
            1–4, 15).
   „   meaning and ministry of, V. 155–56 ; vii. 4. 7–8.
——bow, centre of a, IV. 238 ; v. 15. 33.
      „   meaning of, V. 353 ; ix. 11. 9.
      „   not more enjoyed for a knowledge of optics, III.
              325 ; iv. 17. 42.
——cloud, apertures in, show purest blue sky, I. 272 ; ii. 3.
            4. 20.
      „   beauty of English, V. 154 ; vii. 4. 6.
      „   formation of, V. 146–47 ; vii. 3. 14–16.
      „   obliquity of, V. 160–61 ; vii. 4. 15.
Ramification, V. 54 *seqq.* ; vi. 7. 2 *seqq.*
Ranunculus glacialis pyrenæus, II. 115 ; iii. 1. 13. 11.
Raphael [SYNOPSIS. I. xvii, xxx, xxxii, xxxvi-vii, 4 n, 5, 6, 11, 12,
       37, 87, 95, 116, 120, 130, 147, 163, 175, 367 n, 444.
       II. 8 n, 47, 52, 86, 89, 105, 129, 132, 139, 145, 218,
       232–33, 238, 239, '83 Epil. **III.** 16, 18, 30, 37, 41–2,
       55, 56–9, 59 n, 60–1, 104, 123, 130, 331, 332, 334. 355.
       IV. 1, 49, 53, 59, 376–77, 379. **V.** x, 39, 42, 202–3, 304,
       350 n, 352 n] :—
   architecture of, mere framework, I. 116 ; ii. 1. 7. 29 (om.
      ed. 1, 2).
   author's early reverence for, I. 5 ; i. 1. 1. 4 (ed. 1 only).
      „   „   study of, II. 86 ; iii. 1. 7. 5 ('83 n).
      „   influenced by, V. x ; *pref.* 7.
   chiaroscuro of, I. 180 ; ii. 2. 3. 14 (ed. 1, 2 only).
      „   before colour with, IV. 49 ; v. 3. 18.
   "clear and tasteless poison of," III. 60 ; iv. 4. 18.
   colour of, V. 350 n, 352 n ; ix. 11. 8 n.
   composition, V. 202–3 ; viii. 4. 6.
      „   from the ideal, II. '83 Epil. 9.
   conception, great, I. 11 ; i. 1. 2. 7.
   corruption of, II. 117 ; iii. 1. 14. 14 (ed. 1 only).
   decline of, II. 47 ; iii. 1. 5. 10.
   details of, shells and flowers, I. xxxii ; *pref. ed.* 2. 24.
   engraving from, III. 355 ; App. i.
   figures of, best below life-size, III. 41–2 ; iv. 3. 19.
   finish of (when heaven-taught), II. 89 ; iii. 1. 10. 4.
      „   III. 130 ; iv. 9. 18.

Raphael, *continued :*

flowers in works of, I. 87 ; ii. 1. 7. 9 (om. ed. 1, 2). *See above, s. detail.*

fog hated by, IV. 59 ; v. 4. 2.

foliage of, V. 39 ; vi. 5. 2.

    ,,   distant, V. 42 ; vi. 5. 8.

greatness of, I. xlviii ; *pref. ed.* 2. 42–43.

    ,,   I. 444 ; ii. 6. 3. 13.

holy feeling and light of early works, I. 163 ; ii. 2. 1. 22.

ideal beauty of, II. 140 ; iii. 1. 14. 32.

    ,,   ,, loses beauty's force, III. 37 ; iv. 3. 14.

idealism, example of false (" Charge to Peter "), III. 58 ; iv. 4. 16.

landscape of, I. 95 ; ii. 1. 7. 14 (om. ed. 1, 2).

    ,,   ,, II. 47 ; iii. 1. 5. 10.

    ,,   ,, II. 232–33 ; iii. 2. 5. 10–11.

    ,,   ,, III. 334 ; iv. 18. 14.

    ,,   ,, IV. 60 ; v. 4. 19.

Madonnas of, Italians, not Jewesses, I. 130 ; ii. 1. 7. 37 (om. ed. 1, 2).

Masaccio gives him his figures, Perugino his landscape, III. 334 ; iv. 18. 14.

mountain distances of, IV. 376–77 ; v. 20. 16.

    ,, influence on, IV. 379 ; v. 20. 20.

nativities of, V. 304 ; ix. 8. 1.

Passion, renderings of the, II. 139 ; iii. 1. 14. 31.

Perugino excelled by, I. xvii ; *pref. ed.* 2. 9.

    ,, landscape of, borrowed by, III. 334 ; iv. 18. 14.

picturesque follows on, IV. 1 ; v. 1. 1.

Pisan sculpture, its influence on, IV. 379 ; v. 20. 20.

popularity greatest of his feeblest parts, I. 4 *n* ; i. 1. 1. 1 *n.*

portraiture in his works, II. 129 ; iii. 1. 14. 14.

    ,,   ,,   ,, II. 132 ; iii. 1. 14. 19.

religious art, philosophical ideal, III. 61 ; iv. 4. 20.

rough shade in his work, I. 120 ; ii. 1. 7. 31 (om. ed. 1, 2).

sea-painting of, I. 367 *n* ; ii. 5. 1. 22 *n* (om. ed. 1, 2).

second, more likely than a second Rubens, I. 175 ; ii. 2. 2. 12.

sketches of, V. 202–3 ; viii. 4. 4. 6.

skies of, their subtle gradation, II. 52 ; iii. 1. 5. 18.

study not him, but what he studied, I. 5 ; i. 1. 1. 2.

Raphael, *continued:*
  symbolical works of, III. 104 ; iv. 8. 6.
  works of :

  arabesques (Vatican), I. 12 ; i. 1. 2. 9.
      ,,   ,,   I. 105 ; ii. 1. 7. 22 (om. ed. 1, 2).
  Burning Bush, III. 123 ; iv. 9. 8.
  Cartoons, false realism of, III. 56 ; iv. 4. 14.
      See below, s. Charge to Peter, Miraculous Draught.
  Charge to Peter, I. xxx ; *pref. ed.* 2. 23.
      ,,   ,,   false idealism, III. 58 ; iv. 4. 16.
      ,,   ,,   its background, III. 334 ; iv. 18. 14.
  Holy Family (Uffizii, Tribune), III. 332 ; iv. 18. 12.
  Holy Innocents (Nat. Gall.), II. 139 ; iii. 1. 14. 31.
      ,,   ,,   ,,   ,,   II. 192–93 ; iii. 2. 3. 21.
  Madonna, Ansidei (Nat. Gall., 1171), II. 71 ; iii. 1. 8. 4 (ed.
                                            1 only).
      ,,   del Baldacchino, background, II. 47 ; iii. 1. 5.
                                            10.
      ,,   ,, Cardellino, radiant sky, II. 47 ; iii. 1. 5. 10.
      ,,   dell' Impannata, *ib.* ; *ib.*
      ,,   della Sediola, *ib.* ; *ib.*
      ,,   ,,   ,,   III. 55 ; iv. 4. 12.
      ,,   di San Sisto, I. xvi ; *pref. ed.* 2. 9 (n. ed. 2–4
                                            only).
      ,,   ,,   ,,   false idealism of, III. 61 ; iv. 4. 19.
      ,,   ,,   ,,   symmetry of, II. 71 ; iii. 1. 8. 4
                                            (ed. 1 only).
  Michael the Archangel, II. 238 ; iii. 2. 5. 20.
  Miraculous Draught of Fishes, I. xxx ; *ed. 2 pref.* 23.
      ,,   ,,   ,,   II. 218 ; iii. 2. 4. 12.
      ,,   ,,   ,,   background, III. 334 ; iv. 18.
                                            14.
      ,,   ,,   ,,   ,,   V. 42 ; vi. 5. 8.
      ,,   ,,   ,,   boats in, III. 331 ; iv. 18. 10.
  Nativities, III. 361 ; App. 3.
  S. Catherine, I. xxxii ; *pref. ed.* 2. 24.
      ,,   I. 37 ; i. 2. 1. 5.
      ,,   mouth of, I. 147 ; ii. 1. 7. 47 (ed. 1, 2. 12).
      ,,   ,,   II. 105 ; iii. 1. 12. 10.
      ,,   ,,   II. 239 ; iii. 2. 5. 21 (and '83 *n*).
  S. Cecilia (Bologna), II. 145 ; iii. 1. 15. 6.
      ,,   ,,   II. 233 ; iii. 2. 5. 11.
      ,,   ,,   fiddles in foreground, III. 16 ; iv. 1. 19.
      ,,   ,,   ,,   ,,   III. 18 ; iv. 2. 1.

Raphael : works of, *continued :*

S. Cecilia (Bologna), fiddles in foreground, III. 59 *n* ; iv. 4.
18 *n.*

    ,,   ,,   symmetry of, II. 71 ; iii. 1. 8. 4 (ed. 1
only).

S. John (Tribune), II. 47 ; iii. 1. 5. 10.

Samson and the Lion, II. 218 ; iii. 2. 4. 12.

School of Athens, III. 30 ; iv. 3. 5.

Transfiguration, I. 180 ; ii. 2. 3. 14 (ed. 1, 2 only).

    ,,   ,,   II. 8 *n* ; iii. 1. 1. 7 *n.*

    ,,   ,,   colour in, deficient, IV. 53 ; v. 3. 23.

    ,,   ,,   kicking gracefulness, III. 59 *n* ; iv. 4. 17 *n.*

Rapidity, a quality of execution, I. 40 ; i. 2. 2. 6.

Rarey, on the horse, quoted, V. 284 *n* ; ix. 6. 21 *n.*

Ravines, I. 316 ; ii. 4. 3. 12.

   ,, in lower Alps, IV. 273 ; v. 16. 40-1.

Rays, painting of, by old masters, I. 226-27 ; ii. 3. 1. 18.

Reading aloud, good and bad, IV. 288-89 ; v. 17. 18.

Realism, idealism and, in art, II. 215 ; iii. 2. 4. 9.

   ,, its growth in religious art, III. 51 *seqq.* ; iv. 4. 8 *seqq.*

Reality, no picture reaches the, III. 20 ; iv. 2. 5.

Realization in art, and deception, I. xxxii *n* ; *pref. ed.* 2. 24 *n.*

   ,,   ,,   III. 18 *seqq.* ; iv. 2. 1 *seqq.*

   ,,   ,,   colour *v.* chiaroscuro, IV. 49-50 ; v. 3. 19
seqq.

   ,,   ,,   its growth and influence, III. 51-3 ; iv. 4. 9.

   ,,   ,, ,, relation to colour, III. 148 ; iv. 10. 18.

Reason, moral feelings affecting the, II. 122-23 ; iii. 1. 14. 5.

Recklessness of aim, in great men, V. 253-54 ; ix. 3. 32-3.

Recollection, of natural phenomena, feeble, I. 172 ; ii. 2. 2. 8.

Red, the loveliest of pure colours, IV. 48 ; v. 3. 16. *See s.
Scarlet.*

Reed, in the Bible, III. 241-42 ; iv. 14. 53.

Refinement, analysis of, II. 87 *seqq.* ; iii. 1. 10. 1 *seqq.*

   ,, and toil, V. 360-62 *seqq.* ; ix. 11. 22-3 *seqq.*

   ,, of spiritual and practical minds, V. 310-11 ; ix. 8.
13 *seqq.*

Reflection, essential to the perception of truth, I. 56 ; ii. 1. 2. 5.

Reflections in water, I. 350-51 ; ii. 5. 1. 6-7.

   ,,   ,,   I. 350-54 ; ii. 5. 1. 6-9 (om. ed. 1, 2).

   ,,   ,,   do not repeat what they reflect, I. 380 ; ii.
5. 3. 7.

Reflections in water, *continued :*

„ „ on moving water, elongated, I. 356–57 ; ii. 5. 1. 12 (om. ed. 1, 2).

„ „ surface and, how far jointly visible, I. 376 *seqq.* ; ii. 5. 3. 2 *seqq.*

Reform, not in "heartless abandonment of ancestral custom," III. 312 ; iv. 17. 25.

Reformation, change in ideas of faith, etc., at the, V. 256 *seqq.* ; ix. 4. 2.

„ effect on art, of the, III. 60 ; iv. 4. 18.

„ „ „ V. 256–57 ; ix. 4. 4.

„ „ „ V. 276 ; ix. 6. 4.

„ strength of the, in what, V. 275 *seqq.* ; ix. 6. 1 *seqq.*

Relation, ideas of, I. 14 ; i. 1. 3. 1.

„ „ I. 30–1 ; i. 1. 6. 4.

„ „ I. 32 *seqq.* ; i. 1. 7. 1 *seqq.*

„ „ art's noblest subjects, I. 33 ; i. 1. 7. 3.

„ „ defined, I. 34 ; i. 1. 7. 4.

„ „ object of their study, I. 46 ; i. 2. 3. 6.

„ „ III. 1 ; iv. 1. 1.

„ „ V. 172 *seqq.* ; Parts viii. and ix.

Religion [SYNOPSIS. **I.** xlviii. **II.** '83 *pref.* 6, 150. **III.** 64, 157, 268–69, 318, 358. **IV.** 373, 374, 423. **V.** 228, 239, 241, 321–22] :—

basis of true, II. '83 *pref.* 6.

combination of practice and "theoria," II. 150 ; iii. 1. 15. 12.

desire for some, natural, III. 157 ; iv. 11. 7.

faith and, III. 318 ; iv. 17. 33. *See s. Faith.*

intellectual weakness often seen with intense, V. 228 ; ix. 2. 8 *seqq.*

inquiry into its grounds, how to be made, III. 358 ; App. ii.

mediæval, and contemplation of evil, V. 241 ; ix. 3. 7.

modern, deadness of, I. xlviii ; *pref. ed.* 2. 43.

„ decline of, III. 268–69 ; iv. 16. 10.

mountain influence on, IV. 373 *seqq.* ; v. 20. 12 *seqq.*

northern and southern temper, IV. 374 ; v. 20. 13.

objective and subjective, IV. 423 ; App. iii. 1.

pride of, the worst of all pride, III. 64 ; iv. 4. 24.

seafaring life (*e.g.* Venice) and, V. 239 ; ix. 3. 3.

Religion, *continued:*

    Venice and London (*temp.* Giorgione and Turner), V. 321–22 ; ix. 9. 12–14.

        See s. Advent, Apostles' Creed, Belief, Christ, Cities, Church, Evangelicalism, Faith, Fasting, Free-thought, God, Greece, Immortality, Infidelity, Jesuitism, Man, Manifestation, Monasticism, Monks, Pleading, Prayer, Preaching, Presbyterianism, Protestantism, Puritanism, Revelation, Romanism, Sabbatarianism, Sacrifice, Salvation, Sanctification, Scepticism, Sermons, Superstition, Testimony.

Religious art [SYNOPSIS. **II.** 231. **III.** 30–1, 51 *seqq.*, 53–4, 60–2, 64–5, 267, 269. **IV.** 376] :—

    artists' character, vanity of modern, III. 30–1 ; iv. 3. 6.

      ,,   feeling for their work, III. 53–4 ; iv. 4. 10.

    early and later, III. 51 *seqq.* ; iv. 4. 7 *seqq.*

    excitement created by some, morbid, III. 61 ; iv. 4. 19.

    ideal, growth of, undermines religion, III. 53 ; iv. 4. 9.

      ,,   true ideals of, III. 61–2 ; iv. 4. 20.

    landscape, symmetrical, II. 231 ; iii. 2. 5. 9.

    later, dull in unreality, III. 60 ; iv. 4. 18.

    limited influence of, III. 62 ; iv. 4. 21.

      ,,   ,,   ,, *e.g.* picture in a room, III. 60; iv. 4. 19.

    modern, dangers of, III. 64–5 ; iv. 4. 24.

      ,,   landscape, wholly secular, III. 267 ; iv. 16. 7.

      ,,   no real, III. 269 ; iv. 16. 10.

    steep mountain distances in, IV. 376 ; v. 20. 16.

    "the monk's opera or theatre-going," III. 61 ; iv. 4. 19.

Rembrandt [SYNOPSIS. **I.** 11, 88, 96, 183 *n*, 429 and *n.* **II.** 45, 218. **III.** 39, 274, 337, 343. **IV.** 42–5, 49, 59, 65–6. **V.** ix, 262, 279, 283] :—

    author's early admiration of, V. ix ; *pref.* 7.

    chiaroscuro, I. 180 ; II. 2. 3. 14 (ed. 1, 2 only). *See below, s. etchings.*

      ,,   III. 39 ; iv. 3. 16.

      ,,   and colour-system, IV. 42–5 ; v. 3. 11–13.

      ,,   before colour with, IV. 49 ; v. 3. 18.

      ,,   photographic, IV. 65–6 ; v. 4. 11.

    colour-system of, IV. 48 ; v. 3. 16. *See above, s. chiaroscuro.*

      ,,   sombre, III. 274 ; iv. 16. 18.

      ,,   ,,   and sullen, IV. 59 ; v. 4. 2.

    dogs in his works, V. 283 ; ix. 6. 19.

Rembrandt, *continued :*

    etchings, better than his canvases, I. 96 ; ii. 1. 7. 15 (om.
        ed. 1, 2).

      „   I. 183 *n* ; ii. 2. 2. 20 *n* (om. ed. 1, 2).

      „   chiaroscuro of, I. 429 and *n* ; ii. 6. 1. 31 *n* (om.
        ed. 1, 2).

    excepted by author from Dutch school, I. 11 ; i. 1. 2. 7.

    finish deficient, I. 88 ; ii. 1. 7. 10 (om. ed. 1, 2).

    ideality in treatment (Spotted Shell), II. 218 ; iii. 2. 4. 11.

    landscape of, III. 337 ; iv. 18. 20.

    scriptural subjects of, V. 279 ; ix. 6. 10.

    single truth only in each picture (cf. Veronese), III. 39 ;
        iv. 3. 16.

    tree-drawing of, I. 388 ; ii. 6. 1. 14 (ed. 3, 4 only).

    Turner's study of, III. 343 ; iv. 18. 29.

    unspiritual, V. 262 ; ix. 4. 14.

    vulgarity, etc., of, III. 274 ; iv. 16. 18.

    works of :

        Presentation in the Temple, II. 45 ; iii. 1. 5. 7.

        Spotted Shell, II. 218 ; iii. 2. 4. 11.

        Wife and Himself (Dresden), his greatest work, V. 279 ; ix.
        6. 10.

Remorse, for neglect of friends since dead, I. 7 ; i. 1. 1. 5.

Renaissance [SYNOPSIS. **III.** 67, 68, 198, 270-71, 273-74, 328.
        IV. 380-81, 390-92. **V.** 196] :—

    architecture, IV. 380-81 ; v. 20. 23.

      „   desire for greatness, V. 196 ; viii. 3. 3.

    arts of, III. 68 ; iv. 5. 4.

    climax of, in ugliness and gloom, III. 270 ; iv. 16. 12.

    effect on colour of, III. 273-74 ; iv. 16. 18.

    fatal effects of, III. 274 ; iv. 16. 19.

    grasp of, by Browning and Shakspere, IV. 390-92 ; v. 20.
        33-4.

    landscape, hackneyed type of, III. 198 ; iv. 13. 26.

    painting of mythology, III. 67 ; iv. 5. 3.

    reaction from, in love of nature, III. 270-71 ; iv. 16. 13.

    spirit of the, IV. 392 ; v. 20. 34.

    Turner, and its affectations, III. 328 ; iv. 18. 4.

Repose, artistic, love and value of, II. 70 ; iii. 1. 7. 1.

    „   characteristic of the eternal mind, II. 70 ; iii. 1. 7. 1.

    „   consistent with ideal organic form, II. 116; iii. 1. 13. 12.

Repose, *continued :*
„   expression of, in matter, II. 71 ; iii. 1. 7. 2.
„   implies energy, II. 72 ; iii. 1. 7. 3.
„   in the Laocoon, II. 74 ; iii. 1. 7. 6.
„   „ M. Angelo's Plague of Serpents, II. 74 ; iii. 1. 7. 6 *n.*
„   „ Turner's Rietz, V. 184–87 ; viii. 2. 3 *seqq.*
„   scenery and, I. 288 ; ii. 4. 1. 3.
„   test of great art and beauty, II. 73–4 ; iii. 1. 7. 5.
„   value of, in spiritual work, II. 237 ; iii. 2. 5. 19.
Réposoir, Mt., III. 145 ; iv. 10. 15.
„   „ IV. 254 ; v. 16. 20.
„   „ convent of, IV. 260 ; v. 16. 26.
Repulsiveness, overcome by custom, II. 34 ; iii. 1. 4. 5.
Resegone, Il (Comasque Alps), IV. 162 ; v. 12. 21.
Resemblance, recognition of by single attributes, I. 59–60 ; ii. 1
            2. 8.
„   truth and, III. 135 ; iv. 10. 3.
Reserve, of great artists, V. 199 ; viii. 3. 8.
„   „   „ V. 200 *seqq.* ; viii. 4. 1 *seqq.*
„   of true gentleman, V. 290–92 ; ix. 7. 8. 9.
Resilience, law of (especially in leaves), V. 34–5 ; vi. 4. 14.
„   „   „   „ V. 68 ; vi. 7. 19.
„   „   „   „ V. 71 ; vi. 8. 6.
„   „   „   „ V. 79 ; vi. 8. 12.
„   „   „   „ V. 82 ; vi. 8. 18.
Rest, human love of, II. 70 ; iii. 1. 7. 1.
„   lines of, IV. 292 ; v. 17. 21.
„   „ IV. 302 ; v. 17. 32.
„   „ IV. 328–29 ; v. 18. 13 *seqq.*
Restoration, ruin of, I. 111–12 ; ii. 1. 7. 26 (om. ed. 1, 2).
„   „   I. 123–24 ; ii. 1. 7. 34 (*ib.*).
„   „   II. 88 ; iii. 1. 10. 3.
„   „   III. 98–9 ; iv. 7. 21.
„   „   IV. 13 ; v. 1. 14.
Restraint, and liberty, II. 90 *seqq.* ; iii. 1. 10. 5 *seqq.*
„   beauty of, IV. 284 ; v. 17. 10.
„   „   IV. 288 ; v. 17. 18.   *See s. Moderation.*
Rethel, Alfred, woodcuts of (Death Avenger and Friend), III.
            106–8 ; iv. 8. 8–9.
„   „   „ IV. 410 ; App. i. 5.
Retsch's illustrations, Schiller's Kampf mit dem Drachen, II.
        183 ; iii. 2. 3. 12.

Reuss, the, Lucerne, IV. 344 ; v. 19. 11.
Revelation, divine, V. 223 ; ix. 1. 11–12.
   ,,   leaf's lesson, V. 83 ; vi. 8. 19.
   ,,   narrow English ideas of, III. 151 ; iv. 10. 22
   ,,   national greatness based on, V. 84–5 ; vi. 8. 19.
Reverence. *See s. Religion, Veneration.*
Reynolds, Sir J. [SYNOPSIS. I. xxi *n*, xxvii–viii, xxviii–ix, xxxi–ii, 8,
                48, 67, 88, 214. II. 217. III. 3, 5, 7, 16–17,
                23, 26, 27, 105, 344. IV. 69 and *n*, 79, 247.
                V. 214, 262, 316–17, 346, 350 *n*, 353 *n*]:—
  characteristics of :
      dash and speed of, IV. 69 and *n* ; v. 4. 16 and *n*.
        ,,   ,,   V. 214 ; viii. 4. 21.
      colour of, V. 350 *n* ; ix. 11. 8 *n*.
        ,,   V. 353 *n* ; ix. 11. 8 *n*.
      finish deficient, I. 88 ; ii. 1. 7. 10 (om. ed. 1, 2).
      gentleness of, V. 214 ; viii. 4. 21.
      influence of early life on, V. 318 ; ix. 9. 7.
      mystery and vagueness, IV. 79 ; v. 5. 15.
      poetical temper of, IV. 247 ; v. 16. 11.
      subtlety and tenderness of, IV. 69 *n* ; v. 4. 16 *n.*
      unspiritual, V. 262 ; ix. 4. 14.
  costume of his time, V. 316–17 ; ix. 9. 3.
  lectures wrong, his pictures right, III. 27 ; iv. 3. 2.
  paints sunlight rarely, V. 346 ; ix. 11. 3.
  quoted :
      paper in the *Idler*, III. 3 *seqq.* ; iv. 1. 4 *seqq.*
      on existence of beauty, III. 26 ; iv. 3. 1.
      ,, detail and breadth in art, I. xxxii–iii ; *pref. ed.* 2. 25.
      ,, Dutch school, "slowest intellect succeeds best," III.
          5 ; iv. 1. 5.
      ,, Gainsborough, I. xxi *n* ; *pref. ed.* 2. 13 *n*.
      ,, generalization, I. xxix *seqq.* ; *pref. ed.* 2. 21 *seqq.*
      ,, idealism, I. xxvii–viii ; *pref. ed.* 2. 19–20.
      ,, imitative art, III. 16 ; iv. 1. 19.
      ,,   ,,   III. 23 ; iv. 2. 8.
      ,, Italian school, III. 5 *seqq.* ; iv. 1. 5 *seqq.*
      ,, over-finish, I. 214 ; ii. 2. 5. 1/.
      ,, "paint a cat or a fiddle" (*Idler*, No. 79), I. 22 ; i.
          1. 4. 5.
      ,, poetry and history, III. 7 ; iv. 1. 8.
      ,, rules of picture-making, I. 48 ; ii. 1. 1. 3.

Reynolds, Sir J. : quoted, *continued:*

        on shadows and light, I. 180 ; ii. 2. 3. 13 (ed. 1, 2 only).

        „ technical knowledge, I. 8 ; i. 1. 2. 1.

        „ texture, how to be rendered, II. 217 ; iii. 2. 4. 11.

        „ truth in art, I. 67 ; ii. 1. 3. 8.

        „ Venetian school, III. 16 ; iv. 1. 19.

     squirearchy of, V. 318 ; ix. 9. 7.

     Turner's study of, III. 344 ; iv. 18. 30.

     works of :

        Charity, III. 105 ; iv. 8. 7.

        Holy Family (Nat. Gall., 78), I, xxxi ; *pref. ed.* 2. 23.

Rheims, cathedral of, IV. 275 ; v. 16. 42.

     „   „   IV. 381 ; v. 20. 23.

Rheinfelden bridge, V. 368 *n* ; ix. 11. 30 *n* (pl. 83).

Rhine, basalt borders of the, IV. 260 ; v. 16. 27.

Rhododendron, II. 79 ; iii. 1. 8. 3.

     „   leaf, V. 29–30 ; vi. 4. 8–10.

     „   „ V. 32 *seqq.* ; vi. 4. 12–13.

     „   shoot, V. 107 *n* ; vi. 10. 19 *n.*

     „   type of trefoil tree-structure, V. 21 ; vi. 3. 13.

Rhone, colour of the, I. 354–55 ; ii. 5. 1. 10 (om. ed. 1, 2).

     „   valley of the, IV. 100 ; v. 7. 6.

     „   „   its formation, IV. 174 ; v. 13. 11.

     „   „   „ size, IV. 176 ; v. 13. 12.

     „   „   once a glacier, IV. 178 ; v. 13. 16.

     „   „   IV. 297 ; v. 17. 28 (débris).

     „   „   IV. 337 ; v. 19. 3.

Richard Cœur de Lion, blue eyes of, III. 158 ; iv. 11. 9.

Richardson, love and study of nature by, III. 302 ; iv. 17. 7.

     „   works of :

        Clarissa (unread by author, 1856), III. 313 ; iv. 17. 27.

        Pamela, *ib.* ; *ib.*

Richelieu, subtlety of, V. 295 ; ix. 7. 15.

Richmond, George, in Rome, II. 73 ; iii. 1. 7. 5 ('83 *n*).

———— Hill, view from, IV. 366 ; v. 20. 2. *See s. Turner.*

Riffelhorn, Mt. Cervin from the, IV. 190–91 ; v. 14. 12.

     „   precipices of, IV. 245–46 and *n* ; v. 16. 8–9 and *n.*

Rigi, railway on the, I. 278 ; ii. 3. 4. 31. F.A. *n* (ed. 1–4. 34).

     „ (Turner's Goldau), IV. 332–33 ; v. 18. 22.

Right, two wrongs may make a, in art, II. 161 ; iii. 2. 2. 6 ('83 *n*).

Rio, Forme de l'Art, quoted, II. 132 ; iii. 1. 14. 19.

   ,,   ,,   ,,   ,,   II. 145 ; iii. 1. 15. 6.

   ,,   ,,   ,,   ,,   V. 226 ; ix. 2. 4.

Ripples on water, effect of, I. 355–57 ; ii. 5. 1. 11–14 (om. ed. 1, 2).

Rivalry, baseness of, V. 387 ; ix. 12. 20.

River-gods, Greek, III. 181–82 ; iv. 13. 6–7.

Rivers, finding not cutting their way, IV. 100–1 ; v. 7. 6.

Roberts, David [SYNOPSIS.   I. 125-27, 303, 433.   II. '83 Epil. 1. 14] :—

    at author's birthday dinner, II. '83 Epil. 14.

    author's early imitation of, II. '83 Epil. 1.

    drawing of, exquisite, I. 76 ; ii. 1. 7. 8 *n* (ed. 1, 2 only).

       ,,   of architecture, I. 125 ; ii. 1. 7. 35.

       ,,   ,,   I. 433 ; ii. 6. 2. 1.

    Egyptian temple hieroglyphics, I. 126 ; ii. 1. 7. 35.

    European reputation of, I. 125 ; ii. 1. 7. 35 (om. ed. 1, 2).

    hills of, I. 303 ; ii. 4. 3. 28 (ed. 1–4 only).

    works of :

        European sketches, foliage, I. 396 ; ii. 6. 1. 27 *n* (ed. 1, 2 only).

        Holy Land, I. 125 ; ii. 1. 7. 35 (om. ed. 1, 2).

        Roslin Chapel (1844), I. 127 ; ii. 1. 7. 35 (om. ed. 1, 2).

Robson, G., character of his works, praised, I. 101 ; ii. 1. 7. 20 (om. ed. 1, 2).

   ,,   ,,   ,,   ,,   I. 375*n* ; ii. 5. 2. 12 *n* (mountain-tarns).

   ,,   cloudiness of, IV. 59 ; v. 4. 2.

   ,,   unaffected but uninventive, III. 278 ; iv. 16. 26.

Rochdale manufacturers, V. 358 ; ix. 11. 17.

Rochers des Fys (Col d'Anterne), cliff of, IV. 254 ; v. 16. 20.

Rocks [SYNOPSIS.   I. xxxv, 76, 179, 314, 328-31.   III. 120, 196 *seqq*., 247, 254-55.   IV. 105, 111, 113-15, 120, 122-26, 127-36, 143, 165, 215, 255, 267 *seqq*., 319-20.   V. 127] :—

    chiaroscuro of, I. 330 ; ii. 4. 4. 4 (ed. 1, 2. 6).

    colour of, I. 178–79 ; ii. 2. 2. 16–17.

       ,,   IV. 113–15 ; v. 8. 14–15.

       ,,   IV. 127–36 ; v. 9. 10 *seqq*.

       ,,   IV. 143 ; v. 11. 11.

    crystalline, their composition, IV. 111 ; v. 8. 10.

    curvature of, I. 314–15 ; ii. 4. 3. 10.

       ,,   I. 330 *n* ; ii. 4. 4. 3 *n* (om. ed. 1, 2).

Rocks, *continued :*

    curvature of, IV. 158–60 ; v. 12. 20 *seqq.*

        „   IV. 224–25 ; v. 15. 20.

    different kinds of, I. 328 ; ii. 4. 4. 1.

    division into primary, etc., IV. 105 *seqq.* ; v. 8. 1 *seqq.*

        „   „   „   IV. 165 ; v. 13. 1.

    drawing of, by ancient landscapists, I. 330–31 ; ii. 4. 4. 5
                (ed. 1, 2, § 7).

        „   „ Claude and others, IV. 267 *seqq.* ; v. 16.
                35 *seqq.*

        „   mediæval, III. 254–55 ; iv. 15. 16 (pl. 10).

    feeling for, by mediævals and moderns, IV. 319–20 ;
        v. 18. 2.

    formation of, I. 76 ; ii. 1. 6. 1.

        „   IV. 120 ; v. 9. 1.

    generalization of, impossible, I. xxxiv–v ; *pref. ed.* 2. 27–8.

    highest, the hardest, IV. 165 ; v. 13. 1.

    in Homer, III. 196 *seqq.* ; iv. 13. 24 *seqq.*

        „   III. 247 ; iv. 15. 7.

    nature's finishing off of, III. 120 ; iv. 9. 6.

    structure of, junction of slaty and compact crystallines, IV.
        215 ; v. 15. 12.

    undulated substance of, IV. 122–26 ; v. 9. 5–6.

        „   surface of stratified, V. 127 ; vii. 2. 9.

    white, in Homer and Dante, III. 248 ; iv. 15. 7.

        See s. Dante, Mountains.

Rogers, Samuel, owns " Magdalen " by Titian (now in Nat.
              Gall.), V. 252 ; ix. 3. 29.

    „   „   „ picture by R. Wilson, I. 98 ; ii. 1. 7.
              17 (om. ed. 1, 2).

    „   „   works of, quoted :

                on Amalfi (" Italy "), II. 244 ; Add. 4 (om.
                  ed. 1).

                „ M. Angelo, II. 199 *n* ; iii. 2. 3. 28.

                vignettes and engravings to :

                  by Goodall, I. 183 *n* ; ii. 2. 2. 20 *n* (om.
                    ed. 1, 2).

             „   „ Datur Hora Quieti, I. 155 ;
                  ii. 2. 1. 10.

             „   „ Datur Hora Quieti, I. 183 *n* ;
                  ii. 2. 2. 20 *n* (om. ed.
                  1, 2).

Rogers, Samuel, works of, quoted : *continued:*

vignettes and engravings to, *continued:*

by Jacqueline, II. 225 ; iii. 2. 4. 20 (Poems p. 144).

Poems (pp. 7, 80, 192), sunbeams, I. 226 ; ii. 3. 1. 17.

  ,,   (p. 80), sunbeams, I. 235 ; ii. 3. 2. 11.

See s. Turner (III. Works of) ;— Rogers' " Italy," " Poems."

Rokeby, Turner's love of, IV. 261 ; v. 16. 28.

Romanism [SYNOPSIS. II. 138, 229–30. III. 60–1, 269. IV. 351, 353–55, 359, 375, 424. V. 275–76] :—

art and, III. 60–1 ; iv. 4. 19.

  ,,   tawdry art of, IV. 353–54 ; v. 19. 23.

best points of, due to mountain influence, IV. 375 ; v. 20. 14.

gloom of character, IV. 353 *seqq.* ; v. 19. 23.

idleness encouraged by, IV. 354 ; v. 19. 23.

in lowlands and mountains, IV. 375–76 ; v. 20. 14–15.

logical training of, IV. 424 ; App. iii. 2.

morbid love of horrors, II. 138 ; iii. 1. 14. 29.

  ,,   ,,   ,,   especially modern, IV. 351 ; v. 19. 20.

Protestantism and, division of, III. 269 ; iv. 16. 10.

  ,,   ,,   ,,   IV. 353–55 ; v. 19. 23.

  ,,   ,,   tempers of, compared, IV. 375 ; v. 20. 14.

purgatory, morbid contemplation of, IV. 354 ; v. 19. 23.

Reformation and, V. 275–76 ; ix. 6. 2–4.

representation of God and the Madonna in, II. 229–30 ; iii. 2. 5. 7.

superstition encouraged by, IV. 354 ; v. 19. 23.

Swiss (the Valais), IV. 359 ; v. 19. 29.

Romanesque art up to 1200, III. 215 ; iv. 14. 20.

  ,,   façades, author's love of, II. 220 ; iii. 2. 4. 14.

Romantic association, charm of, peculiar to modern Europe, and why, III. 310 ; iv. 17. 21.

Romanticism, modern, III. 281–82 ; iv. 16. 32.

Rome [SYNOPSIS. I. 5, 97, 165. II. 64 *n*, 170, 220, '83 Epil. 7. 13. III. 71, 109, 145, 156. IV. 372. V. 132, 284, 349 *n*, 357, 369] :—

ancient, intellectual lead of, IV. 372 *seqq.* ; v. 20. 11 *seqq.*

Rome, *continued:*

 ancient, its fall, and the lesson of it, V. 369 ; ix. 11. 31.

  „ no landscape painting in, III. 156 ; iv. 11. 5.

  „ worst days of, art in, III. 71 ; iv. 5. 7.

 art, colour of, bad, V. 349 *n* ; ix. 11. 8 *n.*

  „ horse in, V. 284 ; ix. 6. 22.

  „ modern degraded, I. 5 ; i. 1. 2.

 military asceticism, V. 357 ; ix. 11. 17.

 mountain form, IV. 372 ; v. 20. 11.

 surroundings and works of art in :

   Campagna and country round, bad for young landscapists,
     I. 97 ; ii. 1. 7. 17 (om. ed. 1, 2).

    „ described, I. 165 ; ii. 2. 2. 2.

    „ horse-racing in the, III. 145 ; iv. 10. 14.

   Camuccini Titian, II. 170 ; iii. 2. 2. 19.

   Coliseum, V. 132 ; vii. 2. 14.

   St. Peter's, exaggeration of parts, II. 64 *n* ; iii. 1. 6. 10 *n.*

   Sistine Chapel, ceiling, II. 220 ; iii. 2. 4. 14.

    „   „ frescoes of Botticelli and Perugino (author's
        work on, 1874), II. '83 Epil. 13.

    „   „ life of Moses, II. '83 Epil. 7.

   Temple of Antoninus and Faustina, griffin, III. 109 ; iv. 8.
    11 (pl. 1).

Romney Marsh, IV. 367 ; v. 20. 3.

Roots of a tree, V. 46 ; vi. 6. 4.

Rosa. *See s. Monte Rosa, Salvator Rosa.*

Rose, admired most of flowers, because no shadow in it, IV.
 48 ; v. 3. 16.

 „ artificial, not a rose at all, III. 36 *n* ; iv. 3. 12 *n.*

 „ -colour, of dawn in hill-country, IV. 368 ; v. 20. 4.

 „ leaf of the tree, III. 217–18 ; iv. 14. 24.

 „ petals, form of, V. 38 ; vi. 5. 1.

 „ „ growth of, V. 64–5 ; vi. 7. 14.

 „ scent of, particles making it, V. 118 ; vii. 1. 7.

 „ wild, its beauty, II. 93 ; iii. 1. 11. 1 ('83 Introd. Note).

 „ „ IV. 368 ; v. 20. 5.

      See s. Alpine Rose.

Rosini, Abbé, and author at Pisa, 1845, II. '83 Epil. 9.

Roslin Chapel, drawing of, by D. Roberts, I. 127 ; ii. 1. 7. 35
  (om. ed. 1, 2).

 „ „ III. 328 ; iv. 18. 4.

Rossberg, fall of the, IV. 163 *n* ; v. 12. 22 *n.*

„   „   „   IV. 331–32 ; v. 18. 20–1.

See s. Turner's Goldau (pl. 50)

Rosselli, Cosimo, fresco S. Ambrogio, Florence, II. 60 *n* ; iii. 1. 6. 8 *n.*

Rossetti, symbolical power of, III. 106 ; iv. 8. 7.

Rotterdam, III. 299 ; iv. 17. 4.

„   no Shakspere produced by, IV. 383 ; v. 20. 27.

Roubilliac, tombs by, II. 75 ; iii. 1. 7. 7.

Rouen Cathedral, fretted front of, I. 15 ; i. 1. 3. 2.

„   „   IV. 275 ; v. 16. 42.

„   „   IV. 381 ; v. 20. 22.

„   Church of St. Nicholas, destroyed, II. 7 *n* ; iii. 1. 1. 7 *n.*

„   old buildings at, destroyed, *ib.* ; *ib.*

Rouges, Aiguilles, IV. 206 ; v. 15. 2.

Royal Academy, bad hanging of pictures at, I. 106 *n* ; ii. 1. 7. 22 *n* (om. ed. 1, 2).

„   „   duties of, *ib.* ; *ib. (ib.).*

„   „   notes on pictures in, before 1848, II. 241 ; Add. 1 (om. ed. 1).

„   „   taught Turner nothing but error, III. 327 ; iv. 18. 3.

See s. Author, Leighton, Martin.

Royal road, none to anywhere worth going to, III. 319 ; iv. 17. 35.

Rubbish-heap, plants growing on, V. 105 ; vi. 10. 14.

Rubens [SYNOPSIS. I. 11, 41, 88, 96, 163, 170, 175, 179, 233, 359. II. 2, 88 *n*, 134, 146, 192 *n*. III. 36, 104–5, 123, 193, 333, 337–38. IV. 15. V. x, 39, 100, 214, 262, 277–81, 283, 286, 346] :—

allegory in, V. 279 ; ix. 6. 10.

author's early reverence for, I. 175 ; ii. 2. 2. 12.

„   praise of, in " Modern Painters," Vol. I., regretted, V. x ; *pref.* 7.

calibre of mind, unique, I. 175 ; ii. 2. 2. 12.

character, V. 277–78 ; ix. 6. 8.

chiaroscuro, I. 175 ; ii. 2. 2. 12.

colour, black and yellow its keynotes, I. 179 ; ii. 2. 2. 17.

combines chiaroscuro and colour, I. 180 ; ii. 2. 3. 14 (ed. 1 only).

Cuyp and, V. 275–86 ; ix. 6. 1 *seqq.*

descriptions of his pictures, V. 277–79 ; ix. 6. 6. *seqq.*

Rubens, *continued :*

> distinguished by author from Dutch school, I. 11; i. 1. 2. 7.
>
> dogs in his pictures, V. 283 ; ix. 6. 19.
>
> finish deficient, I. 88 ; ii. 1. 7. 10 (om. ed. 1, 2).
>
>   „   „   through impetuosity, II. 88 *n*; iii. 1. 10. 3 *n.*
>
> flowers of, ill-done, V. 100 ; vi. 10. 5.
>
> glory of, I. 163 ; ii. 2. 1. 22.
>
> grace and mystery deficient, IV. 15 ; v. 1. 17.
>
> horse first much painted by, V. 285 ; ix. 6. 22.
>
> hunting-pieces, V. 277 ; ix. 6. 7.
>
>   „   „   V. 281 ; ix. 6. 13.
>
>   „   „   V. 283 ; ix. 6. 19.
>
> landscape of, I. 96 ; ii. 1. 7. 15 (om. ed. 1, 2).
>
>   „   license, I. 96 ; ii. 1. 7. 15 (om. ed. 1, 2).
>
>   „   I. 184 ; ii. 2. 4. 6 (ed. 1, 2 only).
>
>   „   III. 193 ; iv. 13. 20.
>
>   „   III. 337 ; iv. 18. 20.
>
>   „   and Pre-Raphaelite compared, III. 333 ; iv. 18. 12.
>
>   „   pastoral, V. 279 ; ix. 6. 10.
>
> leaf-drawing of, V. 39 ; vi. 5. 3.
>
> letters of, quoted, V. 214 ; viii. 4. 21.
>
>   „   „   V. 278 ; ix. 6. 8.
>
> martyrdoms, delight in, V. 277 ; ix. 6. 6.
>
> power of, covers other faults, V. 286 ; ix. 6. 23.
>
> profane subjects, his best, V. 277 ; ix. 6. 5.
>
> realistic temper of, III. 104–5 ; iv. 8. 6–7.
>
> religion of, V. 278 ; ix. 6. 9.
>
> "s'amuse à être ambassadeur," II. 2 ; iii. 1. 1. 2.
>
> second, less likely than a second Raphael or Titian, I. 175 ; ii. 2. 2. 12.
>
> sense of beauty deficient, II. 146 ; iii. 1. 15–17.
>
>   „   „   sacrifice to truth, III. 36–7 ; iv. 3. 12.
>
> sensuality of, II. 134 ; iii. 1. 14. 24.
>
> skies of, colour, I. 170 ; ii. 2. 2. 7.
>
>   „   horizons, I. 359 ; ii. 5. 1. 16.
>
> sun in his works, III. 338 ; iv. 18. 23.
>
> sunlight seldom painted by, V. 346 ; ix. 11. 3.
>
> symbolical works of, III. 104–5 ; iv. 8. 6–7.
>
> unspiritual, V. 262 ; ix. 4. 14.

Rubens, *continued:*

unspiritual, no religious feeling, V. 277–78 ; ix. 6. 7–9.

works of :

    Antwerp, "Adoration of Magi," I. 41 ; i. 2. 2. 7.

        ,,   "Crucifixion," II. 191–92 and *n* ; iii. 2. 3. 20 *n.*

        ,,   St. John, V. 277 ; ix. 6. 6.

    Berlin, picture of sunlight, V. 346 *n* ; ix. 11. 3 *n.*

    Brussels, Christ and St. Francis, V. 277 ; ix. 6. 6.

        ,,   Martyrdom of Bishops, *ib.* ; *ib.*

    Cologne, St. Peter's, V. 277 ; ix. 6. 6.

    Dulwich, No. 175, rainbow, I. 96 ; ii. 1. 7. 15 (om. ed. 1, 2).

        ,,   ,,   error of light, I. 175 ; ii. 2. 2. 12.

        ,,   No. 187, Marie de' Medici, III. 105 ; iv. 8. 6.

    Düsseldorf, Madonna, V. 277 ; ix. 6. 6.

    Florence, Pitti, landscape compared with Titian next it, I. 96 ;

        ii. 1. 7. 15 (om. ed. 1, 2).

    London (Nat. Gall.) :—

        No. 66, His own Villa, I. 184 ; ii. 2. 4. 6 (ed. 1, 2 only).

        ,, 67, His own Family as a Holy Family, V. 278 ;

        ix. 6. 9.

        ,, 157, Sunset, I. 96 ; ii. 1. 7. 15 (om. ed. 1, 2).

        ,,   ,,   ,, fleecy clouds, I. 233 ; ii. 3. 2. 9.

    Louvre, sun in work at, I. 97 ; ii. 1. 7. 15 (om. ed. 1–3).

        ,,   ,,   ,,   III. 338 ; iv. 18. 23.

    Munich, Last Judgment, V. 277 ; ix. 6. 6.

    various, Battle of Amazons, V. 277 ; ix. 6. 5.

        ,,   Daniel in Lions' Den, V. 277 ; ix. 6. 7.

        ,,   Waggoner, tree stem from, III. 123 ; iv. 9. 8.

Ruins, continental and English compared, IV. 3 ; v. 1. 3.

  ,,   of ancient monuments, etc., throughout Europe, II. 6 *n* ;

      iii. 1. 1. 7 *n.*

  ,,   pictures of, conventional, I. 119 ; ii. 1. 7. 31 (om. ed. 1, 2).

      See s. Picturesque.

  ,,   plants growing on, V. 105 ; vi. 10. 14.

Rules, of art, genius and inventive power needs none, III. 91–4 ;

    iv. 7. 11–12.

Runnymede, association of ideas and, II. 35 ; iii. 1. 4. 7.

Rupert's, Prince, drop, II. 167 ; iii. 2. 2. 13.

Rural population, to be educated, III. 74 ; iv. 5. 13.

Russia, Emperor of (d. 1855), saying of, during Crimea, IV.

    410–11 ; App. i. 5–6.

Rustic, implied reproach of word, V. 4 ; vi. 1. 4.

Ruysdael [SYNOPSIS. I. 6, 346, 348, 365, 370. **V.** 39, 136]:—
    author's depreciation of, I. 6 ; i. 1. 1, 4.
    clouds of, false, V. 136 ; vii. 2. 19.
    few rough seas of, I. 339 *n* ; ii. 5. 1. 21 *n* (ed. 3 only).
       ,,   ,,   I. 339 ; ii. 5. 1. 22 (ed. 1, 2).
    leaf-drawing of, V. 39 ; vi. 5. 3.
    waterfalls, I. 345–46 ; ii. 5. 1. 2.
       ,,   I. 348 ; ii. 5. 1. 5.
       ,,   I. 365 ; ii. 5. 1. 21.
       ,,   I. 370 ; ii. 5. 2. 2.
    work of, Louvre sea-piece, I. 365 ; ii. 5. 1. 21 (om. ed. 1, 2).

Sabbatarianism, English, III. 151–52 ; iv. 10. 22.
       ,,   ,,   V. 322 ; ix. 9. 13.
Sacrifice, first-fruits, etc., value of the idea, III. 205 ; iv. 14. 7.
    ,, glory of self-, in tree growth, V. 59 ; vi. 7. 7.
Sad-coloured dress, III. 251 ; iv. 15. 13.
Saddleback (Cumberland hills), its formation, I. 316 ; ii. 4. 3.
    12 (om. ed. 1, 2).
Sailors, life of, sea and sky, their companions, V. 4 ; vi. 1. 4.
       ,,   ,, superstition of, V. 239 ; ix. 3. 3.
       ,, love of massive beauty, V. 240 ; ix. 3. 5.
Sails, comparison of leaf forms to, V. 23 *seqq.* ; vi. 4. 1 *seqq.*
Sainsbury, W., editor of "Rubens' Letters," V. 278 *n* ; ix.
    6. 8 *n.*
Saint Anthony, visions of, II. 151 ; iii. 2. 1 (Introd. Note '83,
    § 3).
—— Augustine, II. 71 ; iii. 1. 7. 1.
—— Bernard, by Lake Leman, his indifference to nature, III.
    305 ; iv. 17. 10.
—— Dominic, IV. 373 ; v. 20. 12.
—— Francis of Assisi, love of birds, II. 98 ; iii. 1. 12. 2.
    ,,   ,,   ,, III. 156 ; iv. 11. 6.
    ,,   ,,   ,, IV. 373, 375 ; v. 20. 12, 15.
—— George in Aliga (Church, Venice), III. 335 ; iv. 18. 15
    (pl. 15).
—— Gervais described, III. 145–46 ; iv. 10. 15.
—— Gothard, devil's bridge on, III. 246 ; iv. 15. 5.
    ,,   ,, Faido Pass, IV. 22 ; v. 2. 9 (pl. 20, 21).
    ,,   ,, Saussure on, IV. 422 ; App. ii. 5.
—— Jean de Maurienne, valley of, I. 289–90 ; ii. 4. 1. 5.
    ,,   ,,   ,,   ,, V. 161 ; vii. 4. 17.

Saint Jerome, V. 242 ; ix. 3. 9.
—— Louis, the saintliest king, III. 352 ; iv. 18 (39).
—— Mark's mosaics, II. 220 ; iii. 2. 4. 14.
—— Magdalen in the desert, V. 242 ; ix. 3. 9.
—— Martin's, Savoy, IV. 169 ; v. 13. 6.
—— Mary of Egypt, V. 242 ; ix. 3. 9.
—— Michael's Mount, II. 200 n ; iii. 2. 3. 28 n.
—— Michel (Savoy), limestone ridge, V. 142 ; vii. 3. 11.
   „   „   „   precipice near, V. 161 ; vii. 4. 17.
—— Paul, I. 65 ; ii. 1. 3. 6.
   „   „ presence of, weakly, II. 124 ; iii. 1. 14. 7.
   „   „ representation of (S. Cecilia, Bologna), III. 59 n ·
           iv. 4. 17 n.
   „   „ visions of, II. 151 ; iii. 2. 1 (Introd. Note '83, § 3).
—— Peter, falling before the sword, V. 242 ; ix. 3. 9.
—— Pierre, study and love of nature, III. 302 ; iv. 17. 7.
   „   „   "Virginie," III. 313 ; iv. 17. 27.
—— Sebald, shrine of (Nuremberg), V. 258 ; ix. 4. 6.
—— Simeon Stylites, V. 9 ; vi. 2. 4.
—— Stephen, stoning of, IV. 319 ; v. 18. 2.
—— Veronica, V. 251 ; ix. 3. 26.
Saladin, and Cœur de Lion, IV. 410 ; App. i. 5.
   „   talisman of, IV. 392 ; v. 20. 34.
Salamis, battle of, II. 238 ; iii. 2. 5. 20.
Salève, Mt. (petit), IV. 169 ; v. 13. 6.
Salisbury crags. See s. Edinburgh.
Sallenche, valley of, I. 289 ; ii. 4. 1. 5.
   „   views above, described, III. 145–46 ; iv. 10. 15.
   „   IV. 254 ; v. 16. 20.
Salt-tax, in Swiss history, V. 95 ; vi. 9. 14.
Salvation, a gift, not a reward, II. 149 ; iii. 1. 15. 11.
Salvator Rosa [SYNOPSIS. I. xxv, xxxv, 6, 42, 81, 94, 98, 119, 166,
           186–90, 218, 228, 236, 241, 244, 248–52, 255, 270,
           287, 312–13, 319, 328–32, 349, 366, 413–15. II.
           48, 88, 137, 146, 170, 188 and n, 230. III. 37, 124,
           274, 337, 343. IV. v, 44, 59, 274, 313, 377. V.
           51, 53, 72–4, 78, 136, 232, 255 seqq., 260–64, 266,
           270, 304, 311, 312, 325, 326, 368 n]:—
   Angelico and, contrasted, V. 311 ; ix. 8. 14.
   art teaching in his days, IV. 313 ; v. 17. 47.
   brutality of, II. 48 ; iii. 1. 5. 12.
   „   „   II. 137 ; iii. 1. 14. 29.

Salvator Rosa, *continued:*

  brutality of, II. 146 ; iii. 1. 15. 7.
    „   „   II. 188 and *n* ; iii. 2. 3. 18.
  Calabrian scenery, its influence on, V. 261 ; ix. 4. 13.
  character and training of, V. 260–63 ; ix. 4. 11 *seqq.*
    „   „   passion of, V. 304 ; ix. 8. 1.
    „   „   sensualism of, V. 232 ; ix. 2. 13.
    „   „   spiritual pensiveness of, V. 262 ; ix. 4. 14.
    „   „   temper conquered by evil, V. 312 ; ix. 8. 15.
  chiaroscuro of, I. 186–87 ; ii. 2. 3. 4.
    „   „   I. 189–90 ; ii. 2. 3. 7.
    „   „   I. 180 ; ii. 2. 3. 15 (ed. 1, 2 only).
            See below, s. colour
  clouds of, false, V. 136 ; vii. 2. 19.
    „   „   I. 236 ; ii. 3. 2. 11.
    „   „   I. 241 ; ii. 3. 3. 3.
    „   „   I. 244 ; ii. 3. 3. 7.
    „   generalized, I. 248–51 ; ii. 3. 3. 13–17.
    „   monotonous, I. 255 ; ii. 3. 3. 23.
  colour and light of, IV. 44 ; v. 3. 12.
    „   sombre, III. 274 ; iv. 16. 18.
  death as viewed by, V. 262–64 ; ix. 4. 15–17.
    „   „   „   V. 325 ; ix. 9. 22.
    „   drawing of, V. 368 *n* ; ix. 11. 31 *n.*
  depreciation of, by author, I. *pref. ed.* 3 (only).
    „   „   „   I. 6 ; i. 1. 1. 4 (esp. ed. 1).
    „   „   „   I. 94 ; ii. 1. 7. 14 (om. ed. 1, 2).
  "desperate," IV. 59 ; v. 4. 2.
  Dürer and, V. 255 *seqq.* ; ix. 4. 1 *seqq.*
  education of, V. 260–61 ; ix. 4. 11 *seqq.*
  etching of, "Democritus omnium derisor," V. 51 ; vi. 6. 10.
  execution of, vicious, I. 42 ; i. 2. 2. 9.
    „   „   II. 88 ; iii. 1. 10. 3.
  feebleness, due to lack of love for nature, I. 81–2 ; ii. 1. 7. 5 (om. ed. 1, 2).
  fire of, I. 98 ; ii. 1. 7. 17 (om. ed. 1, 2).
  generalization of foregrounds, etc., I. xxxv ; *pref. ed.* 2. 28.
            See above, s. clouds, and below, s. rocks.
  ghastliness, love of, I. 413–14 ; ii. 6. 1. 11 (om. ed. 1, 2).
  imagination, vigorous, II. 170 ; iii. 2. 2. 19.
  impressiveness, not truth, his aim, I. 42 ; i. 2. 2. 9.

Salvator Rosa, *continued*:

impressiveness, not truth, his aim, V. 270 ; ix. 5. 10.

influence of, no moral, I. xxv ; *pref. ed.* 2. 17.

   „   evil, I. 119 ; ii. 1. 7. 30 (om. ed. 1, 2).

jests of, V. 262 ; ix. 4. 13.

landscape of, I. 413–14 ; ii. 6. 1. 11.

   „   IV. v ; *pref.* 1.

"lurid chasms" of, V. 326 ; ix. 9. 24.

Michelet on "ce damné Salvator," V. 262 ; ix. 4. 14.

mountains of, I. 313–14 *n* ; ii. 4. 3. 9 *n* (om. ed. 1. 2).

   „   I. 319 ; ii. 4. 3. 17.

   „   IV. 274 ; v. 16. 41.

   „   use of by, IV. 377 ; v. 20. 17.

power of, III. 337 ; iv. 18. 20–2.

   „   V. 261–62 ; ix. 4. 13–14.

Reformation and, V. 257 *seqq.* ; ix. 4. 4. *seqq.*

rocks of, I. 218 ; ii. 3. 1. 4.

   „   I. 287 ; ii. 4. 1. 2.

   „   I. 328 *seqq.* ; ii. 4. 4. 1 *seqq.*

   „   I. 329–30 *n* ; ii. 4. 4. 3 *n* (om. ed. 1, 2).

   „   Stanfield's compared with, I. 332 ; ii. 4. 4. 9 (ed. 1, 2. 11).

   „   I. 349 ; ii. 5. 1. 5 (om. ed. 1, 2).

sketches and etchings, better than his pictures, I. 414 ; ii. 6. 1. 12 (om. ed. 1, 2).

skies, I. 228 ; ii. 3. 1. 20. *See above, s. clouds.*

slurred work of, II. 88 ; iii. 1. 10. 3.

spiritual art, its last trace in, V. 262 ; ix. 4. 14.

   „   „   „ V. 266 ; ix. 5. 1.

style of, dashing, III. 343 ; iv. 18. 28.

subjects of, ugly, III. 37 ; iv. 3. 12.

tree-drawing of, I. 413–14 ; ii. 6. 1. 10–11.

   „   „   boughs and branches, V. 50–3 ; vi. 6. 10, 12.

   „   „   „   „ V. 72–4 ; vi. 8, 7, 9.

   „   „   „   „ V. 78 ; vi. 8. 11 (cf. III. pl. 4. fig. 8)

truth, his natural feeling for, I. 413 ; ii. 6. 1. 11.

Turner little affected by him, III. 337 ; iv. 18. 21.

ugliness preferred to beauty by, V. 74 ; vi. 8. 7.

vulgarity of, III. 37 ; iv. 3. 12.

   „   III. 274 ; iv. 16. 18.

   „   III. 337 ; iv. 18. 21.

Salvator Rosa, *continued:*

  water, single instance of well-painted (Pitti Palace), I. 366 ;
    ii. 5. 1. 21 (om. ed. 1, 2).
  wealth, his scorn of, V. 262 ; ix. 4. 14.
  works of :

    Apollo and Sibyl, branch in, V. 78 ; vi. 8. 11 *n.*
    Catiline, V. 311 ; ix. 8. 14.
    Dulwich Gallery, 159, clouds and sky, I. 244 ; ii. 3. 3. 7.
      ,,　　　,,　　　,,　　,,　　I. 270 ; ii. 3. 4. 17.
      ,,　　　,,　　　,, foreground rock, I. 331 ; ii. 4. 4. 7.
      ,,　　　,,　　220, clouds, false, I. 245 ; ii. 3. 3. 8.
      ,,　　　,,　　　,,　　,, monotonous, I. 255 ; ii. 3. 3.
        23.
      ,,　　　,,　　　,,　　,, mountain in, I. 312 ; ii. 4. 3. 8.
      ,,　　　,,　　　,,　　,, rock in foreground, I. 331 ; ii.
        4. 4. 7.
    Florence (Pitti), II. 137 ; iii. 1. 14. 29.
      ,,　　　,, I. 314 *n* ; ii. 4. 3. 9 *n* (om. ed. 1, 2).
      ,,　　　,, Diogenes, II. 170 ; iii. 2. 2. 19.
      ,,　　　,, Peace burning Arms of War, trees in, I. 414 ;
        ii. 6. 1. 11 (om. ed. 1, 2).
      ,,　　　,, S. Anthony, II. 48 *n* ; iii. 1. 5. 12 *n.*
      ,,　　　,,　　　II. 230 *n* ; iii. 2. 5. 7 *n.*
      ,,　　　,, Sea-piece, I. 366 ; ii. 5. 1. 21 (om. ed. 1, 2).
      ,,　　　,,　　　,, II. 188 *n* ; iii. 2. 3. 18 *n.*
      ,,　　　,, Umana Fragilita, grey spectre in, V. 262 ;
        ix. 4. 14.
    Guadagni Palace, I. 414 ; ii. 6. 1. 11 (om. ed. 1, 2).
      ,,　　　,, II. 170 ; iii. 2. 2. 19.
      ,,　　　,, Baptism of Christ, II. 188 *n* ; iii. 2. 3. 18 *n.*
    Mercury and Woodman (Nat. Gall.), impossible colour, I.
      166–67 ; ii. 2. 2. 4.
    Œdipus, trees in, III. 124 ; iv. 9. 9.
      ,,　　　,,　　V. 72–4 ; vi. 8. 7.
    S. Jerome (Brera, Milan), II. 170 ; iii. 2. 2. 19.
    School of Plato, boughs in, V. 72–4 ; vi. 8. 7.
      ,,　　　,, etching of, V. 311 ; ix. 8. 14 (fig. 99).
    Witch of Endor, V. 311 ; ix. 8. 14.

Samaria, Christ and woman of, quoted by Swiss peasant, IV.
  377–78 ; v. 20. 18.
San Miniato, fresco at, II. 8 *n* ; iii. 1. 1. 7 *n.*
Sand, George, study and love of nature, III. 302 ; iv. 17. 7.
  ,,　　　,,　　　,,　　　,,　　　,,　　III. 313 ; iv. 17. 27.

Sand, colours of, in the poets, III. 234–35 ; iv. 14. 45.

   ,,   lines of heaps of, IV. 328 ; v. 18. 14.

   ,,   opal from, V. 176 ; viii. 1. 9.

Sandstone, place of, in scenery, IV. 134 ; v. 11. 1 *seqq.*

Sans-nom, Aiguille, V. 139 ; vii. 3. 4.

Sanctification, true and doctrinal, II. '83 *pref.* 5.

Sap, its action in trees, V. 45 ; vi. 6. 3 *n.*

Sapling, growth of a, V. 57 ; vi. 7. 5.

Sapphire, consummation of clay, V. 176 ; viii. 1. 9.

Satan, representations of, in art, II. 230 *n* ; iii. 2. 5. 7 *n.*   *See s.*
   Lawrence.

Satiety of beauty, IV. 138–39 ; v. 11. 7.

Saul, towering presence of, III. 158 ; iv. 11. 9.

Saussure.   *See s. De Saussure.*

Savonarola, portrait of, by Fra Bartolomeo, II. 129 ; iii. 1.
   14. 14.

Savoy, flower "pain de bon Dieu," IV. 369 *n* ; v. 20. 5 *n.*

   ,,   mountains of, IV. 260 ; v. 16. 26.

   ,,   peasantry, their gloomy life, IV. 338–40 ; v. 19. 4–5.

   ,,   preference for highest pasturages, IV. 104 *n* ; v. 7. 10 *n.*

   ,,   valleys, cultivation of, IV. 132 ; v. 10. 5.

       See s. Annecy, Blanc, Bonneville, Breven, Chambéry, Cha-
          mouni, Chartreuse, Flegère, Reposoir, Sixt, Taconay,
          Tapia, Varens, Vergi.

Scabious-head, IV. 61–2 ; v. 4–5.

Scale, of works of art.   *See s. Size.*

Scamander, river-god, III. 182–84 ; iv. 13. 7–8.

Scandinavia, influence of the pine, V. 94 ; vi. 9. 12.

   ,,   intellect and art of, V. 152 ; vii. 4. 2.

   ,,   origin of northern imagination in, IV. 374 ; v.
                             20. 13.

   ,,   ,,   ,,   ,,   IV. 379 ; v.
                             20. 20.

Scarlet, use of, in Bible, IV. 54–5 ; v. 3. 24.

   ,,   ,,   ,, nature (dawn, sunset, blood), V. 349 ; ix.
              11. 7.

   ,,   ,, by Turner, V. 348–49 and *n* ; ix. 11. 7 and *n.*
             See s. Red.

Scenery, associations connected with, III. 307–9 ; iv. 17. 14
   seqq.

   ,,   its effect on inhabitants, IV. 142–43 ; v. 11. 10.

Scenery, *continued*:

„   its interest rooted in human emotion, V. 218 ; ix. 1. 4.

„   man's presence injures the noblest, I. 217 ; ii. 3. 1. 1.

„   man to *live* amid quiet, not sublime, IV. 139 ; v. 11. 7.

„   northern and southern mountain, compared, III. 248 ; iv. 15. 8.

„   reverence for fair, III. 275 ; iv. 16. 20.

„   ruin of, for commerce, IV. 398 ; v. 20. 42.

„   „   modern, V. 368 *n* ; ix. 11. 30 *n*.   *See s. Quarries.*

„   two aspects of, bright and dark, V. 229–30 ; ix. 2. 10–11.

„   what, most productive of literature, IV. 382 ; v. 20. 25. *See s. Places.*

Scents, different in same flowers, I. 72 ; ii. 1. 5. 2.

„   intemperance as regards, II. 17 ; iii. 1. 2. 7.

Scepticism, causes and nature of modern, III. 265 ; iv. 16. 3–4.

„   „   „   „   III. 268–69 ; iv. 16. 10.

Schaffhausen, Falls of, described, I. 369–70 ; ii. 5. 2. 2.

„   „   „   V. 189–90 ; viii. 2. 10.

„   „   railway bridge over, V. 357 *n* ; ix. 11. 15 *n*.

Schiller, Letters on æsthetic culture (the Laocoon), II. 76 *n* ; iii. 1. 7. 6 *n*.

„   saying of, that sense of beauty is no incentive to duty, II. 148 ; iii. 1. 15. 9.

„   works of, illustrated, II. 183 ; iii. 2. 3. 12.   *See s. Retsch.*

Schöngauer, Martin, drawings after (Harleian MS.), IV. 349–52 ; v. 19. 18–21.

Schreckhorn, I. 292 ; ii. 4. 2. 1.

„   IV. 173 ; v. 13. 9.

Science,* aspects, as well as natures, have their, III. 325 ; iv. 17. 42.

„   danger of, in checking contemplation, III. 325 ; iv. 17. 42.

„   errors of modern, V. 221 ; ix. 1. 9.

„   may mislead as to aspects, IV. 413 ; App. ii. 1.

* *See s.* Botany, Buoyancy, Clouds, Darwinism, Dust, Earth, Faraday, Galileo, Geology, Investigation, Kepler, Locke, Natural History, Optics, Qualities, Rain, Rainbow, Rain-cloud, Reflections, Sea, Shadow, Sky, Storm, Sun, Sunbeam, Sunlight, etc., Vapour, Water, Waves, White.

Science, *continued:*

„ modern interest in, III. 272 ; iv. 16. 16.

„ practical use of, II. 9–10 ; iii. 1. 1. 8.

„ relation to painting of natural, III. 323 ; iv. 17. 39.

„ subservient to life, II. 9 ; iii. 1. 1. 8.

„ true sight hindered by knowledge of, IV. 414 ; App. ii. 1.

„ value of, in rousing from dreams to activity, III. 325 ; iv. 17. 42.

Scoffing, modern tendency to, II. 182 ; iii. 2. 3. 10.

Scorn, love or, which to cultivate, V. 262 ; ix. 4. 14.

Scotch border farmer and old Greek compared, III. 199–200 ; iv. 13. 28.

„ breezes, V. 160 *n* ; vii. 4. 14 *n.*

„ firs, seeds of cones, V. 65 ; vi. 7. 15.

„ „ spray of, V. 86 ; vi. 9. 1.

„ Highland scene described, V. 229–30 ; ix. 2. 11.

„ hillside vegetation, IV. 304–5 ; v. 17. 37.

„ hills and moorland, IV. 97 ; v. 7. 4.

„ „ blue, IV. 132 ; v. 10. 5.

„ mist, V. 144 ; vii. 3. 13.

„ pastor, praise of Highlands, V. 229 ; ix. 2. 11 (F.A. *n*).

„ peasant at Matlock, author's talk with, V. 230–32 ; ix. 2. 12.

„ poetry, pathos of, IV. 374 ; v. 20. 13.

„ „ border ballads, IV. 383 ; v. 20. 27.

Scott, Rev. A. J., author's debt to, V. 312 *n* ; ix. 8. 15 *n.*

Scott, Sir W. [SYNOPSIS. **I.** xxi *n*, 3 *n*, 123, 183 *n*, 268. **II.** 151, 212, 213 *n*, '83 Epil. 13. **III.** 69, 101, 182 *n*, 198, 209–11, 248, 257–58, 263, 269, 274, 276–98, 302, 304, 307, 327–29. **IV.** 29, 347. **V.** 297, 362, 383]:—

aim of, no seriousness in, III. 283 ; iv. 16. 34.

art, his indifference to and ignorance of, III. 282 ; iv. 16. 33.

Cattermole's annual illustrations to, I. 123 ; ii. 1. 7. 33 (om. ed. 1, 2).

classical scenes never thoroughly given by, III. 329 ; iv. 8. 7.

colouring of, bright and pure, III. 274 ; iv. 16. 18.

„ „ its truth, III. 289 ; iv. 16. 42.

„ „ perfect chord instanced, III. 292 ; iv. 16. 43.

death without hope, V. 383 ; ix. 12. 14.

decay of power in later novels, IV. 347 ; v. 19. 15.

ease of, III. 278 ; iv. 16. 27.

Scott, Sir W., *continued:*

education of, neglected, III. 327 and *n* ; iv. 18. 3 *n.*

estimate of himself and his work, III. 277 ; iv. 16. 25.

Gothic architecture loved by, III. 282 ; iv. 16. 33.

    ,,   ,,   where learnt, III. 328 ; iv. 18. 4.

greatest writer of his age, III. 280, 284 ; iv. 16. 30. 35.

healthy virility of his work, II. 213 *n* ; iii. 2. 4. 6 *n.*

imagination of, involuntary remembrance, IV. 29 ; v. 2. 17.

love of liberty, etc., III. 288 ; iv. 16. 40.

loyalty of, III. 288 ; iv. 16. 40.

melancholy of, instanced, III. 294–95 ; iv. 16. 45. *See below, s. poetry.*

moral sense of, seen in *conduct* of his stories, III. 295 ; iv. 16. 45.

nature as illustrated by him, II. '83 Epil. 13.

    ,,   aspect of, as animated, III. 284 *seqq.* ; iv. 16. 36 *seqq.*

    ,,   given as she is, not as she affects him, III. 285 ; iv. 16. 37.

    ,,   love of, intense, because humble and unselfish, III. 286 ; iv. 16. 38.

    ,,   ,,   for its antiquity, freedom, and beauty, III. 289 ; iv. 16. 41.

    ,,   mingled pain and pleasure, III. 297–98 ; iv. 17. 2.

    ,,   ,,   ,,   III. 302–3 ; iv. 17. 8.

    ,,   morals from, melancholy, III. 294 ; iv. 16. 45.

    ,,   most seen in his early works, III. 304 ; iv. 17. 9.

on pride and vanity, III. 294 ; iv. 16. 45.

poetry of, its landscape, III. 263 ; iv. 15. 21.

    ,,   III. 276 ; iv. 16. 23.

    ,,   its sorrowful tone, III. 283 ; iv. 16. 34.

    ,,   no pathetic fallacy in it, III. 285–86 ; iv. 16. 37.

politics of (Jacobite), III. 288 ; iv. 16. 40.

popularity of, instant, and why, I. 3 *n* ; i. 1. 1. 1 *n.*

public treatment of, V. 383 ; ix. 12. 14.

Puritans, liked less than Cavaliers by, III. 288 ; iv. 16. 40.

religion of, vague and deficient, III. 269 ; iv. 16. 10.

    ,,   ,,   ,,   ,,   III. 281 ; iv. 16. 31.

    ,,   ,,   ,,   ,,   III. 295–96 ; iv. 16. 45.

river-spirits in, III. 182 *n* ; iv. 13. 7 *n.*

rocks loved by (contrast Dante), III. 292 ; iv. 16. 43.

romantic love of the past, III. 281–82 ; iv. 16. 32.

    ,,   novels his worst, Scotch his best, *ib.* ; *ib.*

Scott, Sir W., *continued :*

style, mannered, not affected, III. 277 ; iv. 16. 26.

temper, at once light and sorrowful, III. 283 ; iv. 16. 34.

Turner at Abbotsford with, II. 151 ; iii. 2. 1 ('83 Introd. Note 2).

    „   his engravings to, I. 183 *n* ; ii. 2. 2. 20 *n* (om. ed. 1, 2).

    „   „ relation to, III. 276 ; iv. 16. 22. *See s. Turner.*

    „   „   „ (cf. Dante and Giotto), III. 327 ; iv. 18. 2.

typical of his age, III. 198 ; iv. 13. 27.

    „   „ III. 276 ; iv. 16. 23.

    „   „ III. 280 ; iv. 16. 30.

wife's death, Charlotte's coffin, III. 281 ; iv. 16. 31.

works of, Scottish character in (cf. Gotthelf), V. 362 ; ix. 11. 24.

(*a*) novels referred to :

"Antiquary," Heavysterne, III. 282 ; iv. 16. 32.

"Black Dwarf," deformed, not vulgar, V. 297 ; ix. 7. 20.

"Castle Dangerous," skeleton shield, IV. 347 ; v. 19. 15.

"Guy Mannering" greater than "In Memoriam," III. 280 ; iv. 16. 29.

"Heart of Midlothian," Jeanie Deans, III. 282 ; iv. 16. 32.

"Monastery," author's favourite as a child, III. 307 ; iv. 17. 14.

    „ Mysie Happer, II. 151 ; iii. 2. 1 ('83 Introd. Note 2).

    „ Sir P. Shafton, *ib.* ; *ib.*

    „ White Lady of Avenel, III. 101 ; iv. 8. 3.

"Quentin Durward," "Rouge Sanglier," I. xx *n* ; *pref. ed.* 2. 13 *n.*

"Red Gauntlet," III. 282 ; iv. 16. 32.

"Rob Roy" (Fairservice), *ib.* ; *ib.*

(*b*) poems—lines quoted :

"Ah ! what have I to do with pride?" III. 294 ; iv. 16. 45.

"And well the lonely infant knew," III. 287 ; iv. 16. 39.

"As oft awake by lone St. Mary's silent lake," III. 297 ; iv. 17. 2.

"As snow upon the mountain's breast," etc., III. 257 ; iv. 15. 19.

Scott, Sir W. : (*b*) poem**s**—lines quoted, *continued :*

 "Blackford, on whose uncultured breast," III. 283 ; iv. 16. 34.

 Edinboro' (new town and Britomart), III. 282; iv. 16. 33.

  ,, "The wandering eye could o'er it go," III. 290–91 ; iv. 16. 42.

 "Far beneath, where slow they creep," III. 283; iv. 16. 34.

 "Far in the distant Cheviot's blue," III. 248; iv. 15. 8.

 "For I was wayward, bold, and wild," III. 289; iv. 16. 41.

 "Foxglove and nightshade side by side," III. 294; iv. 16. 45.

 Loch Coriskin, I. 268; ii. 3. 4. 14 (ed. 1–4. 15).

 "Mine be the eve of tropic sun," III. 295; iv. 16. 45.

 "Mingled . . . resignation and content," III. 298; iv. 17. 2.

  ,, ,, ,, ,, III. 306 ; iv. 17. 11.

 "Oh ! what a tangled web we weave When first we practise to deceive," III. 295 ; iv. 16. 45.

 "Right up Ben Ledi," etc., III. 69 ; iv. 5. 6 (F.A. *n*).

 Risingham ("Rokeby"), III. 285 ; iv. 16. 36.

  ,, ,, vi. 2–3, III. 293 ; iv. 16. 44.

 "Teith . . . graced the sable strath with green," III. 290; iv. 16. 42.

 "The blackening wave is edged with white," III. 289 ; iv. 16. 42.

 "The foam-globes on her eddies ride," III. 294; iv. 16. 45.

 "The Greta flow to meet the Tees," III. 285 ; iv. 16. 36.

 "The mountain shadows lie . . . Fancy's eye," III. 294; iv. 16. 45.

 "The rocky summits split and rent," II. 212 ; iii. 2. 4. 6.

 "The sultry summer day is done," III. 294-95 ; iv. 16. 45.

 "The summer dawn's reflected hue" (Loch Katrine), III. 293 ; iv. 16. 44.

 "The white pavilions made a show" (Flodden), III. 290; iv. 16. 42.

 "There is a pleasure in the pain," III. 297 ; iv. 17. 2.

 "They saw Lord Marmion's falcon fly," III. 211 ; iv. 14. 13.

Scott, Sir W.: (b) poems—lines quoted, continued:

"Thousand pavilions, white as snow," III. 290; iv. 16. 42.

"'Twas silence all. He laid him down," III. 291; iv. 16. 42.

"'Twere sweet to mark the setting day," III. 295; iv. 16. 45.

"Yon lonely thorn," etc., III. 284; iv. 16. 36.

Scottish Academy (1848), works in, II. 246; Add. 8 (om. ed. 1).

Scribe "Reine d'un jour," V. 296; ix. 7. 16.

Scripture. See s. Bible.

Sculpture,* imagination manifested in, II. 197–98; iii. 2. 3. 26–7.

„ imitation in painting and, I. 20–1; i. 1. 4. 3.

„ landscape in, III. 202; iv. 14. 1.

„ modern, of lace, etc., and the Elgin marbles, I. xxxvi; pref. ed. 2. 29.

„ „ of hair, etc., II. 221; iii. 2. 4. 16.

„ Pisan, influence on later art, IV. 379; v. 20. 20.

„ Renaissance, III. 69–70; iv. 5. 6.

„ suitability of rock for, IV. 116 seqq.; v. 8. 16 seqq.

„ „ „ IV. 135; v. 11. 3.

„ thirteenth century, fidelity to nature, III. 215–22; iv. 14. 20 seqq.

„ „ „ „ V. 53; vi. 6. 12.
See s. Statues.

Scylla, meaning of, V. 235; ix. 2. 17.

Sea [SYNOPSIS. I. 345, 348, 349–50, 352–53, 360 seqq., 366, 387, 395, 397–98, 403. II. 43. III. 203 n. IV. 369, 380 n. V. viii, 151–71, 240]:—

angel of the, V. 151–71; vii. 4. 1 seqq.

author's proposed book on the, V. viii; pref. 5.

beauty of, V. 240; ix. 3. 5.

described, after storm, I. 403–4; ii. 5. 3. 38.

influence of, on artists (Tuscan and Venetian), IV. 380 n; v. 20. 21 n.

its grandeur, IV. 369; v. 20. 6.

„ idea of space a main attraction, II. 43; iii. 1. 5. 3.

„ "tameless unity," I. 345; ii. 5. 1. 1.

* See s. Antinous, Apollo Belvidere, Dannaeker, Elgin, Gladiator, Griffin, Laocoon, M. Angelo, Quercia, Roubilliac, Siena, Tombs, Venus (Milo), Verrocchio.

Sea, *continued* :

　　light on the, how caused, I. 353–54 ; ii. 5. 1. 9 (om. ed. 1, 2).

　　　　　,,　　　　,,　　　　,,　I. 387–88 ; ii. 5. 3. 17.

　　mediæval dislike of the, III. 203 *n* ; iv. 14. 2 *n.*

　　painting the, impossible, never yet done, I. 349 ; ii. 5. 1.
　　　　　5 (om. ed. 1, 2).

　　　　,,　　　,,　many difficulties of, I. 395–96 ; ii. 5. 3. 29
　　　　　　　(om. ed. 1, 2).

　　　　,,　　　,,　of old masters, I. 360 *seqq.* ; ii. 5. 1. 17 *seqq.*
　　　　　　　(om. ed. 1, 2).

　　picture, sea-scape, R.A. 1843, I. 348 ; ii. 5. 1. 5 (om. ed. 1, 2).

　　rendering of, in mosaic and painted glass, etc., I. 366 ; ii.
　　　　5. 1. 22 (om. ed. 1, 2).

　　shadows on the, colour of, apparent, I. 351–52 ; ii. 5. 1. 8
　　　　(om. ed. 1, 2).

　　study it, from the sea, not from the shore, I. 397–98 ; ii. 5.
　　　　3. 31.

　　See s. Foam, Stanfield, Turner, Venice, Water, Waves.

Sebastopol. *See s. Crimea.*

Sedentary life, gloominess and, IV. 355 ; v. 19. 25.

See clearly, say simply, the rarest gift, III. 278 ; iv. 16. 28. *See*
　　s. Sight.

Seed, definition of a, V. 105–6 ; vi. 10. 15.

　　,,　vessels, V. 105–7 ; v. 10. 15–18.

Seers, III. 144 ; iv. 10. 13.

　　,,　and thinkers, III. 279 ; iv. 16. 28.

　　,,　meaning of, V. 178 ; viii. 1. 14.

Seine, chalk côteaux of the, IV. 260 ; v. 16. 27.

　　,,　loved by author, IV. 366 ; v. 20. 2.

Self-command, thought a sign of gentlemanship, V. 292 ; ix.
　　　7. 10.

　　　,,　　　acquired by the vulgar, V. 292 ; ix. 7. 10.

　　　,,　　　essential to the artist, V. 213 ; viii. 4. 20.

　　　,,　　　rarity of, V. 198 ; viii. 3. 5.

Self-deception, refusal of God's warning, IV. 362 ; v 19. 32.

Self-forgetfulness, V. 198 ; viii. 3. 5.

Self-preservation, instinct of, and the sublime, I. 44–5 ; i. 2
　　3. 3.

Selfishness, cannot reason rightly, II. 122 ; iii. 1. 14. 5.

　　　,,　　fatal to an artist, V. 213–14 ; viii. 4. 20–21.

　　　,,　　of indifference to surrounding sorrow, IV. 362–63
　　　　　v. 19. 32.

Selfishness, *continued*:

,,   political, V. 295 ; ix. 7. 15.

,,   vulgarity of, V. 302–3 ; ix. 7. 24.

Sensation, less keen as life advances, II. 33–4 ; iii. 1. 4. 4.

,,   primary, cannot be defined, III. 161–62 ; iv. 12. 1–2 *n*.

Senses, essentials to perfection of the, II. 25 ; iii. 1. 3. 6.

,,   not to be morbidly overtrained, II. 25 ; iii. 1. 3. 6–7.

,,   proportion and distance only, grasped by, I. 25–6 ; i. 1. 5. 5.

,,   their errors, through imagination, I. 57–8 ; ii. 1. 2. 6.

Sensibility, artistic, I. 440 ; ii. 6. 3. 4.

,,   essence of gentlemanship, V. 289 ; ix. 7. 5.

,,   largely a moral quality, I. 55–6 ; ii. 1. 2. 4.

,,   of all noble minds, *ib.* ; *ib.*

,,   perception of facts requires, I. 56–7 ; ii. 1. 2. 5.

,,   to beauty, its degrees and training, I. 55 ; ii. 1. 2. 3.

,,   to colour and form distinct, I. 440 ; ii. 6. 3. 4.

,,   vulgarity of deficient, V. 301–2 ; ix. 7. 23.

,,   want of, in over-regard for appearances, V. 295 ; ix. 7. 16.

See s. Dutch school.

Sensitiveness, of fine natures, V. 289–90 ; ix. 7. 5–6.

,,   ,,   ,,   V. 291–92 ; ix. 7. 9.

,,   ,,   poets, greater and less, III. 169 ; iv. 12. 10.

Sensuality, as affecting the countenance, II. 132 *seqq.* ; iii. 1. 14. 20.

,,   beauty and, II. 13 ; iii. 1. 2. 1 *seqq.*

,,   colour and, II. 133 ; iii. 1. 14. 21 *seqq.*

,,   ,,   III. 71 ; iv. 5. 7.

,,   in art, III. 77 ; iv. 6. 2.

,,   love of beauty consistent with, IV. 348–49 ; v. 19. 17.

Sentimental literature, its place and rank, III. 279–80 ; iv. 16. 29–30.

Septuagint, The, quoted, V. 159 ; vii. 4. 13.

Sequence, unity of, II. 55–7 ; iii. 1. 6. 3–4.

Seriousness, lack of, in modern life, II. 182 ; iii. 2. 3. 10.

,,   of all great men, III. 275 ; iv. 16. 19.

Sermons, on the pregnant meaning of texts, V. 166 *n* ; vii. 4. 25 *n*.

Serpents, character of, V. 295 ; ix. 7. 15.

,,   colour of venomous, dark, IV. 53 ; v. 3. 23.

Serpents, *continued :*

    „   in Greek myths, V. 158 *seqq.* ; vii. 4. 11 *seqq.*

    „   Python and death-worm, V. 355 ; ix. 11. 12.

    „   symbolism of, III. 213–14 ; iv. 14. 17.

Servants, dress of, V. 361 *n* ; ix. 11. 22 *n.*

    „   modern treatment of, III. 184–85 ; iv. 13. 9.

Seventeenth century, no great art in, III. 337 ; iv. 18. 20.

Severn, the river, its size, IV. 176 ; v. 13. 12.

——, Joseph, II. 73 ; iii. 1. 7. 5 ('83 *n*).

Seyton war-cry, "set on," III. 347 ; iv. 18 (33).

Shade, distinctness of, in nature, I. 330 ; ii. 4. 4. 4.

    „   gradation of, necessary, II. 51 ; iii. 1. 5. 17.

    „   sketch of master conceived in colour and, I. 429 ; ii. 6. 1. 31.

    „   want of, in early art, I. 57–8 ; ii. 1. 2. 6.

               See s. Chiaroscuro.

Shadow, absolute and relative qualities of, IV. 37 ; v. 3. 3.

    „   as given by various masters, IV. 49 ; v. 3. 18–19.

    „   colourists' right, chiaroscurists' wrong, IV. 50 ; v. 3. 20.

    „   depth and sharpness of, I. 184–85 ; ii. 2. 3. 1.

    „   forms of cast, strange, IV. 77 ; v. 5. 11.

    „   importance of cast, I. 351 *seqq.* ; ii. 5. 1. 8 *seqq.*

    „   mediæval rejection of, III. 211 ; iv. 14. 13 *seqq.*

    „   negative in colour, V. 348 *n* ; ix. 11. 6 *n.*

    „   painting of, by Italians, Dutch, and Turner, I. 185 *seqq.* ; ii. 2. 3. 2 *seqq.*

    „   „   without any, purist, 1200–1300, III. 78 ; iv. 6. 3.

    „   photographic exaggeration of, IV. 65 ; v. 4. 11.

    „   variety of, in nature, I. 178–79 ; ii. 2. 2. 16.

    „   water and, I. 352–54 ; ii. 5. 1. 9.

    „   „   I. 354–55 ; ii. 5. 1. 10 (om. ed. 1, 2).

Shakspere [SYNOPSIS. I. xxiv, xxxvii, 3 *n*, 16, 65, 403 *n.* **II.** 74, 83, 98–9, 139 *n*, 155, 177, 180–81. **III.** 37–8, 73, 85, 89, 98, 101, 165 *n*, 166 *n*, 193, 227, 235 *n*, 240, 268, 295, 296, 324. **IV.** 317–18, 383–96. **V.** 92, 233, 251, 297] :—

    I. 65 ; ii. 1. 3. 6.

    anachronisms, etc., of, IV. 387–88 ; v. 20. 30.

    architecture of, gold in, IV. 390 ; v. 20. 33.

    armour in, IV. 387–88 ; v. 20. 30.

    art in his time, in England, IV. 389 ; v. 20. 31.

Shakspere, *continued:*

 characters, contrasts and foils in his, III. 37–8 ; iv. 3. 14.

 ,, ,, ,, ,, III. 85 ; iv. 7. 3.

 complete portraiture of, III. 85 ; iv. 7. 3.

 ,, ,, III. 98 ; iv. 7. 20.

 ,, ,, IV. 387 ; v. 20. 30.

 creative genius of, III. 165 *n* ; iv. 12. 6 *n.*

 Dante compared with, IV. 394–95 and *n* ; v. 20. 38 and *n.*

 dress, his indifference to fine, IV. 387–88 ; v. 20. 30.

 fate in, IV. 395 *n* ; v. 20. 38 *n.*

 ,, V. 233 ; ix. 2. 15.

 flowers particularized by, I. xxxvii ; *pref. ed.* 2. 31.

 ,, ,, ,, IV. 386 and *n* ; v. 20. 29 and *n.*

 friars in, IV. 393 ; v. 20. 36.

 grasp of human nature, equal and universal, IV. 384–86 ;
  v. 20. 28–29.

 Greek tragedy and, V. 233 ; ix. 2. 15.

 grotesque in, III. 101 ; iv. 8. 3.

 historical plays, give eternal truth, III. 98 ; iv. 7. 20
       (F.A. *n*).

 ,, ,, ,, ,, IV. 389 ; v. 20. 32.

 imagination of, II. 177–78 ; iii. 2. 3. 4–5.

 jests of, no longer laughable, III. 268 ; iv. 16. 9.

 looks down and on, not up, IV. 396 ; v. 20. 38.

 meadows loved by, III. 240 ; iv. 14. 51.

 mediævalism, not entered into by him, IV. 387 *seqq.* ; v.
  20. 30–31.

 misunderstood, I. 3–4 *n* ; i. 1. 1. 1 *n.*

 monasticism in, IV. 393 ; v. 20. 36.

 mountains disregarded by, III. 193 ; iv. 13. 20.

 ,, influencing him, IV. 383 ; v. 20. 27.

 ,, ,, ,, IV. 385 ; v. 20. 29.

 ,, various quotations on, IV. 393 *seqq.* ; v. 20. 37.

 on *natural* tendencies of men, IV. 395 *n* ; v. 20. 38 *n.*

 pine trees in, IV. 394 *seqq.* ; v. 20. 38 *seqq.*

 plots of, often trivial, IV. 395 ; v. 20. 38.

 religion of (cf. Titian), V. 251 ; ix. 3. 28.

 Renaissance corrupts, IV. 389 ; v. 20. 32.

 repose of, II. 74 ; iii. 1. 7. 5 ('83 *n*).

 scenery essential to him, IV. 385 *seqq.* ; v. 20. 28 *seqq.*

 ,, ,, ,, IV. 396 ; v. 20. 38.

 self-annihilation shows his power, I. xxiv ; *ed.* 2. *pref.* 16.

Shakspere, *continued*:

    stands alone, no second Shakspere, IV. 317–18 ; v. 17. 51

    subject of, his own age, IV. 386–87, 389 ; v. 20. 30, 32.

    sympathy and universality of, III. 98 ; iv. 7. 20.

       ,,   ,,   ,,   IV. 384–86 ; v. 20. 28–9.

  virtue in, IV. 395 ; v. 20. 38.

  woods loved by, III. 227 ; iv. 14. 33.

  works of, quoted or referred to :

      As You Like It, Jaques, first character of the kind, III. 295 ; iv. 16. 45.

         ,,   ,,   ,,   inconsistent temper of, III. 324 ; iv. 17. 41.

         ,,   ,,   Rosalind, III. 227 ; iv. 14. 33.

         ,,   ,,   Touchstone, IV. 385 ; v. 20. 29.

         ,,   ,,   ii. 7, "compact of jars," III. 296 ; iv. 16. 45.

    Coriolanus, ii. 1, "My gracious silence, hail !" II. 155 ; iii. 2. 1. 5.

    Cymbeline, Imogen and Cloten, III. 85 ; iv. 7. 3.

         ,,   iii. 3, "A cell of ignorance," IV. 393 ; v. 20. 37.

         ,,   ,,   "Beastly ; subtle as the fox," *ib.* ; *ib.*

         ,,   iv. 2, "By his top doth take the mountain pine," IV. 394 ; v. 20. 38.

         ,,   ,,   "Wench-like words" (Imogen's brothers), IV. 386 ; v. 20. 29.

         ,,   ,,   "With wild wood-leaves and weeds," *ib. n* ; *ib. n.*

    Hamlet, death of Hamlet, IV. 395 *n* ; v. 20. 38 *n.*

       ,,   Ophelia, IV. 386 ; v. 20. 29.

       ,,   ,,   her death, V. 233 ; ix. 2. 15.

       ,,   i. 5, "Canst work i' the earth so fast ?" III. 166 *n* ; iv. 12. 6.

       ,,   ,,   "More things in heaven and earth," I. 54 ; ii. 1. 2. 1.

       ,,   iv. 5, "There's pansies, that's for thoughts," II. 98 ; iii. 1. 12. 3.

       ,,   ,,   "There's pansies, that's for thoughts," II. 181 ; iii. 2. 3. 7.

       ,,   v. 1, "Here hung those lips," etc., II. 180 ; iii. 2. 3. 7.

    1 *Henry IV.*, iv. 1, Prince Henry to Falstaff, III. 85 ; iv. 7. 3.

         ,,   ,,   "Bated like eagles, . . . golden coats like images," IV. 387 ; v. 20. 30.

    2 *Henry IV.*, i. 2, "Two-and-twenty yards of satin," IV. 388 ; v. 20. 30.

Shakspere : works of, quoted or referred to, *continued :*

   Henry V., generally, IV. 387–88 ; v. 20. 30.

      ,,   i. 2, "Invoke his warlike spirit," III. 89 ; iv. 7. 8.

      ,,   iii. 5, " Rush on his host, as doth the melted snow," IV. 394 ; v. 20. 37.

      ,,   iii. 7, " Tut ! I have the best armour," etc., IV. 387 ; v. 20. 30.

      ,,   ,,   " Stars or suns upon it ?" IV. 388 ; *ib.*

      ,,   iv. 3, " Our gayness and our gilt are all besmirched," IV. 388 ; *ib.*

   Henry VIII., Queen Katharine's death, V. 233 ; ix. 2. 15.

      ,,   i. 1, " The fire that mounts the liquor," II. 139 n ; iii. 1. 14. 31 n.

   Julius Cæsar, IV. 386 ; v. 20. 29.

   King John, Arthur's death, IV. 395 n ; v. 20. 38 n.

      ,,   ,,   V. 233 ; ix. 2. 15.

      ,,   ii. 2, herald's speech, IV. 388 n ; v. 20. 30 n.

   King Lear, I. xxii ; *pref. ed.* 2. 16.

      ,,   Cordelia, and Regan, III. 85 ; iv. 7. 3.

      ,,   ,,   her death, IV. 395 n ; v. 20. 38 n.

      ,,   ,,   ,,   V. 233 ; ix. 2. 15.

   Macbeth, i. 2, "Where the Norweyan banners flout," II. 181 ; iii. 2. 3. 8.

      ,,   iv. 1, "yesty waves," I. 403 n ; ii. 5. 3. 38 n.

      ,,   iv. 3, "He has no children," II. 178 ; iii. 2. 3. 5.

   Merchant of Venice, Portia, III. 73 ; iv 5. 10.

      ,,   ,,   iii. 2, "fair Portia's counterfeit," IV. 389 ; v. 30. 31.

      ,,   ,,   iv. 1, "estimation of a hair," I. 16 ; i. 1. 3. 3.

      ,,   ,,   iv. 1, " You may as well forbid the mountain pines," IV. 394 ; v. 20. 38.

   Merry Wives of Windsor, Falstaff, III. 85 ; iv. 7. 3.

      ,,   ,,   ,,   ,,   IV. 385 ; v. 20. 29.

      ,,   ,,   ,,   ,,   not vulgar, V. 297 ; ix. 7. 20.

      ,,   ,,   ,,   Quickly, IV. 385 ; v. 20. 29.

      ,,   ,,   ,,   Shallow, III. 85 ; iv. 7. 3.

      ,,   ,,   ,,   Slender, IV. 385 ; v. 20. 29.

      ,,   ,,   ,,   v. 6, "chairs of order . . . knighthood's bending knee," IV. 388 ; v. 20. 30.

   Midsummer Night's Dream, Helena, III. 227 ; iv. 14. 33.

      ,,   ,,   ,,   Quince, IV. 385 ; v. 20. 29.

      ,,   ,,   ,,   Titania, III. 101 ; iv. 8. 3.

Shakspere : works of, quoted or referred t *continued :*

   Midsummer Night's Dream, iii. 2, "Taurus' snow," IV. 394 ;
                  v. 20. 37.

     ,,   ,,   ,, iv. 1, "Like far-off mountains
                        turned into clouds," *ib.* ; *ib.*

     ,,   ,,   ,, v. 2, "With this field dew con-
                        secrate," IV. 388 ; v. 20. 30.

   Othello, IV. 386 ; v. 20. 29.
    ,,   IV. 395 ; v. 20. 38 *n.*

   Richard II., iii. 2, "Fires the proud tops of $\left\{\begin{array}{l} \text{IV. 394 ; v.} \\ \text{20. 38.} \\ \text{V. 92 ; vi. 9. 9.} \end{array}\right.$
             the eastern pines,"

   Romeo and Juliet, due to a small accident, IV. 395 *n* ; v. 20.
             38 *n.*

    ,,   ,, i. 3, "By thinking on the frosty Caucasus,"
                IV. 394 ; v. 20. 37.

    ,,   ,, i. 4, Queen Mab speech (fancy), II. 181 ;
                iii. 2. 3. 8.

    ,,   ,, iii. 1, "Oh ! I am fortune's fool," V. 233 ;
                ix. 2. 15.

    ,,   ,, v. 3, "As rich shall Romeo," etc., IV. 389 ;
                v. 20. 31.

   Tempest, Ariel, III. 101 ; iv. 8. 3.

    ,,   ,, his prison of pines (i. 2), IV. 394 ; v. 20. 38.

    ,,   ,, Caliban foil to Miranda, III. 37 ; iv. 3. 14.

    ,,   ,,   ,, idealism, II. 110–11 ; iii. 1. 13. 3.

    ,,   ,, i. 2, "Come unto these yellow sands," III.
                235 *n* ; iv. 14. 45 *n.*

    ,,   ,, v. 1, "by the spurs plucked up the pine," IV.
                394 ; v. 20. 38.

   Twelfth Night, Sir Toby, IV. 385 ; v. 20. 29.

    ,,   ,, Viola, II. 83 ; iii. 1. 9. 5.

    ,,   ,, ii. 3, "excellent good i' faith," III. 142 ; iv.
                10. 11.

   Two Gentlemen, Launce, IV. 385 ; v. 20. 29.

    ,,   ,, Silvia, III. 227 ; iv. 14. 33.

   Winter's Tale, Hermione's statue, ideal of sculpture, IV. 389 ;
             v. 20. 31.

    ,,   ,, Perdita, III. 73 ; iv. 5. 10.

    ,,   ,,   ,, IV. 386 ; v. 20. 29.

    ,,   ,, "O, Proserpina, for $\left.\begin{array}{l} \end{array}\right\}$ II. 99 ; iii. 1. 12. 3.
             the flowers," etc.,

    ,,   ,,   ,,   ,,   ,, II. 180 ; iii. 2. 3. 7.

Shapfells, author's visit as a child to, III. 307 ; iv. 17. 13.

Shark, dorsal fin's action, II. 102 ; iii. 1. 12. 7.

Sharpe, Mr., geologist, opposed to Forbes, IV. 180 *n* ; v. 13. 18 *n*.

Shaw, Henry, engravings of mediæval ornaments, III. xii ; *pref.* 6.

Sheffield Museum, II. '83 Epil. 10.

Shelley [SYNOPSIS. I. xxxvii, 235. II. 180, 210, 212, 213 *n*, 216, 222, '83 Epil. 7, 10. III. 283, 287, 302, 305, 312, 314, 315, 324. V. 383] :—

    death without hope, V. 383 ; ix. 12. 14.

    drowned in Gulf of Spezzia, II. '83 Epil. 7.

    floating paper boats on the Serchio, III. 314 ; iv. 17. 27.

    flowers particularized by, I. xxxvii ; *pref. ed.* 2. 31.

    imagination of (sickly dreaming), II. 213 *n* ; iii. 2. 4. 6 *n*.

    indignation of, at pain and injustice, III. 315 ; iv. 17. 28.

    inspired by the Lac de Chède, I. 353 *n* ; ii. 5. 3. 5 *n* (ed. 1, 2 only).

    love of nature, selfish, III. 287 ; iv. 16. 28.

      „   „   and study, III. 302 ; iv. 17. 7.

      „   „   „   III. 305 ; iv. 17. 10.

    morbid, III. 324 ; iv. 17. 41.

    passionate nature of, III. 3.2 ; iv. 17. 26.

    public neglect of, V. 383 ; ix. 12. 14.

    sad, because impious, III. 283 ; iv. 16. 34.

    works of, quoted :

        Alastor, II. 222 ; iii. 2. 4. 18.

        " Grey rocks did heap," etc., II. 212 ; iii. 2. 4. 6.

        " Hills mingling their flames with twilight," II. 216 ; iii. 2. 4. 10.

        " It feeds the quick growth of the serpent vine," II. 210 ; iii 2. 4. 5.

        " Lamp of life, thy lips are burning," II. 180 ; iii. 2. 3. 7.

        " Shepherded by the slow unwilling wind " (clouds), I. 235 ; ii. 3. 2. 10.

Shenstone, his study and love of nature, III. 302 ; iv. 17. 7.

    „   quoted (" Jessy "), " If thro' the garden," etc., III. 176 ; iv. 12. 16.

Shipping, in time of Nelson, V. viii ; *pref.* 5.

Shooting. *See s. Sport.*

Shoots, of a tree, V. 12 ; vi. 3. 2. *See s. Branch, Stem, Tree, etc.*

Shrewsbury, the river Severn at, IV. 176 ; v. 13. 12.

Sibyl, Apollo and the, V. 355 ; ix. 11. 12.

,,   Deïphobé, V. 363 *n* ; ix. 11. 26 *n*.

Siena, Pisan sculpture at; IV. 379 ; v. 20. 21.

Sierra, Spanish, IV. 162 ; v. 12. 21.

Sight [Synopsis. I. 53–8, 196–97, 204, 212 *n*. II. 4, 16–17, 29, 40.
    III. 278, 299. IV. 16–17, 60 *seqq.*, 73–4, 321–22, 424. V.
    53, 362] :—

    always imperfect, "we never see all a thing," I. 204 ; ii. 2.
                                                        5. 4.

        ,,   ,,   ,,   ,,   ,,   IV. 321 ; v.
                                                        18. 5.

        ,,   ,,   we never see quite clearly, IV. 60 *seqq.* ;
                                v. 4. 4 *seqq.*

    better than scientific knowledge, V. 53 ; vi. 6. 11.

    choice and, do we see what we *choose* to see? IV. 321 ; v.
        18. 4.

    clear sight and simple talk, a rare gift, III. 278 ; iv. 16. 28.

    cultivation needed to ensure truth of, I. 53 *seqq.* ; ii. 1. 2.
                                                    1 *seqq.*

        ,,   musical ear and, IV. 73–4 ; v. 5. 5–6 *seqq.*

    education and, IV. 424 ; App. iii. 3.

        ,,   ,,   V. 362 ; ix. 11. 23.

    focus of the eye, I. 197–98 and *n* ; ii. 2. 4. 2, 4.

    fulness and truth of, distinct, IV. 321–22 ; v. 18. 5.

    keenness of, how tested, II. 40 ; iii. 1. 4. 12.

    knowledge and, contradictions of, I. 57–8 ; ii. 1. 2. 6.

        ,,   ,,   needed for perception of truth, *ib.* ; *ib.*

    paint "what you see," IV. 16–17 ; v. 2. 2–3.

    pleasures of, lofty, II. 16–17 ; iii. 1. 2. 5–6.

        ,,   to be cultivated, II. 29 ; iii. 1. 3. 13.

    powers of, in painting and judging pictures, I. 212 *n* ; ii. 2.
        5. 15 *n* (om. ed. 1, 2).

    present age does not value, II. 4 ; iii. 1. 1. 5.

    thought and, III. 278 ; iv. 16. 28.

        ,,   less great than sight, III. 299 ; iv. 17. 4.

    two objects at different distances cannot be seen at once, I.
        197–98 ; ii. 2. 4. 2–3.

    unconscious often, and so distinct from perception, I. 54–5 ;
        ii. 1. 2. 2.

    use of, continual ; that of hearing, intermittent, I. 54–5 ; ii.
        1. 2. 2.

Sigier, Dante on, III. 89 ; iv. 7. 8.

Silence, of a true gentleman, V. 291 ; ix. 7. 8.

Simmenthal, mountains of the, IV. 142 ; v. 11. 9.

Simon, Mrs. John, drawing by author owned by, II. '83 Epil. 4 *n*.

Simplicity, more difficult than complexity, I. 18 ; i. 1. 3. 5.

    „   of great men, III. 94 ; iv. 7. 13.

    „   quality of execution, I. 40 ; i. 2. 2. 3.

Sin, defined as "missing the mark" (ἁμαρτία), V. 372 ; ix. 12. 2.

  „ disorder of, II. 79 ; iii. 1. 8. 3.

  „ Greek view of, V. 233–34 ; ix. 15. 15.

  „ punishment of, IV. 363 ; v. 19. 32.

  „ self-destruction of, III. 115 ; iv. 8. 21.

  „ washing away of (fountain of love), V. 353 ; ix. 11. 8. *See s. Sinlessness.*

Sinai, any game or sport on? III. 270 ; iv. 16. 11.

Sinbad, origin of, V. 157 ; vii. 4. 9.

Sincerity, essential to great art, III. 38–9 ; iv. 3. 16.

    „   „   „   „   III. 43 ; iv. 3. 21.

    „   „   „   „   V. 214–15 ; viii. 4. 23.

Singing, children to learn, V. 361 *n* ; ix. 11. 22 *n*.

Sinlessness, purity typical of, II. 84 ; iii. 1. 9. 6.

Sion (Valais), character of people, IV. 358–62 ; v. 19. 28–32.

    „   „   IV. 273 ; v 16. 40. *See s. Ardon.*

    „   „   description of town of, IV. 359–60 ; v. 19. 31.

    „   „   effect of tourists on, IV. 398 ; v. 20. 42.

    „   „   its Bishopric, V. 94 ; vi. 9. 13.

Sirius, V. 123 ; vii. 2. 5.

Sistine Chapel, I. 34 ; i. 1. 7. 3.

    „   „   tourists' talk about, I. 59 ; ii. 1. 2. 7.

    „   „   works in :

                Daniel, I. 67 ; ii. 1. 3. 8.

                Jonah, I. 32 ; i. 2. 1. 3 (ed. 1, 2 only).

Sisymbrium Irio, leaf of, V. 105 ; vi. 10. 14.

Sixt, mountains near, IV. 152 ; v. 12. 12.

  „   „   „ IV. 158 ; v. 12. 18.

  „   „   „ IV. 254 ; v. 16. 20.

Size, large, in works of art, II. 222–23 ; iii. 2. 4. 19.

  „   „   „ III. 41–2 ; iv. 3. 19.

  „ love of, in art, V. 196 ; viii. 3. 3.

Sketches, charm of, in their call on the imagination, III. 148 ; iv. 10. 18.

Sketches, *continued :*

„ power felt in pictures and, I. 37–8 ; i. 2. 1. 7.

„ to be encouraged, I. 447 ; ii. 6. 3. 19.

„ use and kinds of, made by great artists, } V. 201 *seqq.*;
experimental, determinant, com- } viii. 4. 3–4
memorative, } *seqq.*

Sky [SYNOPSIS. I. 57, 76–7, 171, 216–20, 223–24, 230, 239, 272, 371.
III. 258. IV. 37–8, 370–71, 414. V. 118–19, 125–26 *n*,
128 *seqq.*] :—

blue of the, how caused, I. 219 ; ii. 3. 1. 5.

„ „ „ V. 118–19 ; vii. 1. 8.

„ „ Italian less than northern, I. 57 ; ii. 1. 2. 5.

„ „ purest, seen only after rain, I. 272 ; ii. 3. 4. 20
(ed. 1–4. 22).

„ „ unpaintable, I. 171 ; ii. 2. 2. 7.

„ „ „ "blue fire," IV. 37 ; v. 3. 3–4.

body of air, not a hard dome, I. 219–20 ; ii. 3. 1. 6–7.

„ „ „ „ IV. 414 ; App. ii. 1.

brightness of, IV. 37–8 ; v. 3. 4.

colours of, their variety, I. 249 ; ii. 3. 3. 14. *See above, s. blue.*

Dante's description, III. 258 ; iv. 15. 20.

depth of, a chief feature, I. 219 ; ii. 3. 1. 7.

engravings of, V. 125–26 *n* ; vii. 2. 6–7.

gradation of colour, I. 222 ; ii. 3. 1. 11.

lessons taught by, I. 216–17 ; ii. 3. 1. 1 *seqq.*

look through, not at it, *ib.* ; *ib.*

man's apathy to its beauties, I. 217 ; ii. 3. 1. 2.

ministering power of the, I. 217 ; ii. 3. 1. 1.

mountain and lowland, IV. 370–71 ; v. 20. 8.

perspective of the, V. 128 *seqq.* ; vii. 2. 10 *seqq.*

reflections of, in water, I. 348 ; ii. 5. 1. 4.

regions of, three, I. 230 ; ii. 3. 2. 2.

space of, more important than its colour, I. 77 ; ii. 1. 6. 2.

transparency of, I. 220 ; ii. 3. 1. 7.

truth of, I. 216 *seqq.* ; ii. 3. 1. 1 *seqq.*

vapour, its effect on, I. 224 ; ii. 3. 1. 13 *seqq.*

Sky-painting, artists to give its ordinary, not its exceptional
effects, I. 218 ; ii. 3. 1. 4.

„ dignity of, redeeming otherwise vulgar pictures,
II. 48 and *n* ; iii. 1. 5. 12 *n*.

„ green, I. 168 and *n* ; ii 2. 2. 5 and *n*.

Sky-painting, *continued :*

„ impossibility of perfect. *See s. Sky, blue.*

„ in early Italian pictures, I. 89, 90 ; ii. 1. 7. 11 (om. ed. 1, 2).

„ „ „ „ II. 46–7 ; iii. 1. 5. 9.

„ in mediæval MS. as a background, III. 215 ; iv. 14. 20.

„ in modern landscape, I. 227 ; ii. 3. 1. 19.

„ „ „ III. 264 ; iv. 16. 1.

Slate, colour of, IV. 131 *seqq.* ; v. 10. 3 *seqq.*

„ qualities of, IV. 129 *seqq.* ; v. 10. 1 *seqq.* *See s. Cleavage.*

Slaty coherents, characteristics of, iv. 129 *seqq.* ; v. 10. 1 *seqq.*

„ „ use of, IV. 133 ; v. 10. 6.

„ crystallines, IV. 120 *seqq.* ; v. 9. 1 *seqq.*

„ „ bank of, IV. 322 ; v. 18. 7 (pl. 48).

Slavery, essential to "classical" ideal life, V. 268 and *n* ; ix. 5. 6 and *n.*

Slime, in streets of manufacturing towns, V. 175–76 ; viii. 1. 7. 8.

Smell. *See s. Scent.*

Smith, Dict. Antiq. s. "Cyrenaica" quoted, V. 330 ; ix. 10. 4.

——, Sydney, "Memoirs" of, on the "Immortal," V. 298 *n* ; ix. 7. 21 *n.*

Smoke, colour of, V. 135 ; vii. 2. 18.

„ -nuisance, III. 188 ; iv. 13. 14.

„ „ "our smoke-paradise," V. 343 ; ix. 10. 24.

„ steam and, clouds of, distinguished by Turner, I. 247 ; ii. 3. 4. 13 (ed. 1–4 only).

Smollett, little love of nature in, III. 314–15 ; iv. 17. 28–9.

„ "Roderick Random," *ib.* ; *ib.*

Snow [Synopsis. I. 304–6. II. 83–4, 96. IV. 253]:—

Alpine, laws of its formation, I. 305–6 ; ii. 4. 2. 20 (om. ed. 1, 2).

beauty of, II. 83–4 ; iii. 1. 9. 5.

„ II. 96 ; iii. 1. 12. 1.

gradations of, unpaintable, IV. 253 ; v. 16. 18.

painting of, rules for, I. 305–6 ; ii. 4. 2. 19–20 (om. ed. 1, 2).

-wreath, described, never painted, I. 303–4 ; ii. 4. 2. 19 (om. ed. 1, 2).

Snowdon, IV. 170 ; v. 13. 8.

Snyders, hunting scenes and dogs, V. 281 ; ix. 6. 13.

„ „ „ „ V. 283 ; ix. 6. 19.

Social improvement, its real question, V. 362–63 ; ix. 11. 25.

Socrates, III. 156 ; iv. 11. 6.

   ,,   death of, V. 183 ; viii. 1. 20.

Softness, and obscurity, essential to greatest art, IV. 64 ; v. 4. 9.

   ,,   ,,   smoothness in art (Stothard, etc.), III. 79 ; iv. 6. 5–6.

Soil, the earth's, changed and renewed by the mountains, IV. 102 *seqq.* ; v. 7. 9 *seqq.*

Solazzino, repainting of Orcagna's "Inferno," II. 137 ; iii. 1. 14. 29.

Soldanella Alpina, II. 96 ; iii. 1. 12. 1 (and F.A. *n*).

   ,,   ,,   II. 115 ; iii. 1. 13. 11.

Soldier, character of the true, IV. 410 ; App. i. 5.

   ,,   the best, not for pay, V. 379 ; ix. 12. 7.

Solomon, character of, II. 103 ; iii. 1. 12. 8 ('83 *n*).

Soot, diamond from, V. 176 ; viii. 1. 9.

Sophocles, Ajax, "green sand," III. 234 ; iv. 14. 45.

   ,,   Antigone, her innocence checks not her fate, V. 233 ; ix. 2. 15.

   ,,   Œdipus Coloneus, on clouds in, V. 157 ; vii. 4. 10.

   ,,   ,,   ,,   ,,   Colonos praised for rain, III. 260 ; iv. 15. 21.

   ,,   ,,   ,,   ,,   forests, III. 226 ; iv. 14. 33.

   ,,   ,,   ,,   ,,   green glades, III. 234 ; iv. 14. 45.

   ,,   ,,   ,,   ,,   wine-coloured ivy, III. 234 ; iv. 14. 43.

Sorrento, ravines of, I. 218 ; ii. 3. 1. 4.

Sorrow, modern and Greek, III. 189 ; iv. 13. 14.

   ,,   source of good, V. 83 ; vi. 8. 18.

Southern and northern character. *See s. Northern.*

Southey on knowledge of and desire to impart truth, I. xix ; *pref. ed.* 2. 12.

Space, child instinct about, II. 42–3 ; iii. 1. 5. 3.

   ,,   idea of infinity, its power, II. 44 ; iii. 1. 5. 5.

   ,,   never truly given till Turner, I. 199 ; ii. 2. 4. 6.

   ,,   no dead, in nature, I. 205 ; ii. 2. 5. 5.

   ,,   truth of, I. 196 *seqq.* ; ii. 2. 4. 1 *seqq.*

   ,,   ,,   I. 202 *seqq.* ; ii. 2. 5. 1 *seqq.*

   ,,   want of, in ancient landscape, I. 272 ; ii. 3. 4. 20.

Spagnoletto, slurred work of, II. 88 ; iii. 1. 10. 3.

Spanish Chapel, Florence, S. Memmi's frescoes, III. 104 ; iv. 8. 6.

Sparta, epitaph, "Go, stranger," etc., III. 347 ; iv. 18. 34.

    „   „   V. 181–82 ; viii. 1. 8.

    „   military asceticism, V. 357 ; ix. 11. 17.

    „   mountains from, IV. 372 ; v. 20. 11.

"Spasmodic" literature, V. 267–68 ; ix. 5. 5.

Species, defined, II. 109 ; iii. 1. 13. 2 (and '83 n).

    „   truths of, beautiful ; idiosyncrasies generally defects,
        I. 64–6 ; ii. 1. 3. 5–7.

Spenser [SYNOPSIS. I. xviii n. II. 30 n, 57 n, 83 n, 134, 141,
        207, '83 Epil. 13. III. 102, 105, 227, 282. V. 124,
        340–42] :—

    as illustrator of nature, II. '83 Epil. 13.

    grotesque of, instanced, III. 102 ; iv. 8. 5.

    love of woods in, III. 227 ; iv. 14. 33.

    scenes of horror in, impossible to painter, II. 207 ; iii.
        2. 4. 2.

    spiritual personification of, III. 105 ; iv. 8. 7.

    works of :

        "Faërie Queen," Belphœbe, etc. (ideas of colour), II. 83 n ; iii.
            1. 9. 5 n.

        „   „   „   „   „   III. 227 ; iv.
            14. 33.

        „   „   Britomart disarming, III. 282 ; iv. 16. 33.

        „   „   „   dress, etc., of, V. 124 ; vii. 2. 6.

        „   „   Envy described, III. 102 ; iv. 8. 5.

        „   „   Eris, V. 340–41 ; ix. 10. 21.

        „   „   Forest of Errour, II. 57 n ; iii. 1. 6. 5 n.

        „   „   Hesperides, V. 342 ; ix. 10. 23.

        „   „   Red Crosse Knight and Errour, II. 187 ;
            iii. 2. 4. 2 (ed. 1 only).

        Hymn to Beauty, "But believe me," etc., II. 30 n ; iii. 1.
            3. 16 n.

        „   „   II. 83 n ; iii. 1. 9. 5 n.

        „   „   II. 141 ; iii. 1. 14. 32.

        quoted, on the nude, "Of all God's works," etc., II. 134 ;
            iii. 1. 14. 23.

        „   „   "Truth is one, and right is ever one," I. xviii n ;
            pref. ed. 2. 10 n.

Spirals, beauty of, II. 65 ; iii. 1. 6. 11.

    „   of thorn, V. 29 ; vi. 4. 8 (pl. 52).

Spirits, evil, how to be represented in art, II. 230 n ; iii. 2.
    5. 7 n.

Spirits, *continued :*
    „   human, unity through love, II. 55 ; iii. 1. 6. 2.
Spiritual beings, four manifestations of, conceivable, II. 226
                     seqq. ; iii. 2. 5. 2 *seqq.*
    „   „   introduction of, into landscape art, V. 217 ;
                     ix. 1. 2.
    „   „   rejected by modern art, V. 262 ; ix. 4. 14.
Spirituality, and purity, II. 86 ; iii. 1. 9. 9.
Splügen, pass of the (Via Mala), III. 245 ; iv. 15. 3.
Sport [SYNOPSIS. II. 98. III. 321. V. 2, 99, 283, 361]:—
    author's views of, V. 285 ; ix. 6. 22.
    deer-parks, V. 99 ; vi. 10. 2.
    evil influence of, II. 98 ; iii. 1. 12. 2 ('83 *n*).
    hunting and racing, III. 321 ; iv. 17. 36.
        „   „   shooting, V. 2 ; vi. 1. 1.
        „   „   „   V. 283 ; ix. 6. 19.
        „   „   „   V. 361 ; ix. 11. 22.
      See s. Horses, Hunting, Race-horses, Racing.
Sporting print, " Fox-hunter's death-bed," V. 285 ; ix. 6. 22.
Spring (season), spent by us in town ! V. 99 ; vi. 10. 2.
    „   of branches, V. 69 *seqq.* ; vi. 8. 3 *seqq.*
Square, four sides of, seldom comprehended, III. ix ; *pref.* 4.
Staffordshire, scenery of, IV. 367 ; v. 20. 3.
Stage-imitation, noble pleasure from, I. 22 ; i. 1. 4. 6.
    „   -peasantry, idea of Alpine life, IV. 340 ; v. 19. 6.
Stanfield, Clarkson [SYNOPSIS. I. 127–29, 156, 179, 200, 238, 258,
                        300–1, 307, 324–25, 331–33, 371, 374–75,
                        426 *n.* II. 244, '83 Epil. 14. IV. 7–8,
                        59]:—
    at author's birthday dinner, II. '83 Epil. 14.
    characteristics of (architecture, etc.), I. 127 *seqq.* ; ii. 1. 7.
      36 (om. ed. 1, 2).
    chiaroscuro of, I. 300 ; ii. 4. 2. 14.
    cirrus clouds, I. 238 ; ii. 3. 2. 13.
    clouds, finest next to Turner's, I. 257 ; ii. 3. 3. 27.
    definiteness of, IV. 59 ; v. 4. 2.
    foliage of, I. 426 *n* ; ii. 6. 1. 28 *n* (om. ed. 1, 2).
    frigidity, want of tone, I. 156 ; ii. 2. 1. 12.
    knowledge and power of, I. 245 ; ii. 3. 4. 7 (ed. 1, 2 only).
        „   „   „   I. 374 ; ii. 5. 2. 10.
    mountain-drawing, Alpine, I. 280 ; ii. 4. 2. 22 (ed. 1, 2
      only).

Stanfield, Clarkson, *continued:*

    mountain-drawing, urged to draw the Alps, I. 307 ; ii. 4.
        2. 21.

      ,,   ,,   I. 324–26 ; ii. 4. 3. 25–6.

    praise of, I. 76 ; ii. 1. 7. 6 (ed. 1, 2 only).

    realistic work of, I. 127, 129 ; ii. 1. 7. 36.

      ,,   ,,   IV. 59 *n* ; v. 4. 2.

    rocks of, I. 179 ; ii. 2. 2. 16.

      ,,   I. 331–32 ; ii. 4. 4. 8.

      ,,   Salvator's and Harding's compared, I. 332–33 ; ii.
           4. 4. 9–10.

    seas of, I. 371 ; ii. 5. 2. 5.

      ,,   I. 374 ; ii. 5. 2. 10.

      ,,   I. 375 ; ii. 5. 2. 12.

    ships and boats "brand new," I. 129 ; ii. 1. 7. 36 (om. ed.
      1, 2).

    space in his pictures, I. 200 ; ii. 2. 4. 6.

    truth of, I. 76 ; ii. 1. 7. 8 *n* (ed. 1, 2 only).

    Turner far above, I. xiii ; *pref.* 2.

    water-painting of, I. 343 ; ii. 5. 2. 2 (ed. 1, 2 only).

    windmill by (and by Turner), IV. 7–8 ; v. 1. 10–11.

    works of :

        Amalfi (R.A. 1848), II. 244 ; Add. 4–5 (om. ed. 1).

        Borromean Islands (St. Gothard), I. 300–1 ; ii. 4. 2. 14–15.

        Botallack Mine, Cornwall, I. 332 ; ii. 4. 4. 8.

        Coast Scenery, Dol, Brittany, IV. 7–8 ; v. 1. 10–11.

        Hastings, East Cliff, I. 332 ; ii. 4. 4. 8.

        Innspruck (*Pictorial Annual*), I. 280 ; ii. 4. 2. 22 (ed. 1
          2 only).

        Ischia, I. 128–29 ; ii. 1. 7. 36 (om. ed. 1, 2).

         ,,   I. 331 ; ii. 4. 4. 8.

        Magra (1847), II. 244 ; Add. 5 (om. ed. 1).

        Suli, hills of (Finden's Byron), I. 326 ; ii. 4. 3. 26.

        Venices, I. 76 ; ii. 1. 7. 9 (ed. 1, 2 only).

         ,,   Ducal Palace, I. 129 ; ii. 1. 7. 36 (om. ed. 1, 2).

        Wreck on Dutch Coast, I. 128 ; ii. 1. 7. 36 (om. ed. 1, 2).

Stars, Canis Major, V. 123 ; vii. 2. 6. *See s. Sirius.*

Statues, colossal (Medici chapel), II. 223 ; iii. 2. 4. 19.

    ,,   tinted or gilded, examples of, II. 216 ; iii. 2. 4. 9.
          See s. Sculpture.

Statute, judgment and, V. 170 ; vii. 4. 34.

Steam, clouds of smoke and, distinguished by Turner, I. 247 ; ii. 3. 4. 13 (ed. 1–4 only).

„ visibility of, V. 118 ; vii. 1. 7.

Steele, quoted on description, III. 150 ; iv. 10. 21.

Steen. *See s. Jan Steen.*

Steino, Gorgon, V. 158 ; vii. 4. 11.

Stem-structure, V. 21–2 ; vi. 3. 14.

„ „ "a messenger to the roots," V. 46 ; vi. 6. 4.

„ „ V. 54 *seqq.* ; vi. 7. 1 *seqq.*

Stewart, Dugald, on imagination and fancy, II. 152–53 ; iii. 2. 1. 3.

„ „ „ „ composition, II. 159 ; iii. 2. 2. 3.

Stockje, Mt., IV. 249, 250 ; v. 16. 13, 15.

Stone-colour, idea of, IV. 136–37, 143 ; v. 11. 5, 11.

„ -cutting, ugliness of most, III. 120 *seqq.* ; iv. 9. 6–7.

Stones, drawing of, IV. 326–27 ; v. 18. 11.

„ lessons from, if patiently sought, IV. 322 ; v. 18. 6.

„ mountains in miniature, IV. 322 ; v. 18. 7.

„ our most familiar servants, IV. 181 ; v. 13. 19.

„ painting of, ancient and modern, IV. 319–21 ; v. 18. 1–3.

„ surfaces of, their beauty, IV. 322–23 ; v. 18. 7.

„ walls of, prison-lessons, V. 4 ; vi. 1. 4.

Storm, description of, near Col de Balme, I. 262 ; ii. 3. 4. 4.

„ elevation and velocity of, I. 260–62 *n* ; ii. 3. 4. 1–4 *n.*

„ gathering, described, I. 279 ; ii. 3. 4. 32 (ed. 1–4. 36).

„ „ „ V. 156 ; vii. 4. 8.

„ smoking of waterfalls, sign of departing, I. 267 *n* ; ii. 3. 4. 13 *n* (ed. 1–4. 14 *n*).

„ violent, never well engraved, I. 275 *seqq.* ; ii. 3. 4. 25 *seqq.* (ed. 1–4. 30).

Stothard, purity of, II. 133 ; iii. 1. 14. 20.

„ „ III. 79 ; iv. 6. 5.

„ Rogers' "Italy," p. 96, engraving to Ginevra, V. 41 ; vi. 5. 6.

Stowe, Mrs., "Sunny Memories," III. 59 *n* ; iv. 4. 18 *n.*

Straight lines, curves more beautiful than, IV. 278 *seqq.* ; v. 17. 3 *seqq.*

Strangeness, as a quality of execution, I. 40–2 ; i. 2. 2. 7.

„ familiarity and, as cause of delight, II. 33–4 ; iii. 1. 4. 4.

Strangeness, *continued:*
    „   familiarity and, as cause of delight, II. 58-9 ; iii.
            1. 6. 6.
Strata, of Matterhorn, IV. 415 ; App. ii. 1.
    „   three types of stratification, IV. 156 *seqq.* ; v. 12. 18 *seqq.*
Stratford-on-Avon, mountain influence on Shakspere, IV. 382–
        83 ; v. 20. 25–7.
Straw Street, and seventh heaven in Dante, III. 89 ; iv. 7. 8–9.
Strawberry-plant, seed of, V. 106 and *n* ; vi. 10. 15–16 and *n.*
Streams, beds of, how hollowed out, I. 391 ; ii. 5. 3. 22.
    „   sculpture of hills by, IV. 145 *seqq.* ; v. 12. 2 *seqq.*
    „   „   „   IV. 223 *seqq.* ; v. 15. 19 *seqq.*
    „   „   „   IV. 277 *seqq.* ; v. 17. 1 *seqq.*
    „   „   „   IV. 293 *seqq.* ; v. 17. 22 *seqq.*
Strength, good breeding and physical, V. 289 ; ix. 7. 5.
Strid, geology of the, IV. 263–66 ; v. 16. 31–3.
Stucco, vileness of, III. 248 ; iv. 15. 9.
Studies from nature, memoranda of great artists, V. 202 *seqq.* ;
        viii. 4. 6 *seqq.*
Stulz (tailor), I. 231 ; ii. 3. 3. 14 (ed. 1, 2 only).
Style in art, greatness of (choice of subject, love of beauty, in-
                vention, sincerity), III. 29–47 ; iv. 3. 5 *seqq.*
    „   not an individual manner, but the one true method,
            I. 101–2 ; ii. 1. 7. 20 (om. ed. 1, 2).
    „   "the grand style," III. 3 *seqq.* ; iv. 1. 4 *seqq.*
                See s. Reynolds.
Subject, choice of, decides rank of artist, III. 29 *seqq.* ; iv. 3.
        5 *seqq.*
    „   „   fettered by fashion and patrons, III. 31–2 ;
                iv. 3. 8.
Subjective, useless word, III. 161–63 ; iv. 12. 1–3.
    „   used wrongly (and so "objective"), IV. 423 ; App.
            iii. 1.
Sublime, wide meaning of the word, I. 44 *seqq.* ; i. 2. 3. 1 *seqq.*
Sublimity, attainment of, in art, I. xxviii ; *pref. ed.* 2. 20.
    „   effect of, on the mind, I. 44 ; i. 2. 3. 1 *seqq.*
    „   effort after, in art, IV. 256–58 ; v. 16. 23–4.
    „   essence of, V. 101 ; vi. 10. 7.
    „   is not always truth, I. 168–69 ; ii. 2. 2. 5.
    „   picturesque, when accidental, IV. 2. 6–7 ; v. 1. 1 *seqq.*
                See s. Burke.
Submission, good of, V. 101 ; vi. 8. 18.

Subtlety, political, V. 295 ; ix. 7. 15.

Success in art, its secret, V. 199 ; viii. 3. 8.

Suckling (Sir J.), Wedding Ballad (" Her lips were red," etc.),
 II. 179 ; iii. 2. 3. 7.

Sue, Eugene, love and study of nature by, III. 302 ; iv. 17. 7.

 „ „ " Mystères de Paris," "je déteste la campagne,'
        III. 313 and *n* ; iv. 17.
        26–27.

 „ „ „ „ Squelette (horrors), IV.
        348 ; v. 19. 16.

Suffering, path to glory, III. 241 ; iv. 14. 53.

 „ selfish indifference to and neglect of, IV. 362–63 ; v.
    19. 32.

Suffolk scenery, no ballads from, IV. 383 ; v. 20. 27.

Suggestiveness, imagination and, II. 184–85 ; iii. 2. 3. 14.

Sun, colour of, given only by Turner, V. 346 ; ix. 11. 3.

 „ dazzling : why, then, not Turner ? I. 174–75 ; ii. 2. 2. 11.

 „ early painting of, by Bonifazio, Claude, etc., III. 337–38 ;
   iv. 18. 22.

 „ rays round the, V. 130 ; vii. 2. 13.   *See s. Sunbeams.*

 „ the tabernacle of the, IV. 92 ; v. 6. 9.

Sunbeams, none from clear sun, I. 225 ; ii. 3. 1. 15.

 „ painting of, by Claude and Turner, I. 223 *seqq.* ; ii.
    3. 1. 13 *seqq.*

 „ radiation of, IV. 414 ; App. ii. 1.

 „ when visible, I. 223 *seqq.* ; ii. 3. 1. 13 *seqq.*

Sunflower, II. 90 ; iii. 1. 10. 4.

Sunlight, cannot be painted, IV. 35 ; v. 3. 1.

 „ on water, I. 352 ; ii. 5. 1. 8 (om. ed. 1, 2).

 „ yellow, not by colourists, V. 346 ; ix. 11. 3.

Sunrise in the Alps, described, I. 280–81 ; ii. 3. 4. 34 (ed.
  1–4. 38).

 „ near London, clouds at, V. 122 *seqq.* ; vii. 2. 4.

 „ sign of Rising Sun, with rays, untrue, I. 225 ; ii. 3.
   1. 15.

Sunset, described, I. 162–63 ; ii. 2. 1. 21.

 „ „ its brilliancy in the high clouds, I. 170–71 ;
    ii. 2. 2. 7.

 „ how rarely *thoroughly* seen, I. 171–72 ; ii. 2. 2. 8.

 „ Longfellow on, III. 185 *n* ; iv. 13. 10 *n.*

 „ no one but Turner can paint, I. 171–72 ; ii. 2. 2. 8.

 „ recollection of, always feeble, *ib.* ; *ib.*

Sunset, *continued :*
„   stormy, described, I. 280 ; ii. 3. 4. 33 (ed. 1–4. 37).
Superiority, degrees of, I. 441 ; ii. 6. 3. 7.
Supernatural, rendering of the, in art, II. 126–27 ; iii. 2. 5. 1–4.
Superstition, in hill-countries, IV. 374 ; v. 20. 13.
„   northern and the pine, V. 94 ; vi. 9. 12.
Surface, beauty of, II. 83 ; iii. 1. 9. 5.
„   of water, imperfectly reflective, I. 350 ; ii. 5. 1. 6.
„   „   unpaintable, I. 376 ; ii. 5. 3. 1.
Surprise, the pleasure of, I. 20 ; i. 1. 4. 2.
Suttee, Hindoo, III. 321 ; iv. 17. 36.
Swammerdam, his work did not pay, V. 379 ; ix. 12. 7.
Swan, beauty of a, II. 57 ; iii. 1. 6. 5.
„   „   its wing at sunset, II. 83 *n* ; iii. 1. 9. 5 *n*.
Swift, " Tale of a Tub " (ix), on anatomy in art, II. 243 ; Add.
   3 (om. ed. 1) ('83 *n*).
Swinburne, Sir J., Callcott owned by, I. 100 ; ii. 1. 7. 18 (om.
   ed. 1, 2).
Switzerland [SYNOPSIS. I. 302, 379. III. 240. IV. 74–5, 139
            seqq., 142–43, 173 *seqq.*, 274–75, 305–7, 338–40,
            344–45, 358–59, 367–68, 382, 396–98. V. 94–7,
            357 *n*, 368 *n*]:—
   cantons of, significance of their names, V. 96 ; vi. 9. 15.
   divisions and geography of, IV. 173 *seqq.* ; v. 13. 10 *seqq.*
   drawings of, average, I. 306–7 ; ii. 4. 2. 20–1 (om. ed. 1, 2).
      „   IV. 274–75 ; v. 16. 42.
      „   tower, IV. 74–5 ; v. 5. 7.
   flowers of (pain du bon Dieu), IV. 368–69 *n* ; v. 20. 5. *See
      s. Botany.*
   forest cantons (under the woods), V. 96–7 ; vi. 9. 15.
   history of (Egeri), V. 94–6 ; vi. 9. 13–14.
   Lac de Chède destroyed, I. 353 *n* ; ii. 3. 3. 5 *n* (ed. 1, 2
      only).
   Lake of Geneva, Clarens railway bridge, V. 357 *n* ; ix.
      11. 15 *n*.
   malaria (Valais), IV. 359 ; v. 19. 30.
   meadows of, III. 240 ; iv. 14. 51.
   no poet produced by, IV. 382 ; v. 20. 25.
   people of : character and life, IV. 142–43 ; v. 11. 10.
      „   „   „   IV. 338–40 ; v. 19. 4–5.
      „   „   „   IV. 344–45 ; v. 19. 10–11.
      „   „   „   IV. 358–59 ; v. 19. 28.

Switzerland, *continued:*

    people of : character and life, IV. 396 ; v. 20. 39.

       ,,   ,,   ,,   V. 94 *seqq.* ; vi. 9. 12–16.

       ,,   feeling for mountains, V. 96 ; vi. 9. 15.

       ,,   *the* Swiss *par excellence* (Helvetii), V. 95 ; vi. 9. 13.

    religion of, V. 95–6 ; vi. 9. 14.

    Romanism and Protestantism, IV. 359 ; v. 19. 29.

    ruin of, by railroads, IV. 396–98 ; v. 20. 40 *seqq.*

       ,,   ,, tourists, *ib.* ; *ib.*

       ,,   modern, V. 368 *n* ; ix. 11. 30 *n.*

    scenery of, best idea of Paradise, IV. 367 ; v. 20. 3.

       ,,   detail of, great, IV. 304–6 ; v. 17. 37–9.

       ,,   ,,   unpaintable, IV. 307 ; v. 17. 40.

       ,,   lowlands described, IV. 139 *seqq.* ; v. 11. 8 *seqq.*
                See s. Fribourg.

       ,,   number of trees in, IV. 307 ; v. 17. 39.

       ,,   unpicturesque ! IV. 307 ; v. 17. 40.

       ,,   ,,   IV. 368 *n* ; v. 20. 4 *n.*
                See s. Alps, Mountains, Places.

Syenites, characteristics of, IV. 113 *seqq.* ; v. 8. 14 *seqq.*

Syllogism, few people can form a, III. ix ; *pref.* 4.

Symbolism in art, its place and value, I. 226–27 *n* ; ii. 3. 1. 18 *n*
                        (om. ed. 1, 2).

   ,,   ,,   ,,   ,,   II. 221–22 ; iii. 2. 4. 17.

   ,,   ,,   ,,   ,,   III. 103–4 ; iv. 8. 6.

   ,,   ,,   imitation changing to, III. 215 ; iv. 14. 19.

   ,,   ,,   mediæval, of clouds and water, III. 222–23 ;
                iv. 14. 28.

   ,,   ,,   passionate expression of (Lombard griffin),
                III. 115 ; iv. 8. 21. *See s. Calais tower.*

   ,,   ,,   symbolical works of great painters, their best,
                III. 104 ; iv. 8. 6.

Symmetry defined, as distinct from proportion, II. 78–9 ; iii. 1. 8. 2.

   ,,   in clouds, I. 232–33 ; ii. 3. 2. 8.

   ,,   ,, mountain form, I. 317 ; ii. 4. 3. 13.

   ,,   ,, nature, necessary in art, II. 78 *seqq.* ; iii. 1. 8. 1 *seqq.*

   ,,   ,, tree-curvature, I. 424 ; ii. 6. 1. 25.

   ,,   ,,   ,,   V. 38 ; vi. 5. 1.

   ,,   **,, tree-stems, V. 63–5 ; vi. 7. 14**

Symmetry, *continued*:

,,   natural number and variety heightened in effect by, I. 232–33 ; ii. 3. 2. 6–8.

,,   true and false, mediæval and modern, III. 210–11 ; iv. 14. 12–13.

,,   type of Divine justice, II. 78–80 ; iii. 1. 8. 1 *seqq.*

,,   use of, in religious art, II. 80 ; iii. 1. 8. 4.

,,   ,,   ,,   ,, IV. 79–80 ; v. 5. 16.

,,   value of, in spiritual pictures, II. 237 ; iii. 2. 5. 18.

Sympathy, characteristics of, II. 100 ; iii. 1. 12. 5.

,,   ,,   II. 182 ; iii. 2. 3. 9.

,,   condition of noble picturesque, IV. 9–11 ; v. 1. 11 *seqq.*

,,   ,,   ,,   ,, IV. 14 ; v. 1. 16.

,,   cunning goes with absence of, V. 293 ; ix. 7. 11.

,,   foundation of true criticism, III. 25 ; iv. 2. 8.

,,   in art, essential to appreciate emotional work, I. 90 ; ii. 1. 7. 11 (om. ed. 1, 2).

,,   ,,   ,,   artist, with nature, III. 24 ; iv. 2. 8.

,,   ,,   its influence on the picturesque, IV. 9–10 ; v. 1. 12.

,,   human, V. 221 ; ix. 1. 9.

,,   necessary to detect passing expression, III. 72 ; iv. 5. 8.

,,   sign of true gentleman, V. 290–91 ; ix. 7. 8.

,,   vulgarity of want of, III. 89 ; iv. 7. 9.

,,   when keenest, II. 182 ; iii. 2. 3. 9.

,,   with humanity, II. 182 ; iii. 2. 3. 9.

,,   ,,   ,, IV. 11 ; v. 1. 13.

,,   ,,   nature, II. 98–9 ; iii. 1. 12. 3 *seqq.*

,,   ,,   ,, III. 187–88 ; iv. 13. 13.

,,   ,,   ,, III. 205 ; iv. 14. 7.

,,   ,,   ,, IV. 14–15 ; v. 1. 16 *seqq.*

System-makers, waste of time by, III. 2 ; iv. 1. 2.

Tabernacle, colours of God's, V. 169 ; vii. 4. 30.

Tabor, Mt., the scene of the Transfiguration, IV. 404–5 ; v. 20. 48. *See s. Hermon.*

Taconay, Mt., clouds over, V. 149 ; vii. 3. 17.

,,   ,,   form and top of, IV. 172 *n* ; v. 13. 8 *n.*

,,   ,,   ,,   ,, IV. 217, 218 ; v. 15. 15–16.

Taconay, Mt., *continued :*

　　,,　　　,,　　　form and top of, IV. 223–4 ; v. 15. 18–19 (pl. 35).

　　,,　　　,,　　　,,　　　,,　　　IV. 298 ; v. 17. 30.

　　,,　　　,,　　　,,　　　,,　　　IV. 329 *n* ; v. 18. 15 *n*.

　　,,　　　,,　　　ridges of, I. 316 ; ii. 4. 3. 12.

Talk, waste of vital power in, III. 107 ; iv. 8. 9.

Tapia (Chamouni), IV. 172 *n* ; v. 13. 8 *n*.

　　,,　　　,,　　　crest of, IV. 217 ; v. 15. 15.

　　,,　　　,,　　　,,　　　IV. 220 *n* ; v. 15. 16 *n*.

　　,,　　　,,　　　,,　　　IV. 223 ; v. 15. 18.

　　,,　　　,,　　　curves at its base, IV. 298 ; v. 17. 30.

　　,,　　　,,　　　slope of, IV. 329 *n* ; v. 18. 15 *n*.

　　,,　　　,,　　　,,　　　IV. 422 ; App. ii. 5.

Taste [SYNOPSIS. I. 29–30, 442, 444.　II. 18, 21–30, 36–7, 88.
　　　III. 69–70.　IV. 283–84.　V. 267] :—

　　defined, I. 29–30 ; i. 1. 6. 1–3.

　　education of, II. 18 ; iii. 1. 2. 8.

　　　　,,　　　possible, II. 23 ; iii. 1. 3. 3.

　　　　,,　　　right temper for, II. 26–7 ; iii. 1. 3. 9.

　　　　,,　　　the word, its meaning, III. 69–70 ; iv. 5. 6.

　　experience a test of, IV. 283–84 ; v. 17. 9.

　　fastidious implies false, II. 28 ; iii. 1. 3. 11.

　　fondness for unfinished works, I. 445 ; ii. 6. 3. 15.

　　　　,,　　　　,,　　　　,,　　II. 88 ; iii. 1. 10. 3.

　　judges in matters of, meaning of term, II. 24 ; iii. 1. 3. 4.

　　judgment and, deliberate and instinctive, I. 30 ; i. 1.
　　　6. 3.

　　meaning of good, V. 267 ; ix. 5. 3–5.

　　men of, described, I. 29–30 ; i. 1. 6. 1.

　　public, its nature, I. 442 ; ii. 6. 3. 8–9.

　　purity of, tested by universality, II. 28 ; iii. 1. 3. 11.

　　reason for our, not to be asked, I. 29 ; i. 1. 6. 1.

　　right, that of the majority? II. 22–3 ; iii. 1. 3. 2.

　　tests of true, and false, II. 21 *seqq.* ; iii. 1. 3. 1. *seqq.*

　　　　,,　　　　,,　　　　,,　　II. 28 ; iii. 1. 3. 11.

　　unconscious association affects, II. 36–7 ; iii. 1. 4. 9.
　　　　　　　　　See s. Classical.

Tayler, Frederic, his sketches better than his pictures, I. 38 ;
　　i. 2. 1. 8.

　　　　,,　　　　,,　　　rain-blue of his water-colours, I. 273 ; ii. 3. 4.
　　　　21 (ed. 1–4. 24).

Taylor, on imagination, II. 157–58 ; iii. 2. 2. 1.

Teaching, example the best, V. 359 ; ix. 11. 20.

    ,,   explanation and hints in, their value, V. 376 *n* ; ix. 12. 4 *n.*

Technical qualities of art. *See s. Execution.*

Tees, banks of, IV. 315 ; v. 17. 48.

Telegraph, value of the, III. 320–21 ; iv. 17. 35–6.

Temperance and intemperance, II. 14–16 ; iii. 1. 2. 3–5.

Tempesta, picturesque landscape of, V. 218 ; ix. 1. 3.

Teniers [SYNOPSIS. I. 6, 227, 335. III. 30, 37. V. 279, 283, 304, 309] :—

    author's depreciation of, I. 6 ; i. 1. 1. 4.

    ,,   want of sympathy with, V. 304 ; ix. 8. 1.

    character of his work, V. 309 ; ix. 8. 11.

    dogs in, unclean, V. 283 ; ix. 6. 19.

    skies of, some fine, I. 227 ; ii. 3. 1. 20.

    subjects of, low, III. 30 ; iv. 3. 5.

    ,,   ugly, III. 37 ; iv. 3. 12.

    unspiritual, V. 279 ; ix. 6. 10.

    work of (Dulwich Gallery, 139), I. 335 ; ii. 4. 4. 13.

Tennyson [SYNOPSIS. II. Epil. 13. III. 165 *n*, 169, 177 *n*, 269, 274, 276, 280, 284–87, 302. IV. 19. V. 180 *n*, 286, 295, 364] :—

    colour of, rich, III. 274 ; iv. 16. 18.

    emotional writing of, III. 280 ; iv. 16. 29.

    finish and melody of, III. 276 ; iv. 16. 23.

    love of nature, dreamy, III. 302 ; iv. 17. 8.

    pastorals of, V. 286 ; ix. 6. 23.

    pathetic fallacy in, III. 177 *n* ; iv. 12. 26 *n.*

    ,,   ,,   III. 284–87 ; iv. 16. 36–8.

    Pre-Raphaelite brethren and, IV. 19 ; v. 2. 5.

    reflective, III. 165 ; iv. 12. 6 *n.*

    religious doubts of, III. 269 ; iv. 16. 10.

    second order of poets (subdued by their feelings), III. 169 ; iv. 12. 10.

    sense of beauty, V. 364 ; ix. 11. 26.

    works of :

        Brook, II. '83 Epil. 13.

        Grandmother, The, " A lie which is half the truth," etc., V. 295 ; ix. 7. 14.

        In Memoriam, less great than " Guy Mannering," III. 280 ; iv. 16. 29.

        ,,   ,,   quoted, III. 287 ; iv. 16. 38.

Tennyson : works of, *continued :*
    In Memoriam, quoted, V. 180 *n* ; viii. 1. 16 *n*.
    Lady of Shalott, "His broad clear brow . . . galaxy," III.
        209 ; iv. 14. 11.
    Maud, quoted, III. 177 *n* ; iv. 12. 15 *n*.
       ,,   ,,   III. 287 ; iv. 16. 39.

Terburg, Gerard, quiet painting of, V. 309 ; ix. 8. 11.
Terrible, contemplation of the, by mountaineers, IV. 344 *seqq.* ;
    v. 19. 9. *seqq.*
   ,,   great men can be, without being licentious, I. 414 ; ii.
        6. 1. 11 (om. ed. 1, 2).
Terror, human, and holy fear, II. 136 ; iii. 1. 14. 27.
Testimony, fear of God and, V. 169–70 ; vii. 4. 33.
Tête Noire, IV. 160 ; v. 12. 21.
Texture, rendering of, in art, II. 217 ; iii. 2. 4. 11.
Thackeray, religious teaching of, III. 269 ; iv. 16. 10.
Thames, its wooded reaches, IV. 369–70 ; v. 20. 7.
   ,,   near London, described, V. 319 ; ix. 9. 8.
Thaumas (son of Nereus), V. 157 ; vii. 4. 9.
   ,,   ,,   ,,   V. 347 ; ix. 11. 4.
Theatre, costliness of modern drama, useless and bad, IV. 341
    and *n* ; v. 19. 6 *n*.
Theoria [SYNOPSIS. II. '83 *pref.* 7, 9–13, 17, 19, 26, 96–8, 103,
    108–9, 149–50, 168] :—
    definition and meaning of, II. 9 ; iii. 1. 1. 8 ('83 *n*).
       ,,   ,,   ,,   II. 13 ; iii. 1. 2. 1.
       ,,   ,,   ,,   II. 17 ; iii. 1. 2. 6.
       ,,   ,,   ,,   II. 26 ; iii. 1. 3. 7.
    faculty of, II. 10–11 ; iii. 1. 1. 10.
       ,,   imagination and, united, II. 168 ; iii. 2. 2. 16.
       ,,   its connection with just judgment, II. 103 ; iii. 1.
            12. 8.
       ,,   ,, function as to vital beauty (charity), II. 96–8 ;
            iii. 1. 12. 1–2.
    happiness of, II. '83 *pref.* 7.
    the service of heaven, II. 149–50 ; iii. 1. 15. 12.
    three operations of, II. 108–9 ; iii. 1. 13. 1.
    universality of Christian, II. 19 ; iii. 1. 2. 10.
Thermopylæ, II. 72 ; iii. 1. 7. 4.
Think, few people ever, V. 179 ; viii. 1. 14. *See s. Thought.*
Thinkers, seers, and sayers, III. 278–79 ; iv. 16. 28.

Thirteenth-century art, fails of deceptive imitation, III. 20 ; iv. 2. 5.

Thistle, leaf of, V. 105 ; vi. 10. 14.

Thomson (poet), lines of, quoted under Turner's pictures, V. 329 ; ix. 10. 3.

————, T., Outline of Geology, IV. 123 *n* ; v. 9. 5 *n*.

Thornbury's Life of Turner, V. 373 ; ix. 12. 3.

Thorns, persons compared to, V. 180 ; viii. 1. 16.

Thought, connection with art, I. 47 *seqq.* ; ii. 1. 1. 1 *seqq.*

        ,,   ,,   ,,   knowledge, I. 52 ; ii. 1. 1. 10.

        ,,   defined, I. 32–3 ; i. 1. 7. 1 *seqq.*

        ,,   false, worse than none at all, I. 50 ; ii. 1. 1. 7. *See s. Think, Thinkers.*

        ,,   highest, most independent of fine words, I. 10 ; i. 1. 2. 5.

        ,,   various, of different minds on same things, III. 300–1 ; iv. 17. 6.

Ticino. *See s. Faido.*

Time, the "sacred verdict" of, its value, I. 1–7 ; i. 1. 1. 1–5.

Tintoret [SYNOPSIS. I. 82-8, 91, 104, 115-16, 146, 213 *n*, 247 *n*, 359, 414, 422 *n*. II. 2, 8 *n*, 48, 79, 80, 88 *n*, 129, 132, 139, 169–71, 186–96, 200 *n*, 205 *n*, 216, 219, 222 *n*, 230 *n*, '83 Epil. 12–14. III. 42, 46, 49, 63, 98, 104–5, 131, 15 , 278, 289, 336, 345, 355. IV. 15, 27 *n*, 29, 59, 64, 67, 308, 317, 324, 377, 380, 408. V. 100, 211 *n*, 220, 246, 251, 254, 350 *n*, 353 *n*]:—

asking to paint new house, II. 89 *n* ; iii. 1. 10. 3 *n*.

author's admiration of, II. '83 Epil. 14.

clouds of, I. 230 *n* ; ii. 3. 3. 13 (ed. 3, 4 only).

    ,,   sublime, II. 222 *n* ; iii. 2. 4. 17 *n*.

colour, and light of, I. 104 ; ii. 1. 7. 21 (om. ed. 1, 2).

    ,,   and no form, like gems, II. 216 ; iii. 2. 4. 10.

    ,,   favourite colours, black and white, III. 289 ; iv. 16. 42.

    ,,   III. 46 ; iv. 3. 26.

    ,,   V. 350 *n* ; ix. 11. 8 *n*.

    ,,   imagination and, V. 353 *n* ; ix. 11. 8 *n*.

delicacy of, III. 42 ; iv. 3. 20.

ease of, III. 278 ; iv. 16. 27.

engraving from, III. 355 ; App. (pl. 17).

execution, its certainty, II. 200 *n* ; iii. 2. 3. 28 *n*.

finish deficient, I. 87 ; ii. 1. 7. 10 (om. ed. 1, 2).

Tintoret, *continued* :

 finish deficient, through impetuosity, II. 88 *n* ; iii. 1. 10. 3 *n*.
  „ III. 131 ; iv. 9. 18.
  „ IV. 69 ; v. 4. 15.
 flowers in, rare, V. 100 ; vi. 10. 5.
 foregrounds of, I. 213 *n* ; ii. 2. 5. 15 *n* (om. ed. 1, 2).
 frescoes, no remnants of any, I. 116 ; ii. 1. 7. 30 (om. ed. 1, 2).
 groundwork of his pictures, often dark, V. 211 *n* ; viii. 4. 17 *n*.
 humour in, none, IV. 15 ; v. 1. 17.
  „ „ or very rare, IV. 408 ; App. i. 3.
 imagination noble, II. 169 ; iii. 2. 2. 17.
   „ unconscious remembrance and, IV. 29 ; v. 2. 17.
   „ unsurpassed, II. 170 ; iii. 2. 2. 19.
   „ „ examples given, II. 186–97 ; iii.
         2. 3. 15 *seqq.*
 landscape, I. 92 ; ii. 1. 7. 12 (om. ed. 1, 2).
  „ grand, II. 79 ; iii. 1. 8. 3 ('83 *n*).
  „ „ but limited, I. 82–4 ; ii. 1. 7. 6–7 (om. ed
       1, 2).
  „ III. 345 ; iv. 18. 31.
  „ vague, IV. 59 ; v. 4. 2.
 modesty of, II. 132 ; iii. 1. 14. 19.
 mountains, first well drawn by, IV. 377 ; v. 20. 16.
  „ loved by him, IV. 380 ; v. 20. 21.
 mystery and softness of, IV. 64 ; v. 4. 9.
 neglect of his works at Venice, II. 8 *n* ; iii. 1. 1. 7 *n*.
  „ „ „ „ III. 150 ; iv. 10. 21.
 negro behind king in work of, IV. 27 *n* ; v. 2. 16 *n*.
 passion as rendered by, II. 139 ; iii. 1. 14. 31.
 perception of, intense, IV. 69 ; v. 4. 15.
 pictures of, the two best, V. 246 ; ix. 3. 17.
 picturesque of, IV. 15 ; v. 1. 17.
 portraiture in works of, II. 129, 132 ; iii. 1. 14. 14. 19.
 power of, I. 87–8 ; ii. 1. 7. 10 (om. ed. 1, 2).
  „ greatest of all, I. 92 ; ii. 1. 7. 12 (om. ed. 1, 2).
  „ IV. 324 ; v. 18. 9.
 qualities of, IV. 308 ; v. 17. 42.
 realistic temper of, III. 104 ; iv. 8. 7.
 religion of (Bible subjects), III. 63 ; iv. 4. 22 (F.A. *n*).
  „ V. 251 ; ix. 3. 28.
 Ridolfi's Life, quoted, II. 2 ; iii. 1. 1. 2.
 saying, " Sempre si fa il mare maggiore," II. 2 ; iii. 1. 1. 2.

Tintoret, *continued :*

sense of space first given by, I. 92 ; ii. 1. 7. 12 (om. ed. 1, 2).

skies of, luminous, II. 48 ; iii. 1. 5. 11.

stands alone, IV. 317–18 ; v. 17. 51.

stones, painting of, I. 146 ; ii. 1. 7. 46 (om. ed. 1, 2).

     „   „   II. 199 ; ii. 3. 28.

subjects of, his own age, III. 98 ; iv. 7. 19–20.

supremacy of, first shown by author, II. '83 Epil. 13.

swift strokes of, III. 42 ; iv. 3. 20.

symbolical works of, III. 104–5 ; iv. 8. 6–7.

symmetrical groups of, II. 80 ; iii. 1. 8. 4.

temper of, II. 194 *n* ; iii. 2. 3. 22 *n*.

Titian less great, more finished, I. 91 ; ii. 1. 7. 12 (om. ed. 1, 2).

trees of, sweet-chestnut (concentric grouping), II. 79 ; iii. 1. 8. 3.

truth of, IV. 69 ; v. 4. 16.

Venice, painting of her architecture by, I. 115 ; ii. 1. 7. 29 (om. ed. 1, 2).

works of :

    Adoration of Magi (Venice), III. 85 ; iv. 7. 2–3.

        „   „   „   III. 131 ; iv. 9. 18.

        „   „   „   IV. 69 ; v. 4. 15.

    Agony in Garden, II. 171 ; iii. 2. 2. 19.

        „   „   II. 194 ; iii. 2. 3. 22.

    Annunciation, its imagination, II. 187–88 ; iii. 2. 3. 17.

    Baptism of Christ, II. 188–90 ; iii. 2. 3. 18–19.

        „   „   II. 197 ; iii. 2. 3. 25.

        „   „   II. 219 ; iii. 2. 4. 13.

    Cenacolo, S. Giorgio Maggiore, IV. 59 *n* ; v. 4. 2 *n*.

    Christ before Pilate, II. 194 ; iii. 2. 3. 22.

    Crucifixion, II. 80 ; iii. 1. 8. 4.

        „   II. 191, 197 ; iii. 2. 3. 20, 25.

        „   II. 219 ; iii. 2. 4. 13.

        „   II. '83 Epil. 12.

        „   V. 220 ; ix. 1. 8.

        „   V. 246 ; ix. 3. 17.

    Death of Abel, I. 84 *n* ; ii. 1. 7. 7 (om. ed. 1, 2).

        „   „   I. 414 ; ii. 6. 1. 11 (om. ed. 1, 2).

        „   „   I. 422 *n* ; ii. 6. 1. 23 *n*.

    Doge Loredano (lion in), II. 220 ; iii. 2. 4. 15.

        „   Mocenigo, I. 115 ; ii. 1. 7. 29 (om. ed. 1, 2).

    Doges in Ducal Palace, III. 104 ; iv. 8. 6.

Tintoret : works of, *continued* :

  Entombment (Parma), II. 186–87 ; iii. 2. 3. 16.

  ,, ,, III. 336 ; iv. 18. 18 (pl. 17).

  Fall of Adam, I. 84 *n* ; ii. 1. 7. 7 *n* (om. ed. 1, 2).

  Flight into Egypt, II. 170 ; iii. 2. 2. 19.

  ,, ,, II. 194 ; iii. 2. 3. 22.

  Golden Calf, II. 222 ; iii. 2. 4. 17.

  ,, ,, IV. 59 *n* ; v. 4. 2 *n*.

  Holy Innocents, II. 139 ; iii. 1. 14. 31.

  ,, ,, II. 193–94 ; iii. 2. 3. 21.

  ,, ,, II. 197 ; iii. 2. 3. 25.

  Last Judgment (S. M. dell' Orto), II. 194–96 ; iii. 2. 3. 23-4.

  Paradise, I. 359 ; ii. 5. 1. 16 (om. ed. 1, 2).

  ,, III. 49 ; iv. 4. 5 (F.A. *n*).

  ,, IV. 67 ; v. 4. 13.

  ,, IV. 68 ; v. 4. 15.

  ,, V. 246 ; ix. 3. 17.

  ,, V. 254 ; ix. 3. 32.

  Plague of Fiery Serpents, II. 197 *n* ; iii. 2. 3. 25 *n*.

  Scuola di S. Rocco, II. '83 Epil. 12.

  ,, ,, II. 194 ; iii. 2. 3. 22.

  ,, ,, II. 200 *n* ; iii. 2. 3. 28 *n*.

  Temptation, II. 171 ; iii. 2. 2. 19.

  ,, II. 181 *n* ; iii. 2. 3. 28 *n*.

  ,, II. 230 ; iii. 2. 5. 7 *n*.

  Venice (S. M. dell' Orto), I. 115 ; ii. 1. 7. 28.

  ,, ,, ,, II. 171 ; iii. 2. 2. 19.

Titian [Synopsis. I. xxx, xxxiii, xlviii, 17, 82-3, 84, 89-91, 95-7, 104-5, 115-16, 132, 143, 146, 157-58, 163, 167, 175, 179, 183 *n*, 213 *n*, 227 *n*, 247 *n*, 367, 396, 416-17, 424 *n*. II. 48, 79, 129, 132-35, 146, 170, 173, 216, 222, 235. III. 19, 21, 47, 131 and *n*, 335-36, 343, 346, 360. IV. 49, 59, 64, 197, 211 *n*, 212 *n*, 230-31, 239, 323-24, 377, 408. V. viii, 39, 42, 80, 99-100, 126 *n*, 178, 190, 211 *n*, 214, 217, 243, 246, 251-54, 273, 277, 280, 283, 298, 300 *n*, 304, 316, 345, 346, 348-50 *n*, 353 *n*, 370 *n*, 383]:—

appreciation of, demanded, III. 19 ; iv. 2. 3.

author's deep study of (1858), V. viii ; *pref.* 4.

 ,, sympathy with, V. 304 ; ix. 8. 1.

architecture of, I. 90 ; ii. 1. 7. 11 (om. ed. 1, 2).

  ,, especially Venice, I. 115 ; ii. 1. 7. 29 (om. ed. 1, 2).

best pictures of, three, V. 246 ; ix. 3. 17.

Titian, *continued :*

blue atmosphere and sky of, V. 99 ; vi. 10. 3.

,,   ,,   ,,   V. 348 ; ix. 11. 6.

Bonifazio influenced by, III. 360 ; App. 3.

Cadore, his birthplace, IV. 377 ; v. 20. 16.

classical revels, V. 273 ; ix. 5. 17.

clouds of, generalized, I. 247 *n* ; ii. 3. 3. 13 *n* (om. ed. 1, 2).

   ,,   their outlines, IV. 230.

   ,,   ,,   V. 126 *n* ; vii. 2. 6 *n*.

coarseness in, no real, II. 133 ; iii. 1. 14. 22.

   ,,   of feature in, V. 251 ; ix. 3. 29.

colour of, and light, I. 104 ; ii. 1. 7. 21 (om. ed. 1, 2).

   ,,   before chiaroscuro (shadows), IV. 49 ; v. 3. 18.

   ,,   exaggerated, I. 91 ; ii. 1. 7. 12 (om. ed. 1, 2).

   ,,   its depth, II. 235 ; iii. 2. 5. 15.

   ,,   praised, II. 133 ; iii. 1. 14. 22.

   ,,   ,,   noble, III. 339 ; iv. 18. 24.

   ,,   ,,   perfect, IV. 324 ; v. 18. 9.

   ,,   ,,   ,,   V. 346 ; ix. 11. 3.

   ,,   ,,   ,,   V. 350 *n* ; ix. 11. 8 *n*.

   ,,   truth of, sacrificed to tone, I. 158–61 ; ii. 2. 1. 15.

   ,,   use of yellow, I. 179 ; ii. 2. 2. 17. *See below, s.*
              distances, flatness of mass.

composition, instance of, V. 190 ; viii. 2. 12.

crests. *See below, s. mountains.*

distances, false, and colour, I. 167 ; ii. 2. 2. 4.

   ,,   I. 184 ; ii. 2. 4. 6 (ed. 1, 2 only).

dogs, in his pictures, V. 283 ; ix. 6. 19.

drapery of, I. 396 ; ii. 5. 3. 29 (om. ed. 1, 2).

   ,,   V. 178 ; viii. 1. 12.

drawing of, I. 183 *n* ; ii. 2. 2. 20 *n* (om. ed. 1, 2).

finish of, III. 131 ; iv. 9. 18.

flatness of mass (colour without form), II. 216 ; iii. 2. 4. 10.

flesh tint, I. 17 ; i. 1. 3. 4.

flowers painted by, less than jewels and fans, V. 100 ; vi.
       10. 4.

foliage, I. 424 *n* ; ii. 6. 1. 24 *n* (om. ed. 1, 2).

   ,,   V. 39 ; vi. 5. 2.

   ,,   V. 42 ; vi. 5. 8.

foregrounds of, I. 105 ; ii. 1. 7. 22 (om. ed. 1, 2).

   ,,   I. 213 *n* ; ii. 2. 5. 15 *n* (om. ed. 1, 2).

form, V. 350 *n* ; ix. 11. 8 *n*. *See above, s. flatness of mass.*

Titian, *continued :*

     frescoes by, no remnants of, I. 116 ; ii. 1. 7. 30 (om. ed. 1, 2).

     gentleness of, V. 214 ; viii. 4. 21.

     Giorgione rivals, III. 346 ; iv. 18. 32.

     glow of, I. 163 ; ii. 2. 1. 22.

     home of.   *See below, s. surroundings.*

     human body, conception of, V. 252–53 ; ix. 3. 30.

     idealism of, in seizing specific character, I. xxxiii ; *pref. ed.* 2. 26.

     imagination of, noble, II. 170 ; iii. 2. 2. 19.

     inscriptions in his pictures, V. 298 ; ix. 7. 21.

     jests rarely if ever, IV. 408 ; App. i. 3.

         „   „   V. 283 ; ix. 6. 20.

     knowledge of landscape, great, I. xxx ; *pref. ed.* 2. 23.

     landscape of, grand but limited, I. 82 ; ii. 1. 7. 6 (om. ed. 1, 2).

         „   I. 95 ; ii. 1. 7. 14 (om. ed. 1, 2).

         „   its emotional character, I. 96 ; ii. 1. 7. 15 (om. ed. 1, 2).

         „   its native qualities, I. 131 ; ii. 1. 7. 37 (om. ed. 1, 2).

         „   „   „   II. 79 ; iii. 1. 8. 3 ('83 *n*).

         „   „   „   III. 335–36 ; iv. 18. 16–18.

         „   leads heroic landscape, V. 217 ; ix. 1. 2.

         „   no agriculture in it, V. 243 ; ix. 3. 11.

         „   no sunshine, I. 96 ; ii. 1. 7. 15 (om. ed. 1, 2).

         „   occasionally vague, IV. 59 ; v. 4. 2.

     leaf-drawing.   *See above, s. foliage.*

     Lefèbre's engravings of, V. 190 ; viii. 2. 12.

     lines of, always noble, IV. 211 *n* ; v. 15. 8 *n*.

     method and vehicles of, unknown, I. 143 ; ii. 1. 7. 45 (om. ed. 1, 2).

     mind of, V. 252 ; ix. 3. 30.

     modesty of, II. 132 ; iii. 1. 14. 19.

     mountains of, best in his deepest works, IV. 230–31 ; v. 15. 27.

        „   „   „   „   IV. 377 ; v. 20. 16.

        „   „   „   „   IV. 380 ; v. 20. 21.

     mystery and softness of, IV. 64 ; v. 4. 9.

     nude studies of, II. 135 ; iii. 1. 14. 24.

         „   „   V. 253 ; ix. 3. 30.

Titian, *continued :*

    nymphs of, V. 304 ; ix. 8. 1.

    portraiture in his works, II. 129 ; iii. 1. 14. 14.

        „   „   „   II. 132 ; iii. 1. 14. 19.

    Poussin, N., and, V. 273 ; ix. 5. 17.

    power of, I. xlviii ; *pref. ed.* 2. 42.

        „   III. 21 ; iv. 2. 5.

        „   cannot be taught, III. 47 ; iv. 3. 27.

    quiet and reserve of, V. 300 *n* ; ix. 7. 23 *n. See s. "royal calm."*

    religion of (cf. Shakspere), V. 251–54 ; ix. 3. 28 *seqq.*

    richness of, V. 345 ; ix. 11. 2.

    "royal calm" of, V. 353 *n* ; ix. 11. 8 *n.*

    sense of human beauty, deficient, II. 146 ; iii. 1. 15. 6.

    shadows of, colour in them, IV. 49 ; v. 3. 19.

    skies of, luminous, II. 48 ; iii. 1. 5. 11.

    solemnity of, V. 383 ; ix. 12. 13.

    stands alone, less so than Rubens, I. 175 ; ii. 2. 2. 12.

    stone-drawing of, IV. 323 *seqq.* ; v. 18. 8 *seqq.*

    supremacy of, in his truth, IV. 324 ; v. 18. 9.

    surroundings of, III. 335 ; iv. 18. 15–16.

        „   „   Venice described, V. 315–16 ; ix. 9. 1.

    tone, truth of colour sacrificed to it, I. 157–58 ; ii. 2. 1. 15.

    trees, I. 146 ; ii. 1. 7. 46 (om. ed. 1, 2).

        „   I. 416–17 ; ii. 6. 1. 14 (om. ed. 1, 2).

        „   use of sweet-chestnut, II. 79 ; iii. 1. 8. 3.

        „   wanting in foreshortening, V. 80 ; vi. 8. 13.

        „   wood-cuts after, IV. 197 ; v. 14. 18. *See above, s. foliage.*

    Turner influenced by, III. 343 ; iv. 18. 28.

    water-painting of, I. 367 ; ii. 5. 1. 23 (om. ed. 1, 2).

    works of :

        Alps from Venice (wood-cut), IV. 230–31 ; v. 15. 27.

            „   „   „   IV. 239 ; v. 15. 34.

        Assumption (Venice Acad.), I. 84 *n* ; ii. 1. 7. 7 *n* (om. ed. 1, 2).

            „   „   „   IV. 212 *n* ; v. 15. 8 *n* (cherub's wing).

            „   „   „   V. 246 ; ix. 3. 17.

            „   „   „   V. 254 ; ix. 3. 32.

            „   „   „   V. 277 ; ix. 6. 5.

            „   „   „   V. 343 ; ix. 10. 25.

Titian : works of : *continued :*

Bacchus and Ariadne (Nat. Gall.) :—

    aquilegia in, I. xxx ; *pref. ed.* 2. 23.

       ,,   I. xxxiii ; *ib.* 26.

    columbine, V. 100 ; vi. 10. 4.

    tone and truth of colour, I. 157–58 ; ii. 2. 1. 15.

    vine-leaves of (Nat. Gall.), III. 131 ; iv. 9. 18.

Bishops (Louvre), V. 280 ; ix. 6. 13.

Camuccini, Rome, II. 170 ; iii. 2. 2. 19.

Desert (Ven. Acad.), I. 79 ; ii. 1. 7. 7 *n* (om. ed. 1, 2).

Entombment (Louvre), II. 48 ; iii. 1. 5. 11.

    ,,   ,,   snail shells in, III. 131 *n* ; iv. 9. 18 *n*.

Europa (Dul. Gall.), I. 158 ; ii. 2. 1. 15.

Faith, architecture poor, I. 115 ; ii. 1. 7. 29 (om. ed. 1, 2).

Flagellation (Louvre), luscious colour, II. 48 ; iii. 1. 5. 11.

Flora, V. 370 *n* ; ix. 11. 32 *n*.

fresco, St. Antonjo, Padua, III. 335 ; iv. 18. 17 (pl. 16).

Holy Family (Nat. Gall.), V. 211 *n* ; viii. 4. 17 *n*.

Lavinia (Berlin), V. viii ; *pref.* 4.

    ,,   ,,   V. 100 ; vi. 10. 4.

    ,,   (Dresden), V. viii ; *pref.* 4.

    ,,   ,,   V. 100 ; vi. 10. 4.

Madonna and Child with St. Andrew, V. 191 ; viii. 2. 12.

    ,,   with St. Peter and St. George, *ib.* ; *ib.*

Magdalen (Barberigo, Venice), II. 133 ; iii. 1. 14. 22.

    ,,   (Nat. Gall.), V. 252 ; ix. 3. 29.

    ,,   (Pitti Palace), II. 133 ; iii. 1. 14. 22.

    ,,   ,,   V. 251–52 ; ix. 3. 28–9.

    ,,   ,,   V. 370 *n* ; ix. 11. 32 *n*.

Marriage of St. Catherine, I. 96 ; ii. 1. 7. 15 (om. ed. 1, 2).

Notomie, V. 370 *n* ; ix. 11. 32 *n*.

portraits, Admiral (Munich), V. viii ; *pref.* 4.

    ,,   girl in white (Dresden), *ib.* ; *ib.*

    ,,   Lady, rose and gold (Dresden), *ib.* ; *ib.*

Presentation of Virgin, V. 246 ; ix. 3. 17.

St. Francis receiving the stigmata) I. 227 *n* ; ii. 3. 1. 18 *n* (om.

  (wood-cut),   )   ed. 1, 2).

    ,,   ,,   ,,   II. 222 ; iii. 2. 4. 18.

St. Jerome (Brera, Milan), its details, I. 91–2 ; ii. 1. 7. 12 (om. ed. 1, 2).

    ,,   ,,   ,, landscape, II. 170 ; iii. 2. 2. 19.

    ,,   ,,   ,,   ,,   II. 173 ; iii. 2. 2. 22.

    ,,   ,,   IV. 377 ; v. 20. 16.

    ,,   ,,   V. 80 ; vi. 8. 13.

St. John (Venice Acad.), II. 129 ; iii. 1. 14. 14.

Titian : works of, *continued* :

St. Peter Martyr (Venice), I. 83 ; ii. 1. 7. 6 (om. ed. 1, 2).

　　　　”　　　　”　　　　”　　clouds in, II. 170 ; iii. 2. 2. 19.

　　　　”　　　　”　　　　”　　　　”　II. 222 ; iii. 2. 4. 17.

　　　　”　　　　”　　　　,　　landscape of, II. 173 *n* ; iii. 2. 2. 22 *n*.

　　　　”　　　　”　　　　”　　trees in, V. 80 ; vi. 8. 13.

　　　　”　　　　”　　　　”　　V. 246 ; ix. 3. 17.

Supper at Emmaus (Louvre), III. 21 ; iv. 2. 5.

　　　　”　　　　”　　　　”　　III. 131 ; iv. 9. 18.

　　　　”　　　　”　　　　”　　V. 280 ; ix. 6. 13.

Tribute Money (Dresden), V. viii ; *pref.* 4.

Venice Acad. next Basaiti, sky, I. 89 ; ii. 1. 7. 11 (om. ed. 1, 2).

Venus, III. 68 ; iv. 5. 4.

Toad-flax, painting of, by Bellini, III. 131 *n* ; iv. 9. 18 *n*.

Tombs, carving of, good and bad, distinguished, II. 76 *n* ; iii. 1. 7. 7 *n*.

Tone [SYNOPSIS. I. 77, 79, 149 *seqq.*, 152–56, 159 *n*, 162. IV. 35 *seqq.*] :—

a secondary truth, I. 77 ; ii. 1. 6. 2.

aerial perspective and, distinct, I. 150 ; ii. 2. 1. 3.

chiaroscuro and, distinct, I. 152 *n* ; ii. 2. 1. 7 *n*.

great colourists and, I. 157 ; ii. 2. 1. 14.

　　　　”　　　　”　　*e.g.* Titian, I. 157–58 ; ii. 2. 1. 14.

lack of, in modern oils, I. 155 ; ii. 2. 1. 12.

less important than space and form, I. 158 *n* ; ii. 2 1. 17 *n* (om. ed. 1, 2).

many united at once in nature, I. 162–63 ; ii. 2. 1. 21.

meaning of, I. 149 *seqq.* ; ii. 2. 1. 1 *seqq.*

　　　　”　　I. 155 *seqq.* ; ii. 2.

of old masters, I. 79 ; ii. 1. 7. 3.

　　”　　　”　　I. 152 ; ii. 2. 1. 5.

　　”　　　”　　I. 180 ; ii. 2. 3. 13 (ed. 1, 2 only).

truth of, IV. 35 *seqq.* ; v. 3. 1 *seqq.*

Tophana, aqua, IV. 352 ; v. 19. 21.

Topographical painting, preciousness of pure, IV. 17–18 ; v. 2. 3–4.

　　　　”　　　　”　　slight exaggeration allowed, V. 207 ; viii. 4. 8 *seqq.*

　　　　　See s. Turner.

Torcello, mosaics of, II. 220 ; iii. 2. 4. 14.

Torrents, force and work of mountain, IV. 145 *seqq.* ; **v. 12. 2** *seqq.*

    ,,   lines of, curved, I. 392 ; ii. 5. 3. 24.

    ,,   ,,   ,,   IV. 330 ; v. 18. 18.

    ,,   mountains furrowed by, I. 316 ; ii. 4. 3. 12.

    ,,   ,,   ,,   IV. 330 ; v. 18. 16.

    ,,   power of, beneficent, IV. 302 ; v. 17. 31.

    ,,   ,,   in cutting a way, IV. 272-74 ; v. 16. 40 *seqq.*

    ,,   ,,   - ,,   ,,   IV. 337 ; v. 19. 3.

    ,,   sculpture of earth by, IV. 277 ; v. 17. 1-2.

Tourists, idea that the least seen is most worth seeing, IV. 186 ; v. 14. 6.

    ,,   in Switzerland, on glaciers, III. 267 ; iv. 16. 6.

    ,,   ,,   ruin of the people by, IV. 168 ; v. 13. 5.

    ,,   ,,   ,,   ,,   IV. 396 *seqq.* ; v. 20. 40 *seqq.*

Tours (S. Julien), old buildings at, destroyed, II. 7 *n* ; iii. 1. 1. 7 *n.*

Towns, life in, IV. 382 ; v. 20. 26.

    ,,   manufacturing, muddy streets of, V. 175-76 ; viii. 1. 7. 8.

Trafalgar, "Royal Sovereign" at, compared to "Modern Painters," Vol. I., and its critics (1843), I. xi ; *pref. ed.* 2. 1.

Transfiguration, the, III. 207 ; iv. 14. 10.

    ,,   ,,   IV. 403 *seqq.* ; v. 20. 47 *seqq.*

    ,,   ,,   Raphael's and the reality, III. 59 *n* ; iv. 4. 17 *n.*

Transcripts from nature, pictures that are, III. 150 ; iv. 10. 21.

Transitions of nature, imperceptible, IV. 129 ; v. 10. 1.

Transparency, in mountain chains, I. 299 ; ii. 4. 2. 13.

    ,,   incompatible with highest beauty, II. 82-4 ; iii 1. 9. 4-5.

    ,,   partial, the most beautiful, *ib.* ; *ib.*

    ,,   the sky, its, I. 219-20 ; ii. 3. 1. 7.

Travelling, imagination soon jaded by seeing too much, III. 145 ; iv. 10. 14

    ,,   railroad, III. 311-12 ; iv. 17. 24-5.

    ,,   to see the Continent, *ib.* ; *ib.*

    ,,   thought and sight, its ends, not pace, III. 321 ; iv. 17. 35.

Treatment, breadth of, V. 198-99 ; viii. 3. 7-8.

Trees [SYNOPSIS. I. 76, 309–10, 407–9, 315–16, 425. II. 164–66.
        III. 122 *seqq.*, 127. IV. 80–1, 286–87, 369–70. V. 4, 5,
        9–12, 21, 46–7, 54, 56 *seqq.*, 60 *seqq.*, 66–7, 74, 76, 82–5,
        86 *seqq.*]:—

    angles of, I. 415 ; ii. 6. 1. 13.
    architecture and, coincidences of structure, V. 21 ; vi.
        3. 14.
    beauty of, V. 81–2 ; vi. 8. 17–18.
    branches of, downward tendency, I. 309–10 ; ii. 4. 3. 4.
        „   thickness of, do not taper, I. 408–9 ; ii. 6
                 1. 2–5.
    capable of feeling ? V. 5 ; vi. 1. 6.
    classical love of, III. 194 ; iv. 13. 22.
        „   „   IV. 79 ; v. 5. 16.
    complexity of, I. 412–13 ; ii. 6. 1. 10.
    diminution and increase of, *ib.* ; *ib.*
    distinguishing, not easy, I. 74–5 ; ii. 1. 5. 8.
    drawing of, by different artists.   *See s. Artists' names.*
        „   common faults, V. 76 ; vi. 8. 10.
        „   conventional till Turner, V. 74 ; vi. 8. 9.   *See
                 s. Turner.*
        „   difficulty of, I. 379 ; ii. 6. 1. 1 (ed. 1, 2 only).
        „   „   especially contours of tops, V.
                 67–8 ; vi. 7. 18.
        „   knowledge of human figure essential to, I. 417 ;
                 ii. 6. 1. 14 (om. ed. 1, 2).
        „   of old masters, I. 407 *seqq.* ; ii. 6. 1. 1 *seqq.*
        „   „   „   I. 425 ; ii. 6. 1. 25.
        „   rules for, by the unimaginative, II. 164–66 ; iii.
                 2. 2. 11.
        „   stems, III. 122 *seqq.* ; iv. 9. 8 *seqq.* (pl. 2, 3, 4).
        „   „   rightly drawn by only Titian and Turner,
                 I. 416 ; ii. 6. 1. 14 (om. ed. 1, 2).
                 See s. Italian school.
        „   to be wayward, III. 127 ; iv. 9. 14.
    European, list of common, I. 408 ; ii. 6. 1. 2.
    growth of, I. 76 ; ii. 1. 6. 1.
        „   its laws, IV. 80–1 ; v. 5. 17.
        „   „   V. 18 ; vi. 3. 12.
        „   its main principle, V. 54 ; vi. 7. 1.
        „   plants and flowers, V. 56 *seqq.* ; vi. 7. 4 *seqq.*
        „   V. 60 *seqq.* ; vi. 7. 10 *seqq.*

Trees, *continued*:

    growth of, V. 66 ; vi. 7. 17 *seqq.*

        ,,   V. 81 ; vi. 8. 15.

    kinds of (shield and sword leaf), V. 9–10 ; vi. 2. 5.

        ,,   ,,   ,,   ,,   V. 86–7 ; vi. 9. 2.

    lessons to be learnt from, V. 82–5 ; vi. 8. 18–20.

    love of, a test of purity of life, V. 4 ; vi. 1. 4.

    lowland and mountain, IV. 369–70 ; v. 20. 7.

        ,,   and pines compared, V. 88 *seqq.* ; vi. 9. 4 *seqq.*

    mechanical aspect of, V. 45 *n* ; vi. 6. 3.

    outlines of, III. 122 ; iv. 9. 8.

    ramification of, I. 409 ; ii. 6. 1. 4–5.

        ,,   V. 62–3 ; vi. 7. 12.

        ,,   V. 66–8 ; vi. 7. 16 *seqq.*

    shoots of, furrows in, V. 47 ; vi. 6. 5 (pl. 51).

        ,,   knots in, their meaning, V. 12 ; vi. 3. 2.

        ,,   types of, V. 11–12 ; vi. 3. 2.

    structure of (trefoil, etc.), V. 21 ; vi. 3. 13.

    symmetrical curves of, I. 424 ; ii. 6. 1. 25.

    tapering of, how caused, I. 408 ; ii. 6. 1. 2.

    thickness of, diminishes only by dividing, I. 408–9 ; ii. 6. 1. 2.

    tops of, contours difficult to draw, V. 67–8 ; vi. 7. 18.

    trunks, "messengers to the roots," V. 46 ; vi. 6. 4.

    wind's action on, "frangas non flectes," I. 415 ; ii. 6. 1. 13.

        ,,   ,,   IV. 286–87 ; v. 17. 14.

                See s. Botany.

Trefoil, in trees and architecture, V. 21 ; vi. 3. 14.

Trient, Gorge du, IV. 273 ; v. 16. 40.

    ,,   ,,   country round, IV. 337 *seqq.* ; v. 19. 3.

    ,,   ,,   tourists' effect on, IV. 398 ; v. 20. 42.

True, means trustworthy, V. 181 *n* ; viii. 1. 17 *n. See s. Truth.*

Trunk, growth of, thicker and higher, V. 55 *seqq.* ; vi. 7. 2 *seqq.*

Trust, defined, V. 181 ; viii. 1. 17.

    ,,   love and, essential to man, V. 381 ; ix. 12. 10.

Truth [SYNOPSIS. I. xviii–xix, 14, 24–8, 39, 46, 51, 53, 56, 62–77, 85, 325, 434, 441. II. 32, 173, 200 *n.* III. 1, 35 *n*, 38, 89, 98, 109, 116, 133, 135, 147, 177, 222, 260, 270, 317–18. IV. 48, 256–7. V. 71, 293–94]:—

    art and :

        beauty, truth not to be sacrificed to, III. 35 *n* ; iv. 3. 12 *n.*

        ,,   ,,   result of doing so, III. 270 ; iv. 16. 12.

Truth: art and, *continued* :

      first quality in execution, I. 39 ; i. 2. 2. 1.

      foundation and test of all art, I. 51 ; ii. 1. 1. 8.

        ,,   *e.g.* does a picture add to recorded truth?
                    I. 85 ; ii. 1. 7. 8 (om. ed. 1, 2).

        ,,   I. 441–42 ; ii. 6. 3. 7.

        ,,   III. 38 ; iv. 3. 16.

        ,,   III. 116 ; iv. 9. 1.

        ,,   III. 147 ; iv. 10. 17.
                    See below, s. ideas.

      imitation and, distinct, I. 24 *seqq.* ; i. 1. 5. 2 *seqq.*

        ,,   inconsistent, I. 27–8 ; i. 1. 5. 6.

      judgment of truth in art, can be got by study, I. 51–2 ;
        ii. 1. 1. 10.

      judgment of truth in art, can be got by study, I. 53 ; ii.
        1. 2. 1.

    attainment of the most precious, IV. 40 ; v. 3. 7.

    beauty and, nothing untrue is beautiful, I. 27–8 ; i. 1. 5–6.

      ,,   though truth is not beauty, II. 32 ; iii. 1. 4. 1.

      ,,   ,,   ,,   ,,   III. 35 *n* ; iv. 3.
                    12 *n.*

    capable always of abuse, I. xviii *n* ; *pref. ed.* 2. 10 *n.*

    choice of, by artists, the essence of style, III. 39 ; iv. 3. 16.

      ,,   ,,   ,,   ,,   IV. 48 ; v. 3. 17.

      ,,   by old masters and moderns, I. 79–81 ; ii. 1. 7. 3.

    classes of, deceptive and inner likeness, III. 135 ; iv. 10. 3.

    colourists' and chiaroscurists', IV. 44 ; v. 3. 12.

      ,,   ,,   IV. 49 ; v. 3. 19.

    difficulty of stating it unassailably, III. 133 ; iv. 10. 1.

    discovery of, difficult, I. 53–5 ; ii. 1. 2. 1–2.

      ,,   intellectual but sharpened by moral sense, I.
        56 ; ii. 1. 2. 4.

    dominion of, entire, *e.g.* pathetic fallacy, III. 177; iv.
      12. 15.

    Greek views of falsehood and, V. 293–94 ; ix. 7. 12 *seqq.*

    grotesque idealism may well convey, III. 103–4 ; iv. 8. 5–6.

    highest, almost impossible to explain, I. 434–35 ; ii. 6. 2. 2.

    ideas of, in art, I. 14 ; i. 1. 3. 1.

      ,,   ,,   I. 24 ; i. 1. 5. 1.

      ,,   the foundation of art, I. 28 ; i. 1. 5. 6.

      ,,   ,, object of their study, I. 46 ; i. 2. 3. 6.

      ,,   III. 1 ; iv. 1. 1.

Truth, *continued :*

imaginative truth, instanced (Two Griffins), III. 109 ; iv.
8. 11.

    „   „   its preciousness, IV. 31 ; v. 2. 21.

    „   „   work, tested by, II. 172–4; iii. 2. 2. 21–2.

imitation and, distinct, I. 24–8 ; i. 1. 5. 2 *seqq.*

infinity essential to, I. 254–55 ; ii. 3. 3. 22.

instinctive discovery of, III. 222 ; iv. 14. 28.

invention demands, V. 215 ; viii. 4. 23.

knowledge of great, goes with desire to impart it, I. xviii ;
pref. ed. 3. 12.

law of, in painting, III. vi ; *pref.* 2.

likeness to nature and, III. 135 ; iv. 10. 3.

many-sided, hence apparent inconsistency, V. 298 *n* ; ix.
7. 21 *n.*

mystery of all great, II. 200 *n* ; iii. 2. 3. 28 *n.*

nature's always varying, I. 58 ; ii. 1. 2. 7.

perception of, its requisites, I. 55–6 ; ii. 1. 2. 3–5.

reception of, slow, I. xix ; *pref. ed.* 2. 12.

refusal to see, obvious, IV. 256–57 ; v. 16. 23.

rendering of, compared to hospitality, IV. 48 ; v. 3. 17.

sacred, how conveyed, III. 317–18 ; iv. 17. 32.

sacrifice of, to decision and velocity, I. 42–3 ; i. 2. 2. 8–9.

simplest, believed last, III. 318 ; iv. 17. 34.

sometimes spoken through evil men, II. 146–47 ; iii. 1.
15. 8.

taught by action only, not talk, V. 71 ; vi. 8. 5.

unity of, I. xviii *n* ; *pref. ed.* 2. 10 *n.*

universal, of great idealists, *e.g.* Shakspere, III. 98 ; iv.
7. 20.

value of, as it is characteristic, I. 67 ; ii. 1. 3. 9.

    „   „   distinctive, I. 65 ; ii. 1. 3. 5.

    „   frequent and rare, I. 68 *seqq.* ; ii. 1. 4. 1 *seqq.*

    „   general and particular, I. 62 *seqq.* ; ii. 1. 3. 1 *seqq.*

    „   „   „   *e.g.* mountain-drawing, I.
325 ; ii. 4. 3. 26.

    „   most important, those which tell us most (specific
form), I. 76 ; ii. 1. 6. 1.

vulgar blindness to its beauty, V. 295 ; ix. 7. 15.

whole, never vulgar, III. 89 ; iv. 7. 9.

Truthfulness of true gentlemen, V. 293 ; ix. 7. 11.

Turin, church of Superga, clouds over, V. 147 ; vii. 3. 16.

Turin, *continued :*

   „   pictures at :

        Vandyck's Children of Charles I., V. 100 ; vi. 10. 5.

        Veronese's Magdalen, V. 282 ; ix. 6. 17.

           „   Queen of Sheba, V. vii ; *pref.* 4.

           „   „   „   V. 249 ; ix. 3. 23.

        Wouvermans' war-piece, V. 307 *seqq.* ; ix. 8. 7 *seqq.*

Turkish "God is great," its meaning, IV. 39 ; v. 3. 6.

Turner, J. M. W.

    I. Personal: Life and Character.   II. As an Artist.   III.
        Works of, referred to.

[SYNOPSIS OF I. AND II.   (For that of III. Works, see pp. 316 *seqq.*)

Vol. I.   xvii–xix, xxiv *n*, xlviii–l ; 33, 52, 62, 89, 92, 104, 121, 129–30,
    133 *seqq.*, 136–48, 152, 155–58, 160–63, 166–71, 174–82, 187 *seqq.*,
    190, 194–95, 199, 200–1, 209, 213 *n*, 215, 220, 225 *seqq.*, 234 *seqq.*,
    239, 250 *seqq.*, 252 *seqq.*, 266 *seqq.*, 274 *seqq.*, 282 *seqq.*, 290, 302,
    305, 321–23, 324, 328–29, 338 *seqq.*, 349, 356, 359–60, 367, 378
    seqq., 383, 388–90, 397–98, 401, 404–5, 416–17, 425, 433–37, 441–
    42, 453–54.

Vol. II.   '83 *pref.* 9 ; 52, 151, 216 ; '83 Epil. 1, 13–14.

Vol. III.   v, x, xii ; 42, 63, 94, 106, 126–27, 129–30, 133, 134–38,
    198 *n*, 215, 246, 251, 276–78, 296, 310, 323, 325–30, 336, 339–44,
    346, 357.

Vol. IV.   1, 7–9, 15–16, 21–5, 27–32, 35, 41–5, 48–50 *n*, 58 *seqq.*, 63,
    68–9, 74–5, 77, 78, 81, 85–6, 183 *n*, 187, 201–2, 233–39, 253, 259–
    64, 273–74, 307–9, 312, 314, 317, 323, 327, 330–34, 411, 419.

Vol. V.   v, vi, viii–xi ; 40–1, 42, 52–3, 67–8, 71, 74, 79–80, 90, 102,
    108, 110, 125–26 *n*, 132 *seqq.*, 137, 142–43, 154, 162, 164, 185
    seqq , 188, 194, 207, 211, 212, 218, 315 *seqq.*, 317–29, 345–50,
    356–57, 364–66 *n*, 369–73, 381–84 *n.*]

    I. Personal : Life and Character.

      anecdotes and sayings of :   *See below, s. character.*

           looking at author's "Falls of Rhine," I. 369 ; ii. 5. 2. 2
             (F.A. *n*).

           „   „   St. Gothard, III. 94 ; iv. 7. 13.

           saying "I never lose an accident," V. 194 ; viii. 2. 15.

           „   "Keep my works together," V. 366 *n* ; ix. 11. 30 *n*.

           „   "Paint your impressions," IV. 237 *n* ; v. 15. 32 *n*.

           supposed saying that author saw in his works things he
             never meant, IV. 237 ; v. 15. 32.

Turner, J. M. W. : *I. Personal : Life and character, continued :*

author and his writings, Turner's feeling for, V. 382 ;
ix. 12. 11.   *See s. II.*

birthplace influences him always, V. 317 *seqq.* ; ix. 9.
4 *seqq.*

boyhood of, *ib.* ; *ib.*

„   at Brentford and Twickenham, V 323 ;
ix. 9. 15.

character :

analysis and anecdotes of, V. 374 *n* ; ix. 12. 4 *n.*
compared with Dante's, V. 364 ; ix. 11. 26.
„   „   „   and Keats'.   *See below, s. mind.*
earnestness, V. 375 *n* ; ix. 12. 4 *n.*
feeling for landscape, II. '83 *pref.* 9.
hopelessness of, V. 355 ; ix. 11. 2.
kindness and truth, V. 374–75 and *n* ; ix. 12. 4 and *n.*
not vulgar, V. 320 ; ix. 9. 9.
reserved, IV. 237 ; v. 15. 32.
sensitiveness, V. 382–83 ; ix. 12. 12.
want of faith, V. 372–75 ; ix. 12. 1–4.

death of, 1851, II. '83 Epil. 14.
and funeral, III. v-vi ; *pref.* 1.
his works praised *then*, I. 453–54 ; ii. 6.
3 ; postscript (om. ed. 1–4).

education of, by his parents, V. 320 *seqq.* ; ix. 9. 10.
„   classical, its effect, III. 330 ; iv. 18. 8.
„   in architecture, V. 329 *n* ; ix. 10. 3 *n.*
See below, s. home.

emotion, at mention of the Wharfe, IV 262 ; v. 16. 29.

estimate of self and his works, III. 277 ; iv. 16. 25.
„   „   seldom praised his own works, IV. 25 ;
v. 2. 13.

first drawing-master, Mr. Lowe, III. 345 ; iv. 18. 31.

geologist as well as painter, I. 290 ; ii. 4. 1. 6.

home-surroundings, III. 330 ; iv. 18. 31.
„   „   contrary influences of admiration
and love of home, IV. 262 ; v.
16. 29.
Giorgione's compared, V. 315 *seqq.* ;
ix. 9. 1 *seqq.*

industry of, even and continuous, V. 328 ; ix. 10. 2.

Turner, J. M. W. : *I. Personal : Life and character, continued :*

influence on, of Italy, I. 137–38 ; ii. 1. 7. 42 (om. ed. 1, 2).

„ „ romantic associations, III. 310 ; iv. 17. 21.

See s. II. Influences.

intellect of, I. 33 ; i. 1. 7. 2.

life of, author's plans as to writing a, V. 373 ; ix. 12. 3 *seqq.*

„ being written, *ib.* ; *ib.*

love of sea and shipping, V. viii ; *pref.* 5.

„ „ „ V. 319 ; ix. 9. 8.

love of sunset light (and his character), V. 364 ; ix. 11. 27.

memory of early impressions, IV. 30 ; v. 2. 18.

mind of, its characteristics, IV. 31–2 ; v. 2. 21.

„ Keats' and Dante's compared, V. 320 ; ix. 9. 9.

movements of :

at Abbotsford with Scott, II. 151 ; iii. 2. 1 ; '83 Introd. Note, 2.

at author's birthday dinner, II. '83 Epil. 4.

first Yorkshire visit, V. 323–24 ; ix. 9. 16–17.

last mountain journey (St. Gothard), III. 246 ; iv. 15. 5.

poetry of, " Fallacies of Hope," V. 325 ; ix. 9. 21.

„ „ „ „ V. 329 ; ix. 10. 3.

„ „ „ „ V. 369 *n* ; ix. 11. 31 *n.*

„ „ „ „ V. 384 *n* ; ix. 12. 15 *n.*

religious training of, V. 321–22 ; ix. 9. 13–14.

Scott (Sir W.) and, II. 151 ; iii. 2. 1 ; '83 Introd. Note, 2.

„ „ III. 276 ; iv. 16. 22.

„ „ cf. Dante and Giotto, III. 327 ; iv. 18. 2.

sense of beauty, V. 363 ; ix. 11. 26.

„ justice, V. 375–76 *n* ; ix. 12. 4 *n.*

sympathy with children, IV. 15 ; v. 1. 17.

will, clear if informal, IV. 81 ; v. 5. 18.

„ condition of bequest to Nat. Gallery, V. vi *seqq.* ; *pref.* 2.

II. As an Artist.

admiration for, a test of our knowledge of nature, I. 436 ; ii. 6. 2. 4.

Turner, J. M. W. : *II. As an Artist, continued :*

  aim of his works, V. 366 *n* ; ix. 11. 30 *n. See below, s. teaching.*

  author's admiration for, 1843–60, increased, V. 372 ; ix. 12. 1.

  „   appeal to, I. 452–53 ; ii. 6. 3. 24.

  „   arrangement of his drawings for National Gallery, 1857–58, V. v *seqq.*; *pref.* 1 *seqq.*

  „   eulogies of, I. 76 ; ii. 1. 7. 6 (ed. 1, 2 only).

  „   „   I. 300 ; ii. 4. 3. 24 (*ib.*).

  „   „   I. 435–37 ; ii. 6. 2. 3–6.

  „   opinion of, would sound like rhapsody, I. 130 ; ii. 1. 7. 37 (om. ed. 1, 2).

  „   prominence given to in "Modern Painters," I. 438 ; ii. 6. 3. 1.

  „   vignettes (early) in imitation of, II. '83 Epil. 1.

  catalogue of his works, Boone's, V. 329 *n* ; ix. 10. 3 *n.*

  „   „   „   planned by author, III. x ; *pref.* 5.

  chiaroscuro of :

    colour and. *See below, s. colour.*
    I. 141 ; ii. 1. 7. 44.
    I. 152–53 ; ii. 2. 1. 7.
    I. 158 ; ii. 2. 1. 16.
    extreme light and shade, always in small quantities, } I. 190–91 ; ii. 2. 3. 8.
    „   „   „   „   I. 194 ; ii. 2. 3. 13.
    inviolable, I. 181 ; ii. 2. 2. 20 (ed. 1–2. 23).
    „   I. 187 *seqq.* ; ii. 2. 3. 5 *seqq.*
    list of effects of light, I. 282 *seqq.* ; ii. 3. 5. 1 *seqq.*
    love of light, I. 423–24 *n* ; ii. 6. 1. 24 *n* (om. ed. 1, 2).
    „   esp. sunset light, V. 364 ; ix. 11. 27.
    shadow by him, more than sunlight by others, V. 356 ; ix. 11. 14.

        See below, s. objects painted by (*shadows, twilight effects*), *and s. tone.*

  classical knowledge, V. 162 ; vii. 4. 18.
  „   pictures bad, I. 138–39 ; ii. 1. 7. 42 (om. ed. 1, 2).
  „   „   „   III. 330 ; iv. 18. 8.

Turner, J. M. W.: *II. As an Artist, continued:*

    colour of :

        I. 121 ; ii. 1. 7. 32 (om. ed. 1, 2).

        best in later (1843) works, I. 180 ; ii. 2. 2. 18.

        blended variety of, I. 177–78 ; ii. 2. 2. 15.

        blue, his use of, I. 167 ; ii. 2. 2. 4.

           ,,   brown, and purple, III. 251 and *n* ; iv. 15. 12 and *n.*

           ,,   storm-blues, V. 211 ; viii. 4. 18.

        brilliancy, less than nature, I. 166 ; ii. 2. 2. 3.

           ,,   the sun more dazzling, I. 174–75 ; ii. 2. 2. 11.

        chiaroscuro and, I. 104 ; ii. 1. 7. 21 (om. ed. 1, 2).

                ,,   I. 170 ; ii. 2. 2. 6.

                ,,   I. 181 ; ii. 2. 2. 20 (ed. 1, 2. 23).

                ,,   IV. 49 ; v. 3. 18.

        drawings, all faultless in colour, I. 181 ; ii. 2. 2. 19.

        failures in, instanced, I. 161 ; ii. 2. 1. 20.

           ,,   ,,   I. 180–81 ; ii. 2. 2. 18.

        form and, I. 143 ; ii. 1. 7. 45 (om. ed. 1, 2).

           ,,   sacrificed to abstract colour, II. 216–17 ; iii. 2. 4. 10.

        gradations of, II. 52 ; iii. 1. 5. 18.

        grey used to subdue vividness, I. 177 ; ii. 2. 2. 14.

        period after 1820, V. 345 ; ix. 11. 2.

        pure, raw, colour used rarely, I. 176 ; ii. 2. 2. 13.

        scarlet shadows, V. 348 ; ix. 11. 6.

           ,,   used as type of death and love, V. 369 *n* ; ix. 11. 31 *n.*

        space and aerial colour (cf. Tintoret), I. 92 ; ii. 1. 7. 12 *n* (om. ed. 1, 2).

           ,,   more than colour, I. 143 ; ii. 1. 7. 45 (om. ed. 1, 2).

        sun-*colour* given by him alone, V. 346 ; ix. 11. 3.

        system of colour, IV. 42–5 ; v. 3. 11–13.

           ,,   ,,   IV. 47–8 ; v. 3. 16.

           ,,   ,,   its basis and character, V. 349–50 *n* ; ix. 11. 8 *n.*

        truth of, I. 166 *seqq.* ; ii. 2. 2. 3 *seqq.*

           ,,   though it looks unnatural, and why, IV. 41–2 ; v. 3. 9. 10.

        yellow, use of, for sunlighted green, I. 170 ; ii. 2. 2. 6.

           ,,   ,,   rather than purple, I. 179–80 ; ii. 2. 2. 17.

    compared with other artists :

        gratitude of other artists to, V. 382 ; ix. 12. 11.

        greater than Callcott or Stanfield, I. viii ; *pref.* 2.

           ,,   ,,   Claude, I. 33 ; i. 1. 7. 2. *See below, s. influences on.*

Turner, J. M. W.: *II. As an Artist, continued:*

  imitations of, monotonous, IV. 308; v. 17. 42.
  inferior to Gainsborough in management of a single tint,
    I. xxi *n*; *ed. 2. pref.* 13 *n.*

  composition of:

    example of, IV. 330; v. 18. 17.
    Faido pass, IV. 25; v. 2. 14 (pl. 21).
    introduction of recollected incident, IV. 27–8; v. 2. 16.
    Loire side (repose), V. 185 *seqq.* ; viii. 2. 3 *seqq.*
    Schaffhausen (tumult), *ib.* ; *ib.*
    sketch of Lausanne, V. 207–8; viii. 4. 9–11.

  contemplative landscape headed by, V. 218 *n*; ix. 1.
    2 *n.*
  conventionality and. *See s. innovations.*
  curvature loved by, I. 133 ; ii. 1. 7. 39.
    „   „   I. 425 ; ii. 6. 1. 26.
    „   „   III. 127 ; iv. 9. 14.
    „   „   IV. 201–2 ; v. 14. 23.
    „   „   IV. 238–39 ; v. 15. 34.
    „   „   IV. 309 ; v. 17. 43.
  delineation and drawing power, III. 136–37 ; iv. 10. 5.
    „   „   „   IV. 58 *seqq.*; v. 4. 1
                                           seqq.

  distance and space:

    first truly expressed by him, I. 199–200 ; ii. 2. 4. 6.
    "never vacant, never distinct," I. 209 ; ii. 2. 5. 11.
    sharp outline, I. 303 ; ii. 4. 2. 18.

  drawings of:

    all faultless in colour, I. 181 ; ii. 2. 2. 19.
    chaster and quieter than his oils, *ib.* ; *ib.*
    critics to study them, *ib.* ; *ib.*
    typical of his age, III. 276 ; iv. 16. 23.

  ease of, III. 278 ; iv. 16. 27.
  effectiveness of his pictures at a distance, I. 200–1 ; ii.
    2. 4. 7.

  engravings of:

    always beautiful, and why, I. 181–82 ; ii. 2. 2. 20.
    "making out" in, ruinous, I. 195 ; ii. 2. 3. 13.
    richness of his work beyond all engraving, V. 43; vi.
      5. 9.

Turner, J. M. W. : *II. As an Artist, continued :*

richness of his work beyond all engraving, V. 110; vi. 10. 20–21.

storms ruined by, I. 275 *seqq.*; ii. 3. 4. 25 *seqq.* (ed. 1–4. 30 *seqq.*).

"white or black?" V. 375 *n*; ix. 12. 4 *n*.

epic poetry, *e.g.* "Carthage," I. 33; i. 1. 7. 2.

errors and failures of :

causes of, I. 142–44; ii. 1. 7. 45 (om. ed. 1, 2).

due to failure of perception, IV. 238; v. 15. 33.

  „ want of faith, V. 372–75; ix. 12. 1–4.

if there were none, he would *be* nature, III. 136; iv. 10. 4.

often are sacrifices to secure other virtues, I. 144; ii. 1. 7. 45 (om. ed. 1, 2).

exception to all rules, I. 345 *n*; ii. 5. 2. 4 *n* (ed. 1, 2 only).

execution of :

its mystery, I. 215; ii. 2. 5. 18.

  „ richness and fineness, beyond engraving, V. 43; vi. 5. 9. *See below, s. method, mystery.*

foregrounds of :

assumed nearness of, I. 213 *n*; ii. 2. 5. 15 *n* (om. ed. 1, 2).

characteristics, I. 338 *seqq.*; ii. 4. 4. 20 *seqq.*

detail and delicacy, III. 129–30; iv. 9. 17.

flowers and foliage in, V. 102; vi. 10. 9.

richness of, beyond engraving, V. 108–10; vi. 10. 19–21.

stones and, IV. 327–28; v. 18. 12.

Gothic never thoroughly understood by, III. 330; iv. 18. 8.

gradations of effect in, I. 277; ii. 3. 4. 28.

  „   „   IV. 74–5; v. 5. 7. *See above, s. colour.*

imagination :

associative (Lib. Stud. "Procris and Cephalus"), II. 171; iii. 2. 2. 20.

apparent, involuntary remembrance, IV. 29; v. 2. 17.

Turner, J. M. W. : *II. As an Artist, continued :*

  gives sublimity to simple subjects, *e.g.* Bolton Abbey, IV.
   262–63 ; v. 16. 30.

  inventive, and truth of impression, IV. 21–4 ; v. 2. 8 *seqq.*
    ,,   ,,   ,,   IV. 332–33 ; v. 18. 23.

inequality of his work, I. 144 ; ii. 1. 7. 45 (om. ed. 1, 2).
infinity, I. 254 *seqq.* ; ii. 3. 3. 22 *seqq.*
 ,, I. 300–1 ; ii. 4. 2. 15.
 ,, V. 42–3 ; vi. 5. 8–9.

influences on : *See s. I. Personal.*

  of Academy teaching, III. 327–28 ; iv. 18. 3.
  ,, classical landscape, III. 198 *n* ; iv. 13. 26 *n.*
  ,, Claude, III. 339–43 ; iv. 18. 25–7.
  ,, ,, excelled by him, I. xvii ; *ed. 2. pref.* 9.
  ,, Dutch school, I. 401 ; ii. 5. 3. 37 (om. ed. 1, 2).
  ,, ,, ,, III. 343–44 ; iv. 18. 29–30.
  ,, English school, *ib.* ; *ib.*
  ,, Gothic and classical architecture, V. 329 *n* ; ix. 10. 3 *n.*
  ,, Poussin, III. 343 ; iv. 18. 28.
  ,, Roman studies, V. 110 ; vi. 10. 21.
  ,, Titian, III. 343 ; iv. 18. 28.
  ,, Vandevelde, I. 349 ; ii. 5. 1. 5.
  ,, Venetian school, III. 336 ; iv. 18. 19.
  ,, Yorkshire hills, I. 133 ; ii. 1. 7. 39.
    ,,   ,, IV. 259 ; v. 16. 25.
    ,,   ,, IV. 317 ; v. 17. 51.
    ,,   ,, IV. 327 ; v. 18. 12.

innovations of :

  against conventional landscape, I. xlviii ; *ed. 2. pref.* 43.
  ,,   ,,   ,,   I. 142 ; ii. 1. 7. 44 (om.
               ed. 1, 2).
  license occasionally criminal, I. 144 ; ii. 1. 7. 45 (om
   ed. 1, 2).
  their audacity from the first, IV. 314–15 ; v. 17. 48.
   See above, s. colour (scarlet shadow).

invention too great to spend long over a single subject,
  IV. 307–8 ; v. 17. 41.
litter loved by him, V. 318 ; ix. 9. 6.
meanings of, secret and symbolic, V. 164 ; vii. 4. 21.
methods of, compared with da Vinci's, IV. 49 *n* ; v.
  3. 19 *n.*

Turner, J. M. W. : *II. As an Artist, continued:*

methods of, original, IV. 35 ; v. 3. 1. *See below, s. mystery.*

mystery of, I. 209–10 ; ii. 2. 5. 11.
„ I. 215 ; ii. 2. 5. 18.
„ I. 437 ; ii. 6. 2. 6.
„ IV. 58 *seqq.* ; v. 4. 1 *seqq.*
„ IV. 68 ; v. 4. 14.
„ V. 42–3 ; vi. 5. 8–9.
„ V. 212 ; viii. 4. 19.
„ V. 377 *n* ; ix. 12. 4 *n*.
 See below, s. objects (mist).

objects and things painted by :

architecture, I. 211 ; ii. 2. 5. 12.
„ I. 434 ; ii. 6. 2. 1.
„ III. 328 ; iv. 18. 4.
„ III. 330 ; iv. 18. 8.
„ V. 329 ; ix. 10. 3.
banks, IV. 309–10 ; v. 17. 43–4.
„ IV. 314–15 ; v. 17. 48.
clergyman only once drawn by, V. 322 *n* ; ix. 9. 13 *n*.
clouds, first to give upper region of, I. 234 ; ii. 3. 2. 10.
„ „ „ „ I. 239 ; ii. 3. 2. 15.
„ instances of, I. 250 *seqq.* ; ii. 3. 3. 16 *seqq.*
„ kinds of, cirrus, I. 234 *seqq.* ; ii. 3. 2. 10 *seqq.*
„ „ „ and cumulus, I. 251–53 ; ii. 3. 3. 19–21.
„ „ cumulus, never painted, V. 137 ; vii. 3. 2.
„ „ „ „ V. 142 ; vii. 3. 10.
„ „ rain-clouds, beyond engraving, I. 266 ; ii. 3. 4. 11.
„ „ „ examples of, *ib.* ; *ib.*
„ „ „ never rightly painted, V. 154 ; vii. 4. 6.
„ knowledge of, III. 106 ; iv. 8. 7.
„ storm-, V. 162 ; vii. 4. 18.
„ supremely *drawn*, V. 160 *seqq.* ; vii. 2. 15 *seqq.*
„ truth of, V. 163 ; vii. 2. 19.
country seats, III. 328–30 ; iv. 18. 4. 7.
death painted by, V. 369 *n* ; ix. 11. 31 *n*.
drapery, always true in line, IV. 238 ; V. 15. 33.
English scenery, affected by love of foreign, IV. 262 ; v. 16. 29.

Turner, J. M. W. : *II. As an Artist, continued :*

    figures of :

          ,,   how placed, I. 121 ; ii. 1. 7. 32 (om. ed.
                         1, 2).

          ,,   want of drawing in, justified, I. 201 ; ii. 2.
                         4. 8.

          ,,   ,,   ,,   ,,   III. 357 ; App. ii.

    foliage. *See below, s. tree-drawing.*

    foregrounds. *See above, s. foregrounds.*

    French subjects, affected by love of home, IV. 262 ; v.
               16. 29.

          ,,   ,,   best of his foreign studies, I. 137 ; ii. 1.
                      7. 41 (om. ed. 1, 2).

    geology of, I. 290 ; ii. 4. 1. 6. *See below, s. mountain-
              drawing.*

    Highland scenery, purple in, III. 251 ; iv. 15. 12.

    Italian and classical works all unsatisfactory (except
        Venice), I. 138 *seqq.* ; ii. 1. 7. 42 *seqq.* (om. ed. 1, 2).

    mist "blazing mist," I. 89 ; ii. 1. 7. 10 (om. ed. 1, 2).

      ,, perfectly given, I. 274–75 ; ii. 3. 4. 24 (ed. 1–4.
          27–8).

    Mont Blanc frequently drawn by, IV. 183 *n* ; v. 14. 3 *n.*

    mountain-drawing of :   *See below, s. snow-painting.*

        IV. 312 ; v. 17. 46.

        best that ever can be done, IV. 317 ; v. 17. 51.

        cleavage, IV. 419 ; App. ii. 4.

        detail and redundancy of, IV. 308 ; v. 17. 41–2.

        effect of height given, I. 320–21 ; ii. 4. 3. 19.

        favourite forms, IV. 259 *seqq.* ; v. 16. 26 *seqq.*

        instant grasp of mountain form, IV. 201 ; v. 14. 22.

        knowledge of structure, IV. 236 ; v. 15. 31.

        lines of rest, IV. 330 ; v. 18. 17.

        massiveness of, I. 133 ; ii. 1. 7. 39 (om. ed. 1, 2).

        Yorkshire hills, his first idea of, IV. 259 ; v. 16. 25.

    precipices (Yorkshire hills), IV. 259 ; v. 16. 25.

        ,,   IV. 274 ; v. 16. 41.

    ravines, IV. 273 ; v. 16. 41.

    reflections, I. 161 ; ii. 2. 1. 20.

        ,,   I. 381 ; ii. 5. 3. 8.

        ,,   I. 382–83 ; ii. 5. 3. 10.

        ,,   I. 400 ; ii. 5. 3. 36 *seqq.*
             See below, s. water.

    rivers, distant, I. 388 ; ii. 5. 3. 18.

    rocks, I. 328–29 ; ii. 4. 4. 1–2.

      ,, III. 333–34 ; iv. 18. 13. *See below, s. stone.*

Turner, J. M. W. : *II. As an Artist, continued :*

seas :

breaking wave not done even by him, I. 397 ; ii. 5. 3.
30 (om. ed. 1, 2).
his rolling seas, I. 398-99 ; ii. 5. 3. 32.
influence of Dutch school, I. 401-2 ; ii. 5. 3. 37 (om. ed.
1, 2).
too grey and opaque, III. 344 ; iv. 18. 30.

shadows :

generally, I. 187 *seqq.* ; ii. 2. 3. 5 *seqq.*
their strange truth, IV. 77 ; v. 5. 11.
too long or short often, IV. 238 *n* ; v. 15. 33 *n*.
See above, s. chiaroscuro, colour.

skies :

brilliancy less than nature's, I. 146 ; ii. 1. 7. 46.
  ,,   ,,   ,,   I. 170 ; ii. 2. 2. 7.
  ,,   ,,   ,,   I. 213 *n* ; ii. 2. 5. 15 *n*.
  ,,   ,,   ,,   I. 250-51 ; ii. 3. 3. 16.
  ,,   ,,   ,,   I. 283 ; ii. 3. 5. 2.
drawn from memory, V. 125-26 *n* ; vii. 2. 6 *n*.
influenced by his London birth, V. 317 ; ix. 9. 4.
spacious always, I. 220 ; ii. 3. 1. 8.

snow-painting :

faulty, I. 305 ; ii. 4. 2. 19 (om. ed. 1, 2).
rare, IV. 253 ; v. 16. 18.
  ,, never of high Alps, V. 137 ; vii. 3. 2.

steam and smoke distinct, I. 247 ; ii. 3. 4. 13 (ed. 1-4
only).
stone-drawing, IV. 24-5 ; v. 2. 13.
      ,,   IV. 323 *seqq.* ; v. 18. 8 *seqq.*
      ,,   IV. 319 ; v. 18. 2.
storms, I. 275 *seqq.* ; ii. 3. 4. 25 *seqq.* (ed. 1-4. 30 *seqq.*).
  ,, ruined by engravers, *ib.* ; *ib. See above, s. clouds.*
sunbeams, I. 223 *seqq.* ; ii. 3. 1. 13 *seqq.*

tree-drawing :

I. 416-18 ; ii. 6. 1. 14-15 (om. ed. 1, 2).
III. 126-27 ; iv. 9. 13-14 (pl. 5).
V. 71 ; vi. 8. 5 *seqq.*
branches, I. 424-25 ; ii. 6. 1. 26.
     ,,   V. 52-3 ; vi. 6. 11 (pl. 61).
     ,,   V. 66-7 ; vi. 7. 17.
     ,,   V. 76-9 ; vi. 8. 11-12.
cypress never specifically drawn by him, I. 140 ; ii. 1. 7.
43 (om. ed. 1, 2).

Turner, J. M. W. : *II. As an Artist, continued :*

    foliage, I. 423–24 *n* ; ii. 6. 1. 24 *n* (om. ed. 1, 2).

        ,,   I. 427 ; ii. 6. 1. 28 (om. ed. 1, 2).

        ,,   I. 135–37 ; ii. 1. 7. 40–1.

        ,,   V. 42–3 ; vi. 5. 8–9.

        ,,   V. 108 ; vi. 10. 19.

    foreshortening, V. 79 ; vi. 8. 12.

    generally grouped, IV. 81 ; v. 16. 18.

    idiosyncrasies, IV. 259 ; v. 16. 26.

    pear-shaped ideal, *ib.* ; *ib.*

        ,,   ,,   V. 68 ; vi. 7. 20.

    stems, V. 80 ; vi. 8. 13.

    unconventional, V. 74 ; vi. 8. 9.

    twilight effects, I. 213 *n* ; ii. 2. 5. 15 *n* (om. ed. 1, 2).

    water-painting :

        I. 378 *seqq.* ; ii. 5. 3. 4 *seqq.*

        calm water, I. 382–83 ; ii. 5. 3. 10.

        distant expanses, I. 387 ; ii. 5. 3. 16.

        moving water, elongated reflections, I. 356–57 ; ii. 5. 1. 12 (om. ed. 1, 2).

        ,,   reflections, I. 360–61 *n* ; ii. 5. 1. 17 *n* (om. ed. 1, 2).

        waterfalls, I. 344 ; ii. 5. 2. 3 (ed. 1–4 only).

        ,,   I. 389–90 ; ii. 5. 3. 20.

        weight in water, I. 390 ; ii. 5. 3. 20.

        ,,   ,,   I. 399 ; ii. 5. 3. 33.

    waves. *See above, s. seas.*

    windmills by Stanfield and by Turner, IV. 7–9 ; v. 1. 10–11.

    perception of :

        if absent, the cause of his errors, IV. 238 ; v. 15. 33.

        its intensity, IV. 69 ; v. 4. 15.

        ,, rightness, constant, IV. 307 ; v. 17. 41.

        ,,   ,,   ,,   IV. 312 ; v. 17. 46.

        ,,   ,,   ,,   IV. 332–33 ; v. 18. 23.

        ,, and accuracy, V. 53 ; vi. 6. 11.

        ,,   ,,   *e.g.* on glacier motion, V. 89–90 ; vi. 9. 6.

    perspective of, I. 433 ; ii. 6. 2. 1.

        ,,   ,, lectures on, R.A., V. 376 *n* ; ix. 12. 4 *n*.

    picturesque in, IV. 1 *seqq.* ; v. 1. 1 *seqq.*

Turner, J. M. W.: *II. As an Artist, continued:*

    picturesque in, noble, his wide sympathy, IV. 15 ; v. 1.
       17. *See s. Ruins.*

    pine, he cannot enter into its spirit, I. 135 ; ii. 1. 7. 40.
      ,,   ,,   ,,   ,,   V. 90 ; vi. 9. 7.

    pre-Raphaelitism and :

      not opposed, III. 136–38 ; iv. 10. 5–6.
      thus author praises both, *ib.* ; *ib.*
      Turner the true head of pre-Raphaelitism, IV. 63 ; v.
        4. 8.

    progress of his work :

      course, generally, I. 133 *seqq.* ; ii. 1. 7. 39 *seqq.* (om.
        ed. 1, 2).
      ,,   ,,   I. 436–37 ; ii. 6. 2. 5.
      early works, enforced artificialness, III. 328–29 ; iv.
        18. 5–6.
      ,,   ,,   first period, V. 328–30 ; ix. 10. 1–3.
      ,,   ,,   little colour in, V. 345 ; ix. 11. 1.
      ,,   ,,   models for young artists, I. 447–48 ; ii. 6.
        3. 20.
      English drawings, I. 133–34 ; ii. 1. 7. 39 (om. ed. 1, 2).
      last drawings made with unabated power, IV. 333 ; v.
        18. 24.
      later manner, I. 146 ; ii. 1. 7. 46 (om. ed. 1, 2).
      1840 first culmination of power, I. 135 ; ii. 1. 7. 46 (ed.
        3, 4 only).
      1843 best in colour, I. 180 ; ii. 2. 2. 18.
      ,,   period of all, IV. 333 ; v. 18. 23.
      1845 failure of power begins, III. v ; *pref.* 1.
      1846 works during, I. *ed.* 3, *pref.* 3 (ed. 3 only).

    public appreciation and criticism of :

      critics ignorant, esp. of colour, I. 152 ; ii. 2. 2. 1 (ed.
        1, 2 only).
      ,, to study his *drawings*, I. 181 ; ii. 2. 2. 19.
      duty of press to him, I. 452–53 ; ii. 6. 3. 24.
      embittering effect on him, III. v ; *pref.* 1.
      extravagance charged against him, IV. 187 ; V. 14. 8.
      falsehood   ,,   ,,   I. 52 ; ii. 1. 1. 10.
      ,,   ,,   ,,   I. 441 ; ii. 6. 3. 7.
      finest works not understood, I. 404 ; ii. 5. 3. 38.
      his bright imageries above criticism, III. 63 ; iv. 4. 23.
      life shortened by criticism (*Blackwood*), IV. 411 ; App. i. 6.
      power blunted by it, V. 382–83 ; ix. 12. 11–14.

Turner, J. M. W. : *II. As an Artist, continued:*

       rightness of his work, wrongness of his critics (hence
          " Modern Painters "), V. ix–xi ; *pref.* 7–8.

       study needed to understand, I. xxii *n* ; *pref. ed.* 2. 13 *n.*

       unpopular and grand (cf. Æschylus), I. xxiv *n* ; *pref. ed.*
          2. 16 *n.*

       works of, to be viewed as a whole, I. 161 ; ii. 2. 1. 20.

redundancy of, never monotonous, IV. 308 ; v. 17. 42.

repose, how expressed by, V. 187 ; viii. 2. 5.

    „   instanced, I. 384 ; ii. 5. 3. 12.

ruins, love of, V. 364–65 ; ix. 11. 28.

scientific knowledge, instanced, I. 253 ; ii. 3. 3. 20.

        „   „   limited, IV. 238 ; v. 15. 33.
        See below, s. truth to nature.

sensibility, the root of his greatness, IV. 261 ; v. 16. 28.

    „   V. 317 ; ix. 9. 5.

simplicity of line, IV. 261 ; v. 16. 27.

size of his best works (18 in. × 12 in.), III. 42 ; iv. 3. 19.

sketches and memoranda of, V. 207 ; viii. 4. 8 *seqq.*

    „   „   „   V. 367–68 *n* ; ix. 11. 30 *n.*

stones, love of, IV. 24–5 ; v. 2. 13. *See above, s
stone-drawing.*

supremacy of :

    I. xix ; *pref. ed.* 2. 12.

    father of modern art, I. 137 ; ii. 1. 7. 12 (ed. 1, 2 only).

    first declared by author, II. '83 Epil. 13.

        „   „   „   V. 357 ; ix. 11. 16.

    „ to express emotions caused by landscape, III. 326 ;
        iv. 17. 43.

    heads all landscape, I. *pref. ed.* 3 (ed. 3 only).

        „   „   III. 215 ; iv. 14. 20.

        „   „   III. 296 ; iv. 16. 45.

        „   „   III. 323 ; iv. 17. 39.

        „   „   esp. contemplative, V. 218 *n* ; ix.
        1. 2 *n.*

    is the only perfect landscapist, I. 441–42 ; ii. 6. 3. 6–8.

    may be excelled one day, I. 144 ; ii. 1. 7. 45 (om. ed. 1, 2).

    paints things never done before (clouds, mountains,
        stones), I. 146 ; ii. 1. 7. 46 (om. ed. 1, 2).

    works of " the loveliest imagery of nature ever done," V.
        356 ; ix. 11. 14.

Turner, J. M. W. : *II. As an Artist, continued :*

  sympathy of, wide and general, IV. 15 ; v. 1. 17.
  teaching of :

    deepest thought of his slightest passages, I. 382 ; ii. 5. 3. 9.
    gives aspects, Bacon essences, III. 325–26 ; iv. 17. 43.
    nature as viewed by him, IV. 85 ; v. 5. 22.
      ,,   ,,   ,,   IV. 86 ; v. 6. 1.
    on discord and Eris, V. 341–42 ; ix. 10. 22.
    paints man's labour, sorrow, and death, V. 325 *seqq.* ; ix. 9. 20 *seqq.*
    pride of man as viewed by, V. 365 ; ix. 11. 29.
    rendering of death (crimson skies), IV. 333 ; v. 18. 24.
      ,,   ,,   V. 325–26 ; ix. 9. 22–3.
    "rose and canker," V. 356 ; ix. 11. 13 *seqq.*
    Venice, Rome, and Carthage, ideals of, V. 368–69 ; ix. 11. 31.

  thoroughness of, as great as possible, V. 374 *n* ; ix. 12. 4 *n.*
  tone in his pictures :

    attainment of truth of tone, I. 152–53 ; ii. 2. 1. 7.
    drawings better than earlier oils in, I. 155–56 ; ii. 2. 1. 12–13.
    early works lacking in, *ib.* ; *ib.*
    example of, the "Folkestone," *ib.* ; *ib.* (ed. 1, 2 only).
    perfect after 1833, *ib.* ; *ib.*
    relation of, to Claude's, *ib.* ; *ib.*
      ,,   ,,   Cuyp's, *ib.* 160–61 ; *ib.* 20.
    sometimes faulty in detail of colour, *ib.* ; *ib.*
    unites several tones in one picture, *ib.* 162 ; *ib.* 21.

  topography of, IV. 16–34 ; v. 2. 2–24.
  truth to nature :

    ,,   ,,   I. xlix ; *pref. ed.* 2. 46.
    due to perception, not science, I. 322 ; ii. 4. 3. 21.
      ,,   ,,   ,,   V. 53 ; xi. 6. 11.
    general remarks, I. 433 *seqq.* ; ii. 6. 2. 1 *seqq.*
    he alone has painted nature in her own colours, IV. 42 ; v. 3. 9.
    his sense of truth, V. 364 ; ix. 11. 26.
    never sacrificed to effect, I. 158 ; ii. 2. 1. 16.
    summed up by him, III. 135 ; iv. 10. 3.
    yet unlike nature, III. 133 ; iv. 10. 2.

Turner, J. M. W. : *II. As an Artist, continued :*

ugliness and dirt, painted and tolerated by, V. 317–18. ix. 9. 5–6.

universality and completeness of, I. 441–42 ; ii. 6. 3. 6–8.

variety of, and particular truth, I. 62–3 ; ii. 1. 3. 2.

„   never repeats himself, gives in each picture a final truth, I. 266 ; ii. 3. 4. 12.

vehicles of :

fading of his oils, not of his drawings, I. 145 *n* ; ii. 1. 7. 46 *n* (om. ed. 1, 2).

„   „   I. 421 *n* ; ii. 6. 3. 24 (ed. 1 only).

„   „   V. 356 ; ix. 11. 14.

„   „   V. 370 ; ix. 11. 31.

vignettes, true and free from "niggling," V. 40–1 ; vi. 5. 6.

III. Works of : *   [Synopsis. I. 33, 84 *n*, 98–9, 104, 115, 133–42, 143–47, 154–57, 161–63, 168 *n*, 170–71, 175–77, 180–82 *n*, 187–89, 194–95, 209–11 *n*, 225–26, 234–37, 250–53, 255–57, 266–71, 273–74, 276–77, 280 *n*, 283–85, 290, 293–95, 300–1, 302–3, 305, 311, 315, 318, 319, 321–22, 323–24, 329, 338–39, 341–44, 356, 359–60, 365, 367, 373, 378–79, 394, 397–99, 400, 402, 404–6, 417–18, 423 *n*, 425, 433. II. 171, 173, 184–86, 214–15, 221–25, 241, Epil. 3. 9. 13. III. 106, 123, 126–30, 134, 198 *n*, 245–46, 251, 327–29, 333–34, 336. IV. vi, 7–9, 15, 24, 27, 29–30, 74–5, 81, 202, 232–34, 238–39, 262–64, 273–74, 308–10, 312, 315, 317, 327, 331–34. V. vi *n*, viii, 42–3, 66–8, 71, 76–9, 90, 108–10, 124–25 *n*, 130, 132, 142, 161–64, 184, 185 *n*, 188 *seqq.*, 190–92, 202–7 *n*, 211 *n*, 317–22, 322 *n*, 323 *n*, 325, 329 *seqq.*, 337 *seqq.*, 345 *seqq.*, 347, 350 *n*, 356, 363–66 *n*, 340–41 *n*, 383, 385] :—

Acro-Corinth	cirrus clouds in tree	Finden's Bible Large picture	I. 235 ; ii. 3. 2. 10
Æsacus and Hesperie		Large picture	I. 417 ; ii. 6. 1. 15 (*ib.*)
„ „	heroic foliage	Lib. Stud.	I. 135 ; ii. 1. 7. 40 (om. ed. 1, 2)

* Most of the works in the above list will be found to come under one or other of the following heads :—

Academy and other Large Pictures. *See s.* Æsacus, Apollo and Python, Approach to Venice, Bamborough, Battle of Nile, Carthage, Childe Harold, Chryses' Prayer, Cicero's Villa, Coniston Fells, Crossing

Turner, J. M. W. : *III. Works of, continued :*

Æsacus and Hesperie	solemnity; effect of Italy	Lib. Stud.	I. 137; ii. 1. 7 42 (*ib.*)
,, ,,	foliage	,, ,,	I. 424 *n*; ii. 6. 1. 24 *n* (*ib.*)
,, ,,		,, ,,	II. 173; iii. 2. 2. 22
,, ,,		,, ,,	V. 365-6; ix. 11. 29
Alnwick	very fine	England and Wales, 9	I. 134; ii. 1. 7. 39 (om. ed. 1, 2)
,,	effect of light	,, ,,	I. 285; ii. 3. 5. 2.
Alps at Daybreak	chiaroscuro	Rogers' Poems, p. 192	I. 195; ii. 2. 3. 13

the Brook, Daphne and Leucippus, Deluge, Departure of Regulus, Egypt Tenth Plague, Fire at Sea, Flight into Egypt, Fountain of Fallacy, Giudecca, Glaucus and Scylla, Golden Boughs, Greenwich Hospital, Hannibal crossing the Alps, Hero and Leander, Hesperides, Houses of Parliament, Italy (Ancient and Modern), Ivy Bridge, Juliet and her Nurse, Lake Avernus, Lincoln Cathedral, Llanberis, Malmesbury, Mercury and Argus, Murano, Napoleon, Narcissus and Echo, Nelson's Death, Old Téméraire, Ostend, Palestrina, Peterborough Cathedral, Port Ruysdael, Rosenau, San Benedetto, Sea-piece, Shylock, Slave-ship, Snowstorm, Snowstorm Avalanche, etc., Sun of Venice, Tintern Abbey, Ulysses and Polyphemus, Venice, Walhalla, Waterloo, Whalers.

CAMPBELL'S POEMS. *See s.* At Summer Eve, Andes, Beech Tree's Petition, Hohenlinden, Last Man.

ENGLAND AND WALES. *See s.* Alnwick, Bedford, Blenheim, Bolton, Buckfastleigh, Carew, Colchester, Coventry, Cowes, Dartmouth Cove, Devonport, Dudley, Durham, Ely, Eton, Folkestone, Fowey, Gosport, Great Yarmouth, Hampton Court, Harlech, Kenilworth, Kilgarren, Langharne, Llanberis, Llanthony, Longships Lighthouse (Land's End), Lowestoft, Malvern, Nottingham, Oakhampton, Orford, Penmaen-Mawr, Richmond, St. Michael's Mount, Salisbury, Saltash, Stonehenge, Tees, Trematon, Ulleswater, Upnor, Warwick, Winchelsea, Windsor. *And see below, s.* YORKSHIRE SERIES (WHITTAKER'S RICHMONDSHIRE).

FINDEN'S BIBLE. *See s.* Acro-Corinth, Assos, Babylon, Bethlehem, Corinth, Egypt, Engedi, Mount Lebanon, Pyramids, Sidon, Sinai, Solomon's Pools.

HAKEWELL'S ITALY. *See s.* Alps from Turin, Hakewell, Isola Bella.

KEEPSAKE. *See s.v. and s.* Arona, Chateau de la Belle Gabrielle, Florence, Marly.

LIBER STUDIORUM. *See s.v. and s.* Æsacus, Basle, Ben Arthur, Blair Athol, Bonneville, Chepstow, Dumblane, Dunstanborough, Egypt, English Castle, Farmyard, Grande Chartreuse, Greenwich, Grenoble, Hedging and Ditching, Holy Island, Interior of a Church, Jason, Juvenile Tricks, Inverary, Isis, Kirkstall Crypt, Lauffenbourg, Lindisfarne, Little Devil's Bridge, Lost Sailor, Marine Dabblers, Mer de Glace, Morpeth Tower, Peat Bog, Pembury Mill, Procris and Cephalus, Raglan, Rape of Europa, Rivaulx, Rizpah, St. Catherine's Hill (Guildford), St. Gothard, Solway

Turner, J. M. W.: *III. Works of, continued:*

Alps at Daybreak	rays of sun and clouds	Rogers' Poems,	I. 226 ; ii. 3. 1. 17
,, ,,	cirrus clouds and mist	,, ,,	I. 236–37; ii. 3. 2. 12
,, ,,	sunrise colours	,, ,,	I. 280 ; ii. 3. 4. 34 (ed. 1–4. 37)
,, ,,	effect of light	,, ,,	I. 283 ; ii. 3. 5. 2
Alps from Turin	mountains	,, ,,	I. 293 ; ii. 4. 2. 4
Amalfi	clouds	Hakewell's Italy	III. 134 ; iv. 10. 3
		Rogers' Italy, p. 216	I. 253–54; ii. 3. 3. 21
Amboise (Chateau)	chiaroscuro	Rivers of France	I. 194 ; ii. 2 3. 13
Amboise	,,	,, ,,	*ib.* ; *ib.*
,,	,,	,, ,,	I. 285 ; ii. 3. 5. 2

Moss, Source of Arveron, Spenser's "Faërie Queen," Strawyard, Thun, Tyre, Via Mala, Watercress Gatherers, Watermill, Winchelsea, Young Anglers.

MILTON. *See s.v. and s.* Lycidas, Temptation on the Mountain.

RIVERS OF FRANCE. *See. s.v. and s.* Amboise (Chateau), Amboise, Beaugency, Blois (and Blois, Chateau), Caudebec, Chaise de Gargantua, Chateau Gaillard, Clairmont, Clairmont and Mauves, Havre, Honfleur, Jumièges, Light-towers of the Héve, Loire, Mantes, Montjean, Orleans, Paris (Pont Neuf), Quillebœuf, Quillebœuf and Villequier, Rietz, Rouen, St. Cloud, St. Denis, St. Julien, Seine and Marne, Seine, Tours, Troyes, Vernon.

ROGERS' ITALY. *See s.v. and s.* Amalfi, Aosta, Bridge with Pines, Como, Farewell, Felucca, Galileo's Villa, Lake Albano, Lake of Geneva, Lucerne, Marengo, Pæstum, Perugia, Ruins, St. Bernard, St. Maurice, Tell's Chapel, Venice.

ROGERS' POEMS. *See s.v. and s.* Alps at Daybreak, Boy of Egremond, Datur hora Quieti, Human Life, Jacqueline, Loch Lomond, Lodore, Pleasures of Memory, Rialto, St. Anne's Hill, St. Herbert's Isle, Sunset Behind Willows, Tornaro's Brow, Twilight, Voyage of Columbus.

SCOTT, SIR W. NOVELS. *See s.* Antiquary, Brienne, Chiefswood, Dunstaffnage, Fontainebleau, Fort Augustus, Glencoe, Piacenza, Rhymer's Glen, Tantallon, Venice.—POEMS. *See s.* Armstrong's Tower, Caerlaverock, Derwentwater, Dryburgh, Jedburgh, Junction of Greta and Tees, Loch Achray, Loch Coriskin, Loch Katrine, Mayburgh, Melrose, Skiddaw.

VARIOUS DRAWINGS. *See s.* Baden, Bingen, Calais, Calder Bridge, Chamouni, Constance, Dazio Grande, Delphi, Faido Pass, Goldau, Hastings (battle of), Lucerne, Nemi, Oberwesel, Pas de Calais, Rheinfelden, Schaffhausen, Seckingen, Shipwreck studies, Sketches, Sunset, Swiss subjects, Swiss Wall-tower, Trossachs, Uri, Venice, Via Mala, Zurich, Zug.

YORKSHIRE SERIES (WHITTAKER'S RICHMONDSHIRE). *See s.* Aske Hall, Brignal, Hardraw, Heysham, Ingleborough, Junction of Greta and Tees, Kirkby Lonsdale, Richmond, Simmer Lake, Tees (Upper Fall), Wycliffe, Yorkshire, Zurich.

Turner, J. M. W. : *III. Works of, continued :*

Ancient Italy	*See below, s. Italy*		I. 195 ; ii. 2. 3. 13
Andes Coast	chiaroscuro	Campbell (pl. 2)	I. 274 ; ii. 3. 4. 23 (ed. 1-4. 26)
,, ,,	clouds	,, ,,	I. 279 n ; ii. 3. 4. 32 n (ed. 1-4. 36)
,, ,,	mountains	,, ,,	I. 294 ; ii. 4. 2. 5
Antiquary	clouds and precipices	Scott .	I. 280 n ; ii. 3. 4. 32 (ed. 1-4. 36)
,,	storm scene	,,	I. 406 n ; ii. 5. 3. 40 n
Aosta	mountains	Rogers' Italy	I. 294 ; ii. 4. 2. 5
Apollo and Python	colour of clouds	R.A., 1811	V. 345 *seqq.* ; ix. 11. 1 *seqq.*
,, ,,		,, ,,	V. 347 ; ix. 11. 4
Apollo and Sibyl	*See below, s. Bay of Baiæ*	,, ,,	V. 356 ; ix. 11. 14
Approach to Venice (from Fusina)	exquisite colour	R.A., 1844	I. 146 ; ii. 1. 7. 46 (om. ed. 1, 2)
Armstrong's Tower	chiaroscuro (shadows)	Scott	I. 188 ; ii. 2. 3. 5
Arona and St. Gothard	distant mountains	Keepsake, 1829	I. 300-1 ; ii. 4. 2. 14-15
Aske Hall	trees	Yorkshire	I. 417 ; ii. 6. 1. 15 (om. ed. 1, 2)
,, ,,	branch of tree		V. 76-9 ; vi. 8. 11-12
Assos	twilight	Finden's Bible	I. 213 n ; ii. 2. 5. 15. n (om. ed. 1, 2)
,,	effect of light	,, ,,	I. 285 ; ii. 3. 5. 2
At Summer Eve	chiaroscuro	Campbell (pl. 1)	I. 195 ; ii. 2. 3. 13
Babylon	clouds	Finden's Bible	I. 250 ; ii. 3. 3. 16
Baden		Nat. Gall.	V. vii ; *pref.* 3
Bamborough	failure, over-detail		I. 144 ; ii. 1. 7. 45 (om. ed. 1, 2)
,,	breaking wave		I. 397 ; ii. 5. 3. 30 (om. ed. 1, 2)
Basle	unsatisfactory	Lib. Stud.	I. 134 ; ii. 1. 7. 40 (om. ed. 1, 2)
Battle of Nile		R.A., 1799	V. 329 ; ix. 10. 3.
Bay of Baiæ (with Apollo and the Sibyl)	crude colour, over-detail	R.A., 1823	I. 140 ; ii. 1. 7. 43 (om. ed. 1, 2)
,, ,,	foreground	,, ,,	I. 343 ; ii. 4. 4. 29
,, ,,		,, ,,	III. 330 ; iv. 18. 8
,, ,,	foreground	,, ,,	V. 110 ; vi. 10. 20
,, ,,		,, ,,	V. 355 ; ix. 11. 12
Beaugency	chiaroscuro	Rivers of France	V. 363 ; ix. 11. 26
			I. 194 ; ii. 2. 3. 13
Bedford	coarse and conventional	,, ,, England and Wales	I. 283 ; ii. 3. 5. 2
			I. 134 ; ii. 1. 7. 39 (om. ed. 1, 2)
Beech-tree's petition	shadows	Campbell	I. 187-88 ; ii. 2. 3. 5
Ben Arthur	noble lines of hills	Lib. Stud.	I. 103 ; ii. 1. 7. 39 (om. ed. 1, 2)
,, ,,	stones		IV. 326-27 ; v. 18. 11-12
Ben Lomond	clouds	Rogers' Poems, p. 203	I. 274 ; ii. 3. 4. 23 *See s. Loch Lomond*
Bethlehem	clouds	Finden's Bible	I. 275 ; ii. 3. 3. 26
Bingen	effect of light		I. 284 ; ii. 3. 5. 2
Blair Athol	trees	Lib. Stud.	I. 417 ; ii. 6. 1. 15 (om. ed. 1, 2)
Blenheim	effect of light	Eng. and Wales, 16	I. 284 ; ii. 3. 5. 2

Turner, J. M. W. : *III. Works of, continued :*

Blois	chiaroscuro	Rivers of France	I. 194 ; ii. 2. 3. 13
,, Chateau	,,	,, ,,	*ib.* ; *ib.* and pl. 85
,, ,,	distance	,, ,,	I. 211 *n* ; ii. 2. 5. 12 *n*
,, ,,	twilight	,, ,,	I. 213 *n* ; ii. 2. 5. 15 *n* (om. ed. 1, 2)
,, ,,	,,	,, ,,	I. 285 ; ii. 3. 5. 2
Bolton Abbey	trees	Eng. and Wales, 1	I. 417 ; ii. 6. 1. 15
,, ,,	,,	,, ,,	III. 126–28 ; iv. 9. 13–15
,, ,,	cliffs	,, ,,	III. 333–34 ; iv. 18. 13 (pl. 12)
,, ,,	,,	,, ,,	IV. 233 *n* ; v. 15. 30 *n*
,, ,,	,,	,, ,,	IV. 262–63 ; v. 16. 30–2
Bonneville	foreground	Lib. Stud.	I. 135 ; ii. 1. 7. 40 (om. ed. 1, 2)
,,	colour	Allnutt's	I. 141 ; ii. 1. 7. 44 (om. ed. 1, 2)
	,,	Birmingham	
Boy of Egremond	chiaroscuro	Rogers' Poems, p. 184	I. 195 ; ii. 2. 3. 13
,, ,,	torrent	,, ,,	I. 394 ; ii. 5. 3. 28
Bridge with pines		Rogers' Italy, p. 183	IV. 263 ; v. 16. 32
			I. 139 ; ii. 1. 7. 43 (om. ed. 1, 2)
Brienne	chiaroscuro (shadows)	Scott	I. 188 ; ii. 2. 3. 5
,,	,,		I. 195 ; ii. 2. 3. 13
Brignal Banks		Yorkshire	IV. 333–34 ; v. 18. 24
,, Church	trees	,,	I. 417–18 ; ii. 6. 1. 15 (om. ed. 1, 2)
Buckfastleigh	effect of light	Eng. and Wales, 4	I. 283 ; ii. 3. 5. 2
,,	kite-flying	,, ,,	IV. 15 ; v. 1. 17
Caerlaverock	luminous twilight	Scott's Poems, vol. 4	I. 213 *n* ; ii. 2. 5. 15 *n* (om. ed. 1, 2)
,, ,,	,,	,, ,, ,,	I. 280 ; ii. 3. 4. 33 (ed. 1–4. 37)
Calais	effect of light		I. 285 ; ii. 3. 5. 2
Calder Bridge	quiet beauty	E. Bicknell	I. 141 ; ii. 1. 7. 44 (om. ed. 1, 2)
Caldron Snout Fall	effect of light		I. 284 ; ii. 3. 5. 2
Caligula's Bridge	"nonsense picture"	R.A., 1831	I. 139 ; ii. 1. 7. 42 (om. ed. 1, 2)
			V. 363 ; ix. 11. 26
Carew Castle	effect of light	Eng. and Wales, 17	I. 284 ; ii. 3. 5. 2
Carthage (Building)	toy-boats in foreground	R.A., 1815	I. 33 ; i. 1. 7. 2
,, ,,	over-accumulation	,,	I. 138 ; ii. 1. 7. 42 (om. ed. 1, 2)
,, ,,	bad in colour	,,	I. 144 ; ii. 1. 7. 45 (*ib.*)
,, ,,	tone, and foreground	,,	I. 156 ; ii. 2. 1. 13
,, ,,	colour deficient	,,	I. 181 ; ii. 2. 2. 18
,, ,,	,,	,,	III. 330 ; iv. 18. 8
,, ,,	,,	,,	V. 368–69 ; ix. 11. 31
,, (Fall)	bad in colour	,,	I. 138 ; ii. 1. 7. 42 (om. ed. 1, 2)
,, ,,	tone	,,	I. 156 ; ii. 2. 1. 13
,, ,,	false in colour	,,	I. 181 ; ii. 2. 2. 18
,, ,,	meaningless composition	,,	III. 330 ; iv. 18. 8
	scarlet in	,,	V. 369 *n* ; ix. 11. 31 *n*
Caudebec	effect of light	Rivers of France	I. 285 ; ii. 3. 5. 2
,,	mountain and river	,, ,,	I. 321 ; ii. 4. 3. 20
,,	river	,, ,,	I. 388 ; ii. 5. 3. 18

Turner, J. M. W. : *III. Works of, continued :*

Chaise de Gargantua	water	Rivers of France	I. 385 ; ii. 5. 3. 14
Chamouni	pines	Lib. Stud.	I. 135 ; ii. 1. 7. 40 (om. ed. 1, 2)
,,		Fawkes' (Farnley)	I. 128 ; ii. 1. 7. 41 (ed. 3-4 only)
,,	study of gneiss	Author's coll.	III. 134 ; iv. 10. 3 *See s. Grande Chartreuse*
Chateau de la Belle Gabrielle	trees in bough	Keepsake	I. 418 ; ii. 6. 1. 15 V. 66 ; vi. 7. 17 (fig. 55)
Chateau Gaillard	chiaroscuro	Rivers of France	I. 194 ; ii. 2. 3. 13
Chepstow	architecture	Lib. Stud.	I. 135 ; ii. 1. 7. 40 (om. ed. 1, 2)
	pensive symbolism	,, ,,	V. 365 ; ix. 11. 29
Chief's-wood Cottage	trees	Scott ,,	I. 418 ; ii. 6. 1. 15
Childe Harold		R.A., 1832	V. 363 ; ix. 11. 26
Chryses' Prayer		R.A., 1811	V. 355 ; ix. 11. 12
Cicero's Villa	"nonsense picture"	R.A., 1839	I. 139 ; ii. 1. 7. 42 (om. ed. 1, 2)
,, ,,	colour deficient	,, ,,	I. 144 ; ii. 1. 7. 45 (*ib.*)
,, ,,	tone	,, ,,	I. 156 ; ii. 2. 1. 13
Clairmont	effect of light	Rivers of France	I. 285 ; ii. 3. 5. 2
,, and Mauves	hills	,, ,,	I. 322 ; ii. 4. 3. 22
Coblentz			*See s. Ehrenbreitstein*
Colchester	tone	England and Wales	I. 144 ; ii. 2. 1. 12 (ed. 1, 2 only)
	tint, delicate and full	,, ,,	I. 168 ; ii. 2. 2. 22 (ed. 1, 2 only)
Cologne	tone	,, ,,	I. 144 ; ii. 2. 1. 12 (ed. 1, 2 only)
Como	clouds	Rogers' Italy	I. 252 ; ii. 3. 3. 18
Coniston Fells	poetical quotation	R.A., 1798	V. 329 ; ix. 10. 3.
Constance	level mist	Brantwood in 1878	I. 389 ; 2. 5. 3. 19
Corinth	effect of light	Finden's Bible	I. 284 ; ii. 3. 5. 2
Coventry	storm	Eng. and Wales, 17	I. 270 ; *seqq.* ; ii. 3. 4. 16-19 (ed. 1-4. 18-21)
,,	passage of repose	,, ,,	*ib.* ; *ib.*
,,	effect of light	,, ,,	I. 284 ; ii. 3. 5. 2.
Cowes	tone	,, ,, 8	I. 144 ; ii. 2. 1. 12 (ed. 1, 2 only)
,,	effect of light	,, ,, ,,	I. 285 ; ii. 3. 5. 2
,,	summer twilight	,, ,,	I. 384 ; ii. 5. 3. 12
,,	water	,, ,,	I. 386 ; ii. 5. 3. 15
Crossing the Brook	hybrid composition	R.A., 1815	I. 138 ; ii. 1. 7. 42 (om. ed. 1, 2)
,, ,,	tone	,, ,,	I. 156 ; ii. 2. 1. 13
,, ,,	not a fine piece of colour	,, ,,	I. 180 ; ii. 2. 2. 18
,, ,,	trees	,, ,,	I. 418 ; ii. 6. 1. 15
Daphne and Leucippus	capital in foreground		I. 212 and *n* ; ii. 2 5. 14 and *n*
,, ,,	hills		I. 311 ; ii. 4. 3. 6
,, ,,	,,		I. 318 ; ii. 4. 3. 16
,, ,,	meaningless classicism		III. 330 ; iv. 18. 8
,, ,,	mountains		IV. 308 ; v. 17. 42
,, ,,	foreground		V. 110 ; vi. 10. 20

Turner, J. M. W. : *III. Works of, continued :*

Dartmouth	rays of sun	Rivers of England	I. 225 ; ii. 3. 1. 15
,, Cove	trees	Ergland and Wales	I. 418 ; ii. 6. 1. 15
Datur hora quieti	tone	Rogers' Poems, end	I. 155 ; ii. 2. 1. 10
,, ,,	chiaroscuro	,, ,,	I. 195 ; ii. 2. 3. 13
,, ,,	effect of light	, ,,	I. 284 ; ii. 3. 5. 2
,, ,,		,, ,,	V. 187 ; viii. 2. 5
Dazio Grande (St. Gothard)	torrent ,,	,, ,,	I. 394 ; ii. 5. 3. 28
,, ,,			II. '83 Epil. 3
,, ,,			IV. 24 ; v. 2. 13
Delphi	sunrise		I. 280 ; ii. 3. 4. 33 (ed. 1-4. 37)
Deluge	engraving, very rare	R.A., 1813	I. 367 ; ii. 5. 1. 22 (om. ed. 1, 2)
Departure of Regulus	"nonsense picture"	Brit. Inst., 1837	I. 139 ; ii. 1. 7. 42 (om. ed. 1, 2)
Derwentwater, Skiddaw	rippled calm	Scott	I. 387 ; ii. 5. 3. 16
Devil's Bridge (St. Gothard)		Lib. Stud.	IV. 28 ; v. 2. 16
Devonport Dockyards	tone	Eng. and Wales, 8	I. 144 ; ii. 2. 1. 12 (ed. 1, 2 only)
,, ,,	sky	,, ,,	I. 168 *n* ; ii. 2. 2. 5 *n*
,, ,,	water calm	,, ,,	I. 383 ; ii. 5. 3. 10
Dryburgh	river	Scott	I. 388 ; ii. 5. 3. 18
Dudley	tone	Eng. and Wales, 19	I. 144 ; ii. 2. 1. 12 (ed. 1, 2 only)
,,	engraver's additions	,, ,,	I. 183 *n* ; ii. 2. 2. 20 *n* (om. ed. 1, 2)
,,	effect of light		I. 285 ; ii. 3. 5. 2
Dumblane	architecture	Lib. Stud.	I. 135 ; ii. 1. 7. 40 (om. ed. 1, 2)
Dunbar	sea	Scott's Prov. Ants.	I. 398 ; ii. 5. 3. 32
Dunstaffnage	rain-clouds	Scott's Novels, vol. 24	I. 277 ; ii. 3. 4. 28 (ed. 1-4. 33)
,,	distance	,, ,,	I. 303 ; ii. 4. 2. 18
Dunstanborough	architecture	Lib. Stud.	I. 135 ; ii. 1. 7. 40 (om. ed. 1, 2)
,, ,,		,, ,,	V. 365 ; ix. 11. 29
Durham	tone	England and Wales	I. 144 ; ii. 2. 1. 12 (ed. 1, 2 only)
,,	effect of light	,, ,	I. 284 ; ii. 3. 5. 2
,,	trees	,, ,,	I. 418 ; ii. 6. 1. 15
Egypt, Fifth Plague	failure	Finden's Bible	I. 138 ; ii. 1. 7. 42 (om. ed. 1, 2)
			V. 329 ; ix. 10. 3
,, Tenth Plague	cramped	Lib. Stud.	I. 138 ; ii. 1. 7. 42 (om. ed. 1, 2)
,, ,, ,,		,, ,,	V. 325 *n* ; ix. 9. 21 *n*
,, ,, ,,		,, ,,	V. 329 ; ix. 10. 3
,, ,, ,,	fine, but uninteresting	Large work, R.A., 1802	I. 138 ; ii. 1. 7. 42 (om. ed. 1, 2)
Ehrenbreitstein (Coblentz)	sunset mist	Brantwood in 1878	I. 256 ; ii. 3. 4. 29 (ed. 1-4 only)
,, ,,	water		I. 361 ; ii. 5. 3. 19 (om. ed. 1, 2 only)
,, ,,			II. '83 Epil. 3
Ely	architecture	Eng. and Wales, 16	I. 434 ; ii. 6. 2. 1
Engedi	twilight	Finden's Bible	I. 213 *n* ; ii. 2. 5. 15 *n* (om. ed. 1, 2)
,,			I. 285 ; ii. 5. 3. 2
English Lowland Castle	exquisite work	Lib. Stud.	I. 135 ; ii. 1. 7. 40 (om. ed. 1, 2)

Turner, J. M. W. : *III. Works of, continued :*

Eton College	coarse and conventional	Eng. and Wales, 12	I. 134 ; ii. 1. 7. 39 (om. ed. 1, 2)
Faido Pass (St. Gothard)		Brantwood, 1878	IV. 24 *seqq.* ; v. 2. 13 *seqq.* (pl. 21)
" "			IV. 233 ; v. 15. 30
Farewell	sharpness of distance	Rogers' Italy	I. 302–3 ; ii. 4. 2. 18
Farmyard (poultry)	simple domesticity	Lib. Stud.	I. 135 ; ii. 1. 7. 40 (om. ed. 1, 2)
" (white horse)			*See s. Strawyard*
Felucca, The (moonlight)		Rogers' Italy, p. 223	I. 257 ; ii. 3. 3. 26
Fire at Sea	damaged in cleaning	Nat. Gall.	V. 211 *n* ; viii. 4. 18 *n*
Flight into Egypt	sky	R.A.	I. 257 ; ii. 3. 3. 26
Florence	light, and details	Keepsake, 1828	I. 140 ; ii. 1. 7. 43 (om. ed. 1, 2)
"	effect of light	" "	I. 284 ; ii. 3. 5. 2
Folkestone	gathering darkness	England and Wales	I. 257 ; ii. 3. 3. 26
"	effect of light	" "	I. 285 ; ii. 3. 5. 2
Fontainebleau	distance	Scott	I. 211 *n* ; ii. 2. 5. 12 *n*
Fort Augustus	lower mountains	Scott's Novels, vol. 26	I. 323 ; ii. 4. 3. 23
Fountain of Fallacy	colour faded	Brit. Inst., 1839	I. 139 ; ii. 1. 7. 42 (om. ed. 1, 2)
Fowey Harbour	effect of light	England and Wales	I. 283 ; ii. 3. 5. 2
" "	sea	" "	I. 398 ; ii. 5. 3. 32
" "		" "	V. 161 *n* ; vii. 4. 15 *n*
Galileo's Villa		Rogers' Italy, p. 115	I. 139 ; ii. 1. 7. 43
" "		" "	I. 257 ; ii. 3. 3. 26
Garden of Hesperides			*See below, s. Hesperides*
Giudecca Canal	colour of water	R.A., 1841	I. 384 ; ii. 5. 3. 11 *See s. Venice*
Glaucus and Scylla		" "	III. 198 *n* ; iv. 13. 26 *n*
Glencoe	clouds	Scott	I. 277 ; ii. 3. 4. 28 (ed. 1–4. 33)
"	distance	"	I. 303 ; ii. 4. 2. 18
"	hills	"	I. 311 ; ii. 4. 3. 6
Goldau	sunset storm	Brantwood, 1878	I. 280 ; ii. 3. 4. 33
"	" " and lake		I. 389 ; ii. 5. 3. 19
"			II. '83 Epil. 3
"	engraved in "Modern Painters"		IV. vi ; *pref.* 2
"			IV. 331–34 ; v. 18. 20–5
"			V. 369 *n* ; ix. 11. 31 *n*
Golden Bough and Sibyl	mountains	Nat. Gall.	IV. 308 ; v. 17. 42
Gosport "	rain-blue	Eng. and Wales, 11	V. 355 ; ix. 11, 12
" "			I. 273 ; ii. 3. 4. 22 (ed. 1–4. 25)
Grande Chartreuse, Mill near			I. 134 ; ii. 1. 7. 40 (om. ed. 1, 2)
" "	bough-drawing	Lib. Stud.	I. 417 ; ii. 6. 1. 15 (om. ed. 1, 2)
" "	close foliage	" "	I. 424 *n* ; ii. 6. 1. 24 *n* (om. ed. 1, 2)
" "		" "	II. '83 Epil. 9
" "		" "	III. 337 ; iv. 18–19
" "			IV. 273 ; v. 16. 41
" "			V. 365 ; ix. 11. 28

Turner, J. M. W. : *III. Works of, continued*.

Great Yarmouth	sea	Eng. and Wales, 7	I. 406 *n*; ii. 5. 3. 40 *n*
Greenwich Hospital	architecture		I. 135; ii. 1. 7. 40 (om. ed. 1, 2)
Grenoble to Chambéry	vintagers	Lib. Stud.	I. 135, 136; ii. 1. 7. 40 (*ib.*)
Hakewell's Italy	generally, detailed work		I. 134; ii. 1. 7. 39 (om. ed. 1, 2)
Hampton Court	chiaroscuro	Eng. and Wales, 7	I. 188; ii. 2. 3. 5
Hannibal crossing Alps	unsatisfactory condition	R.A., 1812	I. 137; ii. 1. 7. 41 (om. ed. 1, 2)
Hardraw Fall		Yorkshire	IV. 327; v. 18. 12
Harlech	mist	Eng. and Wales, 21	I. 256; ii. 3. 4. 29 (ed. 1–4 only)
Hastings	trees	Views in Sussex	II. 214; iii. 2. 4. 6
Havre	cirrus clouds	Rivers of France	I. 237; ii. 3. 2. 13
Hedging and Ditching	simple domesticity	Lib. Stud.	I. 135; ii. 1. 7. 40 (om. ed. 1, 2)
,, ,,	trees	,, ,,	I. 417; ii. 6. 1. 15 (om. ed. 1, 2)
			V. 365; ix. 11. 28
Hero and Leander	fine and unconventional	R.A., 1837	I. 139; ii. 1. 7. 42 (om. ed. 1, 2)
,, ,,	shadows		I. 187; ii. 2. 3. 5
,, ,,	clouds		I. 257; ii. 3. 3. 26
,, ,,	breaking waves		I. 397; ii. 5. 3. 30
,, ,,	steps		I. 434; ii. 6. 2. 1
,, ,,	damaged in cleaning (National Gallery)		V. 211 *n*; viii. 4. 18 *n*
Hesperides' Dragon		Brit. Inst., 1806	III. 106; iv. 8. 7
,, Garden			III. 329; iv. 18. 6.
,, ,,			V. 317; ix. 9. 4
,, ,,			V. 330 *seqq.*; ix. 10. 3 *seqq.*
,, ,,			V. 337 *seqq.*; ix. 10. 15 *seqq.* (pl. 78)
,, ,,			V. 369; ix. 11. 31
,, ,,			V. 383; ix. 12. 13
,, ,,			V. 387; ix. 12. 20
Heysham and Cumberland Hills	rain-clouds	Yorkshire	I. 274; ii. 3. 4. 23 (ed. 1–4. 26)
Hohenlinden	effect of light	Campbell, p. 87	I. 283; ii. 3. 5. 2.
Holy Isle		Lib. Stud.	III. 329; iv. 18. 6.
Honfleur	chiaroscuro	Rivers of France	I. 195; ii. 2. 3. 13
,,	hills	,, ,,	I. 322; ii. 4. 3. 22
Houses of Parliament (Burning)	effect of light		I. 285; ii. 3. 5. 2
,, ,,	chiaroscuro		I. 195; ii. 2. 3. 13
Human Life, vignette	distance	Rogers' Poems, p. 63	I. 211 *n*; ii. 2. 5. 12 *n*
,, ,,	effect of light		I. 283; ii. 3. 5. 2
Ingleborough		Yorkshire	IV. 262; v. 16. 29
Interior of a Church	architecture	Lib. Stud.	I. 135; ii. 1. 7. 40 (om. ed. 1, 2)
,, ,, ,,	ethical meaning		V. 322 *n*; ix. 9. 13 *n*
Inverary	fir trees	,, ,,	V. 71; vi. 8. 6 (fig. 56)
Isis			V. 191; viii. 2. 13
Isola Bella		Hakewell's Italy	III. 134; iv. 10. 3
Italian Studies (Rome and Naples)		Nat. Gall.	V. 212–13; viii. 4. 19

Turner, J. M. W. : *III. Works of, continued:*

Italy, Ancient	"nonsense picture"	R.A., 1838	I. 139; ii. 1. 7. 42 (om. ed. 1, 2)
„ Modern	English, foliage		I. 139 seqq.; ii. 1 7. 43 (ib.)
„ „	engraving, Art Union		I. 182 n; ii. 2. 2. 20 n (ib.)
„ „	architecture	„ „	I. 404; ii. 6. 2. 1 (ed. 1, 2 only)
„ „	„		III. 123; iv. 9. 8
„ „	mountains		IV. 308; v. 17. 42
Ivy Bridge	foreground and detail		I. 141; ii. 1. 7. 44 (om. ed. 1, 2)
„ „	torrent		I. 395; ii. 5. 3. 28
„ „	butterfly		III. 130; iv. 9. 17
Jacqueline	mountains	Rogers' Poems, p. 145	I. 294-97; ii. 4. 2. 5-9
			II. 225; iii. 2. 4. 20
Jason	figure, and rocks	Lib. Stud. „	I. 138; ii. 1. 7. 42 (om. ed. 1, 2)
„	dragon	„ „	II. 184-85; iii. 2. 3. 13-14
„	„ trees	„ „	II. 214; iii. 2. 4. 6
„		„ „	III. 106; iv. 8. 7
		„ „	III. 337; iv. 18. 19
Jedburgh	chiaroscuro	Scott	I. 195; ii. 2. 3. 13
Juliet and her Nurse	„ later manner	R.A., 1836	I. 143-44; ii. 1. 7. 45-6
„ „	effect of light	„ „	I. 285; iii. 3. 5. 2
Jumièges	rain-cloud	Rivers of France	I. 266-67; ii. 3. 4. 12
	water		I. 386; ii. 5. 3. 15
Junction of Greta and Tees	foreground débris	Yorkshire	I. 342; ii. 4. 4. 26
„ „	torrent	„	I. 394; ii. 5. 3. 28
„ „	kite-flying		IV. 15; v. 1. 17
		„ Scott	IV. 327; v. 18. 12
Juvenile Tricks	trees	Lib. Stud.	I. 417; ii. 6. 1. 15 (om. ed. 1, 2)
„ .		„ „	IV. 15; v. 1. 17
Keepsake (drawing for)	trees	B. G. Windus	I. 137; ii. 1. 7. 41 (om. ed. 1, 2)
Kelso	„	Scott	I. 388; ii. 6. 1. 14 (ed. 1, 2 only)
Kenilworth	tone	Eng. and Wales	I. 144; ii. 2. 1. 12 (ed. 1, 2 only)
„	effect of light	„ „	I. 284; ii. 3. 5. 2
Kilgarren	finest work	„ „ 6	I. 134; ii. 1. 7. 39 (om. ed. 1, 2)
Killiecrankie	waterfall	Scott	I. 393; ii. 5. 3. 25
Kirkby Lonsdale Churchyard	effect of light	Yorkshire	I. 283; ii. 3. 5. 2
„ „	trees	Yorkshire series	I. 417; ii. 6. 1. 15
„ „		„ „	IV. 15; v. 1. 17
			IV 333; iv. 18. 24
Kirkstall Crypt		Lib. Stud.	V. 365; ix. 11. 29
Lake Albano	effect of light	Rogers' Italy	I. 284; iii. 3. 5. 2
„ of Geneva	clouds	„ „	I. 253; ii. 3. 3

Turner, J. M. W. : *III. Works of, continued :*

Lake of Geneva	effect of light	Rogers' Italy	I. 283 ; ii. 3. 5. 2
„ „ Lucerne			*See below,* s. Lucerne
„ „ Zug	companion to "Goldau"		V. 369 n ; ix. 11.31 n
Langharne	sea	Eng. and Wales, 16	I. 398-401 ; ii. 5. 3. 32-6
Last Man, vignette	sunset and clouds	Campbell	I. 280 ; ii. 3. 4. 33 (ed. 1-4. 37)
Lauffenbourg	unsatisfactory	Lib. Stud.	I. 135 ; ii. 1. 7. 40 (om. ed. 1, 2)
„		„ „	III. 336 ; iv. 18. 19
„		„ „	V. 191 ; viii. 2. 12
„	original (Nat. Gall.)	„ „	V. vii ; *pref.* 3
Lebanon			*See* s. Mt. Lebanon
Liber Studiorum	copying of, recommended		V. 192 ; viii. 2. 14
„ „	domestic subjects		I. 135 ; ii. 1. 7. 40
„ „	foliage		I. 135-36 ; ii. 1. 7. 40
„ „	foregrounds		I. 105 ; ii. 1. 7. 22 (om. ed. 1, 2)
„ „	frontispiece (Europa)		V. 366 ; ix. 11. 30
„ „	influence of Claude and Titian		III. 336 ; iv. 18. 19
„ „	lessons on labour, love, pride		V. 364-66 ; ix. 11. 28 seqq.
„ „	right exaggeration in		II. 225 ; ii. 2. 4. 21
„ „	ruins in, numerous		V. 365 ; ix. 11. 28
„ „	subjects, Eng. mostly		I. 135 ; ii. 1. 7. 40 } (om. ed. 1, 2)
„ „	„ Eng. the best		I. 135 ; *ib.* }
„ „	„ Italian		*ib.* ; *ib.* (*ib.*)
„ „	„ Swiss, his best of Switzerland		I. 137 ; ii. 1. 7. 41 (*ib.*)
„ „	trees of		I. 417 ; ii. 6. 1. 15 (*ib.*)
Light-towers of the Héve	chiaroscuro	Rivers of France	I. 195 ; ii. 2. 3. 13
Lincoln Cathedral		R.A., 1795	V. 329 ; ix. 10. 3
Lindisfarne		Lib. Stud.	V. 365 ; ix. 11. 29
Little Devil's Bridge over the Russ	praised	„ „	I. 134 ; ii. 1. 7. 40 (om. ed. 1, 2)
			IV. 27-8 ; v. 2. 16
Llanberis	unexaggerated gloom	R.A.	I. 98-9 ; ii. 1. 7. 17 (om. ed. 1, 2)
„	clouds over Snowdon	Eng. and Wales, 18	I. 274 ; ii. 3. 4. 23 (ed. 1-4. 26)
„	effect of light	„ „	I. 284 ; ii. 3. 5. 2
„			V. 351 n ; ix. 11. 8 n (pl. 80)
Llanthony	finest work	„ „ 20	I. 134 ; ii. 1. 7. 39 (om. ed. 1, 2)
„	stones in foreground	„ „	I. 183 n ; ii. 2. 2. 20 n (*ib.*)
„	gray colour—rain	„ „	I. 267 ; ii. 3. 4. 13 (ed. 1-4. 14)
„	foreground rocks	„ „	I. 341 ; ii. 4. 4. 25
„	torrent		I. 393 ; ii. 5. 3. 26
Loch Achray	distance	Scott	I. 303 ; ii. 4. 2. 18
„ Coriskin	clouds and rain	„	I. 268 ; ii. 3. 4. 14-15
„ „	hills	„	I. 311 ; ii. 4. 3. 5
„ „		„	IV. 232-33 ; v. 15. 29
„ Katrine	hill drawing	„	I. 312 ; ii. 4. 3. 6
„ „	rippled calm	„	I. 387 ; ii. 5. 3. 16

Turner, J. M. W. : *III. Works of, continued :*

Loch Lomond	chiaroscuro	Rogers' Poems, p. 203	I. 195 ; ii. 2. 3. 13
" "	clouds	" "	I. 274 ; ii. 3. 4. 23 (ed. 1-4. 26)
" "	rippled calm	" "	I. 387 ; ii. 5. 3. 16
Lodore "	chiaroscuro	" " p. 36	I. 195 ; ii. 2. 3. 13
Loire Scene	precipice and sunset	Rivers of France	I. 194 ; ii. 5. 3. 13
Loire-side, subjects	additions in engravings	" "	V. 184-85 n; viii. 2. 2
Longships Lighthouse, Land's End	grey tones (original drawing)	Eng. and Wales, 20	I. 168 ; ii. 2. 2. 22 (ed. 1, 2 only)
" "			I. 267 ; ii. 3. 4. 12 n (ed. 1-4. 14)
" "	clouds at twilight	" "	I. 269 ; ii. 3. 4. 15 (*ib.* 16)
" "	greys	" "	I. 373 ; ii. 5. 2. 9
, "	sea	" "	I. 398 ; ii. 5. 3. 32
" "	breakers	" "	I. 400-1 ; ii. 5. 3. 35-6
Lost Sailor		Lib. Stud.	V. 368-69 n ; ix. 11. 31 n
Lowestoft	effect of light	Eng. and Wales, 22	I. 283 ; ii. 3. 5. 2
"	grey	" "	I. 373 ; ii. 5. 2. 9
"	sea	" "	I. 406 n; ii. 5. 3. 40 n
Lucerne (1845)	town from lake	drawing	I. 388 ; ii. 5. 3. 19 II. '83 Epil. 3
" (Mt. Pilate)			IV. 238-39; v. 15.34
"			IV. 315-16; v.17. 49
" Lake	mist	Rogers' Italy	I. 256 ; ii. 3. 4. 29 (ed. 1-4 only)
" "		" "	I. 279 ; ii. 3. 4. 32 (ed. 1-4. 36)
" "		" "	I. 388 ; ii. 5. 3. 19
Lycidas, vignette	sea	Milton	I. 400 ; ii. 5. 3. 35
Malmesbury Abbey		R.A., 1792	V. 329 ; ix. 10. 3
Malvern Abbey	effect of light	Eng. and Wales, 13	I. 284 ; ii. 3. 5. 2
Mantes	" "	Rivers of France	I. 285 ; ii. 3. 5. 2
Marengo, Battle of	geology	Rogers' Italy	I. 290 ; ii. 4. 1. 6
"	distance		I. 303 ; ii. 4. 2. 18
Marine Dabblers		Lib. Stud.	IV. 15 ; v. 1. 17
Marly	trees in (from Tintoret's Death of Abel)	Keepsake	I. 84 ; ii. 1. 7. 7 (om. ed. 1, 2)
" "			I. 422 ; ii. 6. 1. 23
Mayburgh	chiaroscuro	Scott	I. 195 ; ii. 2. 3. 13
Mer de Glace	aiguilles		I. 133 ; ii. 1. 7. 39 (om. ed. 1, 2)
" "	ice-cold and slippery	Lib. Stud.	I. 305 ; ii. 4. 2. 19 (om. ed. 1, 2}
" "	Aiguille Charmoz	" "	IV. 202 ; v. 14. 23
Melrose	chiaroscuro	Scott	I. 195 ; ii. 2. 3. 13
"	river	"	I. 388 ; ii. 5. 3. 18
Mercury and Argus	truth of tone	R.A., 1836	I. 154 ; ii. 2. 1. 9
" "	delicate colour of sky		I. 176-77; ii. 2. 2. 13
" "	engraving		I. 182 n; ii. 2. 2. 20 n
" "	distance		I. 209-10; ii. 2. 5. 11
" "	cirrus clouds		I. 235 ; ii. 3. 2. 10
" "	effect of light		I. 284 ; ii. 3. 5. 2
" "	foreground		I. 338 ; ii. 4. 4. 19
" "	"		I. 343 ; ii. 4. 4. 29
" "	stream in		I. 394 ; ii. 5. 3. 27

Turner, J. M. W.: *III. Works of, continued:*

Mercury and Argus	foliage in foreground		I. 423; ii. 6. 1. 24
,, ,,	trees		I. 396; ii. 6. 1. 26 (ed. 1, 2 only)
,, ,,			V. 68; vi. 7. 20
Milton	generally, chiaroscuro		I. 195; ii. 2. 3. 13
,,			*See s. Lycidas Temptation*
Mill near Grande Chartreuse (Lib. Stud.)	*See s. Grande Chartreuse*		
Montjean	effect of light	Rivers of France	I. 285; ii. 3. 5. 2
Morecambe Bay	*See s. Heysham*		
Morpeth Tower		Lib. Stud.	V. 365; ix. 11. 29
Mount Lebanon (S. Antonio)	geology	Finden's Bible	I. 312; ii. 4. 3. 7
,, ,,			V. 164; vii. 4. 21
Murano and Cemetery	faultless	R.A., 1842	I. 146; ii. 1. 7. 46 (om. ed. 1, 2)
Napoleon	colour faulty	R.A., 1842	I. 161; ii. 2. 1. 20
,,	less brilliant than nature		I. 170–73; ii. 2. 2. 7–9
,,	colour		I. 180; ii. 2. 2. 17
,,	cirrus cloud		I. 235; ii. 3. 2. 10
,,	effect of light		I. 284; ii. 3. 5. 2
,,	foreground rocks		I. 329; ii. 4. 4. 2
,,			IV. 333; v. 18. 24
,,	clouds		V. 134; vii. 2. 16
,,			V. 366 *n*; ix. 11. 30 *n*
,,			V. 369 *n*; ix. 11. 31 *n*
Narcissus and Echo		R.A., 1804	V. 329; ix. 10. 3
Nelson's Death			V. 319; ix. 9. 8
Nemi	foliage		I. 135; ii. 1. 7. 46 (ed. 3, 4 only)
,,	mist		I. 256; ii. 3. 4. 29 (ed. 1–4 only)
,,	effect of light		I. 284; ii. 3. 5. 2
,,	water		I. 361; ii. 5. 3. 19 (ed. 1, 2 only)
Nottingham	effect of light	England and Wales	I. 284; ii. 3. 5. 2
,,	reflection in water	,, ,,	I. 381–82; ii. 5. 3. 8–9
,,	drawings 1795–1833	,, ,,	IV. 30; v. 2. 19
,,		,, ,,	IV. 30; v. 2. 19 (pl. 22–3)
Oakhampton	finest work	,, ,,	I. 134; ii. 1. 7. 39 (om. ed. 1, 2)
,,	tone	,, ,,	I. 144; ii. 2. 1. 12 (ed. 1, 2 only)
,,	clouds	,, ,,	I. 274; ii. 3. 4. 23 (ed. 1–4. 26)
,,	effect of light	,, ,,	I. 283; ii. 3. 5. 2
,,	leafy foreground		I. 423; ii. 6. 1. 24
Oberwesel	foliage	Windus	I. 135; ii. 1. 7. 46 (ed. 3, 4 only)
,,	mist		I. 256; ii. 3. 4. 29 (ed. 1–4 only)
,,	effect of light		I. 284; ii. 3. 5. 2
,,	hill drawing		I. 324; ii. 4. 3. 24
,,	water		I. 361; ii. 5. 3. 19 (ed. 1, 2 only)
Old Téméraire	chiaroscuro	R.A., 1839	I. 143–44 *n*; ii. 1. 7 45–6 *n* (om. ed. 1, 2)

Turner, J. M. W. : *III. Works of, continued :*

Old Téméraire	union of different tones	R.A., 1839	I. 162–63; ii. 2. 1. 21
,, ,,	less brilliant than nature	,, ,,	I. 171; ii. 2. 2. 7
,, ,,	engraving of (Finden)	,, ,,	I. 182 *n*; ii. 2. 2.20 *n* (om. ed. 1, 2)
,, ,,	cirrus clouds	,, ,,	I. 235; ii. 3. 2. 10
,, ,,	effect of light	,, ,,	I. 284; ii. 3. 5. 2
,, ,,		,, ,,	IV. 333; v. 18. 24
,, ,,	clouds	,, ,,	V. 134; vii. 2. 16
,, ,,		,, ,,	V. 319; ix. 9. 8
Orford (Suffolk)	effect of light	England and Wales	I. 283; ii. 3. 5. 2
Orleans	chiaroscuro	Rivers of France	I. 194; ii. 2. 3. 13
Ostend	sea	R.A., 1844	I. 402; ii. 5. 3. 37 (om. ed. 1, 2)
Pæstum	storm	Rogers' Italy	I. 277; ii. 3. 4. 28 (ed. 1–4. 33)
,,	effect of light	,, ,,	I. 284; ii. 3. 5. 2 V. 163; vii. 4. 20
Palestrina	raw white, long avenue	R.A., 1830	I. 140; ii. 1. 7. 43 (om. ed. 1, 2)
Paris, Pont Neuf	distance	Rivers of France	I. 211 *n*; ii. 2. 5. 12 *n*
Pas de Calais	reflection of buoy		I. 359; ii. 5. 1. 16 (om. ed. 1, 2)
,, ,,	sea and colour		I. 402; ii. 5. 3. 37 (om. ed. 1, 2)
Peat Bog		Lib. Stud.	III. 336; iv. 18. 19 V. 365; ix. 11. 28
Pembury Mill	quiet domesticity	,, ,,	I. 135; ii. 1. 7. 40 (om. ed. 1, 2)
Penmaen Mawr	foreground rocks	England and Wales	I. 343; ii. 4. 4. 28
Perugia	chiaroscuro	Rogers' Italy, p. 168	I. 187; ii. 2. 3. 5
Peterborough Cathedral		R.A., 1795	V. 329; ix. 10. 3
Piacenza	effect of light	Scott	I. 284; ii. 3. 5. 2
,,	mountains		I. 315; ii. 4. 3. 10
Pilatus			*See s. Lucerne*
Pleasures of Memory	chiaroscuro	,,	I. 187; ii. 2. 3. 5
,, ,,		,,	I. 195; ii. 2. 3. 13
,, ,,	effect of light	Rogers' Poems, opp. title	I. 188; ii. 3. 5. 2
,, ,,	trees		I. 418; ii. 6. 1. 15 (om. ed. 1, 2)
Port Ruysdael	sea	Birchnell's Leg., 1846 R.A., 1844	I. 402; ii. 5. 3. 37 (om. ed. 1, 2)
Procris and Cephalus	foliage	Lib. Stud.	I. 135; ii. 1. 7. 40 (om. ed. 1, 2)
,, ,,	effect of Italy	,, ,,	I.137; ii. 1. 7. 42 (*ib.*)
,, ,,	trees	,, ,,	I.417; ii. 6. 1. 15(*ib.*)
,, ,,	foliage	,, ,,	I. 424 *n*; ii. 6. 1. 24 *n* (*ib.*)
,, ,,	noble imagination	,, ,,	II. 171; iii. 2. 2. 20
,, ,,	rays of light	,, ,,	II. 222; iii. 2. 4. 18
,, ,,		,, ,,	II. '83 Epil. 9
,, ,,		,, ,,	III. 337; iv. 18. 19 V. 366; ix. 11. 29
Pyramid, Caius Cestius	effect of light	Byron	I. 285; ii. 3. 5. 2
Pyramids, Egypt near the	clouds	Finden's Bible	I. 257; ii. 3. 3. 26

Turner, J. M. W. : *III. Works of, continued* :

Quillebœuf	yellow and black study	Rivers of France	I. 180 ; ii. 2. 2. 17
,,	sea	,, ,,	I. 400 ; ii. 5. 3. 34
Quillebœuf and Villequier	chiaroscuro	,, ,,	I. 195 ; ii. 2. 3. 13
Raglan		Lib. Stud.	V. 365 ; ix. 11. 29
Rape of Europa		,, (frontispiece)	V. 366 ; ix. 11. 30
,, Proserpine			I. 139 ; ii. 1. 7. 42 (om. ed. 1, 2)
Rheinfelden			V. vii ; *pref.* 3
Rhine subjects			V. 368 n; ix. 11. 30 n
			IV. 317 ; v. 17. 51
Rhymers' Glen	shadow	Scott	I. 188 ; ii. 2. 3. 5
,, ,,	waterfall		I. 393 ; ii. 5. 3. 25
Rialto	chiaroscuro	Rogers' Poems, p. 95	I. 257 ; ii. 3. 3. 26
,,	moonlight clouds		I. 195 ; ii. 2. 3. 13
,, and Bridge of Sighs	effect of light	,, ,,	I. 285 ; ii. 3. 5. 2
Richmond (Middlesex)	,, ,,	England and Wales	I. 284 ; ii. 3. 5. 2
Richmond (Yorkshire)	girl and dog, rain-cloud	Yorkshire	I. 277 ; ii. 3. 4. 28 (ed. 1-4. 33)
,, ,,	,, ,,		IV. 15 ; v. 1. 17
,, ,,	,, ,,		IV. 312 ; v. 17. 46
,, ,,	foreground ,,		V. 42 ; vi. 5. 9 (pl. 55)
,, from the moors			V. 108-10 ; vi. 10. 19-20 (pl. 61-2)
,, Castle	leaf-cluster		V. 192 ; viii. 2. 14
,, ,,	hills		III. 245 ; iv. 15. 3-4
Rietz, near Saumur		Rivers of France	V. 184 ; viii. 2. 2 (pl. 73)
Rivaulx	architecture	Lib. Stud.	I. 135 ; ii. 1. 7. 40 (om. ed. 1, 2)
		,, ,	V. 365 ; ix. 11. 29
Rivers of France	Cousens' plates	,, ,	I. 137 ; ii. 1. 7. 40
,, ,,			I. 183 n; ii. 2. 2. 20 n (om. ed. 1, 2)
,, ,,			IV. 317 ; v. 17. 51
Rizpah	no local character	,, ,,	I. 138 ; ii. 1. 7. 42 (om. ed. 1, 2)
,,		,, ,,	III. 337 ; iv. 18. 19
,,		,, ,,	IV. 15 ; v. 1. 17
,,		,, ,,	V. 325 n; ix. 9. 21 n
,,		,, ,,	V. 366 ; ix. 11. 29
Rogers' Italy and	moonlights		I. 137 ; ii. 1. 7. 41 (om. ed. 1, 2)
,, ,,			I. 139; ii. 1. 7. 43 (*ib.*)
,, Poems	Goodall's plates		I. 183 n; ii. 2. 20 n (*ib.*)
,, ,,	,, ,, fail in rendering snow		I. 305; ii. 4. 2. 19(*ib.*)
Rome, from the Forum	failure of colour		I. 144 ; ii. 1. 7. 45 (om. ed. 1, 2)
,, ,,			V. 368-69; ix. 11. 31
Rosenau (Prince Albert's chateau)	surface of water	R. A., 1841	I. 378 ; ii. 5. 3. 4
Rouen	distance	Rivers of France	I. 211 n; ii. 2. 5. 12 n
,, Cathedral	façade	,, ,,	I. 434 ; ii. 6. 2. 1
,, from St. Catherine's Hill	clouds	,, ,,	I. 255 ; ii. 3. 3. 24
,, ,,	river	,, ,,	I. 388 ; ii. 5. 3. 18
,, ,,	sky	,, ,,	V. 132 ; vii. 2. 15
Ruins		Rogers' Italy, p. 168	I. 188 ; ii. 2. 3. 5

Turner, J. M. W. : *III. Works of, continued:*

St. Anne's Hill	shadows on tree-trunk	Rogers' Poems, p. 91	I. 187 ; ii. 2. 3. 5
			IV. 81 ; v. 5. 18
St. Bernard, Great	clouds	,, Italy, p. 11	I. 279 ; ii. 3. 4. 32 (ed. 1–4. 36)
St. Catherine's Hill (Guildford)	architecture	Lib. Stud.	I. 135 ; ii. 1. 7. 40 (om. ed. 1, 2)
St. Cloud, Lantern of	chiaroscuro	Rivers of Fra..ce	I. 195 ; ii. 2. 3. 13
St. Denis ,,	barred clouds	,, ,,	I. 284 ; ii. 3. 5. 2
			I. 280 ; ii. 3. 4. 33 (ed. 1–4. 37)
St. Gothard	effect of light	,, ,,	I. 285 ; ii. 3. 5. 2
	magnificent	Lib. Stud.	I. 134 ; ii. 1. 7. 40 (om. ed. 1, 2)
,,	rocks in	,, ,,	I. 330 n; ii. 4. 4. 3 n (ib.)
,,	noblest plate of all	,, ,, unpublished	III. 246 ; iv. 15. 5
,,			IV. 28 ; v. 2. 16
,,	subjects generally		IV. 273 ; v. 16. 41
,,	mountain lines		IV. 308–10 ; v. 17. 42–3 (pl. 29, 37)
,,			IV. 317 ; v. 17. 51
,,	his last perfect drawing		IV. 333–34 ; v. 18. 24–5
,,	litter of stones		V. 318 ; ix. 9. 6
,,			V. 367 n; ix. 11. 30 n
			See s. Arona, Dazio Grande, Devil's Bridge, Faido
St. Herbert's Isle	effect of light	Rogers' Poems, p. 40	I. 285 ; ii. 3. 5. 2
St. Julien, Tours	chiaroscuro	Rivers of France	I. 194 ; ii. 2. 3. 13
St. Maurice ,,	,, black stork	Rogers' Italy	I. 285 ; ii. 3. 5. 2
			I. 195 ; ii. 2. 3. 13
,,	clouds		I. 279 ; ii. 3. 4. 32 (ed. 1–4. 36)
,,	waterfall		I. 393 ; ii. 5. 3. 25
St. Michael's Mount	clouds		I. 142 ; vii. 3. 10
	rain-cloud	Eng. and Wales, 24	I. 277 ; ii. 3. 4. 28 (ed. 1–4. 33)
,, ,,	,, ,,	,, ,,	I. 280 n; ii. 3. 4. 32 n (ed. 1–4. 36 n)
Salisbury	symbols of rair	England and Wales	V. 162 seqq. ; vii. 4. 18 seqq.
Saltash	effect of light	,, ,,	I. 284 ; ii. 3. 5. 2
,,	water		I. 380 ; ii. 5. 3. 6
San Benedetto looking toward Fusina	colour	R.A., 1843	I. 146 ; ii. 1. 7. 46 (om. ed. 1, 2)
,, ,,	colour of water	, ,,	I. 384 ; ii. 5. 3. 11
,, ,,	clouds in		V. 132–34 ; vii. 2. 16
Saxon Ruin	architecture	Lib. Stud.	I. 135 ; ii. 1. 7. 40 (om. ed. 1, 2)
Scarborough	mussel shells	Harbours of Eng.	III. 130 ; iv. 9. 17
Schaffhausen		drawing, N.G.	V. vii ; *pref.* 3
,,	composition		V. 188 seqq. ; viii. 2. 8 seqq.
Scott Illustrations	engravings by Miller		I. 183 n; ii. 2. 2. 20 n (om. ed. 1, 2)
Sea-piece	grand distance	Ellesmere Collection	I. 402 ; ii. 5. 3. 37 (om. ed. 1, 2)
Seckingen		drawing, N.G.	V. vii ; *pref.* 3.
Seine and Marne, Confluence of	chiaroscuro	Rivers of France	I. 195 ; ii. 2. 3. 13
,, ,,	water	,, ,,	I. 385 ; ii. 5. 3. 14
Seine, Mantes to Vernon	chiaroscuro	,, ,,	I. 195 ; ii. 2. 3. 13

Turner, J. M. W.: *III. Works of, continued:*

Shipwreck Studies			V. vi *n*; *pref.* 2 *n*
Shylock, Venice	distance fine		I. 211 *n*; ii. 2. 5. 12 *n*
,,	cirrus clouds		I. 234; ii. 3. 2. 10
,,	effect of light		I. 284; ii. 3. 5. 2
Sidon	breaking wave	Finden's Bible	I. 397; ii. 5. 3. 30
			(om. ed. 1, 2)
Sighs, Bridge of			*See s. Rialto*
Simmer Lake, Ask-rig	mist	Yorkshire	I. 256; ii. 3. 4. 29
			(ed. 1–4 only)
Sinai		Finden's Bible	V. 164; vii. 4. 21 (pl. 86)
Sketch (Dawn)	colour-symbolism		V. 369 *n*; ix. 11. 31 *n*
Sketches, Earliest	Clifton, Bristol, Oxford		V. 323 *n*; ix. 9. 16 *n*
,, (Lausanne)	road to Fribourg	National Gallery	V. 207–9; viii. 4. 8 *seqq.*
,, (N.G.)	no experiments		V. 202; viii. 4. 4
,, memoranda	sunrise	,	V. 203–7; viii. 4. 7
Skiddaw	chiaroscuro	Scott	I. 195; ii. 2. 3. 13
,,	,,	,,	I. 283; ii. 3. 5. 2
,,	mountains	,,	I. 323; ii. 4. 3. 23
Slave Ship	chiaroscuro	R.A., 1840	I. 143–45 *n*; ii. 1. 7. 45–6 *n*
			(om. ed. 1, 2)
,,	tone	,, ,,	I. 156; ii. 2. 1. 13
,,	colour	,, ,,	I. 161; ii. 2. 1. 20
,,	,,	,, ,,	I. 180; ii. 2. 2. 17
,,	rain-cloud	,, ,,	I. 277; ii. 3. 4. 28
			(ed. 1–4. 33)
,,	effect of light	,, ,,	I. 284; ii. 3. 5. 2
,,	sea, his noblest	,, ,,	I. 404–5; ii. 5. 3. 39–40
			II. 224; iii. 2. 4. 20
,,	colour-symbolism	,, ,	IV. 333; v. 18. 24
,,	rain-cloud	,, ,,	V. 160–61; vii. 4. 15–16
,,	colour-symbolism	,, ,,	V. 369 *n*; ix. 11. 31 *n*
Snowstorm	colour, warm grey	R.A., 1842	I. 180; ii. 2. 2. 17
,,	greys	,, ,,	I. 373; ii. 5. 2. 9
,,	sea and mist	,, ,,	I. 404; ii. 5. 3. 38
,,	story of (Kingsley)		V. 375 *n*; ix. 12. 4 *n*
,, Avalanche and Inundation	clouds, etc.	R.A., 1837	I. 137; ii. 1. 7. 41
			(om. ed. 1, 2)
	mountains		I. 319; ii. 4. 3. 17
Solomon's Pools	clouds in	Finden's Bible	I. 251–52; ii. 3. 3. 17
,, ,,	effect of light	,, ,,	I. 284; ii. 3. 5. 2
,, ,,	clouds	,, ,,	V. 130; vii. 2. 13 (fig. 83)
Solway Moss		Lib. Stud.	III. 336; iv. 18. 19
Source of Arveron	stones	,, ,,	IV. 327; v. 18. 11
,,	pine-trees	,, ,,	V. 89; vi. 9. 6
Spenser's "Faërie Queen"	effect of Italy	,, ,,	I. 137; ii. 1. 7. 42
			(om. ed. 1, 2)
Splugen		Brantwood	II. '83 Epil. 3
			IV. 334; v. 18. 25
Stonehenge	clouds (badly engraved)	England and Wales	I. 276–77; ii. 3. 4. 26–8
			(ed. 1–4. 31–3)
,,	effect of light		I. 284; ii. 3. 5. 2
,,	symbolism		V. 162–63; vii. 4. 18–20
Strawyard (white horse)	quiet domesticity	Lib. Stud.	I. 135; ii. 1. 7. 40
			(om. ed. 1, 2)
Sun of Venice	colour	R.A., 1843	I. 146; ii. 1. 7. 46 (*ib.*)

Turner, J. M. W. : *III. Works of, continued :*

Sun of Venice	water, etc.	R.A., 1843	I. 383 ; ii. 5. 3. 11
Sunset Behind Willows	tone	Rogers' Poems	I. 156 ; ii. 2. 1. 13
Swiss subjects	details	Farnley drawings	I. 134 ; ii. 1. 7. 39 (om. ed. 1, 2)
,, ,,	earliest	Drawings, 1804–6	*ib.* ; *ib.* 40 (*ib.*)
,, ,,	deficient		I. 136–37 ; *ib.* 41 (*ib.*)
,, ,,	his best of Switzerland	Lib. Stud.	I. 137 ; *ib.* (*ib.*)
,, ,,	fine in colour	Drawings, 1842	I. 146 ; *ib.* 46 (*ib.*)
, ,,	magnificent	,, ,,	I. 388 ; ii. 5. 3. 19 II. '83 Epil. 3 IV. 317 ; v. 17. 51
Swiss Wall-tower			IV. 74–5 ; v. 5. 7
Tantallon Castle	sea	Scott's Prov. Ant.	I. 400 ; ii. 5. 3. 35
Tees, Chain Bridge	water	Eng. and Wales, 24	I. 390–93 ; ii. 5. 3. 21–5
,, ,,	trees	,, ,,	I. 418 ; ii. 6. 1. 15
,, Lower Fall	foreground rocks		I. 342 ; ii. 4. 4. 26
,, ,, ,,	waterfall		I. 393 ; ii. 5. 3. 25
,, Upper Fall	foreground rocks	Yorkshire, vol. i.	I. 339 *seqq.* ; ii. 4. 4. 21–7
,,			I. 343 ; ii. 4. 4. 27
,,	water		I. 389 *seqq.* ; ii. 5. 3. 20
,,		,, ,,	IV. 328 ; v. 18. 12 *See s. Junction of Greta and Tees*
Tell's Chapel		Rogers' Italy, p. 8	I. 315 ; ii. 4. 3. 10
Temple of Jupiter	"nonsense picture"		I. 139 ; ii. 1. 7. 42 (om. ed. 1, 2)
,, ,,			III. 329 ; iv. 18. 6
Temple of Minerva, Cape Colonna			V. 163–64 ; vii. 4. 20
Temptation on Mountain		Milton	II. 224 ; iii. 2. 4. 20
Thun	unsatisfactory	Lib. Stud.	I. 135 ; ii. 1. 7. 40 (om. ed. 1, 2)
Tintern Abbey		R.A., 1794, 1795	V. 329 ; ix. 10. 3
Tivoli	trees		I. 140 ; ii. 1. 7. 43
Tornaro's Brow	chiaroscuro	Rogers' Poems, p. 80	I. 226 ; ii. 3. 1. 17
,, ,,	cirrus clouds	,, ,, ,,	I. 235 ; ii. 3. 2. 11
Tours	effect of light	Rivers of France	I. 285 ; ii. 3. 5. 2
Towers of the Héve	,, ,,	,, ,,	I. 285 ; ii. 3. 5. 2
Trafalgar			V. 319 ; ix. 9. 8
Trematon Castle		England and Wales	I. 284 ; ii. 3. 5. 2
Trossachs	a bad work, praised by public	Grundy's	I. 141 *n* ; ii. 1. 7. 44 (om. ed. 1–4)
Troyes	chiaroscuro	Rivers of France	I. 195 ; ii. 2. 3. 13
,,	,,	,, ,,	I. 285 ; ii. 3. 5. 2
Twilight	,,	Rogers' Poems, p. 7	I. 226 ; ii. 3. 1. 17
,,	,,	,, ,, ,,	I. 285 ; ii. 3. 5. 2
,,		,, ,, ,,	I. 418 ; ii. 6. 1. 15 (om. ed. 1, 2)
Tyre at Sunset		Lib. Stud. frontispiece	V. 366 ; ix. 11. 30
Ulleswater	water surface	England and Wales	I. 342 ; ii. 4. 4. 26
,,			I. 379 ; ii. 5. 3. 5
,,			IV. 327 ; v. 18. 12
Ulysses and Polyphemus		R.A., 1829	IV. 333 ; v. 18. 24

Turner, J. M. W. : *III. Works of, continued :*

Ulysses and Polyphemus			V. 347 ; ix. 11. 4
,, ,,			V. 369 *n* ; ix. 11 31 *n*
Upnor Castle	effect of light	England and Wales	I. 283 ; ii. 3. 5. 2
,,	water		I. 380 ; ii. 5. 3. 6
Uri, Lake of	hill-drawing		I. 324 ; ii. 4. 3. 24
Venice	generally	various	I. 76 ; ii. 1. 7. 40 (ed. 1, 2 only)
,,	vagueness of	,,	I. 115 ; ii. 1. 7. 29 (om. ed. 1, 2)
,,	grandeur	,,	I. 140 ; ii. 1. 7. 43 (*ib.*)
,,	fading	,, Academy works	I. 145 *n* ; ii. 1. 7. 46 *n* (*ib.*)
,,	colour	,, 1845	I. 146 ; ii. 1. 7. 46 (*ib.*)
,,		,, 1843	I. 180 ; ii. 2. 2. 17
,,	distances	,,	I. 211 *n* ; ii. 2. 5. 12 *n* ib. ; *ib.*
,,	,,	Rogers' Italy	
,,	effects of light	various	I. 284 ; ii. 3. 5. 2
,,	reflections, white sails		I. 356 ; ii. 5. 1. 12 (om. ed. 1, 2)
,,	ripples	Scott's Novels, 10	I. 338 ; ii. 5. 1. 14 (ed. 1, 2 only)
,,	architecture		III. 330 ; iv. 18. 8
,, Grand Canal		Miller, 1834	V. 125 *n* ; vii. 2–6 *n*
,, Campo Santo	sky	R.A., 1842	V. 132 ; vii. 2. 15 (pl. 67)
			See s. Approach, Giudecca, Murano, Rialto, Shylock, Sun of Venice, San Benedetto
Vernon	water	Rivers of France	I. 386 ; ii. 5. 3. 15
Via Mala			III. 245–46 ; iv. 15. 4–5
,, ,,	subjects generally		IV. 273 ; v. 16. 41
,, ,,	noblest of Lib. Stud.	Lib. Stud.	V. 368 *n* ; ix. 11. 31 *n*
Voyage of Columbus	Italian subject		I. 139 ; ii. 1. 7. 43 (om. ed. 1, 2)
	clouds and sky	Rogers' Poems	I. 257 ; ii. 3. 3. 26
,, ,,	effect of light	,, ,,	I. 283 ; ii. 3. 5. 2
,, ,,		,, ,,	II. 215 ; iii. 2. 4. 7
,, ,,	phantom vignette	,, ,,	II. 221 ; iii. 2. 4. 16
,, ,,		,, ,,	III. 106 ; iv. 8. 7
Walhalla	cracked as soon as painted	R.A., 1843	I. 145 *n* ; ii. 1. 7. 46 *n* (om. ed. 1, 2)
Warwick	effect of light	England and Wales	I. 284 ; ii. 3. 5. 2
,,	trees	,, ,,	I. 418 ; ii. 6. 1. 15
Watercress Gatherers	quiet domesticity	Lib. Stud.	I. 135 ; ii. 1. 7. 40 (om. ed. 1, 2)
Waterloo	rain-cloud	R.A., 1818	I. 277 ; ii. 3. 4. 28 (ed. 1–4. 33)
	effect of light		I. 285 ; ii. 3. 5. 2
Watermill	beautiful and solemn	Lib. Stud.	I. 135 ; ii. 1. 7. 40 (om. ed. 1, 2)
			V. 364 ; ix. 11. 28
Whalers	inferior works	R.A., 1845	I. 146 ; ii. 1. 7. 46 (om. ed. 1, 2) ib. ; *ib.* (*ib.*)
Wharfe, Shores of	,, ,,	,, ,,	*See s. Bolton Abbey*

Turner, J. M. W. : *III. Works of, continued :*

Whitby	lonely arches		III. 329 ; iv. 18. 6
Winchelsea Gate	detail and fulness	Lib. Stud.	I. 135 ; ii. 1. 7. 40 (om. ed. 1, 2)
,, ,,	pensive suggestiveness		V. 365 ; ix. 11. 29
,,	lightning	England and Wales	I. 182 n ; ii. 2. 2. 20 n (om. ed. 1, 2)
,,	storm	,, ,,	I. 276 ; ii. 3. 4. 26 (ed. 1-4. 31)
	,, effect of light	,, ,,	I. 284 ; ii. 3. 5. 2
Windmill and Lock	composition	Lib. Stud.	IV. 7-9 ; v. 1. 10-11
,, ,,	solemnity	,, ,,	V. 364 ; ix. 11. 28
Windsor Castle from Eton	coarse and conventional	England and Wales	I. 134 ; ii. 1. 7. 39 (om. ed. 1, 2)
Wycliffe nr. Rokeby		Yorkshire	IV. 327 ; v. 18. 12
Yorkshire series	drawings among his best		I. 133-34 ; ii. 1. 7. 39 (om. ed. 1, 2)
,, ,,	culminating point		I. 140-41 ; ii. 1. 7. 44
,, ,,	engravings		I. 183 n ; ii. 2. 2. 20 n (om. ed. 1, 2)
,, ,,	clear reflections		I. 378 n ; ii. 1. 5. 3. 4 n (*ib.*)
,, ,,	foregrounds		I. 424 n ; ii. 6. 1. 24 n (*ib.*)
Young Anglers	tree	Lib. Stud.	III. 245 ; iv. 15. 4 V. 76 ; vi. 8. 10 (fig. 61)
Zug, Lake of	water		I. 389 ; ii. 5. 3. 19
,, ,,	symbolism		V. 369 n ; ix. 11. 30 (pl. 87)
Zurich	lake		I. 389 ; ii. 5. 3. 19

Turner (W.), of Oxford, mountain-drawings of, I. 327 and n ;
      ii. 4. 3. 28 and n (om. ed. 1-4).
      ,,   ,,   ,,   unaffected but uninventive, III. 278 ;
            iv. 16. 26.
————'s "Elements of Chemistry," II. 162 ; iii. 2. 2. 8.
Tuscan school, central source of European art, IV. 379 ; iv. 20. 20.
      ,,   ,,   sea and mountain influence on, IV. 380 n ; v. 20.
            21 n.
            See s. Italian school.
Twickenham, Turner at, III. 328 ; iv. 18. 4.
      ,,   ,,   V. 323 ; ix. 9. 15.
Twilight, effect of, I. 213 n ; ii. 2. 5. 15 n (om. ed. 1, 2).
      ,, emotional beauty of, II. 43-4 ; iii. 1. 5. 4.
Tylor, Alfred, F.G.S., the late, on river curvature, II. 66 ; iii. 5.
      6. 12 ('83 n).
Types or lessons :
      beauty, II. 31 ; iii. 1. 3. 16.
      ,,   II. 93 ; iii. 1. 11. 1.

Types, *continued:*

    beauty, V. 165 ; vii. 4. 24.

    buds, III. 217–18 ; iv. 14. 24.

    colour, V. 349–54 and *n* ; ix. 11. 8–9 *n.*

    crags, IV. 227 ; v. 15. 23.

    crystallization, V. 174–75 ; viii. 1. 6

    grass, III. 240–43 ; iv. 14. 53.

    infinity, II. 44–5 ; iii. 1. 5. 5.

        „   IV. 84 ; v. 5. 21.

    leaf growth, V. 34–5 ; vi. 4. 14 *seqq.*

        „   V. 59 ; vi. 7. 7.

        „   V. 83–4 ; vi. 8. 19 *seqq.*

    light, II. 81 ; iii. 1. 9. 1.

    mica-flake, IV. 252 ; v. 16. 17.

    moderation, II. 87–92 ; iii. 1. 10. 1 *seqq.*

    mountain, V. 144 ; vii. 4. 12.

        „   decay, IV. 335 ; v. 18. 26.

        „   „   IV. 364 ; v. 19. 33.

    mythological, V. 158–59 ; vii. 4. 12.

        „   V. 330–33 ; ix. 10. 4 *seqq.*

    purity, II. 81–6 ; iii. 1. 9. 1 *seqq.*

    rainbow, V. 353 ; ix. 11. 9.

    rush, III. 241 ; iv. 14. 53.

    sky, II. 42–5 ; iii. 1. 5. 3 *seqq.*

    stones, weeds, etc., V. 180 ; viii. 1. 16.

    sunlight, V. 354 ; ix. 11. 9.

    symmetry, II. 78–80 ; iii. 1. 8. 1 *seqq.*

    trees, V. 57–8 ; vi. 7. 5.

        „   V. 81–5 ; vi. 8. 17 *seqq.*

Typhon, locks of, V. 157 ; vii. 4. 10.

      „   „   V. 160 ; vii. 4. 15 (pl. 72).

      „   meaning of, V. 335 ; ix. 10. 12.

      „   „   V. 337 ; ix. 10. 15.

Tyrants, always of some use, III. 279 ; iv. 16. 28.

Tyrol, pure Romanism of the, IV. 376 ; v. 20. 15.

Uccello, Paolo, battle of S. Egidio by (Nat. Gall.), V. 5 ; vi. 1. 6.

      „   „   „   „   compared with the Wouvermans at Turin, V. 308 ; ix. 8. 9.

Ugliness, its place in art, IV. 27 *n* ; v. 2. 16 *n.*

    „   love of, *e.g.* in old German art, IV. 348 ; v. 19. 17.

Ugliness, *continued*:

„ of man, on the increase, III. 159 ; iv. 11. 9.

„ positive nature of, III. 27 ; iv. 3. 2.

See s. Dress, Nature.

Ugolino, dream of (Dante), III. 256 ; iv. 15. 17.

Ulm, twisted fountain of, V. 22 ; vi. 3. 14.

Umber, use of, by old schools, III. 250 ; iv. 15. 10–11.

Unbelief. *See s. Infidelity.*

Uncertainty, advantages of, IV. 72 ; v. 5. 3.

"Uncle Tom's Cabin" referred to, III. 71 ; iv. 5. 7.

Unconsciousness of genius, III. 94 ; iv. 7. 12.

Undulation of mountain form, IV. 158–60 ; v. 12. 20.

„ „ rocks, IV. 122, 124 ; v. 9. 5. 6.

Unity, apparent proportion a cause of, II. 61–2 ; iii. 1. 6. 10.

„ „ „ „ „ II. 69 ; iii. 1. 6. 17.

„ artistic, and false ideal, III. 56 ; iv. 4. 15.

„ beauty of, IV. 288 ; v. 17. 18.

„ essential to beauty, II. 55 ; iii. 1. 6. 2.

„ glory and constancy of, II. 55 ; iii. 1. 6. 2.

„ imagination associative and, II. 161–62 ; iii. 2. 2. 7.

„ kinds of (subject, origin, sequence, membership), II. 55–7 ; iii. 1. 6. 3.

„ of membership, essential to great art, II. 163 ; iii. 2. 2. 9.

„ of two similar things by a third and different one, II 56–7 ; iii. 1. 6. 4.

„ type of Divine comprehensiveness, II. 54 ; iii. 1. 6. 1.

„ „ „ „ „ II. 56 ; iii. 1. 6. 3.

„ „ „ „ „ II. 60–1 ; iii. 1. 6. 8.

„ „ „ „ „ II. 161 ; iii. 2. 2. 6.

„ „ „ „ „ II. 163 ; iii. 2. 2. 9.

„ variety connected with, II. 57 ; iii. 1. 6. 5.

See s. Nature.

Unterwalden, pine hills of, V. 97 ; vi. 9. 16.

Urbane, implied meaning of word, V. 4 ; vi. 1. 4.

Urbino, art of district of, IV. 379 ; v. 20. 21.

Uri, Canton of, no poet from, IV. 382 ; v. 20. 25.

„ scenery of Bay of, V. 96–7 ; vi. 9. 16.

Utilitarians, a misnomer, II. 4–5 ; iii. 1. 1. 5.

Utility, beauty is not, II. 33 ; iii. 1. 4. 2.

„ meaning of, defined, II. 3 *seqq.* ; iii. 1. 1. 3. *seqq.*

Utility, *continued :*

„　the most materially useful, the least noble work, II. 9–10 ; iii. 1. 1. 8.

Uwins' (R.A. 1848) "Vineyard in S. France," II. 245 ; Add. 6 (om. ed. 1, 2).

Val d' Aosta, Alps from Turin, clouds on, V. 142 ; vii. 3. 11.

„　　„　described, IV. 185 ; v. 14. 6.

„　　„　people of, their character, IV. 352–53 ; v. 19. 22.

Val Ferret, IV. 185 ; v. 14. 6.

Valais, the, I. 316 *n* ; ii. 4. 3. 12 (om. ed. 1, 2).

„　　„　IV. 198 ; v. 14. 19.

„　　„　hills of, IV. 191 ; v. 14. 12.

„　　„　limestones of, IV. 272 ; v. 16. 40.

„　　„　map of, IV. 173 ; v. 13. 10.

„　　„　people of, IV. 358–62 ; v, 19. 28. 32.

„　　„　　„　V. 94 ; vi. 9. 13.

„　　„　tourists' effect on, IV. 398 ; v. 20. 42.

Valleys, excavations of, not by rivers, IV. 100 ; v. 7. 6.

„　formation of English and French, IV. 314–15 ; v. 17. 48.

„　gloom in, IV. 344–45 ; v. 19. 11.

　　　See s. Alps, Chamouni, Cluse, France, Frütigen, Grindel wald, etc., etc.

Vallombrosa, pastures of, III. 208 ; iv. 14. 10.

Valorsine, country near, IV. 337 ; v. 19. 3.

Valuable things—sun, air, life, III. 319 ; iv. 17. 35.

Van Eyck, grotesque idealism of, III. 150 ; iv. 10. 21.

„　his definiteness, IV. 66 ; v. 4. 12.

„　　„　sense of beauty, deficient, IV. 353 ; v. 19. 22.

„　　„　strength, *ib.* ; *ib.*

Vandevelde [SYNOPSIS. I. xlviii, 348–49, 361, 365, 369, 379–80, 406 *n*. III. 344]:—

author's abuse of, I. xlviii ; *pref. ed.* 2. 42.

libels on the sea, I. 348–49 ; ii. 5. 1. 4, 5 (om. ed. 1, 2).

seas of, I. 365 ; ii. 5. 1. 20 (om. ed. 1, 2).

„　I. 406 *n* ; ii. 5. 3. 40 *n* (ed. 1, 2. 39 *n*).

shadows on water, I. 369 ; ii. 5. 2. 1.

Turner's study of, I. 349 ; ii. 5. 1. 5 (om. ed. 1, 2).

„　　„　III. 344 ; iv. 18. 30.

Vandevelde, *continued*:

work of:

    No. 113, Dulwich Gallery ⎫ I. 361 ; ii. 5. 1. 17 (om. ed. 1, 2).
    (showing reflections ⎬ I. 338 ; ii. 5. 1. 15–18 (ed. 1, 2 only).
    in water), ⎭ I. 379–80 ; ii. 5. 3. 6.

Vandyck [SYNOPSIS. I. 11. V. 100, 262, 277, 279, 285, 300–1 *n*]:—

delicacy of, V. 301 *n* ; ix. 7. 23 *n*.

flowers in, slight, V. 100 ; vi. 10. 5.

horse well painted first by, V. 285 ; ix. 6. 22.

not religious or spiritual, V. 262 ; ix. 4. 14.

    „   „   „   V. 277 ; ix. 6. 5.

not to be classed with Dutch school, I. 11 ; i. 1. 2. 7.

scriptural subjects of, V. 279 ; ix. 6. 10.

works of:

    Equestrian portrait (author's diary quoted), V. 300 *n* ; ix. 7. 23 *n*.

    King Charles I., children of (Turin), V. 100 ; vi. 10. 5.

Vanity, fatal to art and artist, I. 85 ; ii. 1. 7. 8.

    „   „   „   „ I. 88 ; ii. 1. 7. 10 (om. ed. 1, 2).

    „   „   „   „ V. 213–14 ; viii. 4. 20. 21.

    „ right and wrong, V. 296 ; ix. 7. 18.

Vapour, clouds and, V. 113–14 ; vii. 1. 2.

    „   „   V. 121 ; vii. 2. 1.

    „   „   V. 135–36 ; vii. 2. 18.

    „   „   V. 141 ; vii. 3. 7.

    „ visibility of, V. 146–47 ; vii. 3. 15. *See s. Clouds.*

Varens, Aiguille de, III. 145–46 ; iv. 10. 5.

    „   „   IV. 169 ; v. 13. 6.

    „   „   IV. 254 ; v. 16. 20.

Variety, best when united with symmetry, I. 232 ; ii. 3. 2. 8.

    „ harmonious, II. 57 ; iii. 1. 6. 5.

    „ necessary, *ib.* ; *ib.*

    See s. Nature, characteristics of.

Varley, John, deep feeling of, I. 163 *n* ; ii. 2. 1. 21 *n*.

    „   „ hill-drawings of, I. 303 ; ii. 4. 3. 28 (ed. 1–4 only)

    „   „ painting of water, I. 343 ; ii. 5. 2. 2 (ed. 1–4 only).

    „   „ works of, I. 448 ; ii. 6. 3. 22.

Vasari, on painting what we see, and what we expect to see, I. xxix ; *pref. ed.* 2. 23.

Vasari, *continued :*

,,   pleasure of, at Ghirlandajo's window (S. M. Novella), I. 109 ; ii. 1. 7. 25 (om. ed. 1, 2).

,,   simplicities of, on art, III. 20 ; iv. 2. 4.

Vatican, arabesques, I. 105 ; ii. 1. 7. 22 (om. ed. 1, 2).

,,   frescoes, chiaroscuro, I. 180 ; ii. 2. 3. 14 (ed. 1, 2 only).

,,   "Torso," its perfection, I. 434 ; ii. 6. 2. 2.

Vaud, Pays de, IV. 367 ; v. 20. 3.

Vegetation, author's study of, in "Modern Painters," how written, V. viii ; *pref.* 5.

,,   classified into tented and building plants, V. 7–9 ; vi. 2. 2–3.

,,   delight of, in expansion, III. 216–18 ; iv. 14. 21. 24.

,,   forest, V. 151–52 ; vii. 4. 2.

,,   hill-side, IV. 305 ; v. 17. 37.

,,   ideal form of, various, II. 112–14 ; iii. 1. 13. 7–9.

,,   ,,   ,,   destroyed by cultivation, II. 114 ; iii. 1. 13. 10.

,,   its ministry to man, V. 2–3 ; vi. 1. 2. 3.

,,   our pleasure is proportionate to its vitality, II. 99 ; iii. 1. 12. 4.

,,   process of form in, V. 86–7 ; vi. 9. 2.

,,   sculpture of, V. 39 ; vi. 5. 4.

,,   truth of, I. 405 *seqq.* ; II. 6. 1. 1 *seqq.*

        See s. Flowers.

Vehicles, of artists, often their own secret, I. 142–43 ; ii. 1. 7. 45 (om. ed. 1, 2). *See s. Turner, s.v.*

Veiento, scenery round, I. 165 ; ii. 2. 2. 2 (*ed.* 1, 2. 3).

Velasquez, "dogs and surly kings" of, V. 280 ; ix. 6. 13.

,,   feeling for dogs, V. 283 ; ix. 6. 19.

,,   flowers in, rare, V. 100 ; vi. 10. 5.

,,   gentleness of, V. 214 ; viii. 4. 21.

,,   never jests, V. 283 ; ix. 6. 20.

,,   noble portraits of, III. 43 ; iv. 3. 21

,,   sunlight seldom painted by, V. 346 ; ix. 11. 3.

,,   truth and colour of, V. 353 *n* ; ix. 11. 8 *n.*

Velocity of execution. *See s. Execution.*

Veneration, inculcated by science, III. 272 ; iv. 16. 16.

,,   the highest moral feeling, I. 14–15 ; i. 1. 3. 2.

Venga Medusa," mountain cloud, V. 142 ; pl. 70. *See s Dante* (2).

Venice—(a) *Miscellaneous;* (b) *Particular buildings and pictures;* (c) *Venetian school.*

(a) *Miscellaneous:*

    Alps from, IV. 230 ; v. 15. 27.

    character of people (" The Wings of the Lion," V. 358
        seqq. ; ix. 3. 1 *seqq.*) :—

        contempt of agriculture, V. 242–43 ; ix. 3. 10–11.

        mind of, perfect, V. 253 ; ix. 3. 31.

        pride, its causes, *ib.* ; *ib.*

    description of, frescoed and gilded, I. 116–17 ; ii. 1. 7.
        30 (om. ed. 1, 2).

      „   Giorgione's home, V. 315 *seqq.* ; ix. 9.
                    1 *seqq.*

      „   „   „ V. 324 ; ix. 9. 18.

    destruction of, I. 116–17 ; ii. 1. 7. 30 (om. ed. 1, 2).

      „   by the French, of 166 churches, I. 117 ;
              ii. 1. 7. 30 (om. ed. 1, 2).

      „   „ neglect and ruin of palaces, II. 8 *n* ;
              iii. 1. 1. 7 *n.*

      „   „ restoration, I. 114 ; ii. 1. 7. 28 (om.
              ed. 1, 2).

    enchanted voice of, V. 371 ; ix. 11. 32.

    equestrian statues, V. 285 ; ix. 6. 22.

    fall of, its lesson, V. 369–71 ; ix. 11. 31–2.

    fishermen, bronzed limbs of, I. 364 ; ii. 5. 1. 19 (om.
        ed. 1, 2).

    fishing-boat (felucca) sails, I. 383–84 ; ii. 5. 3. 11.

      „   „   „ IV. 250 ; v. 16. 15.

    frescoes of palaces in old days, I. 116 ; ii. 1. 7. 30 (om.
        ed. 1, 2).

    glass, V. 64 ; vi. 7. 14.

      „ blowing of, metaphor on education, IV. 426 ;
        App. iii. 4.

    modern degradation, I. 364 ; ii. 5. 1. 19 (om. ed. 1, 2).

    opera (1850) of " Death and the Cobbler," IV. 347 ; v.
        19. 14.

    painting of, by Canaletto and modern artists, I. 76 ; ii
        1. 7. 7 *seqq.* (ed. 1, 2 only).

    poverty despised by, V. 318 ; ix. 9. 7.

    quarrels with the Pope, V. 238–39, 244 ; ix. 3. 2. 3, 12

    religion, and the sea life of, V. 239 ; ix. 3. 3.

Venice : (a) *Miscellaneous, continued* :
    religion up to Tintoret, V. 244–46 ; ix. 3. 12 *seqq.*
        „   „   V. 321 ; ix. 9. 12.
    streets of, ugly manners in modern, IV. 347 ; v. 19. 15.
    view from Titian's house, I. 82 ; ii. 1. 7. 6 (om. ed. 1, 2).
    water, reflections in (author's diary), I. 351 ; ii. 5. 1. 7
        (om. ed. 1, 2).
    whitewash (inscription over Giorgione fresco), I. 116 ;
        ii. 1. 7. 30 (om. ed. 1, 2).

(b) *Particular buildings and pictures* :
    Academia, Basaiti, golden sky, I. 89 ; ii. 1. 7. 11 (om.
        ed. 1, 2).
        „   Bellini's (Gentile) S. ⎫ I. 114 ; ii. 1. 7. 28
                 Mark's,   ⎭   (om. ed. 1, 2).
        „   „   „   „   II. 220 ; iii. 2. 4. 14.
        „   modern landscapes, I. 84 ; ii. 1. 7. 7 (om.
                 ed. 1, 2).
        „   Tintoret's "Death of Abel," I. 84 *n* ; ii. 1.
                 7. 7 *n* (om. ed. 1, 2).
        „   „   "Fall of Adam," *ib.* ; *ib.* (*ib.*).
        „   Titian's Assumption, *ib.* ; *ib.* (*ib.*).
        „   „   Desert, I. 84 ; ii. 1. 7. 7 (*ib.*).
        „   „   S. John, II. 129 ; iii. 1. 14. 14.
    Barberigo Palace, Titian's Magdalen, II. 133 ; iii. 1.
        14. 22.
    Ca' Dario, marbles, I. 118 ; ii. 1. 7. 30 (om. ed. 1, 2).
    Ca' d' Oro, use of gold on, I. 117 *n* ; ii. 1. 7. 30 *n* (om.
        ed. 1, 2).
    Ca' Trevisan, marbles, I. 118 ; ii. 1. 7. 30 (om. ed. 1, 2).
    Ducal Palace, capital, bear's head and honeycomb, II.
        199 ; iii. 2. 4. 5 (ed. 1 only).
        „   „   Rio façade, "Stones of Venice," quoted,
                 V. 299 *n* ; ix. 7. 21 *n*.
    Fondaco de' Tedeschi, remains of ⎫ I. 116 ; ii. 1. 7. 30
        Giorgione fresco,   ⎭   (om. ed. 1, 2).
        „   „   „   V. 370 ; ix. 11. 32.
    Piazzetta, Sansovino side, I. 115 ; ii. 1. 7. 29 (om. ed. 1, 2).
    Rialto, market-boats of the, at dawn, I. 364 ; ii. 5. 1. 19
        (om. ed. 1, 2).
    S. Francesco della Vigna, Bellini in, I. 90 ; ii. 1. 7. 11
        (om. ed. 1, 2).

Venice : (*b*) *Particular buildings and pictures, continued* :

    S. Giovanni e Paolo, Titian's Peter Martyr in, II. 170 ;
        iii. 2. 2. 19.

    S. Grisostomo, Bellini's S. Jerome in, I. 90 ; ii. 1. 7. 11
        (om. ed. 1, 2).

        „   „   „   II. 129 ; iii. 1.
        14. 14.

        „   ’   „   II. 230 ; iii. 2.
        5. 8.

    S. Maria dell' Orto, Cima da Conegliano in, I. 86 ; ii.
        1. 7. 9 (om. ed. 1, 2).

        „   „   Tintorets in, I. 115 ; ii. 1. 7. 28
        (om. ed. 1, 2).

        „   „   II. 171 ; iii. 2. 2. 19.

    S. Mark's Church, capitals of, II. 220 ; iii. 2. 4. 15.

        „   „   cloisters, mosaics, II. 60 ; iii. 1.
        6. 8.

        „   „   corner of, contains more than whole
        modern cathedral, II. 220–21 ;
        iii. 2. 4. 15.

        „   „   fresco of the Annunciation, II. 187 ;
        iii. 2. 3. 17.

        „   „   mouldings of, use of gold on, I.
        117 *n* ; ii. 1. 7. 30 *n* (om. ed.
        1, 2).

        „   „   outer porch, mosaic of deluge, I.
        366–67 ; ii. 5. 1. 22 (om. ed.
        1, 2).

        „   „   restoration, II. 88 ; iii. 1. 10. 3.

        „   „   „   of mosaics, II. 220 ;
        iii. 2. 4. 14.

        „   „   tower, II. '83 Epil. 4.

        ’   „   view of, I. 211 ; ii. 2. 5. 13.

    Convent, Giotto's Passion, II. 138 ; iii. 1.
        14. 29.

        „   Place, and S. Paul's Churchyard compared,
        V. 322 ; ix. 9. 14.

    Scuola di San Rocco, author and J. D. Harding at, II.
        '83 Epil. 12.

        „   „   ruin of, II. 8 *n* ; iii. 1. 1. 7 *n*.

        „   „   Tintoret's Flight into Egypt, II.
        170 ; iii. 2. 2. 19.

Venice : (b) *Particular buildings and pictures, continued :*

   Scuola di San Rocco, Tintoret's Temptation, II. 170 ;
                               iii. 2. 2. 19.

        „   „   „   various, II. 194 ; iii.
                                2. 3. 22.

(c) *Venetian school :*

   animals in their pictures, *e.g.* dogs, V. 281 ; ix. 6. 14.
     „   and horses, V. 284–85 ; ix. 6. 22.
   characteristics and aim of, V. 238 *seqq.* ; ix. 3. 1 *seqq.*
     „   compared with Greek art, V. 241–42 ;
                     ix. 3. 6–8.
     „   last *believing* school of Italy, V. 244 ;
                     ix. 3. 12.
     „   moral power of, not seen by author till
                     1858, V. vii. x ; *pref.* 4. 7.
     „   mountain and sea influence on, IV. 380 ;
                     v. 20. 21.
   colour-system of, IV. 45–8 ; v. 3. 14–16.
     „   „   love of massive colour, V. 238 ; ix.
                     3. 2.
     „   „   V. 350 *n* ; ix. 11. 8 *n.*
   conquest of evil, its highest spirit, V. 232 *seqq.* ; ix. 2.
        13 *seqq.*
   decline of, how caused, V. 252–54 ; ix. 3. 30–33.
   feeling for beauty, V. 325 ; ix. 9. 19.
   foliage of, almost faultless, I. 83 ; ii. 1. 7. 7 (om. ed.
        1, 2).
   landscape of, II. 233 *n* ; iii. 2. 5. 11 *n.*
     „   distances of, II. 48 ; iii. 1. 5. 11.
     „   ends with Tintoret, 1594, III. 337 ; iv.
                     18. 20.
     „   influence of, slight, and why, I. 83–4 ; ii.
                     1. 7. 7 (om. ed. 1, 2).
     „   „   on Claude, III. 340, 342 ;
                     iv. 18. 25. 27.
     „   „   on Turner, III. 336 ; iv. 18.
                     18–19.
     „   no marine effects in, I. 367 ; ii. 5. 1. 23
                     (om. ed. 1, 2).
     „   pride of, V. 243 ; ix. 3. 10–11.
     „   solemnity of, soothing, I. 84 ; ii. 1. 7. 7
                     (om. ed. 1, 2).

Venice : (c) *Venetian school*, landscape of, *continued* :

      ,,   solemnity of, I. 142 ; ii. 1. 7. 44 (om. ed. 1, 2).

      ,,   sunlight and twilight, how given by, *ib.* ; *ib.* (*ib.*).

      ,,   ,,   rarely painted by, V. 346 ; ix. 11. 3.

      methods of painting, V. 210–12 ; viii. 4. 17–18.

      model for young landscapists, dangerous as a, I. 83 ; ii. 1. 7. 7 (om. ed. 1, 2).

      Pisan sculpture, its influence on, IV. 380 ; v. 20. 20.

      portraits of, *e.g.* doges, their modest dignity, II. 132 ; iii. 1. 14. 19.

      ,,   praying, V. 245 ; ix. 3. 15–16.

      religious art, familiarity of treatment, *e.g.* animals at Christ's feet, V. 246–47 ; ix. 3. 18.

      ,,   lack of expression in, III. 33 ; iv. 3. 10.

      ,,   naturalist, III. 84–5 ; iv. 7. 2–3.

Venus and marriage, V. 333 ; ix. 10. 8.

—— de Medici, III. 72 ; iv. 5. 8.

  ,,   ,,   what it would be like in granite, IV. 117 ; v. 8. 17.

—— of Milo, I. 434 ; ii. 6. 2. 2.

Vergi, Montagne de, IV. 260–61 ; v. 16. 26–7.

Vernet, Horace, works of, III. 97 ; iv. 7. 18.

Verona, Can Grande's house and tomb, IV. 5 ; v. 1. 5.

  ,, Cathedral, griffin from, III. 109 ; iv. 8. 11 (pl. 1).

  ,, San Zeno, leaf scroll, V. 53 ; vi. 6. 12.

  ,,   ,, twisted shafts, V. 22 ; vi. 3. 14.

  ,, view of mountains from, IV. 372 ; v. 20. 11.

  ,,   ,,   ,,   ,, IV. 379 ; v. 20. 20.

Veronese [SYNOPSIS. I. xlviii, 90, 104, 116, 124, 247 *n*, 393–96. II. 48, 217. III. 18, 21, 33, 36–9, 42, 45, 65, 93–4, 104, 131, 339. IV. 15, 43–7, 64, 69, 308, 324, 377–80, 408. V. vii, 42, 74, 100, 191, 212, 214, 219, 244, 246–51, 278, 281–83, 350 *n*, 370 *n*] :—

    character and qualities of work :

        III. 21 ; iv. 2. 5.

        V. 251 ; ix. 3. 27.

        V. 321 ; ix. 9. 11.

        IV. 308 ; v. 17. 42.

Veronese : character and qualities of work, *continued :*

    beauty and sense of contrast, III. 36–7 ; iv. 3. 12–14.

    breadth of (cf. Rembrandt), III. 39 ; iv. 3. 16.

    colour and chiaroscuro of, I. 104 ; ii. 1. 7. 21 (om. ed. 1, 2).

    „   „   „ I. 180 ; ii. 2. 3. 14 (ed. 1, 2 only).

    „   „   „ IV. 43–7 ; v. 3. 11–12. 14.

    „   „   „ IV. 49 ; v. 3. 18.

    colour delicate, I. 393 ; ii. 5. 3. 26.

    „ perfect, V. 350 *n* ; ix. 11. 8 *n.*

    composition of, noble, III. 339 ; iv. 18. 24.

    delicacy of, III. 42 ; iv. 3. 20.

    finish, III. 131 ; iv. 9. 18.

    gentleness of, V. 214 ; viii. 4. 21.

    greatness of, I. xlviii ; *ed.* 2, *pref.* 42.

    love of mountains, small, IV. 377, 380 ; v. 20. 16. 21.

    ludicrous element in, IV. 408 ; App. i. 3.

    „ jests always, always within truth, V. 283 ; ix. 6. 20.

    perception of, intense, IV. 69 ; v. 4. 15.

    power of, IV. 324 ; v. 18. 9.

    religious feeling of, V. 246 ; ix. 3. 17.

    sacred pictures of, lack expression, III. 33 ; iv. 3. 10.

    silver tenderness of, I. 163 ; ii. 2. 1. 21.

    sincerity of manner, III. 45 ; iv. 3. 25.

    softness and mystery of, IV. 64 ; v. 4. 9.

    swift strokes of, III. 42 ; iv. 3. 20.

    symbolical works of, III. 104 ; iv. 8. 6.

    tragic feeling of, not deep, IV. 15 ; v. 1. 17.

    unconscious of his method, III. 93–4 ; iv. 7. 12.

details of his works :

    animals in his portraits, III. 18 ; iv. 2. 1.

    architecture of, I. 90 ; ii. 1. 7. 11 (om. ed. 1, 2).

    architectural drawing, I. 116 ; ii. 1. 7. 29 (om. ed. 1, 2).

    clouds of, generalized, I. 247 *n* ; ii. 3. 3. 13 *n* (om. ed. 1, 2).

    dogs in his pictures, V. 281 *seqq.* ; ix. 6. 14 *seqq.*

    „ fur of, compared with Landseer, II. 217 ; iii. 2. 4. 11.

    drapery of, I. 396 ; ii. 5. 3. 29 (om. ed. 1, 2).

Veronese : details of his works, *continued :*

    foliage of, V. 42 ; vi. 5. 8.

        ,,   V. 74 ; vi. 8. 8–9 (pl. 57).

    foregrounds of, V. 100 ; vi. 10. 5.

    pearl-painting of, V. 211–12 ; viii. 4. 18.

    skies of, luminous, II. 48 ; iii. 1. 5. 11.

  engravings of, by Lefèbre, V. 191 ; viii. 2. 12.

  frescoes of (Venice), all perished, I. 116 ; ii. 1. 7. 30 (om. ed. 1, 2).

  works of :

      Ascent to Calvary (St. Veronica), Dresden, V. 251 ; ix. 3. 26.

      Cupid and two mastiffs, V. 281 ; ix. 6. 14. 15.

      Europa (flowers in), Dresden, V. 100 ; vi. 10. 5.

        ,,   ,,   ,,   V. 191 ; viii. 2. 12.

      Family of Darius (Nat. Gall.), V. 212 ; viii. 4. 18.

      His own family (cf. Rubens'), Dresden, V. 247–49 ; ix. 3. 19. 21.

      ,,   ,,   ,,   ,,   ,,   V. 278 ; ix. 6. 9.

      ,,   ,,   hope, dark veiled, V. 385 ; ix. 12. 18.

      Holy Family, Brussels, V. 250 ; ix. 3. 25.

      Magdalen, Turin, V. 282 ; ix. 6. 17.

        ,,   washing Christ's Feet, III. 21 ; iv. 2. 5.

        ,,   ,,   ,,   ,,   III. 33 ; iv. 3. 10.

      Marriage in Cana (drapery), Louvre, III. 131 ; iv. 9. 18.

      ,,   ,,   IV. 69 ; v. 4. 15.

      ,,   ,,   V. 219 ; ix. 1. 5.

      ,,   ,,   V. 244 ; ix. 3. 13.

      ,,   ,,   (his best picture), V. 246 ; ix. 3. 17.

      ,,   ,,   (aim of), V. 282 ; ix. 6. 16.

      Marsyas, V. 370 *n* ; ix. 11. 32 *n.*

      Queen of Sheba, Turin, V. vii ; *pref.* 4.

      ,,   ,,   ,,   V. 249 ; ix. 3. 23.

      Supper at Emmaus, III. 33 ; iv. 3. 10.

      ,,   ,,   III. 65 ; iv. 4. 24.

      ,,   ,,   V. 282 ; ix. 6. 18.

      Susannah and the Elders, Louvre, V. 74 *n* ; vi. 8. 8 *n.* 9.

      ,,   ,,   ,,   ,,   V. 282 ; ix. 6. 17.

      Triumph of Venice, V. 191 ; viii. 2. 12.

Verrocchio. Andrea del, I. 131 ; ii. 1. 7. 37 (om. ed. 1, 2).

    ,,   ,,   his "Baptism of Christ," II. 189 ; iii. 2. 3. 18.

Verte, Aiguille, II. 159 ; iii. 2. 2. 3.

Vesta, sphere of, V. 333 ; ix. 10. 8.

Vesuvius, cloud over, IV. 147 ; v. 12. 5.

Vevay, author's love of, IV. 366 ; v. 20. 2.

    ,,   hills near, IV. 329 *n* ; v. 18. 15 *n*.

    ,,   orchards and narcissus, III. 235 ; iv. 14. 46.

Via Mala, significance of term, III. 245 *seqq.* ; iv. 15. 3 *seqq.*

Vice various, virtue one, I. xvii *n* ; *pref. ed.* 2. 10 *n* (ed. 2, 3 only).

Village beauty, III. 74 ; iv. 5. 11.

Villeneuve, mountains of, IV. 260 ; v. 16. 26.

    ,,   ,,   limestone bank above, IV. 304–5 ; v. 17. 36–7 (pl. 40).

                         See s. Chillon.

Vindonissa, ramparts of, V. 139 ; vii. 3. 4.

Vine, docile grace of the, V. 88 ; vi. 9. 4.

    ,,   gadding, V. 111 ; vi. 10. 23.

Vinet, Alex., "Vital Christianity" quoted, II. 125 *n* ; iii. 1. 14. 9 *n.*

Violet, V. 107 *n* ; vi. 10. 19 *n.*

Virgil, influence of, on Dante, III. 199 ; iv. 13. 27.

    ,,   ,,   Homer on, *ib.* ; *ib.*

    ,,   quoted on Eris and Hesperides, V. 341–42 ; ix. 10. 22.

    ,,   ,,   ,,   Laocoon (Æn. II.), II. 75 *n* ; iii. 1. 7. 6 *n.*

    ,,   ,,   ,,   "over-roofed and hanging rocks," IV. 268 , v. 16. 37.

Virginia Water, Turner and, III. 328 ; iv. 18. 4.

Virtue, beauty and, in animals and men, II. 106 ; iii. 1. 12. 10.

    ,,   Byron on the unity of, I. xvii *n* ; *pref. ed.* 2. 10 *n* (ed. 2, 3 only).

            See s. Countenance, Ethical subjects.

Visions of delirium and high imagination, II. 151 ; iii. 2. 1 (Introd. Note '83, § 3).

Volcanic convulsions of the world, still possible ? IV. 147–48 ; v. 12. 5.

    ,,   rocks, their formation, IV. 121 ; v. 9. 3.

Volpato's engraving of Raphael's Parnassus, V. 42 ; vi. 5. 8.

Vosges, mountains of the, IV. 160 ; v. 12. 20.

Voza, the (plain of Arve), I. 268 ; ii. 4. 1. 5 (ed. 1 only).

Vulgarity, defined, V. 287 *seqq.* ; ix. 7. 1 *seqq.*

    ,,   ,,   V. 289 ; ix. 7. 4.

    ,,   essence and signs of (deathful selfishness), V. 301–3 ; ix. 7. 23–4.

Vulgarity, *continued :*

„ examples of, V. 295–96 ; ix. 7. 16 *seqq.*

„ inconceivable by greatest minds, III. 89-90 ; iv. 7. 9.

„ perfect truth has no, III. 90 ; iv. 7. 9.

„ seen in love of mere physical beauty, III. 72 ; iv. 5. 8.

„ the worst, that of education, III. 73 ; iv. 5. 10.

See s. Digby (Sir K.), Dutch school, Emerson, Gentleman.

Vulgate, Gen. iii. 8, "in medio ligni Paradisi," IV. 364 ; v. 19. 33.

„ Job xxxvi. 29, "Si voluerit extendere nubes," V. 155 ; vii. 4. 7.

Waagen, "Art and Artists in England" (ii. 151), on Turner, quoted, IV. 71 and *n* ; v. 5. 1 and *n.*

Wales, hill scenery of, IV. 132 ; v. 10. 5.

Walker's "Itinerant," Turner's "Nottingham" in, IV. 30 ; v. 2. 19.

Wallis (artist), snow-scenes by, I. 303–4 *n* ; ii. 4. 2. 19 *n.*

Walpole, Horace, his affectation about art, III. 20 ; iv. 2. 4.

War, evil of, V. 83 ; vi. 8. 18.

„ for honour's sake, V. 268 ; ix. 5. 6.

„ involves injustice somewhere, III. 349 ; iv. 18. 36.

„ love of, less than of old, III. 157–59 ; iv. 11. 8–9.

„ „ „ „ III. 273 *n* ; iv. 16. 16 *n.*

„ modern fear and the art of, *ib.* ; *ib.*

„ neglect of natural beauty and mediæval, V. 4–5 ; vi. 1. 5–6.

„ often productive of more good than evil, III. 346 ; iv. 18. 33.

„ Napoleon I. *See s. Crimean War.*

Warner's "Fair Rosamond" quoted, "With that she dashed her on the lips," II. 179 ; iii. 2. 3. 7.

Warwickshire scenery, and Shakspere, IV. 383, 385 ; v. 20. 27. 29.

„ trees, pines, IV. 394 ; v. 20. 38.

Water [SYNOPSIS. I. 315–16, 345–60, 369 *seqq.*, 376, 389–92. III. 222–23, 249. IV. 99, 224, 369. V. 116 *seqq.*] :—

aqueous erosion of hills, I. 315 ; ii. 4. 3. 11.

„ action on mountain crests, IV. 224 *seqq.* ; v. 15. 19 *seqq.*

clouds and globules of, V. 116 *seqq.* ; vii. 1. 5 *seqq.*

Water, *continued*:

    colour of, causes of local, I. 350 *seqq.*, 354 ; ii. 5. 1. 6–9
        (om. ed. 1, 2).

       ,,   lakes and streams, III. 249 ; iv. 15. 9.

    -falls, action of, described, I. 389–90 ; ii. 5. 3. 20.

    functions of, I. 345 ; ii. 5. 1. 1.

    laws of its phenomena, I. 350–58 ; ii. 5. 1. 6–15.

    marvel of, infinite, I. 345 ; ii. 5. 1. 1.

    motion of, caused by the mountains, IV. 99 *seqq.* ; v. 7. 6
        seqq.

    mountains and lowlands, IV. 369 ; v. 20. 6.

    painting of, ancient, modern, and Turner, I. 345, 369, 376 ;
        ii. 5. 1. 1 *seqq.*, 2. 1 *seqq.*, 3. 1 *seqq.*

       ,,   difficulty of, I. 346 ; ii. 5. 1. 2. *See s. Wave.*

       ,,   ideal of, I. 347–48 ; ii. 5. 1. 4 (om. ed. 1, 2).

       ,,   laws for, I. 392–93 *n* ; ii. 5. 3. 25 *n* (om. ed. 1, 2).

       ,,   like trying to paint a soul, I. 345 ; ii. 5. 1. 1.

       ,,   smooth surface especially, I. 376 *seqq.* ; ii. 5. 3.
           1 *seqq.*

       ,,   swift execution needed, I. 371 ; ii. 5. 2. 4.

       ,,   various artists' effects, I. 360 *seqq.* ; ii. 5. 1. 17
           seqq.

    plains formed by, I. 289 ; ii. 4. 1. 5.

    proverb, " If water chokes," etc., III. 311 ; iv. 17. 23.

    reflections in, I. 350–51 ; ii. 5. 1. 6–7.

       ,,   I. 352–54 ; ii. 5. 1. 9 (om. ed. 1, 2).

       ,,   I. 355 *seqq.* ; ii. 5. 1. 11 *seqq.*

       ,,   eye cannot see at once surface and, I. 376 ;
           ii. 5. 3. 2.

    rippled, effects of, I. 355–57 ; ii. 5. 1. 11–14 (om. ed.
        1, 2).

    running, its action, I. 391 ; ii. 5. 3. 22.

    shadows, none on clear water, I. 351 ; ii. 5. 1. 8.

    sunlight on, its effect, I. 352 ; ii. 5. 1. 8.

    symbolism of, mediæval, III. 223 ; iv. 14. 28.

    truth of, I. 345 *seqq.* ; ii. 5. 1. 1 *seqq.*

       See s. Foam, Sea, Streams, Torrents, Waves.

Water colour, easily gives transparent rain blue, I. 273 ; ii. 3. 4
        21 (ed. 1–4. 24).

    ,,   ,,   effect of light on, I. 145 *n* ; ii. 1. 7. 46 *n*.

    ,,   ,,   modern, methods of, V. 350 *n* ; ix. 11. 8 *n*.

    ,,   ,,   ,,   skies of, true, I. 227 ; ii. 3. 1. 19.

Water Colour Society (1846), foliage drawing, I. 427 ; ii. 6. 1. 28 (om. ed. 1, 2).

Water-cress, Derbyshire, V. 231 ; ix. 2. 12.

Waterloo, battle of, V. 326 ; ix. 9. 22.

    ,,   ,,   etchings, I. 97 ; ii. 1. 7. 16 (om. ed. 1, 2).

    ,,   Bridge, granite of, IV. 241 ; v. 16. 4.

Watts (G. F.), symbolical power of, III. 106 ; iv. 8. 7.

Waves, character, massiveness of, III. 170–71 ; iv. 12. 11.

    ,,   curves of, I. 397–98 ; ii. 5. 3. 31.

    ,,   ,,   questions on, V. viii ; *pref.* 5.

    ,,   devouring and terrible (cf. mountains), IV. 104 ; v. 7. 10.

    ,,   edges of, often dark and sharp, I. 254 ; ii. 3. 3. 21.

    ,,   grander than any torrent, IV. 369 ; v. 20. 6.

    ,,   Greek rendering of, II. 221 ; iii. 2. 4. 17.

    ,,   Homeric epithets of, III. 178–79 ; iv. 13. 2.

    ,,   painting of, difficult, I. 346 ; ii. 5. 1. 2.

    ,,   ,,   ,,   I. 395–98 ; ii. 5. 3. 29–31 (om. ed. 1, 2).

    ,,   size of, exaggerated, II. 224 ; iii. 2. 4. 20.

Wayside," "By the, V. 42 ; vi. 5. 9 (pl. 55).

Weather, English, wet, worth painting, V. 151 ; vii. 4. 1.

    ,,   of importance to animals ? I. 216 ; ii. 3. 1. 1 (F.A. *n*).

Wealth, kinds of, III. 319–20 ; iv. 17. 35.

    ,,   pursuit of, degrading, V. 268 ; ix. 5. 6.

    ,,   ,,   desire for, V. 387 ; ix. 12. 20.

      See s. Money.

Webster (artist), his subjects base, III. 30 ; iv. 3. 5.

Wedgwood's ware, III. 321 ; iv. 17. 36.

    ,,   ,,   III. 332 ; iv. 18. 12.

Weeds, V. 105 ; vi. 10. 14.

    ,,   people compared to, V. 180 ; viii. 1. 16.

Weisshorn, peak of, IV. 187 ; v. 14. 10.

    ,,   ,,   IV. 249 ; v. 16. 13.

Wells, cathedral of, IV. 381 ; v. 20. 22.

Westminster Abbey, distant view of, I. 210 ; ii. 2. 5. 12.

    ,,   Bridge, I. 213 *n* ; iii. 2. 5. 15 *n.*

    ,,   Duke of, Paul Potter in gallery of, II. 242 ; Add 2 (om. ed. 1).

Westmoreland, scenery of, IV. 367 ; v. 20. 3.

Wetterhorn, IV. 173–75 ; v. 13. 9. 11.

    ,,   IV. 187 ; v. 14. 10.

Wharfe, shores of, IV. 315 ; v. 17. 48 (pl. 12).

„ Turner's love of, IV. 261–62 ; v. 16. 28–9.

„ Wordsworth quoted, "Wharfe as he moved along,' etc., IV. 264 ; v. 16. 32.

Whelp, Shakspere's use of word, III. 88 ; iv. 7. 8.

White, Adam, naturalist, note to author, I. xxx n ; pref. ed. 2 (22 n. om. ed. 1–4).

„ (colour), effect of light and shade on, IV. 36–7 ; v. 3. 2.

Whitewash, and restoration, II. 88 ; iii. 1. 10. 3.

„ in modern Italy, III. 248 ; iv. 15. 9.

Wilkie, popular, and why, I. 4 n ; i. 1. 1. 1 n.

„ praised, I. 10 ; i. 1. 2. 7 (ed. 1, 2 only).

„ qualities of, clearness and definiteness, IV. 59 ; v. 4. 2.

„ Turner's study of, III. 344 ; iv. 18. 30.

Willow, the most graceful English tree, V. 75 ; vi. 8. 10.

Wilson, Richard, characteristics of, I. 97 ; ii. 1. 7. 17 (om. ed. 1, 2).

„ „ chiaroscuro of, I. 180 ; ii. 2. 3. 15 (ed. 1, 2 only).

„ „ classicalism of, hybrid, I. 131 ; ii. 1. 7. 37 (om. ed. 1, 2).

„ „ ideal landscape of, IV. 202 ; v. 14. 23.

„ „ sunshine of, imperfect colour, V. 346 ; ix. 11. 3.

„ „ Turner's study of, III. 344 ; iv. 18. 30.

„ „ works of :

Mæcenas' villa (Nat. Gall.), I. 98 ; ii. 1. 7. 17 (om. ed. 1, 2).
Niobe (Nat. Gall.), II. 221 ; iii. 2. 4. 16.

Winckelmann, on the Laocoon, II. 76 n ; iii. 1. 7. 6 n.

Wind, on Yorkshire moors, V. 160 n ; vii. 4. 14 n.

Windmills, picturesque, of Stanfield and Turner, IV. 7 seqq. ; v. 1. 10 seqq. (pl. 19).

Windows, English and French, finish of, III. 118 ; iv. 9. 4.

„ pictures not to be mere, III. 134 seqq., 138 ; iv. 10. 3 seqq. 6.

Windus, B. G., gallery of :

Harding in, I. 100 ; ii. 1. 7. 24 (ed. 3, 4 only).
Turner's drawing of trees (for "Keepsake"), I. 137 ; ii. 1. 7. 41 (om. ed. 1, 2).

„ Nemi, I. 146 ; ii. 1. 7. 46 (om. ed. 1, 2).

Windus, B. G. : gallery of, *continued*:
   Turner's Oberwesel, *ib.* ; *ib. (ib.).*
   „   „   and Nemi, I. 256 *n*; ii. 3. 4. 29 *n* (ed. 1–4 only).
   „   Rhine, I. 125 ; ii. 1. 7. 39 (ed. 3–4 only).

Wine, good judgment of, worth learning, II. 25 ; iii. 1. 3. 6 ('83 *n*).
Wing, beauty of a bird's, its elements, IV. 210–12 ; v. 15. 8.
Winkelried, V. 196 ; viii. 3. 4.
Winter, drawings of, generally failures, I. 303 ; ii. 4. 2. 19 (om. ed. 1, 2).
Wit, finish belies gaiety in, III. 268 ; iv. 16. 9.
Wittenberg, V. 95 ; vi. 9. 14.
Wood, description of a, by Homer, III. 195 ; iv. 13. 23.
   „   „   „ northerns and southerns (Dante, Homer, Shakspere), III. 226–27 ; iv. 14. 33.
   „   domestic use of marble and, IV. 392 ; v. 20. 35.
   ——— -cutting, Dürer's and modern, IV. 228 ; v. 15. 25.
Woollett, engraving of Pars' Mer de Glace, IV. 202 ; v. 14. 23.
Wordsworth [Synopsis. I. 4 *n*, 88, 96 *n*, 188, 217, 219, 225, 234, 269–70, 443, 451 *n*. II. 4 *n*, 12 *n*, 42, 59, 71, 73 *n*, 99, 103, 110, 158, 210–15. III. 13, 44, 141, 165 *n*, 175–77, 183, 233, 266–69, 276, 277, 287, 298, 301, 302–6, 309, 310–11, 315, 357, 359. IV. 264. V. 286] :—
   aim and motive of his work, III. 304 ; iv. 17. 9.
   author's debt to, III. 359 ; App. 3.
   characteristics of :
      I. 443 ; ii. 6. 3. 11.
      anxious feeling, III. 269 ; iv. 16. 10.
      conceit and jealousy of, III. 277 ; iv. 16. 25.
      egotism, spoils his love of nature, III. 287 ; iv. 16. 38.
      fancy and imagination, II. 210–13 ; iii. 2. 4. 5 *seqq.*
      imagination, III. 44 ; iv. 3. 22.
      love of nature, corrections of his impressions, II. 42 ; iii. 1. 5. 2 ('83 *n*).
      „   dreaming, III. 302–3 ; iv. 17. 8.
      „   simplicity and, III. 304 ; iv. 17. 9.
      narrowness of mind, III. 302 ; iv. 17. 7.
      not allegorical, III. 183 ; iv. 13. 7.
      penetrative depths of, III. 276 ; iv. 16. 23.

Wordsworth : characteristics of, *continued :*

  reflective, III. 165 *n* ; iv. 12. 6 *n.*

  simplicity of, affected, III. 277 ; iv. 16. 26.

     „ anticipated by motive, III. 315–16 ; iv.
        17. 29–30.

  description of a cloud, II. 71 ; iii. 1. 7. 2.

   „ „ a foreground, I. 88 ; ii. 1. 7. 10 (om. ed. 1, 2).

   „ „ rays of sun, I. 234 ; ii. 3. 2. 9.

   „ „ skies, I. 219 ; ii. 3. 1. 7.

  pastorals of, V. 286 ; ix. 6. 23.

  plants loved by, II. 99 ; iii. 1. 12. 3.

  popularity of, limited, and why, I. 4 *n* ; i. 1. 1. 1 *n.*

  sonnets of, I. 419 ; ii. 6. 23 (ed. 1 only).

    „ to Beaumont and Haydon, not Reynolds and
       Turner, III. 141–42 ; iv. 10. 9.

  to be studied, III. 357 ; App. 2.

  Turner's truth illustrated by, I. 188 ; ii. 2. 3. 5.

  works of, quoted or referred to :

   (*a*) Conversations, III. 277 ; iv. 16. 25.

    Ellen, III. 176–77 ; iv. 12. 16.

    on activity (Exc., v. 608–25) }
     „ („ vi. 102–214) } III. 233 ; iv. 14. 41.

    „ emotions of youth, II. 36 ; iii. 1. 4. 8 ('83 *n*).

     „ and delight in nature, III. 305–6 ; iv. 17. 11.

    Intimation of Immortality, *ib.* ; *ib.*

     „   „ III. 309 ; iv. 17. 19.

    on railways in lake district, II. 12 ; iii. 1. 1. 11 (note
     at end).

    poem on the imagination, II. 110 ; iii. 1. 13. 3 ('83 *n*).

     „ „ „ II. 158 ; iii. 2. 2. 1.

    preface to his poems, II. 215 ; iii. 2. 4. 8.

   (*b*) "A Pagan suckled in some creed outworn," III. 269 ; iv.
    16. 10.

    "Accuse me not of arrogance, If having walked with
     nature," Title-page of each vol.

    "An abyss In which the everlasting stars abide" (Exc.,
     Bk. ii.), I. 219 ; ii. 3. 1. 7.

    "Be as a presence," etc. (Exc., iv. 520–25), I. 269 ; ii. 3.
     4. 15 (ed. 1–4. 17).

    "Beauty of its star-shaped," I. 88 ; ii. 1. 7. 10 (om. ed.
     1, 2).

    "Beneath an old **grey** oak—**as** violets lie," II. **72** ; iii.
     1. 7. 2.

Wordsworth : works of, quoted or referred to, *continued :*

"Custom lies upon us," etc., II. 59 ; iii. 1. 6. 6.

"   ,,   ,,   " III. 311 ; iv. 17. 23.

"on the Daisy," II. 211 ; iii. 2. 4. 5.

"   ,,   ,, " III. 138 ; iv. 10. 5.

"Filling more and more with crystal light," II. 118 ; iii. 1. 13. 15.

"Fresh from God's hands" (of a child), III. 310 ; iv. 17. 22.

"Heaven lies about us in our infancy," II. 42 ; iii. 1. 5. 2 (om. ed. 2).

"Huge trunks . . . fraternal four of Borrowdale," III. 301 ; iv. 17. 6.

"In such high home of visitation . . . thought was not," II. 122 ; iii. 1. 14. 5.

"In such high home of visitation . . . thought was not," III. 305 ; iv. 17. 11.

"It doth not love the shower," etc., II. 99 ; iii. 1. 12. 3.

"Lie round me scattered like a flock of sheep," II. 72 ; iii. 1. 7. 2.

"Multitudes of little floating clouds," I. 234 ; ii. 3. 2. 9.

"Nature never did betray the heart that loved her," I. 451 *n* ; ii. 6. 3. 23 *n*.

"Not for these I raise The songs of thanks and praise," II. 37 ; iii. 1. 5. 2 (ed. 2 only).

"Oh, move, thou cottage, from behind yon oak," III. 175 ; iv. 12. 15.

"Perhaps to himself at that moment he said," III. 13 ; iv. 1. 14.

"Rays of light, now suddenly diverging" (Exc., ix.), I. 225 ; ii. 3. 1. 15.

"Remoter charm by thought supplied," III. 298 ; iv. 17. 2.

"Tempered and allayed by sympathies," II. 98 ; iii. 1. 12. 2.

"That heareth not," etc. (on clouds), II. 71 ; iii. 1. 7. 2.

"That universal instinct of repose,   } II. 73*n*; iii.
"The life where hope and memory are as one," } 1. 7. 4 *n*.

"The clouds that gather round the setting sun," I. 96 *n* ; ii. 1. 7. 15 *n* (om. ed. 1, 2).

"The river glideth at its own sweet will," III. 266 ; iv. 16. 5.

"The tall pine, the shadow" (Exc., ii.), I. 188 ; ii. 2. 3. 5.

"'Tis my faith that every flower enjoys the air it breathes," II. 98 ; iii. 1. 12. 3.

Wordsworth : works of, quoted or referred to, *continued :*

"Too bright, too good, For human nature's daily food," I. 217 ; ii. 3. 1. 1.

"True to the kindred spirits of heaven and home," II. 103 ; iii. 1. 12. 9.

"We live by admiration, hope, and love," II. 4 *n* ; iii. 1. 1. 5 *n.*

"Wharfe as he moved along, To matins joined a mournful voice," IV. 264 ; v. 16. 32.

"Yew trees," II. 214 ; iii. 2. 4. 6.

Work, each man has his God-appointed, I. 85 ; ii. 1. 7. 8 (om. ed. 1, 2).

„ good, is always enjoyed work, V. 301 *n* ; ix. 7. 23 *n.*

„ once well done, done once for all, IV. 14 *n* ; v. 1. 15 *n.*

„ pay and, "best work always for nothing," V. 379 ; ix. 12. 7.

„ purse or curse, no good work done for, V. 379, 381 ; ix. 12. 7. 10.

„ want of, V. 162 *n* ; vii. 4. 17 *n.*

Working Men's College, drawing by pupil, V. 76 ; vi. 8. 10 (pl. 58).

World, the better, the only *real* one, V. 385 ; ix. 12. 19.

„ children of this, V. 386 ; ix. 12. 19.

„ fighting with, and getting on in, V. 385–86 ; ix. 12. 18–19.

„ great men neglected by, till they are gone, } I. 7 ; i. 1. 1. 5.

„   „   „   „   III. v–vi ; *pref.* 1.

„ "sojourning city," I. 110 ; ii. 1. 7. 26 (om. ed. 1, 2).

„ system of, one in great things and small, V. 381 ; ix. 12. 10.

See s. Earth.

Wornum, R. (Nat. Gall.), and the Turner drawings, V. v, vii ; *pref.* 1, 3.

Wouvermans [SYNOPSIS. I. 87. V. 39, 41, 136, 218, 305–11] :—

author has no sympathy with, V. 304 ; ix. 8. 1.

character of his work, I. 87 ; ii. 1. 7. 10 (om. ed. 1, 2).

„   „   „   V. 309 ; ix. 8. 11.

compared with Angelico, V. 309–11 ; ix. 8. 12–13.

delights in things carnal, V. 307, 310 ; ix. 8. 7. 12.

false clouds of, V. 136 ; vii. 2. 19.

landscape of, hybrid, V. 218 ; ix. 1. 3.

Wouvermans, *continued :*
  landscape of, hybrid, V. 305 ; ix. 8. 2.
  leaf-drawing of, V. 39, 41 ; vi. 5. 3, 7.
  works of :

  > Munich, Pinacothek, landscape, No. 208, V. 305–7 ; ix
  > 8. 2–6.
  > Turin, war-piece, V. 307 *seqq.* ; ix. 8. 7 *seqq.*

Writers, great, ambiguity of, IV. 77–8 ; v. 5. 12–13.
  „   quoted or referred to :

  > Addison, Æschylus, Alison, Anacreon, Arabian Nights,
  > Aristophanes, Aristotle, Bacon, Balzac, Baxter, Bell,
  > Beranger, Blitzius, Boileau, Brown, Browning,
  > Bunsen, Bunyan, Burke, Burns, Byron, Carlyle,
  > Cary, Cayley, Cervantes, Chaucer, Coleridge,
  > Constantin, Cooper, Crabbe, Dante, De la Vigne,
  > De Stendhal, Dickens, Digby, Dumas, Edgeworth,
  > Emerson, Euripides, Fénélon, Feuillet, Genlis,
  > Goethe, Goldsmith, Gotthelf, Hazlitt, Helps, Her-
  > bert, Herodotus, Hesiod, Holmes, Hood, Hooker,
  > Howitt, Humboldt, Hunt, James, Jameson, John-
  > son, Kant, Keats, Kingsley, Lamartine, Le Sage,
  > Lindley, Lindsay, Link, Linnæus, Locke, Longfellow,
  > Lowell, Lucian, Macaulay, Mallet, Marmontel,
  > Metastasio, Michelet, Mill, Milnes, Milton, Molière,
  > North (Blackwood), Palgrave, Pascal, Plato, Pope,
  > Radclyffe, Richardson, Rio, Rogers, Sainsbury, Sand,
  > Schiller, Scott (A.J.), Scott (W.), Scribe, Shakspere,
  > Shelley, Shenstone, Smith, Smollett, Sophocles,
  > Southey, Spenser, Steele, Stewart, Stowe, Sue,
  > Swift, Taylor, Tennyson, Thackeray, Thomson,
  > Tylor, Vasari, Vinet, Virgil, Waagen, Walker, Wal-
  > pole, Warner, Winckelmann, Wordsworth, Young,
  > Zanetti.

Writing, careful, needs careful reading, III. 5–6 ; iv. 1. 5.
  „   difficulty of, simply, III. 278 ; iv. 16. 28.
  „   waste of time generally, III. 316 ; iv. 17. 31.

Xanthias, referred to, I. xxii ; *pref. ed.* 2. 13.

Yellow, purple and, the use of, I. 179 ; ii. 2. 2. 17.
  „   qualities of, V. 322 ; ix. 11. 7.

Yolande of Navarre, her missal, III. 221 (pl. 9).

Yorkshire, formation of limestone hills, IV. 106 ; v. 8. 2.

    ,,   hills, influence on Turner, I. 133 ; ii. 1. 7. 39.

    ,,   ,,   ,,   ,,   IV. 259 ; v. 16. 25.

    ,,   ,,   ,,   ,,   V. 323–24 ; ix. 9. 16.

    ,,   valleys, IV. 315 ; v. 17. 48.

    ,,   winds and clouds, on the moors, V. 160 n ; vii. 4. 14 n.

    ,,   Yoredale shales, geology of, IV. 264–66 ; v. 16. 33–4.

Young, colour in, " In melancholy dipped *embrowns* the whole," III. 250 ; iv. 15. 11.

    ,,   love and study of nature, III. 302 ; iv. 17. 7.

    ,,   solitude of, III. 314 n ; iv. 17. 27.

    ,,   works of, quoted, " Where shall I find him ? angels, tell me where," III. 174 ; iv. 12. 15.

    ,,   worldliness of, III. 314 ; iv. 17. 27.

Youth, age and, each their ideal, II. 117 ; iii. 1. 13. 15.

    ,,   sense of beauty keenest in, II. 42 ; iii. 1. 5. 2.

Zanetti, on Giorgione's frescoes, quoted, V. 370 and n ; ix. 11 32 and n.

Zermatt, character of its people, V. 94 ; vi. 9. 13.

    ,,   Matterhorn from, IV. 190 ; v. 14. 12.

    ,,   ,,   ,,   IV. 244 ; v. 16. 7.

    ,,   ,,   ,,   IV. 248 ; v. 16. 11.

    ,,   St. Nicholas' valley, rock from, IV. 123 ; v. 9. 5.

    ,,   villages, morgues in, IV. 345 ; v. 19. 11.

Zeuxis, leaf-drawing of, V. 39 ; vi. 5. 2.

    ,,   Centaur of, II. 203 ; iii. 2. 3. 29.

    ,,   ,,   V. 284 ; ix. 6. 21.

Zmutt Glacier (Red Glacier), IV. 190 ; v. 14. 12.

    ,,   ,,   ,,   described, IV. 249 ; v. 16. 13.

Zoilus, I. xiii ; *pref. ed.* 2. 3.

Zuccaro's frescoes (Florence), II. 220 ; iii. 2. 4. 14.

Zumloch quartz, IV. 417 ; App. ii. 3.

Zurich, and Swiss Reformers, V. 95 ; vi. 9. 14.

BIBLIOGRAPHY·

BIBLIOGRAPHY

VOLUME I.

Edition I., 1843.

"MODERN PAINTERS : Their Superiority in the Art of Land-scape Painting to all the Ancient Masters proved by Examples of the True, the Beautiful, and the Intellectual, from the Works of Modern Artists, especially from those of J. M. W. Turner, Esq., R.A. By A Graduate of Oxford. [Quotation from Wordsworth as motto.] 8vo, pp. xxxi, 420. London : Smith, Elder & Co., 65, Cornhill. 1843."

This was an octavo volume in dark green or purple cloth, lettered on the back with the words "Modern Painters : Their Superiority in the Art of Landscape Painting to the Ancient Masters," enclosed in the device of the sun rising over the sea, which has figured in all subsequent editions of the book, up to and including that of 1873.

The larger sized page and familiar pale green binding was not adopted until Volume II. and the third edition of Volume I., both of which appeared in 1846.

The quotation from Wordsworth will be found on the title-page of every edition of every volume of the work. It is indicated below thus : [*].

Edition II., 1844.

Similar and practically identical with the first edition, pp. lxxxviii, 423. A long "Preface to the Second Edition" is added, and there are a few differences in the text.

Edition III., 1846.

"MODERN PAINTERS. Volume I., containing Parts I. and II. By A Graduate of Oxford. Third Edition. Revised by

the Author.   [*] pp. lxiv, 422.   London : Smith, Elder & Co.,
etc. 1846."

This edition was considerably revised, containing a " Preface
to the Third Edition," omitted in the fourth and all later
editions. It was also the first of this volume in which the
page was enlarged.

This and all later volumes of the book were lettered simply
" Modern Painters, Volume I., II.," etc.

Edition IV., 1848.

" MODERN PAINTERS. Volume I., containing Parts I. and II.
By A Graduate of Oxford. [*] Fourth Edition, pp. lxiv, 422.
London : Smith, Elder & Co. 1848."—This edition varies but
little from the third.

Edition V., 1851.

" MODERN PAINTERS. Volume I., containing Parts I. and II.,
' Of General Principles and of Truth.' By John Ruskin, Author
of ' The Stones of Venice,' ' The Seven Lamps of Architecture,'
etc., etc. [*] Fifth Edition. Revised by the Author. Pp. lxiv,
423. London : Smith, Elder & Co. 1851."

This edition was the first volume of the book bearing the
author's name (although his anonymity had ceased with the
publication of " The Seven Lamps of Architecture. By John
Ruskin, Author of ' Modern Painters,' " in 1849). It was fully
revised from the fourth edition, and contained an added postscript on the death of Turner, dated " Denmark Hill, June,
1851."

Edition VI., 1856. }
Edition VII., 1867. } Reprints of the Fifth Edition.

VOLUME II.

Edition I., 1846.

" MODERN PAINTERS. Volume II., containing Part III.,
Sections 1 and 2, ' Of the Imaginative and Theoretic Faculties.'

By A Graduate of Oxford. [*] pp. xvi, 217. London : Smith, Elder & Co., etc. 1846."

The enlarged page was first used in this volume as explained in the "Advertisement" thus :—"The illustrations preparing for the third volume of this work having rendered a large page necessary, the present volume, and the third edition of the first volume (in preparation), are arranged in a corresponding form."

The "Addenda" at pp. 216–17 of this edition consisted of four notes afterwards embodied in the text or omitted, their place being taken in the second and later editions by quite other matter under the same heading.

Edition II., 1848.

Same title-page (but for "Second Edition") as in Edition I., pp. xvi, 220. This edition was revised.

Edition III., 1851.

"MODERN PAINTERS. Volume II., etc., as above. By John Ruskin, Author of 'The Stones of Venice,' 'The Seven Lamps of Architecture,' etc., etc. Third Edition. Revised by the Author. [*] pp. xvi, 224. London : Smith, Elder & Co. 1851."

Edition IV., 1856. } Reprints of the Third Edition.
Edition V., 1869. }

Supplementary Edition, 1883.

"MODERN PAINTERS. Volume II., 'Of Ideas of Beauty' and 'Of the Imaginative Faculty.' By John Ruskin, LL.D. (Honorary Student of Christ Church, etc., etc.). [*] Re-arranged in two volumes, and revised by the Author. George Allen, Sunnyside, Orpington, Kent. 1883." (Second Edition, 1885.)

The first of these volumes (pp. xx, 360) contains a new preface, and Part III., Section 1 of the one-volume edition re-arranged with various additional notes as Part II. in three new sections, thus :—

> Sec. 1. "Of the Theoretic Faculty," chaps. 1–4, being chaps. 1–4 of the 1-vol. edition.
>
> „ 2. "Of Typical Beauty," chaps. 1–7, being chaps. 5–11 of the 1-vol. edition.
>
> „ 3. "Of Vital Beauty," chaps. 1–4, being chaps. 12–15 of the 1-vol. edition.

The second of them (pp. vi, 248) contains Part III., Section 2 of the single volume edition, re-arranged with additional notes, including a long Introductory Note (pp. 1–5), as Part III., "Of the Imaginative Faculty." The "Addenda" are also reprinted, with an Epilogue (pp. 225–48).

All the new matter of this edition is included in Volume II. of the "Complete Edition" (1888).

VOLUME III.

Edition I., 1856.

"MODERN PAINTERS. Volume III., containing Part IV., 'Of Many Things.' By John Ruskin, M.A., Author of 'The Stones of Venice,' 'The Seven Lamps of Architecture,' etc., etc. [*] pp. xvi, 348. London, etc. 1856."

This volume contains 18 plates, including the frontispiece, and various woodcuts. The preface is dated "Denmark Hill, Jan., 1856."

There was a second edition in 1867, but the text of this volume has remained unchanged.

VOLUME IV.

Edition I., 1856.

"MODERN PAINTERS. Volume IV., containing Part V., 'Of Mountain Beauty.' By John Ruskin, M.A., Author, etc., etc. [*] pp. xi, 411. London, etc. 1856."

This volume contains 35 plates, including the frontispiece, and various woodcuts. The preface is dated "Denmark Hill, March, 1856."

There was a second edition in 1867, but the text of this volume also has remained unchanged.

Portions of it, however, were reprinted with additions and slight alterations in " Cœli Enarrant " and " In Montibus Sanctis" (see below).

VOLUME V

Edition I., 1860.

" MODERN PAINTERS. Volume V., completing the work, and containing Parts VI., ' Of Leaf Beauty ;' VII., ' Of Cloud Beauty ;' VIII., ' Of Ideas of Relation—1. Of Invention Formal ;' IX., 'Of Ideas of Relation—2. Of Invention Spiritual.' By John Ruskin, M.A., etc., etc.   [*] pp. xvi, 384.   London etc., etc.   1860."

This edition contains, besides many woodcuts, a frontispiece and 34 other steel engravings, plates 51 to 84, and one unnumbered plate, " Monte Rosa Sunset," p. 343.

There was no further edition of this volume until the new edition of all five volumes in 1873 ; but a passage from the last chapter was reprinted, with some additions, in the Turner Notes of 1878 (see Complete Edition).

EDITIONS OF ALL FIVE VOLUMES.

A. 1873. " MODERN PAINTERS. Volume I., etc., etc. By John Ruskin. LL.D., Author of ' The Stones of Venice,' etc., etc. [*] A New Edition. London : Smith, Elder & Co., 15, Waterloo Place. 1873."

Vol. I.,   pp. lxiii, 423.
  „ II.,   „ xvi, 224.
  „ III.,   „ xix, 348.
  „ IV.,   „ xii, 411.
  „ V.,   „ xvi, 384.

In Volume I. of this edition is added a preface, limiting the edition to a thousand copies, and signed by the author's own hand.   Beyond this the work is a reprint without alteration from the last editions of the different volumes of the work.

B. 1888. " MODERN PAINTERS.   Volume I., etc., etc.   By

John Ruskin, LL.D., etc., etc.   Complete Edition.   George Allen, Sunnyside, Orpington, Kent.   1888."

    Vol. I.,   pp. lxiii, 425.
      " II.,   " xxvii, 264.
      " III., " xix, 351.
      " IV., " xii, 420.
      " V.,   " xvi, 364.

This edition is a reprint of that of 1873, with no alterations of text, except in the case of wrong references or obvious errors. The prefaces and one or two other passages are divided into numbered sections for the sake of the references in the Index contained in this volume.

The fifth volume of this edition contains three hitherto unpublished plates, viz., 85, Chateau de Blois (facing p. 157); 86 and 87, Lake of Zug and Dawn after the Wreck (between pages 340 and 341); and an Epilogue dated "Chamouni, Sunday, September 16th, 1888."

The edition is brought up to date, containing, in the form of appendices, almost all the various notes and other matter added by the author in reprints of portions of the work, especially in the two-volume (1883) edition of the second volume, " In Montibus Sanctis," " Cœli Enarrant," and " Frondes Agrestes."

SELECTIONS FROM "MODERN PAINTERS."

" *In Montibus Sanctis:* Studies of Mountain Form and of its Visible Causes, collected and completed out of ' Modern Painters.' By John Ruskin, etc., etc.   George Allen, Sunnyside, Orpington, Kent.   1884–85."

1884. Part I., pp. viii, 40, contains a preface, dated "Brantwood, 16th September, 1884;" Chapter I., "Of the Distinctions of Form in Silica" (*read before the Mineralogical Society, July 24th,* 1884), and a Postscript to Chapter I.

1885. Part II., pp. 41–85, contains Chapter II., "The Dry Land" (being a reprint of Vol. IV., Chap. vii., with some added notes and a postscript), and Chapter III., "Of the Materials of Mountains" (being a reprint of part of Vol. IV., Chap. viii., with similar added notes and postscript).

(No further parts of this work have been issued.)

" *Cœli Enarrant:* Studies of Cloud Form and of its Visible Causes, collected and completed out of 'Modern Painters.' By John Ruskin, etc., etc. George Allen, Sunnyside, Orpington, Kent, 1885 "

Part I., pp. viii, 32, contains a preface, dated "Oxford, November 8th, 1884 ;" Chap. I., "The Firmament," being Chap. vi. of Vol. IV., and Chapter II., "The Cloud-Balancings," being Chap. i. of Part VII. in Vol. V., with one or two added notes.

(No further parts of this work have been issued.)

"*Frondes Agrestes:* Readings in 'Modern Painters,' chosen at her pleasure by the Author's friend, the Younger Lady of the Thwaite, Coniston. G. Allen, Orpington. 1875. pp. vii, 184."

With a preface, dated "Herne Hill, 5th December, 1874," and 34 occasional foot-notes.

The preface is reprinted below ; * the foot-notes will be found in the appendices of "additional matter" to each volume of the "Complete Edition" (1888).

The following table gives the references to the different

---

* " PREFACE.—I have been often asked to republish the first book of mine which the public noticed, and which, hitherto, remains their favourite, in a more easily attainable form than that of its existing editions. I am, however, resolved never to republish the book as a whole ; some parts of it being, by the established fame of Turner, rendered unnecessary ; and others having been always useless, in their praise of excellence which the public will never give the labour necessary to discern. But, finding lately that one of my dearest friends, who, in advanced age, retains the cheerfulness and easily delighted temper of bright youth, had written out, for her own pleasure, a large number of passages from 'Modern Painters,' it seemed to me certain that what such a person felt to be useful to herself, could not but be useful also to a class of readers whom I much desired to please, and who would sometimes enjoy, in my early writings, what I never should myself have offered them. I asked my friend, therefore, to add to her own already chosen series, any other passages she thought likely to be of permanent interest to general readers ; and I have printed her selections in absolute submission to her judgment, merely arranging the pieces she sent me in the order which seemed most convenient for the reciprocal bearing of their fragmentary meanings, and adding here and there an explanatory note ; or, it may be, a deprecatory one, in cases where my mind had changed. That she did me the grace to write every word with her own hands, adds, in my eyes, and will, I trust, in the readers' also, to the possible claims of the little book on their sympathy ; and although I hope to publish some of the scientific and technical portions of the original volumes in my own large editions, the selections here made by my friend under her quiet woods at Coniston—the Unter-Walden of England—will, I doubt not, bring within better reach of many readers, for whom I am not now able myself to judge or choose, such service as the book was ever capable of rendering, in the illustration of the powers of nature, and intercession for her now too often despised and broken peace.—*Herne Hill, 5th December,* 1874."

passages contained in "Frondes Agrestes," those marked by
an asterisk being those to which the notes are added :—

Section I.—Principles of Art.

1.	i. 25-6.	I. i. 6. 1, 2.
2.	ii. 23.	III. i. 3. 9.
3.	ii. 8-9.	III. i. 1. 8.
4.*	ii. 25.	III. i. 3. 13.
5.*	iii. 93.	IV. 7. 16.
6.*	iii. 66-7.	IV. 5. 6.
7.*	iii. 92.	IV. 7. 15.
8.*	iii. 59-60.	IV. 4. 22.

Section II.—Power and Office of Imagination.

9.*	iii. 47.	IV. 4. 5.
10.*	iii. 21.	IV. 2. 7.
11.	iii. 266.	IV. 16. 24.
12.*	iii. 94-5.	IV. 7. 19, 20.
13.*	iii. 265-66, 269.	IV. 16. 23, 29.
14.*	ii. 185.	III. i. 3. 13.
15.	iii. 85.	IV. 7. 8.
16.	iii. 287-88.	IV. 17. 3.
17.	iii. 136-37.	IV. 10. 8.
18.ˣ	iv. 134-37.	V. 11. 8, 9.
19.*	iv. 353.	V. 20. 2.
20.*	iii. 2-3.	V. 1. 2, 3.

Section III.—Illustrative: The Sky.

21.*	i. 201.	II. iii. 1. 1, 2, 3
22.*	v. 140.	VII. 4. 6.
23.	i. 208.	II. iii. 1. 13.
24.*	{ v. 106-7-11	VII. i. 2, 3, 9.
	iv. 68-70.	V. 5. 2-5.
25.*	i. 258-60.	II. iii. 4. 31-4.
26.*	iv. 83-9.	V. 6. 2-9.

Section IV.—Illustrative: Streams and Sea.

27.	i. 320.	II. v. 1. 1.
28.	v. 139.	VII. 4. 5.
29.*	i. 343.	II. v. 2. 3.
30.*	iv. 139-41.	V. 12. 1, 2, 3.
31.*	i. 375.	II. v. 3. 38.

Section V.—Illustrative: Mountains.

32.*	iv. 90-100.	{ V. 7 except 5, 1st par. ; and 2nd par. of 9.
33.	i. 267.	II. iv. 1. 3.
34.**	iv. 120.	V. 9. 6.
35.*	iv. 169.	V. 13. 11-14.
36.*	iv. 126-27.	V. 10. 4, 5.
37.	iv. 244-46.	V. 16. 16, 17.

Section VI.—Illustrative: Stones.

38.	iv. 311.	V. 18. 6.
39.	iv. 295.	V. 17. 37-8.

40.	iii. 117.	IV. 9. 6.
41.	iv. 132.	V. 11. 6.
42.	iv. 129-30.	V. 11. 2.
43.	iv. 125.	V. 10. 3.
44.	iv. 324.	V. 18. 26.

Section VII.—Illustrative: Plants and Flowers.

45.	v. 3-4.	VI. 1. 34.
46.	v. 78.	VI. 8. 20.
47.*	v. 84-6.	VI. 9. 7-9.
48.	v. 89-90.	VI. 9. 15-16.
49.	i. 153-54.	II. ii. 2. 2.
50.	v. 94.	VI. 10. 7.
51.	v. 91-2.	VI. 10. 2, 3.
52.	iv. 46.	V. 3. 16.
53.	v. 109.	VII. i. 6.
54.*	{ i. 281.	I. iv. 2. 19.
	ii. 86.	III. i. 12. 1.
55.	ii. 104.	III. i. 13. 10, 11.
56.	iv. 100.	VI. 10. 18.
57.	iii. 230-33.	IV. 14. 51, 53.
58.	v. 102.	VI. 10. 24.
59.	v. 102-3.	VI. 10. 24.
60.	v. 103.	VI. 10. 25.

Section VIII.—Education.

61.	v. 332.	IX. 11. 20, 21.
62.	iii. 306.	IV. 17. 32.
63.*	iii. 308.	IV. 17. 34.
64.	iii. 300.	IV. 17. 24.
65.	v. 333-34.	IX. 11. 22.
66.	v. 329.	IX. 11. 15.
67.	iii. 295.	IV. 17. 13.
68.	iii. 309.	IV. 17. 35.
69.	iii. 2.	IV. 1. 2.
70.	iii. 333.	IV. 18. 32.
71.	i. 79.	II. i. 7. 8.
72.*	ii. 48-9.	III. i. 6. 2.
73.*	ii. 87.	III. i. 12. 2.
74.*	ii. 87.	III. i. 12. 2.
75.	iv. 310.	V. 18. 5.

Section IX.—Moralities.

76.*	v. 149.	VII. 4. 22.
77.	iii. 53-5.	IV. 4. 16.
78.	ii. 123-24.	III. i. 14. 27.
79.	ii. 135-36.	III. i. 15. 11.
80.	ii. 112.	III. i. 14. 5.
81.	ii. 113.	III. i. 14. 9.
82.	ii. 114.	III. i. 14. 10.
83.	ii. 63.	III. i. 7. 1.
84.	i. 6.	I. i. 1. 5.
85.	ii. 68.	III. i. 7. 7.
86.	iv. 326.	V. 19. 3, 4.
87.*	v. 210-11.	IX. 2. 11.
88.	i. xxxvii-viii.	{ I. pref. to 2nd edition.
89.	iv. 365.	VI. 20. 18.
90.	iv. 387-end.	V. 20. 45-end.

NOTES

NOTES TO VOLUME I

Preface to the Second Edition (1844).

P. xvii, § 9, line 19, "conception of their being excelled," eds. 2, 3, 4 add a note as follows :—"One or two fragments of Greek sculpture, the works of Michael Angelo, considered with reference to their general conception and power, and the Madonna di San Sisto, are all that I should myself put into such a category ; not that even these are without defect, but their defects are such as mortality could never hope to rectify."

P. xviii, § 10, last line, note, "various and multitudinous," eds. 2 and 3 add, "'Vice,' says Byron, in *Marino Faliero*, 'must have variety ; but Virtue stands like the sun, and all which rolls around drinks life from her aspect.'"

P. xxii, § 13, line 5, "its consequences," eds. 2 and 3 add, "How long must art and its interests sink, when the public mind is inadequate to the detection of this effrontery of incapacity ! In all kindness," etc.

P. xxx, § 23, eds. 2, 3, 4 omit the foot-note.

P. xliii, § 38, line 22, for "solitary," ed. 2 reads, "neglected."

P. xliv, § 39, note, line 6, "saint-worship, deprives," eds. 2, 3, and 4 read, "saint-worship, excommunicates himself from all benefit of the Church, and deprives," etc.

P. xliv, § 39, note, line 16, for "so ludicrous . . . conveys," eds. 2 and 3 read, "so laughable and lamentable, that they are at once, on all, and to all, students of the gallery a satire and a warning."

P. xlix, § 45, end, "indifference to him," ed. 2 (only) adds the following note :—"The disadvantageous prominence given in some of the following pages to Mr. Maclise, was entirely owing to my knowing him to have many friends, and multitudinous admirers, and to my feeling that were his powers exerted in a right direction, he might infinitely elevate and advance our school of art. I am sorry for the harshness with which I have spoken, for it has hurt the feelings of many for whose judgment I have the most true respect ; but I have not cancelled the passage because I have not altered my opinion. I cannot help feeling that there is, in many of the creations of Maclise's imagination, a strange character of savage recklessness, which, however striking, animated, and impressive in characters to which it properly belongs, is grievously out of place in anything approaching to ideal subject. I may be entirely wrong in this feeling, but so long as it remains unchanged, I cannot refrain from beseeching Mr. Maclise to devote his vivid imagination and vigorous powers of hand to creations of more tenderness, repose, and dignity ; and above all, not to condescend, capable as he is of kindling his canvas with life, and stamping it with character, to spend his time in imitating the sparkle of wine-glasses, and elaborating the fractures of nutshells."

Preface to the Third Edition (1846), omitted in all other editions.

" It is with much regret, and partly against my own judgment, that I republish the following chapters in their present form. The particular circumstances (stated in the first preface) under which they were originally written, have rendered them so unfit for the position they now hold, as introductory to a serious examination of the general functions of art, that I should have wished first to complete the succeeding portions of the essay, and then to write another introduction of more fitting character. But as it may be long before I am able to do this, and as I believe what I have already written may still be of some limited and practical service, I have suffered it to re-appear, trusting to the kindness of the reader to look to its intention rather than its temper, and forgive its inconsideration in its earnestness.

" Thinking it of too little substance to bear mending, wherever I have found a passage which I thought required modification or explanation, I have cut it out ; what I have left, however imperfect, cannot, I think, be dangerously misunderstood : something I have added, not under the idea of rendering the work in any wise systematic or complete, but to supply gross omissions, answer inevitable objections, and give some substance to passages of mere declamation.

"Whatever inadequacy or error there may be, throughout, in materials or modes of demonstration, I have no doubt of the truth and necessity of the main result ; and though the reader may, perhaps, find me frequently hereafter showing other and better grounds for what is here affirmed, yet the point and bearing of the book, its determined depreciation of Claude, Salvator, Gaspar, and Canaletto, and its equally determined support of Turner, as the greatest of all landscape painters, and of Turner's recent works as his finest, are good and right ; and if the prevalence throughout of attack and eulogium be found irksome or offensive, let it be remembered that my object thus far has not been either the establishment or the teaching of any principles of art, but the vindication, most necessary to the prosperity of our present schools, of the uncomprehended rank of their greatest artist, and the diminution, equally necessary, as I think, to the prosperity of our schools, of the unadvised admiration of the landscape of the seventeenth century. For I believe it to be almost impossible to state in terms sufficiently serious and severe the depth and extent of the evil which has resulted (and that not in art alone, but in all matters with which the contemplative faculties are concerned) from the works of those elder men. On the Continent, all landscape art has been utterly annihilated by them, and with it all sense of the power of nature. We in England have only done better because our artists have had strength of mind enough to form a school withdrawn from their influence.

"The points are somewhat farther developed in the general sketch of ancient and modern landscape which I have added to the first section of the second part. Some important additions have also been made to the chapters on the painting of the sea. Throughout the rest of the text, though something is withdrawn, little is changed; and the reader may rest assured that if I were now to bestow on this feeble essay the careful revision which it much needs, but little deserves, it would not be to alter its tendencies, or modify its conclusions, but to prevent indignation from appearing virulence on the one side, and enthusiasm partizanship on the other."

Preface to New Edition (1873), omitted in later edition.

" I have been lately so often asked by friends on whose judgment I can rely, to permit the publication of another edition of 'Modern Painters' in its original form, that I have at last yielded, though with some violence to my own feelings; for many parts of the first and second volumes are written in a narrow enthusiasm, and the substance of their metaphysical and religious speculation is only justifiable on the ground of its absolute honesty. Of third, fourth, and fifth volumes, I indeed mean eventually to rearrange what I think of permanent interest for the complete edition of my works, but with fewer and less elaborate illustrations; nor have I any serious grounds for refusing to allow the book once more to appear in the irregular form which it took as it was written, since of the art-teaching and landscape descriptions it contains I have little to retrench, and nothing to retract.

"This final edition must, however, be limited to a thousand copies, for some of the more delicate plates are already worn—that of the Mill Stream in the fifth volume, and of the Loire Side very injuriously; while that of the Shores of Wharfe had to be retouched by an engraver after the removal of the mezzotint for reprinting. But Mr. Armytage's, Mr. Cousens', and Mr. Cuff's magnificent plates are still in good state; and my own etchings, though injured, are still good enough to answer their purpose.

"I sign with my own hand this preface to every copy, thus certifying it as containing the best impressions of the original plates now producible, and belonging to the last edition of the book in its complete form.

"JOHN RUSKIN."

[Autograph.]

P. 4 (i. 1, 1, 1),* note, three lines from end, for "Orcagna, Angelico," eds. 1 and 2 read, "Cimabue, Fra Bartolomeo."

P. 6 (i. 1, 1, 4), line nineteen, "imagination. And let it be understood," etc., ed. 1 runs thus, "imagination. And let it be that in all

* These numbers refer to part, section, chapter, and paragraph.

questions respecting the art of the fourteenth and fifteenth centuries, we ought not to class the historical and landscape painters together, as possessing anything like equal rank in their respective walks of art. It is because I look with the most devoted veneration upon M. Angelo, Raffaelle, and Da Vinci, that I do not distrust the principles which induce me to look with contempt on Claude, Salvator, and Gaspar Poussin. Had I disliked all, I should have believed in and bowed before all; but in my admiration of the greater, I consider myself as having warrant for the repudiation of the less. I feel assured that they cannot with reason be admired together,—that the principles of art on which they worked are totally opposed, and that the landscape painters of the old school have been honoured only because they had in them a shadow and semblance of the manner of the nobler historical painters, whose principles in all points they directly reversed. But be this as it may, let it be understood . . ."

P. 11 (i. 1, 2, 7), twelve lines from end, "polished into inanity," eds. 1 and 2 insert, "A pencil scratch of Wilkie's on the back of a letter is a great and a better picture—and I use the term picture in its full sense—than the most laboured and luminous canvas that ever left the easel of Gerard Dow. A finished," etc.

P. 15 (i. 1, 3, 2), eds. 1–4 omit the foot-note referring to "The Stones of Venice."

P. 15 (i. 1, 3, 3), eds. 1 and 2 omit from marginal note the words, "The meaning of the word 'excellence.'"

P. 20 (i. 1, 4, 2), eds. 1 and 2 omit the foot-note reference to Aristotle; while ed. 3 adds to it the quotation, "συλλογισμός ἐστιν, ὅτι τοῦτο ἐκεῖνο," omitted in eds. 4 et seqq.

P. 21 (i. 1, 4, 3), four lines from end, for "were the hero or his horse," eds. 1 and 2 read, "be a Madonna or a lemon-peel."

P. 21 (i. 1, 4, 4), six lines from end, after "sensual pleasure," eds. 1 and 2 add, "and one precisely of the same order and degree, whether it be received from the bristles of a boar or the tears of a Magdalen."

P. 27 (i. 1, 5, 5), "This gentleman . . . projection," eds. 1 and 2 read, "Had I wished to know if the anatomy of the limbs was faithfully marked —if their colour was truly expressive of light, and beautiful in itself—if the composition of the picture was perfect, or its conception great—I might as well have inquired of one of the Flanders mares in the stable at the Fleur de Blé, as of this gentleman. He could only . . . projection."

P. 36 (i. 2, 1, 3), "in the other felt," eds. 1 and 2 continue, "Supposing ourselves even capable of ascertaining in our own persons the truth of what is often by sculptors affirmed of the Laocoon, that the knowledge developed in it must have taken a lifetime to accumulate, we should yet scarcely receive from that statue the same sensation of power with which we are at once impressed by him who hurled the mighty prostration of the limbs of the Jonah along the arch of the Sistine."

[This is the reference to M. Angelo mentioned in § 4, and made unintelligible in later editions by the omission of this sentence.]

P. 38 (i. 2, 1, 8), "The power involved . . . enduring." In eds. 1 and 2 this sentence ran thus:—" The power involved in such a picture, and the ideas and pleasures following on the estimate of it, are unquestionably far higher than can legitimately be traced in, or received from the works of any other mere water-colour master now living."

P. 43 (i. 2, 2, 9), foot-note, line 6 from end, " such, on the other hand, the softness," etc. In eds. 1 and 2 this is as follows:—" Such is every effort on the part of the engraver to give roughness or direction of surface by wriggling or peculiarly directed lines, and such the softness and smoothness which are the great attraction of Carlo Dolci. These are the exhibitions of particular powers and tricks of the hand and fingers, in total forgetfulness of any end whatsoever to be attained thereby, and would scarcely deserve the pains of criticism were it not for the unreasonable delusion that makes even men of taste and feeling suppose that to be right in an engraving, which they would cry out against as detestable and intolerable in a drawing. How long are our engravers to be allowed to go on murdering the foreground of our great artists, twisting and wriggling and hatching and scratching over the smooth stones and glossy leaves, until St. Laurence's gridiron is a jest to the martyrdom of the eye, 'making out' everything that the artist intentionally concealed, and smothering everything that he made refined or conspicuous? When shall we have an engraver who will touch his steel as if he had fingers and feeling?"

P. 46 (i. 2, 3, 6), for "originators of just thought," eds. 1 and 2 read, "originators of new and just thought; as it is new, leading us to observe the powers of fancy and imagination; as it is just, the force of moral truth."

P. 48 (ii. 1, 1, 3), "crown of the connoisseur," eds. 1 and 2 continue, "and of those 'standard' pictures with which half the walls of Europe are covered, and for the manufacture of which recipes are to be found in most works on art. 'Take one-eighth light, three-eighths middle tint, four-eighths shadow; mix carefully, flavour with cochineal, cool with ultramarine, and serve up sentiment.' Nay, even where a high ideal has been sought for, the search seldom produces more than one good picture, on which a few clever but monotonous changes are rung by the artist himself, and innumerable discords by his imitators, ending in the multiplication *ad nauseam* of the legitimate landscape ragout, composed of a large tree, a bridge, a city, a river, and a fisherman."

P. 51 (ii. 1, 1, 7). The note referring to "The Stones of Venice" was added in ed. 5.

P. 79 (ii. 1, 7, 2), line 11, "judgment of art. It is strange, that . . . ," eds. 1 and 2 read, "judgment of art. We have no eye for colour—we perceive no intention in composition—we do not know anything about form —we cannot estimate excellence—we do not care for beauty—but we know whether it deceives. It is a strange thing that . . ."

P. 80 (ii. 1, 7, 3), "Cuyp, . . . but he has no sense of beauty," eds. 1 and 2 read, "Cuyp, . . . but then he has not the slightest idea of the meaning of the word 'beautiful.'"

P. 80 (ii. 1, 7, 4), line 6, "mind of the spectator," eds. 1 and 2 read, "spectator, and chiefly of forcing upon his feelings those delicate and refined truths of specific form, which are just what the careless eye can least detect or enjoy, because they are intended by the Deity to be the constant objects of our investigation that they may be the constant sources of our pleasure."

P. 81 (ii. 1, 7, 5), "supported on a stick instead of a trunk." Almost all the rest of this chapter (§§ 5-47) was not included in eds. 1 and 2, which contained instead briefer passages §§ 6-11 as follows :—

"[§ 6. And with the feeling of modern artists.] Who, that has one spark of feeling for what is beautiful or true, would not turn to be refreshed by the pure and extended realizations of modern art! How many have we —how various in their aim and sphere—embracing one by one every feeling and lesson of the creation ! David Cox, whose pencil never falls but in dew—simple-minded as a child, gentle, and loving all things that are pure and lowly, content to lie quiet among the rustling leaves, and sparkling grass, and purple-cushioned heather, only to watch the soft white clouds melting with their own motion, and the dewy blue dropping through them like rain, so that he may but cast from him as pollution all that is proud, and artificial, and unquiet, and worldly, and possess his spirit in humility and peace. Copley Fielding, casting his whole soul into space—exulting like a wild deer in the motion of the swift mists, and the free far surfaces of the untrodden hills—now wandering with the quick, pale, fitful sun-gleams over the dim swells and sweeps of grey downs and shadowy dingles, until, lost half in light and half in vapour, they melt into the blue of the plain as the cloud does into the sky—now climbing with the purple sunset along the aerial slopes of the quiet mountains, only known from the red clouds by their stillness—now flying with the wild wind and sifted spray along the white, driving, desolate sea ; but always with the passion for nature's freedom burning in his heart, so that every leaf in his foreground is a wild one, and every line of his hills is limitless. J. D. Harding, brilliant and vigorous, and clear in light as nature's own sunshine —deep in knowledge, exquisite in feeling of every form that nature falls into —following with his quick, keen dash the sunlight into the crannies of the rocks, and the wind into the tangling of the grass, and the bright colour into the fall of the sea-foam—various, universal in his aim—master alike of all form and feature of crag, or torrent, or forest, or cloud ; but English, all English at his heart, returning still to rest under the shade of some spreading elm, where the fallow deer butt among the bending fern, and the quiet river glides noiselessly by its reedy shore, and the yellow corn sheaves glow along the flanks of the sloping hills. Clarkson Stanfield, firm and fearless, and unerring in his knowledge—stern and decisive in his truth—perfect and certain in composition—shunning nothing, concealing nothing, and falsifying nothing—never affected, never morbid, never failing—conscious of his strength, but never ostentatious of it—acquainted with every line and hue of the deep sea—chiselling his waves with unhesitating knowledge of every curve of their anatomy, and every moment of their motion—building his mountains rock by rock, with wind in every fissure and weight in every stone—and modelling the masses of his sky with the strength of tempest in their every fold. And Turner—glorious in conception—unfathomable in knowledge—solitary in power—with the elements waiting upon his will, and the night and the morning obedient to his call, sent as a prophet of God to reveal to men the mysteries of His universe, standing, like the great angel of the Apocalypse, clothed with a cloud, and with a rainbow upon his head, and with the sun and stars given into his hand."

"[§ 7. The character of Venice as given by Canaletti.] But I must not anticipate my subject—what I have asserted must be proved by deliberate investigation of facts, and in no way left dependent on feeling or imagination. Yet I may, perhaps, before proceeding into detail, illustrate my meaning more completely by a comparison of the kind of truths impressed upon us in the painting of Venice by Canaletti, Prout, Stanfield, and Turner.

"The effect of a fine Canaletti is, in its first impression, dioramic. We fancy we are in our beloved Venice again, with one foot, by mistake, in the clear, invisible film of water lapping over the marble steps of the foreground. Every house has its proper relief against the sky—every brick and stone its proper hue of sunlight and shade—and every degree of distance its proper tone of retiring air. Presently, however, we begin to feel that it is lurid and gloomy, and that the painter, compelled by the lowness of the utmost light at his disposal to deepen the shadows, in order to get the right relation, has lost the flashing, dazzling, exulting light, which was one of our chief sources of Venetian happiness. But we pardon this, knowing it to be unavoidable, and begin to look for something of that in which Venice differs from Rotterdam, or any other city built beside canals. We know that house, certainly; we never passed it without stopping our gondolier, for its arabesques were as rich as a bank of flowers in spring, and as beautiful as a dream. What has Canaletti given us for them? Five black dots. Well; take the next house. We remember that too; it was mouldering inch by inch into the canal, and the bricks had fallen away from its shattered marble shafts, and left them white and skeleton-like; yet, with their fretwork of cold flowers wreathed about them still, untouched by time, and through the rents of the wall behind them there used to come long sunbeams, greened by the weeds through which they pierced, which flitted and fell, one by one, round those grey and quiet shafts, catching here a leaf and there a leaf and gliding over the illumined edges and delicate fissures, until they sank into the deep dark hollow between the marble blocks of the sunk foundation, lighting every other moment one isolated emerald lamp on the crest of the intermittent waves, when the wild sea-weeds and crimson lichens drifted

and crawled with their thousand colours and fine branches over its deca
and the black, clogging, accumulated limpets hung in ropy clusters from
the dripping and tinkling stone. What has Canaletti given us for this?
One square red mass, composed of—let me count—five-and-fifty, no; six-
and-fifty, no; I was right at first—five-and-fifty bricks, of precisely the
same size, shape, and colour, one great black line for the shadow of the
roof at the top, and six similar ripples in a row at the bottom! And this
is what people call 'painting nature'! It is, indeed, painting nature—as
she appears to the most unfeeling and untaught of mankind. The
bargeman and the bricklayer probably see no more in Venice than Canaletti gives—heaps of earth and mortar, with water between—and are just
as capable of appreciating the facts of sunlight and shadow, by which he
deceives us, as the most educated of us all. But what more there is in
Venice than brick and stone—what there is of mystery and death, and
memory and beauty—what there is to be learned or lamented, to be loved
or wept—we look for to Canaletti in vain.

   "[§ 8. By Prout.] Let us pass to Prout. The imitation is lost at once.
The buildings have nothing resembling their real relief against the sky;
there are multitudes of false distances; the shadows in many places have
a great deal more Vandyke-brown than darkness in them; and the lights
very often more yellow-ochre than sunshine. But yet the effect on our eye
is that very brilliancy and cheerfulness which delighted us in Venice itself,
and there is none of that oppressive and lurid gloom which was cast upon
our feelings by Canaletti.* And now we feel there is something in the
subject worth drawing, and different from other subjects and architecture.
That house is rich, and strange, and full of grotesque carving and character—that one next to it is shattered and infirm, and varied with picturesque rents and hues of decay—that farther off is beautiful in proportion,
and strong in its purity of marble. Now we begin to feel that we are in
Venice; this is what we could not get elsewhere; it is worth seeing, and
drawing, and talking and thinking of,—not an exhibition of common
daylight or brick walls. But let us look a little closer; we know those
capitals very well; their design was most original and perfect, and so
delicate that it seemed to have been cut in ivory;—what have we got for
them here? Five straight strokes of a reed pen! No, Mr. Prout, it is not
quite Venice yet.

   "[§ 9. By Stanfield.] Let us take Stanfield then. Now we are farther

---

   * "It will be observed how completely I cast aside all mere *mechanical* excellence as unworthy of praise. Canaletti's *mechanism* is wonderful,—Prout's, the
rudest possible; but there is not a grain of feeling in the one, and there is much in
the other. In spite of all that can be alleged of the mannerism and imperfections of
Prout as an artist, there is that in his drawings which will bring us back to them
again and again, even after we have been rendered most fastidious by the exquisite
drawing and perfect composition of the accomplished Roberts. There is an appreciation of realization of continental character in his works—a locality and life which
have never yet been reached by any other of our architectural draughtsmen—and
they are the sign of deep feeling and high genius, by whatever faults of manner
they may be attained or accompanied; and we shall think ourselves in danger of
losing our right feeling for art, and for nature too, when we find ourselves unable to
turn occasionally from the refined grace of Roberts, and the absolute truth of
Stanfield, to linger with Prout on the sunny side of a Flemish street, watching the
fantastic peaks of its gables in the sky, and listening for the clatter of the sabot."

still from anything like Venetian tone; all is cold and comfortless, but there is air and good daylight, and we will not complain. And now let us look into the buildings, and all is perfection and fidelity; every shade and line full of feeling and truth, rich and solid, and substantial stone; every leaf and arabesque marked to its minutest curve and angle; the marble crumbling, the wood mouldering, and the waves splashing and lapping before our eyes. But it is all drawn hard and sharp, there is nothing to hope for or find out, nothing to dream of or discover; we can measure and see it from base to battlement, there is nothing too fine for us to follow, nothing too full for us to fathom. This cannot be nature, for it is not infinity. No, Mr. Stanfield, it is scarcely Venice yet.

"[§ 10. By Turner.] But let us take, with Turner, the last and greatest step of all. Thank heaven, we are in sunshine again,—and what sunshine! Not the lurid, gloomy, plague-like oppression of Canaletti, but white, flashing fulness of dazzling light, which the waves drink and the clouds breathe, bounding and burning in intensity of joy. That sky,—it is a very visible infinity,—liquid, measureless, unfathomable, panting and melting through the chasms in the long fields of snow-white, flaked, slow-moving vapour, that guide the eye along their multitudinous waves down the islanded rest of the Euganean hills. Do we dream, or does the white forked sail drift nearer, and nearer yet, diminishing the blue sea between us with the fulness of its wings? It pauses now; but the quivering of its bright reflection troubles the shadows of the sea, those azure, fathomless depths of crystal mystery, on which the swiftness of the poised gondola floats double, its black beak lifted like the crest of a dark ocean bird, its scarlet draperies flashed back from the kindling surface, and its bent oar breaking the radiant water into a dust of gold. Dream-like and dim, but glorious, the unnumbered palaces lift their shafts out of the hollow sea,—pale ranks of motionless flame,—their mighty towers sent up to heaven like tongues of more eager fire,—their grey domes looming vast and dark, like eclipsed worlds,—their sculptured arabesques and purple marbles fading farther and fainter, league beyond league, lost in the light of distance. Detail after detail, thought beyond thought, you find and feel them through the radiant mystery, inexhaustible as indistinct, beautiful, but never all revealed; secret in fulness, confused in symmetry, as nature herself is to the bewildered and foiled glance, giving out of that indistinctness, and through that confusion, the perpetual newness of the infinite, and the beautiful.

"Yes, Mr. Turner, we are in Venice now.

"[§ 11. The system to be observed in comparing works with reference to truth.] I think the above example may, at least, illustrate my meaning, and render clear the distinction which I wish the reader always to keep in mind, between those truths which are selected as a means of deception, and those which are selected for their own sake. How few of the latter are usually given by the old masters, I shall proceed to show; but in so doing I shall not take particular instances of local character like the above, but shall confine myself to those general truths of nature which are common to all countries and times, and which are independent of local or national characters, partly because the works of the old masters are for the most part intended not to be particular portraiture, but ideal or general nature; and partly because the representation of the local character of scenery will more properly be considered under the head of ideas of relation, as it necessarily bears the same relation to ideal landscape which the representation of individual character does to that of the ideal human form, animated by its perfect and generic mind. At present, therefore, I leave out of the question all consideration of peculiar and local character, though, in doing so, I omit one of the chief and most essential qualities of truth in at least one-half of the works of our greatest modern master, and I am content to take that which is universal in the moderns, and compare it with that which is suffered to be universal in the ancients. And when we have investigated the nature and desirableness of ideas of relation, we will take up those parts of the works of both schools which are local, and observe how the knowledge of specific character is used to awaken and direct the current of particular thought. In the execution of our immediate task, we shall be compelled to notice only a few of the most striking and demonstrable facts of nature. To trace out the actual sum of truth or falsehood in any one work, touch by touch, would require an essay on every department of physical science, and then a chapter to every inch of canvas. All that can be done is to take the broad principles and laws of nature, and show, in one or two conspicuous instances, where they have been observed, and where violated, and so to leave the reader to find out for himself how the observation and violation have been continued in every part, and down to the most delicate touches. I can do little more than suggest the right train of thought and mode of observation; to carry it fully out must be left to the feeling and the industry of the observer. [§ 12. Difficulty of demonstration in such subjects.] And as some apology for the most inadequate execution even of what I have here attempted, it should be considered how difficult . . . ." [See now p. 137].

P. 86 (ii. 1, 7, 9), note, for "was perhaps thinking . . . like manna," eds. 3 and 4 read, briefly, "had, I imagine, a view also to its chemical property."

P. 92 (ii. 1, 7, 12). The note referring to "The Stones of Venice" was added in ed. 5.

P. 96 (ii. 1, 7, 15). The quotation in the note was placed in eds. 3 and 4 in the body of the text, after the words "imitative truth in it."

P. 97 (ii. 1, 7, 15), ed. 3 omitted the words "and in one in the Louvre . . . appears in another."

P. 108 (ii. 1, 7, 24), "colour and texture; but partly," eds. 3 and 4 read, "colour and texture; a large drawing in the possession of B. G. Windus, Esq., of Tottenham, is of great value as an example of his manner at the period; a manner not only careful, but earnest, and free from any kind of affectation. Partly . . . ."

P. 119 (ii. 1, 7, 31), line 22, for "I remember Mackenzie, and Haghe," eds. 3 and 4 read, "I have Mackenzie in my eye."

Pp. 121 and 130 (ii. 1, 7, 32 and 37). The note referring to "The Stones of Venice" was added in ed. 5.

P. 130 (ii. 1, 7, 37), lines 2 and 4 from foot, for "Nicolo," ed. 3 reads, "Nino."

P. 134 (ii. 1, 7, 39), for "examples, as well as some of the drawings . . . of Farnley," eds. 3 and 4 read, "examples. The most perfect gem in execution is a little bit on the Rhine, with reeds in the foreground, in the possession of B. G. Windus, Esq., of Tottenham; but the Yorkshire drawings seem to be, on the whole, the most noble representatives of his art at this period."

P. 137 (ii. 1, 7, 41), line 21, for "of the drawings above alluded to . . . my present space," eds. 3 and 4 read, "The Valley of Chamounix, in the collection of Walter Fawkes, Esq., I have never seen; it has a high reputation." And in line 27, for "berg," eds. 3 and 4 read, "land."

P. 141 (ii. 1, 7, 44), eds. 3 and 4 omit italics and foot-note.

P. 146 (ii. 1, 7, 46), line 3, "to the exhibition of them . . . Benedetto," eds. 3 and 4 read, at greater length, "to the exhibition of them. But his powers did not attain their highest results till towards the year 1840, about which period they did so suddenly, and with a vigour and concentration which rendered his pictures at that time almost incomparable with those which had preceded them. The drawings of Nemi, and Oberwesel, in the possession of B. G. Windus, Esq., were among the first evidences of this sudden advance; only the foliage in both these is inferior; and it is remarkable that in this phase of his art, Turner has drawn little foliage, and that little badly—the great characteristic of it being its power, beauty, and majesty of colour, and its abandonment of all littleness and division of thought to a single impression. In the year 1842 he made some drawings from recent sketches in Switzerland; these, with some produced in the following years, all of Swiss subjects, I consider to be, on the whole, the most characteristic and perfect works he has ever produced. The Academy pictures were far inferior to them, but among these, examples of the same power were not wanting, more especially in the modern pictures of Venice, the Sun of Venice, going to Sea, the San Benedetto."

P. 147 (ii. 1, 7, 47), after the end of the last paragraph but one ("concluding section"), eds. 1 and 2 add a further paragraph:—
"It would be needless, after having explained a given truth, to repeat the same phrases, 'observe it here' or 'trace it there,' with respect to all the works in which it may happen to occur. I shall illustrate each truth from the works of the artist by whom I find it most completely and constantly given; commonly, therefore, from those of the father of modern art, J. M. W. Turner, and I shall then name the other artists in whom its faithful rendering is also deserving of praise."
To the last paragraph eds. 1 and 2 add marginal note, "§ 13. General plan of investigation," and at its close the words, "Architecture will be slightly noticed in the concluding section of the present part; more fully in the following parts of the work."

P. 155 (ii. 2, 1, 12), after "intense fire of summer noon," eds. 1 and 2 add, "The Cowes, Devonport with the Dockyard, Colchester, Okehampton,

Folkestone, Cologne, Kenilworth, Durham, and Dudley might be instanced as cases of every effect of the most refined and precious tone, which we might fearlessly, if not triumphantly, compare with the very finest works of the old masters. And the difference," etc.

P. 156 (ii. 2, 1, 13), line 6 from end, for "shall find few pictures . . . which do," eds. 1 and 2 read, "shall not find a single . . . which does."

P. 158 (ii. 2, 1, 18), eds. 1 and 2 omit the foot-note.

P. 162 (ii. 2, 1, 21), eds. 1 and 2 begin this section, "I do not doubt the comparison."

P. 164 (ii. 2, 2, 1), eds. 1 and 2 insert a further paragraph at the beginning of this chapter as follows :—

"[§ 1. Incompetence of the later critics of Turner's colour.] There is nothing so high in art but that a scurrile jest can reach it, and often, the greater the work, the easier it is to turn it into ridicule. To appreciate the science of Turner's colour would require the study of a life, but to laugh at it requires little more than the knowledge that yolk of egg is yellow and spinage green—a fund of critical information on which the remarks of most of our leading periodicals have been of late years exclusively based. We shall, however, in spite of the sulphur and treacle criticisms of our Scotch connoisseurs, and the eggs and spinage of our English ones, endeavour to test the works of this great colourist by a knowledge of nature somewhat more extensive than is to be gained by an acquaintance, however familiar, with the apothecary's shop, or the dinner-table."

P. 169 (ii. 2, 2, 5), line 21, after "by local falsehood" ed. 1 continues, "It is quite true that in this particular department of art, colour, one error may often be concealed by another, and one falsehood made to look right, by cleverly matching another to it; but that only enables us to be certain, that when we have proved one colour to be false, if it looks right, there must be something else to keep it in countenance, and so we have proved two falsehoods instead of one. And indeed truth is only," etc.

P. 169 (ii. 2, 2, 5), ed. 1 omits the last paragraph of this section, "Whatever depth . . . σκιᾷ."

P. 174 (ii. 2, 2, 10, end), for "do not ask . . . enjoy," eds. 1 and 2 read, "do not talk about truth."

P. 175 (*ib.* 12), lines 14–17, for "But I have . . . sudden streak," eds. 1 and 2 read, "Whenever therefore I see anything attributed to him artistically wrong, or testifying a want of knowledge of nature, or of feeling for colour, I become instantly incredulous; and if ever I advance anything . . . affirmed to be his as such, it is not so much under the idea that it can be his, as to show what a great name can impose upon the public. The landscape I speak of has, beyond a doubt, high qualities in it; I can scarcely make up my mind whether to like it or not, but at any rate it is something which the public are in the habit of admiring and taking upon trust to any extent. Now the sudden streak . . ."

P. 176 (*ib.* 13), line 11 from foot, eds. 1 and 2 number this paragraph "[§ 15. His great tenderness in all large spaces of colour"] and begin it as follows :—" And it is, perhaps, herein that the chief beauty, excellence, and truth of Turner's colour, as distinguished from the absurd, futile, and fatal efforts which have been made to imitate it, chiefly lies. For Nature, in the same way, never uses raw colour ; there is a tenderness and sub- dued tone about her purest hues, and a warmth, glow, and light in her soberest. It is instructive . . ."

P. 177 (*ib.* 13, end), eds. 1 and 2 conclude this paragraph thus : "ultra- marine ; skies, in which the raw, meaningless colour is shaded steadily and perseveringly down, passing through the pink into the yellow as a young lady shades her worsted, to the successful production of a very handsome oil-cloth, but certainly not of a picture.
" But throughout . . ."

P. 179 (*ib.* 16, end), eds. 1 and 2 conclude this paragraph thus : ". . . stone ; while no artist, dead or living, has ever attained the constant and perfect realization of the great principle of nature—that there shall be nothing without change : with him, and with him only, every individual stroke of the brush has in itself gradations and degrees of colour ; and a visible space of monotony is a physical impossibility. Every part is abundant and perfect in itself, though still a member of the great whole ; and every square inch contains in itself a system of colour and light, as complete, as studied, and as wonderful as the great arrangement of that to which it is subordinate.
" What I am about," etc.

P. 181 (*ib.* 19, end), eds. 1 and 2 here proceed with a considerable additional passage as follows : " . . . colour is based, but it would be absurd at present to occupy more time with so inexhaustible a subject ; the colour of these inimitable drawings must be considered when we examine them individually, not separated from what it illustrates. Taken generally, the chief characteristics of Turner's colour, whether in drawings or paintings, considered only with respect to truth, and without reference to composition or beauty, of which at present we can take no cognizance, are those above pointed out, which we shall briefly recapitulate.
" [§ 22. The perfection and importance of his greys. Recapitulation.] 1. Prevalence, variety, value, and exquisite composition of greys. The grey tones are, in the drawings especially, the most wonderful as well as the most valuable portions of the whole picture. Some of the very first-rate drawings are merely harmonies of different kinds of grey : ' Longships Lighthouse, Land's End,' for instance. Several appear to have been drawn entirely with modulated greys first, and then sparingly heightened with colour on the lights ; but whatever the subject, and however brilliant the effect, the grey tones are the foundation of all its beauty.
" 2. Refinement, delicacy, and uncertainty in all colours whatsoever. Positive colour is, as I before said, the rarest thing imaginable in Turner's works, and the exquisite refinement with which variety of hue is carried

into his feeblest tints is altogether unparalleled in art. The drawing of Colchester, in the England series, is an example of this delicacy and fulness of tint together, with which nothing but nature can be compared. But I have before me while I write a drawing of the most vigorous and powerful colour, with concentrated aerial blue opposed to orange and crimson. I should have fancied at a little distance, that a cake of ultramarine had been used pure upon it. But, when I look close, I discover that all which looks blue in effect is in reality a changeful grey, with black and green in it, and bluer tones breaking through here and there more or less decisively, but without one grain or touch of pure blue in the whole picture, except on a figure in the foreground, nor one grain, nor touch of any colour whatsoever, of which it is possible to say what it is, or how many are united in it. Such will invariably be found the case, even with the most brilliant and daring of Turner's systems of colour.

"3. Dislike of purpose, and fondness for opposition of yellow and black, or clear blue and white.

"[§ 23 (as § 20 in later editions).] 4. Entire subjection of the whole system of colour to that of chiaroscuro. I have not before noticed this, because I wished to show how true and faithful Turner's colour is, as such, without reference to any associated principles. But the perfection and consummation of its truth rests in its subordination to light and shade—a subordination . . ."

P. 182 (ii. 2, 2, 20), line 3, eds. 1 and 2 omit the foot-note.

P. 182 (ii. 2, 2, 20), line 5, for "Were it necessary," eds. 1, 2, 3, and 4 read, "He paints in colour, but he thinks in light and shade; and were it necessary."

P. 183 (ii. 2, 2, 20), line 8, "deserved disgrace. With him the hue," eds. 1 and 2 continue, "For no colour can be beautiful, unless it is subordinate; it cannot take the lead without perishing—in superseding the claims of other excellences, it annihilates its own. To say that the chief excellence of a picture is its colour, is to say that its colour is imperfect. In all truly great painters, and in Turner more than all, the hue."

Eds. 3 and 4 read here, "deserved disgrace. With him, as with all the greatest painters, and in Turner more than all, the hue."

Ib., *ib.*, line 10, for "the chief source," eds. 1, 2, 3, and 4 read, "the source nor the essence."

P. 184 (ii. 2, 3, 1), line 4, for "we speak of these. At present," eds. 1 and 2 read, "we speak of them—we must not bring their poetry and their religion down to optics. I cannot watch the sun descending on Sinai, or stand in the starry twilight by the gates of Bethlehem, and begin talking of refraction and polarization. It is your heart that must be the judge here—if you do not *feel* the light, you will not see it. When, therefore, I have proved to you what is beautiful, and what God intended to give pleasure to your spirit in its purity, we will come to Turner as the painter of light—for so emphatically he should be called—and, picture by picture, we will trace at once the truth and the intention.

"But at present . . ."

P. 191 (ii. 2, 3, 9), line 13, "able to manufacture," eds. 1 and 2 read, "able to paint lanterns and candles, the principle here laid down is exceedingly correct; or if it means being able to manufacture."

P. 193 (ii. 2, 3, 11), line 8, eds. 1–4 read, "her great rule, to give precisely the same quantity of deepest shade which she does of highest light, and no more; points . . ."

P. 194 (ii. 2, 3, 13), eds. 1 and 2 insert between § 12 and § 13 of the later editions the following passages :—

"[§ 13. General falsehood of the old masters in this respect.] Now observe how totally the old masters lost truth in this respect by their vicious trickery in trying to gain tone. They were glad enough to isolate their lights, indeed; but they did even this artificially, joining them impercep-tibly, as Reynolds says, with the shadows, and so representing, not a point of illuminated objects on which light strikes and is gone, but a lantern in the picture, spreading rays around it, and out of it. And then to gain the deceptive relief of material objects against extended lights, as noticed in Chapter I. of this section, § 4, they were compelled to give vast spaces of deep shadow, and so entirely lost the power of giving the points of dark-ness. Thus the whole balance of every one of their pictures is totally destroyed, and their composition as thoroughly false in chiaroscuro, as if they had given us no shade at all, because one member, and that the most important of the shadows of the landscape, is totally omitted. Take the Berghem, No. 132, Dulwich Gallery, which is a most studied piece of chiaroscuro. Here we have light isolated with a vengeance! Looking at it from the opposite side of the room, we fancy it must be the repre-sentation of some experiment with the oxy-hydrogen microscope; and it is with no small astonishment that we find on closer approach, that all the radiance proceeds from a cow's head! Mithra may well be inimical to Taurus, if his occupation is to be taken out of his hands in this way! If cattle heads are to be thus phosphorescent, we shall be able to do without the sun altogether.

"But even supposing that this were a true representation of a point of light, where are our points of darkness? The whole picture, wall, figures, and ground, is one mass of deep shade, through which the details are, indeed, marvellously given when we look close, but which totally precludes all possibility of giving a single point or keynote of shade. Now nature, just as far as she raised the white cow's head above all the middle tint in light, would have put some black on the cow's head, or hole in the wall, or dark piece of dress, something, it matters not what—below all the middle tint in darkness,—just as violent and just as conspicuous in shade, as the head is violent and conspicuous in light. Consequently, Berghem has given us only two members of the system of chiaroscuro, of which nature has appointed that there shall always be three.

"[§ 14. Excellence of the chiaroscuro of M. Angelo, P. Veronese, and Rubens.] I have chosen this picture for illustration, because it is a very clever and careful work by a master, not, in his ordinary works, viciously disposed to tricks of chiaroscuro. But it must be evident to the reader, that in the same way, and in a far greater degree, those masters are false who are commonly held up as the great examples of management of chiaroscuro. All erred, exactly in proportion as they plunged with greater ardour into the jack-a-lantern chase. Rembrandt most fatally and constantly; and (of course I speak of quantity, not of quality, of shade) next to him, Correggio; while the Florentines and Romans kept right just because they cared little about the matter, and kept their light and shade in due subordination to higher truths of art. Thus Michael Angelo's chiaroscuro is, perhaps, the most just, perfect, unaffected, and impressive existing. Rafaelle's early works are often very truthful in quantity, though not in management,—the Transfiguration totally wrong. The frescoes of the Vatican, before their blues gave way, must have been very perfect. But Cagliari, and Rubens in his finest works, are the only two examples of the union of perfect chiaroscuro with perfect colour. We have no lantern-lights in their works, all is kept chaste and shed equally from the sky, not radiating from the object; and we have invariably some energetic bit of black, or intense point of gloom, commonly opposed to yellow to make it more conspicuous, as far below all the rest of the picture as the most brilliant lights are above it.

"[§ 15. Errors of the landscape painters.] Among the landscape painters, Cuyp is very often right; Claude, sometimes, by accident, as in the Seaport, No. 14 in our own Gallery, where the blue stooping figure is a beautifully-placed keynote of gloom. Both the Poussins, Salvator, and our own Wilson, are always wrong, except in such few effects of twilight as would, even in reality, reduce the earth and sky to two broad equalized masses of shade and light. I do not name particular works, because if the facts I have above stated be once believed, or proved, as they may be, by the slightest observation, their appreciation is easy, and the error or truth of works self-evident."

P. 195 (ii. 2, 3, end), eds. 1 and 2 add a final "§ 17 Recapitulation," as follows:—

"Such, then, are the two great principles by which the chiaroscuro of our greatest modern masters differs from that of the more celebrated of the ancients. I need scarcely again point out the farther confirmation resulting from the examination of them, of my assertion that ideas of imitation were incompatible with those of truth. We have now seen that to obtain *one* truth of tone necessary for the purposes of imitation, the old masters were compelled to sacrifice, first, real relation of distances, then truth of colour, and finally, all legitimate chiaroscuro,—sacrifices which, however little they may be felt by superficial observers, will yet prevent the real lover of nature from having the slightest pleasure in their works, while our great modern landscape painter, scorning all deceptive imitation, states boldly the truths which are in his power, and trusts for admiration, not to the ill-regulated feelings, which are offended because his statement must be imperfect, but to the disciplined intellect, which rejoices in it for being true."

P. 196 (ii. 2, 4, 1), the foot-note was omitted in eds. 1 and 2.

P. 198 (ii. 2, 4, 4), foot-note, eds. 1 and 2 omit the last three lines, "On the other hand . . . towards the distance."

P. 199 (ii. 2, 4, 5), "representing space," eds. 1 and 2 proceed as follows :—

"And that they did not, must be felt by every observer in cases where varied forms of sky or distance join with near foliage or foreground, when, though the near leaves may be made almost black for force, and the encountering sky or hills toned into the most exquisite purity of atmosphere, nothing can prevent the eye from feeling the intersection and junction of the lines, and an inextricable confusion of parts, which I have sometimes heard critics expatiating upon as harmony of composition and unity of arrangement, when, in fact, it is destruction of space. Some exceptions occur when the background has been considered of small importance, and has been laid in merely to set off near objects ; and often very beautiful exceptions in the bits of landscape, thrown in by great masters as the background to their historical pictures, usually a thousand times better than the laboured efforts of the real landscape painters.* [§ 6. Exception in the landscape of Rubens.] But only Rubens affords us instances of anything like complete observation of the principle in entire landscape. The distance of the picture of his own villa, in the National Gallery, is no small nor unimportant part of the composition ; the chief light and colour of the picture are dedicated to it. But Rubens felt that, after giving the very botany and ornithology of his foreground, he could not maintain equal decision, nor truthfully give one determined outline in the distance. Nor is there one ; all is indistinct, and confused, and mingling, though every thing, and an infinity of things, too, is told ; and if any person will take the trouble to keep his eye on this distance for ten minutes, and then turn to any other landscape in the room, he will feel them flat, crude, cutting, and destitute of space and light. Titian, Claude, or Poussin, it matters not, however scientifically opposed in colour, however exquisitely mellowed and removed in tone, however vigorously relieved with violent shade, all will look flat canvas beside this truthful, melting, abundant, limitless distance of Rubens. [§ 7. But modern artists, etc.] But it was reserved for modern art to take even a bolder step in the pursuit of truth. To sink the distance for the foreground was comparatively easy ; but it implied the partial destruction of exactly that part of the landscape which is most interesting, most dignified, and most varied ; of all, in fact, except the mere leafage and stone under the spectator's feet. Turner introduced a new era . . . " etc.

P. 199 (ii. 2, 4, 6), line 7 ("always the sign of vice in art"), eds. 1 and 2 add this foot-note here :—

"That is to say, if they are systematically and constantly used. Soft

* "It is particularly interesting to observe the difference between the landscape of Nicholas Poussin when it is a background and when it is a picture, not with reference to the point at present under discussion, but to general grandeur and truth of conception. When it is a background, it almost draws us away from the figures ; when it is a picture, we should be glad of some figures to draw us away from it. His backgrounds are full of light, pure in conception, majestic in outline, graceful in detail, and in every way instructive and delightful—take No. 295 in the Dulwich Gallery for instance. But his landscapes sometimes sink almost as low as Gaspar's, and are lightless, conventional, false, and feeble—only just less so than those of the professed landscape painters, and that is saying little enough for them."

and melting lines are necessary in some places, as, for instance, in the important and striking parts of the outline of an object which turns gradually, so as to have a large flat surface under the eye just when it becomes relieved against space, and so wherever thick mist is to be expressed, or very intense light; but in general, and as a principle of art, lines ought to be made tender by graduation and change as they proceed, not by slurring. The hardest line in the world will not be painful if it be managed as nature manages it, by pronouncing one part and losing another, and keeping the whole in a perpetual state of transition. Michael Angelo's lines are as near perfection as mortal work can be; distinguished, on the one hand, from the hardness and sharpness of Perugino and the early Italians, but far more, on the other, from the vicious slurring and softness which Murillo falls into when he wishes to be fine. A hard line is only an imperfection, but a slurred one is commonly a falsehood. The artist whose fault is hardness *may* be on the road to excellence—he whose fault is softness *must* be on the road to ruin."

P. 200 (ii. 2, 4, 6), lines 1 and 6, the foot-notes are omitted in eds. 1 and 2.

P. 200 (ii. 2, 4, 6), line 19, for "Thus, Callcott's Trent is," eds. 1 and 2 read, "Thus, Callcott's magnificent Trent (perhaps the best picture, on the whole, he has ever painted) is."

P. 201 (ii. 2, 4, 8), eds. 1 and 2 add the following paragraph at the end of the chapter :—

"The laborious completeness of the figures and foregrounds of the old masters, then, far from being a source of distance and space, is evidently destructive of both. It may, perhaps, be desirable on other grounds; it may be beautiful and necessary to the ideal of landscape. I assert at present nothing to the contrary; I assert merely that it is mathematically demonstrable to be untrue."

P. 205 (ii. 2, 5, 6), line 21, "windows. There is no suggestion," eds. 1 and 2 read, "windows. The light side is blank, No. 1; the dark side is blank, No. 2; and the windows are blanks, Nos. 3, 4, 5. There is not a shadow of a suggestion . . ."

Pp. 212–13 (ii. 2, 5, 15), eds. 1 and 2 omit the foot-note.

P. 214 (ii. 2, 5, 17), "A single dusty roll . . . doomsday. What Sir J. Reynolds," eds. 1 and 2 here read as follows :—" Of all errors, therefore, too much making out is the most vicious; because it in fact involves every other kind of error, denying one-half of the truths to be stated, while it misrepresents those which it pretends to state. He who pretends to draw all the leaves of an oak, denies five while he expresses three, and expresses those three falsely. He alone who defines none, can suggest all. [§ 17. Swift execution, etc.] We shall see, hereafter, in examining the qualities of execution, that one of its chiefest attractions is the power of rightly expressing *infinity;* and that the pleasure which we take in the swift strokes of a great master is not so much dependent on the swiftness or decision of them, as on the expression of infinite mystery by the mere breaking, crumbling, or dividing of the touch, which the labour of months could not have reached, if devoted to separate details. One of Landseer's breaking, scratchy touches of light is far more truly expressive of the infinity of hair, than a week's work could make a painting of particular hairs; and a single dusty roll . . . doomsday. And thus while the mind is kept intent upon wholeness of effect, the hand is far more likely to give faithful images of details, than if the mind and hand be both intent on the minutiæ. What Sir J. Reynolds . . . "

P. 214 (ii. 2, 5, 18), line 28, for " It is more agreeable that," eds. 1 and 2 read, " It is more agreeable that a nostril or an ear should be suggested by a single dash of the pencil than that they should be made out with microscopic accuracy,—more agreeable that."

Ib. (*ib.*), line 34, for "impressive," eds. 1 and 2 read, "impressive; it will lose only what is monotonous and uninteresting, if not disagreeable."

P. 215 (ii. 2, 5, 18, end), line 11, after " followed her," eds. 1 and 2 continue thus :—" And thus we have two great classes of error in landscape painting : the first, the attempting to give all details distinctly, which is the error of children, mechanics, and the Dutch school; the second, the omitting details altogether, which is commonly the error of an impetuous, intellectual, but uncultivated mind, and is found in whatever is best of the Italian school. (Claude's foregrounds come under the same category with the Dutch.) Both destroy space and beauty, but the first error is a falsehood, the second only an imperfection."

Ib. (*ib.*, § 19, end), eds. 1 and 2 add the following :—" Let me, however, point back for a moment to the result of our present examination of general truths. We have found the old masters excel us in one particular quality of colour—probably the result merely of some technical secret, and in one deceptive effect of tone, gained at the expense of a thousand falsehoods and omissions. We have found them false in aerial perspective, false in colour, false in chiaroscuro, false in space, false in detail; and we have found one of our modern artists faithful in every point, and victorious in every struggle, and all of them aiming at the highest class of truths. For which is the most important truth in a painting—for instance, of St. Mark's, Venice,—the exact quality of relief against the sky, which it shares with every hovel and brick-kiln in Italy, or the intricacy of detail and brilliancy of colour which distinguish it from every other building in the world? Or with respect to the street of Poussin, is it of more importance that we should be told the exact pitch of blackness which its chimneys assume against the sky, or that we should perceive the thousands of intricate and various incidents which in nature would have covered every cottage with history of Italian life and character? Our feelings might answer for us in an instant ; but let us use our determined tests. The one truth is uncharacteristic, unhistorical, and of the secondary class ; the others are characteristic, historical, and of the primary class. How incalculably is the balance already in favour of modern art !"

P. 217 (ii. 3, 1, 1, end), for "its appeal to what is immortal . . . mortal is essential," eds. 1 and 2 read, "it is surely meant for the chief teacher of what is immortal in us, as it is the chief minister of chastisement or of blessing to what is mortal."

Ib. (ii. 3, 1, 2, end), last line, for "extraordinary; and yet it is not," eds. 1 and 2 read, "extraordinary, when the heavens force themselves on our attention with some blaze of fire, or blackness of thunder, or awaken the curiosity of idleness, because the sun looks like a frying-pan, or the moon like a fool.

"But it is not . . . "

P. 218 (ii. 3, 1, 4), lines 26 and 30, "of the old masters," eds. 1 and 2 continue, "representative of round, cushion-like swellings and protuberances associated in a very anomalous and unintelligible manner, with legs, arms, and cart-wheels; or if this be saying too much, at least the beauty of the natural forms is so little studied, that such representations are received either for truth, or for something better than truth. Whatever there may be in them of the poetical, I believe I shall be able to show that there is a slight violation of the true.

"And I shall enter . . . judges. Its other component parts of subject can be open to the criticism of comparatively but few. What I may."

P. 222 (ii. 3, 1, 11), line 1, for "Again, look," eds. 1 and 2 read, "And, by-the-bye, while we are talking of graduations of colour, look at."

P. 223 (ii. 3, 1, 11, end), line 2, "about the sun," eds. 1 and 2 add, "yet people call such an absurdity as this 'truth;' and laugh at Turner, because he paints crimson clouds."

P. 223 (ii. 3, 1, 13), line 34, "effects take place," eds. 1 and 2 add a foot-note: 'I shall often be obliged, in the present portion of the work, to enter somewhat tediously into the examination of the physical causes of phenomena, in order that in the future, when speaking of the beautiful, I may not be obliged to run every now and then into physics, but may be able to assert a thing fearlessly to be right or wrong, false or true, with reference for proof to principles before developed. I must be allowed, therefore, at present, to spend sometimes almost more time in the investigation of nature than in the criticism of art."

P. 226–27 (ii. 3, 1, 18), eds. 1 and 2 omit the foot-note.

P. 227 (*ib.*, *ib.*), "in the study," eds. 1 and 2 add, "of the perfect and deeply-based knowledge of such phenomena which is traceable in all works of Turner, we shall see farther instances in the following chapter."

P. 236 (ii. 3, 2, 11, end), "never leave it more?" eds. 1 and 2 add, "And yet you will say that these men painted nature, and that Turner did not!"

P. 241 (ii. 3, 3, 4), line 9 from foot, for "local vapour, as vapour rendered locally visible by a fall of temperature," eds. 1 and 2 read, "solid bodies borne irregularly before the wind, as they are the wind itself, rendered visible in parts of its progress by a fall of temperature in the moisture it contains."

P. 242 (ii. 3, 3, 4), line 15, "Another resultant phenomenon," to "gradually into storm" (line 32), was omitted in eds. 1 and 2.

P. 244 (ii. 3, 3, 7), line 16, for "but it is *false*. I do not take," eds. 1 and 2 read, "I do not intend at present to dispute that circular sweeps of the brush, leaving concentric lines distinctly indicative of every separate horse-hair of its constitution, may be highly indicative of masterly handling. I do not dispute that the result may be graceful and sublime in the highest degree, especially when I consider the authority of those vaporescent flourishes, precisely similar in character, with which the more sentimental of the cherubs are adorned and encompassed in models of modern penmanship; nay, I do not take."

P. 244 (ii. 3, 3, 8), line 5 from foot, the words "of the seventeenth century" were omitted in eds. 1 and 2.

P. 247 (ii. 3, 3, 13), eds. 1 and 2 omit the foot-note; while in eds. 3 and 4 it ran thus: "Here . . . Veronese—excepting only Tintoret and the religious schools."

P. 248 (ii. 3, 3, 13), line 31, for "to Salvator," eds. 1 and 2 read, "to Berghem, to Cuyp."

P. 249 (ii. 3, 3, 14), line 16, "impertinent winds. There is no," eds. 1 and 2 read, "impertinent winds. Stulz could not be more averse to the idea of being ragged. There is no."

P. 252 (ii. 3, 3, 19). The whole of this section ("I would draw . . . inhabited by fire") was entirely different in ed. 1 (only), where it ran thus :— "[§ 19. Compared with the clouds of Backhuysen.] It is instructive to compare with this such a sky as that of Backhuysen, No. 75, Dulwich Gallery, where we have perfectly spherical clusters of grape-like, smooth, opaque bodies, which are evidently the results of the artist's imaginative powers, strained to their highest pitch in his study, perhaps, however, modified and rendered more classical and ideal by his feeling of the beautiful in the human form, at least in that part of it which is in Dutchmen most peculiarly developed. There are few pictures which are so evidently in-door work as this, so completely in every part bearing witness to the habit of the artist of shutting his eyes and soul to every impression from without, and repeating for ever and ever without a sensation of imperfection, a hope or desire of improvement, or a single childish, contemptible, and impossible conception. It is a valuable piece of work, as teaching us the abasement into which the human mind may fall when it trusts to its own strength, and delights in its own imagination."

Pp. 253–54 (ii. 3, 3, 21), line 2 from foot, "possible. I name this vignette, etc.," ed. 1 (only) reads here as follows : "possible. But even here the great outline of the mass is terminated by severe right lines, four sides of an irregular hexagon, and the lesser cloud is peaked like a cliff. But I name this vignette not only because . . . indicated in spite of the most ponderous forms, and because it is as faithful as it is bold in the junction of those weighty masses with the delicate, horizontal lines of the lower air, but because it is a characteristic example," etc.

P. 256 (ii. 3, 3, 25, end), "real infinity," eds. 1 and 2 read, "real infinity, ending, as in the works of one of our artists most celebrated for *sublimity* of conception (the general admiration of whose works, however ill-founded, I can perfectly understand, for I once admired them myself), in morbid and meaningless tautology."

P. 258 (ii. 3, 3, 28). The foot-note was, as its date (1851) implies, omitted in eds. 1-4.

P. 264 (ii. 3, 4, 6), line 16, "no form at all," eds. 1 and 2 conclude the § thus : "no form at all, and that the result, however admirable or desirable it may perhaps, on principles hitherto undeveloped, be hereafter proved, is in all cases, and from all hands, as far as the representation of nature is concerned, something which only ought not to amuse by its absurdity, because it ought to disgust by its falsehood."

P. 264 (ii. 3, 4, 7), line 19, "De Wint, or even," eds. 1 and 2 read, "De Wint, the spongy breadth of Cattermole, or even."

Ib. (ii. 3, 4, 7), line 22, for "utter scorn. But one," eds. 1 and 2 read, "utter scorn. The works of Stanfield, here, as in all other points, based on perfect knowledge, would enable us to illustrate almost every circumstance of storm, and should be our text-book, were it not that all he has done has been farther carried by a mightier hand. But one."

P. 265 (ii. 3, 4, 10), line 24, "storm tones," eds. 1 and 2 omit the foot-note, and read, "storm tones : so surely as Copley Fielding attempts the slightest hint at cloud form, beyond the edgeless ray, which is tossed and twisted in the drift of the rain, does he become liny, hard, and expressionless,—so surely as he leaves the particular greys and browns whose harmony can scarcely be imperfect, and attempts the slightest passage of red colour, much more when he plunges into the difficulties of elaborate and elevated composition, does he become affected, false, and feeble."

P. 267 (ii. 3, 4, 12, end), "speak home at once," eds. 1 and 2 continue, "once ; but let it be especially observed how we have, added to all this, just where the rainbow melts away, the wreath of swift and delicate cloud-form, left in decisive light, which Fielding could only have rendered in darkness, and even then with little more than the bare suggestion of imperfect outlines ; while Turner has given us in every flake a separate study of beautiful and substantial form."

P. 267 (ii. 3, 4, 12-13). Between § 12 and § 13 eds. 1-4 insert an additional "[§ 13. Illustration of the nature of clouds in the opposed forms of cloud and steam]," as follows : "But there is yet added to this noble composition an incident which may serve us at once for a further illustration of the nature and forms of cloud, and for a final proof how deeply and philosophically Turner has studied them.

"'We have, on the right of the picture, the steam and the smoke of a passing steamboat. Now steam is nothing but an artificial cloud in the process of dissipation; it is as much a cloud as those of the sky itself, that is, a quantity of moisture rendered visible in the air by imperfect solution. Accordingly, observe how exquisitely irregular and broken are its forms, how sharp and spray-like; but with all the facts observed which were pointed out in Chap. II. of this Section, the convex side to the wind, the sharp edge on that side, the other soft and lost. Smoke, on the contrary, is an actual substance, existing independently in the air; a solid, opaque body, subject to no absorption or dissipation but that of tenuity. Observe its volumes; there is no breaking up nor disappearing here; the wind carries its elastic globes before it, but does not dissolve nor break them.* Equally convex and void of angles on all sides, they are the exact representations of the clouds of the old masters, and serve at once to show the ignorance and falsehood of these latter, and the accuracy of study which has guided Turner to the truth.'"

P. 269 (ii. 3, 4, 15), for "In the Long Ships . . . we have clouds," eds. 1 and 2 read, "The Long Ships Lighthouse, Land's End, is, perhaps, a finer instance of the painting of the rain-cloud than any yet given. Taken as a whole, it is, perhaps, the noblest drawing of Turner's existing. The engraving is good, as a plate, but conveys not the slightest idea of the original. We have here clouds."

P. 269 (ii. 3, 4, 15), line 13, "transparent veil, but," eds. 1 and 2 read, "transparent veil, like Fielding's rain, but."

Ib. (*ib. ib.*), line 10 from foot, at "It is this untraceable," etc., eds. 1–4 add a marginal note, § **17**: "The individual character of its parts."

P. 270 (ii. 3, 4, 16), in eds. 1–4 the marginal note runs, "Deep studied form of swift rain-cloud in the Coventry."

P. 271 (ii. 3, 4, 19), ed. 1 (only) opens this section thus: "Find me such a magnificent statement of all truth as this among the old masters, and I will say their works are worth something. But I have not quite done," etc.

P. 272 (ii. 3, 4, 19, end), ed. 1 (only) omits the last sentence, "Engravers . . . rest of the sky," of this paragraph.

Ib. (ii. 3, 4, 20), line 8, for "purest," ed. 1 (only) reads, "purest and most perfect."

Ib. (*ib. ib.*), line 10 from foot, opposite "of this effect," etc., eds. 1–4 have a marginal note, "§ (23). Absence of this effect in the works of the old masters."

---

* It does not do so until the volumes lose their density by inequality of motion, and by the expansion of the warm air which conveys them. They are then, of course, broken into forms resembling those of clouds.

P. 275 (ii. 3, 4, 24), line 10, opposite " But the aerial, etc.," eds. 1-4 have a marginal note, "[§ . His effects of mist so perfect that, if not at once understood, they can no more be explained or reasoned on than nature herself.]"

P. 275 (ii. 3, 4, 24, end), "nor nature inform," eds. 1-4 here insert a further paragraph :—

"[§ 29. Various instances.] It would be utterly absurd, among the innumerable passages of the kind given throughout his works, to point to one as more characteristic or more perfect than another. The 'Simmer Lake, near Askrig,' for expression of mist pervaded with sunlight,—the 'Lake Lucerne,' a recent and unengraved drawing, for the reception of near mountain form, not into dark, but into luminous cloud, the most difficult thing to do in art,—the 'Harlech' for expression of the same phenomena, shown over vast spaces in distant ranges of hills,—the 'Ehrenbreitstein,' a recent drawing, for expression of mist rising from the surface of water at sunset, and, finally, the glorious 'Oberwesel' and 'Nemi,' * for passages of all united, may, however, be named, as noble instances, though in naming five works I insult five hundred."

P. 278 (ii. 3, 4, 30-1), marginal note, "old masters," eds. 1-4 read, "old masters. Morning on the plains," and omit marginal note to § 31.

P. 279 (ii. 3, 4, 31, end), line 1, "upon the plain," eds. 1 and 2 add note "Vignette to Milton : Temptation on the Mountain."

P. 280, foot-note [3], eds. 1 and 2 omit words, "Goldau . . . order."

P. 289 (ii. 4, 1, 5), line 9 from foot, for "hills to the south-east," ed. 1 reads, "hills of the Voza," and ed. 2, "hills of the Pavillon."

P. 290 (ii. 4, 1, 6), line 6, for "Let the reader now open," eds. 1 and 2 read, "If what I have said has been well understood, I need only bid the reader open."

P. 293 (ii. 4, 2, 3). The end of this paragraph, "; and this last condition. . . . Swiss geologists," is omitted in eds. 1-4.

P. 294 (ii. 4, 2, 4). At the end of this paragraph eds. 1 and 2 have a further sentence : "Admire it or not. It is such a concentration of Alpine truth as could only have been put together by one as familiar with these snowy solitudes as their own eagles."

P. 296 (ii. 4, 2, 7-8). Between these two paragraphs eds. 1 and 2 insert the following :—

"[§ 8. The perfection of Turner's vignette 'Jacqueline']. But open at the 145th page of Rogers' Poems. I said little of this vignette just now, when talking of structure, that I might insist upon it more forcibly as a piece of effect. Of all the pieces of mountain elevation that ever were put upon paper, perhaps this is the most soaring and impressive. The dreamy faintness of their mighty strength, the perfect stillness and silence of their distant sleep, and the fulness of sunlight in which they are bathed and

---

* In the possession of B. G. Windus, Esq., of Tottenham.

lost, bear away the mind with them like a deep melody; and through all this,—through the aerial dimness out of which they rise like spectres, are told the facts and forms which speak of their reality like their own echoes. [§ 9. Its peculiar expression of Alpine facts.] For instance, the highest range of rock on the extreme left is precisely the place where, in nature, there would be a little plateau or level, retiring back to the foot of the supreme summit; and as surely as there would be such a level, a kind of breathing time in the mountain before it made its last spring, so surely would that little plain be loaded with a glacier, so surely would that glacier advance to the brow of the precipice, and so surely would it hang over it, in the white tongue which, in the vignette, descends over the precipice exactly under the highest snowy peak. Now they are these little touches of exquisite, deep, and finished truth, which mark the vastness of Turner's intellect; they are just those which never can be generally appreciated, owing to the unavoidable want of the knowledge required to meet them. Observe how much this single bit of white tells us. It tells us that there is a glacier above those cliffs, of consistence and size; it tells us, therefore, that there is a comparatively level space on which the fallen snow can accumulate; and it tells us, therefore, that the white summits are a mile or two farther back than the rocks below them; and to make all this doubly clear, the black moraine invariably left by the falling snow at the edge of such a plain, where it first alights, is marked by the dark line crossing, nearly horizontally, under the central peak. All this speaks home at once, if we have but knowledge enough to understand it; and, be it remembered, this same white and dark touch would be equally a dead letter to us in nature herself, if we had not. A person among the Alps for the first time in his life would probably not even notice the little tongue of ice hanging over the precipice, much less would he comprehend how much it told. It could only be someone long acquainted with mountains who could tell you the width of the plateau, and how many chamois were likely to be upon it. I might name many other works of Turner, in which the same deep Alpine truth is carried out; but this alone would be sufficient to prove his unapproached superiority, at least over the ancients. What the moderns have done we shall see presently."

Eds. 1 and 2 then continue, "Although, however."

P. 302 (ii. 4, 2, 16), line 3, "from a rock," eds. 1–4 here insert two sentences: "There are three trees on the Mont Salève, about eight miles from Geneva, which from the city, as they stand on the ridge of the hill, are seen defined against the sky. The keenest eye in the world could not tell them from stones."

P. 303 (ii. 4, 2, 19, 20). These two §§ are omitted in eds. 1 and 2, which have in their place the following :—"[§ 21. Review of the Alpine drawings of modern artists generally. The great excellence of J. D. Harding.] Such, then, are the chief characteristics of the highest peaks and extreme distances of all hills, which we see that the old masters, taken as a body, usually neglected, and, if they touched, maligned. They fortunately did little, as whatever they did was wrong; and prudently affirmed little, as whatever they affirmed was false. The moderns have generally done all that they have done, well; but, owing to the extreme difficulty of managing or expressing the brilliancy of snow, and the peculiar character of the vertical and severe lines, which are not, under ordinary circumstances, attractive to an artist's eye, we cannot point to so many or so various examples of truth as in other cases. But nothing can be more accurate than the knowledge, or more just than the feelings of J. D. Harding, whenever he touches Alpine scenery; and he takes the bull by the horns far more frequently than any other of our artists. His magnificent 'Wengern Alp,' and his 'Chamouni,' engraved in the illustrations to Byron, are quite unequalled, even by Stanfield. [§ 22. The apparent carelessness of Stanfield in such subjects. True feeling of Copley Fielding.] The latter artist, indeed, we know not from what cause, fails, or at least falls short of what we should expect from him, more frequently in subjects of this kind than in anything else he touches. He usually makes the snowy summits a subordinate part of his picture, and does not appear to dwell upon them with fondness or delight, but to get over them as a matter of necessity. We should almost imagine that he had never made careful studies of them, for even in the few touches he gives, the intelligent drawing for which he is usually distinguished is altogether wanting. No man, however, in such subjects has suffered more from engravers; the plate of 'Innspruck,' in the *Picturesque Annual*, might have been opposed to Turner's work as an instance of want of size and dignity in Alpine masses, and want of intelligence in the drawing of the snow, the dark touches on which are altogether impressive; and, as there is no distinction in them of dark side from shadow, might be taken for rocks, or stairs, rather than for shades indicative of form. But these parts, in the originals, are delicately and justly drawn, though slightly, and have very high qualities of size and distance. We shall, moreover, in speaking of the lower mountains, have better grounds for dwelling on the works of this master, as well as on those of Copley Fielding, who has most genuine feeling for hill character, but has never grappled with the central summits."

P. 313 (ii. 4, 3, 8–9), line 15, for "series of concave curves. Yet if we go on," eds. 1 and 2 read, "series of concave curves, like those of a heap of broken plates and dishes, exhibiting on the whole as complete a piece of absurdity as ever human fingers disgraced themselves by producing.
"And yet not quite, neither, for if we go on."

Ib. (ii. 4, 3, 9), line 29, "There is no cast shadow." Here, eds. 1–4 read, at greater length, as follows : "Rocks with pale-brown light sides, and rich-green dark sides, are a phenomenon perhaps occurring in some of the improved passages of nature among our Cumberland lakes ; where I remember once having seen a bed of roses, of peculiar magnificence, tastefully and artistically assisted in effect by the rocks above it being painted pink to match ; but I do not think that they are a kind of thing which the clumsiness and false taste of nature can be supposed frequently to produce, even granting that these same sweeps of the brush could, by any exercise of imagination, be conceived representative of a dark, or any other side, which is far more than I am inclined to grant, seeing that there is no cast shadow."

P. 316 (ii. 4, 3, 12), eds. 1 and 2 omit the foot-note.

P. 316 (ii. 4, 3, 12), lines 27 and 28, for "Saddleback," eds. 1 and 2 read, "Glaramara," while for "du Taconay," eds. 1 and 2 read, "du Coté."

P. 322 (ii. 4, 3, 22), "Dulwich Gallery," eds. 1 and 2 here proceed: "We have here a mass of mountain intended to retire from us, but the clumsy workman, not being able to indicate this achievement upon their surfaces, is compelled to have recourse to the usual tyro's expedient of drawing edge behind edge, like the scenes of a theatre, and these same unlucky edges only multiply the exhibition of his weakness, for having evidently no power of indicating roundness or solidity in any of them, he has trusted entirely, like an awkward schoolboy, to making the outline hard and bright, and shading the body of each gradually as it comes down, which is so far from accomplishing his purpose that it has made the edges, if anything, rather nearer than any other part of the hills, and instead of promontories we have pasteboard scenes. There is no detail," etc.

P. 322 (ii. 4, 3, 22), line 37, "fall to the bottom," eds. 1 and 2 here proceed: "Now there is no doubt nor capability of dispute about such painting as this; it is the work of a mere tyro, and a weak and childish tyro, ignorant of the common laws of light and shadow; it is what beginners always do, and always have done, but what, if they have either sense or feeling, they soon cease to do. I could not point," etc.

P. 324 (ii. 4, 3, 24, end), eds. 1 and 2 conclude this paragraph as follows: "sweetness. It will only be when we can feel as well as think, and rejoice as well as reason, that I shall be able to lead you with Turner to his favourite haunts,—to bid you walk with him along slopes of the waving hills, with their rich woods bending on their undulations like the plumage on a bird's bosom, and up the hollow paths of silent valleys, and along the rugged flanks of heaving mountains, passing like a cloud from crag to crag, and chasm to chasm, and solitude to solitude, among lifted walls of living rock, mighty surges of tempestuous earth, dim domes of heaven-girded snow, where the morning first strikes, and the sunset last lingers, and the stars pause in their setting, and the tempest and the lightning have their habitations, to bid you behold in all that perfect beauty,—which is known only to love,—that truth infinite and divine which is revealed only to devotion.

"I can scarcely," etc.

P. 326 (ii. 4, 3, 27), "Copley Fielding . . . as long as he keeps," eds. 1 and 2 read, "Copley Fielding is our next greatest artist in the drawing of the inferior mountains. His mountain *feeling* is quite perfect; nothing can be more delicate than his perceptions of what is graceful in the outline, or of what is valuable in the tenderness of aerial tone. But, again, as with his clouds, so with his hills; it is all feeling, and no drawing. As long as he keeps."

P. 327 (ii. 4, 3, 28), the end of the chapter from "Some of the best . . . William Turner of Oxford," including the foot-note, was not in eds. 1–4, where the chapter ended thus: "very slight. His colour is very beautiful; indeed both his and Fielding's are far, far more refined than Stanfield's. We wish he could oftener take up some wild subject, dependent for interest on its mountain forms alone, as we should anticipate the highest results from his perfect drawing; and we think that such an exercise, occasionally gone completely through, would counteract a tendency which we perceive in his present distances, to become a little thin and cutting, if not incomplete.

"[Callcott's work, when he takes up a piece of hill scenery, is very perfect in all but colour.] The late G. Robson was a man most thoroughly acquainted with all the characteristics of our own island hills; and some of the outlines of John Varley showed very grand feeling of energy of form." [Eds. 3 and 4 omit the bracketed words.]

P. 329 (ii. 4, 4, 3), foot-note, eds. 1 and 2 omit the foot-note, and contain the afterwards omitted passage referred to in it as follows:—

". . . impressed on rocks. [§ 4. The true outlines are all angular.] Again, the grand outlines of rocks are all angular. Water-worn and rounded they may be, or modulated on the surface as we shall presently see, but their prevailing lines and shadows are still rectilinear. In the Napoleon —I can illustrate by no better example, for I can reason as well from this as I could with my foot on the native rock—the great outlines of the foreground are all straight, firm, and decided; its planes nearly level, though touched with tender modulations by the washing of the waves, and the complicated fracture above spoken of, though its edges are entirely rounded off, retains all the character of the right lines of which it was originally composed. [§ 5. Salvator's are all curved.] But I think it would be difficult to show any strokes of the brush on any rock painted by the old masters, by Salvator especially, not curvilinear. And the circular," etc.

P. 331 (ii. 4, 4, 7), line 30, "symbolical of rock. The forms," eds. 1 and 2 here read to the end of the paragraph as follows: "symbolical of rock. I should be glad of other opinions on the subject; but, on the whole, I believe that much more is to be said against it botanically than geologically, and that the hypothesis most favourable to Salvator would furnish us, in this piece of drawing, with one of the first examples existing of concentrated geological falsehood. The forms . . . meant for rock; not to speak of the blocks on the other side of the river in the same picture, whose shapeless, daubed, shadowless concavities are to the full as offensive and absurd, though not quite so ambiguous."

P. 332 (ii. 4, 4, 8), line 12, "characteristic than others," eds. 1–4 read, "characteristic than others; [for he is a man who never fails, and who is constantly presenting us with more highly wrought example of rock truth]; but his Ischia, in the present British Institution, may be taken as a fair average. The Bottallack Mine," etc.

[Eds. 3 and 4 omit the bracketed words.]

P. 333 (ii. 4, 4, 10), lines 23–28, "but it is much to be regretted . . . everything," eds. 1 and 2 omit this passage and the foot-note, reading instead, "forcibly, especially in oils, where his decision of execution is very remarkable. And, indeed, there are few of our landscape painters who, though they may not possess the intimate and scientific geological knowledge of Stanfield and Harding, are not incomparably superior in every quality of drawing to every one of the old masters, though, as it is paying them but a poor compliment to say that they do not contradict nature in every particular, I should rather say, who are not intelligent, truthful, and right in all their work, as far as it goes."

P. 335 (ii. 4, 4, 13), line 28, between paragraphs 13 and 14, eds. 1 and 2 insert the two following paragraphs :—

"[§ 16. And of Copley Fielding.] Now I may point in contradistinction to this to one of Copley Fielding's down or moor foregrounds, and I may tell you that its curves are right and true, and that it is the real ground of nature, such as she produces fresh designs and contours of with every shower ; the foreground of his 'Bolton Abbey,' in last year's Academy, is a good instance ; and yet I can scarcely tell you wherein its truth consists, except by repeating the same sentences about continuity and variety of curves, which, after all, are things only to be felt and found out for yourself, by diligent study of free nature. No words will explain it, unless you go and lie for a summer or two up to your shoulders in heather, with the purple, elastic ground about you defined against the sky like fantastic mountains. After you have done this you will feel what truth of ground is, and till then I cannot in such fine points as these tell it you; but the facts are not the less certain because they are inexplicable. The ground of Teniers is anatomically wrong, and that of Fielding right, however little one person may be able to feel that they are so, or another to explain why.

"[§ 17. The foreground of Both.] It is an easier matter, however, to point out the fallacy of pieces of ground undisguised by vegetation, such as Both's foreground in No. 41 of the Dulwich Gallery. If this were meant for rock it would come under the same category with Salvator's above mentioned, but its evident brown colour seems to mark it for earth ; and I believe that no eye can help feeling that the series of peaks with hollow curves between them which emerge from the grass in the centre, are such as could not support themselves for ten minutes against an April shower. Concave descending curves can only be obtained in loose soil when there is some knotted and strong protection of roots and leaves at the top, and even then they are generally rough and broken ; but whenever earth is exposed, as here, it is reduced, either by crumbling in heat, or by being washed down in rain, to convex forms furrowed by little ravines, and always tending as they descend to something like an even slope. Hence nature's ground never by any chance assumes such forms as those of Both, and if—which it would be most difficult to do—a piece of even the toughest clay were artificially reduced to them, with the first noon-day sun, or first summer shower, she would have it all her own way again."

P. 337 (ii. 4, 4, 17), line 2, for "foregrounds," eds. 1-4 read, "beautiful foregrounds."

Ib. (ii. 4, 4, 18), line 17 from foot, "in fact . . . impotent," eds. 1 and 2 read, "in fact, the whole arrangement is precisely, in foreground, what we before saw in Claude's hills ; the impotent," etc.

P. 340 (ii. 4, 4, 23), line 5, "and yet of which one deep," eds. 1-4 read, "and yet throughout indicating that perfect parallelism which at once explained to us the geology of the rock, and falling into one grand mass, treated with the same simplicity of light and shade, which a portrait painter adopts in treating the features of the human face, which, though each has its own separate chiaroscuro, never disturb the wholeness and grandeur of the head, considered as one ball or mass. So here, one deep," etc.

P. 341 (ii. 4, 4, 24), line 9, "carried out," eds. 1 and 2 add, "You must work and watch for this ; it is not to be taught by words."

P. 342 (ii. 4, 4, 26), line 27, "study, chiselled," eds. 1-4 read, "study (and has evidently been drawn from nature), chiselled."

P. 343 (ii. 4, 4, 27, end), line 15, eds. 1 and 2 here insert a further paragraph :—

"I may, perhaps, illustrate the particular qualities of modulation in ground, which are so remarkable in Turner, by a little bit of accidental truth in Claude. In the picture before spoken of, with the three banks, the little piece of ground above the cattle, between the head of the brown cow and the tail of the white one, is well articulated, just where it turns into shade. The difference between this and the hard edges of the banks on the left, can scarcely but be felt."

Ib. (ii. 4, 4, 29), last line, "knowledge. Often as I," eds. 1 and 2 add, "knowledge. But if we once comprehend the excellence of the drawings, we shall find that these ideal works are little more than glorious combinations of the minor studies, combinations uniting the gathered thought and disciplined knowledge of years. It is impossible to go into them in writing, the mind itself is lost in the contemplation of their infinity, and how shall words express or follow that which to the eye is inexhaustible? Often as I . . . "

P. 346 (ii. 5, 1, 2), line 3, eds. 1 and 2 omit the words, "to paint the actual play of hue on the reflective surface, or."

Ib. (ii. 5, 1, 4-18). Of these sections §§ 4-17 * are omitted in eds. 1 and 2, which contain instead the following :—

"[§ 4. General rules which regulate the phenomena of water. First,

---

* In ed. 3 *et seqq.* these sections remain unaltered, with the following exceptions : p. 351, § 7, ed. 3 omits the paragraph, "A boat swinging . . . bright green," and for "I have inserted the last two paragraphs because they," reads, "I have left the passage about the white and red stripe because it ;" p. 359, § 16, line 13, for "the garden : not leading," etc., eds. 3 and 4 read, "garden. Not, for Tintoret, the leading to the gate with consolation and counsel ; his strange ardour of conception is seen here as everywhere. Full . . .'

its universality of reflection.] We must first state a few of the constant and most important laws which regulate the appearance of water under all circumstances. They are not dependent merely on experience or observation, but are all demonstrable from the mechanical properties of water and light.

"I. Nothing can hinder water from being a reflecting medium, but dry dust or filth of some kind on its surface. Dirty water, if the foul matter be dissolved or suspended in the liquid, reflects just as clearly and sharply as pure water, only the image is coloured by the hue of the mixed matter, and becomes comparatively brown, or dark.*

"[§ 5. How modified by ripple.] II. If water be rippled, the side of every ripple next to us reflects a piece of the sky, and the side of every ripple farthest from us reflects a piece of the opposite shore, or of whatever objects may be beyond the ripple. But as we soon lose sight of the farther sides of the ripples on the retiring surface, the whole rippled space will then be reflective of the sky only. Thus, where calm distant water receives reflections of high shores, every extent of rippled surface appears as a bright line interrupting that reflection with the colour of the sky.

"[§ 6. How prolonged and broken.] III. When a ripple, or swell, is seen at such an angle as to afford a view of its farther side, it carries the reflection of objects farther down than calm water would. Therefore all motion in water elongates reflections, and throws them into confused vertical lines.

"IV. Rippled water, of which we can see the farther side of the waves, will reflect a perpendicular line clearly, a bit of its length being given on the side of each wave, and easily joined by the eye. But if the line slope, its reflection will be excessively confused and disjointed, and if horizontal, nearly invisible.

"[§ 7. How changed in relation of parts.] V. Every reflection is the image of the reverse of just so much of the objects beside the water as we could see if we were placed as much under the level of the water as we are actually above it. [We cannot see the reflection of the top of a flat stone, because we could not see the real top of the stone if we were under the level of the water; and]† if an object be so far back from the bank, that if we were five feet under the water level we could not see it over the bank, then, standing five feet above the water, we shall not be able to see its image under the reflected bank.

"[§ 8. VI. Not affected by distance.] But if the object subtend the proper angle for reflection it does not matter how great its distance may be. The image of a mountain fifty miles off is as clear, in proportion to the clearness of the mountain itself, as the image of a stone on the beach, in proportion to the clearness of the stone itself.

---

* (Note in ed. 2, only).—"Brown, as in the case of mountain waters coloured by morasses; or dark, as in lowland estuaries fouled with fine soluble mud. If the foul matter be insoluble, as when streams are charged with sand, or yellow alluvial soil, the reflection is paled and nearly destroyed by its prevalent colour, *beneath* the eye, while it remains clear at a distance from the eye. For full explanation of this and other phenomena of water, especially of rule vii., *vide* Rippingille's *Artist's and Amateur's Magazine* for November 1843.

† Bracketed matter omitted in ed. 2.

"[§ 9. Water receives no shadow.] There is no shadow on clear water. Every darkness on it is reflection, not shadow. If it have rich colouring matter suspended in it, or a dusty surface, it will take [a feeble] * shadow, and where [there is even very faint and variable] † positive colour, as in the sea, it will take something like shadows in distant effect, but never near. Those parts of the sea which appear bright in sunshine, as opposed to other parts, are composed of waves of which every one conveys to the eye a little image of the sun, but which are not themselves illumined in doing so, for the light on the wave depends on your position, and moves as you move; it cannot, therefore, be positive light on the object, for you will not get the light to move off the trunk of a tree because you move away from it. The horizontal lines, therefore, cast by clouds on the sea, are not shadows, but reflections. Optical effects of great complication may take place by means of refraction and mirage, but it may be taken for granted that if ever there is a real shadow, it is cast on mist, and not on water. And on clear water, near the eye, there never can be even the appearance of a shadow, except by a delicate tint on the foam, or transmitted through the body, as through air.

"[§ 10. Works of Canaletti. His management of ripple equally false in near water.] These rules are universal and incontrovertible. Let us test them by some of the simplest effects of ancient art. Among all the pictures of Canaletti . . . [as in eds. 3 *et seqq.*] symbolical of ripple. On the water so prepared, he fixes his gondolas in very good perspective, and thus far no objection is to be made to the whole arrangement. But a gondola, as everybody knows, is a very long, shallow boat, little raised above the water, except at the extremities, but having a vertical beak, and rowed by two men, or sometimes only one, *standing.* Consequently, wherever the water is rippled, as by Canaletti, we have, by our fourth rule, only a broken and indistinct image of the horizontal and oblique lines of the gondola, but a tolerably clear one of the vertical beak, and the figures, shooting down a long way under or along the water. What does Canaletti give us? A clear, dark, unbroken reflection of the whole boat, *except* the beak and the figure, which cast none at all. A worthy beginning.

"[§ 11. And indistinct.] And as the canal retires back from the eye, Canaletti very properly and geometrically . . . smooth water. Now by our second rule . . . quiet lake. Exemplary Canaletti!

"[§ 12. He erred not from ignorance, but impotence.] Observe, I do not suppose Canaletti, frequently as he must have been afloat on these canals, to have been ignorant of their everyday appearance. I believe him to be a shameless asserter of whatever was most convenient to him; and the convenience of this, his scientific arrangement, is indisputable. For in the first place, it is one of the most difficult," etc., as in later editions.

P. 363 (ii. 5, 1, 18), line 11, "an ignorant artist." Here eds. 1 and 2 have this note: "The exquisite accuracy of Canaletti's imitations of chiaroscuro in architecture in no degree proves him an artist. Any mechanic can imitate what is quiet and finite. It is only when we have

* Omitted in ed. 2.
† Ed. 2, "it has itself a,"

motion and infinity, as in water, that the real powers of an artist are tried. We have already seen that Canaletti could not give the essential truths— the infinite, that is to say—even of architecture ; and the moment he touches any higher subject his impotence is made manifest."

P. 363 (ii. 5, 1, 18), line 25, "detection," eds. 1 and 2 add, "and he has not reckoned without his host."

Ib. (*ib.*), in eds. 1 and 2 this § is entitled "§ 13. His falseness of colour," and, omitting the first two sentences of later editions, "Now in all . . . pardoned in him," runs thus :—

"Now, what possibly can be expected from any part of the works of a man who is either thus blind to the broadest facts, perpetually before his eyes, or else who sits down to try how much convenient lying the public can digest ? It would be wasted time to look in him for fine truth, when he thus starts in direct defiance of the most palpable. But if it be but remembered."

Ib. (*ib. ib.*, end), "by the thousand," eds. 1 and 2 add, "not less fatally, though, of course, less demonstrably, than in the broad cases presented by his general arrangement."

P. 364 (ii. 5, 1, 19), "Venice is sad and silent now," etc. From here to the end of the chapter (except the paragraph, "The seas of Claude . . . exceedingly few," on p. 366) is omitted in eds. 1 and 2. In § 21, at "sea-piece of Ruysdael's in the Louvre," there is this note in ed. 3 only :—

"In the last edition of this work was the following passage :—"I wish Ruysdael had painted one or two rough seas. I believe if he had he might have saved the unhappy public from much grievous victimizing, both in mind and pocket, for he would have shown that Vandevelde and Backhuysen are not quite sea deities.' The writer has to thank the editor of Murray's 'Handbook of Painting in Italy' for pointing out the oversight. He had passed many days in the Louvre before the above passage was written, but had not been in the habit of pausing long anywhere except in the last two rooms, containing the pictures of the Italian school. The conjecture, how-ever, shows that he had not ill-estimated the power of Ruysdael ; nor does he consider it as in anywise unfitting him for the task he has undertaken, that for every hour passed in galleries he has passed many days on the sea-shore."

P. 364 (ii. 5, 1, 19), in place of the above, "Venice is sad," etc., to end of chapter, eds. 1 and 2 contain the following passages :—

"[§ 14. Illustration from Turner of the truth.] I shall not insult any of the works of modern art by comparing them with this, but I may as well illustrate, from a vignette of Turner, the particular truth in the drawing of rippled water of which we have been speaking. There is a ripple in the 'Venice,' given among the illustrations to Scott's works, on which we see that the large black gondola on the right casts but a faint reflection from its body, while the upward bend of the beak throws a long and decided one. The upright figures on the left cast white light on the water, but the boat in which they are standing has no reflection except at the beak, and there a dark one. The two behind show the same thing.

"[§ 15. The calms of Vandevelde.] Let us next look at a piece of calm water by Vandevelde, such as that marked 113 in the Dulwich Gallery. There is not a line of ripple or swell in any part of this sea; it is absolutely windless. Nothing can prevent the sea, when in such a state as this, from receiving reflections, because it is too vast and too frequently agitated to admit of anything like dry dust or scum on its surface, and however foul and thick a Dutch sea may be in itself, no *internal* filth can ever take away the polish and reflective power of the surface. Nor does Vandevelde appear to suppose it can, for the near boat casts its image with great fidelity, which being prolonged downwards, informs us that the calm is perfect. But what is that underneath the vessel on the right? A grey shade, descending like smoke a little way below the water, not of the colour of the hull, having no drawing nor detail in any part of it, and breaking off immediately, leaving the masts and sails totally unrecorded in the water. [§ 16. Their various violations of natural laws.] We have here two kinds of falsehood. First, while the ship is nearly as clear as the boats, the reflection of the ship is a mere mist. This is false by Rule VI. Had the ship been misty, its shadow might have been so; not otherwise. Secondly, the reflection of the hull would in nature have been as deep as the hull is high (or, had there been the slightest swell on the water, deeper), and the masts and sails would all have been rendered with fidelity, especially their vertical lines. Nothing could by any possibility have prevented their being so, but so much swell in the sea as would have prolonged the hull indefinitely. Hence, both the colour and the form of Vandevelde's reflections are impossible.

"[§ 17. Also proceeded from impotence, not from ignorance.] Here again, as in the case of Canaletti, I do not suppose Vandevelde to have been ignorant of these common truths; but purposely and wilfully to have denied them, because he did not know how to manage, and was afraid of them. He evidently desired to give an impression of great extent of surface between the boat and the ships, and thought that if he gave the reflection the eye would go under the water instead of along it; and that, as the tops of the masts would come down to the nearest part of the surface, they would destroy the evidence of distance, and appear to set the ship *above* the boat instead of *beyond* it. And I doubt not, in such awkward hands, that such would indeed have been the case. I think he estimated his own powers with great accuracy and correctness, but he is not on that account to be excused for casting defiance in the teeth of nature, and painting his surface with grey horizontal lines, as is done by nautically disposed children; for no destruction of distance in the ocean is so serious a loss as that of its liquidity. It is better to feel a want of extent in the sea, than an extent which we might walk upon or play at billiards upon. [§ 18. Their painful effect even on unobservant eyes.] And though Vandevelde's eye and feeling were too blunt to suffer much pain from his wilful libelling of nature, he ought not to have reckoned upon general blindness. Unobservant eyes may, indeed, receive almost any degree of error for truth, under particular circumstances; but I cannot believe that any person who has ever floated on calm sea, can stand before this picture without feeling that the whole of the water below the large ship looks like vapour or smoke. He may not know why, he may not miss the reflection, nor expect it, but he *must* feel that something is wrong, and that the image before him is indeed 'a painted ship—upon a painted ocean.' Perhaps the best way of educating the eye for the detection of the falsehood is to stand before the mill of Hobbima, No. 131, in which there is a bit of decently painted water, and glance from one picture to the other, when Vandevelde's will soon become by comparison a perfect slate-table, having scarcely even surface or space to recommend it ; for, in his ignorance of means to express proximity, the unfortunate Dutchman has been reduced to *blacken* his sea as it comes near, until by the time he reaches the frame it looks perfectly spherical, and is of the colour of ink. What Vandevelde *ought* to have done, and how both the falsehood of his present work, and the destruction of surface which he feared, might have been avoided altogether, I shall show in the third chapter of this section.

"[§ 19. Singular mistake of Cuyp in casting half-a-dozen reflections from one object.] I might thus proceed through half the pieces of water-painting of the old masters which exist, and point out some new violation of truth, some peculiar arrangement of error, in every one ; sometimes, indeed, having little influence on the general effect, but always enough to show us that the painter had no real knowledge of his subject, and worked only as an imitator, liable to fall into the most ridiculous mistakes the moment he quitted his model. In the picture of Cuyp, No. 83, Dulwich Gallery, it is exceedingly difficult to understand under what kind of moral or intellectual delusion the painter was induced to give the post at the end of the bank on the left, its *numerous* and radiating reflections or shadows ; for, in the first place, the sun is not apt to cast half-a-dozen shadows at the same time, neither is water usually disposed to reflect one line in six directions ; and, in the second place, supposing that in some melancholy state of bewilderment the painter had supposed these shadows to be indicative of radiating light proceeding from the sun, it is difficult to understand how he could have cast the shadow of the ship in the distance in a line, which, if produced, would cut half of the shadows of the post at right angles. This is a slight passage, and one not likely to attract attention ; but I do not know anything more perfectly demonstrative of an artist's entire ignorance. I hope, however, and think it probable—for Cuyp *had* looked at nature, and I can scarcely suppose him capable of committing anything so gross as this—that the shadows of the post may be a picture-dealer's improvement, and that only the one cast by the ship is Cuyp's.

"[§ 20. And of Paul Potter, in casting no reflections from half-a-dozen objects.] Again, in the picture attributed to Paul Potter, No. 176, Dulwich Gallery, I believe most people must feel, the moment they look at it, that there is something wrong with the water ; that it looks odd, and hard, and like ice or lead ; and though they may not be able to tell the reason of the impression—for when they go near they will find it smooth and lustrous, and prettily painted,—yet they will not be able to shake off the unpleasant sense of its being very like a plate of bad mirror set in a model landscape among moss, rather than like a pond. The reason is that, while this water receives clear reflections from the fence and hedge on the left, and is everywhere smooth and evidently capable of giving true images, it yet reflects none of the cows.

"[§ 21. Painting of water in motion. Ruysdael.] We can scarcely expect after finding such errors as these in the painting of ordinary smooth water, to receive much instruction or pleasure from the efforts of the old masters at the more difficult forms and features of water in motion. If, however, all form and feature be abandoned, and falling water be selected at the moment, and under the circumstances when it presents nothing to the eye but a few breaking flakes of foam on the surface of a dark and colourless current, it is then far easier to paint than when it is smooth, and accordingly we find Claude and Poussin succeeding in it well, and throwing a bit of breaking foam over their rocks with good effect; and see Ruysdael carrying the matter farther, and rendering a low waterfall completely, with great fidelity. It is true that he divests his water of colour, and is often wanting in transparency, but still there is nothing radically wrong in his work, and this is saying much. What falling water may be, and ought to be, we shall see in the following chapter.

"[§ 22. Painting of rough sea. Vandevelde and Backhuysen.] I wish Ruysdael had painted one or two rough seas. I believe if he had, he might have saved the unhappy public from much grievous victimizing, both in mind and pocket, for he would have shown that Vandevelde and Backhuysen are not quite sea-deities. As it is, I believe there is scarcely such another instance to be found in the history of man, of the epidemic aberration of mind into which multitudes fall by infection, as is furnished by the value set upon the works of these men. All others of the ancients have real power of some kind or another, either solemnity of intention, as the Poussins, or refinement of feeling, as Claude, or high imitative accuracy, as Cuyp and Paul Potter, or rapid power of execution, as Salvator; there is something in all which ought to be admired, and of which, if exclusively contemplated, no degree of admiration, however enthusiastic, is unaccountable or unnatural. But Vandevelde and Backhuysen have *no* power, no redeeming quality of mind; their works are neither reflective, nor eclectic, nor imitative; they have neither tone, nor execution, nor colour, nor composition, nor any artistical merit to recommend them; and they present not even a deceptive, much less a real, resemblance of nature. Had they given us staring green seas, with hatchet edges, such as we see 'Her Majesty's Ship So-and-So' fixed into by the heads or sterns in the outer room of the Academy, the thing would have been comprehensible; there is a natural predilection in the mind of man for green waves with curling tops, but not for clay or wool, and the colour, we should have thought, would have been repulsive even to those least cognizant of form. [§ 23. Their errors of colour and shadow.] Whatever may be the chilliness, or mistiness, or opacity of Dutch climate and ocean, there is no water, which has motion in it, and air above it, which ever assumes such a grey as is attributed to sea by these painters; cold and lifeless the general effect may be, but at all times it is wrought out by variety of hue in all its parts; it is a grey caused by coldness of light, not by absence of colour. And how little the authority of these men is worthy of trust in matters of effect, is sufficiently shown by their constant habit of casting a coal-black shadow half way across the picture on the nearest waves; for, as I have before shown, water itself *never* takes any shadow at all, and the shadow upon foam is so delicate in tint and so broken in form as to be scarcely traceable. The men who could allow themselves to lay a coal-black shadow upon what never takes any shadow at all, and whose feelings were not hurt by the sight of falsehood so distinct, and recoiled not at the shade themselves had made, can be little worthy of credit in anything that they do or assert. [§ 24. And powerless efforts in rendering spray.] Then their foam is either deposited in spherical and tubular concretions, opaque and unbroken, on the surfaces of the waves, or else, the more common case, it is merely the whiteness of the waves shaded gradually off, as if it were the light side of a spherical object, of course representing every breaker as crested, not with spray, but with a puff of smoke. Neither let it be supposed that, in so doing, they had any intention of representing the vaporous spray taken off wild waves by violent wind. That magnificent effect only takes place on large breakers, and has no appearance of smoke except at a little distance; seen near, it is dust. But the Dutch painters cap every little cutting ripple with smoke, evidently intending it for foam, and evidently thus representing it because they had not sufficient power over the brush to produce the broken effect of real spray. Their seas, in consequence, have neither frangibility nor brilliancy; they do not break, but evaporate; their foam neither flies, nor sparkles, nor springs, nor wreathes, nor curdles, nay, it is not even white, nor has the effect of white, but of a dirty efflorescence or exhalation, [§ 25. Their impossible insertion of vessels], and their ships are inserted into this singular sea with peculiar want of truth; for, in nature, three circumstances contribute to disguise the water-line upon the wood;—when a wave is thin, the colour of the wood is shown a little through it; when a wave is smooth, the colour of the wood is a little reflected upon it; and when a wave is broken, its foam more or less obscures and modifies the line of junction; besides which, the wet wood itself catches some of the light and colour of the sea. Instead of this, the water-line of the Dutch vessels is marked clear and hard all round; the water reflecting nothing, showing nothing through it, and equally defined in edge of foam as in all other parts. [§ 26. And impossible curves of surge.] Finally, the curves of their waves are not curves of *projection*, which all sea lines are, but the undulating lines of ropes, or other tough and connected bodies. Whenever two curves, dissimilar in their nature, meet in the sea, of course they both break, and form an edge; but every kind of curve, catenary or conic, is associated by these painters in most admired disorder, joined indiscriminately by their extremities. This is a point, however, on which it is impossible to argue, without going into high mathematics, and even then the nature of particular curves, as given by the brush, would be scarcely demonstrable; and I am the less disposed to take much trouble about it because I think that the persons who are really fond of these works, are almost beyond the reach of argument. I can understand why people like Claude, and perceive much in their sensations which is right and legitimate, and which can be appealed to, and I can give them credit for perceiving more in him than I am a present able to perceive; but when I hear of persons *honestly* admiring Backhuysen or Vandevelde, I think there must be something physically wrong or wanting in their perceptions. At least, I can form no estimate of what their notions or feelings are, and cannot hope for anything of principle or opinion common between us, which I can address or understand.

"[§ 27. The seas of Claude. Their truthfulness.] The seas of Claude are the finest pieces of water painting in ancient art. I do not say I like them because they appear to me selections of the particular moment when the sea is most insipid and characterless; but I think that they are exceedingly true to the forms and time selected, or at least that the fine instances of them are so, of which there are exceedingly few. Anything and everything is fathered upon him, and he probably committed many mistakes himself, and was occasionally right rather by accident than by knowledge.

"Claude and Ruysdael, then, may be considered as the only two men among the old masters who could paint anything like water in extended spaces or in action. The great mass of landscape painters, though they sometimes succeeded in the imitation of a pond or a gutter, display, whenever they have space or opportunity to do so, want of feeling in every effort, and want of knowledge in every line."

P. 369 (ii. 5, 2, 1), line 2, for "suggestively, if not faithfully," eds. 1 and 2 read, "respectably and faithfully, if not beautifully."

Ib. (ii. 5, 2, 1), line 23, "expression of repose," eds. 1 and 2 add, "He is a little too apt to mistake the affected for the poetical. Some of his evening passages of sea-shore with calm seas are very perfect, and he is peculiarly daring and successful in the treatment of extensive rippled surface."

Ib. (ii. 5, 2, 2), eds. 1–4 entitle this section, "§ 2. The calm rivers of De Wint, J. Holland," etc., and read, "Hundreds . . . calm water. De Wint is singularly powerful and certain, exquisitely bright, and vigorous in colour. The late John Varley produced some noble passages. I have seen, some seven years ago, works by J. Holland, which were, I think, as near perfection as water-colour can be carried—for *bonâ fide* truth, refined and finished to the highest degree. [But he has since that time produced more pictures every year; and his fate appears irrecoverable, unless by a very strong effort and a total change of system. I need scarcely refer to the calms of Stanfield and Callcott, of whose excellence it is better to say nothing than little. I only wish that they both, especially the latter, would be a little less cold.]*

"[§ 3. The character of bright, and violent, falling water.] But the power of modern artists is not brought out until they have greater difficulties to struggle with. Stand for half-an-hour," etc.

P. 370 (ii. 5, 2, 3), line 4 from foot, for "and rich in colour, if he would," eds. 1–4 read, "and unequalled in colour, except by Turner. None of our water-colour painters can approach him in the management of the variable hues of clear water over weeded rocks; but his feeling for it often leads

---

* Eds. 3 and 4 omit the passage bracketed [*sic*] above.

him a little too far, and, like Copley Fielding, he loses sight of simplicity and dignity for the sake of delicacy or prettiness. His waterfalls are, however, unequalled in their way ; and if he would," etc.

P. 371 (ii. 5, 2, 4), for " J. D. Harding is, I think, nearly unequalled in," eds. 1 and 2 read, " J. D. Harding is, I think, of all men living, and therefore, certainly, of all who have ever lived, the greatest master in," etc., adding as a foot-note, " Turner is an exception to all rules, and whenever I speak generally he is to be considered as such."

P. 372 (ii. 5, 2, 6–7), App., " Study of chiaroscuro. There is indeed one fresh point," eds. 1, 2, and 3 read, " study of chiaroscuro in an exceedingly ill-chosen grey. Besides, the perpetual repetition of the same idea is singularly weakening to the mind. Fielding, in all his life, can only be considered as having produced *one* sea picture. The others are duplicates. He ought to go to some sea of perfect clearness and brilliant colour, as that on the coast of Cornwall or of the Gulf of Geneva, and study it in broad daylight, with no black clouds or drifting rain to help him out of his difficulties. He would then both learn his strength and add to it."
" [§ 8. Its high aim at character.] But there is one point," etc.

P. 373 (ii. 5, 2, 9), line 13 from foot, for " The Land's End," etc., eds. 1, 2, and 3 read, " nor is Mr. Fielding without a model in art, for the Land's End . . . "

P. 374 (ii. 5, 2, 10), line 3 from foot, " to learn how to conceal," eds. 1 and 2 read, " to learn what is now in *his* art the one thing wanting—how to conceal."

P. 377 (*ib.*, *ib.*, 3), line 15 from foot, for " induce an effort of clearness which, perhaps, the artist," eds. 1 and 2 read, " make everybody inclined to cry out—the moment they come before the picture—' Dear me, what excessively clear water !' when, perhaps, in a lowland study, clearness is not a quality which the artist," etc.

P. 378 (*ib.*, *ib.*), line 4, for " ordinary," eds. 1 and 2 read, " right and natural."

P. 378 (ii. 5, 3, 4), eds. 1 and 2 omit the foot-note.

P. 379 (ii. 5, 3, 5), line 17, " close to us," eds. 1 and 2 add in foot-note : " The ' Lac de Chède' *was* (alas for the word ! it was destroyed by an eboulement three years ago), to my mind, the loveliest thing in Switzerland ; a pool of emerald water, clearer than the mountain air around it, and yet greener than the pine boughs whose gloom it imaged, full of bright, forest-like weeds, and peopled by multitudes of lustrous, gliding, innocent serpents, unearthly creatures, which gave it more of the Greek feeling of divinity than is now perhaps left in the whole wide world. It was probably the groundwork of many of Shelley's noblest descriptive passages."

Ib. (*ib.*, *ib.*, 6), last line, " distant water," eds. 1 and 2 add a foot-note, " In all this reasoning I suppose knowledge in the reader of the optical mode in which reflections are produced; otherwise it can scarcely be understood."

Pp. 383–84 (ii. 5, 3, 11), this section ("After all, . . . reflective blue") is shorter and quite different in eds. 1 and 2, which read, "If, then, we consider what will be the effect of the constant observation of all natural laws, down to the most intricate and least apparently important, an observation carried out not merely in large or broad cases, but in every spot or shade of the slightest passages of reflection; if we add to this all that attainment of intricacy and infinity which we have generally described as characteristic of Turner's execution universally; if we suppose, added to this, all that radiance and refinement which we observed to be constant in his colours, brought by the nature of the subject up to their utmost brilliancy and most delicate states of perpetual transition and mystery; if we suppose all this, aided by every mechanical means of giving lustre and light that art can supply, used with the most consummate skill; and if we suppose all this thought, beauty, and power applied, manifested, and exerted to produce the utmost possible degree of fulness and finish that can be concentrated into given space, we shall have some idea of Turner's painting of calm water universally."

P. 386 (ii. 5, 3, 14), line 22 from foot, "meets the shore. In the," eds. 1 and 2 read, "meets the shore. But it is only by persons who have not carefully watched the effect of a steamer's wake when she is running close by shore that the exquisite accuracy with which all this is told and represented is at all appreciable. In the . . ."

P. 386 (ii. 5, 3, 15), last line, "faculties of the mind," eds. 1 and 2 add, "There is almost a deep truth, which must be reasoned upon and comprehended in them before their beauty can be felt."

P. 388 (ii. 5, 3, 19). This section ("But all these . . . twilight") is shorter and quite different in eds. 1 and 2, which read, "Of Turner's more difficult effects of calm surface associated with rising mist, it is impossible to speak partially; we must consider them as associated with effects of light, and many other matters difficult of investigation, only to be judged of by contemplating each picture as a whole. The 'Nemi,' 'Oberwesel,' and 'Ehrenbreitstein' have been already instanced (Sect. III., Chap. IV.), the latter being especially remarkable for its expression of water surface, seen not through but under mist. The 'Constance' is a more marvellous example than all, giving the vast lake, with its surface white with level mist lying league beyond league in the wan twilight, like a fallen space of moony sky."

P. 389 (ii. 5, 3, 20), eds. 1 and 2, the first two sentences of this section ("it will be remembered . . . its forms") run as follows:—"But we must pause to observe Turner's victory over greater difficulties. The chief peculiarity about his drawing of falling or running water, is his fearless and full rendering of its forms."

P. 391 (ii. 5, 3, 23), "takes the shape" is not italicized in eds. 1–4, "leopard; if it meet . . . sea waves forwards" (p. 392). This passage in eds. 1 and 2 runs thus :—"leopard. The finest instance that I know, of this state of water, is the course of the Dranse near Martigny. That river has just descended a fall of six thousand feet in twenty miles, without, as far as I know, one break, stop, or resting-place in the whole distance; and its velocity and power are at last so tremendous that, if it meets a rock seven or eight feet above the level of its bed, it will neither part nor foam, nor express any concern about the matter, but clears it in a smooth dome of water, without apparent exertion, coming down again as smoothly on the other side, the whole surface of the surge being drawn into parallel lines by its extreme velocity, but quite foamless, except in places where the form of the bed opposes itself at some direct angle to such a line of fall and causes a breaker, so that the whole river has the appearance of a deep and raging sea."

P. 392 (ii. 5, 3, 24), line 17, "grace," eds. 1 and 2 add, "little broken by foam."

Ib. (*ib.*, *ib.*), line 22, "of beautiful line," eds. 1 and 2 read, "of the line of beauty quite unbroken by edges, except here and there where a rock rises too high to be cleared and causes a breaker."

P. 392 (ii. 5, 3, 25), "We see therefore . . . most beautiful forms," eds. 1 and 2 read, "And now we can understand the peculiar excellence of Turner's torrent drawing. With his usual keen perception of all that is most essential in nature; of those qualities and truths which tell us most about the past as well as the present, he seizes on these curved lines of the torrent, not only as the most beautiful forms."

Ib. (*ib.*, *ib.*), last line, for "attribute," eds. 1-4 read, "exclusive attribute." Eds. 1 and 2 omit the foot-note, and eds. 3 and 4 the word "exclusively" in the first line of it.

P. 393 (ii. 5, 3, 26), line 17, "dusty vapour," eds. 1 and 2 add a foot-note : "Compare note, Sect. III., Chap. IV., § 13."

P. 394 (ii. 5, 3, 27), line 22, "basin," eds. 1 and 2 add, "presenting us, in the rest of their progress, with that most difficult of all appearances for a painter to render,—a torrent descending steeply as it retires from us."

Ib. (*ib.*, *ib.*), line 25, "recorded exactly," eds. 1 and 2 read, "recorded, each recorded with unequalled fidelity, and each recorded exactly."

P. 394 (ii. 5, 3, 28), line 37, "A still finer example," etc. From here to the end of § 30 (p. 369) is omitted in eds. 1 and 2, which read, "But it is time for us to pass to the contemplation of Turner's drawing of the sea."

Pp. 397-98 (ii. 5, 3, 31). In eds. 1 and 2 this section appears as "[§ 29. His drawing of the sea. The essential ideas characteristic of the ocean"], and begins as follows :—"The idea of the sea which an unobservant landsman obtains by standing on the beach is a peculiarly limited and imperfect one. The curl of the breakers under ordinary circumstances is uniform and monotonous, both in its own form, and in its periodical repetition. The size of the waves out at sea is neither seen nor compre-hended ; and the image carried away is little more than that of an extensive field of large waves, all much resembling each other, moving gradually to the beach, and breaking in the same lines and forms.

"But such is not the real nor essential character of the sea. Afloat . . . all the rest ; and the breaker, whose curl, seen from the land, had something of smallness and meanness in its contours, presents . . . velo-city and power. If, in such a position, whether in a boat, or on some isolated rock (the last by far the best) on a rocky coast, we abandon our-selves for hours to the passive reception of the great and essential impres-sions of that which is around us, the only way of arriving at a true feeling of its spirit, the three great ideas which we shall carry away with us will be those of recklessness, power, and breadth ;—[§ 30. Are recklessness, power, and breadth.]—recklessness manifested in the . . . falling. When we see the waves successively."

P. 398 (ii. 5, 3, 31-2), "recoils and recovers. Aiming," etc., eds. 1 and 2 read, "recoils and recovers. Finally, the sensation of breadth is peculiarly impressed, not by the extent of sea itself, but by the enormous sweep and hollow of every wave, of which no idea whatever can be formed from the beach, and by the grand unity of the curves of the breakers, which now appear to fall, not in curls, but in precipices.

"[§ 31. How Turner renders them in the 'Hero and Leander.'] Now they are those grand characters of the sea which Turner invariably aims at, and never rests satisfied unless he has given ; and, in consequence, even in his coast seas, he almost always . . . as in the 'Langharne,' 'Land's End,' 'Fowey,' and 'Dunbar.' But never failing to give at least one example of every truth, he has presented us with one most studied representation of a rolling sea, as seen from the shore, in the 'Hero and Leander.' The drawing of the approaching and falling breakers, under the moonlight, in this picture, must, I believe, remain, like the memory of some of the mighty scenes of nature herself, impressed for ever on the minds of all who have once seen it.

"[§ 32. In the 'Langharne.'] But it is on such wild coast seas as those of the 'Land's End' and 'Langharne' that Turner's power is chiefly con-centrated. The latter."

Pp. 401-2 (ii. v. 3, 37). This section ("The greater number . . . earlier time") is omitted in eds. 1 and 2. In its last sentence, for "It is instruc-tive," eds. 3 and 4 read, "It is thus of peculiar truth and value ; and instructive."

P. 403 (ii. v. 3, 58), foot-note. Eds. 1 and 2 omit this foot-note, and have this one :—

    *   "'The yesty waves
Confound and swallow navigation up.'—*Macbeth*, Act iv. Sc. 1."

P. 406 (ii. 5, 3, 40), foot-note 2, "multitudinous waves," eds. 1 and 2 add, "the ποντίων κυμάτων ἀνήριθμον γέλασμα," and for the last sentence of the note, "There is hardly . . . of sea," read, "You may tire yourself by walking over the extent of that shore."

P. 407 (ii. 6, 1, 1). In eds. 1 and 2 this section is entitled, "Extreme difficulty of representing foliage, and ease with which the truth of its representation may be determined."

P. 407 (ii. 6, 1, 1), line 15, "principally consists . . . to demonstrate," etc. Here eds. 1 and 2 read thus: "principally consists. And it is a daring choice; for of all objects that defeat and defy the utmost efforts of the painter to approach their beauty, a noble tree is the most inimitable; and I scarcely know a more hopeless state of discouragement—a more freezing and fettering sensation of absolute impotence, than that which comes over the artist in his forest walks, as he sees the floor, and the pillars, and the roof of the great temple, one labyrinth of loveliness, one wilderness of perfections, with the chequering sunbeams dancing before him like mocking spirits; and the merry leaves laughing and whispering about him in the pride of their beauty, as knowing that he cannot catch nor imitate one ray, nor one form of their hues and their multitude.

"Although, however, there is insuperable difficulty in the painting of foliage, there is, fortunately, little difficulty in ascertaining the comparative truth of the representation; for wherever specific form and character is organized and complete, it is easy, without requiring any laborious attention or extraordinary knowledge in the reader, to demonstrate," etc.

P. 410 (ii. 6, 1, 7), line 13, for "this piece," eds. 1 and 2 read, "this precious piece," and line 5, for "This latter is a representation," eds. 1 and 2 read, "This is a fine example of the general system of bough-drawing of the Italian school. It is a representation."

P. 411 (ib., ib., 8), line 4, at "Turner" eds. 1 and 2 add a note, "Compare § 12" (§ 13 in later eds.).

P. 412 (ib., ib., 9), foot-note. Eds. 1 and 2 omit this note.

P. 412 (ib., ib., 10), line 16, "from which they spring. Precision," eds. 1–4 here read thus: "from which they spring. Where a bough divides into two equal ramifications, the diameter of each of the two is about two-thirds that of the single one, and the sum of these diameters, therefore, one-fourth greater than the diameter of the single one. Hence, if no boughs died or were lost, the quantity of wood in the sprays would appear one-fourth greater than would be necessary to make up the thickness of the trunk. But the lost boughs remove the excess, and therefore, speaking broadly, the diameters of the outer boughs put together would generally just make up the diameter of the trunk. Now mathematical precision."

Pp. 413–14 (ii. 6, 1, 11). From "but the most gross examples. . . . Not so with Claude" (inclusive) is omitted in eds. 1 and 2, in which § 12 appears as § 11. "But it is only by looking over the sketches of Claude."

P. 414 (ii. 6, 1, 12), line 38, for "the landscape," eds. 1–4 read, "the windy landscape," and line 19, for "are masterly; yet that," eds. 1 and 2 read, "are masterly. I believe it will, some time or another, if people ever begin to think with their own heads, and see with their own eyes, be the death-warrant of Gaspar's reputation, signed with his own hand. That."

P. 415 (*ib.*, *ib.*, 13), the italics were first added in ed. 5.

Pp. 416–17 (*ib.*, *ib.*, 14, 15). These two sections are omitted in eds. 1 and 2, while in them (p. 417, lines 2–4), for "Albert Dürer has given . . . but misses," eds. 3 and 4 read, "Rembrandt and Albert Dürer have given . . . but both miss," etc.

In place of them eds. 1 and 2 read as follows :—

"[§ 13. Unity of all truth in the works of Turner. Crossing the Brook."] In passing to the works of Turner I have little more to do than to name the most characteristic pictures, for the truths I have been pointing out are so palpable and evident that the reader can decide for himself in a moment where they exist, and where they are wanting. The 'Crossing of the Brook' will probably be the first which will occur to the minds of those best acquainted with Turner's works, and indeed the stems on the extreme left of the picture, especially the fainter ones entangled behind the dark tree, and the vistas of interwoven boughs which retire in the centre, are above all praise for grace and truth. These, and the light branches on the left in the 'Mercury and Argus,' may be given as standards of the utmost possible refinement and fidelity in tree-drawing, carried out to the last fibres of the leaflets. I am desirous, however, where it is possible, to give references to engravings as well as to original works, and neither of these have been so well rendered by the engraver as a little passage of thicket on the right in the 'Chain-bridge over the Tees,' of the England series. This piece of drawing is peculiarly expressive of the complexity, entanglement, and aerial relation of which we have just been speaking. The eye is lost in its exquisite multiplicity, yet you can go through among the boughs, in and out, catching a leaf here and a sunbeam there, now a shadow and now a stem, until you come out at the cliff on the other side, and there is not one of those countless stems at the same distance with another, not one that you do not leave behind you before you get to the next, however confused and entangled you may be with their intersections and their multitude. Compare this with Gaspar's tree in 'La Riccia,' and decide for yourself which is truth. One, infinite, graceful, penetrable, interwoven, sun-lighted, alive ; the other, three brown strokes of paint, at precisely the same distance from the eye, without one intersection, without one cast shadow, and without one ramification to carry the foliage.

"[§ 14. 'Chiefswood Cottage, 'Chateau de la Belle Gabrielle,' etc.] The vignette of 'Chiefswood Cottage,' in the illustrations to Scott, is peculiarly interesting as an illustration of all that we have been saying of the tapering of trunks. One stem, on the left, is made to taper in perspective, by receding from the eye, as well as by sending off quantities of brushwood at its base, and observe how it contrasts with and sets off the forms of all the others. Look at the stems of the dark trees on the right, how they rise without the least diminution, although so tall, till they fork ; note the exquisite observance of proportion in the diminution of every spray at the very instant of dividing, the inconceivable and countless complexity, depth, aerial recession, and grace of the sprays themselves. This vignette and the 'Chateau de la Belle Gabrielle' always appear to me about the two most finished pieces of bough-drawing that Turner has produced. We should, however, associate with them the group of waving willows in the 'Warwick' (England series), the 'Dartmouth Cove,' with its dark, gnarled trunk and delicate springing stems above the flag (also a picture to be closely studied with reference to bough-anatomy); the branching stems above the river in the 'Durham,' the noble group of full-grown trees in the 'Kelso,' and, perhaps grander than all, the tall mass of foliage in the 'Bolton Abbey.'"

P. 418 (ii. 6, 1, 16), "Let us, however, pass," etc. Eds. 1 and 2 give this section as "[§ 15. Character of leafage. Its singular inequality."], and for the first two sentences of it read the following :—

"Such being the truth of the stems and branches, as represented by modern painters, let us see whether they are equally faithful in foliage, and whether the old masters atone by the leaves for the errors of the stems. Nature's great aim, in arranging her leaves, as in everything else, is to get symmetry and variety together, to make the symmetry be *felt*, but only the variety *seen*. Consequently, though she ranges her leaves on their individual sprays with exquisite regularity, she always contrives to disguise that regularity in their united effect. For as in every group of leaves," etc.

P. 419 (ii. 6, 1, 17, end), for "stalks," eds. 1 and 2 read, "roots ; " and after "claw," they add, "and behold a tree ! "

P. 422 (ii. 6, 1, 22), line 28, "each," eds. 1 and 2 add note, "Compare Sect. II., Chap. IV., § 16," and below (§ 23) they omit the foot-note.

Pp. 423–24 (ii. 6, 1, 24), eds. 1 and 2 omit the long foot-note.

P. 425 (ii. 6, 1, 26), line 20, "moderns," eds. 1 and 2 add, " The tree in the 'Mercury and Argus' is the most perfect example I remember of the pure ideal form."

P. 426 (ii. 6, 1, 27, end). From here to the end of the chapter is omitted in eds. 1 and 2, which contain instead the two following sections and foot-note :—

"[§ 26. Connection in foliage between truth and beauty.] Let me then close the investigation of the truth of nature with this link between the true and the beautiful, for we may always assume that the ideal or perfect form of any object is the most beautiful it can possibly assume, and that it can be only diseased taste in us, which dislikes it, if we ever find ourselves doing so. And I shall prove hereafter that this perfect form of trees is not only the most beautiful which *they* can assume, but one of the most perfect which can be presented to the eye by any means or object. And especially in foliage, nothing can be true which is not beautiful, so that we shall be far better able to trace the essential qualities of truth in tree-drawing, and especially the particular power of Turner, when we are able to speak of grace as well as advocacy.

"[§ 27. Foliage of Harding, Fielding, and other modern painters.] We have before expressed our admiration of the works of J. D. Harding for general drawing of trees, and we may once again refer to them as an illustration of every truth we have been pointing out in foliage. We only wish they were carried a little farther and finer. We should enjoy a little more of the making out which we find in Claude's foreground, to give greater value to his brilliant execution; and we should like a little more attention paid to specific character of trees, and to the designing of the boughs. Harding's boughs are always *right*, always flexible and growing; but they are not always so put together that we wonder how anything so beautiful could ever have been conceived. There is not a distinct design of perfect beauty in every spray, which there always is in nature.

"Callcott's foliage is very refined and ideal, very faultless, though apt to be dreadfully cold in colour. Stanfield is sometimes awkward, though not exactly wrong; he inserted his stone-pine into the road at Pozzuoli like a sign-post. Copley Fielding is very wild, intricate, and graceful, wanting only in dignity; he should also remember that leaves, here and there, both have and show sharp edges. Creswick I have already noticed. Cattermole is very grand in his conception of form; and many others of our water-colour painters have produced instructive passages." *

P. 427 (ii. 6, 1, 28), eds. 3 and 4 omit the second and third foot-notes.

P. 431 (ii. 6, 1, 33), line 15, "affected," eds. 3 and 4 add, "This is bitterly to be regretted, for few of our artists would paint foliage better, if he would paint it from nature, and with reverence."

P. 432 (ii. 6, 1, 34), line 5, "more honour," eds. 3 and 4 add a further sentence and paragraph thus :—"I have much pleasure in Creswick's works, and I am always glad to see them admired by others.

"[§ 35. Conclusion. Works of J. Linnell and S. Palmer.] I shall conclude this sketch of the foliage art of England, by mention of two artists, whom I believe to be representative of a considerable class, admirable in their reverence and patience of study, yet unappreciated by the public, because they do what is unrecommended by dexterity of handling. The forest studies of J. Linnell are peculiarly elaborate, and, in many points, most skilful. They fail, perhaps, of interest, owing to the over fulness of detail and a want of generalization in the effect; but even a little more of the Harding sharpness of touch would set off their sterling qualities, and make them felt. A less known artist, S. Palmer, lately admitted a member of the Old Water Colour Society, is deserving of the very highest place among faithful followers of nature. His studies of foreign foliage especially are beyond all praise for care and fulness. I have never seen a stone pine or a cypress drawn except by him; and his feeling is as pure and grand as his fidelity is exemplary. He has not, however, yet, I think, discovered what is necessary and unnecessary in a great

---

* "It may not, perhaps, be out of place to protest against the mode in which the foliage is executed in Mr. Moon's publication of Roberts' Eastern Sketches. So magnificent a work should have been put only into first-rate hands, and there is much about it unsatisfactory in every way; partly from attempting too much, but chiefly from the incapability of the hands employed in the landscape. No one but Harding should have executed the foliage; and, at any rate, a good draughtsman should have been secured for the foreground. I know not whose work they are; but they are a libel on Mr. Roberts, whose foliage is always beautiful and artistical, if not very carefully studied."

picture; and his works, sent to the Society's rooms, have been most unfavourable examples of his power, and have been generally, as yet, in places where all that is best in them is out of sight. I look to him, nevertheless, unless he lose himself in over reverence for certain conventionalisms of the older schools, as one of the probable renovators and correctors of whatever is failing or erroneous in the practice of English art."

P. 433 (ii. 6, 2, 1), lines 7–23, "because enough . . . disgraceful," eds. 1 and 2 here read thus: "because there is nothing in the nature of the thing itself, with which the ordinary observer is not sufficiently acquainted to be capable of forming a pretty accurate judgment of the truth of its representation; and the difference between one artist and another in architectural drawing does not depend so much upon knowledge of actual form, in which it is here impossible grossly to err, as on the representation of that form with more able application of the general laws of chiaroscuro and colour, or with greater precision and delicacy of execution. The difference between Roberts and Turner, as architectural draughtsmen, does not depend on any greater knowledge in one or another of the channelling of triglyphs, or the curvature of volutes, but on the application of general principles of art to develop and adorn such truths. [§ 2. Because dependent only on the artist's mode of execution, and knowledge of general principles.] The execution which is good and desirable in drawing a stone on the ground channelled by frost is equally good and desirable in drawing a stone in a building channelled by the chisel. He who can do the one can far more easily do the other, for architecture requires only a simple and straightforward application of those rules of which every other material object of a landscape has required a most difficult and complicated application. It is disgraceful to misrepresent them, but it is no honour to draw them well. It is disgraceful," etc.

P. 434 (ii. 6, 2, 1), lines 5–11, "I may, however, refer for . . . intricacy of parts. I have then only," etc., eds. 1 and 2 here begin a new paragraph, and read thus:—

"[§ 3. Notice of a few characteristic examples of Turner's architecture.] I may, however, refer to what has been already said upon the subject in Sect. II., Chap. IV., §§ 6, 12, 13 (and note), and 14, and I may point for . . . intricacy of parts. The 'Modern Italy' may be adduced as a standard of the drawing of architectural distance. But so much of the excellence of all these pictures depends, partly on considerations of principles of beauty, not yet developed, partly on expression of local character, and yet systematised illustration of part by part, of which we cannot yet take cognizance, that we should only do harm by entering on close criticism of their works at present. I have, then, only."

P. 436 (ii. 6, 2, 4), line 2, for "that feeling," eds. 1 and 2 read, "it would be unjust if it could, for that feeling," etc.

Ib. (*ib.*, *ib.*), line 4, "years of labour. There is," eds. 1–4 insert a further passage thus: "years of labour. [§ 5. There is nothing in his works which can be enjoyed without knowledge.] And there is, indeed, nothing in Turner—not one dot nor line—whose meaning can be understood without knowledge; because he never aims at several impressions, but at the deep final truth, which only meditation can discover, and only experience recognize.   There is nothing done or omitted by him which does not imply such a comparison of ends, such a rejection of the least worthy (as far as they are incompatible with the rest), such careful selection and arrangement of all that can be united, as can only be enjoyed by men capable of going through the same process and discovering the reasons for the choice.   [§ 6. And nothing which knowledge will not enable us to enjoy.]   And, as there is nothing in his works which can be enjoyed without knowledge, so there is nothing in them which knowledge will not enable us to enjoy.   There is."

P. 444 (ii. 6, 3, 13), line 10, "green-room," eds. 1 and 2 add here this foot-note: "We have very great respect for Mr. Maclise's power as a draughtsman, and if we thought that his errors proceeded from weakness we should not allude to them, but we most devoutly wish that he would let Shakespeare alone.   If the Irish ruffian who appeared as 'Hamlet' last year had been gifted with a stout shillelah, and if his state of prostration had been rationally accounted for by distinct evidence of a recent 'compliment' on the crown; or if the maudlin expressions of the young lady christened 'Ophelia' had been properly explained by an empty gin bottle on her lap, we should have thanked him for his powerful delineation both of character and circumstance.   But we cannot permit him thus to mislead the English public (unhappily too easily led by any grinning and glittering fantasy), in all their conceptions of the intention of Shakespeare."

P. 445 (ii. 6, 3, 16), last line, "thirty," eds. 1–4 omit the foot-note.

P. 448 (ii. 6, 3, 22), line 37, "Now we should like . . . most original" (p. 450).   This page and a half is omitted in ed. 1 only, which reads simply, "Now we should like to see our artists working out, with all exertion of their concentrated powers, and application of their most extensive knowledge, such tints of simple and marked individual sentiment as they may get from nature at all places and at all times."

P. 450 (ii. 6, 3, 23), in ed. 1 (only) this paragraph was quite different, being as follows :—

"[§ 23. What should be their general system.]   Let them take for their subjects some touch of single unadulterated feeling, out of the single and serious parts of nature, looking generally for peace and solemnity rather than for action or magnificence, and let each of their subjects so chosen be different from all the others, but yet part of the same system with all the others, having a planned connection with them, as the sonnets of Wordsworth have among themselves; and then let each of these chants or sonnets be worked out with the most laborious completeness, making separate studies of every inch of it, and going to nature for all the important passages, for she will always supply us with what we want a thousand times better than we can ourselves; and let only seven or eight such pictures be painted in the year, instead of the forty or fifty careless repetitions which we see our more prolific water-colour painters produce at present; and there can be little doubt that the public will soon understand the thing, and enjoy it, and be quite as willing to give one hundred guineas for each complete and studied poem as they are now to give twenty for a careless or meaningless sketch.   And artists who worked on such a principle would soon find that both their artistical powers, and their fancy, and their imagination, were incalculably strengthened by it, and that they acquired by the pursuit of what was simple, solemn, and individual, the power of becoming, when they chose, truly magnificent and universal."

P. 452 (ii. 6, 3, 24), lines 15–31, "And now but one word . . . but of faith," ed. 1 (only) for this passage reads briefly, "With respect to the great artist whose works have formed the chief subject of this treatise, the duty of the press is clear.   He is above all criticism, beyond all animadversion, and beyond all praise.   His works are not to be received as in any way subjects or matters of opinion, but of Faith."

P. 453 (*ib.*, *ib.*), line 2, "completed poems," ed. 1 (only) adds, "poems, using no means nor vehicle capable of any kind of change.   We do not presume to form even so much as a wish, or an idea, respecting the manner or matter of anything proceeding from his hand.   We desire only that he would follow."

Ib. (*ib.*, *ib.*), last line, eds. 1 and 2 omit the foot-note.

P. 453–4, eds. 1–4 omit this Postscript.

NOTES TO VOLUME II

P. vii, Advertisement, eds. 1 and 2 read, "The illustrations in preparation for the third volume of this work having rendered a large page necessary, the present volume and the new edition of the first volume are arranged in a corresponding form.

"The following chapters," etc.

Ed. 1 also reads "Olympiads" for "years" in this Advertisement.

P. 6 (iii. 1, 1, 6), note 2, 1883 addition. This is not a note of 1856, as it was first added in the second (1848) edition of this volume.

P. 6 (*ib.*, 7), l. 16, eds. 1 and 2 read, "sagene" for "net"; and "strength of England" for "strength."

Ib., note 2, l. 5, eds. 1 and 2 om. "at the corner of the market-place."

P. 9 (*ib.*, 7), l. 6, for "we might," ed. 1 has, "we, foul and sensual as we are, might."

Ib. (*ib.*, 8), l. 16, ed. 1 reads, "All science and art may be divided into that which is subservient to life, or which is the object of it."

Ib. (*ib.*), l. 4 from foot, for "admits that whatever branch," ed. 1 reads, "proves and accepts the proposition, that whatever part."

P. 12 (*ib.*, 11), note. In ed. 1 this note was printed among the *Addenda*, at the end of the volume (pp. 216–17).

Ib. (*ib.*, 4), l. 21, after "intemperate," ed. 1 adds "(ἀκόλαστοι)."

Ib. (*ib.*), l. 24, ed. 1 reads, "and so are actually ἀκόλαστοι, in many instances and acts which lower not."

P. 15 (*ib.*), l. 9, for "mere passion," ed. 1 reads, "mere passion and impulse."

Ib. (*ib.*), l. 21 from foot, after "intemperate," ed. 1 adds, "or ἀκόλαστοι," and omits "for the time."

P. 16 (*ib.*, 5), l. 24, for "melody," ed. 1 reads, "music."

Ib. (*ib.*, 6), l. 5, for "self-sufficiency," ed. 1 reads, "permanence and self-sufficiency, where no other sensual pleasures are permanent or self-sufficient."

P. 18 (*ib.*, 7), l. 2, for "the sense . . . son," ed. 1 reads, "that of Isaac concerning his son."

P. 21 (iii. 1, 3, 1), l. 8 from foot, ed. 1 here reads thus, "What canon or text is there . . . beautiful? To what authority, when men are at variance with each other on this subject, shall it be deputed to judge which is right? or is there any such authority or canon at all?

"For it does not . . . taste, it is frequently denied, when we press to particulars, by the assertion of each individual that he has a right to his opinion—a right which is sometimes claimed even in moral matters, though then palpably without foundation, but which does not appear," etc.

P. 23 (*ib.*, 2), l. 14, for "a vain command . . . affections," ed. 1 reads, "which, if men . . . affections, would be the command of an impossibility."

Ib. (*ib.*, 3), l. 33, "characters," ed. 1 reads, "agreeable or disagreeable qualities."

P. 25 (*ib.*, 7), ll. 34-9, ed. 1 omits from "If then, . . . individual," reading, "That, then, which is required."

P. 26 (*ib.*), l. 13, ed. 1 adds a further sentence to this paragraph thus:— "And yet this dwelling upon them comes not up to that which I wish to express by the word Theoria, unless it be accompanied by the perception of their being a gift from and manifestation of God, and of all those nobler emotions before described, since not until so felt is their essential nature comprehended."

P. 28 (*ib.*, 12-13), ed. 1 adds a sentence, and reads as follows: "fears famine. I have seen a man of true taste pause for a quarter of an hour to look at the channelling that recent rain had traced in a heap of cinders.

"And here is evident another reason of that duty which we owe respecting our impressions of sight, namely, to discipline ourselves to the enjoyment of those which are eternal in their nature, not only because these are the most acute, but because they are the most easily . . ."

P. 35 (*ib.*, 6), l. 14, "cultivation," ed. 2 here adds a foot-note, given in ed. 1 among the *Addenda* at the end (p. 216), as follows:—

"Some confusion may arise in the mind of the reader on comparing this passage with others in the course of the volume; such as the second paragraph in the next chapter, in which the instinctive sense of beauty is asserted as existing in the child. But it is necessary always to observe the distinction made in the second chapter between the instinctive, or æsthetic, and the real, or theoretic perceptions of Beauty; and farther, it is to be remembered, that every elevated human instinct is in a manner put under voluntary power, and when highly cultivated, appears in increasing purity and intensity in each succeeding generation, or, on the other hand, diminishes until the race sinks into degradation nearly total, out of which no general laws may safely be deduced."

Ib. (*ib.*), last line, for "are . . . Alison," eds. 1 and 2 read, "are rare"; p. 36, l. 3, they omit "and placed in logical form"; and

p. 36, l. 4, for "to involve , . . . syllogisms," they read, "to fall into . . . forms."

P. 37 (*ib.*, 9), l. 11, "ourselves," eds. 1 and 2 omit "which will not . . . complicated beauty," and continue, "Let the eye but rest on some rude or uncouth form"; and l. 19, for "boughs" read "forms."

P. 42 (*ib.*, 2). The quotation on this page is different in ed. 2 (only), where the following is substituted :—

> "Not for these I raise
> The songs of thanks and praise,
> But for these obstinate questionings
> Of sense, and outward things,
> Fallings from us : vanishings,
> Blank misgivings of a creature
> Moving about in worlds not realized."

P. 43 (*ib.*, 3), l. 11, ed. 2 (alone) omits these lines, reading, "but I am certain"; and again, at the beginning of § 5, reads, "peculiar to themselves, for this, whatever it be, must be one of the primal and most effectual motives."

P. 44 (*ib.*, 5), l. 32, ed. 2 (only) omits the word "sensual."

P. 48, foot-note, l. 3, ed. 1 reads, "manifested with little, comparatively, that is offensive."

P. 50 (iii. 1, 5, 15), l. 37, for "browsing," eds. 1 and 2 read, "cattle."

P. 51 (*ib.*), l. 7, for "light," ed. 1 reads, "light, which is most intense when it impinges at the highest angle."

P. 55 (iii. 1, 6, 2), ll. 11–13 from foot, ed. 1 reads, "and so to the perfection of beauty in lines, or colours, or forms, or masses, or multitudes, the appearance of some species of Unity is, in the most determined sense of the word, essential."

P. 56 (*ib.*, 3), l. 4, for "impulse" ed. 1 reads, "inspiration."

P. 56 (*ib.*), l. 17, for "the melody . . . lines," ed. 1 has, "and it is the melody of sounds and the beauty of continuous lines."

P. 64, foot-note, l. 11, ed. 1 reads, "giving long legs and enormous wings to the smaller tribes, and short and thick proportion to the larger."

P. 67 (iii. 1, 6, 13, end), ed. 1 reads, "influence at all, which is the same as to conclude that there is no such thing as music, because there are more melodies than one."

P. 74 (iii. 1, 7, 5), l. 5, ed. 1 reads, "inspiration vanishes in the tottering affectations or tortured insanities of modern times. There is . . . inconsistency or absence of thought . . . evil choice of subject;

over-accumulation of materials, whether in painting or literature, the shallow and unreflecting nothingness of the English schools of art, the strained and disgusting horrors of the French, the distorted feverishness of the German :—pretence, over-decorations, over-divisions of parts in architecture, and again in music, in acting," etc.

Pp. 74-6, foot-note. The last two sentences of this foot-note appear in ed. 1 as a note in the *Addenda*, thus :—" It ought to have been noticed respecting the Virgilian conception of the Laocoon, that no fault . . . "

P. 76, foot-note, for "and the ruder, often the nobler," ed. 1 has, "a certain rudeness and incompleteness of finish is very noble in all." And the last sentence runs thus :—" There is a monument put up lately by a modern Italian sculptor in one of the side chapels of Santa Croce ; the face fine and the execution dexterous. But it looks as if . ."

P. 79 (iii. 1, 8, 3), l. 26, eds. 1 and 2 insert after "for instance," " —(whence the perfect beauty of the Alpine rose)—."

P. 80 (*ib.*, 4), l. 6, ed. 1 reads, "in like order. The Rafaelle at Blenheim, the Madonna di San Sisto, and all the works of Perugino, Francia, and John Bellini, present some such form, and the balance, at least, is preserved, even in pictures necessitating . . ."

P. 82 (iii. 1, 9, 4), l. 37, ed. 1 reads, "rendered difficult by the host of associated ideas connected with it, for the ocular sense . . is infinitely enhanced . . ."

P. 84 (*ib.*, 6), l. 25, ed. 1 reads, "to his abstract nature. And if the idea of sin is incapable of being formed with respect to Him, so also is its negative, for we cannot form an idea of negation where we cannot form an idea of presence. If, for instance, one could conceive of taste or flavour in a proposition of Euclid, so also might we of insipidity, but if not of the one, then not of the other. So that in speaking of the goodness of God, it cannot be that we mean anything more than His Love, Merciful-ness, and Justice, and these attributes I have shown to be expressed by other . . . in matters. Neither can I trace any more distinct relation between this idea . . . openness, of which I have already spoken as more expressed . . ."

P. 87 (iii. 1, 10, 2), l. 22, for "constant," ed. 1 has "eternal."

P. 88 (*ib.*, 3), foot-note, l. 3, ed. 1 reads, "it is) but of thought ; either impatient, which there was necessity to note swiftly, or impetuous, which it was well to note in mighty manner, as pre-eminently . . . with Tintoret, and often with Michael Angelo, and in lower," etc.

P. 93 (iii. 1, 11, 1), ll. 7 and 5 from foot, for "evidence within reach," ed. 1 has, "conceivable evidence," and later reads, "to show, in some measure, the inherent worthiness and glory of God's works, and something of the relations they bear to each other and to us, leaving," etc.

P. 94 (*ib.*, 2), l. 3, ed. 1 has, "necessary consequence of the perfection."

P. 95 (*ib.*, 4), note. Ed. 1 adds at the end of this note, "The conclud-ing book of the Ethics should be carefully read. It is all most valuable."

P. 97 (iii. 1, 12, 1), l. 13, ed. 1 reads, "of those that wallow or of those that soar; of the fiend-hunted swine by the Gennesaret lake, or of the dove returning to its ark of rest."

Ib. (*ib.*, 2), ll. 13 *seqq.*, ed. 1 reads, "Wherefore, it is evident that even the ordinary . . . he needs not, and which live not for his uses; nay, he has seldom grace to be grateful even to those that love and serve him, while on the other hand . . . more truly. Wherefore it is good."

P. 98 (*ib.*), l. 13, ed. 1 has, "added teaching of that gift, which we have from things beneath us, in thanks for the love they cannot equally return, that anguish."

Ib. (*ib.*), end of § 2, "necessities," ed. 1 adds this note: "I would have Mr. Landseer, before he gives us any more writhing otters, or yelping packs, reflect whether that which is best worthy of contemplation in a hound be its ferocity, or in an otter its agony, or in a human being its victory, hardly achieved even with the aid of its more sagacious brutal allies, over a poor little fish-catching creature, a foot long."

Ib. (*ib.*, 3), l. 29, ed. 1 reads, "breathes, neither do I ever crush or gather one without some pain), yet . . . giving happiness, and we cannot feel the desire of that which we cannot conceive, so that if we conceive not of a plant as capable of pleasure, we cannot desire to give it pleasure, that is, we cannot love it in the entire sense of the term.

"Nevertheless, the sympathy . . . so to love, as with Shelley of the sensitive plant, and Shakspeare always."

P. 99 (*ib.*, 4), l. 19, for "strength in the plant," ed. 1 has, "enjoyment in the particular individual plant itself."

Ib. (*ib.*), ll. 18-23, ed. 1 reads, "parts jointed on one to another . . . growing out of each other (note the singular imposition in many of them, the prickly pear for instance, of the fruit upon the body of the plant, so that it looks like a swelling or disease), and often farther opposed by harsh truncation of line, as in the cactus truncato-phylla."

P. 101 (*ib.*, 5), l. 9 from foot, ed. 1 reads, "become useful; it lives not for itself, and its beauty is gone . . . regained only in part when."

P. 101 (*ib.*), l. 20, ed. 1 reads, "of all utility which is based . . . of any creature, for in such ministering to each other as is consistent."

P. 102 (*ib.*, 7), ll. 36 *seqq.*, ed. 1 reads, "As, therefore, it appears from all evidence that it is the sense . . . organic form, it is evident from reason, as demonstrable by experience, that those forms . . . sensation. Hence we find gradations of beauty, from the apparent impenetrableness of hide," etc.

P. 103, note, ed. 1 adds the previous line, "Type of the wise,—who soar but never roam."

P. 104 (*ib.*, 9), ed. 1 reads, "There is much difficulty in the way . . . typical beauty, which are among them, as it seems, arbitrarily distributed; so that . . . cruel are often clothed . . . covert of the reeds and fens. But that mind only is fully disciplined in its theoretic power, which can when it chooses, throwing off the sympathies and repugnancies with which the ideas of *distinctiveness* or innocence . . . of animal powers to our own can pursue."

P. 104 (*ib.*, 10), l. 33, ed. 1 reads, "Which moral perfections, that they are indeed productive in proportion to their expression of instant beauty instinctively felt, is best proved by comparing those parts of animals in which they are definitely expressed."

P. 105 (*ib.*), l. 3, the words "(as pre-eminently in the chameleon)" were omitted in the 1883 edition.

P. 107 (*ib.*, 12), l. 7 and l. 26, ed. 1 has, "touchstone faithfulness," and, "every day the theoretic faculty entirely destroyed."

P. 111 (iii. 1, 13, 5), l. 34, ed. 1 has, "I apprehend that, although in respect of size, age, and kind of feeling, there may be some differences between them, yet of those."

P. 121 (iii. 1, 14, 3), l. 8, ed. 1, "on the fresh modes of attaining it, as well as on what he produced as a perfect example of it, chiefly."

P. 122 (*ib.*, 5), l. 3, ed. 1, "The second point to be considered in the influence of mind upon body is the mode of operation and conjunction of the moral feelings on and with the intellectual powers, and then their conjoint influence on the bodily form. Now the operation."

P. 124 (*ib.*, 8), l. 13, ed. 1 has, "owing to the apparent inconsistency of certain excellences and beauties to which they tend, as, first, of different . . ."

Pp. 124-5, foot-note. This note is omitted in ed. 1.

P. 125 (iii. 1, 14, 10), last line, ed. 1, "equal perfection, according to the functions of the creatures, so that there is an ideal of authority."

P. 126 (*ib.*), l. 11, ed. 1, "prevalent recurrence; added to which causes of distinctive character are to be taken into account the difference of age and sex, which, though . . . influence, cannot be banished."

P. 128 (*ib.*, 13), l. 9 from foot, ed. 1 has, "want of truth, which in these days it often in some measure does, for we indeed find faces about us with want enough of life or wholesome character in them to justify anything."

P. 129 (*ib.*, 14), l. 8, ed. 1 has, "and portraiture in real, downright necessity of modes, even in their noblest works"; and l. 17, "where they ought not, as Lippi and the corrupted Rafaelle; and is found often at exceeding disadvantage among men."

P. 130 (*ib.*, 15), l. 3, "If, then, individual . . ." Here ed. 1 has a fresh paragraph, thus :—"(§ 16. The right use of the model.) So far, then, of the use of the model and the preciousness of it in all art, from the highest to the lowest. But the use of the model is not all. It must be used in a certain way, and on this choice of right or wrong way all our ends are at stake, for the art which is of no power without the model, is of pernicious and evil power if the model be wrongly used. What the right use is has been at least exhibited, if not fully explained, in the argument by which we arrived at the general principles.

"The right ideal is to be reached . . ."

Ib. (*ib.*, 16), l. 22. After " toward God," ed. 1 inserts " (Nemesis)."

P. 131 (*ib.*, 18), l. 20, for " vice of all," ed. 1 has, " story of all sin."

P. 132 (*ib.*, 20), l. 3 from foot, for " scent of common," ed. 1 has, " foul scent of human flesh."

P. 133 (*ib.*, 22), l. 33, ed. 1 has, " who, though of little feeling, and often " ; and l. 37, " who had nobler and more serious intellect " ; and § 23, p. 134, l. 7, " are preferable, as in the Francia of our own gallery."

P. 134 (*ib.*, 24), l. 22, ed. 1 has, " profess, whence much may be forgiven to Rubens (as to our own Etty), less, as I think, to Correggio, who, with less apparent and evident coarseness, has " ; and (l. 36) omits " excepting always Etty."

P. 137 (*ib.*, 29), l. 22, for " conceived " ed. 1 has, " dwell for an instant."

P. 138 (*ib.*, 30), l. 27, ed. 1, " These, then, are the four passions whose presence, in any degree, on the human face is degradation. But of all passion it is to be generally observed," and § 31, p. 139, l. 13, for " lowering," ed. 1 has, " evaporating."

P. 141 (*ib.*, 32), note. Ed. 1 quotes eight lines :—

> "Each corse lay flat, lifeless and flat,
> And by the holy rood
> A man all light," etc.

P. 142 (iii. 1. 15, 1), l. 2, " however scanty," ed. 1 has, " though most feeble in its grasp, and scanty."

P. 148 (*ib.*, 9), l. 8, ed. 1 reads, " and I proceed, therefore, to notice that other and opposite error of Christian men in thinking that there is little use or value in the operation of the theoretic faculty ; not that I at present feel myself capable, or that this is the place for the discussion of that vast question of the operations of Taste (as it is called) on the minds of man, and the national value of its teaching, but I wish shortly to reply to that objection which might be urged to the real moral dignity."

Ib. (*ib.*), l. 16, ed. 1, " few so utterly lost but that they receive."

P. 166 (iii. 2, 2, 12), l. 17 from foot, ed. 1, " way, the worse he gets on."

P. 180 (iii. 2, 3, 7), " lamp of life," etc. This appears to be quoted from memory. See Shelley's "Prometheus Unbound," Act. II., Sc. 5, where it runs :—

> "Child of light, thy limbs are burning
> Through the vest that seems to hide them," etc.

Mrs. Shelley's (1839) edition read "lips" for "limbs," but "Lamp of life" is a confusion of the first lines of the first and last verses of the song.

P. 182 (*ib.*, 9), l. 6, "laugh at."   Ed. 1 adds, "The ἀνήριθμον γέλασμα of the sea is on its surface, not in the deep.   And thus."

P. 185 (*ib.*, 14), l. 6, for "mind," ed. 1 has, "imagination"; and l. 11, after "suggestiveness," adds, "and on the absolute right choice of the critical moment."

P. 187 (*ib.*, 16), l. 2, ed. 1, "Jerusalem or of the valley of Jehoshaphat."

P. 193 (*ib.*, 21), l. 36, ed. 1, "in a second : two others are farther in flight, they reach the edge of a deep river,—the water is beat into a hollow by the force of their plunge ;—close to us," . . . (p. 194, l. 7) "effort to save. Their shrieks ring in our ears till the marble seems rending around us, but far back."

P. 195 (*ib.*, 23), l. 31, for "single group," ed. 1, "dozen people at a time."

P. 202 (*ib.*, 29), l. 3, ed. 1, "mean this, the true foundation of all art which exercises eternal authority over men's minds ; (all other imagination than this is either secondary and contemplative, or utterly spurious ;) the base."

P. 207 (iii. 2, 4, 2), l. 11, "grossness," ed. 1 adds, "as in the description of the combat of the Red Cross Knight with Errour."

P. 217, foot-note, ed. 1 omits the last twelve lines of this note, and briefly reads, "Mourner, and to all in which the character and inner life of animals are developed. But all lovers of art must regret to find Mr. Landseer wasting his energies on such inanities as the 'Shoeing,' and sacrificing colour, expression, and action to an imitation of glossy hide."

P. 219 (iii. 2, 4, 13), l. 5, ed. 1 has, "in such circumstances I think it necessary, always provided it be based, as in the instances given I conceive it to be, upon thorough knowledge of the creature symbolised and wrought out by a master hand, and these conditions being observed, I believe it to be right and necessary in architecture to modify all animal forms by a severe architectural stamp, and in symbolical use of them to adopt a typical form, to which practice the contrary and its evil consequences are ludicrously . . ."

P. 221 (*ib.*, 15), line 1, "modern cathedrals," ed. 1 adds, "; and of the careful finish of the work this may serve for example, that one of the capitals of the Doge's palace is formed of eight heads of different animals, of which one is a bear's with a honeycomb in the mouth, whose carved *cells* are hexagonal."

P. 222 (*ib.*, 18), l. 28, after "valuable," ed. 1 adds, "(in the Cephalus they would be utterly destructive,)."

P. 224 (*ib.*, 20), ll. 20 and 23, ed. 1 has, "enormous breaker . . . sail, with Christ and His twelve disciples in it."

P. 241. These addenda are not contained in ed. 1, but are to be found in all other editions, although, in the Epilogue of the 1883 edition in two small volumes, they are referred to as "given, I believe, only in the second edition."

The first edition had, however, two pages of other Addenda, consisting of four notes, of which (*a*) the first was afterwards inserted in the body of the work, at p. 10; (*b*) the second was so inserted at p. 31 in edition 2, but omitted in later editions. See these notes above. (*c*) The third consisted of the two penultimate sentences of the long note on the "Laocoon" at p. 67: "It ought, however, to have been noticed respecting the Virgilian conception of the Laocoon that no fault is to be found . . . action of the coils." (*d*) The fourth was a long note referred to at p. 185, and ran as follows :—

"It is painful to trace upon the walls of the exhibitions lately opened in London, the universal evidence of the mode of study deprecated in this passage ; and to observe the various kinds of wreck which are taking place in consequence with many of our most promising artists. In the British Institution I saw only three pictures in which there was evidence of desire and effort to render a local passage of Nature faithfully. These were, first, a hayfield in a shower (I cannot, at this moment, refer to the painter's name) ;* with a wooden bridge and a single figure in the foreground, whose sky, in rainy, shattered, transparent grey, I have seldom seen equalled, and whose distance and foreground were alike carefully studied, the one obscure with the dusty vapour rising out of the heat of the shower, the other rich in broad and luxuriant leafage ; (the foaming water on the left was, however, too cold and false in its reflections). The second was a sky of Lauder's, evidently taken straight from nature (which, with the peculiar judgment frequent in hanging committees, was placed at the top of the central room), but which was in great measure destroyed by the intrusion of a lay figure and dramatic sea ; the third a forest study by Linnell. Among the various failures, I am sorry to have to note the prominent one of Turner's ; a strange example of the way in which the greatest men may at times lose themselves, from causes it is impossible to trace. Happily, this picture cannot be construed into a sign of generally declining power, for I have seen three drawings executed at the same period, in which the artist's mind appears at its full force. Nothing, however, could be more unfortunate than the central portion of the picture in the Institution, a heavy mass of hot colour being employed in the principal shade, and a strange meaningless green spread over the delicate hues of the distance, while the shadows on the right were executed with pure and crude blue,

* See pp. 223–24 of later editions.

such as I believe cannot be shown in any other work whatsoever of the great painter. I am also sorry to have to warn so good a painter as Mr. Goodall of his being altogether on a wrong road; the false chiaroscuro, exaggerated and impossible aerial perspective, and morbid prettiness and polish of complexions, in his large picture, are means of attracting vulgar notice which he certainly does not need, and which if he continues to employ them, must end, and that speedily, in his sinking irrecoverably beneath the rank which it was the hope of all lovers of English art to see him attain and hold.

"One more picture I must mention, as a refreshing and earnest study of truth, yet unexhibited, but which will appear in the Royal Academy; a seashore by Collins, where the sun, just risen and struggling through gaps of threatening cloud, is answered by the green, dark, transparent sea, with a broad flake of expanding fire. I have never seen the oppression of sunlight in clear, lurid, rainy atmosphere more perfectly or faithfully rendered, and the various portions of reflected and scattered light are all studied with equal truth and solemn feeling."

THE END

Printed by BALLANTYNE, HANSON & Co.
Edinburgh & London

Ruskin Reprints

Uniform with this volume

Cloth *limp, Gilt Tops,* **2s. 6d.** ⎫
Leather *limp, Gilt Tops,* **3s. 6d.** ⎬ *per vol. net*

Sesame and Lilies. Three Lectures and long Preface.

The Crown of Wild Olive. Essays on Work, Traffic, and War, etc.

The Two Paths. On Decoration and Manufacture.

Time and Tide. On Laws of Work.

Lectures on Art. Delivered at Oxford in 1870.

A Joy For Ever. On the Political Economy of Art.

The Queen of the Air. A Study of Greek Myths

The Ethics of the Dust. On the Elements of Crystallization.

The Elements of Drawing. With 50 Illustrations.

The Eagle's Nest. On the Relation of Natural Science to Art.

Munera Pulveris. On the Elements of Political Economy.

Frondes Agrestes. Readings in "Modern Painters."

Mornings in Florence

LONDON: GEORGE ALLEN

I

Ruskin Reprints

Uniform with this volume

Cloth *limp, Gilt Tops,* **2s. 6d.**⎱ *per vol. net*
Leather *limp, Gilt Tops,* **3s. 6d.**⎰

S. Mark's Rest.   The History of Venice.

The Stones of Venice.   Vol. I.   Selections
for Travellers.

The Stones of Venice.   Vol. II.   Selections
for Travellers.

**The price of the Volumes marked with an
asterisk (*) will, owing to the inclusion of all
the Illustrations, be**

Cloth . . 3s. 6d. net
Leather . 4s. 6d. net

* The Seven Lamps of Architecture

Modern Painters.   Vol. I.

Modern Painters.   Vol. II.

* Modern Painters.   Vol. III.

* Modern Painters.   Vol. IV.

* Modern Painters.   Vol. V.

Other Volumes to follow

LONDON: GEORGE ALLEN